America's
TEST KITCHEN

ALSO BY THE EDITORS AT AMERICA'S TEST KITCHEN

The America's Test Kitchen Family Cookbook

The Best of America's Test Kitchen 2007

THE BEST RECIPE SERIES:
The Best 30-Minute Recipe
The Best Light Recipe
The Cook's Illustrated Guide to Grilling & Barbecue
Best American Side Dishes
The New Best Recipe
Cover & Bake
Steaks, Chops, Roasts & Ribs
Baking Illustrated
Restaurant Favorites at Home
The Best Vegetable Recipes
The Best Italian Classics
The Best American Classics
The Best Soups & Stews

THE TV COMPANION SERIES:
Test Kitchen Favorites
Cooking at Home with America's Test Kitchen
America's Test Kitchen Live!
Inside America's Test Kitchen
Here in America's Test Kitchen
The America's Test Kitchen Cookbook

834 Kitchen Quick Tips

To order any of our books, visit us at
http://www.cooksillustrated.com
http://www.americastestkitchen.com
or call 800-611-0759

WELCOME TO
AMERICA'S TEST KITCHEN

THIS BOOK HAS BEEN TESTED, WRITTEN, AND edited by the folks at America's Test Kitchen, a very real 2,500-square-foot kitchen located just outside of Boston. It is the home of *Cook's Illustrated* magazine and *Cook's Country* magazine and is the Monday-through-Friday destination for more than two dozen test cooks, editors, food scientists, tasters, and cookware specialists. Our mission is to test recipes over and over again until we understand how and why they work and until we arrive at the "best" version.

We start the process of testing a recipe with a complete lack of conviction, which means that we accept no claim, no theory, no technique, and no recipe at face value. We simply assemble as many variations as possible, test a half dozen of the most promising, and taste the results blind. We then construct our own hybrid recipe and continue to test it, varying ingredients, techniques, and cooking times until we reach a consensus. The result, we hope, is the best version of a particular recipe, but we realize that only you can be the final judge of our success

(or failure). As we like to say in the test kitchen, "We make the mistakes, so you don't have to."

All of this would not be possible without a belief that good cooking, much like good music, is indeed based on a foundation of objective technique. Some people like spicy foods and others don't, but there is a right way to sauté, there is a best way to cook a pot roast, and there are measurable scientific principles involved in producing perfectly beaten, stable egg whites. This is our ultimate goal: to investigate the fundamental principles of cooking so that you become a better cook. It is as simple as that.

You can watch us work (in our actual test kitchen) by tuning in to *America's Test Kitchen* (www.americastestkitchen.com) on public television or by subscribing to *Cook's Illustrated* magazine (www.cooksillustrated.com) or *Cook's Country* magazine (www.cookscountry.com), which are each published every other month. We welcome you into our kitchen, where you can stand by our side as we test our way to the "best" recipes in America.

THE BEST MAKE-AHEAD RECIPE

A BEST RECIPE CLASSIC

THE BEST MAKE-AHEAD RECIPE

A BEST RECIPE CLASSIC

BY THE EDITORS OF

COOK'S ILLUSTRATED

PHOTOGRAPHY
DANIEL J. VAN ACKERE

ILLUSTRATIONS
JOHN BURGOYNE

AMERICA'S TEST KITCHEN

BROOKLINE, MASSACHUSETTS

America's Test Kitchen
17 Station Street
Brookline, MA 02445

ISBN-13: 978-1-933615-14-1
ISBN-10: 1-933615-14-1
Library of Congress Cataloging-in-Publication Data
The Editors of Cook's Illustrated

The Best Make-Ahead Recipe
How To Cook Now To Save Time Later

1st Edition
ISBN-13: 978-1-933615-14-1
ISBN-10: 1-933615-14-1
(hardcover): U.S. $35; Can. $43.95
I. Cooking. I. Title
2007

Manufactured in the United States of America

10 9 8 7 6 5 4 3 2 1

Distributed by America's Test Kitchen, 17 Station Street, Brookline, MA 02445

Senior Editor: Lori Galvin
Senior Food Editor: Julia Collin Davison
Associate Editors: Rachel Toomey and Sarah Wilson
Assistant Editor: Elizabeth Wray Emery
Test Cooks: Bryan Roof and Megan Wycoff
Series Designer: Amy Klee
Art Director: Carolynn DeCillo
Designer: Matthew Warnick
Photography: Daniel J. van Ackere
Food Styling: Marie Piraino
Illustrator: John Burgoyne
Senior Production Manager: Jessica Lindheimer Quirk
Copyeditor: Ann Martin Rolke
Proofreader: Debra Hudak
Indexer: Elizabeth Parson

Pictured on front of jacket: Individual Chocolate Soufflé (page 360)
Pictured on back of jacket: Breaded Chicken Breasts Stuffed with Goat Cheese and Thyme (page 276), Overnight Sour Cream Coffeecake (page 328), Rigatoni with Beef Ragù (page 118), Slow-Cooker Beef Stew (page 142), and Make-Ahead Mashed Potatoes (page 59)

CONTENTS

PREFACE

MY FIRST JOB, AT THE PRINCELY WAGE OF
75 cents per hour, was to help Charlie Bentley do
the afternoon milking. Sure, we'd hay when the sun
was shining, fix tractors, and, at the end of the summer, grab a corn knife and go down the rows, but
the one job you had to do every day, twice a day,
was the milking.

The barn was set just off the main road and
next to a still-famous trout stream that ran into the
Battenkill. The cows came down off the moun-
tain pastures and walked through a large culvert
underneath the road, then made their way to the
red barn. One of my jobs was to herd the cows in,
something with which they needed little help. I
carried an old leather milking strap (used to hang
the milker from their backs) and slapped the odd
straggler on the rump, but, for the most part, this
was an easy way to make my two or three dollars
a day.

The barn itself wasn't much to look at. It had a
poured concrete floor, stanchions to hold the cows
in place during milking, and two gutters in the
floor for the waste. That was another less-appealing
but character-building part of my job: shoveling
out the gutters, filling the large manure bucket, and
then pushing the bucket on the overhead track out
to the spreader.

One day early on in my milking career, I went
to herd the cows and when I got back to the barn
I realized that I had forgotten to open the door.
To my surprise and embarrassment, the herd had
broken through the worn slats—one side was
barely hanging by one hinge and the other side
lay smashed into splinters on the floor. This was
the opposite of "closing the barn door after the
cows got out" but just as humiliating. A little bit of
advance planning would have spared me the disappointment I found in Charlie's eyes. Vermonters
never dress you down; they just turn quiet, their
faces freeze into granite, and they refuse to look
you in the eye. Believe me, I would have preferred
to have been taken out to the woodshed, but I did
learn a valuable lesson.

As with farming, a bit of planning makes cooking enormously easier and more enjoyable. I don't
mean just organizing menus and doing the shopping for the week on Sunday. This book is about
rethinking casseroles so they can be frozen and then
simply thrown into a hot oven at the last minute.
And how to engineer a coffeecake or muffin batter
than can withstand the freezer without turning out
dry and dull when baked. And even something as
simple as making a large batch of beef stew. Do you
really have to brown each and every piece of stew
meat? (No, you don't.)

We have done the work, so you don't have to
wonder how to make recipes well ahead of time or
in larger quantities, or how to use leftovers without
always resorting to a catchall soup or stew.

That is not to say I am not a short-order cook
at heart. I am. I love to see what is in the root cel-
lar or the garden and make up a last-minute meal.
But all my years in the kitchen have taught me
that the best meals come from good planning and
solid culinary knowledge. With this cookbook in
hand, you can still throw things together at the last
minute. But now you can be certain that dinner is
going to be a great success. Good short-order cooks
have known this for generations. It is all in what
you do ahead of time that makes the last-minute
preparation appear effortless and taste great.

I have learned my lesson. These days, I open
the barn doors before I get the cows, and I have
a freezer full of homemade frozen dinners and
leftover big batches of soups and stews. After all,
I don't want Charlie to be disappointed when he
drops by for dinner.

Christopher Kimball
Founder and Editor
Cook's Illustrated and *Cook's Country*
Host, *America's Test Kitchen*

1

APPETIZERS

APPETIZERS

WHEN WE'RE PREPARING AND SERVING appetizers, that's usually not all we're doing. We're also answering the front door, pouring drinks, and catching up with old friends who know their way to our kitchen. Appetizers are, after all, party food. If we're the hosts, we can bet that having lots of time alone in the kitchen is an unlikely proposition. Therefore our goal was to develop recipes that would allow you to do most (if not all) of the prep work in advance, so that you can actually relax and enjoy being with your guests.

In our research for this chapter, we quickly realized that most recipes fall into one of two categories: those that are make-ahead by design and those that are not. The natural make-ahead recipes are typically cold appetizers such as dips, spreads, and other items that actually benefit from a little time in the fridge. Making them ahead of time allows their flavors to deepen and meld, as is the case with Marinated Feta Cheese with Lemon and Shallot (page 16) and Chicken Liver Pâté (page 18). Our goals for these recipes were to pinpoint the absolute best ways to make them ahead of time and to determine just how far in advance they could be made.

Our main focus for this chapter, however, was on those recipes that didn't have any obvious make-ahead solutions. Most of these recipes were for hot appetizers—the dishes that keep you in the kitchen during the party. Take crab cakes for example. To serve really good ones at a party, you'd typically have to fry the cakes at the last minute, as the guests are arriving—a total mess and hassle. If you're like us, you don't want your guests standing at the stove with you when you're scrambling to finish up a hot appetizer. But with our Cocktail Crab Cakes (page 22), a tray of crab cakes goes directly from the fridge (or freezer) into the oven. We developed a creative oven-frying method that allows you to do all of the prep a day ahead with no messy frying. We used the same fridge-to-oven method for everything from Roasted Artichoke Dip (page 6) to Mini Empanadas (page 25). We completely assembled these recipes before storing them, leaving little work to do at the last minute. In fact, we were surprised to discover just how well this technique worked for a variety of appetizers that require time in the oven.

Other recipes required a slightly different approach. For our Rustic Caramelized Onion Tarts with Blue Cheese and Walnuts (page 35), we found that partially baking the dough before storing the tart gave us the crisp crust we wanted, and still allowed us to assemble and top the tart ahead of time. If we assembled the tart and stored it without taking this step, the crust became soggy.

We've also included recipes for a variety of accompaniments such as marinated olives, spiced almonds, relishes, and dips—all easily made in advance and perfect for rounding out any cocktail party menu (see our menu ideas on pages 5, 16, and 29). With these make-ahead recipes at hand, we guarantee your next gathering will be a fun, stress-free affair.

HOT ARTICHOKE DIP

A STAPLE OF PARTY BUFFETS IN THE seventies, hot artichoke dip is an ode to convenience cooking. There are various permutations of this recipe, but most involve a simple concoction of canned artichokes, mayonnaise, and Parmesan cheese all combined in the food processor. The mixture is then poured into a baking dish, topped with buttery bread crumbs, and baked. What results should be a creamy, tangy, crowd-pleasing dip ready to be scooped up with crackers, breadsticks, or crudités. Unfortunately, all too often the dip is one-dimensional and there is nary a hint of real artichoke flavor. We wanted to dust off what has become something of a relic and give the flavors a fresher, less dated spin. And we also wanted a dip where all the work could be done in advance.

Right off the bat, we knew we'd need to find a replacement for the tinny-tasting canned artichoke hearts this recipe typically relies on. Fresh artichokes were too expensive and too much effort for the return (not to mention the fact that we would need to use up to 6 pounds). First, we turned to jarred marinated artichokes (packed in oil with herbs and spices), but they made our dip overseasoned and greasy. Even when the artichokes were well rinsed, our dip still tasted of the marinade. We had much better success with frozen artichokes. Following the directions on the package, we cooked the artichokes in boiling water until just tender. They had a fresh, clean artichoke flavor, much preferred to that of the marinated and acrid canned varieties. Certainly this was an improvement, but their flavor was a bit muted. We decided to try roasting the artichokes with olive oil, salt, and pepper until just tender and browned on the edges. This simple technique was a revelation, deepening and intensifying their flavor.

With the artichokes settled, we turned to the dip's other key ingredients: mayonnaise and Parmesan cheese. Typical recipes for this dip use a 1 to 1 ratio of mayo to cheese, however tasters found this amount of cheese made for a grainy dip. We tested the dip with lower and lower amounts of cheese until we hit upon the perfect ratio of mayonnaise to cheese—2 to 1. The only issue with the new ratio is that the dip lacked creaminess. Looking back to some other recipes we dug up in our research, we noticed that some included sour cream or cream cheese (in addition to the mayonnaise). We gave it a try, adding a small amount of each to two separate dips. Tasters found that sour cream was too tangy and thinned the dip's texture, making it almost soupy. However, cream cheese was just the breakthrough we needed, and a small amount gave the dip the creamy body it lacked.

Our dip was coming together, but it still needed some tweaking. We wanted to keep the simplicity of the artichoke dip intact, so we looked to flavors that would complement, not obscure, the existing flavors. Sautéed onion and garlic were a natural pairing with the artichokes and cheese. Lemon juice lent the dip a fresh brightness and zing missing from the original dip. After trying a variety of herbs, the woodsy flavor of fresh thyme won tasters over and a pinch of cayenne gave the dip a welcome bit of heat.

We now had a well-balanced, complex dip with bright flavors, but we still needed to address the topping—typically a mixture of butter and bread crumbs. Tasters were not too keen on this plain topping, however. Most complained that the topping's flavor was "just plain boring" and its texture sandy, messy, and "not crisp enough." Going

MAKE IT A MENU

Marinated Black and Green Olives

Warm Spiced Almonds

Roasted Tomato and Goat Cheese Tarts

Crispy Garlic and Rosemary Polenta Triangles with Herbed Goat Cheese

Sicilian Eggplant Relish with crostini

Roasted Artichoke Dip with Italian breadsticks

on a suggestion from a fellow test cook, we discovered that a bit of Parmesan cheese mixed with the bread crumbs did the trick. The cheese added a welcome boost in flavor and aided in making the topping crisp and more cohesive. This meant no more crumbs falling all over the place. Finally, we had a dip with fresh, sophisticated flavors that was anything but a relic. Now we needed to see how it would hold up if made in advance.

Freezing this dip turned out to be a complete disaster. We assembled each batch in a casserole dish and wrapped it tightly with plastic wrap. After a week in the freezer, we removed them and tested thawing and then reheating the dips a number of different ways. But none of these techniques worked, and our dip really never came back to life. Every dip that we froze and reheated emerged from the oven as a greasy broken mess. Admitting defeat, we decided to see how it would hold when refrigerated.

Overall, we found that the flavors and ingredients in our dip held up well in the refrigerator. Making sure the dip baked up with a crisp topping was our biggest concern though. We were wary of storing the dip with the crumb topping intact, as we figured the topping would soak up moisture from the dip and never crisp up when it came time to bake. Happily, we discovered our recipe didn't require an extra step of holding the topping separately and adding it later, as it crisped and browned just fine—even after sitting on top of the dip for a couple of days. In the end, we discovered that three days was about the limit for storing this dip. Stored any longer, and the dip developed an overwhelming garlic and onion flavor.

Roasted Artichoke Dip

SERVES 10 TO 12

It's important that the cream cheese be at room temperature, otherwise it will not mix well. Also, this dip is best served warm, so make sure it comes out of the oven just as your guests are starting to arrive. Serve with crackers or small toasted baguette slices.

TOPPING
2   slices high-quality white sandwich bread, quartered
2   tablespoons grated Parmesan cheese
1   tablespoon unsalted butter, melted

DIP
2   (9-ounce) boxes frozen artichokes (do not thaw)
2   tablespoons olive oil
    Salt and ground black pepper
1   medium onion, minced
2   medium garlic cloves, minced or pressed through a garlic press (about 2 teaspoons)
1   cup mayonnaise
4   ounces cream cheese, at room temperature
1   ounce Parmesan cheese, grated (about ½ cup)
2   tablespoons juice from 1 lemon
1   tablespoon minced fresh thyme leaves
    Pinch cayenne pepper

1. FOR THE TOPPING: Pulse the bread in a food processor to coarse crumbs, about 6 pulses. Toss the bread crumbs with the Parmesan and butter; set aside.

2. FOR THE DIP: Adjust an oven rack to the middle position and heat the oven to 450 degrees. Line a baking sheet with foil. Toss the artichokes with 1 tablespoon of the oil, ½ teaspoon salt, and ¼ teaspoon pepper, and spread out over the prepared baking sheet. Roast the artichokes, stirring occasionally, until browned at the edges, about 25 minutes. Let the artichokes cool and then chop coarse.

TESTING NOTES

CHOOSING THE RIGHT CHOKE

We found that the type of artichokes you use in the Roasted Artichoke Dip can make all the difference.

Fresh Artichokes

Too much work

Fresh artichokes taste great; however, they simply take too much time to prep and cook for this dip (and they aren't cheap either). We wanted something simpler.

Canned Artichokes

No flavor

The canning process and the watery packing liquid rob canned artichokes of any flavor. When made into a dip, tasters said it "tasted like nothing" and "if it didn't say 'Artichoke Dip' on the top of the tasting sheet, I wouldn't know what I was eating."

Jarred Marinated Artichokes

Not a shortcut

These artichokes are usually marinated in an Italian-style vinaigrette. When we used them straight out of the jar, tasters said the dip took on a "nasty flavor" that was "all over the place." When we rinsed them, tasters thought the dip still tasted of the marinade.

THE WINNER: Frozen Artichokes

In our first test, frozen artichokes tasted a bit watery when cooked following the package instructions but we discovered that roasting them in the oven for 20 minutes not only helped to evaporate the excess water, but intensified their flavor—resulting in a dip that was the hands-down favorite. Tasters remarked, "This is what artichoke dip is supposed to taste like!"

QUICK AND EASY CREAMY DIPS

ADDING GREAT VARIETY TO ANY COCKTAIL PARTY TABLE, CREAMY DIPS ARE EASILY MADE IN advance. In fact they're actually better when made ahead of time, because their flavors have a chance to fuse, resulting in a well-balanced dip. With our Creamy Dip Base, you can whip up any number of fresh-flavored dips by stirring in one of our flavor add-ins, depending on your mood, the season, or the confines of your pantry.

Creamy Dip Base
MAKES ABOUT 1½ CUPS

Mix ¾ cup mayonnaise, ¾ cup sour cream, and 1 tablespoon lemon juice together, then stir in a flavor add-in (see below), and season with salt and pepper to taste. Allow the dip to sit for at least 15 minutes for the flavors to meld. The dip will keep, covered and refrigerated, for up to 2 days. Be sure to reseason the dip with salt, pepper, and additional lemon juice to taste before serving.

➤ FLAVOR ADD-INS
Blue Cheese–Scallion Dip
Add 1 ounce mild blue cheese (such as Stella), crumbled (about ¼ cup), 2 thinly sliced scallions, and 1 teaspoon freshly ground black pepper.

Sun-Dried Tomato and Basil Dip
Add ¼ cup finely chopped sun-dried tomatoes and 2 tablespoons minced fresh basil leaves.

Jalapeño-Lime Dip
Add lime juice (instead of fresh lemon juice) to the dip base, ¼ cup chopped pickled jalapeño chiles, and 2 thinly sliced scallions.

Tapenade Dip
Add ¼ cup minced kalamata olives, 1 teaspoon minced garlic, and 1 tablespoon minced fresh parsley leaves.

Curry-Cilantro Dip
Add 1 minced shallot, 2 teaspoons curry powder, and 2 tablespoons minced fresh cilantro leaves.

3. Meanwhile, heat the remaining 1 tablespoon oil in a 10-inch skillet over medium-high heat until just shimmering. Add the onion and cook until softened, 5 to 7 minutes. Stir in the garlic and cook until fragrant, about 30 seconds. Transfer the onion mixture to a large bowl and set aside.

4. Stir the mayonnaise, cream cheese, Parmesan, lemon juice, thyme, and cayenne into the onion mixture until uniform, smearing any lumps of cream cheese against the side of the bowl with a rubber spatula. Gently fold in the chopped artichokes and season the mixture with salt and pepper to taste. Transfer the mixture to an ungreased 8-inch square baking dish and smooth the top. Sprinkle the bread crumbs evenly over the top.

5. To store: Cover the baking dish tightly with plastic wrap and refrigerate for up to 3 days.

6. To serve: Adjust an oven rack to the middle position and heat the oven to 400 degrees. Unwrap the dip and bake, uncovered, until hot throughout and the bread crumbs are golden brown, 20 to 25 minutes. Let cool for 5 minutes before serving.

TO SERVE RIGHT AWAY
Bake the assembled dip as directed in step 6.

➤ VARIATION
Roasted Artichoke Dip with Spinach
Removing the excess moisture from the spinach is crucial here; we found it best to wrap the thawed spinach in paper towels and squeeze out as much liquid as possible.

Follow the recipe for Roasted Artichoke Dip, reducing the amount of artichokes to 1 box. Add 1 (10-ounce) box frozen chopped spinach, thawed and squeezed dry, to the pan along with the garlic in step 3.

RELISHES AND SPREADS

HAVING THE RIGHT ACCOMPANIMENTS CAN MAKE OR BREAK A GREAT COCKTAIL PARTY SPREAD. But making a good variety of accompaniments for an hors d'oeuvres table the day of a party can be a real hassle. While you should be setting up the bar or dressing the table with linens, you're still chopping herbs or dicing onions. Here are some great recipes that hold well when made several days in advance and are sure to turn some heads.

Olivada

MAKES ABOUT 1¾ CUPS

Olivada is the Italian version of tapenade, the French olive paste. We prefer rich, meaty kalamata olives for this recipe, although you can use any high-quality brined black olives here. See page 193 for our tasting of green olives. This spread is great served as a condiment on a cheese board with toasted baguette slices, but can also be used as a topping for pasta.

1	cup pitted kalamata olives (see note)
1	cup pitted brined green olives (see note)
4	anchovy fillets, rinsed, patted dry, and minced
3	tablespoons extra-virgin olive oil
1	tablespoon capers, rinsed and minced
2	teaspoons minced fresh rosemary
1	medium garlic clove, minced or pressed through a garlic press (about 1 teaspoon)
2	tablespoons minced fresh basil leaves (for serving)

1. Pulse the olives, anchovies, oil, capers, rosemary, and garlic together in a food processor until the mixture is finely minced and forms a chunky paste, about ten 1-second pulses.

2. To STORE: Transfer the mixture to an airtight container and refrigerate for 1 hour or up to 1 week.

3. To SERVE: Bring the olivada to room temperature and stir in the basil before serving.

Caramelized Onion Jam with Dark Rum

MAKES ABOUT 1 CUP

This jam is great served as a condiment on a cheese board with toasted bread or crackers. Keep a close eye on the onions during the final few minutes of browning so that they don't scorch.

1	tablespoon unsalted butter
1	tablespoon vegetable oil
2	pounds onions (about 4 medium), chopped medium
1	teaspoon light brown sugar
	Salt
1	tablespoon water
2	teaspoons dark rum
1	teaspoon minced fresh thyme leaves
½	teaspoon cider vinegar
	Ground black pepper

1. Melt the butter with the oil in a 12-inch nonstick skillet over medium-low heat. Stir in the onions, brown sugar, and ½ teaspoon salt. Cover and cook, stirring occasionally, until the onions are softened and have released their juices, about 10 minutes.

2. Remove the lid, increase the heat to medium-high, and continue to cook, stirring often, until the onions are deeply browned, 10 to 15 minutes.

3. Off the heat, stir in the water. Transfer the mixture to a food processor and add the rum, thyme, and vinegar. Pulse the mixture to a jam-like consistency, about 5 pulses. Season with salt and pepper to taste.

4. To STORE: Transfer the jam to an airtight container and refrigerate for 1 hour or up to 1 week.

5. To SERVE: Bring the jam to room temperature before serving.

Sicilian Eggplant Relish

MAKES ABOUT 2½ CUPS

Do not peel the eggplant here; the skin softens during cooking and helps prevent the eggplant from breaking apart completely. Serve with garlic crostini or pita chips. This relish can also be used as a topping for pasta.

3	tablespoons olive oil
1	medium eggplant (1 pound), cut into ¼-inch dice
	Salt and ground black pepper
1	medium onion, minced
1	tablespoon tomato paste
2	medium garlic cloves, minced or pressed through a garlic press (about 2 teaspoons)
2	anchovy fillets, rinsed, patted dry, and minced
1	tablespoon minced fresh oregano leaves, or 1 teaspoon dried
	Pinch red pepper flakes
¼	cup balsamic vinegar, plus extra to taste
2	tablespoons minced fresh parsley leaves
1	tablespoon sugar
½	teaspoon grated zest from 1 lemon

1. Heat 1 tablespoon of the oil in a 12-inch nonstick skillet over high heat until just smoking. Add half of the eggplant, ¼ teaspoon salt, and ⅛ teaspoon pepper and cook, stirring often, until the eggplant begins to soften and brown, about 3 minutes. Transfer the eggplant to a medium bowl. Return the skillet to high heat and repeat with 1 more tablespoon of the oil, the remaining eggplant, ¼ teaspoon salt, and ⅛ teaspoon pepper; transfer to the bowl.

2. Add the remaining 1 tablespoon oil to the skillet and return to medium heat until just shimmering. Add the onion and cook until softened, 5 to 7 minutes. Stir in the tomato paste and cook until it is incorporated and begins to brown, about 1 minute. Stir in the garlic, anchovies, oregano, and pepper flakes and cook until fragrant, about 30 seconds.

3. Return the eggplant to the pan, cover, and cook over medium-low heat until the eggplant is very soft, about 8 minutes. Off the heat, stir in the vinegar, parsley, sugar, and lemon zest, and season with salt and pepper to taste.

4. To STORE: Transfer the relish to an airtight container and refrigerate for 1 hour or up to 3 days.

5. To SERVE: Bring the relish to room temperature and season with additional vinegar, salt, and pepper to taste before serving.

Roasted Red Pepper Spread

MAKES ABOUT 2 CUPS

Serve this dip with pita chips, fresh pitas cut into wedges, or baguette slices.

12	ounces jarred roasted red peppers, drained, rinsed, and patted dry
1	cup walnuts, toasted
¼	cup coarsely ground plain wheat crackers
3	tablespoons juice from 1 lemon, plus extra as needed
2	tablespoons extra-virgin olive oil
1	tablespoon mild molasses
1	teaspoon honey
½	teaspoon ground cumin
⅛	teaspoon cayenne pepper
	Salt

1. Process all of the ingredients except the salt together in a food processor until smooth, about ten 1-second pulses. Season with salt to taste.

2. To STORE: Transfer the spread to an airtight container and refrigerate for 1 hour or up to 3 days.

3. To SERVE: Season with additional salt and lemon juice to taste. Serve either cold or at room temperature.

BAKED BRIE
EN CROÛTE

WITH ITS GLOSSY, GOLDEN PASTRY CRUST and rich, creamy interior, baked Brie en croûte became a cocktail-party favorite in the 1980s. It's a dish that satisfies all cravings, since the cheesy filling is often balanced with a sweet fruit jam. To make it, puff pastry dough is simply wrapped around a small wheel of Brie. In our favorite version, the dough is pleated around the Brie in such a way as to create an exposed space on top of the cheese. After a stint in the oven to bake the "croûte" and heat the cheese, the Brie is removed from the oven and the open well on top is filled with jam.

Right off the bat we knew this recipe had great make-ahead potential: Simply wrap the Brie with the pastry, refrigerate or freeze until needed, and it's ready to go straight to the oven at a moment's notice. But before we could determine what adjustments needed to be made to the recipe to make it ahead of time, we knew we needed to start at the beginning and figure out what makes a great baked Brie in the first place.

Beginning with the cheese, we were hit with an unexpected twist. In the past when choosing Brie, we have always recommended selecting a cheese that was pliant to the touch and whose edges have started to brown ever so slightly. At this stage, the Brie should be a little runny and at its peak flavor. We assumed that this would be the best type to use for Brie en croûte. We were wrong. After baking the encased Brie at this stage of ripeness, we found that when we cut into the cheese, it ran into a shallow, oily pool around a hollow shell of puff pastry. Wondering if the cheese was too ripe, we attempted the same recipe with a less-mature piece of cheese that was still soft, yet would spring back when pressed. (The rind was snow white with no hint of coloration.) The result of this test was what we wanted—a molten center of cheese that was spreadable but didn't run once baked.

Next we turned to fine-tuning the other elements of the dish. Whether to use homemade puff pastry or frozen was our first question, and it didn't take long to answer. While we would agree that homemade puff pastry, which is made with 100 percent butter, tastes better than frozen commercial versions—which normally contain all vegetable shortening—we also knew the amount of time and effort involved in making homemade was just not worth it, especially when a good frozen substitute can be found at any well-stocked supermarket.

Just as with pie dough, it's important when baking puff pastry to preheat the oven and to make sure your temperature gauge is accurate. The water contained in the dough must steam so that the dough separates into delicate, flaky layers. If the temperature is too low, the pastry won't have enough lift, and you won't achieve those flaky layers; if it's too hot, the outer layers of the puff pastry overcook before the inside cooks through. We found that preheating the oven to 400 degrees provided just enough heat for the maximum "puff" and proper browning. (A brush of egg wash before going into the oven also aided in giving our pastry good color and shine.)

We weren't too surprised to learn that we could simply wrap the cheese and hold it in the refrigerator for up to three days. But we were amazed that the cheese could be frozen for up to a month. When tasted side-by-side, tasters could not tell the difference between a Brie that had been frozen and one that had been refrigerated. They thought for sure that the harsh environment of the freezer would wreak havoc on the soft cheese's fine texture.

WRAPPING THE BRIE
IN PUFF PASTRY

1. Lift the pastry up over the cheese, pleating it at even intervals and leaving an opening in the center where the Brie is exposed.

2. Press the pleated edge of pastry up into a rim, which will later be filled with the preserves or jelly.

One final note on the advanced preparation: Although we found that chilled Brie could go straight from the fridge to the oven, the same cannot be said for Brie stored in the freezer. We find it's best to thaw the cheese in the fridge for 24 hours before baking.

FREEZE IT

Baked Brie en Croûte

SERVES 8 TO 10

The texture of the baked Brie will depend on the brand, type, and age of Brie you buy; it may melt completely or may merely soften. If the Brie melts completely (easy to identify after it's baked), let it cool for 30 to 40 minutes before serving, or else it will be very soupy and hard to eat. Nearly any flavor of preserves, jelly, or chutney can be used. Serve with crackers, small toasted pieces of baguette, or wedges of apple or pear.

1	(9½ by 9-inch) sheet frozen puff pastry, thawed (see the box)
1	large egg, beaten
1	(8-ounce) wheel soft Brie
1	large egg, beaten (for baking)
¼	cup apricot preserves, orange marmalade, or hot pepper jelly

1. Line the bottom of a pie dish (or cake pan) with parchment paper; set aside. Roll the puff pastry out to a 12-inch square on a lightly floured work surface. Using another pie dish or other round guide, trim the pastry into a 9-inch circle with a paring knife. Brush the edges of the pastry circle lightly with the beaten egg. Place the Brie in the center of the circle and, following the illustrations on page 10, wrap it in the pastry, leaving a small opening in the top. Transfer the Brie to the prepared pie dish.

2. To STORE: Wrap the pie dish with plastic wrap, being careful not to press down the pleating or rim of the puff pastry, and refrigerate for up to 3 days, or freeze for up to 1 month.

3. To SERVE: If frozen, let the Brie thaw in the refrigerator for 24 hours. Adjust an oven rack to the middle position and heat the oven to 400 degrees. Unwrap the Brie and brush the pastry with the beaten egg. Bake until the exterior is a deep golden brown, 30 to 35 minutes.

4. Transfer the cheese to a wire rack and, using the tip of a paring knife, cut into the top of the Brie to check its consistency. If the cheese is just softened, let it sit for 5 minutes before serving; if the cheese is melted and soupy, you will need to let it sit and cool until thickened for 30 to 40 minutes before serving. Spoon the preserves into the exposed center of the Brie as it cools.

TO SERVE RIGHT AWAY

Place the wheel of Brie in the freezer until firm (30 to 60 minutes) before wrapping in pastry as described in step 1. Bake as directed in step 3.

TEST KITCHEN TIP: Puff Pastry

Puff pastry is super-flaky dough characterized by dozens of buttery layers. It is made by wrapping a simple pastry dough around a square of cold butter, rolling the dough, folding the dough over numerous times, and chilling the dough for at least one hour between each fold (creating multiple layers). When the dough is baked, the water in the butter creates steam, which prompts the dough to puff into flaky, delicate layers.

Puff pastry is too difficult to make for all but the most accomplished baker. Thankfully, Pepperidge Farm Puff Pastry Sheets are available in virtually every supermarket and work well. Each 1-pound package contains two 9½ by 9-inch sheets. Because the dough is frozen, however, it must be defrosted before it can be worked; otherwise it can crack and break apart. We have found that thawing the dough in the refrigerator overnight is the best method, but it takes some forethought. Countertop defrosting works fine too, but don't rush it. Depending upon the ambient temperature, it may take between 30 and 60 minutes. The dough should unfold easily, but feel firm. If the seams crack, rejoin them by gently rolling them smooth with a rolling pin. And if the dough warms and softens, place it in the freezer until once again firm.

11

CHEESE STRAWS

CHEESE STRAWS ARE A SIMPLE APPETIZER that never fails to impress. In fact, a recipe for them, called Parmesan Cheese Pastry Twists, is usually printed on the back of the Pepperidge Farm Puff Pastry box. By design, the prepared, unbaked straws are easily made ahead and held in the fridge or freezer, on deck for their brief spell in the oven. However, after making this old standby according to the directions on the box, we knew we could do better.

First, we wanted more cheese flavor. While the back-of-the-box recipe called for only ¼ cup cheese, we found it took a full cup of grated Parmesan to produce straws with bold cheese flavor. We then tried a few other cheeses, including Asiago, smoked cheddar cheese, and Manchego. While all of the cheeses melted just fine, only the Parmesan and Asiago retained their full-flavored punch after baking. The other cheeses, although potent on their own, tasted bland against the rich dough. We also tried adding various herbs and spices, such as fresh thyme, smoked paprika, and chili powder, but tasters preferred the batches seasoned with just a little salt and black pepper.

To form the straws, we found it much easier to work with pastry that wasn't fully thawed. When left just a bit icy, the dough came to room temperature as we rolled it out. The recipe on the box forms the straws by cutting the dough into two pieces and sandwiching the cheese between them.

We tried pressing the cheese into just one side of a single piece of dough, but there was simply not enough surface area to hold a cup of cheese. In the end, we found it was better (and simpler) to press the grated cheese onto both sides of a single piece of dough. The exposed cheese would then melt and toast as the pastry puffed in the oven.

However, our straws were not going directly into the oven. After placing the twisted straws on baking sheets, we simply wrapped them up with plastic and into the fridge they went. When it was time to bake the straws, it was as easy as unwrapping them and popping the baking sheets in a hot oven. After about 10 minutes in a 425-degree oven, our straws emerged with a crisp, airy texture and an undeniable cheese flavor that was a hit all around. We had the same great results when storing the straws in the freezer—a storage method we admired even more.

The freezer was our favorite for two reasons: First, we were able to hold the straws for longer—about a week was optimal. Anything much longer than a week and the unbaked straws started picking up off-flavors from the freezer. Second, there was the space-saving bonus of freezing. We discovered that after the baking sheets had been in the freezer for a few hours, we could transfer the completely frozen straws to a zipper-lock bag. This allowed us to make and store larger amounts of cheese straws—a big plus if you're planning on having a large party.

EQUIPMENT: **Cheese Graters**

Whether you are dusting a plate of pasta or grating a full cup of cheese to use in a recipe, a good grater should be efficient and easy to use. After grating more than 10 pounds of Parmesan, we concluded that success is dependent on a combination of sharp grating teeth, a comfortable handle or grip, and good leverage for pressing the cheese onto the grater.

Our favorite model was a flat grater based on a small, maneuverable woodworking tool called a rasp. Shaped like a ruler, but with lots and lots of tiny, sharp raised teeth, the Microplane Grater can grate large quantities of cheese smoothly and almost effortlessly. The black plastic handle, which we found more comfortable than any of the others, also earned high praise. Other flat graters also scored well. What about box graters? They can deliver good results and can do more than just grate hard cheese—but if grating hard cheese is the task at hand, a box grater is not our first choice.

THE BEST GRATER

The Microplane Grater has very sharp teeth and a solid handle, which together make grating cheese a breeze. This grater also makes quick work of ginger and citrus zest.

Cheese Straws

MAKES 14 STRAWS

These straws are easier to make when the pastry is not fully thawed, but still a bit firm. Frozen, refrigerated, or freshly made straws will all bake in roughly the same amount of time. For an attractive presentation, stand the baked cheese straws straight up in a tall glass.

1	(9½ by 9-inch) sheet frozen puff pastry, thawed on counter for 10 minutes
2	ounces Parmesan or Asiago cheese, grated (about 1 cup)
¼	teaspoon salt
¼	teaspoon ground black pepper

1. Line 2 baking sheets with parchment paper; set aside. Place the puff pastry on a sheet of parchment and sprinkle it with ½ cup of the Parmesan, ⅛ teaspoon of the salt, and ⅛ teaspoon of the pepper. Place another sheet of parchment over the top and, using a rolling pin, press the cheese into the dough by gently rolling the pin back and forth. Without removing the parchment, carefully flip the dough over, cheese-side down. Remove the top layer of parchment and repeat with the remaining ½ cup Parmesan, ⅛ teaspoon salt, and ⅛ teaspoon pepper. Measure the piece of dough and continue to roll it out to a 10½-inch square, if necessary.

2. Remove the top sheet of parchment and, following the illustrations on page 14, use a sharp knife or pizza cutter to cut the dough into fourteen ¾-inch-wide strips. Gently twist each strip of dough and then transfer it to the prepared baking sheets, spacing the strips about 1 inch apart.

3. TO STORE: Wrap each baking sheet tightly with plastic wrap and refrigerate for up to 3 days, or transfer to the freezer for up to 1 month. (After the straws are completely frozen, about 4 hours, they can be transferred to a zipper-lock bag to save space in the freezer. Transfer back to a parchment-lined baking sheet before baking.)

4. TO SERVE: Adjust the oven racks to the upper-middle and lower-middle positions and heat the oven to 425 degrees. When the oven is ready,

INGREDIENTS: Parmesan Cheese

When it comes to grated Parmesan cheese, there's a wide range of options—everything from the whitish powder in plastic containers to imported cheese that costs up to $17 a pound. You can buy cheese that has been grated, or you can pick out a whole hunk and grate it yourself. We wondered if the "authentic" Parmigiano-Reggiano imported from Italy would be that much better when tasted side by side with a domestic Parmesan at half the price.

The samples in our tasting included five pregrated Parmesan cheeses (domestic and imported), three wedges of domestic Parmesan, a wedge of Grana Padano (an Italian grating cheese considered a Parmesan type), one of Reggianito (another Parmesan-type cheese from Argentina), and two of Parmigiano-Reggiano. All of the cheeses were tasted grated, at room temperature.

Most of the cheeses in the tasting—except the Parmigiano-Reggiano—were extremely salty. In fact, Parmigiano-Reggiano contains about two-thirds less sodium than other Parmesans. This is because the wheels of Parmigiano-Reggiano are so large that they do not become as saturated with salt during the brining process that is one of the final steps in making the cheese. (The average wheel is about 9 inches high and 16 to 18 inches in diameter and weighs 75 to 90 pounds; domestic Parmesan wheels average 24 pounds.)

One domestic Parmesan scored well enough to be recommended. This was Wisconsin-made DiGiorno. The other less expensive options paled in comparison with the real thing. The pregrated cheeses received especially low ratings and harsh comments from our panel. Most were much too salty and marred by odd off-flavors. Most everyone agreed that these poor imitations could actually ruin a dish.

THE BEST PARMESANS

Nothing compares with real Parmigiano-Reggiano (left). If you can, buy a piece freshly cut from a large wheel. Expect to spend $12 to $17 per pound. Priced at just $8 per pound, domestically made DiGiorno Parmesan (right) is surprisingly good and it is our best buy.

remove the baking sheets from the refrigerator or freezer, unwrap, and bake the straws until fully puffed and golden brown, 8 to 13 minutes, switching and rotating the trays halfway through the baking time. Let the straws cool on a wire rack for 5 minutes before serving. (The cheese straws, completely cooled, can be stored in an airtight container at room temperature for up to 2 days.)

TO SERVE RIGHT AWAY

Bake the prepared cheese straws as described in step 4.

MAKING CHEESE STRAWS

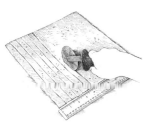

1. Using a sharp knife or pizza cutter, cut the dough into fourteen ¾-inch-wide strips.

2. Holding 1 strip of dough at each end, gently twist the dough in opposite directions and transfer it to a parchment-lined baking sheet. Repeat with the remaining dough, spacing the strips about 1 inch apart.

Marinated Black and Green Olives

MAKES ABOUT 3 CUPS

These olives are a cinch to prepare, and make a great addition to any party spread. Remember to put out a small bowl for the pits. Sambuca is a sweet, licorice-flavored Italian spirit. You can substitute ouzo, a Greek spirit with a similar taste. The chilled marinated olives can be refrigerated, wrapped tightly in plastic wrap, for up to 1 week. Remove from the refrigerator at least 30 minutes before serving.

1½	cups large, brine-cured green olives with pits
1½	cups large, brine-cured black olives with pits
3	shallots, sliced thin
2	tablespoons Sambuca (see note)
¼	cup extra-virgin olive oil
3	garlic cloves, crushed
1	teaspoon grated zest from 1 orange
1	teaspoon minced fresh thyme leaves
1	teaspoon red pepper flakes
¾	teaspoon salt
	Pinch cayenne pepper

Rinse the olives thoroughly, drain, and pat dry. Toss the olives with the remaining ingredients. Cover and refrigerate for at least 12 hours. Remove from the refrigerator at least 30 minutes before serving.

MARINATED FETA CHEESE

MARINATING FETA IN AN HERB-INFUSED OIL is a great way to boost the briny cheese's flavor, and it makes an impressive appetizer you can serve at a moment's notice. Though marinated feta can be used a number of ways (on salads, in pastas, etc.), as a party food it is best folded into a wedge of warm pita bread, while the leftover oil is perfect for dipping. But store-bought marinated feta is often overpriced and the flavors can be dull. We set out to develop a great recipe for marinated feta that could not only be made days ahead of time, but would actually benefit from the advance preparation.

We started by assembling a basic recipe that included sliced shallot, oregano, feta cheese, and olive oil. Our first task was finding the best way to infuse the oil with flavor. Basically there are two ways of doing this, the first being to toss all of the ingredients together and refrigerate. The other is a bit more complicated and requires that you slowly cook the oil over low heat with the shallot and oregano, let the mixture cool before tossing it with the feta, and then refrigerate. We found that tasters preferred feta marinated with the cooked oil. The oil had a nice round, mellow shallot flavor that complemented the fragrant oregano. Gently heating the oil was responsible for unlocking, yet tempering, the flavor of the ingredients. In contrast, the feta marinated in the uncooked oil had a pungent, raw shallot flavor and little oregano presence. It was clear that infusing the oil by heating it with the other ingredients was the way to go.

We were definitely on the right track, but we wondered if we could find a way to infuse the feta with even more flavor during marinating. Combining the feta cubes with the cooled infused

oil produced decent results, but tasters complained that the flavors of the oil and the feta remained too distinct. In other words, the cheese wasn't soaking up the flavors of the oil as much as we had hoped. A couple of test cooks recommended heating the cheese a little bit with the oil, thinking that the cheese would expand slightly when heated so that when it cooled and contracted, it would pull some of the flavorful oil inside (much like a sponge).

We tried cooking the cheese gently with the oil.

QUICK TOASTED ALMONDS

INSTEAD OF BUYING CANNED ALMONDS—WHICH ARE OFTEN TOO SALTY—FOR YOUR next party, we recommend toasting your own. It only takes about eight minutes in a skillet on the stovetop to create toasted almonds with incredibly fresh flavor. Best of all, you can season them with a variety of herbs and spices more interesting than the ubiquitous store-bought smoked variety. Bottom line: You simply can't buy almonds this good. Even better, you can make these almonds five days in advance, making them a perfect choice for a hassle-free cocktail party.

Simple Toasted Almonds
MAKES 2 CUPS

1   tablespoon extra-virgin olive oil or unsalted butter
2   cups skin-on raw whole almonds
1   teaspoon salt
¼   teaspoon ground black pepper

Heat the oil in a large nonstick skillet over medium-high heat until just shimmering. Add the almonds, salt, and pepper and, if desired, one of the flavor combinations below. Toast the almonds over medium-low heat, stirring often, until fragrant and the color deepens slightly, about 8 minutes. Transfer them to a plate lined with paper towels and allow them to cool before serving. The almonds can be stored in an airtight container for up to 5 days.

Rosemary Almonds
Add ½ teaspoon dried rosemary to the skillet with the almonds.

Warm Spiced Almonds
Use unsalted butter rather than olive oil, and add 2 tablespoons sugar, ½ teaspoon ground cinnamon, ⅛ teaspoon ground cloves, and ⅛ teaspoon ground allspice to the skillet with the almonds.

Spanish-Style Almonds
Smoked paprika is a special type of paprika with a strong smoky flavor—it can be found at specialty food import shops and in mail-order spice catalogs.
Add ¾ teaspoon smoked Spanish paprika to the skillet with the almonds.

Chinese Five-Spice Almonds
Add 1 teaspoon Chinese five-spice powder to the skillet with the almonds.

Orange-Fennel Almonds
Add 1 teaspoon grated orange zest and ½ teaspoon ground fennel seeds to the skillet with the almonds.

After the oil was adequately infused, we added the feta cubes and cooked them for a few minutes. We then let the cheese and oil sit until it came to room temperature and then refrigerated the mixture. The next day we found that this technique only worked partway. The drawback was that the cheese cubes had melted too much, forming amorphous little blobs. On the flip side, our hunch was correct, as the cheese did soak up some of the flavorful oil. We looked for an even gentler way of cooking the cheese and discovered that removing the hot oil from the heat before adding the cheese worked perfectly. The residual heat of the oil softened the cheese just enough without melting it. Covering the pot with a lid helped retain the heat long enough for this process to take place, and then as the oil and cheese cooled, the feta slowly drew in some of the infused oil.

With our basic technique determined, we now turned our attention to adding some complexity to the infused oil. In addition to the oregano and shallot, our tasters liked a bit of spicy heat from red pepper flakes and the citrusy bouquet of fresh lemon zest. We also decided to reserve a little of the oil to add after the infused oil and feta cooled. While the infused oil was spiked with great flavor, we found that after gently cooking for 18 minutes, the oil lost a bit of its own character. We found the addition of fresh oil to be a welcome flavor boost, and it really brought the flavors of the marinade together.

As for the feta itself, we found a dizzying number of cheese options at our local supermarkets and cheese shops. Depending on the feta's country of origin and the animal from which it was made, it can vary widely in taste and texture. However, we were pleased to find that we had success with artisanal varieties as well as supermarket feta.

Marinated feta holds well in the refrigerator for about one week. (Freezing it and rethawing it didn't work so well though. The cheese emerges with an odd texture.) We found that it's best to let it come up to room temperature before serving, as the oil congeals in the fridge.

Marinated Feta Cheese with Lemon and Shallot
SERVES 8 TO 10

Both supermarket and higher-quality imported feta work well here. Even after the feta has been eaten, the remaining flavorful oil is great for dipping with bread. Serve with wedges of warm pita bread or slices of baguette.

1¼	cups extra-virgin olive oil
1	medium shallot, halved and sliced thin
1	tablespoon minced fresh oregano leaves
1	teaspoon grated zest from 1 lemon
¼	teaspoon red pepper flakes
8	ounces feta cheese, cut into ½-inch cubes (about 2 cups)

1. Cook 1 cup of the oil, shallot, oregano, lemon zest, and pepper flakes in a small saucepan over low heat until the shallots are softened, about 18 minutes. Remove the saucepan from the heat and stir in the feta. Cover and let sit until the mixture reaches room temperature, about 1½ hours. Stir in the remaining ¼ cup oil.

2. TO STORE: Transfer the mixture to an airtight container and refrigerate for up to 1 week.

3. TO SERVE: Let the mixture sit at room temperature until the oil liquefies, about 1 hour, before serving.

TO SERVE RIGHT AWAY
Serve after adding the remaining oil at the end of step 1.

Marinated Feta Cheese with Orange, Green Olives, and Garlic

Use high-quality brine-cured green olives here.

Follow the recipe for Marinated Feta Cheese with Lemon and Shallot, substituting 1 teaspoon grated orange zest for the lemon zest, and 2 garlic cloves, sliced, for the shallot. Stir ½ cup coarsely chopped pitted green olives (about 4 ounces) into the oil with the feta.

CHICKEN LIVER PÂTÉ

A RELATIVELY SIMPLE PUREE OF CHICKEN livers, butter, and aromatics, great chicken liver pâté has a smooth, mellow flavor and a fine texture that melts to a creamy consistency as you eat it. Unfortunately, bad renditions of this dish are all too common, with a potent offal flavor that permeates every bite—not to mention a dry, chalky texture. We knew this recipe had great make-ahead potential, as it actually benefits from some time in the refrigerator, which gives the flavors a chance to meld. Our goal was to develop a foolproof recipe for this classic appetizer.

To start, we found it necessary to buy the freshest chicken livers we could find and to trim them well of fat and connective tissue. Old, untrimmed livers produced a spread that was overbearingly metallic tasting, with stringy, fibrous bits. Although most recipes we researched employed similar cooking techniques, we found a few small tricks that made all the difference between good and bad liver puree. First, most recipes cook the livers through until they are no longer pink in the middle (15 to 20 minutes). However, we found that a shorter cooking time—about 6 minutes—leaves them with a rosy interior and produces a much better spread. When liver is overcooked, the texture turns chalky and mealy and the delicate nuances of its flavor are lost. But when cooked quickly, the liver retains its soft, creamy texture and a clean, mellow flavor that blends easily with other ingredients.

Another problem we found with a number of recipes is that they call for a laundry list of ingredients to flavor the pâté. After testing some of these recipes, tasters agreed that the resulting pâtés had a muddied character that squelched the chicken livers' subtle, mellow flavor. Therefore, "simple is best" became our guiding principle. To round out the flavor of the liver mixture, tasters liked a simple combination of shallots and fresh thyme. Shallots were preferred for their gentle, sweet allium flavor, which didn't overwhelm the liver puree. (Onion didn't do much for tasters and garlic hogged the spotlight with its assertive flavor.) Tasters found rosemary too strong and piney, and although sage proved promising at first, tasters eventually decided that the herb's flavor was a bit medicinal tasting. Fresh thyme—found in most every recipe we researched—was a perfect match with the other flavors in the pâté.

Because of the livers' short cooking time, we knew the shallots would need a head start. We started by sautéing the shallots and thyme in butter, then added the livers for a quick sear. We then added wine—vermouth being our favorite choice for its complex flavor—and allowed the livers to finish cooking at a gentle simmer as the liquid reduced to a light syrup. Transferring the mixture straight from the sauté pan to the food processor, we quickly transformed it into a smooth puree. At this point we seasoned the pâté with salt, pepper, and a bit of brandy, which served to heighten and unify the pâté's flavors. The pâté was then transferred to a bowl, covered with plastic wrap, and refrigerated until set.

As for storing the pâté once set, we discovered that freezing was out of the question. The pâté wept when thawed and the texture was slightly grainy. When we tried to refrigerate it, we discovered that the top layer of the pâté turned an unsightly greenish-gray color and developed a slight metallic flavor (which some tasters didn't mind). Traditionally, this style of pâté is capped with clarified butter to guard against oxidation, a step we didn't think necessary. Instead, we found that simply pressing plastic wrap against the surface of the pâté worked to minimize oxidation—though not entirely eliminate it. Therefore, when we were ready to serve our pâté, we simple scraped away the discolored top layer.

Chicken Liver Pâté

MAKES ABOUT 2 CUPS

Pressing plastic wrap against the surface of the pâté helps minimize any discoloration due to oxidation. Serve with toasted slices of baguette, toast points, or crackers.

8	tablespoons (1 stick) unsalted butter
3	medium shallots, sliced (about 1 cup)
1	tablespoon minced fresh thyme leaves
	Salt
1	pound chicken livers, rinsed and patted dry, fat and connective tissue removed
¾	cup dry vermouth
2	teaspoons brandy
	Ground black pepper

1. Melt the butter in a 12-inch skillet over medium-high heat until the foaming subsides. Add the shallots, thyme, and ¼ teaspoon salt and cook until the shallots are lightly browned, 3 to 5 minutes. Add the chicken livers and cook, stirring constantly, about 1 minute. Add the vermouth and simmer until the livers are cooked but still have a rosy interior, 4 to 6 minutes more.

2. Using a slotted spoon, remove the livers from the pan and transfer them to a food processor. Continue to simmer the vermouth mixture over medium-high heat until it is slightly syrupy, about 2 minutes longer, then add to the processor.

3. Add the brandy to the processor, and process the mixture until very smooth, about 2 minutes, stopping to scrape down the sides of the bowl with a rubber spatula as needed. Season the pâté with salt and pepper to taste. Transfer to a clean serving bowl and smooth the top.

4. TO STORE: Lay plastic wrap flush to the surface of the pâté and refrigerate until firm, about 6 hours or up to 3 days.

5. TO SERVE: Let the pâté sit at room temperature until slightly softened, about 30 minutes. Scrape off the discolored top ¼ inch of the pâté, if desired, before serving.

TO SERVE RIGHT AWAY

Refrigerate the pâté until firm, about 6 hours. Bring to room temperature before serving.

POTTED SHRIMP

A COMMON WAY TO PRESERVE SHRIMP IN Great Britain and Northern Europe, potted shrimp are whole peeled shrimp that have been cooked and stored in a large amount of butter (the mixture is usually packed into ceramic crocks, or "pots"). The preparation uses little in the way of seasoning and, when stored this way, the shrimp retain their quality and flavor for a number of days—a natural make-ahead dish. The shrimp are then extracted from the butter and sometimes used in pastas and sautés, though more traditionally they are eaten on a warm piece of toast.

The American version of potted shrimp yields a chunky (or smooth) butter-based spread used to slather on crackers or toasted slices of baguette. Typically, in the American version, chopped cooked shrimp is mixed with any number of seasonings and melted butter—though far less butter than the European preparation, which calls for equal parts butter and shrimp! Some recipes call for coarsely chopping the shrimp, while others use a food processor to pulverize the cooked shrimp and butter into a paste.

For some of us here in the test kitchen, potted shrimp was commonplace on our family tables around the holiday season. Easily made a couple of days in advance, potted shrimp is an elegant spread that can miss the mark if not prepared correctly. Bad versions can be dry (not enough butter), underseasoned, and lacking good shrimp flavor. We wanted a spread that balanced the subtle sweetness of shrimp with the dairy richness of butter.

First we needed to decide on a texture for our potted shrimp. Should it be chunky or smooth? Gathering some recipes from our library that reflected both styles, we headed into the kitchen to find the answer. One called for lightly sautéing a pound of peeled shrimp with some aromatics in a little bit of butter. The shrimp were then cooled enough to handle, chopped coarsely, placed in a dish, mixed with melted butter to cover, and refrigerated until set. Another sautéed the shrimp in a similar way, but then transferred the hot shrimp to a food processor. Then, with the food processor running, chunks of butter were added. The butter, slowly melted by the hot shrimp in the food

SHRIMP COCKTAIL

SHRIMP COCKTAIL IS ONE OF THE EASIEST RECIPES TO MAKE AHEAD OF TIME AND CAN be prepared two days in advance. Nonetheless, we're amazed how often those rubbery precooked shrimp from the supermarket freezer section show up at parties. For cocktail shrimp with perfect texture and great flavor, try our classic recipe below. Each of the sauces below makes enough for 1 pound extra-large shrimp.

Best Shrimp Cocktail
SERVES 6 TO 8

Serve these shrimp with one of the sauces below. They also go well with Creamy Chipotle Sauce (page 23).

2	teaspoons juice from 1 lemon
2	bay leaves
1	teaspoon salt
1	teaspoon black peppercorns
1	teaspoon Old Bay Seasoning
1	pound extra-large shrimp (21 to 25 per pound), peeled and deveined

1. Bring the lemon juice, bay leaves, salt, peppercorns, Old Bay, and 4 cups water to a boil in a medium saucepan for 2 minutes. Remove the pot from the heat and add the shrimp. Cover and steep off the heat until the shrimp are firm and pink, about 7 minutes. Drain the shrimp and plunge them immediately into ice water. Discard the bay leaves and peppercorns.

2. To STORE: Drain the shrimp and transfer them to a medium bowl. Wrap the bowl tightly with plastic wrap and refrigerate for up to 2 days.

3. To SERVE: Arrange the shrimp on a cold platter with a sauce for dipping.

TO SERVE RIGHT AWAY
Refrigerate the shrimp for at least 1 hour, until they are thoroughly chilled.

Classic Cocktail Sauce

1	cup ketchup
2	tablespoons juice from 1 lemon
2½	teaspoons prepared horseradish
2	teaspoons hot sauce
½	teaspoon salt
¼	teaspoon ground black pepper

Combine all of the ingredients in a small serving bowl. Season with extra horseradish, hot sauce, salt, and pepper to taste. Cover and refrigerate the sauce to blend the flavors, at least 30 minutes and up to 3 days.

Spicy Caribbean Dipping Sauce

¼	cup juice from 4 limes
¼	cup packed light brown sugar
2	scallions, minced
1	large jalapeño chile, seeds and ribs removed, chile minced
1½	tablespoons minced or grated fresh ginger
¼	teaspoon garlic powder
	Salt and ground black pepper

Combine the lime juice, sugar, scallions, chile, ginger, and garlic powder in a small serving bowl and season the sauce with salt and pepper to taste. Cover and refrigerate the sauce to blend the flavors, at least 30 minutes and up to 2 days.

Soy-Ginger Dipping Sauce

¼	cup soy sauce
¼	cup honey
2	tablespoons rice vinegar
1	tablespoon minced fresh cilantro leaves
1	teaspoon minced or grated fresh ginger
½	teaspoon toasted sesame oil
¼	teaspoon garlic powder
⅛	teaspoon red pepper flakes

Combine all of the ingredients in a small serving bowl. Cover and refrigerate the sauce to blend the flavors, at least 30 minutes and up to 2 days.

processor, whipped together with the shrimp to form an emulsified paste.

We tasted these recipes side by side and learned that tasters preferred the smooth version. They admired its texture, describing the paste as velvety and creamy with good shrimp flavor in every bite. The chunky recipe just wasn't cohesive enough. The butter and shrimp flavors seemed too discrete, and the spread didn't hold well on a cracker—one bite, and small pieces of shrimp crumbled everywhere.

With the texture of our potted shrimp decided, we now turned our attention to determining the best way to cook the shrimp. We already knew that the way shrimp is cooked has a great effect on flavor, and we wondered how this would impact our spread. Although there are numerous ways to cook shrimp, we focused on two of the most common methods: poaching and sautéing. We made two versions of our spread, one with shrimp that were poached in a court-bouillon (a flavorful broth made from water, herbs, and spices), and another made with shrimp that were pan-seared over high heat in a small amount of oil. The flavor difference in the two spreads was dramatic, and the clear winner was the one made with pan-seared shrimp. While the poached shrimp had a subtle, delicate (some might even say bland) flavor, the pan-seared shrimp was just the opposite. The high-heat sauté added some great caramelization to the shrimp, which intensified their flavor and sweetness and added a welcome complexity to the finished spread. (Tossing the shrimp with a tiny amount of sugar before sautéing them further aided the caramelization process.)

Our potted shrimp recipe was developing nicely; however, we still wanted to fine-tune the texture. Up until this point, we had been using one stick of butter for 1 pound of shrimp. Tasters however, requested that the texture of the spread be even creamier. We tried adding a few tablespoons of cream cheese to one version and heavy cream to another. Neither of these was the solution, as the cream cheese dulled the shrimp flavor and heavy cream made the texture too loose. We found that simply adding a few extra tablespoons of butter

was the answer. The extra butter made the spread creamier, without overwhelming the shrimp's delicate flavor.

As far as flavoring our spread, we wanted to keep things simple, using the *fond* (the tasty browned bits left in the pan after sautéing the shrimp) as a starting point. The mellow sweetness of shallot was a nice addition to our spread, more so than the overpowering flavors of either garlic or onion. After transferring the cooked shrimp to the food processor, we sautéed the shallot in the shrimp fond. Once the shallot was soft, we deglazed the pan with a mixture of sherry and fresh lemon juice (two natural pairings with shrimp). We then reduced the mixture a bit to concentrate the flavors and added it to the food processor with the shrimp. Adding an extra dose of lemon juice and sherry before whipping the butter added welcome bright notes.

Potted shrimp will keep, refrigerated, for up to three days. Also, it's best to let the spread sit on the counter for half an hour or so before serving. Letting it sit at room temperature makes it softer and easier to spread. As far as freezing potted shrimp is concerned, we don't recommend it. After freezing a couple of batches, we found that they just didn't thaw correctly. The shrimp flavor turned a bit fishy and the texture of the spread was unappetizingly wet and grainy.

~

Potted Shrimp

MAKES ABOUT 2¼ CUPS

Make sure to remove the tail shells from the shrimp before cooking. Serve this spread with toasted slices of baguette or toast points. The potted shrimp can also be used as a compound butter to add flavor to cooked fish, chicken, or even pasta.

1	pound extra-large shrimp (21 to 25 per pound), peeled and deveined
	Salt and ground black pepper
⅛	teaspoon sugar
2	tablespoons vegetable oil
12	tablespoons (1½ sticks) unsalted butter, cut into 12 pieces

1 medium shallot, minced (about 3 tablespoons)
¼ cup plus 1 teaspoon dry sherry
2 tablespoons plus ½ teaspoon juice from
   1 lemon
   Pinch cayenne pepper

1. Pat the shrimp dry with paper towels, then toss with ¼ teaspoon salt, ¼ teaspoon pepper, and the sugar. Heat 1 tablespoon of the oil in a 12-inch skillet over high heat until just smoking. Add half of the shrimp, quickly distribute them into a single layer, and cook without moving for 1 minute. Stir the shrimp and continue to cook until they are slightly curled and cooked through, about 1 minute longer. Transfer the shrimp to a medium bowl. Return the skillet to high heat and repeat with the remaining 1 tablespoon oil and remaining shrimp; transfer to the bowl.

2. Add 1 tablespoon of the butter to the skillet and melt over medium-high heat until the foaming subsides. Add the shallot and cook until softened about 2 minutes. Stir in ¼ cup of the sherry, 2 tablespoons of the lemon juice, and the cayenne and cook until the mixture is slightly syrupy, about 2 minutes.

3. Process the shrimp with any accumulated juice, the sherry mixture, the remaining 1 teaspoon sherry, and the remaining ½ teaspoon lemon juice in a food processor until the mixture is finely chopped, about 6 pulses.

4. With the food processor running, add the remaining butter 1 piece at a time, and continue to process until the mixture is smooth, about 2 minutes, stopping to scrape down the sides of the bowl as needed. Season the mixture with salt and pepper to taste. Transfer it to a clean bowl and smooth the top.

5. To STORE: Lay plastic wrap flush to the surface of the shrimp and refrigerate for up to 3 days.

6. To SERVE: Let the potted shrimp sit at room temperature until slightly softened, about 30 minutes, before serving.

TO SERVE RIGHT AWAY

Refrigerate the potted shrimp until firm, about 6 hours. Bring to room temperature before serving.

COCKTAIL CRAB CAKES

GOOD CRAB CAKES ARE ALWAYS ONE OF the first appetizers to disappear at a party. But pan-frying bite-sized crab cakes for a house full of guests is an ambitious undertaking. Not only does the technique require a semipermanent stay in front of the stove during the party, it's just plain messy. We wanted to develop a simple technique for making cocktail party–sized crab cakes. More importantly, we wanted to find a way to prepare the crab cakes ahead of time, so that the cakes need only be cooked or reheated before guests arrived.

To begin, we reviewed our basic method for making regular-sized crab cakes. Fresh crabmeat is gently mixed with a dry binder (such as bread crumbs), a wet binder (typically egg), and seasonings. The cakes are formed and then chilled to allow the binders a chance to stiffen a bit, which helps hold the cakes together during cooking. Once chilled, the cakes are dusted with flour and fried until golden brown.

From the start we knew that the key to great crab cakes was top-quality crabmeat. We tested all the various options and found that fresh blue crabmeat, preferably "jumbo lump"—which indicates the largest pieces and highest grade, was best. (We also agreed that fresh pasteurized crabmeat works well in a pinch.) As for the best dry binder, we discovered that crushed saltines worked great. The crushed-up crackers added more flavor than other binders and—unlike bread crumbs—didn't make our crab cakes pasty. We also found that a little goes a long way; though some recipes call for up to ¾ cup of dry binder, we found that about ⅓ cup was all we needed for our recipe.

Mayonnaise keeps the crabmeat moist, while egg helps the crab, cracker crumbs, and seasonings meld together both before and during cooking. For seasonings, we found that simple was best. Old Bay Seasoning (a traditional pairing with crab) and finely minced scallion tops were great complements to the sweet complexity of the crabmeat. Divvying up the mixture into 1-tablespoon portions gave us perfect cocktail-sized crab cakes, 1½ inches in diameter and ½ inch thick. With this size, our recipe easily yielded 36 mini cakes.

Our biggest challenge came next. How were we going to make these cakes in advance? The answer seemed to be to fry the cakes ahead of time, store them, and then reheat them in the oven. Even though we knew frying so many crab cakes would be a hassle, we reasoned that it would be worth the effort if all we had to do was recrisp them in the oven just before serving.

After forming and chilling a batch of crab cakes, we dusted them with flour and pan-fried them. When the cakes were just cooked through, we transferred them to a baking sheet lined with parchment, wrapped the baking sheet tightly with plastic wrap, and refrigerated the crab cakes overnight. The next day, we popped the tray of crab cakes into the oven. The results were dismal and frankly a waste of great (read: expensive) crabmeat. Tasters complained that the cakes were soggy and greasy with a chewy exterior—the dusting of flour had lost its crispness and turned into a tough skin.

Frustrated, we tried the same make-ahead method again, but this time we coated the crab cakes with fine bread crumbs instead of flour. Frying the cakes in advance was a time-consuming

task, but at least this time it paid off—the bread crumbs were a success. After a brief stint in a very hot oven (500 degrees), our cocktail-party crab cakes emerged golden brown with a crisp exterior. A step in the right direction to be sure, however there were still some complaints that the cakes were a tad greasy. Also, we were not completely sold on the idea of having to do all the messy frying for this recipe. We sought alternative methods and came up with oven-frying, a technique we've had success with for other recipes in the test kitchen.

To oven-fry food—whether it be chicken, eggplant, or in this case crab cakes—you coat the food with lightly toasted bread crumbs, which have been tossed with a generous amount of oil. The coated item is then placed on a rack over a baking sheet, and into the oven it goes. The rack promotes even browning of the oil-coated crumbs, which emerge from the oven with a crispy "fried" texture.

We discovered that this technique worked beautifully for our crab cakes. These oven-fried cakes came together in no time and were just as crisp and flavorful as the time-consuming pan-fried ones. We could form and coat our cakes with the crumbs the night before (they're best made up to 24 hours ahead of time), and refrigerate them on the rack so that the next day all we had to do was remove the baking sheet from the fridge, slide them into the oven, and bake. We also were surprised and pleased to discover that these crab cakes freeze well and will hold for up to one month.

TEST KITCHEN TIP:

Speedy Saucing

Dolloping small amounts of sauce or cheese spread onto (or into) small appetizers can be a time-consuming process. We found that using a homemade pastry bag fashioned out of a sturdy, zipper-lock bag makes the task easier and faster, and ensures that you can sauce and serve a hot appetizer, such as Cocktail Crab Cakes (right) or Crispy Polenta Triangles (page 31), before they cool off.

Spoon the mixture into a zipper-lock bag. Snip a small piece from one bottom corner of the bag, then gently squeeze the filling through the hole onto (or into) the appetizers.

FREEZE IT

Cocktail Crab Cakes

MAKES 36 MINI CAKES

If the baked bread crumbs turn a bit clumpy in the oven, let them cool then rub them between your hands to make them finer. If you can't find jumbo lump crabmeat, you can use fresh pasteurized. Frozen and refrigerated cakes will bake in roughly the same amount of time. Serve these cakes with just a squeeze of fresh lemon juice or try them with our Creamy Chipotle Sauce (page 23) or Tartar Sauce (page 23).

4 slices high-quality white sandwich bread, quartered

3 tablespoons vegetable oil

Salt and ground black pepper
1 pound jumbo lump crabmeat, picked over to remove cartilage or shells (see note)
4 saltines, crushed (about 6 tablespoons)
4 scallions, green parts only, minced
1½ teaspoons Old Bay Seasoning
Pinch cayenne pepper
6 tablespoons mayonnaise
1 large egg, lightly beaten
1 lemon, cut into wedges (for serving)

1. Adjust an oven rack to the lower-middle position and heat the oven to 300 degrees. Pulse 2 slices of the bread in a food processor to coarse crumbs, about 6 pulses; transfer the crumbs to a large bowl. Repeat with the remaining bread and transfer to the bowl (you should have about 3½ cups crumbs). Toss the crumbs with the oil, ⅛ teaspoon salt, and ⅛ teaspoon pepper. Spread the crumbs on a rimmed baking sheet and bake, stirring occasionally, until lightly browned and dry, about 20 minutes. Let the crumbs cool to room temperature, then transfer to a shallow dish; set aside.

2. Gently toss the crab, 4 tablespoons of the cracker crumbs, scallions, Old Bay, and cayenne together in a large bowl. Gently fold in the mayonnaise using a rubber spatula. Season the crab mixture with salt and pepper to taste. Gently fold in the egg. If necessary, add the remaining 2 tablespoons cracker crumbs as needed until the mixture just clings together.

3. Line a baking sheet with parchment paper; set aside. Using a tablespoon measure, portion and form the crab mixture into 36 tablespoon-sized cakes roughly 1½ inches in diameter and ½ inch thick. Place the cakes on the prepared baking sheet, cover with plastic wrap, and refrigerate for at least 30 minutes.

4. Line another rimmed baking sheet with foil, place a wire rack on top, and spray the rack with vegetable oil spray. When the crab cakes are chilled, coat them completely with the toasted bread crumbs, pressing gently on the crumbs to adhere. Lay the breaded crab cakes on the prepared wire rack.

5. To store: Cover the crab cakes tightly with plastic wrap and refrigerate for up to 24 hours, or freeze for up to 1 month. (After the cakes are completely frozen, about 4 hours, they can be transferred to a zipper-lock bag to save space in the freezer. Transfer back to a greased wire rack on a lined baking sheet before baking.)

6. To serve: Adjust an oven rack to the middle position and heat the oven to 500 degrees. Unwrap the crab cakes and bake until the crumbs are golden brown and the cakes are firm, 12 to 15 minutes. Following the illustration on page 22, pipe a small amount of sauce over each cake before serving, or serve with lemon wedges.

TO SERVE RIGHT AWAY
Bake the breaded crab cakes as directed in step 6.

Creamy Chipotle Sauce
MAKES ABOUT 1 CUP

½ cup mayonnaise
½ cup sour cream
2 tablespoons minced fresh cilantro leaves
2–3 teaspoons minced chipotle chile in adobo sauce
2 teaspoons juice from 1 lime
1 medium garlic clove, minced or pressed through a garlic press (about 1 teaspoon)
Salt and ground black pepper

Combine the mayonnaise, sour cream, cilantro, chipotle, lime juice, and garlic in a small bowl and season with salt and pepper to taste. Cover and refrigerate the sauce to blend the flavors, at least 30 minutes or up to 2 days.

Tartar Sauce
MAKES ABOUT 1 CUP
If cornichons are not available, substitute 2 tablespoons minced dill pickles.

¾ cup mayonnaise
3 large cornichons, chopped fine, plus 1 teaspoon cornichon juice
1 tablespoon minced scallion
1 tablespoon minced red onion
1 tablespoon rinsed capers, minced
Salt and ground black pepper

Combine the mayonnaise, cornichons and juice, scallion, onion, and capers in a small bowl and season with salt and pepper to taste. Cover and refrigerate the sauce to blend the flavors, at least 30 minutes or up to 4 days.

EMPANADAS

WHEN DECIDING ON RECIPES FOR THIS chapter, we were drawn to empanadas for their inherent make-ahead quality. Prevalent throughout Latin America and Spain, empanadas are filled pastries similar to turnovers. (The word "empanada" actually comes from the Spanish verb *empanar*, which translates as "to bake in pastry.") Because the dough can be made, rolled, cut, and filled in advance, we figured we could assemble these pastries, store them, and bake them when ready. The advantage of having all the prep work done ahead of time was alluring—but first we needed a great recipe.

A selection of cookbooks—including some from Chile, Mexico, Argentina, Spain, and Colombia—yielded a dizzying amount of empanada recipes. And although the dough recipes were all pretty similar, the filling variations were endless. Depending on the country of origin or the preferences of the person making them, savory empanadas might contain seafood, beef, chicken, cheese, or vegetables, while a sweet version might be filled with sweet potatoes or fruit. We decided to focus our attention first on the dough and then we would narrow down our filling choices.

To make empanadas, lard or vegetable shortening (such as Crisco) is typically warmed until liquid and then mixed with flour (and sometimes water) to form a dough. This method for adding fat to flour was unfamiliar to us, so we were curious about the results. Tasters complained that the dough made their fingers greasy, which was a surprise, considering the ratio of fat to flour was an average of 1 to 3—moderate for pastry dough. There were also complaints that the pastry was bland and tough. We knew we would have to try a different approach.

We found great results using a classic pie dough preparation, which cuts cold fat into the flour.

MAKING EMPANADAS

1. Place about 1 teaspoon of the filling in the center of each dough round and moisten the edge of the dough round with water, using either your finger or a pastry brush.

2. Fold the dough in half over the filling, making a half-moon shape.

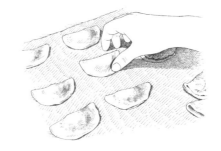

3. Pinch the seam along the edge to secure.

4. Using a dinner fork, crimp the sealed edge to secure.

The mixture is then combined with ice water by hand until a dough forms. This method produces a pastry that bakes up with tender flakiness. And because it requires butter (which is responsible for the flakiness), we now also had a pastry with more flavor. But we proceeded cautiously. We didn't want the richness of the pastry to steal the show; instead, it should accentuate and complement the filling. With this in mind we tested a number of different fat to flour ratios and found that 1 to 3 gave us the balance we wanted. Our pastry was now tender with a touch of flaky richness (and more flavor) that wouldn't overwhelm the filling.

As we discovered early on in our research, there are many styles of fillings for empanadas—and many of them call for hard-to-find Latin American ingredients. Wanting to make our empanada recipe accessible to the American home cook, we decided to keep things simple with a basic beef and cheese filling. Most recipes we found for beef empanadas called for ground beef. Rounding up as many types of ground beef as we could find in our local markets, we made batches of empanadas using ground round, chuck, and sirloin with varying degrees of leanness. Ground round was dry with an off, livery flavor, and tasters were not impressed with the dull flavor of the sirloin. In the end, we agreed that 85 percent lean ground chuck had the best beef flavor and moisture content.

We started by sautéing aromatics (minced onion and garlic), then adding the beef and cooking it until well done. We then cooled the mixture and folded in shredded cheese. According to our research, the ideal beef empanada filling is wet and the crumbled meat should be enveloped in a thick sauce. Ours was moist but still a bit on the crumbly side. We found we could achieve the ideal saucy texture by adding a modest amount of low-sodium beef broth (¾ cup) after cooking the beef partway. The broth simmered with the beef mixture and reduced to a consistency that was moist, but not runny.

With the basics in place, we now focused our attention on boosting the filling's flavor. One tablespoon of tomato paste did much to heighten the beefiness of the filling, while fresh oregano added a nice layer of complexity. For spices, tasters approved of a combination of cumin, clove, and cayenne. And a small amount of sugar added a good balance of sweetness to the savory filling. Finally, tasters decided that a neutral melting cheese, such as Monterey Jack, was best. We also decided to create a variation using ground turkey, raisins, and olives.

As we suspected, these empanadas can be prepared ahead of time with great results. You can make and hold these meat-filled pastries three days in advance if you're refrigerating them, and they keep beautifully in the freezer for up to a month. When they're ready to go into the oven, we prefer to brush them with a little egg wash. The egg gives the baked pastry a great shine and golden brown color—an attractive invitation for your guests to dig in.

FREEZE IT

Mini Empanadas
MAKES 48 EMPANADAS

If your kitchen is very warm, refrigerate all of the dough ingredients for 30 minutes before making the dough. If the dough ever becomes too soft and/or sticky to work with, simply return it to the refrigerator until firm; a dough scraper also comes in handy here. There should be plenty of dough to cut out and make 48 empanadas without having to reroll any dough scraps; we found the rerolled scraps of dough to be very tough.

3¾ cups (18¾ ounces) unbleached all-purpose flour, plus more for dusting the work surface

1 tablespoon sugar

1½ teaspoons salt

12 tablespoons (1½ sticks) unsalted butter, cut into ½-inch cubes and frozen for 10 minutes

1¼ cups ice water

1 recipe Empanada Filling (pages 26–27), chilled

1 large egg, beaten

1. Process the flour, sugar, and salt together in a food processor until combined, about 6 seconds. Scatter the butter pieces over the flour mixture and pulse until the mixture resembles coarse crumbs with butter bits no larger than small peas, about 16 pulses.

2. Transfer the flour mixture to a large mixing bowl. Working with ¼ cup of water at a time, sprinkle the water over the flour mixture and stir it in using a rubber spatula, pressing the mixture against the side of the bowl to form a dough, until no small bits of flour remain (you may not need to use all of the water).

3. Turn the dough out onto a clean work surface and divide it into 2 equal pieces. Press each dough half into a cohesive ball, then flatten the ball into a 6-inch disk. Wrap each disk in plastic and refrigerate until firm but not hard, about 2 hours or up to 2 days.

4. Line 2 baking sheets with parchment paper; set aside. Remove 1 disk of dough from the refrigerator (if refrigerated for longer than 2 hours, let sit at room temperature until malleable). Roll the dough out on a lightly floured work surface into an 18-inch circle about ⅛ inch thick. Using a 3-inch round biscuit cutter, cut out 24 rounds and transfer them to the prepared baking sheet, discarding the dough scraps; wrap the baking sheet with plastic wrap and refrigerate. Repeat with the second disk of dough and the second prepared baking sheet.

5. Working with the first batch of dough rounds, follow the illustrations on page 24 to fill, seal, and shape the empanadas using roughly 1 teaspoon of the chilled filling per empanada. Crimp the edges of the empanadas using a fork, and arrange them on a fresh, parchment-lined baking sheet. Wrap the baking sheet tightly with plastic wrap and refrigerate while making a second batch of empanadas using the remaining dough rounds and filling.

6. To store: Make sure each baking sheet is covered tightly with plastic wrap and refrigerate for up to 3 days, or freeze for up to 1 month. (After the empanadas are completely frozen, about 8 hours, they can be transferred to a zipper-lock bag to save space in the freezer. Transfer back to parchment-lined baking sheets before baking.)

7. To serve: Adjust 2 oven racks to the upper-middle and lower-middle positions and heat the oven to 425 degrees. Unwrap the empanadas and brush with the egg. Bake until golden brown, about 25 minutes, switching and rotating the trays

halfway through the baking time. Let cool for 5 minutes before serving.

TO SERVE RIGHT AWAY

Bake the empanadas as directed in step 7, reducing the baking time to about 20 minutes.

Beef and Cheese Empanada Filling

ENOUGH FOR ABOUT 48 MINI EMPANADAS

The filling can be made while the empanada dough rests in the refrigerator.

l	tablespoon olive oil
l	medium onion, minced
l	tablespoon tomato paste
2	medium garlic cloves, minced or pressed through a garlic press (about 2 teaspoons)
l	teaspoon minced fresh oregano leaves, or ¼ teaspoon dried
l	teaspoon ground cumin
	Pinch ground cloves
	Pinch cayenne pepper
½	pound (85 percent lean) ground chuck
¾	cup low-sodium beef broth
l	teaspoon sugar
	Salt and ground black pepper
2	ounces Monterey Jack cheese, shredded (about ½ cup)

1. Heat the oil in a 12-inch nonstick skillet over medium-high heat until just shimmering. Add the onion and cook until softened, 5 to 7 minutes. Stir in the tomato paste, garlic, oregano, cumin, cloves, and cayenne and cook until fragrant, about 30 seconds. Stir in the beef and cook, breaking up the clumps with a wooden spoon, until no longer pink, about 4 minutes.

2. Stir in the broth, reduce the heat to low, and simmer until the mixture is moist but not wet, about 8 minutes. Off the heat, stir in the sugar and season with salt and pepper to taste. Transfer the mixture to a medium bowl, cover with plastic wrap, and refrigerate until completely cool, about 1 hour. Stir in the cheese and continue to chill until needed, up to 3 days.

Turkey Empanada Filling with Raisins and Olives

ENOUGH FOR ABOUT 48 MINI EMPANADAS

The filling can be made while the empanada dough rests in the refrigerator. Ground pork or 85 percent lean ground beef can be substituted for the turkey.

1	tablespoon olive oil
1	medium onion, minced
1	tablespoon tomato paste
2	medium garlic cloves, minced or pressed through a garlic press (about 2 teaspoons)
2	teaspoons paprika
1	teaspoon minced fresh thyme leaves, or ¼ teaspoon dried
	Ground white pepper
½	pound (93 percent lean) ground turkey
¾	cup low-sodium beef broth
⅓	cup raisins, chopped
⅓	cup pitted brine-cured green olives, chopped
1	teaspoon sugar
	Salt

1. Heat the oil in a 12-inch nonstick skillet over medium-high heat until just shimmering. Add the onion and cook until softened, 5 to 7 minutes. Stir in the tomato paste, garlic, paprika, thyme, and ⅛ teaspoon pepper. Cook until fragrant, about 30 seconds. Stir in the turkey and cook, breaking up the clumps with a wooden spoon, until no longer pink, about 4 minutes.

2. Stir in the broth and raisins, reduce the heat to low, and simmer until the mixture is moist but not wet, about 8 minutes. Off the heat, stir in the olives and sugar and season with salt and pepper to taste. Transfer the mixture to a medium bowl, cover with plastic wrap, and refrigerate until completely cool, about 1 hour or up to 3 days.

BAKED STUFFED MUSHROOMS

SMALL ENOUGH TO EAT IN ONE BITE, STUFFED mushrooms are a welcome addition to any cocktail party. But the amount of work required to make them is often a drawback—who wants to spend all that time right before a party assembling and stuffing individual mushroom caps? That's why stuffed mushrooms seemed like a natural make-ahead choice to us: Stuff the mushrooms a day or so ahead of time and then simply bake them for a few minutes just before serving.

We already knew from previous tests that the mushrooms caps would need to be roasted. Roasting the caps prior to stuffing and baking allowed them to release their moisture and prevented the assembled hors d'ouevres from becoming soggy. By roasting the mushroom caps gill side down first, we were able to drain much of their natural moisture before flipping them over and roasting the other side. As a bonus, roasting intensified the earthy mushroom flavor.

Our main focus, then, would be on the filling: What type of filling would hold up best when prepared in advance? In our research, we came across a variety of fillings, but essentially they all fell into one of three categories. Bread-crumb fillings (made with either fresh or dried crumbs) are typically seasoned with herbs and Parmesan; mushroom fillings are based on a classic French duxelles (a cooked mixture of finely chopped mushrooms and shallots seasoned with herbs); and cheese fillings use soft, creamy cheese such as goat cheese or cream cheese. We tested all three types using a simple procedure: Roast the mushroom caps, fill them, refrigerate overnight, and then bake them the next day.

Overall, we found that each type of stuffing had good flavor, but only the cheese filling held up overnight and baked up well. The filling was simple—just softened cheese flavored with some fresh herbs and a little salt and pepper. Even better, it was quick to throw together (the other filling styles required a lot of preparation) and easy to work with. Best of all, the warm, soft cheese was a real crowd pleaser when paired with the roasted, earthy mushroom caps. By contrast, the bread-crumb filling baked up into an unappealing dense plug of stuffing, while tasters were even more turned off by the mushroom filling—which looked unattractive and oozed with each bite.

With a style of filling decided on, we now focused on the specifics. We tested different types of soft, creamy cheeses such as mascarpone, ricotta, cream cheese, and goat cheese. Tasters felt strongly that the rich, tangy character of the goat cheese was a perfect match with the roasted mushroom caps. However, some tasters felt that the tartness of the goat cheese was a tad overpowering, so we added a small amount of extra-virgin olive oil to mellow its tartness. Tasters liked the simplicity of this filling's flavors, so we decided the only other ingredient it needed was an herb that accentuated the goat cheese–mushroom pairing, and fresh thyme was a perfect match.

With the filling agreed upon, we decided to add a crumb topping, as tasters wanted a textural contrast to the soft bite of the mushroom cap and creamy stuffing. We tried topping the stuffed caps with a fresh bread-crumb mixture (with olive oil and garlic for flavor) before they entered the oven. The results were poor. The mushrooms were done heating through before the crumbs had a chance to brown, leaving a mess of soft, pale crumbs. But toasting the bread crumbs prior to topping the mushrooms worked perfectly, giving our stuffed caps some much-needed crunch.

One last question remained: Should we hold the crumbs separately from the stuffed mushroom caps to prevent the crumbs from becoming soggy overnight? We were afraid that the crumbs would draw moisture from the filling, thus hindering them from crisping in the oven. After a little experimenting, we were happy to find that we could go ahead and sprinkle the crumbs on top, as they crisped and browned just fine.

These mushrooms keep well in the fridge and will hold for up to three days. The freezer was a different story, as batches of frozen stuffed mushroom caps baked up with a rubbery texture. Therefore, we don't recommend freezing these hors d'oeuvres ahead of time.

Baked Stuffed Mushrooms with Goat Cheese and Thyme

MAKES 24 MUSHROOMS

Be sure to buy mushrooms with caps that measure between 1½ and 2 inches in diameter (before roasting).

1	slice high-quality white sandwich bread, quartered
6	tablespoons extra-virgin olive oil
9	medium garlic cloves, minced or pressed through a garlic press (about 3 tablespoons) Salt and ground black pepper
24	(1½- to 2-inch wide) white mushroom caps, wiped clean
4	ounces goat cheese, softened
1	teaspoon minced fresh thyme leaves

1. Adjust an oven rack to the middle position and heat the oven to 300 degrees. Pulse the bread in a food processor to coarse crumbs, about 6 pulses. Toss the crumbs with 1 tablespoon of the oil, 1 tablespoon of the garlic, ⅛ teaspoon salt, and ⅛ teaspoon pepper. Spread the crumbs on a rimmed baking sheet and bake, stirring occasionally, until lightly browned and dry, about 20 minutes; set aside to cool.

2. Increase the oven temperature to 450 degrees and line a baking sheet with foil. Mix 4 more tablespoons of the oil with the remaining 2 tablespoons garlic, ¼ teaspoon salt, and ⅛ teaspoon pepper, then toss with the mushroom caps. Lay the caps, gill side down, on the prepared baking sheet. Roast the mushrooms until they release their juices, about 20 minutes. Flip the caps over and continue to roast until the liquid has evaporated completely and the mushrooms are brown all over, about 10 minutes longer. Remove the mushrooms from the oven, flip gill side down, and set aside to drain any excess moisture.

3. Line a second baking sheet with foil; set aside. Mix the goat cheese, thyme, and remaining tablespoon oil together until smooth, and season with salt and pepper to taste. Transfer the cheese mixture to a small zipper-lock bag and, following the illustration on page 22, snip off a corner of the bag using scissors. Pipe about 1 teaspoon of the goat cheese mixture into each mushroom cap and top with the bread crumbs. Transfer the stuffed mushrooms to the prepared baking sheet.

4. TO STORE: Wrap the baking sheet tightly with plastic wrap and refrigerate for up to 3 days. (If you don't have room for a baking sheet in your refrigerator, you can stack the stuffed mushrooms inside a casserole dish—one on top of the

other—as long as the layers are separated by sheets of parchment paper.)

5. To serve: Adjust an oven rack to the middle position and heat the oven to 450 degrees. Unwrap the mushrooms and bake until the mushrooms and filling are hot and the crumbs are crisp, about 10 minutes.

TO SERVE RIGHT AWAY

Bake the stuffed mushrooms as directed in step 5.

➤ VARIATION

Baked Stuffed Mushrooms with Blue Cheese and Scallions

Follow the recipe for Baked Stuffed Mushrooms with Goat Cheese and Thyme, substituting 3 ounces softened cream cheese and 1 ounce crumbled blue cheese for the goat cheese, and 1 thinly sliced scallion for the thyme.

CRISPY POLENTA TRIANGLES

WHETHER SERVED SOFT AND PORRIDGE-LIKE or cooled until firm and then grilled, baked, or sautéed, polenta offers myriad flavoring opportunities. And since we were looking for a cheesy, bite-sized appetizer that could be made ahead with a minimum of fuss, we turned to polenta as a starting point. Our goal was to make a flavorful polenta, let it firm up, and then a day or so later cut it into triangles, bake it in a hot oven, and top it with cheese.

We started our testing using both instant and traditional polenta. While the traditional polenta had a richer corn flavor, we realized that once we added other ingredients to the polenta that subtlety would be lost. So to keep things simple and save some time in the process, we stuck with the instant polenta. Once the polenta had thickened to a porridge consistency, we added some basic flavorings and then poured it into a 13 by 9-inch baking dish. We then placed it in the refrigerator, uncovered. We found that this step—rather than covering it and trapping in steam—kept the polenta dry, ensuring firm and crisp polenta triangles when baked the next day.

With the basics of the polenta determined, we turned our attention to the flavorings. We wanted soft yet bright flavors that would accent, rather than overwhelm, the polenta. Turning first to sun-dried tomatoes, we found them to be overpowering no matter how few we added. Since mushrooms are a classic pairing with polenta, we gave them a try, but on their own they didn't impart enough flavor to the polenta—in fact, you really couldn't taste them at all.

Next up was a lemon-flavored polenta, which was a step in the right direction. In our first lemon test, we added 3 tablespoons of lemon zest, which made the polenta so lemony that tasters thought it was cake! We kept lowering the amount until we got to 1 teaspoon, which provided a nice balance of corn and lemon flavors. We then decided to add a little garlic and some fresh chives to create a more complex flavor and also to emphasize the savory.

We thought that kalamata olives might also fit the bill. We had to be careful not to puree the olives, or the polenta turned an unappetizing black when we added them. But if we left the olives in large slices they dried out in the oven and lost their flavor. The answer was to mince them until they still had texture, but would mix into the polenta evenly. The addition of a little fresh oregano complemented the briny olives perfectly.

Lastly, we wanted a simple version so we stuck with the basics: garlic and fresh herbs. Raw garlic was too harsh and overpowered the polenta, but sautéing it gave us the rich, mellow garlic flavor we sought. After trying fresh thyme, rosemary, parsley, chives, and oregano, we settled on the heady mix of fresh rosemary and garlic.

Happy with our flavor combinations, we were almost ready to decide on a topping that would work with any of the polenta flavors. But first, should our polenta triangles be baked or oven-fried? Oven-frying can be time-consuming, so we were pleased to discover that we could achieve the crispness we were looking for by simply spraying the baking pan with cooking spray and baking the triangles in a very hot oven for just 25 to 30 minutes. This gave us the perfect golden brown exterior on both the top and the bottom while the interior, although firm, was still appealingly tender.

Next came the cheese. First up was Parmesan, which we thought would add a pleasing texture and depth of flavor. The results were mixed; these triangles browned well and tasted good, but in just a few minutes out of the oven they became grainy and oily. Melting cheeses such as Asiago turned a nice golden brown and looked promising, but were actually our least favorite because of their rubbery texture.

Turning to softer cheeses, we tested both goat and feta cheese, eliminating the feta immediately because after 20 minutes of cooking it was dry, hard, and almost burnt. The goat cheese, which was an ideal accent to all three polenta flavors, lost so much moisture after 20 minutes of baking that it turned to a grainy mess. But because we liked the flavor so much, we attempted to solve this problem. We tried adding olive oil to the cheese before baking it, but the oil cooked the cheese even more and ran out onto the pan during cooking. Spreading the cheese on top the day before so that it was cold when it went in the oven didn't work either. We wanted the goat cheese just barely warm, so we decided to top the polenta with the cheese after it was baked. This was the ideal solution: The texture was perfect, and tasters loved the temperature contrast between the cheese and the triangles. We stuck to adding 1 tablespoon of olive oil to the goat cheese to help it soften quickly. We also added some freshly chopped parsley to the cheese for color and freshness. To speed up the process of topping 24 triangles with cheese, we

POLENTA FLAVOR ADD-INS

Garlic and Rosemary

6 medium garlic cloves, minced or pressed through a garlic press (about 2 tablespoons)
3 tablespoons olive oil
1½ teaspoons minced fresh rosemary

Cook the garlic and oil in a small nonstick skillet over low heat, stirring often, until the garlic is golden and fragrant, about 10 minutes. Off the heat, stir in the rosemary and let cool until needed. Stir into the Crispy Polenta Triangles as directed in step 2.

Olive and Oregano

½ cup minced kalamata olives
3 medium garlic cloves, minced or pressed through a garlic press (about 1 tablespoon)
2 teaspoons minced fresh oregano leaves

Stir the ingredients into the Crispy Polenta Triangles recipe as directed in step 2.

Lemon and Chive

3 tablespoons unsalted butter, cut into 3 pieces
2 tablespoons minced fresh chives
3 medium garlic cloves, minced or pressed through a garlic press (about 1 tablespoon)
1 teaspoon grated zest from 1 lemon

Stir the ingredients into the Crispy Polenta Triangles as directed in step 2.

piped it on using a zipper-lock bag—which was not only much faster and less messy than spooning the cheese on, but also made for an attractive presentation.

~~

Crispy Polenta Triangles with Herbed Goat Cheese

MAKES 48 BITE-SIZED POLENTA TRIANGLES

Be sure to buy instant polenta, which has a much shorter cooking time. The polenta triangles can be arranged on the baking sheets up to 3 hours before their final baking in step 6.

4	cups water
	Salt
I	cup instant polenta
I	Polenta Flavor Add-In (page 30)
	Ground black pepper
8	ounces goat cheese, softened
I	tablespoon olive oil
3	tablespoons minced fresh parsley leaves

1. Line the bottom of a 13 by 9-inch baking dish with parchment paper and coat lightly with vegetable oil spray; set aside. Bring the water to a boil, covered, in a heavy-bottomed 4-quart saucepan over high heat. Reduce the heat to low, stir in 1 teaspoon salt, then pour the polenta into the water in a very slow stream, while stirring in a circular motion with a wooden spoon.

2. Reduce the heat to low and cook uncovered, stirring often, until the polenta is soft and smooth, 3 to 5 minutes. Off the heat, stir in a flavor add-in, and season with salt and pepper to taste. Pour into the prepared baking dish and refrigerate, uncovered, until firm and sliceable, about 1 hour.

3. When the polenta is firm, use the tip of a paring knife to slice it into twenty-four, 2 by 2¼-inch rectangles. Slice each rectangle in half on the diagonal into 2 bite-sized triangles. Mix the goat cheese with the oil and parsley, then transfer to a small zipper-lock bag.

4. To STORE: Cover the dish of sliced polenta tightly with plastic wrap. Refrigerate the polenta and goat cheese mixture for up to 2 days.

5. To SERVE: Adjust an oven rack to the lowest position and heat the oven to 500 degrees. Line 2 baking sheets with foil and spray them with vegetable oil spray; set aside. Let the goat cheese mixture stand at room temperature to soften (to soften quickly, microwave on 50 percent power for 10 to 20 seconds). Transfer the polenta triangles to the prepared baking sheets (don't crowd the triangles or they won't crisp).

6. Bake the polenta, 1 tray at a time, until crisp and golden, 20 to 25 minutes. Transfer the hot polenta triangles to a warm serving platter. Following the illustration on page 22, snip off the corner of the goat cheese bag using scissors and pipe about 1 teaspoon of the goat cheese on top of each polenta triangle before serving.

TO SERVE IMMEDIATELY
Bake the cut polenta triangles as described in steps 5 and 6.

~~~~~

ROASTED TOMATO TART

A TOMATO TART MAKES AN IDEAL APPETIZER, at least in theory. Typically a pastry crust topped with a simple combination of tomatoes and cheese, it is impressive in appearance and substantial enough to feed a crowd. But in reality, the problems with tomato tarts are many. The moisture in the tomatoes almost always guarantees a soggy crust, and the tarts are often tasteless, their spectacular open faces offering false promises of vine-ripened tomato flavor. But the biggest drawback to making a tomato tart would have to be the time involved in making the pastry crust. We wanted to simplify this tart without sacrificing flavor, and also find a way to make it in advance without settling for a soggy crust.

Our make-ahead goal from the beginning was to completely construct the tarts before storing them— the idea being that when party time approached, all we had to do was heat them in the oven. But first we needed to streamline the preparation of these time-consuming tarts, and we knew that the homemade pastry crust would have to go. Looking for a quick alternative, we focused our attention on store-bought puff pastry. We knew we would need to prebake the crust to protect it from the moisture of the tomatoes, and discussed prebaking the crusts and then storing them separately from the topping ingredients. But we ruled out this method because it required too much effort the day you bake the tarts, and we wanted to do as much advance preparation as possible.

Following the recipe on the back of the puff pastry box, we baked our tart shell at 400 degrees. Here we ran into our first problem. The shell was too frail to support a heavy, wet filling. Baked at 350 degrees, the shell was noticeably squatter and drier—and better suited to a heavy filling—but it was also unpleasantly tough and chewy. We wondered whether a two-step baking method might be more successful: a high temperature for initial lift and browning, then a lower temperature to dry out the shell for maximum sturdiness. When started at 425 degrees (until puffed and light golden) and finished at 350 degrees (until well browned), the crust was flaky yet rigid enough to hold the toppings. We wondered, however, if this beautiful crust would hold up in the refrigerator once topped with tomatoes and cheese.

An egg wash baked onto the crust provided a fairly effective moisture barrier against the toppings, but we thought we could do even more to prevent the crust from getting soggy. We wondered if the type of cheese we used might make a difference. Though mozzarella is often found on tomato tarts, we tested a variety of cheeses and found that goat cheese added that extra layer of protection we wanted, shielding the delicate tart shell from the moisture of the tomatoes. In addition, tasters liked the creamy consistency of the goat cheese—and also appreciated its tanginess, which was a nice contrast to the rich, buttery pastry shell. But we had to make sure that the goat cheese was evenly spread across the bottom of the tart shell, otherwise the tomatoes' moisture would still soak the crust. To be able to spread the goat cheese in an even layer, it was crucial that it be thoroughly softened. In addition, we discovered that a little bit of olive oil mixed into the cheese made it even easier to spread, and also contributed a welcome accent of flavor. With the goat cheese layer laid down, our tart was ready for the tomatoes.

At this point, the tart screamed for fresh summer tomatoes, but we wanted to make this recipe year-round. When tomatoes aren't in season, we usually find two options available at the supermarket: the vibrantly red specimens that deliver mealy texture and almost no discernible flavor, and the cherry tomato. Though a little tart in the off-season, cherry tomatoes offer great flavor any time of year. We immediately looked to roasting them to concentrate and sweeten their flavor.

We found plenty of recipes that called for two to three hours of roasting, an unnecessary amount of time in our opinion. In addition, these recipes produced tomatoes with a leathery texture that made them seem oven-dried rather than slow-roasted. We wanted a quicker recipe and a juicier end result, and found that roasting the tomatoes at 350 degrees proved to be just right. These tomatoes became sweet and concentrated in just about 30 minutes.

But when we started to assemble our tart, we

PREPARING TOMATO TART

1. Using the tip of a paring knife, cut a ½-inch border around the edge.

2. Press down the center of the shell, so that it rests about ¼ inch lower than the edge.

3. Gently spread the goat cheese in the center of the tart shells, leaving the raised edge clean.

4. Gently spoon the tomatoes evenly over the cheese, without disturbing the edge.

noticed the tomatoes had a tendency to slide right off the crust—using store-bought puff pastry had saved us an enormous amount of time, but unlike a homemade pastry crust it had no edge to keep the toppings intact. As it turned out, the solution was simple: We could make our own raised edge by cutting a border around the baked pastry shell and then pressing down the center of shell, so that it rested about ¼ inch lower than the edge.

With the toppings for our tart securely in place, we now turned our attention to finding the right complements to the tomatoes and goat cheese. Garlic was a must, and we wanted to add it the easy way, by roasting it along with the tomatoes. Pressed and minced garlic proved to be too overwhelming, but thinly sliced garlic was just right. Although onions added a harsh flavor, delicate shallots were sweet enough to pair with the tomatoes. And because the sweetness level of tomatoes tends to vary, we added a small amount of sugar to the recipe. (The sugar can be easily reduced or even omitted when using sweeter tomatoes.) A modest amount of balsamic vinegar added to the tomatoes before roasting also helped to boost their flavor.

These tarts will hold in the refrigerator for up to one day but no longer (however, even making the tart a day in advance is a huge help when preparing for a party). After about a day, the flaky quality of the puff pastry starts to deteriorate. Also, we had no luck with freezing: The crust baked up crumbly and dense instead of flaky and light.

Once the tarts are assembled—whether you are refrigerating them for later or baking them right away—they only require a short stay in a hot oven. Baked quick and hot to warm the crust and toppings (425 degrees turned out to be the best temperature) and finished with a sprinkling of fresh basil leaves, our tart was ready to take center stage.

Roasted Tomato and Goat Cheese Tarts

MAKES TWO 9 BY 4½-INCH TARTS,
SERVING 8 TO 10

Be gentle with the baked tart shells; baked puff pastry is delicate and will break apart if handled roughly. We prefer Pepperidge Farm Puff Pastry because it is the most widely available brand; however, any brand of puff pastry cut into two 9- by 4½-inch rectangles can be substituted.

TART SHELLS
1   (9½ x 9-inch) sheet frozen puff pastry, thawed (see page 11) and cut into two 9 by 4½-inch rectangles
1   large egg, lightly beaten

FILLING
1   pint cherry tomatoes (about 12 ounces)
3   tablespoons extra-virgin olive oil
2   teaspoons balsamic vinegar
1   medium shallot, halved and sliced thin
3   large garlic cloves, sliced thin
½   teaspoon sugar
    Salt and ground black pepper
8   ounces fresh goat cheese, softened
1   large egg, lightly beaten
1   tablespoon chopped fresh basil leaves

1. FOR THE TART SHELLS: Adjust an oven rack to the middle position and heat the oven to 425 degrees. Line a baking sheet with parchment paper. Lay the pastry rectangles on the prepared baking sheet, brush with the egg, and poke thoroughly with a dinner fork. Bake the shells for about 10 minutes, rotating the baking sheet halfway through the baking time. Decrease the oven temperature to 350 degrees and continue to bake the shells until golden brown and crisp, 10 to 15 minutes longer, rotating the baking sheet again halfway through the baking time. Transfer the baking sheet to a wire rack and let the shells cool. Keep the oven temperature at 350 degrees.

2. FOR THE FILLING: Toss the tomatoes with 1 tablespoon of the oil, vinegar, shallot, garlic, sugar, ½ teaspoon salt, and ¼ teaspoon pepper, and transfer to a 13 by 9-inch baking dish. Roast the tomatoes, without stirring, until the skins are slightly shriveled but the tomatoes have retained their shape, about 30 minutes. Set the tomatoes aside to cool.

3. Mix the goat cheese with the remaining 2 tablespoons oil until smooth, and season with salt and pepper to taste. Following the illustrations on page 32, use the tip of a paring knife to cut

a ½-inch border around the edge of the cooled pastry shells. Press the centers of the pastry shells down to rest about ¼ inch lower than the edges. Divide and spread the goat cheese mixture evenly over the sunken centers of both shells, leaving the raised edges clean. Gently spoon the roasted tomatoes evenly over the cheese on each shell.

4. To STORE: Carefully wrap the baking sheet with plastic wrap and refrigerate for up to 24 hours.

5. To SERVE: Adjust an oven rack to the middle position and heat the oven to 425 degrees. Brush the edges of the tarts liberally with the egg. Bake until the shells are a deep golden brown and the toppings are hot, 10 to 15 minutes, rotating the baking sheet halfway through the baking time. Transfer the baking sheet to a wire rack, and let cool for 5 minutes. Sprinkle with the basil and slice each tart into about 10 pieces before serving.

TO SERVE RIGHT AWAY
Bake the assembled tarts as directed in step 5, reducing the baking time to 8 to 12 minutes.

➤ VARIATION

Roasted Artichoke and Goat Cheese Tarts
Follow the recipe for Roasted Tomato and Goat Cheese Tarts, increasing the oven temperature for the filling in step 3 to 450 degrees. Substitute 1 (9-ounce) box frozen artichoke hearts, not thawed, for the cherry tomatoes. Toss the artichokes with the oil and seasonings as directed in step 2, and roast, stirring occasionally, until the artichokes are browned at the edges, about 25 minutes; set aside to cool and use in place of the tomatoes in step 3.

RUSTIC CARAMELIZED ONION TART

RECIPES FOR CARAMELIZED ONION TART take many forms: Some are eggy and quiche-like, with a rich, buttery pastry crust, while others are more similar to pizza and supported by a thin cracker-like crust. Often the onions are accompanied by additional toppings—and preparations for the tart vary as well (a flambéed tart was the most interesting one we encountered). We wanted an appetizer version of this tart, one that could easily be sliced up into multiple pieces and eaten out of hand. And while we wanted to make this tart in advance, we also wanted to streamline the process.

Right from the start we focused our attention on developing a fairly lean dough for the base. While buttery pastry-style doughs were satisfying and flavorful, most of our tasters thought they were too rich for an appetizer when topped with the caramelized onions. In fact, tasters' favorite version of the tarts they sampled was a recipe for pissaladière—a rustic Provençal free-form onion tart with a crisp crust made from a dough similar to pizza dough. Agreeing to base our tart on the rustic style of pissaladière, we wondered how we might simplify the making of it. Since the onions are the essential component of this tart, we decided to focus our attention on the slow process of caramelizing them—and if we were serious about keeping this tart simple, this meant we would have to find a speedier alternative to homemade crust. Having had success with store-bought pizza dough in other recipes (such as Stromboli on page 310) we decided to give it a shot here.

Since pizza dough is relatively lean, it is sturdier than a rich, buttery dough and we had a good feeling that we'd be able to build these tarts ahead of time, store them, and bake them right before serving. But before diving into the make-ahead aspects of this tart, we first needed to develop a solid working recipe.

Crust shaping and baking technique were the issues at hand here—we wanted it to be rustic in appearance and also crisp. After testing a couple of shaping techniques we determined the best way to shape our dough was stretching it by hand. A rolling pin allowed us to form a perfectly uniform dough, but when we used our hands to make a free-form oval we arrived at the rustic texture and shape we were after. And baking the tart directly on a pre-heated baking stone at 500 degrees ensured a crisp crust every time. In addition, we found that stretching and shaping the dough with oil-coated hands helped give our dough a little more crunch. So did brushing the dough with yet more olive oil before adding the toppings—this extra application of oil further ensured a cracker-like exterior.

With the crust resolved, we turned our attention to the star of the show: the caramelized onions. When it comes to caramelizing onions, we found that most recipes subscribe to one of two methods—low and slow or fast and furious—yet neither works. Low (heat) and slow dries out the onions before they have a chance to darken, while fast and furious (high heat) leaves the onions crunchy and burnt tasting. The solution was to use a combination of low and high heat, starting the onions over medium-low heat so that they release their juices and soften and then increasing the heat to medium-high until they become caramelized.

A nonstick skillet works best for caramelizing onions. The low sides of a skillet allow the steam to evaporate rather than interfere with browning, while the nonstick surface ensures that the caramelization sticks to the onions, not the pan. Stirring in just a bit of water once we removed the onions from the heat prevented them from clumping.

Our tart was coming together, however, tasters felt that it needed a little pizzazz. A sprinkling of crumbled blue cheese went a long way toward boosting the flavor and, because of its complex piquancy, it was noticeable against the backdrop of the rich, sweet onions. Finally, toasted walnuts added a welcome crunch, contrasting nicely with the soft texture of the onions and cheese.

With a solid, well-defined recipe under our belts, we explored different methods for the make-ahead element. The obvious starting point was building the tarts on stretched, uncooked dough, refrigerating it, and then sliding it onto the hot baking stone the next day. Our results using this method were less than favorable. Although we wound up with a crisp bottom, there was an unappetizingly soggy layer of dough underneath the onions. Another option was to form the dough and caramelize the onions—then hold them separately overnight and assemble the tart right before baking it. We didn't want to go down this path though. We thought there was much more make-ahead value in completely constructing the tarts prior to storing, so all that was left to do was stick them in the oven right before serving.

Taking the suggestion of a fellow test cook, we tried partially baking the dough before building and storing it. This turned out to be a great solution. We discovered that a 3-minute stint on a hot baking stone was enough time to partially cook the pizza dough. The baked exterior of the crust held up much better than the raw dough against the moist caramelized onion topping. Our make-ahead rustic tarts now baked up perfectly crisp.

These tarts will hold in the refrigerator for up to three days, however, we could not get frozen versions to bake properly. When reheated, the tart crusts turned tough and the onions had an off-putting, dense texture.

Rustic Caramelized Onion Tarts with Blue Cheese and Walnuts

MAKES TWO 14 BY 8-INCH TARTS, SERVING 14 TO 16

These tarts are not made in a tart pan, but rather are free form and rustic in shape. Note that parchment paper is a must for this recipe. For pizza dough, you can either make your own (see our recipe on page 312), use store-bought, or buy some from your favorite local pizzeria.

2	tablespoons olive oil, plus extra for greasing hands and brushing the dough
2	pounds onions (about 4 medium), halved and sliced 1/4 inch thick
1	teaspoon brown sugar
1/2	teaspoon salt
1	tablespoon water
1	pound pizza dough (see note), divided into 2 equal pieces
	Ground black pepper
1	cup walnuts, toasted and coarsely chopped
4	ounces blue cheese, crumbled (about 1 cup)
2	scallions, sliced thin

1. Adjust an oven rack to the lowest position, set a baking stone on the rack, and heat the oven to 500 degrees. Heat 2 tablespoons of the oil in a 12-inch nonstick skillet over medium-low heat until just shimmering. Stir in the onions, sugar, and salt. Cover and cook, stirring

occasionally, until the onions are softened and have released their juices, about 10 minutes. Remove the lid, increase the heat to medium-high, and continue to cook, stirring often, until the onions are deeply browned, 10 to 15 minutes. Off the heat, stir in the water, then transfer the onions to a bowl and refrigerate.

2. Meanwhile, cut two 20-inch lengths of parchment paper and set aside. Coat your fingers and palms generously with olive oil. Working with 1 piece of dough at a time and following the illustrations below, hold the dough up and gently stretch it to a 12-inch length. Place the dough on the parchment sheet and gently dimple the surface of the dough with your fingertips. Using your oiled palms, push and flatten the dough into a 14 by 8-inch oval. Brush the dough with oil and season with pepper.

3. Slip the parchment with the dough onto a pizza peel (or inverted baking sheet), then slide it onto the hot baking stone. Bake until the dough is cooked through with some spots of light browning on the bottom, about 3 minutes. (If large bubbles form during baking, pop them with the tip of a knife.) Remove the tart shell from the oven with the peel (or pull the parchment onto a baking sheet). Transfer the tart shell along with the parchment paper to a baking sheet, and set aside. Repeat this process with the second piece of dough.

4. Scatter the caramelized onions, walnuts, and blue cheese evenly over both the tarts, leaving a ½-inch border around the edge of each tart shell.

5. To STORE: Wrap each baking sheet with plastic wrap and refrigerate for up to 3 days.

6. To SERVE: At least 1 hour before baking the tarts, adjust an oven rack to the lowest position, set a baking stone on the rack, and heat the oven to 500 degrees. Working with 1 tart at a time, slip the parchment with the tart onto a pizza peel (or inverted baking sheet), then slide it onto the hot baking stone. Bake until the tart is a deep golden brown, about 9 minutes.

7. Remove the tart from the oven with the peel (or pull the parchment onto a baking sheet). Transfer the tart to a cutting board and slide the parchment out from under the tart; let cool for 5 minutes. While the first tart cools, bake the second tart. Sprinkle with the scallions and cut into 16 pieces before serving.

TO SERVE RIGHT AWAY
Bake the assembled tarts as described in step 6, reducing the baking time to about 7 minutes.

➤ VARIATION

Rustic Caramelized Onion Tarts with Provençal Flavors
Follow the recipe for Rustic Caramelized Onion Tarts with Blue Cheese and Walnuts, omitting the walnuts, blue cheese, and scallions. Scatter ½ cup coarsely chopped pitted niçoise olives and 8 anchovy fillets, rinsed, patted dry, and chopped coarse, over the tarts with the onions, then sprinkle each tart with ½ teaspoon minced fresh thyme leaves and ¼ teaspoon fennel seeds. Store and bake as directed. Before serving, sprinkle the tarts with 1 tablespoon minced fresh parsley.

MAKING A RUSTIC TART

1. Hold the dough up and stretch it.

2. Dimple the dough with your fingers.

3. Push the dough into an oval.

4. Sprinkle with toppings.

2

SIDE DISHES

SIDE DISHES

BLANCHED GREEN BEANS TOSSED WITH olive oil or a tray of simple roasted potatoes seasoned with just salt may be fine during the week, but for holidays and entertaining you want something special. But it's just these kinds of meals that are so stressful, and side dishes that require last-minute cooking don't help. Our goal in this chapter, then, was simple. We wanted to develop side dishes that could be made at least a day in advance with minimal last-minute work. Can you imagine being able to make a big batch of mashed potatoes for Thanksgiving dinner the day before? Or creamy polenta that doesn't require 20 minutes of vigilant pot stirring just when you need to be attending to your main course? And what about those perennial favorites that everyone assumes can be made ahead, like potato or pasta salad? If you're like us, you've made or eaten salads that are mushy or just plain lackluster. We were after make-ahead side dishes every bit as good as those made in the frantic last minutes before a meal is ready to be served.

As we began to cook our way through this chapter, it became clear to us that you can't simply take regular side-dish recipes and make them ahead of time. Unlike stews or chilis, which usually taste better after sitting overnight, side dishes usually taste worse when refrigerated and then reheated the next day. Cooked starches have a tendency to set up and become firm, while vegetables turn soggy and mushy; in general, without some adjustment to the recipe, many side dishes made in advance wind up tasting like really bad leftovers. For example, in order to successfully develop our Make-Ahead Mashed Potatoes (page 59), we found it necessary to alter nearly every aspect of our favorite recipe including the cooking and mashing methods and the cream-to-butter proportions. Our make-ahead Creamy Polenta (page 67) requires a dramatically different ratio of liquid to polenta (compared to a traditional recipe) in order to prevent it from turning into a solid brick overnight. And in order to serve up fresh (not soggy) Stuffed Plum Tomatoes (page 41), we lined the tomatoes with a flavorful layer of goat cheese, which not only tasted great but kept the crumb stuffing from absorbing the moisture from the tomatoes.

Across this chapter you'll find a wide range of make-ahead side dishes that will be useful for special occasions—from old standards like Classic Scalloped Potatoes (page 54) and Sweet Potato Casserole (page 52) to more exotic recipes such as Baked Stuffed Onions with Sausage and Swiss Chard (page 43) and Indian-Spiced Rice Pilaf (page 65). There are casual summer side dishes here as well, such as All-American Potato Salad (page 75) and Summer Garden Pasta Salad (page 79) that not only taste great when made a day ahead of time, but will also be more durable on a picnic table. Our secrets? For potato salad, the trick is to add additional mayonnaise (with a little milk) right before serving; for pasta salad, we found that adding only half the dressing up front and the rest as needed just before serving kept the texture of the pasta from becoming soggy. Many recipes here are geared to serve a crowd, since that's when side dishes tend to become an issue. But we also have provided some simple guidelines for blanching a variety of vegetables along with compound butters and vinaigrettes that can dress them and keep things interesting enough for a special occasion and simple enough for everyday.

STUFFED TOMATOES

STUFFED TOMATOES CAN BE REAL LOOKERS with their bright red tomato bases filled with golden, garlicky bread crumbs, chopped basil, and grated Parmesan cheese. Sadly, their appeal usually fades after the first bite reveals the dull, soggy, and flavorless truth. So our goal here was simple: a stuffed tomato that tasted as good as it looked, and could be made ahead of time without complication.

We began our testing by following the directions called for in most cookbook recipes: Stuff a hollowed-out, raw, beefsteak tomato with a bread-crumb filling and bake it at 375 degrees for 30 minutes. As expected, the outcome was disappointing: All these recipes delivered a wet stuffing and wan flavor. We concluded that the same element that makes a tomato taste wonderfully juicy when ripe—water—was the source of its demise when stuffed and baked.

We decided to try swapping plum tomatoes for

beefsteak tomatoes because plum tomatoes have a naturally lower moisture content that might eliminate this water issue altogether. Unfortunately, the stuffed plum tomatoes were nearly as soggy; however, we liked their meaty, sweet flavor and smaller portion size (ideal for a side dish). We hoped to find a way to make them work.

So we tried oven drying them prior to stuffing, rationalizing that the slow, low heat of the oven would concentrate their sweetness and vaporize the water. But while these tomatoes were laden with rich flavor notes, they were also shrunken and collapsed and in no condition to hold any stuffing. Next we tried salting—a trick we often use to draw the moisture out of cucumbers, cabbage, and eggplant. After coring and seeding the tomato halves, we sprinkled the insides with salt, and let them rest upside down on a stack of paper towels. Within 30 minutes, the paper towels had absorbed a tremendous amount of liquid. In addition, the salt brightened and enhanced the tomatoes' flavor. We found that kosher salt worked best here because the larger crystals are easier to sprinkle and disperse more evenly over the tomatoes than regular table salt.

Now we were ready to tackle the stuffing itself. First we tested store-bought bread crumbs against homemade toasted bread crumbs made from white sandwich bread. The fine texture of the store-bought crumbs was gritty and tasted stale compared to the homemade crumbs, which tasted clean and sweet. The bonus of grinding your own crumbs from sandwich bread is that you can make them a bit larger and more rustic—perfect for a stuffed tomato. In terms of flavor, we found olive oil, garlic, Parmesan cheese, and fresh basil to be crucial additions to the toasted crumbs.

The tomatoes were tasting pretty good at this point; however, they still seemed a bit plain and the crumbs were slightly soggy. We tried adding shredded mozzarella, but its flavor was too bland and the stringy texture it added was odd. Testing out a few other cheeses, we finally landed on a surprising and winning idea. In the hollow of the tomato, underneath the cover of garlicky bread crumbs, we spread some goat cheese lightly flavored with olive oil and basil. Nearly hidden from view inside the

tomato, the creamy goat cheese centers both surprised and impressed the tasters. And as an added bonus, the goat cheese helped prevent the crumbs from absorbing any juice released by the tomatoes and this helped the stuffing remain super-crisp, even when the tomatoes were made a day or two ahead of time. In fact, storing the stuffed tomatoes for up to two days in the refrigerator turned out to be no problem. Although we worried that the basil would turn dark and slimy, it held up surprisingly well. As for baking these beauties straight from the refrigerator, we found that a 325-degree oven worked best. This moderate temperature gave the tomatoes time to soften (but not overcook) while the goat cheese heated through and the crumbs crisped up perfectly.

TEST KITCHEN TIP: Crust On

When we make fresh bread crumbs from sliced sandwich bread, we always leave the crust on because it adds valuable flavor and helps to increase the yield. One slice of bread with crust makes roughly 1 cup of crumbs, while one slice of crustless bread yields about ½ cup of crumbs.

Stuffed Plum Tomatoes

SERVES 8

Do not overprocess the bread into fine, even crumbs; the rustic texture of coarse, slightly uneven bread crumbs is preferable here. To scoop out the seeds and ribs from the tomatoes, we found it easiest to use a sharp-edged spoon, such as a measuring spoon, grapefruit spoon, or melon baller. The recipe can be easily doubled.

2	slices high-quality white sandwich bread, quartered
3	medium garlic cloves, minced or pressed through a garlic press (about 1 tablespoon)
3	tablespoons extra-virgin olive oil
¼	cup Parmesan cheese, grated
¼	cup chopped fresh basil leaves Kosher salt and ground black pepper
8	medium, firm, ripe plum tomatoes (3 to 4 ounces each)
6	ounces goat cheese, softened

1. Adjust an oven rack to the middle position and heat the oven to 300 degrees. Pulse the bread in a food processor to coarse crumbs, about 6 pulses. Toss the crumbs, garlic, and 2 tablespoons of the oil together. Spread the crumbs on a rimmed baking sheet and bake, stirring occasionally, until lightly browned and dry, about 20 minutes; set aside to cool. When cool, toss the crumbs with the Parmesan, 2 tablespoons of the basil, and season with salt and pepper to taste; set aside.

2. Meanwhile, slice the tomatoes in half lengthwise, and scoop out the inner ribs and seeds following the illustration below. Sprinkle the insides of the tomatoes with 1½ teaspoons kosher salt, then lay them cut sides down on several layers of paper towels. Let them stand at room temperature to drain, 30 to 60 minutes.

3. Mix the goat cheese with the remaining 1 tablespoon oil and remaining 2 tablespoons basil. Season the goat cheese mixture with salt and pepper to taste, then transfer to a small zipper-lock bag.

4. Pat the inside of the tomatoes dry with paper towels. Following the illustrations on page 22, pipe about 1 teaspoon of the goat cheese into the bottom of each tomato Spoon the bread crumbs into the tomatoes, pressing on them to adhere to the cheese. Arrange the tomatoes in a 13 by 9-inch baking dish.

5. To store: Cover the dish tightly with plastic wrap and refrigerate for up to 2 days.

PREPARING PLUM TOMATOES FOR STUFFING

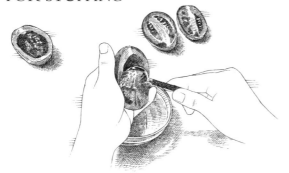

Cut the tomato in half lengthwise and, using a sharp-edged spoon, scoop out the seeds and inner flesh.

6. To serve: Adjust an oven rack to the middle position and heat the oven to 325 degrees. Remove the plastic wrap and bake the tomatoes until the cheese is heated through and the crumbs are crisp, 15 to 20 minutes.

TO SERVE RIGHT AWAY

Bake the tomatoes as directed in step 6.

BAKED STUFFED ONIONS

STUFFED ONIONS ARE THE OFT-OVERLOOKED sibling of stuffed bell peppers and stuffed zucchini. But as a side dish, stuffed onions can really shine; their earthy, caramelized flavor pairs perfectly with grilled or roasted meats. After doing some initial research, we uncovered lots of stuffed onion recipes from all over the world and tested a few of them out before getting started on our own recipe.

None of the initial recipes we tried hit a home run in terms of flavor and texture, but we definitely saw promise. Overall, about half of the recipes turned out onions that were very dry with tough, wrinkled exterior skins, while the other half were so wet that the fillings bordered on onion soup. All of the recipes parcooked the onion shells before stuffing them, although they all used different parcooking methods. The types of fillings varied considerably from recipe to recipe; some were based on rice (much like a stuffed pepper), while others used either sausage or bread cubes as the main ingredient. Our most disappointing finding was that only one of the recipes chopped up the onion cores and included them in the filling—the others simply ignored or discarded them. In addition, all of these recipes were quite time-consuming (the onion coring process was a serious pain) and produced stuffed onions too large for a side dish.

Starting in on our own recipe, we first wanted to figure out how to make the size of the onions more side-dish appropriate and simplify the coring process. Rather than serving one onion per person, we decided it was better to serve just half of a large onion per person. As for the coring issue, we found our answer when we stopped thinking of the onions as edible "bowls" made from a cored onion half, and started thinking of them as hollowed-out, bottomless onion shells (made of a layer of three onion rings—see the illustration at right). And by using this shell, we were able to complete all of the onion prep before the parcooking stage; raw onions are much less slippery and easier to handle than those that have already been cooked.

Moving on, we then tested various parcooking methods, including steaming, boiling, microwaving, roasting, and browning-then-braising. Microwaving, steaming, and boiling produced similar bland, mushy results, while roasting turned the onion shells dry and tough. The brown/braise technique, however, worked well and provided an attractively caramelized rim with a slightly softened and lightly flavored interior. Testing various liquids for the braising, including wine, water, and broth, we found that the broth tasted best and lent a hearty flavor to the onions. Using a 12-inch nonstick skillet, we streamlined this brown-then-braise technique into a stovetop operation that takes only a few minutes.

With the onion shells figured out, we focused next on the filling. Not wanting to ignore or discard the onion cores, we decided it best to reduce their volume and intensify their flavor by caramelizing them (done in the same skillet used to brown and braise the shells). And since we really favored the addition of Italian sausage in our earlier tests, we decided to add it to the caramelized onions. We then tried binding the filling together using bread crumbs or bread cubes (both fresh and dried), but nothing worked. All of the bread binders merely turned the filling dense and gummy and tasters always preferred filling when left unbound. Spinach added a fresh flavor and some welcome color to the sausage-and-onion combo, but the earthy, rustic flavor of Swiss chard brought the house down. (White chard works better than red here because the red color leaches into the filling and turns it pink.) Tasters didn't like the addition of cheese (we tried Parmesan and Gruyère), but did like a hint of sherry vinegar.

PREPPING ONIONS FOR STUFFING

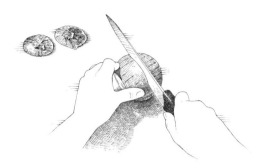

1. Trim off both the root and stem end of the onions, then slice the onions in half through the middle. Remove and discard the brown papery onion skins along with the tough, outermost layer of onion.

2. Remove the core from each onion half (by pushing it out from the other side), leaving just 3 of the outermost layers to form a bottomless shell. Finely chop the onion cores and reserve for use in the filling.

Once stuffed, we found that the onions held well for about 2 days, beyond which they begin to turn mealy and taste funny. Baking the onions straight from the fridge, we tested various oven temperatures and baking times, finding that a moderate 350-degree oven worked best at heating the onions through while browning the tops just slightly.

Baked Stuffed Onions with Sausage and Swiss Chard
SERVES 8

Try to buy white-stemmed Swiss chard if you can; red-stemmed chard can turn the filling an unappealing pink color. Balsamic or red wine vinegar can be substituted for the sherry vinegar. The onions pair well with roasted or grilled meats.

2 tablespoons olive oil

4 large yellow onions (3 to 4 inches across), prepped following the illustrations on page 43

½ cup low-sodium chicken broth

6 ounces sweet Italian sausage, casings removed
Salt

3 medium garlic cloves, minced or pressed through a garlic press (about 1 tablespoon)

1 pound Swiss chard (1 medium bunch), stems discarded and leaves chopped medium (about 8 cups)

2 teaspoons sherry vinegar
Ground black pepper

1. Line a 13 by 9-inch baking dish with foil and set aside. Heat 1 tablespoon of the oil in a 12-inch nonstick skillet over medium heat until shimmering but not smoking. Lay 4 of the onion rings in the skillet, wide ends down, and cook until their edges are browned, 2 to 3 minutes. Transfer the onion rings to a plate without separating any of the layers, and repeat with the remaining 1 tablespoon oil and onion rings.

2. After the second batch of rings is browned, return the first batch to the skillet (they will overlap). Add the broth, cover, and continue to cook over medium heat until the onions are softened, about 5 minutes. Transfer the onions to the prepared baking dish, browned edges facing up. Pour the onion steaming broth into a small bowl and set aside.

PREPARING LEAFY GREENS

To prepare Swiss chard, kale, collard, and mustard greens, hold each leaf at the base of the stem over a bowl filled with water and use a sharp knife to slash the leafy portion from either side of the thick stem into the bowl.

3. Pinch the sausage off into small pieces, and add it to the skillet. Add the chopped onion cores and ½ teaspoon salt to the skillet, cover, and cook over medium heat, stirring occasionally, until the onions are softened, about 10 minutes. Uncover and continue to cook until the onions are golden and dry, 5 to 10 minutes longer.

4. Stir in the garlic and cook until fragrant, about 30 seconds. Stir in the chard leaves and reserved onion steaming broth. Cook, tossing the chard until wilted, about 2 minutes. Off the heat, stir in the vinegar and season with salt and pepper. Spoon the filling into the center of the onion rings.

5. TO STORE: Cover the dish with plastic wrap and refrigerate for up to 2 days.

6. TO SERVE: Adjust an oven rack to the middle position and heat the oven to 350 degrees. Remove the plastic wrap and bake the onions until the filling is hot and bubbling, about 45 minutes.

TO SERVE RIGHT AWAY

Bake the stuffed onions as directed in step 6, decreasing the cooking time to about 25 minutes.

YEAR-ROUND ROASTED VEGETABLES

OTHER THAN CASSEROLES AND SALADS, there aren't too many options when it comes to make-ahead vegetable side dishes. But casseroles and salads don't always fit the bill; we wanted something that would work year-round and be appropriate served alongside a range of main courses, both homey and elegant. After extensive research we realized that the ease and versatility of roasted vegetables was what we were after. Not only do roasted vegetables fit into any menu, but they can be served either hot or at room temperature, making them a valuable addition to our make-ahead repertoire.

To start, we cooked a few roasted vegetable recipes from other cookbooks and tasted some take-out versions from various prepared-food counters and salad bars. Tasting them at room temperature, we found them all pretty dismal. Gone was the fresh, clean taste of the vegetables and, worse yet, we were left with bland, slimy pieces of overcooked vegetables. A few recipes tossed the cooked vegetables with a vinaigrette in an attempt to add flavor, but this just made everything greasy.

Starting in on our own recipe, we learned quickly that choosing the right vegetables makes a big difference. Thin leafy vegetables such as leeks, radicchio, and chard don't work because their texture turns slimy when served cold, while root vegetables such as potatoes and parsnips turn starchy and mealy. We had better luck with vegetables such as asparagus, fennel, zucchini, eggplant, and tomatoes.

Focusing next on the roasting method, we tried simply tossing the vegetables with some olive oil in a large dish and roasting them in a 350-degree oven until tender. The various vegetables, however, turned out consistently mushy, and cranking up the oven temperature did little to improve things. In order to get that roasted flavor, we needed to get the vegetables to brown in the oven. But in order to get them brown, we were forced to overcook them, at which point their texture and flavor were lost. Roasting the vegetables one variety at a time helped slightly, but the vegetables still tasted bland, their flavor cooked out.

We then considered other cooking methods such as broiling, steaming, sautéing, and grilling. Steaming made the vegetables taste waterlogged, and we found the hassle of setting up a grill to make a simple side dish just too time-consuming. Neither broiling nor sautéing provided the ultimate answer alone, but rather the ideal solution was to use both methods. We liked the flavor of some vegetables (zucchini, eggplant, asparagus, and fennel) when they were broiled. The high heat of the broiler cooked these vegetables so quickly that they didn't have time to lose their fresh flavor or turn mushy, while giving them a slight char that translated into a nice "roasted" flavor when served at room temperature. After testing multiple batches, we found that the secret to preserving their texture was to undercook them slightly under the broiler. (The vegetables retained some heat and continued to cook for several minutes after being removed from the oven.)

Alternatively, we preferred to sauté the onions until slightly caramelized, then stir in the tomatoes until just wilted. The tomatoes released a little liquid which, with the sautéed onions, made a clean tasting sauce of sorts. Using cherry tomatoes also added a little extra sweetness and we liked how they held their shape and texture. Pairing the broiled vegetables off into two groups, we came up with two flavorful vegetable combinations, each of which are tossed with the sautéed onion and cherry tomato mixture to make a salad.

Roasted Zucchini and Eggplant Medley
SERVES 8

Undercooking the vegetables is crucial; they will continue to cook after they are removed from the oven. Leaving the skins on the eggplant and zucchini helps keep the vegetables from being mushy after they have cooled. Toasted pine nuts make a nice garnish.

3	medium zucchini (about 1½ pounds), scrubbed, quartered lengthwise, and sliced crosswise into ¾-inch-wide pieces
¼	cup extra-virgin olive oil, plus extra for serving
	Salt and ground black pepper
1	large eggplant (about 1½ pounds), cut into 1-inch cubes
1	medium onion, minced
1	tablespoon minced fresh thyme, or 1 teaspoon dried
3	medium garlic cloves, minced or pressed through a garlic press (about 1 tablespoon)
1	pint cherry tomatoes (about 12 ounces), quartered
¼	cup coarsely chopped fresh basil leaves
1	tablespoon juice from 1 lemon

1. Adjust an oven rack 6 inches from the broiler element and heat the broiler. Line a rimmed baking sheet with foil, and spray it with vegetable oil spray (or use nonstick foil).

2. Toss the zucchini with 1 tablespoon of the oil, ¼ teaspoon salt, and a pinch of pepper and spread it into an even layer over the prepared

INGREDIENTS: High-End Extra-Virgin Olive Oils

In 2001, we tasted inexpensive supermarket oils and proclaimed DaVinci ($12.99 per liter) our favorite. In subsequent tastings, DaVinci has continued its dominance over other mass-market brands. But what if price isn't your first consideration? Does more money buy better olive oil?

When Americans want extra-virgin olive oil, we generally buy Italian. But a growing number of extra-virgin olive oils from other countries now fill store shelves, including more offerings from Spain, the top olive-growing nation, and Greece. There are even oils from California. Gathering 10 best-selling boutique extra-virgin olive oils from a variety of countries, priced at $20 to $56 per liter, we stripped them of their stylish labels and put them through the rigors of a blind tasting.

Sipped straight up from little cups, the extra-virgin olive oils in our lineup offered a pleasingly wide range of flavors, from fruity and "olive-y" to mild, buttery, and mellow to powerfully green, grassy, and pungent. Why does olive oil have such a wide-ranging flavor profile? Experts agree that the type of olive, the time of harvest (earlier means greener, more bitter, and pungent; later, more mild and buttery), and processing are the biggest factors. As one expert pointed out, olive oil is really just olive juice, and the quickest, gentlest extraction yields the truest flavors. The best-quality oil comes from olives picked at their peak and processed as quickly as possible without heat (which can coax more oil from the olives but at the expense of flavor).

The big loser in our tasting was DaVinci, our favorite inexpensive oil, which finished dead last. Although disappointed, we weren't really surprised. This oil may be better than the other inexpensive options, but it couldn't compete with high-end products. At least when it comes to olive oil, high prices buy more than just pretty bottles.

We were surprised, however, that tasters were not impressed with the high-end Italian oils, which finished in fifth through eighth place. Our two top finishers came from Spain, the third from Greece. We needed to explain these unexpected findings.

As we tallied our tasting results, we realized that our two favorite oils—both praised by tasters for their fairly assertive yet well-balanced flavor—were made with a blend of olives. The Columela and Núñez de Prado oils are a mix of intense Picual and mild Hojiblanca olives (the Núñez also adds delicate-flavored Picudo olives), creating a "fruity" olive oil with no elements that were perceived as too strong tasting—or too mild. By contrast, the other two Spanish oils we tasted, L'Estornell and Pons, were made with only the mild-mannered Arbequina olive, and they rated much less favorably.

Darrell Corti, owner of Corti Brothers store in Sacramento, California, and chairman of olive-oil judging at the Los Angeles County Fair (the top domestic and international olive oil competition in the United States), told us that producers often blend extra-virgin oils from olives with distinct flavors to create the overall flavor profile they want. According to Corti, the best oil is often made from a blend of varietals; the blend may consist of several oils, each one made from a single varietal (known as monocultivar, or single-olive, oils), or from a "field blend," in which different types of olives are picked and then processed together to create a single oil.

Was blending the answer we sought? Maybe not. Ranking nearly as high as the top Spaniards was a Greek oil, Terra Medi, made only with Koroneiki olives. It is not a blend, yet its balanced character and fruity, rounded flavor, with no harsh notes, made it similar in profile to the two top oils. Additionally, while some of the so-so Italian oils were made from single varietals, others were blends. So blending alone doesn't guarantee great oil.

The choice of olives is one factor that makes a particular oil more or less appealing. With their characteristic green, intense olive flavor and peppery aftertaste, the Italian oils had a few vocal supporters, but the majority of tasters felt that the oils' harsh pungency overwhelmed the olive flavor.

In the end, balance turned out to be the key factor that determined the winners of our tasting, and we found it in Spanish oils, not Italian oils. Our tasters preferred oils of medium-fruity intensity. Italian oils generally fall into the intense category.

For everyday use (particularly for recipes where olive oil is heated or must compete with strong flavors), we'll stick with DaVinci, but for drizzling over foods just before serving, the test kitchen is ready for an oil change. The top-ranked Columela is our new test-kitchen favorite when we want an extra-virgin olive oil with high-end flavor but don't want to break the bank to pay for it.

THE BEST EXTRA-VIRGIN OLIVE OIL

A blend of intense Picual and mild Hojiblanca olives, Columela Extra-Virgin Olive Oil took top honors for its fruity flavor and excellent balance.

baking sheet. Broil the zucchini, stirring occasionally, until lightly charred around the edges but slightly underdone, 7 to 10 minutes. Gently transfer the cooked zucchini to a wide, shallow serving dish (or casserole dish). Repeat with the eggplant, 1 more tablespoon of the oil, and additional salt and pepper; transfer to the serving dish.

3. Heat the remaining 2 tablespoons oil in a 12-inch nonstick skillet over medium heat until shimmering but not smoking. Add the onion, thyme, and ¼ teaspoon salt and cook until lightly browned, about 10 minutes. Stir in the garlic and cook until fragrant, about 30 seconds. Off the heat, stir in the tomatoes. Gently scatter the onion and tomato mixture into the dish with the broiled vegetables.

4. To STORE: Cover the dish with plastic wrap, poke several vent holes, and refrigerate for up to 2 days.

5. To SERVE: Let the vegetables come to room temperature, about 1 hour. Alternatively, you can microwave them at 50 percent power for 1 to 2 minutes. Sprinkle the basil and lemon juice over the top. Season with salt and pepper to taste, and drizzle with additional olive oil (if desired) before serving.

TO SERVE RIGHT AWAY

After scattering the onion and tomato mixture into the dish in step 3, cover the vegetables and let them sit for about 10 minutes. You can either serve the vegetables warm, or let them cool to room temperature. Sprinkle with the basil, lemon juice, and additional olive oil (if desired) before serving.

➤ VARIATION

Roasted Asparagus and Fennel Medley
Thick spears of asparagus work best here.

Follow the recipe for Roasted Zucchini and Eggplant Medley, substituting 2 medium fennel bulbs (about 1½ pounds), trimmed of stalks, cored, and sliced into ¼-inch-thick strips, and 2 bunches thick asparagus (about 2 pounds), tough ends trimmed, sliced on the bias into 2- to 3-inch lengths, for the zucchini and eggplant. Season and broil the fennel and asparagus, 1 vegetable at a time, as directed in step 2 (the broiling times are the same).

PREPARING FENNEL

1. Cut off the stems and feathery fronds. (The fronds can be minced and used for a garnish.)

2. Trim a very thin slice from the base and remove any tough or blemished outer layers from the bulb.

3. Cut the bulb in half through the base. Use a small, sharp knife to remove the pyramid-shaped core.

4. Lay the cored fennel on a work surface and, with the knife parallel to the cutting board, cut the fennel in half crosswise. With the knife perpendicular to the cutting board, cut the fennel pieces lengthwise into ¼-inch-thick strips.

TRIMMING TOUGH ENDS FROM ASPARAGUS

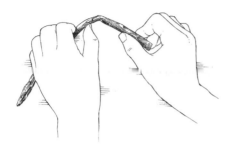

In our tests, we found that the tough, woody part of the stem will break off in just the right place if you hold the spear the right way. With one hand, hold the asparagus about halfway down the stalk; with the thumb and index fingers of the other hand, hold the spear about an inch up from the bottom. Bend the stalk until it snaps.

PUREED BUTTERNUT SQUASH

WITH ITS SILKY-SMOOTH TEXTURE AND earthy, lightly sweetened flavor, pureed butternut squash is a serious crowd pleaser for kids and adults alike. Most recipes for pureed squash are similar in that they cook the squash until tender, then puree it with some butter and/or heavy cream in a food processor. Our questions about making pureed squash were fairly straightforward: Does the cooking method matter? What kind of dairy tastes best? Are there any tricks to making and reheating the puree?

To start, we pitted four cooking methods against one another, including roasting, steaming, braising, and microwaving. Looking both for ease and the best flavor, we found that roasting took too long (over an hour), while steaming and braising washed away some of the distinct squash flavor, producing a less flavorful puree. Microwaving, however, in addition to being one of the easiest cooking methods, won tasters over for producing a clean, sweet squash flavor.

Next, we fussed with the best way to prep the squash for the microwave. We tried microwaving it whole, halved, and cut into large chunks. Microwaving the squash whole was a disaster—it cooked unevenly and the puree tasted seedy. Microwaving squash halves worked better; however,

TEST KITCHEN TIP:
Don't Buy Precut Squash

Don't be tempted to use packages of prepared squash slices (bags of peeled and cubed squash are even worse). The squash is usually dried out and woody.

we found it was hard to microwave more than one squash at a time, thus limiting the size and yield of our recipe. Microwaving the peeled chunks of squash, luckily, worked very well. Not only did the squash cook evenly if given a simple tossing halfway through cooking, but we could cook two or even three heads of squash at the same time if needed. Don't try to save time by buying prepeeled chunks of squash here (believe us, we tried); they are much less flavorful.

The surprising thing about microwaving the squash was the amount of liquid released while cooking—we drained nearly 1 cup of squash liquid out of the bowl before pureeing. (We tasted the liquid and found it had a slightly bitter flavor, which is why we did not opt to include it in the puree.)

Lastly, we found that the squash puree needed only a small amount of dairy to help round out its flavor and add some complexity. Testing various types of dairy including butter, heavy cream, half-and-half, and sour cream, we found the ideal dairy addition to be a combination of butter and half-and-half; it added enough richness to the puree without overpowering the squash flavor. One squash (about 2 pounds) only needs 2 tablespoons of butter and 2 tablespoons of half-and-half.

The puree both refrigerates and freezes well. Reheating the puree in the microwave works best; however, we did note a slight starchy texture when it was reheated. Stirring in a pat or two of fresh butter before serving helped to smooth this out. Rather than add more butter to the recipe overall, we found it better to leave out half of the butter in the initial puree, and add it just before serving.

Pureed Butternut Squash

SERVES 8 TO 10

You can substitute delicata squash for the butternut squash.

2   medium butternut squash (about 4 pounds), peeled, seeded, and cut into 1½-inch chunks (see the illustrations below)
¼   cup half-and-half
4   tablespoons (½ stick) unsalted butter
    Brown sugar
    Salt and ground black pepper

1. Place the squash in a large microwave-safe bowl. Cover the bowl tightly with plastic wrap and microwave on high until the squash is tender and easily pierced with a dinner fork, 15 to 20 minutes, stirring the squash halfway through the cooking time.

2. Carefully remove the plastic wrap (watch for scalding steam). Drain the squash in a colander, then transfer it to a food processor. Add the half-and-half, 2 tablespoons of the butter, 2 tablespoons brown sugar, and 1 teaspoon salt. Process until smooth, about 20 seconds, stopping to scrape down the sides of the bowl as needed.

3. TO STORE: Transfer the puree to an airtight container and refrigerate for up to 4 days, or freeze for up to 1 month. (If frozen, thaw completely in the refrigerator for 1 day before reheating.)

4. TO SERVE: Transfer the puree to a microwave-safe bowl and cover tightly with plastic wrap. Microwave on high power, stirring occasionally, until hot, 3 to 5 minutes. Stir in the remaining 2 tablespoons butter, and season with additional sugar, salt, and pepper to taste.

TO SERVE RIGHT AWAY

Add all of the butter to the hot, cooked squash in the food processor, and season with salt, pepper, and additional sugar to taste before serving.

➤ VARIATIONS

Pureed Butternut Squash with Sage and Toasted Almonds

Follow the recipe for Pureed Butternut Squash; while the squash cooks in the microwave, cook 2 tablespoons of the butter with 1 teaspoon minced fresh sage in a small skillet over medium-low heat until fragrant, about 2 minutes. Substitute the sage butter for the butter added to the food processor in step 2. Sprinkle with ½ cup toasted sliced almonds before serving.

Pureed Butternut Squash with Orange

Follow the recipe for Pureed Butternut Squash, adding 2 tablespoons orange marmalade to the food processor with the butter in step 2.

PREPPING BUTTERNUT SQUASH

With its tough outer skin, bulbous base filled with seeds and fibers, and long, skinny neck, preparing butternut squash can be a formidable task. Follow these key steps, however, and you'll be ready to cut the squash into evenly sized pieces.

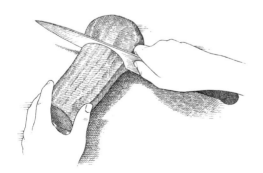

1. Cut off both ends of the squash, remove the skin with a vegetable peeler, and cut the squash in half, separating the bulb from the neck.

2. Cut the bulb in half through the base and remove the seeds with a spoon. Cut peeled and seeded squash as directed in recipes.

Pureed Butternut Squash with Honey and Chipotle Chiles

For a spicier flavor, use the higher quantity of chile.

Follow the recipe for Pureed Butternut Squash, substituting honey for the brown sugar and adding 1½–2½ teaspoons minced chipotle chile in adobo sauce to the food processor with the butter in step 2.

SWEET POTATO CASSEROLE

EVERY THANKSGIVING, WITHOUT FAIL, MILLIONS of households across the country prepare the butter-laden, overspiced, marshmallow-topped side dish we all know and love as Sweet Potato Casserole. It's as much a side of nostalgia as it is a side dish, but with all of that fat, sugar, and spice, the flavor of the sweet potatoes gets lost. Very lost. Thinking that the supporting ingredients ought to play second fiddle to the potatoes while still giving a fond nod to the familiar notion of a sweet potato casserole, we set out to update this home-style classic while testing its ability to go from the fridge to the oven.

Most of the recipes we researched added a great deal of sugar, cream, butter, and eggs to mashed sweet potatoes. Toppings, we were pleased to find, ranged far beyond marshmallows to include everything from a simple scattering of nuts to such glorifications as canned pineapple rings, maraschino cherries, cornflakes, Rice Krispies, bread crumbs, and streusel. Of all the test recipes that we prepared and tasted, the streusel-topped casserole stole the show. The streusel's crisp texture and bittersweet flavor—dark brown sugar balanced by slightly bitter pecans—held the filling's richness at bay.

Three-quarters of the recipes we found called for canned sweet potatoes. They have all the spunk of wet cardboard, so we ruled them out from the start. Custom calls for a vibrantly orange casserole, so choosing the appropriate potato was easy: Garnets, Jewels, or Beauregards are intensely colored and, in fact, sweeter than most pale varieties.

In terms of precooking the potatoes, the choices were boiling, microwaving, and roasting. The first two methods produced bland potatoes. Roasting was a different story. Although it took 1 to 1½ hours at 400 degrees, depending on the potatoes' girth, roasting produced a rich, earthy, intensely sweet flavor that made it worth every minute. Once the potatoes cooled briefly, it was quick work to scrape the soft flesh free of the papery skins.

Like peanut butter, sweet potato casserole typically comes in two styles: chunky and smooth. While the rustic appeal of the former was favored by some testers, most thought that a smooth-textured filling would better complement a crunchy streusel topping. We couldn't get the potatoes smooth enough when mashing by hand, so we resorted to heavy machinery. Both a hand-held and a standing mixer were efficient, but we wanted to try one more option: the food processor. Expecting the worst (food processors turn regular potatoes into wallpaper paste in seconds), we tossed the roasted potatoes into the processor workbowl and let it rip. Instead of dissolving into a starchy mass, as white potatoes would, they quickly became silky smooth.

INGREDIENTS: **Sweet Potatoes**

It's an age-old culinary question: What is the difference between a yam and a sweet potato? Answer: It depends on where you live. In U.S. markets, a "yam" is actually a mislabeled sweet potato. If you can get a glimpse of the box it's shipped in, you'll see the words "sweet potato" printed somewhere, as mandated by the U.S. Department of Agriculture. In other parts of the world, "yam" refers to a true yam, a vegetable having no relation to the sweet potato.

Sold under the label "ñame" (ny-AH-may) or "igname" here in the United States, a true yam has a hairy, off-white or brown skin and white, light yellow, or pink flesh. This tuber is usually sold in log-shaped chunks that weigh several pounds each. Unlike a sweet potato, a true yam tastes bland and has an ultra-starchy texture. It cannot be used as a substitute for sweet potatoes.

Once you get the sweet potatoes home, remove them from any plastic produce bag. Do not wash the sweet potatoes until you are ready to use them because this exposes the vulnerable skin and causes them to go bad more quickly. Refrigeration is also a no-no; it causes the core of the potato to gradually change texture until it resembles a soft, damp cork. The best storage is a dark, well-ventilated spot.

But now the creamy filling proved a bit too smooth to suit the topping. Tasters suggested a mix of potato chunks and smooth puree, so we reserved half of the roasted potatoes and folded them into the puree just before baking; bites of dense potato were thus suspended throughout the puree. This amalgamated texture proved not only to pair perfectly with the crunchy topping but also to heighten the sweet potato flavor.

Roasting had so intensified the flavor of the sweet potatoes that the excessive amounts of sugar traditionally added to the filling had became superfluous. Any more than a few tablespoons of white granulated sugar (brown sugar muddied the flavors) made the filling saccharine. This almost negligible amount of sweetener served as seasoning, rounding out the potatoes' earthiness and mitigating their slightly sour tang.

Any cook knows that fat generally equals flavor, but in this case we found the opposite to be true. Heavy cream—usually added to the casserole's filling—muted the intensity of the potatoes. We thought we could simply reduce the volume, but this made the filling stiff and gummy. Switching to whole milk made the filling too lean, so we split the difference and chose half-and-half. It contributed richness without being cloying. Five tablespoons of butter (most recipes included a full stick, or more) further smoothed things out.

Recipes typically add whole eggs to the filling, but we thought they made our casserole too stiff. Without any eggs, however, the filling was too loose and lacked depth of flavor. Yolks alone proved to be the solution. We tried as few yolks as one and as many as a half-dozen; four proved ideal, giving the casserole just enough body to let it be scooped neatly with a serving spoon.

Warm spices like cinnamon, ginger, and cloves made the casserole taste like pie. Nutmeg, however, in conjunction with a generous grind of black pepper, nicely offset the rich sweetness of the potatoes. Vanilla—a stiff shot of it—added surprising dimension by picking up floral undertones. Many recipes add orange juice and/or zest, but tasters found the flavors distracting. A splash of lemon juice delivered brightness without a citrusy flavor.

ARE THEY DONE YET?

Sweet potatoes take longer to roast than you might think—up to 1½ hours in a 400-degree oven. Here are two ways to determine whether they are properly cooked:

SQUEEZE

PEEK

Although the outside might be tender, the center can still be firm. Before removing sweet potatoes from the oven, squeeze them with a pair of tongs—they should give all the way to the center, without resistance.

If you have doubts, cut sweet potatoes in half lengthwise. If you see whitish marbling (uncooked starches that are firm to the touch), press the halves back together, wrap the potatoes individually in foil, and continue roasting until the marbling disappears.

The winning streusel from our first round of tests was a simple blend of flour, brown sugar, pecans, and softened butter (melted butter made the streusel too hard and crunchy). Although well liked, it was too sweet. We thought we could simply reduce the sugar and call it a day, but this yielded a bland-tasting, sandy streusel. Increasing the butter failed to improve things, and adding more nuts did little good. Streusel may be a simple blend of ingredients, but, as we were finding, they must be in perfect balance if they are to yield perfect results. After making a dozen batches in which we varied each ingredient by miniscule amounts, we finally arrived at an ideal ratio of 2 parts nuts to 1 part each of flour and brown sugar—very nutty and only lightly sweetened.

We worried that getting the streusel crisp while heating the filling through would be hard to do without multiple oven temperatures and partially covering the casserole, especially when baking it straight from the refrigerator. We needn't have worried. A moderate 375-degree oven heated the filling through without drying it while also crisping up (but not burning) the topping.

Sweet Potato Casserole

SERVES 10 TO 12

Try to buy potatoes that are uniform in size and avoid pota-toes larger than 1½ pounds; they require a longer roasting time and tend to cook unevenly. If the potatoes are smaller, the baking time will be shorter. Because natural sugar levels in sweet potatoes vary greatly depending on variety, size, and season, it's important to taste the filling before adding sugar (remember that the streusel topping is quite sweet). If you can find them, Beauregard, Garnet, or Jewel sweet potato varieties have the best texture for this recipe.

FILLING

5	tablespoons unsalted butter, melted, plus more for the greasing dish
7	pounds sweet potatoes (6 to 8 medium), scrubbed and poked several times with the tip of a paring knife
4	teaspoons juice from 1 lemon
1	tablespoon vanilla extract
2	teaspoons salt
½	teaspoon ground nutmeg
½	teaspoon ground black pepper
	Granulated sugar
4	large egg yolks
1½	cups half-and-half

STREUSEL

½	cup all-purpose flour
½	cup packed dark brown sugar
¼	teaspoon salt
5	tablespoons unsalted butter, cut into 5 pieces and softened
1	cup pecans

1. FOR THE FILLING: Adjust an oven rack to the lower-middle position and heat the oven to 400 degrees. Butter a 13 by 9-inch baking dish; set aside. Line a baking sheet with foil, and space the potatoes evenly on the sheet. Bake the potatoes until they are very tender and can be squeezed easily with tongs (see the photos on page 51), 1 to 1½ hours, turning them over halfway through the baking time.

2. FOR THE STREUSEL: While the potatoes bake, process the flour, brown sugar, and salt in a food processor until blended, about 4 seconds. Sprinkle the butter pieces over the flour mixture and pulse until a crumbly mass forms, 6 to 8 pulses. Sprinkle the nuts over the mixture and continue to pulse until combined but some large nut pieces remain, 4 to 6 pulses. Transfer the streusel to a medium bowl and set it aside; set the food processor workbowl aside.

3. When the potatoes are tender, remove them from the oven and cut them in half lengthwise; let cool for about 10 minutes to release their steam. Using an oven mitt or a folded kitchen towel to hold the hot potatoes, scoop out all of the flesh from each potato half into a large bowl (you should have about 8 cups).

4. Transfer half of the cooked potato flesh to the food processor. Add the melted butter, lemon juice, vanilla, salt, nutmeg, and pepper and process until smooth, about 20 seconds. Season the mixture with sugar to taste. With the processor running, slowly add the yolks and half-and-half through the feed tube and continue to process until blended and uniform, about 20 seconds.

5. Mash the remaining half of the cooked potato flesh into coarse 1-inch chunks using a rubber spatula, then stir in the pureed potato mixture until well combined. Transfer the mixture to the prepared baking dish and spread into an even layer. Sprinkle the streusel evenly over the top, breaking up any large pieces with your fingers.

6. TO STORE: Wrap the dish tightly with plastic wrap and refrigerate for up to 2 days.

7. TO SERVE: Adjust an oven rack to the middle position and heat the oven to 375 degrees. Remove the plastic wrap and bake, uncovered, until the topping is well browned and the filling is slightly puffy around the edges, 60 to 70 minutes. Let cool for 10 minutes before serving.

TO SERVE RIGHT AWAY

Bake the casserole, uncovered, until the topping is well browned and the filling is slightly puffy around the edges, 40 to 45 minutes. Let cool for 10 minutes before serving.

SCALLOPED POTATOES

SCALLOPED POTATOES—THINLY SLICED POTA-
toes layered with cream and baked until they are
bubbling and browned—are always popular. They
do not, however, fit easily into a make-ahead time
frame (as potatoes rarely do) because they require
a fair amount of prep. Our goal was simple: Make
the best possible scalloped potatoes with foolproof,
make-ahead instructions.

Using a standard scalloped potato recipe (raw
russet potatoes are layered in a casserole dish with
cream and aromatics), we first tested the difference
between storing an unbaked casserole (with raw
potatoes) versus storing a fully baked casserole.
Before tasting them on the second day, we then
baked the raw casserole until the potatoes were
completely tender, and reheated the prebaked casserole. Neither casserole impressed us. The cold,
raw casserole took over 2½ hours to bake through
and had a downright funky flavor with a grey-
colored top layer (the top layer of potatoes was not
covered by sauce and had turned dark overnight).
It also occurred to us (as we tasted this example)
that storing raw potatoes in cream overnight might
present some food safety issues—this method was
definitely out. The prebaked, then reheated casserole fared a bit better, but the flavors were quite
dull and the texture of the potatoes had turned
mushy by the time the casserole was fully heated
through (reheating took about 1 hour). Cooking
the potatoes before storing the casserole overnight
was the obvious lesson learned here, but the cook-
ing/reheating method needed serious work.

To fix the problem of mushy, overcooked potatoes in the prebaked version, we wondered if we
could just parbake the casserole initially. Bad idea.
The outside edges of a casserole cook through much
more quickly than the center, so that by the time the
potatoes in the center of the casserole had cooked
through in the reheating phase, the outside edges
had turned to a complete mash. In order to produce
evenly cooked make-ahead scalloped potatoes, we
needed to parcook all of the potatoes to the same
degree—that is, the potatoes needed to be parcooked
before they were assembled into the casserole dish.

Parboiling the potatoes first in water, then
layering them into the casserole dish with a flour-
thickened sauce was a method touted in several
other recipes we researched, so we tried it. The
potatoes in this casserole all reheated to a tender,
nonmushy texture on the second day, but they
tasted hollow and washed out while the flour-
thickened sauce tasted stodgy. Working with this
idea, we wondered if we could parboil the potatoes
in the sauce, then pour the entire mixture into
the baking dish—bingo! The potatoes parcooked
evenly on top of the stove and actually took on the
flavor of the sauce. The two keys we noted to making this method work were to gently parsimmer
(rather than parboil) the potatoes in the sauce, and
stir them often as they cooked. The method also
boasted two big bonuses: We only needed to use
one pot for the recipe, and the potatoes released
their natural starch into the sauce, thus negating the
need for the stodgy-tasting flour.

Up until now, we had been using russet potatoes (the classic choice for scalloped potatoes) but
just to make sure we weren't missing anything, we
tested our recipe with all-purpose and Yukon Gold
potatoes. While Yukon Gold and all-purpose potatoes weren't bad, tasters found them a bit waxy and
preferred the earthy flavor of the russets. We also
noted that the russets formed tighter, more cohesive layers owing to their higher starch content.

Heavy cream is the classic, diet-defying sauce
for scalloped potatoes because it doesn't break as
it bubbles away in the oven (as an all-milk or all-
half-and-half sauce does), but rather it thickens to
a silky, luxurious texture. We found the three cups
of cream required to make enough sauce for a
13 by 9-inch casserole dish of scalloped potatoes,
however, simply absurd. Also, many tasters disap-
proved of the overly fatty flavor and thick texture
of a sauce made entirely with heavy cream. To
relieve some of this heaviness, we tried replacing
some of the cream with a number of less fatty
liquids, including half-and-half, milk, and broth.
The half-and-half- and milk-augmented sauces
worked OK (they didn't break), but the potatoes
still tasted a bit heavy and dairy-rich. The chicken
broth–augmented potatoes, on the other hand,
were fantastic. The broth nicely mitigated some of

the cream's heaviness without adding a chickeny flavor or making the sauce taste bland. After trying a variety of broth-to-cream ratios, we landed on a 50–50 split. To further flavor the sauce, we found onion and some garlic to be crucial, while both thyme and bay leaves added a potato-friendly herb flavor that was neither showy nor distracting.

Testing the durability of this casserole, we found that it held well in the refrigerator for up to two days, beyond which time the flavors became too muted and the potatoes began to turn mealy. Throwing a batch into the freezer, we were surprised to find that it reheated like a dream. While a frozen casserole must be completely thawed before baking, we found no problem baking a casserole straight from the refrigerator. A combination of covered and uncovered baking time in a 400-degree oven is ideal for reheating this chilled casserole, and a sprinkling of cheddar over the top helps the potatoes emerge from the oven with an attractive golden crown. The dish is extremely hot straight out of the oven and can be sloppy to serve, but a 10-minute rest is all that's needed for the potatoes and sauce to cool off a little and cohere.

FREEZE IT
Classic Scalloped Potatoes
SERVES 8 TO 10

Slicing the potatoes ⅛ inch thick is crucial for the success of this dish. Use a mandoline, V-slicer (see page 55 for more information), or food processor fitted with a ⅛-inch slicing blade, or slice the potatoes carefully by hand using a very sharp knife. If the potato slices discolor as they sit, put them in a bowl and cover with the cream and chicken broth.

4   tablespoons (½ stick) unsalted butter
2   medium onions, minced
4   medium garlic cloves, minced or pressed
      through a garlic press (about 4 teaspoons)
1   tablespoon minced fresh thyme leaves,
      or 1 teaspoon dried
2½   teaspoons salt
½   teaspoon ground black pepper
1½   cups low-sodium chicken broth
1½   cups heavy cream

3   bay leaves
5   pounds russet potatoes (about 9 medium),
      peeled and sliced ⅛ inch thick
8   ounces cheddar cheese, shredded
      (about 2 cups)

1. Melt the butter in a large Dutch oven over medium-high heat. Add the onions and cook until softened and lightly browned, about 8 minutes. Add the garlic, thyme, salt, and pepper and cook until fragrant, about 30 seconds.

2. Stir in the broth, cream, and bay leaves. Stir in the potatoes, 1 handful at a time, and bring to a simmer. Cover, reduce the heat to medium-low, and continue to simmer, stirring often, until the potatoes are mostly tender (a paring knife can be slipped into and out of a potato slice with little resistance), about 15 minutes.

3. Discard the bay leaves. Pour the potato mixture into a 13 by 9-inch baking dish and press gently into an even layer.

4. TO STORE: Cover the dish with plastic wrap and poke several vent holes with the tip of a paring knife. Refrigerate for up to 2 days, or freeze for up to 1 month. (If frozen, thaw completely in the refrigerator, at least 24 hours, before baking.)

5. TO SERVE: Adjust an oven rack to the middle position and heat the oven to 400 degrees. Remove the plastic wrap, sprinkle the cheddar evenly over the top, and cover the dish tightly with foil. Bake until the mixture is just warm, 30 to 40 minutes. Remove the foil and continue to cook until the cheese is golden brown, and the sauce is bubbling, 30 to 40 minutes longer. Let cool for 10 minutes before serving.

TO SERVE RIGHT AWAY
Sprinkle the cheddar over the top of the casserole and bake, uncovered, until bubbling around the edges and the top is golden, 20 to 30 minutes. Let cool for 10 minutes before serving.

➤ VARIATIONS
Scalloped Potatoes with Chipotle Chiles and Smoked Cheddar
Follow the recipe for Classic Scalloped Potatoes,

adding 3 tablespoons minced chipotle chiles in adobo sauce to the pot with the garlic in step 1, and substituting 8 ounces smoked cheddar cheese, shredded (about 2 cups), for the regular cheddar.

Scalloped Potatoes with Mushrooms and Gruyère

Follow the recipe for Classic Scalloped Potatoes, adding 1 pound shiitake or cremini mushrooms, cleaned and sliced thin, to the butter along with the onions in step 1; cook until the moisture released by the mushrooms has evaporated, about 15 minutes. Substitute 8 ounces Gruyère, shredded (about 2 cups), for the cheddar.

PROPERLY SLICED POTATOES

When the potatoes were cut thicker than ⅛ inch (left), they slid apart when served, yet when cut much thinner (right), the layers melted together, producing a mashed potato–like texture. At exactly ⅛ inch (center), the potatoes held their shape, yet remained flexible enough to form tight, cohesive layers. Although it is possible to cut ⅛-inch slices by hand, it is far easier when using a food processor or mandoline.

EQUIPMENT: Mandolines and V-Slicers

What's cheaper than a food processor and faster (if not also sharper) than a chef's knife? A mandoline. This hand-operated slicing machine comes in two basic styles: the classic stainless-steel model, supported by legs, and the plastic hand-held model, often called a V-slicer. We put both types of machines—ranging in price from $5.99 to $169—to the test. To determine the winners, we sliced melons, cut carrots into julienne (matchstick pieces), cut potatoes into batonets (long, skinny, french-fry pieces), and sliced potatoes into thin rounds. Then we evaluated three aspects of the mandolines: ease of use, including degree of effort, adjustment ease, grip/handle comfort, and safety; quality, including sturdiness and uniformity/cleanliness of slices; and cleanup.

Of the five plastic models we tested, three of them were good choices. The Progressive Mandoline ($27.99) was easy to use and clean, whereas the New Benriner ($32.95) scored highest in comfort and durability. Although the safety guard that holds the food on the Pyrex Kitchen Slicer ($5.99) did not glide easily, it's easy to overlook this flaw given the low price, making it our best buy.

We also tested two classic stainless-steel mandolines. The deBuyer mandoline from Williams-Sonoma ($169) was controversial. Shorter testers had difficulty gaining leverage to cut consistently; some melon slices were ⅛ inch thicker on one side. However, the safety mechanism, sturdiness, and adjustment mechanism were lauded by taller testers. With some practice, all testers were able to produce perfect slices, julienne, and batonet with the Bron Coucke mandoline ($99). This machine has fewer parts to clean and switch out than its plastic counterparts and requires less effort to operate once the user becomes familiar with it. Still, the quality comes at an awfully high price.

BEST BUY

Plastic mandolines (also called V-slicers) may not be as sturdy as stainless-steel versions, but their quality far exceeds the minimal dollar investment. At a mere $5.99, the Pyrex Kitchen Slicer is our best buy.

THE BEST CLASSIC MANDOLINE

Of the two stainless-steel mandolines tested, we preferred this model made by Bron Coucke. Note, however, that it costs 10 times more than a good V-slicer.

MAKE-AHEAD MASHED POTATOES

MASHED POTATOES ARE THE ULTIMATE SIDE dish for all of the big holidays such as Thanksgiving and Christmas. But standing over a pot of boiling water hoping that you are not making the mashed potatoes too soon nor too late, while at the same time keeping an eye on your gravy, pies, roast, and an assortment of other side dishes, can be one of the most stressful parts of holiday cooking. We figured that being able to make a large batch of mashed potatoes a day ahead of time without sacrificing any flavor or texture would be a lifesaver for any time-crunched cook.

To start, we turned to our classic recipe for mashed potatoes, which calls for boiling 2 pounds of russets in their skins, then peeling them and passing them through a ricer or a food mill. One stick of melted butter and 1 cup of half-and-half are then gently folded into the processed potatoes, resulting in the smoothest, creamiest, richest-tasting mashed potatoes you ever dreamed of. These were everything we wanted our make-ahead mashed potatoes to be. Unfortunately, storing these mashed potatoes overnight and simply reheating them didn't work; they turned into something else entirely with a dry, super-grainy texture and off-flavors. Based on this failure, it was clear to us that we needed to start from the beginning and retest everything we thought we knew about mashed potatoes in order to find a great make-ahead version.

Could we solve any of these second-day texture issues by using a different type of potato? We tested mashes made with several lower-starch potatoes, such as Yukon Gold, red, and white potatoes against those made with our standard: russet potatoes. The Yukon Golds were the worst of the lot: stiff, heavy, and a little gluey. The red and white potatoes both had slightly better textures than the russets; they were smoother, less grainy, and felt almost velvety on the tongue. While their texture was better, their flavors were not; the red potatoes tasted dirty and a bit stinky (one taster described the taste as fishy), while the white potatoes tasted hollow and bland. Only russets provided the classic, mashed potato flavor, and despite their graininess, everyone preferred them.

We quickly discovered that buying the potatoes loose, rather than in 5-pound bags, is better because the quality of prebagged russet potatoes is very inconsistent. The potato sizes within the bags can vary widely, and several times we found them wet and rotting (old, soft potatoes make for a grainy, less-flavorful mash). By contrast, when we chose them ourselves from the bin of loose baking potatoes, we were able to pick the best of the lot—evenly sized, firm, nongreen, bruise- and rot-free potatoes. The resulting difference in the quality of the final mashed potatoes makes a few extra minutes spent shopping well worth the effort.

Next we wondered if using heavy cream instead of half-and-half (used in our classic recipe) would make any difference in the texture of the reheated potatoes. Those made with half-and-half lacked depth of flavor and tasted almost watery when reheated, while those made with cream tasted richer and less grainy. Up to now, we had been following a ratio of one stick of butter for 2 pounds of potatoes, but we wondered if we should review this—especially since we were now using heavy cream instead of half-and-half. Testing various ratios of cream to butter, we found it best to cut the ratio of butter by more than half; additional butter made the potatoes just too heavy and obscured the earthy potato flavor.

Up until now, we had been adding just enough cream to make a decent-textured mash (not too watery, not too stiff), but found that the mashed potatoes continued to absorb liquid overnight; mashed potatoes that were at the perfect consistency the day they were made would be dry and stiff when reheated the following day. To eliminate this problem, we found we needed to make the initial consistency of the mashed potatoes quite loose. To confuse the issue further, we noted that various tasters preferred mashed potatoes with different consistencies (some liked them stiffer, while others liked them looser). Plus the quality of the potatoes as well as how carefully they were scooped out of their skins affected how much cream was necessary. Luckily, our final solution to this problem turned out to be quite simple. First, adjust the consistency of the mashed potatoes to your preferred texture. Then, add an additional ½ cup of cream to make them looser so as to accommodate their overnight storage. When reheated the following day, the consistency will once again be ideal.

Next, we wondered if the order or time in which the butter and cream were added to the potatoes would make a difference. Adding the butter first made the potatoes grainier, and left an oily texture on the tongue. Adding the cream first made the mash taste creamier and less mealy. Wondering if some or all of the dairy should be stirred into the reheated mashed potatoes before serving for a fresher flavor, we tested a variety of batches side by side—the results were dramatic. Storing a batch of cooked, mashed potatoes without any butter or cream was a disaster. The reheated potatoes refused to incorporate evenly with the dairy and resulted in a chunky, gritty texture. Adding just a portion of the cream or butter to the reheated potatoes fared a little better, but these potatoes didn't taste nearly as smooth and cohesive as the batch where all of the dairy had been incorporated while the potatoes were freshly mashed and still hot. As we learned the hard way, there is little you can do to enhance the texture of mashed potatoes once they have cooled down.

Our make-ahead potatoes had gotten marginally better since we started, but we were still plagued by an annoying grainy texture. Up until now, we had been faithfully using our standard mashed potato–cooking method: boiling the potatoes in their skins in gently simmering water until tender, then peeling them and ricing them back into the warm pot used for cooking. It was time to put this method to the test against some other cooking methods, including peeling, slicing, and rinsing the potatoes before simmering, twice-boiling the potatoes (a technique touted in a few other books), and even microwaving the raw potatoes in a large bowl (we thought they would steam themselves). While none of these methods proved perfect, one method clearly stood above the others—microwaving. Although we were not fond of microwaving the potatoes on high for about 45 minutes and the texture of the final mash was a little rubbery, we had finally lost that annoying grainy issue.

TESTING NOTES

GETTING THE TEXTURE RIGHT

We found that the hardest part of making mashed potatoes in advance was achieving a smooth, silky texture. Here is how we did it.

1. Microwave, then Bake the Potatoes
This two-step process, rather than just boiling the potatoes, prevents the reheated mashed potatoes from tasting grainy.

2. Beat the Potatoes
After the cooked flesh is scooped out of the baked potatoes, we found it necessary to beat them in a standing mixer until smooth. Merely mashing the flesh wasn't enough and left unwelcome lumps.

3. Add Cream, then Butter
Adding the cream and butter quickly to already smooth, beaten potatoes is key for a silky—not gluey—texture.

4. Add Extra Cream
To prevent the mashed potatoes from drying out as they sit overnight, it's necessary to make them quite soupy. Add cream to your desired serving consistency, then add an additional ½ cup of cream to accommodate their overnight storage.

Taking a closer look at why the microwave had worked better, we wondered if it was because most of the water had been eliminated; the microwave was basically a waterless cooking method. We then tested two other potato-cooking methods that didn't submerge the potatoes in water: steaming and baking. Steaming 5 pounds of potatoes turned out to be a logistical problem requiring a large pot, a large steamer, and a cook with tough skin who could stir the 5 pounds of steaming potatoes as they cooked. Baking the potatoes then mashing them was much easier—we simply baked the potatoes until tender, then cut them open while hot and scraped out the potato flesh. The final consistency of mashed potatoes made from baked potatoes was nearly as good as that of those made from microwaved potatoes.

Next we tried baking the potatoes at different oven temperatures (at 350, 400, and 450 degrees) as well as microwaving them first briefly and then baking them.

The differences were astounding. The potatoes that were cooked at the higher heat were dry, clumpy, and had less flavor. The ones baked at 350 were decent, but could not compete with the ones that had been partially microwaved and then baked. The part microwave/part baking method was not only the fastest (it took just 46 minutes to be exact), but it produced super-silky mashed potatoes that packed great potato flavor; these were the best make-ahead potatoes yet.

Unfortunately, this new cooking method presented us with yet a new problem. Lots of small, dry chunks of potato were making it through the ricer and refusing to incorporate with the dairy, resulting in tough bits that marred the final texture. To solve this issue, we focused on the potato-mashing

> **TEST KITCHEN TIP:**
> **Buying Good Russets**
> Don't use a 5-pound bag of russet potatoes for this recipe, but rather buy loose, evenly sized baking potatoes; the bags tend to include a wild array of sizes (and quality levels), which means that the potatoes won't cook at the same rate.

technique itself. We tried twice-ricing the cooked potatoes, ricing them directly into hot liquid (so the potatoes would incorporate with the liquid without having a chance to clump), and lastly whipping them in a standing mixer. Whipping was the only method that got rid of the chunks, but it also tended to turn the potatoes a bit gluey. Smashing the potatoes up a little by hand before whipping helped reduce the whipping time (and corresponding gluey texture), and using the paddle attachment rather than the whip attachment also helped. Working with the paddle, we noted that it was best to beat just half of the cooked potatoes on high speed, then slowly add the remaining potatoes until all the clumps were gone and the potatoes were uniformly smooth. Lastly, we found that stirring the cream and butter into the beaten potatoes by hand, rather than in the mixer, ensured that the mash would not be gluey.

We had one final issue to conquer: reheating. We played around with putting the mashed potatoes in a casserole dish, then reheating them in the oven, but it just wasn't as easy or fast as reheating them in a bowl in the microwave. We then reheated various batches of mashed potatoes in the microwave at different powers, and made some interesting finds. At 100 percent power, the mashed potatoes took only 8 minutes to reheat, but the potatoes around the sides of the bowl began to dry out and seep fat. At 50 percent power, the potatoes took almost 30 minutes to reheat, but the mashed potatoes at the sides of the bowl were fine. Cutting the difference between the two heat levels, we found that medium-high power (or 75 percent) was ideal; it only took 14 minutes to reheat and it didn't ruin the potatoes around the edges. Stirring the potatoes halfway through the reheating time is absolutely necessary, as is making sure that the plastic wrap is well ventilated to allow the steam to escape.

We were pretty sure we had achieved our goal of make-ahead potatoes that tasted as good as those made the same day, but just to make sure we held a side-by-side tasting. The results? No one could tell the difference between the make-ahead mashed potatoes, and those that were made the same day!

Make-Ahead Mashed Potatoes

SERVES 8 TO 10

Be sure to bake the potatoes until they are completely tender; err on the side of over- rather than undercooking. You can use a hand-held mixer instead of a standing mixer, but the potatoes will be lumpier.

5	pounds russet baking potatoes (about 9 medium), scrubbed and poked several times with a fork
3	cups heavy cream, hot
8	tablespoons (1 stick) unsalted butter, melted
	Salt and ground black pepper

1. Adjust an oven rack to the middle position and heat the oven to 450 degrees.

2. Microwave the potatoes on high power for 16 minutes, turning them over halfway through the cooking time. Transfer the potatoes to the oven and place them directly on the hot oven rack. Bake until a skewer glides easily through the flesh, about 30 minutes, flipping them over halfway through the baking time (do not undercook).

3. Remove the potatoes from the oven, and cut each potato in half lengthwise. Using an oven mitt or a folded kitchen towel to hold the hot potatoes, scoop out all of the flesh from each potato half into a medium bowl. Break the cooked potato flesh down into small pieces using a fork, potato masher, or rubber spatula.

4. Transfer half of the potatoes to the bowl of a standing mixer fitted with the paddle attachment. Beat the potatoes on high speed until smooth, about 30 seconds, gradually adding the rest of the potatoes to incorporate, until completely smooth and no lumps remain, 1 to 2 minutes, stopping the mixer to scrape down the sides and bottom of the bowl as needed.

5. Remove the bowl from the mixer and gently fold in 2 cups of the cream, followed by the butter and 2 teaspoons salt. Gently fold in up to ½ cup more of the cream as needed to reach your desired serving consistency. Once the desired serving consistency is reached, gently fold in an additional

½ cup cream (the potatoes will be quite loose; see Testing Notes on page 57).

6. TO STORE: Transfer the mashed potatoes to a large microwave-safe bowl and cover tightly with plastic wrap. Refrigerate for up to 2 days.

7. TO SERVE: Poke lots of holes in the plastic wrap with the tip of a knife, and microwave at medium-high (75 percent) power until the potatoes are hot, about 14 minutes, stirring gently halfway through the reheating time.

MASHED POTATO CASSEROLE

MASHED POTATO CASSEROLES TRANSFORM THE humble potato into a side dish that is more than the sum of its parts. Smooth, cheesy, and topped off with a crunchy topping, this casserole screams comfort food. But could it be made in advance? This stick-to-your-ribs side dish is usually ruined by loads of cream cheese and such lackluster additions as pimientos and canned beans. Our goal was to redesign the casserole into a convenient make-ahead side dish that could be prepared up to 2 days in advance and reheated without any fussing. We wanted it to be a homey and simple accompaniment for an assortment of main dishes.

Although we had devised a technique for make-ahead mashed potatoes that involved baking the potatoes and then mashing them, we figured we could forgo this step since we were making a casserole. Betting that we could, we started out with our classic mashed potato recipe, which calls for boiling whole potatoes in their skins until tender, then peeling and mashing them. This somewhat fussy technique yields great flavor and a silky texture in fresh mashed potatoes, but these qualities become less noticeable when the potatoes are incorporated into a cheesy casserole. To make the cooking and mashing method easier, we began peeling the potatoes before cooking. Cutting the raw, peeled potatoes into chunks makes them cook faster, but we found that slicing the raw potatoes ensured that they cooked both quickly and evenly.

Based on our initial testing of mashed-potato casseroles, we already knew that the secret to keeping the potatoes creamy and smooth was to mix them with a variety of dairy products. Butter and milk were obvious shoo-ins because they added good flavor and helped loosen the mashed potatoes to a softened consistency. But using butter and milk alone didn't work; the potatoes tasted dry and grainy (much like leftover mashed potatoes). Sorting through the myriad dairy products called for in other recipes, we tested sour cream, cream cheese, cottage cheese, and cheddar cheese in various batches. The cream cheese added a velvety texture, but it gave the potatoes an unpleasant flavor. The cottage cheese left warm, curdled chunks behind, while the cheddar tasted good, but didn't incorporate well into the mashed potatoes or prevent them from turning grainy. Sour cream turned out to be the tasters' favorite, adding a nice richness and refreshing tang. When we added too much, however, its flavor became overpowering. Just 1 cup of sour cream paired with 5 pounds of potatoes was plenty.

Several recipes called for the addition of whole eggs and egg yolks, so we tried casseroles made with eggs to see what they would add. As it turned out, they subtracted more then they added. The whole egg casserole and the egg yolk version were both exceedingly dry and eggy tasting, so we nixed eggs from the ingredient list.

Looking for ways to increase the overall flavor of the casserole, we tried adding powdered mustard, but found that the fresher, more pronounced flavor of Dijon tasted better. To liven up the mash even more, we added some cheddar cheese along with a pinch of cayenne. Although we didn't have luck stirring the cheddar into the potatoes because it didn't incorporate well (and also its flavor got lost), we found that sprinkling it over the top of the casserole worked perfectly. Lastly, to complete the dish, we sprinkled a bread-crumb topping over the cheese. This casserole not only holds well for days in the refrigerator before baking, but the potatoes reheat to a smooth, creamy consistency and retain all of their flavor.

Mashed Potato Casserole
SERVES 8 TO 10

For a slightly spicy version, substitute pepper Jack cheese for the cheddar. Slicing the potatoes, rather than cutting them into chunks, ensures that they will cook more evenly. For the smoothest texture, err on the side of overcooking the potatoes rather than undercooking them.

TOPPING

4	slices high-quality white sandwich bread, quartered
2	tablespoons unsalted butter, melted
¼	cup minced fresh parsley leaves
	Salt and ground black pepper

CASSEROLE

5	pounds russet potatoes (about 9 medium), peeled, sliced into ¾-inch-thick rounds, and rinsed thoroughly
2½	cups whole milk, warmed
1	cup sour cream
8	tablespoons (1 stick) unsalted butter, melted
2½	teaspoons Dijon mustard
1	medium garlic clove, minced or pressed through a garlic press (about 1 teaspoon)
⅛	teaspoon cayenne
	Salt and ground black pepper
8	ounces extra-sharp cheddar cheese, shredded (about 2 cups)

1. FOR THE TOPPING: Adjust an oven rack to the middle position and heat the oven to 300 degrees. Pulse the bread in a food processor to coarse crumbs, about 6 pulses. Toss the crumbs with the butter, and spread them out over a rimmed baking sheet. Bake, stirring occasionally, until golden and dry, about 20 minutes. Let the crumbs cool, then toss with the parsley and season with salt and pepper to taste; set aside.

2. FOR THE CASSEROLE: Meanwhile, place the potatoes in a large Dutch oven and cover by 1 inch of water. Bring to a boil over high heat, then reduce to a simmer and cook until the potatoes are tender (a paring knife can be slipped into and out of the center of the potatoes with very little resistance), about 15 minutes.

3. Drain the potatoes in a colander. Set a food mill (or ricer) over the now empty, but still warm, saucepan. Working in batches, drop the potatoes into the hopper of the food mill and process the potatoes into the saucepan. Stir in the milk, sour cream, butter, Dijon, garlic, and cayenne until uniform. Season with salt and pepper to taste.

4. Spread the potato mixture into a 13 by 9-inch baking dish. Sprinkle the cheddar cheese evenly over the top, followed by the bread crumbs.

5. TO STORE: Cover the dish tightly with plastic wrap and refrigerate for up to 2 days.

6. TO SERVE: Adjust an oven rack to the middle position and heat the oven to 350 degrees. Remove the plastic wrap and cover the dish tightly with foil. Bake for 20 minutes. Remove the foil and continue to bake until the casserole is heated through and the crumbs are crisp, 20 to 30 minutes longer.

TO SERVE RIGHT AWAY

Bake the casserole in a 350-degree oven, uncovered, until hot throughout, 25 to 30 minutes.

➤ VARIATION

Mashed Potato Casserole with Bacon, Blue Cheese, and Caramelized Onions
Follow the recipe for Mashed Potato Casserole, omitting the cheddar. While the potatoes cook, fry 6 slices of bacon (about 6 ounces), minced, in a 12-inch nonstick skillet until crisp. Transfer the bacon to a paper towel–lined plate, and discard all but 1 tablespoon of the bacon fat. Combine the reserved bacon fat, 3 medium onions, minced, and 1 tablespoon sugar in the skillet and cook over medium heat, stirring often, until the onions are very soft and deeply browned, 20 to 30 minutes. Off the heat, stir in 4 ounces blue cheese, crumbled (about 1 cup); set aside. Substitute the bacon and caramelized onion mixture for the cheddar in step 4.

TWICE-BAKED POTATOES

THIS SIMPLE DISH—ESSENTIALLY BAKED russet potatoes from which the flesh has been

HALVING TWICE-BAKED POTATOES

THIS WAY   NOT THIS WAY

Most potatoes have two relatively flat, blunt sides, and two curved sides. Halve the baked potatoes lengthwise so the flat sides will be down when the shells are stuffed; this makes them much more stable on the baking sheet during the final baking.

removed, mashed with dairy ingredients and seasonings, mounded back into the shells, and baked again—offers a good range of both texture and flavor in a single bite. Done well, the skin is chewy and substantial without being tough, with just a hint of crispness to play off the smooth, creamy filling. In terms of flavor, cheese and other dairy ingredients make the filling rich and tangy, a contrast with the mild, slightly sweet potato shell.

Because twice-baked potatoes are put into the oven twice, we found it best to bake them for just an hour, rather than the usual 75 minutes needed for regular baked potatoes. Oiling the skins before baking promotes crispness, not something you necessarily want in plain baked potatoes, but a trait we came to admire in creamy twice-baked potatoes.

Twice-baked potatoes usually are filled with a mixture of well-mashed potato, shredded cheese, and other dairy ingredients, including one or more of the usual suspects: butter, sour cream, cream cheese, yogurt, ricotta, cottage cheese, milk, cream, and buttermilk. Various herbs and spices also often show up, as well as diced meats and sautéed vegetables.

To get an idea how we wanted to flavor our filling, we prepared 10 different recipes with various ingredient combinations. In a rare display of accord, all our tasters agreed on a few general observations. First, everyone preferred tangy dairy products, such as sour cream, yogurt, and buttermilk, to sweet ones, such as milk, cream, and ricotta. Second, the use of only one dairy ingredient produced a rather dull, one-dimensional filling. Another one added depth of flavor and complexity. Third, nobody favored anything too fatty, a preference that left the addition of large amounts of butter (some recipes use up to a full stick for four potatoes) and cream cheese out of the running. Dozens of further tests helped us refine our filling to a rich, but not killer, combination of sharp cheddar, sour cream, and just 4 tablespoons of butter. We learned to season the filling aggressively with salt and pepper. To make these the ultimate twice-baked potatoes, we found bacon, sautéed onions, and a final sprinkling of fresh scallions crucial.

Storing these stuffed potatoes in the refrigerator or the freezer presented no problems, although we had been concerned that they would taste dry or that the skins would become limp. Critical to reheating them successfully right from the fridge or the freezer is using a wire rack and a very hot oven, so that the filling remains hot and the skins crisp.

FREEZE IT

Twice-Baked Potatoes with Bacon, Cheddar, and Scallions

SERVES 8

Buying evenly sized potatoes will help ensure that they cook at the same rate. Be sure to leave a layer of potato inside the potato skins; it helps them retain their shape when stuffed and baked.

4   medium russet potatoes (7 to 9 ounces each), scrubbed, dried, rubbed lightly with vegetable oil, and poked several times with a fork

4   slices (about 4 ounces) bacon, minced

1   medium onion, minced

6   ounces sharp cheddar cheese, shredded (about 1½ cups)

1   cup sour cream

4   tablespoons (½ stick) unsalted butter, softened
    Salt and ground black pepper

2   scallions, sliced thin

1. Adjust an oven rack to the upper-middle position and heat the oven to 400 degrees. Place the potatoes directly on the hot oven rack and bake until the skins are crisp and deep brown and a skewer easily pierces the flesh, about 1 hour, flipping them over halfway through the baking time. Transfer the potatoes to a wire rack and let cool slightly, about 10 minutes.

2. Meanwhile, fry the bacon in a small nonstick skillet over medium-high heat until crisp, about 8 minutes. Transfer the bacon to a paper towel–lined plate, leaving the fat in the skillet. Add the onion to the skillet and return it to medium heat, occasionally stirring until the onion is softened and lightly browned, about 10 minutes; set aside.

3. Cut each potato in half lengthwise, so that the flat sides rest on the work surface (see illustrations on page 61). Using an oven mitt or a folded kitchen towel to hold the hot potatoes, scoop out the flesh from each potato half into a medium bowl, leaving ¼ to ½ inch thickness of flesh in each shell. Transfer the potato shells to a large baking dish.

4. Mash the potato flesh with a fork or rubber spatula until smooth. Stir in 1 cup of the cheddar, sour cream, butter, and sautéed onions, and season with salt and pepper to taste. Spoon the mixture into the potato shells, mounding it slightly at the center. Sprinkle with the remaining ½ cup cheese and the crisp bacon.

5. To store: Cover the dish tightly with plastic wrap and refrigerate for up to 2 days or freeze for up to 1 month. (After the potatoes are completely frozen, about 4 hours, they can be transferred to a zipper-lock bag to save space in the freezer.)

6. To serve: Adjust an oven rack to the middle position and heat the oven to 500 degrees. Set a wire rack over a foil-lined rimmed baking sheet. Lay the refrigerated or frozen potatoes on the rack and bake until the shells are crisp and the filling is heated throughout, 15 to 25 minutes. Sprinkle with the scallions before serving.

TO SERVE RIGHT AWAY

Bake the potatoes as directed in step 6, reducing the baking time to about 10 minutes.

Twice-Baked Potatoes with Bacon, Blue Cheese, and Caramelized Onions

For more caramelized onion flavor, add an extra onion.

Follow the recipe for Twice-Baked Potatoes with Bacon, Cheddar, and Scallions, substituting 2 ounces blue cheese, crumbled (about ½ cup), for the cheddar. Add 1 tablespoon brown sugar to the onions in step 2; cook until they are very soft and deeply browned, about 20 minutes.

Southwestern Twice-Baked Potatoes

Follow the recipe for Twice Baked Potatoes with Bacon, Cheddar, and Scallions, substituting 6 ounces pepper Jack cheese, shredded (about 1½ cups), for the cheddar. Add 3 medium garlic cloves, minced or pressed through a garlic press, to the onions during their final minute of cooking in step 2. Add 1 teaspoon minced chipotle chile in adobo sauce to the mashed potato mixture in step 4.

RICE PILAF

WHEN WE THOUGHT ABOUT MAKE-AHEAD side dishes that every cook would want in their repertoire, we definitely ranked a rice dish very near the top; a simple and flavorful rice pilaf seemed like our best bet—both because we thought it would likely hold and reheat well, given that the rice is cooked in hot oil before being simmered in hot liquid, and because it pairs well with a myriad of main courses. Our questions about making a pilaf ahead of time were fairly straightforward: Would the type of rice or ratio of rice to water change? Would we need to tweak our traditional pilaf cooking method? And what reheating method was best?

The logical first step in developing a make-ahead rice pilaf was to figure out the best type of rice. We immediately limited our testing to long-grain rice, since medium- and short-grain rice inherently produce a rather sticky, starchy product and we were looking for fluffy, separate grains. Plain long-grain white rice worked well in our pilaf, but basmati rice was even better: Each grain was separate, long, and fluffy, and the rice had a fresh, delicate fragrance. That said, we would add that you can use plain long-grain rice if basmati is not available.

Most sources indicate that the proper ratio of rice to liquid for long-grain white rice is 2 to 1, but we found that many cooks use less water and we wondered how an overnight stay in the refrigerator would affect things. After testing every possible ratio from 1 to 1 to 2 to 1 in our overnight tests, we found that we got the best rice using a ratio directly in the middle. A ratio of 1½ cups of water for every cup of rice was perfect. Scaling the recipe up to serve a good number of people (or to have enough for several mid-week meals), we landed on 3 cups of rice to 4½ cups of liquid. The most surprising thing about make-ahead rice pilaf is that, unlike other starchy side dishes that require extra liquid, this ratio stays the same whether you're serving the pilaf right away or storing it in the fridge for several days.

With our rice to water ratio set, we were ready to test the traditional cooking method, which calls for rinsing the rice, sautéing it in some fat, then adding the liquid and simmering. Various recipes we researched declared all these steps to be essential in producing the ultimate pilaf with separated, light, and fluffy grains. We did find that rinsing the rice made a slight difference in texture if eating the pilaf right away (the grains were more separated and shiny), but noted that this small difference seemed to disappear as the rice sat overnight and was reheated. Sautéing the rice, however, had an important impact on both the flavor and texture of the pilaf, even when reheated. Coating the rice with oil before adding the water helped to ensure

STEAMING RICE

After the rice is cooked, cover the pan with a clean kitchen towel, replace the lid, and allow the pan to sit for 10 minutes.

that the grains remained separate, and sautéing them added a great toasted flavor.

Most recipes for rice pilaf cook the rice in the water until the water is gone (at which point the rice is still underdone), then remove the pot from the heat and let the rice steam until tender. Wondering if this steaming time should be shortened since we were going to reheat it later, we tested several batches with various steaming times. Surprisingly, the understeamed rice tasted equally underdone when reheated, while the fully steamed rice tasted tender, separated, and not at all overdone.

We also decided to try placing a clean kitchen towel between the pan and the lid during the steaming time and found that this produced the best results of all. It seems that the towel (or two layers of paper towels) prevents condensation and absorbs the excess water in the pan during steaming, producing drier, fluffier rice. Also, we found that thoroughly tossing the rice with a fork before storing helped to ensure a fluffier pilaf when reheating.

The addition of flavorings, seasonings, and other ingredients is what gives pilaf its distinctive character. We found that dried spices, ginger, garlic, and onion, for example, are best sautéed with the onions before the raw rice is added, while fresh herbs and toasted nuts should be added to the pilaf just before serving to maximize their freshness, flavor, and texture (in the case of nuts). Dried fruits such as currants and apricots can be incorporated just before steaming the rice, which gives them enough time to heat through and plump up without becoming soggy, while the more delicate texture of dates requires them to be added with the herbs and nuts just before serving.

Finally, we tried various reheating methods including the oven, the stovetop, and the microwave; the microwave method was by far the easiest. Comparing different microwave power levels for reheating the pilaf, we found that the only difference was the overall reheating time. A higher power, in our opinion, was better because it was faster. Usually when we reheat things in the microwave, we like to vent the plastic so that the steam and condensation can escape, thus preventing the food getting wet and soggy. For the pilaf, however, we found it better to wrap the plastic tightly over the bowl and leave it unvented. Trapping the steam is crucial to rehydrating the cold, dry rice back to a tender pilaf. While we made and reheated entire batches of rice at a time, you can easily reheat smaller portions of the pilaf using the same method; and by making a big batch initially, you have enough small portions of rice for several dinners throughout the week.

Rice Pilaf
SERVES 10 TO 12

We noted the best flavor and texture with basmati rice; however, long-grain rice can be substituted. The recipe (and the variations) can be cut in half and cooked in a large saucepan to serve 4 to 6 people—the cooking time will remain the same.

4	tablespoons (½ stick) unsalted butter
1	medium onion, minced
	Salt
3	cups basmati rice
4½	cups water
1	bay leaf
	Ground black pepper

1. Melt the butter in a Dutch oven over medium heat. Add the onion and salt, and cook until softened, 5 to 7 minutes. Stir in the rice and cook, stirring occasionally, until the rice is fragrant and the edges begin to turn translucent, about 3 minutes.

2. Stir in the water and bay leaf and bring to a boil over medium-high heat. Cover, reduce the heat to low, and cook until all the water is absorbed, about 15 minutes.

3. Remove the pot from the heat, drape a clean kitchen towel underneath the lid, and let stand, covered, for 10 minutes.

4. To STORE: With a fork, gently toss the rice and transfer to a large, microwave-safe bowl, discarding the bay leaf. Cover the bowl tightly with plastic wrap and refrigerate for up to 2 days.

5. To SERVE: Keep the bowl tightly covered with plastic wrap and microwave on high power until the rice is hot, 12 to 14 minutes. Fluff the rice with a fork and season with salt and pepper to taste.

TO SERVE RIGHT AWAY

Let the rice stand off the heat as described in step 3, then fluff the rice with a fork and season with salt and pepper to taste.

➤ VARIATIONS

Rice Pilaf with Currants and Cinnamon

Follow the recipe for Rice Pilaf, adding 2 medium garlic cloves, minced or pressed through a garlic press (about 2 teaspoons), 1 teaspoon ground turmeric, and ½ teaspoon ground cinnamon to the pot after sautéing the onion in step 1. Cook until just fragrant, about 30 seconds. Sprinkle ½ cup dried currants over the cooked rice before letting the rice stand in step 3.

Indian-Spiced Rice Pilaf with Dates and Parsley

Follow the recipe for Rice Pilaf, adding 2 medium garlic cloves, minced or pressed through a garlic press (about 2 teaspoons), 1 tablespoon minced or grated fresh ginger, ¼ teaspoon ground cinnamon, and ¼ teaspoon ground cardamom to the pot after sautéing the onion in step 1. Cook until just fragrant, about 30 seconds. Before serving, stir in ½ cup chopped dried dates and 3 tablespoons minced fresh parsley leaves.

Saffron Rice Pilaf with Apricots and Almonds

Follow the recipe for Rice Pilaf, adding ½ teaspoon saffron with the onion in step 1. Sprinkle ½ cup chopped dried apricots over the cooked rice before letting the rice stand in step 3. Before serving, stir in ½ cup toasted slivered almonds.

CREAMY POLENTA

POLENTA IS MOST OFTEN SERVED IN ITS SOFT, velvety form and is rarely thought of as a make-ahead option because it turns into a solid brick as it sits overnight. Our goal was simple: We wanted to develop a recipe for make-ahead polenta that was as creamy in texture as the classic stovetop recipe that must be made and served immediately.

Starting off in the grocery store, we learned that there are two types of dried polenta—traditional polenta (basically uniformly coarse-ground cornmeal) and instant or quick-cooking polenta (polenta that has been partially cooked, then dried, and simply requires a brief reconstitution with boiling water). Giving both a whirl, we found that neither kept their soft, creamy texture overnight. While the instant polenta cooked in mere minutes, it had a milder, somewhat bland flavor that tasters didn't like in a side dish, compared to the full corn flavor of traditional polenta. (We do, however, like to use instant polenta in our Crispy Polenta Triangles, page 31.) Unfortunately, making traditional polenta is like a 30-minute arm wrestling match with Arnold Schwarzenegger; its thick, sticky consistency requires constant stirring in order to prevent it from scorching on the bottom of the pan. We obviously had our work cut out for us.

Working with the traditional polenta, our first task was to learn how to keep it from setting up overnight. We tried undercooking it (reasoning that we were making our own version of instant polenta) and overcooking it (reasoning that we would infuse more moisture in the cornmeal so it wouldn't dry out); neither worked. The partially cooked polenta was nearly impossible to rehydrate to a smooth consistency, while the overcooked polenta still turned stiff, but took on an unappealing gummy texture. We then tried adding extra fat (butter and oil) to the polenta to help keep it loose, but that just made it taste greasy. Next, we tested cooking the polenta in broth or milk (rather than water) to see if either would slow down the polenta's rate of moisture absorption as it sat overnight. The milk-and-broth-cooked polenta still turned into a brick, but tasters did like the extra flavor they added (so we set the idea aside for later).

As a last-ditch effort to make creamy make-ahead polenta, we made one final batch in which we increased the amount of liquid by one and a half times in order to make the polenta very soupy (traditional polenta uses a ratio of about 4 cups of liquid to 1 cup of polenta). Our theory was that either the polenta had an insatiable thirst for liquid as it sat overnight (in which case we were out of options), or that it would stop absorbing liquid after a certain point and stay creamy. Luckily, we found that the

EQUIPMENT: Large Saucepans

In the test kitchen (and at home), most of us reach for a 3- to 4-quart saucepan more than any other because its uses go beyond boiling water. Which begs an obvious question: Does the brand of pan matter? With prices for these large saucepans ranging from $24.99 for a Revere stainless-steel model with thin copper cladding at the base up to $140 for an All-Clad pan with a complete aluminum core and stainless-steel interior and exterior cladding, a lot of money is riding on the answer. To let us offer guidance, we tested eight models, all between 3 and 4 quarts in size, from well-known cookware manufacturers.

The tests we performed were based on common cooking tasks and designed to highlight specific characteristics of the pans' performance. Sautéing minced onions illustrated the pace at which the pan heats up and sautés. Cooking white rice provided a good indication of the pan's ability to heat evenly as well as how tightly the lid sealed. Making pastry cream let us know how user-friendly the pan was—was it shaped such that a whisk reached into the corners without trouble, was it comfortable to pick up, and could we pour liquid from it neatly? These traits can make a real difference when you use a pan day in and day out.

Of the tests we performed, sautéing onions was the most telling. In our view, onions should soften reliably and evenly (and with minimal attention and stirring) when sautéed over medium heat. In this regard, the All-Clad, Calphalon, KitchenAid, and Sitram pans all delivered. The Chantal and Cuisinart pans sautéed slightly faster, necessitating a little more attention from the cook, but still well within acceptable bounds. Only the Revere and Farberware Millennium sautéed so fast that we considered them problematic.

Incidentally, the Revere and Farberware pans that sautéed onions too fast for us were the lightest pans of the bunch, weighing only 1 pound 10 ounces and 2 pounds 6 ounces, respectively. This indicates that they were made from thinner metal, which is one reason they heat quickly. On the flip side of the weight issue, however, we found that too heavy a pan, such as the 4-pound Calphalon, could be uncomfortable to lift when full. The ideal was about 3 pounds; pans near this weight, including the All-Clad, KitchenAid, Chantal, Sitram, and Cuisinart, balanced good heft with easy maneuverability.

While none of the pans failed the rice test outright, there were performance differences. In the Sitram, Revere, and Farberware pans, the rice stuck and dried out at the bottom, if only a little bit. Although this did not greatly affect the texture, the flavor, or the cleanup, we'd still choose a pan for which this was not an issue.

Every pan in the group turned out perfect pastry cream. During this test, we did observe one design element that made it easy to pour liquid from the pan neatly, without dribbles and spills. A rolled lip that flares slightly at the top of the pan helped control the pour. Only two pans in the group did not have a rolled lip: the All-Clad and the Calphalon.

So which pan do you want to buy? That depends largely on two things: your budget and your attention span. Based on our tests, we'd advise against really inexpensive pans—those that cost less than $50. For between $50 and $100, you can get a competent pan such as the Chantal, Sitram, or Cuisinart. The only caveat is that you may have to watch them carefully; they offer less room for error than our favorite pans, made by All-Clad, Calphalon, and KitchenAid.

THE BEST LARGE SAUCEPANS

The All-Clad (left), Calphalon (center), and KitchenAid (right) saucepans are our favorites, but they are not flawless. The Calphalon ($110) is heavy, both it and the All-Clad pan ($140) lack rolled lips, and the KitchenAid pan ($119) has a relatively short curved handle. However, these three pans provide moderate, steady heat, even when you are distracted.

soupy polenta set up to lovely creamy consistency overnight. We found that we needed to increase the liquid by more than 50 percent to achieve the right consistency for make-ahead polenta. And as a bonus, cooking the soupy polenta was easier because the extra liquid made it much easier to stir and less likely to stick to the bottom of the pot.

The polenta now had the right overall consistency, but it tasted a little dull and watery. Remembering the flavorful milk and broth test we had done earlier, we tried cutting the water with some milk, chicken broth, and vegetable broth. The broths added a strong flavor that masked the corn flavor of the polenta, but milk added a nice creamy flavor without being overpowering. Testing various ratios of milk to water, we found that too much milk turned the polenta a bit slimy—just 2 cups of milk to 7½ cups of water is plenty using 1½ cups of polenta. Finishing the polenta with just a little butter and raw garlic added a nice rich flavor but, disappointingly, stirring in grated Parmesan cheese made the polenta much too stiff.

Up until now, we had been reheating the polenta in a bowl in the microwave, then whisking it smooth. The reheated texture of the polenta, however, had been a tad gluey. Storing the polenta in a casserole dish and reheating it more gently in the oven without stirring solved this problem. The casserole dish also presented the opportunity for yet more flavor in the way of toppings, including adding back the Parmesan. By sprinkling finely grated Parmesan over the top of the casserole, we were able to include its flavor without ruining the soft, creamy texture of the polenta underneath. Plus the lightly browned cheese topping looked pretty—this dish could go right on the table. This polenta now had it all—great texture, authentic flavor, and good looks.

As a final note, we found that the cheese also made a sturdy layer onto which we could easily sprinkle heavier toppings without having them sink down into the soupy polenta. By adding some sautéed cherry tomatoes or sautéed mushrooms over the top of the cheese, we suddenly took this plain, creamy polenta side dish to a whole new level, without adding much in the way of work.

Creamy Polenta

SERVES 8 TO 10

The polenta will seem very loose initially, but don't worry; it will set up as it sits overnight. In order for the Parmesan to melt and brown nicely on top of the casserole, we found it best to use finely grated fresh Parmesan rather than pre-grated cheese, which has a coarse, granular texture; finely grating the Parmesan is easy to do using the fine holes of a box grater or a Microplane grater.

7½	cups water
2	cups whole milk
	Salt
1½	cups (9 ounces) polenta
4	tablespoons (½ stick) unsalted butter
1	medium garlic clove, minced or pressed through a garlic press (about 1 teaspoon)
	Ground black pepper
2	ounces Parmesan cheese, finely grated (about 1 cup, see note)

1. Bring the water and milk to a boil in a partially covered, heavy-bottomed Dutch oven over medium-high heat. Add 1½ teaspoons salt, and very slowly pour the polenta into the boiling liquid while stirring constantly in a circular motion with a wooden spoon (see the illustration on page 69).

2. Reduce to a simmer over low heat and cook, stirring often, until the polenta no longer has a raw cornmeal taste, all of the liquid has been absorbed, and the mixture has a uniformly smooth but very loose consistency, 20 to 25 minutes.

3. Off the heat, stir in the butter and garlic and season with salt and pepper to taste. Pour the polenta into a 13 by 9-inch baking dish. Sprinkle the Parmesan evenly over the top.

4. To STORE: Wrap the dish tightly with plastic wrap, poke several vent holes in the plastic, and refrigerate for up to 2 days.

5. To SERVE: Adjust an oven rack to the middle position and heat the oven to 450 degrees. Remove the plastic wrap and lightly pat the cheese with paper towels to absorb any condensation that has accumulated. Bake uncovered until the polenta is bubbling and the cheese is nicely browned, 30 to 40 minutes.

TO SERVE RIGHT AWAY

Reduce the amount of water to 5½ cups and the amount of milk to 1 cup; cook the polenta until thick and smooth but still pourable, about 30 minutes. Stir in the butter and garlic as described in step 3. You then have two options for serving:

1) Transfer the polenta to a broiler-safe baking dish, sprinkle the Parmesan evenly over the top, and broil until golden browned, 5 to 10 minutes, or 2) Stir the Parmesan directly into the polenta in the saucepan and serve immediately.

POLENTA TOPPINGS

POLENTA IS OFTEN A FOIL FOR A STEW OR ROASTED VEGETABLES, BUT ON THOSE occasions where it is a stand-alone side dish, it's nice to dress it up a little. Here are two toppings you can sprinkle over our make-ahead polenta recipe (on top of the cheese) before it goes in the refrigerator. Add the herbs just before serving.

Sautéed Cherry Tomato and Basil Topping

Fresh minced tarragon makes a nice substitute for the basil.

- 3 tablespoons olive oil
- 1 medium onion, minced
- 1 tablespoon minced fresh thyme leaves, or 1 teaspoon dried
  Salt
- 6 medium garlic cloves, minced or pressed through a garlic press (about 2 tablespoons)
- 2 pints cherry tomatoes (about 1½ pounds), quartered
  Ground black pepper
- ¼ cup minced fresh basil leaves

Heat the oil in a 12-inch nonstick skillet over high heat until shimmering but not smoking. Add the onion, thyme, and ½ teaspoon salt, and cook until softened and lightly browned, 5 to 7 minutes. Stir in the garlic and cook until fragrant, about 30 seconds. Stir in the cherry tomatoes and cook until heated through, about 1 minute. Remove from the heat and season with salt and pepper to taste. Gently spoon the tomatoes evenly over the Parmesan-topped polenta in step 3 of the master recipe. Store and reheat the polenta as directed in steps 4 and 5. Sprinkle with the basil before serving.

Sautéed Mushroom and Chive Topping

Goat cheese tastes great with this topping; if desired substitute 4 ounces of crumbled goat cheese (about 1 cup) for the Parmesan in the recipe for Creamy Polenta.

- 3 tablespoons olive oil
- 1 pound cremini mushrooms, wiped clean and sliced ¼ inch thick
- 1 medium onion, minced
- 1 tablespoon minced fresh thyme leaves, or 1 teaspoon dried
  Salt
- 6 medium garlic cloves, minced or pressed through a garlic press (about 2 tablespoons)
  Ground black pepper
- 3 tablespoons minced fresh chives

Heat the oil in a 12-inch nonstick skillet over high heat until shimmering but not smoking. Add the mushrooms, onion, thyme, and ½ teaspoon salt, and cook until the mushrooms have released their liquid, shrunk dramatically, and are well browned, 15 to 20 minutes. Stir in the garlic and cook until fragrant, about 30 seconds. Remove from the heat and season with salt and pepper to taste. Gently spoon the mushrooms evenly over the Parmesan-topped polenta in step 3 of the master recipe. Store and reheat the polenta as directed in steps 4 and 5. Sprinkle with the chives before serving.

MAKING POLENTA

When the water comes to a boil, add the salt, then pour the polenta from a measuring cup into the water in a very slow stream, all the while stirring in a circular motion with a wooden spoon to prevent clumping.

BOSTON BAKED BEANS

HEADY WITH SMOKY PORK AND BITTERSWEET molasses, Boston baked beans are an example of a side dish that actually gains in flavor when made at least a day ahead of time. A close reading of recipes—and there are thousands out there—made it clear that authentic Boston baked beans are not about fancy seasonings; they are about developing intense flavor by means of the judicious employment of canonical ingredients (beans, pork, molasses, mustard, and sometimes onion) and slow cooking. Tasters quickly rejected recipes with lengthy lists of untraditional ingredients and short cooking times.

The most important item on the shopping list is, of course, the beans, the classic choice being standard dried white beans in one of three sizes: small white beans, midsize navy or pea beans, or large great Northern beans. While the latter two choices were adequate, tasters preferred the small white beans for their dense, creamy texture and their ability to remain firm and intact over the course of a long simmer. (The two larger sizes tended to split.) Per the test kitchen's previous findings, we found that there is no need to soak beans before cooking, so we gladly skipped that step. We did test canned white beans and were not impressed by their lackluster performance. Within two hours of baking, they had turned to mush and lacked the full flavor of the dried beans.

Next came the meat. Some type of cured pork is essential for depth of flavor and lush texture, though its flavor should never dominate. While traditionalists swear by salt pork, we first tried fleshier pork brisket, which is a meatier version of salt pork. Its flavor was enjoyable, but tasters felt the beans lacked richness—the brisket was too lean. Not surprisingly, salt pork scored high with tasters, although some felt the flavor was too mild. Bacon, a more modern choice, was deemed "too smoky and overwhelming" for most, though the heartier pork flavor was appreciated. On a whim, we put both salt pork and bacon into the pot and found the perfect solution. The bacon brought the desired depth to the beans, and the salt pork muted the bacon's hickory tang. Twice as much salt pork as bacon proved the right balance.

In traditional recipes, the salt pork is cast raw into the beans (often as a large piece) and melts into the sauce, but during tests it failed to render completely. Gelatinous chunks of fatty pork bobbing among the beans left even the most carnivorous taster cold. We first diced the pork into smaller bits, but this was only a partial success; unmelted fat remained. Next, we browned it in the Dutch oven prior to adding the beans, and the results were surprising: This simple step (and one not recommended in any of the recipes we'd found) made the flavor of the beans significantly fuller and better than anything we had

BUYING SALT PORK

FATTY

LEAN

The salt pork shown at top has a high ratio of fat to meat and is preferable in this recipe to leaner, meatier salt pork like the piece shown at the bottom.

SORTING DRIED BEANS WITH EASE

It is important to rinse and pick over dried beans to remove any stones or debris before cooking. To make this task easier, sort dried beans on a white plate or cutting board. The neutral background makes any unwanted matter easy to spot and discard.

yet tasted. Apparently, the melted fat more readily flavored the cooking liquid, and the browned bits of meat tasted richer.

While yellow onion was a controversial ingredient in classic recipes, we sensed its flavor could be important, and our intuition proved right. Tasters loved its sweetness and the full flavor it lent the beans, especially once sautéed in the rendered pork fat. Tasters favored a fine dice so that the onion all but disappeared by the time the beans were ready.

Next we tackled the final two ingredients: mustard and molasses. Dry mustard, the classic choice, had worked fine up until now, but most of the test kitchen felt home cooks were more likely to have prepared mustard on hand and that it provided a perk (vinegar), which cut the beans' sweetness. We tested several varieties, including Dijon, German whole-grain, "yellow," and "brown." They all brought a unique angle to the beans, but brown mustard—Gulden's, in particular—was best, imparting a pleasant sharpness without calling attention to itself. Even with the mustard's tang, though, we found it necessary to add vinegar for acidity. Most classic recipes include cider vinegar from the start of the cooking time (if at all), but we found the acidity stayed sharper when it was added to the beans once finished. A scant teaspoon proved enough to cut the molasses's sweetness and accent the other flavors.

The molasses, we discovered, would take some

finessing, as its brutish flavor and intense sweetness dominated the beans when added carelessly. After tasting batches made with mild, full-flavored (also known as "robust"), and blackstrap varieties, most tasters preferred the subtler tones of the mild variety. We settled on just ½ cup baked with the beans for a balance of moderate sweetness and palate-cleansing bitterness. An additional tablespoon added after cooking gently reemphasized its character.

All that was left to do now was tweak the cooking time. For testing purposes, we had cooked the beans at 250 degrees for six to seven hours. While pleased with the results, we were curious to see what other temperatures might accomplish. We knew that, to a certain extent, flavor and texture were in opposition. The longer the beans cooked, the better the sauce's flavor, but past a certain crucial moment of equilibrium, time worked against the beans, turning them to mush.

We tested cooking temperatures in increments of 25 degrees between 200 and 350 degrees and met with interesting results. At 200 degrees, the beans took upward of eight hours to cook and were still on the crunchy side. At 350 degrees, the beans percolated vigorously and exploded. Midpoints of 275 and 300 degrees were more successful. The beans were creamy textured and the sauce full flavored. With little difference in the outcome when either temperature was used, we chose 300 degrees, which made the beans cook faster, finishing in just about five hours—less time than we had thought possible.

While pleased with the texture and flavor, we still wanted a thicker sauce—soupy beans were not acceptable. We discovered that it was not simply a matter of reducing the volume of water, however, as this led to unevenly cooked beans. We had been cooking the beans start to finish covered with a lid, which had prevented the cooking liquid from

> **TEST KITCHEN TIP: Full of Beans**
> If you can't find small white beans, you can substitute larger-sized beans such as navy, pea, or great Northern; however, these larger beans tend to split as they cook.

reducing effectively. When we removed the lid for the last hour in the oven, we got the results we were looking for—the sauce had reduced to a syrupy, intensified state that perfectly napped the beans.

Boston Baked Beans

SERVES 6 TO 8

This recipe can be scaled up to serve a crowd if you use a large Dutch oven (at least 7¼ quarts)—simply double all of the ingredients.

4	ounces salt pork, trimmed of rind and cut into ½-inch cubes
2	slices (about 2 ounces) bacon, cut into ¼-inch pieces
I	medium onion, minced
9	cups water
I	pound (about 2½ cups) dried small white beans, rinsed and picked over (see the illustration on page 70)
½	cup plus I tablespoon mild molasses
I½	tablespoons prepared brown mustard, such as Gulden's
	Salt
I	teaspoon cider vinegar
	Ground black pepper

1. Adjust an oven rack to the lower-middle position and heat the oven to 300 degrees. Cook the salt pork and bacon in a large Dutch oven over medium heat, stirring occasionally, until lightly browned and most of the fat is rendered, about 7 minutes. Add the onion and continue to cook, stirring occasionally, until the onion is softened, 5 to 7 minutes.

2. Stir in the water, beans, ½ cup of the molasses, mustard, and 1½ teaspoons salt. Increase the heat to medium-high and bring to a boil. Cover the pot, transfer it to the oven and bake, stirring occasionally, until the beans are tender, about 4 hours. Remove the lid and continue to bake until the liquid has thickened to a syrupy consistency, 1 to 1½ hours longer.

3. Remove the beans from the oven. Stir in the remaining 1 tablespoon molasses, vinegar, and season with salt and pepper to taste.

4. TO STORE: Let the beans cool at room temperature for 1 hour, then transfer them to an airtight container and refrigerate for up to 4 days.

5. TO SERVE: Transfer the beans to a pot and reheat over medium-low heat, stirring often, until hot, about 30 minutes.

TO SERVE RIGHT AWAY

Serve the beans after seasoning in step 3.

➤ VARIATION

Barbecued Baked Beans

Barbecued baked beans are slow-simmered, oven-cooked beans that are similar to Boston baked beans. Barbecued baked beans are a bit brasher in flavor, however, so they stand up better to the big flavors of grilled and barbecued foods.

4	slices (about 4 ounces) bacon, chopped coarse
I	medium onion, minced
4	medium garlic cloves, minced or pressed through a garlic press (about 4 teaspoons)
8	cups water
I	pound (about 2½ cups) dried navy beans, rinsed and picked over (see the illustration on page 70)
I	cup strong black coffee
½	cup plus I tablespoon barbecue sauce
¼	cup packed dark brown sugar
I½	tablespoons prepared brown mustard, such as Gulden's
I	tablespoon mild molasses
½	teaspoon hot sauce
	Salt and ground black pepper

1. Adjust an oven rack to the lower-middle position and heat the oven to 300 degrees. Cook the bacon in a large Dutch oven over medium heat, stirring occasionally, until lightly browned and most of the fat is rendered, about 7 minutes. Add the onion and continue to cook, stirring occasionally, until the onion is softened, 5 to 7 minutes. Stir in the garlic and cook until fragrant, about 30 seconds.

2. Stir in the water, beans, coffee, ½ cup of the barbecue sauce, brown sugar, mustard, molasses, hot sauce, and 2 teaspoons salt. Increase the heat to medium-high and bring to a boil. Cover the pot, transfer it to the oven, and bake, stirring occasionally, until the beans are tender, about 4 hours. Remove the lid and continue to bake until the liquid has thickened to a syrupy consistency, 1 to 1½ hours longer.

3. Remove from the oven and stir in the remaining tablespoon barbecue sauce. Season with salt and pepper to taste.

4. To STORE: Let the beans cool at room temperature for 1 hour, then transfer them to an airtight container and refrigerate for up to 4 days.

5. To SERVE: Transfer the beans to a pot and reheat over medium-low heat, stirring often, until hot, about 30 minutes.

TO SERVE RIGHT AWAY
Serve the beans after seasoning in step 3.

ALL-AMERICAN POTATO SALAD

NO ONE IN THEIR RIGHT MIND WOULD try to make potato salad at the last minute—it simply requires too much prep, not to mention some necessary chilling time before serving. But then again, potato salad made more than just a few hours ahead of time usually tastes bland and dried out. Potato salad isn't hard to make, but we needed to find a few make-ahead tricks that would enable it to withstand a few extra days in the refrigerator without losing its flavor or creamy consistency.

To start, we carefully tested five different classic potato salad recipes here in the test kitchen, and not one escaped serious critique. Making them all on day one then tasting them all on day two, we found that all the salads turned quite dry and pasty overnight. As for flavor, three of the salads tasted hopelessly bland, while the fourth was too tart from an excess of vinegar, and the fifth tasted like potato candy, having been seasoned with ⅓ cup sugar. These results inspired us to create our own recipe, but we didn't want to reinvent the wheel. Our goal was simply to nail down a good, solid formula for this summer side dish and figure out how to help

the salad maintain its texture and flavor over the course of several days. Ideally, our salad would be able to boast flavorful, tender potatoes punctuated by crunchy bits of onion and celery, and a dressing with a hint of sweetness and a measure of acidity.

We began with the most basic issue: the potatoes. Recipe writers and home cooks are divided on which potatoes are best for potato salad. Most insist on waxy Red Bliss or boiling potatoes, which hold their shape well during cooking. Some like golden-fleshed, moderately starchy Yukon Golds, while a minority maintain a preference for russets. We boiled up each of these common supermarket candidates and made bare-bones potato salads for a panel of tasters. Obviously, the potatoes differed texturally. But they had one thing in common: They were all incredibly bland.

While developing other recipes for potato salad, the test kitchen has found that seasoning the potatoes while they're hot maximizes flavor. For our next round of tests, then, we splashed the hot potatoes with vinegar before proceeding with our recipe. The russets, being the driest, sponged up the vinegar and tasted great. In contrast, the other potatoes were still a little too mild tasting after the vinegar soak. (See "Why Russets Rule" on page 74 for an explanation.) Although russets were called for in only a small minority of the 30 or more potato salad recipes we had collected, their capacity to soak up vinegar gave them a lot of credibility with us, as it allowed their flavor to shine even after a few days in the fridge. Yes, they do crumble a bit when mixed, but tasters found this quality charming, not alarming. Their starchy, rich texture reminded many tasters of the hefty deli-style potato salads they had grown up with.

As for the type of acid, we experimented first with drizzles of lemon juice and pickle juice. The citrus tones offered by the lemon juice seemed out of place in potato salad and tended to fade quickly as the salad sat, while pickle juice wasn't acidic enough for most tasters. Among red wine vinegar, cider vinegar, and white vinegar, the clear loser was cider vinegar, whose distinctive fruity flavor led to an early dismissal in the tasting. Two tablespoons of plain white vinegar got the most votes for its clean, clear acidity.

Next we needed to determine whether the potatoes should be peeled and cut before or after boiling. Predictably, potatoes boiled in their skins were rich and earthy; those peeled and cut before boiling exhibited slightly less flavor. But peeling and cutting steaming-hot potatoes (a requirement if the potatoes are to be properly seasoned) is a tricky proposition. Thankfully, once the potatoes were dressed, the flavor differences between those boiled with and without their jackets were practically unnoticeable. It's also easier to judge the doneness of a small chunk than it is a whole russet potato, which can turn mushy on the exterior while the inner layer remains firm.

With our cooking technique settled, we turned our focus to flavor. Though the vinegar bath was helpful, we wanted to try further enhancing flavor by spiking the boiling water with potent ingredients. A quartered onion and smashed garlic clove went nearly undetected, as did chicken broth. Finally, we added a few glugs of vinegar to a pot of boiling potatoes, wondering if it would be more effective than seasoning the potatoes post cooking. After nearly an hour of simmering, the potatoes were still not tender. A quick consultation with our science editor reminded us that acid reinforces the pectin in potatoes, making them resistant to breaking down on exposure to heat. We decided to leave well enough alone and to stick with salted water as the boiling medium.

TEST KITCHEN TIP: Foolproof Hard-Cooked Eggs

Hard-cooking an egg can be a crapshoot because there's no way to monitor the cooking progress or test for doneness. Although an overcooked or undercooked egg is not a horrible disaster, it is avoidable—here's how.

Place 6 large eggs in a medium saucepan, cover with 1 inch of water, and bring to a boil over high heat. As soon as the water boils, remove the pan from the heat, cover, and let sit for 10 minutes. Meanwhile, fill a medium bowl with ice water. Transfer the hot eggs to the ice water bath with a slotted spoon and let sit for 5 minutes before peeling. (This recipe is easy to double or triple as long as you use a pot large enough to hold the eggs in a single layer, covered by an inch of water.)

INGREDIENTS: Mayonnaise

Although we love homemade mayonnaise on occasion, we realize that it's not always convenient to whip up a batch, so we set up a tasting of seven nationally available brands of commercially prepared mayonnaise along with Kraft Miracle Whip. Even though the U.S. Food and Drug Administration does not recognize Miracle Whip as a real mayonnaise, we included it in our tasting because of its resounding popularity. Why is Miracle Whip considered a salad dressing and not a mayonnaise? The FDA defines mayonnaise as an emulsified semisolid food that is at least 65 percent vegetable oil by weight, is at least 2.5 percent acidifying ingredient (vinegar and/or lemon juice) by weight, and contains whole eggs or egg yolks. Miracle Whip, which is also sweeter than regular mayo, weighs in with only 40 percent soybean oil. (Water makes up the difference.)

A good mayonnaise will have clear egg flavor and a touch of acidity to offset the significant amount of fat from the added oil. Our tasters liked Hellmann's for having that balance, and Kraft was thought to be "flavorful but not overpowering." Which one should you buy? We recommend Hellmann's, but the difference between the two contenders is not overwhelming.

Finally, is it possible for a light mayo to be as flavorful as the full-fat original? We put five brands to the test: Kraft Light Mayonnaise, Hellmann's Light Mayonnaise, Miracle Whip Light Salad Dressing, Spectrum Light Canola Mayonnaise, and Nayonaise (a soy-based sandwich spread), all with a fat content of 3 to 5 grams per serving. We also threw the winner of the full-fat tasting into the mix (Hellmann's Real Mayonnaise, 11 grams of fat per serving).

The results? Last place went to Nayonaise. Tasters were unanimous in thinking it bore no resemblance to mayonnaise. Miracle Whip and Spectrum didn't fare much better. Tasters thought Kraft was too sweet. Hellmann's Light came in second place, very nearly beating out the winner, Hellmann's Real Mayonnaise. Although the light version had a pastier texture than regular Hellmann's, the bright, balanced flavors were similar.

THE BEST MAYONNAISE

Hellmann's (left) took top honors in our tasting. Among the reduced-fat mayonnaises tested, Hellmann's Light (right) was the clear winner.

Turning our attention to the other salad ingredients, we knew that celery was a must, and one rib fit the bill. Among scallions, shallots, and red, yellow, white, and Vidalia onions, red onion was

SCIENCE: Why Russets Rule

In our potato salad recipe, we found that russets absorbed more vinegar than Red Bliss or any other potato variety tested. We wanted to find out why.

Our first guess was that Red Bliss potatoes must be more dense than russet potatoes, thus the vinegar would penetrate more slowly. The density, or specific gravity, of a potato can be measured in a salt brine. If the potato is more dense than the saltwater, it will sink; if it is less dense, it will float. Our first test did not work out as planned. Although russet potatoes are known for being fluffy when cooked, they are in fact more dense than Red Bliss potatoes.

Flummoxed, we decided to find out just how much more vinegar the russets were absorbing. After taking careful measurements, we found that they were soaking up about 10 percent more vinegar than the Red Bliss. We wondered if this small amount of vinegar—10 percent of 2 tablespoons—could really make a difference in flavor. Hoping to get a look at what was happening inside the potatoes, we added dye to the vinegar for our next test. What we expected to see was more dye along the edges of the russets when compared to the Red Bliss. But when we cut open the cubes of potato, we found that the russets had faults running through the middle that were filled with colored liquid, while the Red Bliss did not (see photo).

A russet potato has weaker cell walls, making it more apt to fall apart and become mealy when cooked. This structural weakness works well in our potato salad, as the cracks and crevices provide avenues for the flavorful vinegar to penetrate deep into the center of the potato chunks.

SINK OR SWIM?

A dense russet potato sinks in saltwater, while the less dense Red Bliss potato bobs to the surface.

the winner for its spark of color, bright taste, and ability to hold well without turning stinky. We also considered pickles—in our opinion, a mandatory ingredient. Bread and butter, dill, and kosher pickles were in the running with gherkins and sweet pickle relish. Each had its devotees, but we decided on pickle relish, which requires no preparation and gives the potato salad a subtle sweetness. In terms of seasonings, we pitted dry mustard (ground mustard seed) against prepared mustard and noted that the pungent dry mustard sparkled in combination with the other ingredients and held its flavor for days, while prepared mustard fell flat. Garlic added a likable sting but was deemed inappropriate for the master recipe. Lastly, hard-cooked eggs created some controversy, considered obligatory by some and a mistake by others—we leave the choice to the cook.

While nailing down the flavors of the salad, we hit upon an unusual finding. Our intuition told us to test celery seed, a spice that has fallen out of favor. The seed of a type of wild celery known as smallage, celery seed didn't merely add strong celery flavor but instead provided an underlying complexity and depth. Potato salad made without celery seed tasted hollow in comparison to salad containing a scant teaspoon. Now we won't make potato salad without it, much less a make-ahead potato salad.

We knew we wanted a classic mayonnaise-based dressing to bind the potatoes with the flavorings, but unfortunately, the mayonnaise seemed to get soaked up readily by the potatoes when the salad sat for longer than just a few hours. As with our Deli-Style Macaroni Salad (page 77), we tried loosening up the salad before serving with various ingredients including oil, water, buttermilk, sour cream, and milk, but tasters had a strong preference for the clean, unadulterated flavor of plain mayonnaise here. Rather than loading up the salad with tons of mayonnaise (more than the potatoes could possibly soak up), we found it best to leave out half of the mayo in the salad initially, then stir in the remaining half just before serving. Lastly, we noted that the salad tastes best when not served straight from the fridge, but when allowed to sit at room temperature for about an hour.

All-American Potato Salad

SERVES 10 TO 12

This recipe can easily be doubled. If only celery salt is available (note that the recipe calls for celery seed), use the same amount, but omit the salt in the dressing. When testing the potatoes for doneness, it may help to simply taste a piece; do not overcook the potatoes or they will become mealy and will break apart. Also, the potatoes must be just warm, or even fully cooled, when you add the dressing. If you find the potato salad a little dry for your liking, add up to 2 tablespoons more mayonnaise.

5	pounds russet potatoes (about 9 medium), peeled and cut into ¾-inch cubes
	Salt
¼	cup distilled white vinegar
2	cups mayonnaise
2	medium celery ribs, minced
½	cup sweet pickle relish
⅓	cup minced red onion
¼	cup minced fresh parsley leaves
1½	teaspoons celery seed
1	teaspoon dry mustard
	Ground black pepper
4	large hard-cooked eggs, peeled and cut into ¼-inch cubes (optional)

1. Place the potatoes in a large Dutch oven and cover by 1 inch of water. Bring to a boil over medium-high heat. Add 1 tablespoon salt, reduce the heat to medium, and simmer, stirring occasionally, until the potatoes are tender (a paring knife can be slipped into and out of the center of the potatoes with very little resistance), about 8 minutes.

2. Drain the potatoes in a colander and transfer them to large bowl. Gently stir in the vinegar and let stand until the potatoes are just warm, about 20 minutes.

3. Meanwhile, stir together 1 cup of the mayonnaise with the celery, pickle relish, onion, parsley, celery seed, dry mustard, ¼ teaspoon pepper, and ½ teaspoon salt in a small bowl.

4. Using a rubber spatula, gently fold the mayonnaise mixture and eggs (if using) into the potatoes.

5. To store: Cover tightly with plastic wrap and refrigerate for up to 2 days.

6. To serve: Let the salad stand at room temperature about 1 hour. Gently fold in the remaining 1 cup mayonnaise and season with salt and pepper to taste.

TO SERVE RIGHT AWAY

Stir the remaining 1 cup mayonnaise into the potatoes in step 4, cover tightly with plastic wrap, and refrigerate until chilled, about 1 hour.

EQUIPMENT: Vegetable Peelers

For years, the Oxo Good Grips peeler has been a standard in our test kitchen. But two new peelers on the market led us back into the kitchen for another look. Oxo's new I-Series line includes a redesigned vegetable peeler that we found to be exceptionally sharp. The blades are replaceable (much like razor blades that click on and pop off). I-Series vegetable peelers have a more slender handle, which solves the only problem we had with the original Good Grips peeler: it was a bit bulky. Nonetheless, the I-Series peeler is heavier, tipping the scale at nearly a quarter pound. The balance of extra weight falls to the blade end, which seems to allow the peeler to do some of the work for you.

Similar in appearance to Oxo's Good Grips peeler is the Messermeister serrated-blade peeler. We were surprised that what we thought would be a novelty peeler could rival and even replace a Good Grips at the usual peeling tasks. What makes this peeler exceptional is its ability to peel ripe peaches and tomatoes, which even the noticeably sharper I-Series peeler was reluctant to do effectively. The Messermeister's narrow black rubber handle, however, makes it difficult to get a good grip.

So what peeler should you reach for? We'll be reaching for the Oxo I-Series. With replaceable blades and solid construction, this peeler will have a home in our kitchen for many years to come. That is, until Oxo introduces a new peeler.

THE BEST VEGETABLE PEELER

The Oxo I-Series peeler ($10) is our new favorite.

Garlicky Potato Salad with Tomatoes and Basil

Follow the recipe for All-American Potato Salad, omitting the pickle relish, parsley, dry mustard, and hard-cooked eggs. Add 1 medium garlic clove, minced or pressed through a garlic press (about 1 teaspoon), to the mayonnaise mixture in step 3. Stir in 1 pint cherry tomatoes (about 12 ounces), halved, and 1 cup chopped fresh basil leaves before serving.

Potato Salad with Horseradish and Dill

Follow the recipe for All-American Potato Salad, omitting the pickle relish, parsley, and dry mustard. Add 3 to 4 tablespoons prepared horseradish to the mayonnaise mixture in step 3. Stir in ½ cup minced fresh dill before serving.

MACARONI SALAD

ALTHOUGH MACARONI SALAD SEEMS AS though it would be a natural make-ahead recipe, we noted that its texture suffers dramatically when made more than a few hours in advance. The noodles absorb all of the moisture out of the mayonnaise, leaving the salad with a strange sticky, greasy texture.

To start fixing this problem, we focused first on the pasta. We noted a big difference between salads made with pasta cooked to an al dente texture and pasta that was cooked through until completely tender. Although both salads absorbed most of the dressing overnight, the al dente pasta chilled to an unappealing stiff texture, while completely tender pasta chilled to a pleasant bouncy texture. Wondering if we could solve the dressing absorption issue by overcooking the pasta past tender (thinking that the pasta would absorb more water during cooking, and therefore take less from the dressing) we tried boiling it even longer. No luck. The overcooked pasta had a mushy texture when chilled and turned out an equally dry salad.

Running with the completely tender, but not overcooked pasta, we found it important to add more salt than usual to the cooking water. While the pasta will taste a little salty on its own, it will be perfectly seasoned when mixed with the other salad ingredients and served cold. We found that 2 tablespoons of salt to 4 quarts of water was just right to season 1 pound of pasta.

Next, we tested when to toss the mayonnaise dressing with the macaroni: Should the pasta be hot, cooled to room temperature, or rinsed until cool? The hot pasta soaked up the dressing within seconds and tasted strange, while both batches of pasta that were allowed to cool first worked better. Rinsing the pasta after cooking became our favorite method because it was faster than letting the pasta cool down on its own, and it produced a slightly softer texture. Patting the macaroni dry after rinsing is not necessary because the macaroni absorbs the extra moisture overnight. As for the dressing itself, we found that the potency of a large shallot plus a hefty amount of lemon juice was necessary to give this salad some spark and brightness; additional lemon juice was needed just before serving as well to boost the overall seasoning and flavor.

Although we were making strides, the macaroni salad still tasted fairly dry the next day. No matter how we treated the macaroni, it seemed to have an insatiable thirst for the mayonnaise dressing as it chilled overnight. Left with no other option, we decided it best to toss the pasta with the dressing just before serving. To keep the undressed pasta from sticking together as it chilled, we tossed it with a little oil. Our first attempt with this method showed promise—the chilled pasta and dressing came together seamlessly and produced a great-looking salad. The flavor, however, was a little drab and the dish did not taste cohesive. We then made a batch in which we tossed the rinsed, oiled pasta with the flavorings and vegetables, saving just the mayonnaise to add before serving. This was the best version yet, with a great, unified flavor.

With our new method in hand, we still had one more issue to iron out. The resulting salad wasn't dry, but it was stiff and needed to be loosened up. We tried adding more oil or more mayonnaise, but this just made the salad greasy. We tried adding water, but it merely dulled the creamy flavor of the dressing. A little buttermilk worked well, but it added a unique tangy flavor not associated with classic macaroni salad (but it works well in our ranch variation). Finally we figured out that loosening the salad with a little milk was the answer. It thinned out the consistency of the dressing without watering down or adding too much flavor. The surprise ending to all of our testing is that the macaroni salad now had incredible staying power far beyond what we expected. By chilling the macaroni thoroughly overnight without the dressing, then tossing it with mayonnaise and milk, we managed to produce a salad that stays moist for days, or at the very least, a few hours on a picnic table.

Deli-Style Macaroni Salad

SERVES 12 TO 14

Cooking the pasta until it is completely tender is crucial here—uncooked pasta becomes tough as it sits in the salad overnight.

	Salt
1	pound elbow macaroni
1	large shallot, minced (about ¼ cup)
5	tablespoons juice from 2 to 3 lemons
2	tablespoons vegetable oil
2	teaspoons Dijon mustard
¼	teaspoon garlic powder
	Ground black pepper
2	hard-cooked eggs (see page 73), peeled and chopped coarse
1	medium celery rib, minced
3	tablespoons sweet pickle relish
2	tablespoons minced fresh parsley leaves
1½	cups mayonnaise
½	cup whole milk

1. Bring 4 quarts of water to a boil in a large pot. Stir in 2 tablespoons salt and the pasta and cook until completely tender. Drain the macaroni in a colander, then rinse until cool.

2. Meanwhile, combine the shallot, 3 tablespoons of the lemon juice, oil, Dijon, garlic powder, ½ teaspoon salt, and a pinch pepper in a large bowl.

3. Toss the rinsed pasta with the shallot mixture, then stir in the eggs, celery, pickle relish, and parsley.

4. TO STORE: Cover the bowl tightly with plastic wrap and refrigerate for up to 3 days.

5. TO SERVE: Stir the mayonnaise, milk, and remaining 2 tablespoons lemon juice into the salad and season with salt and pepper to taste.

TO SERVE RIGHT AWAY

Refrigerate the pasta salad as described in step 4 until just well chilled, about 3 hours, before tossing with the mayonnaise, milk, and lemon juice as described in step 5.

➤ VARIATIONS

Macaroni Salad with Ranch Flavors

	Salt
1	pound elbow macaroni
1	large shallot, minced (about ¼ cup)
5	tablespoons juice from 2 to 3 lemons
2	tablespoons vegetable oil
½	teaspoon garlic powder
	Pinch cayenne
	Ground black pepper
¼	cup minced red bell pepper
1	medium celery rib, minced
2	tablespoons minced fresh dill
2	tablespoons minced fresh cilantro leaves
1	cup mayonnaise
½	cup sour cream
½	cup buttermilk

1. Bring 4 quarts of water to a boil in a large pot. Stir in 2 tablespoons salt and the pasta and cook until completely tender. Drain the macaroni in a colander, then rinse until cool.

2. Meanwhile, combine the shallot, 3 tablespoons of the lemon juice, oil, garlic powder, cayenne, ½ teaspoon salt, and a pinch pepper in a large bowl.

3. Toss the rinsed pasta with the shallot mixture, then stir in the bell pepper, celery, dill, and cilantro.

4. TO STORE: Cover the bowl tightly with plastic wrap and refrigerate for up to 3 days.

5. TO SERVE: Stir the mayonnaise, sour cream, buttermilk, and remaining 2 tablespoons lemon juice into the salad and season with salt and pepper to taste.

TO SERVE RIGHT AWAY

Refrigerate the pasta salad as described in step 4 until just well chilled, about 3 hours, before tossing with the mayonnaise, sour cream, buttermilk, and lemon juice as described in step 5.

Southwestern Macaroni Salad

For a spicier salad, add the higher amount of chipotle chiles.

	Salt
1	pound elbow macaroni
1	large shallot, minced (about ¼ cup)
5	tablespoons juice from 5 limes
2	tablespoons vegetable oil
2–3	tablespoons minced chipotle chiles in adobo sauce
½	teaspoon garlic powder
	Ground black pepper
1	medium celery rib, minced
3	scallions, sliced thin
2	tablespoons minced fresh cilantro leaves
1½	cups mayonnaise
½	cup milk

1. Bring 4 quarts of water to a boil in large pot. Stir in 2 tablespoons salt and the pasta and cook until completely tender. Drain the macaroni in a colander, then rinse until cool.

2. Meanwhile, combine the shallot, 3 tablespoons of the lime juice, oil, chipotle, garlic powder, ½ teaspoon salt, and a pinch pepper in a large bowl.

3. Toss the rinsed pasta with the shallot mixture, then stir in the celery, scallions, and cilantro.

4. To STORE: Cover the bowl tightly with plastic wrap and refrigerate for up to 3 days.

5. To SERVE: Stir the mayonnaise, milk, and remaining 2 tablespoons lime juice into the salad and season with salt and pepper to taste.

TO SERVE RIGHT AWAY

Refrigerate the pasta salad as described in step 4 until just well chilled, about 3 hours, before tossing with the mayonnaise, milk, and lime juice as described in step 5.

PASTA SALADS

FOR CERTAIN OCCASIONS, A FRESH PASTA salad with vegetables and a vinaigrette dressing is a nice alternative to a mayonnaise-based macaroni salad. Unfortunately, we found that most vinaigrette-based pasta salads don't hold up well for very long. Within just a few minutes, the pasta tends to soak up the dressing like a sponge, while the vegetables turn mushy or off-colored as they sit. Obviously, we needed to employ some make-ahead tricks in order to give this dish a longer shelf life.

Starting with the pasta, we noted that it needed to be boiled until fully tender—much like the macaroni in our make-ahead macaroni salad. When the pasta was just cooked to al dente, it took on a tough, chewy texture when chilled; overcooked pasta, on the other hand, turned mushy. Tasters also liked pasta that was cooked in seriously salty water, so we doubled our standard seasoning ratio of salt to water. Unlike with our macaroni salad, however, we found that it was not beneficial to rinse the pasta after cooking. Rinsing the pasta before chilling it results in a softer texture that is fine for macaroni salad but not great with pasta salads where the pasta must stand up to the vegetables. Also, tossing the hot pasta with a portion of the vinaigrette, rather than letting the pasta cool off first, made for a more flavorful salad.

With the pasta figured out, we moved onto the vegetables and found that simply stirring a variety of vegetables into the hot pasta and vinaigrette presented some problems. Green vegetables, such as broccoli, asparagus, or beans, turned an unappealing army-green color, while delicate vegetables, such as zucchini, turned mushy. Also, we weren't keen on including any vegetables that required

> **TEST KITCHEN TIP:**
> **Preventing Oily Pasta Salads**
> When we drain our pasta for pasta salads, we reserve some of the pasta cooking water to add to the dressing. The diluted dressing keeps the salad moist overnight without making the salad oily or disturbing the overall flavors.

parcooking—it was just too much work for a simple pasta salad. In the end, we liked the fresh flavors (and bright colors) of cherry tomatoes, bell peppers, and shredded carrots; they all taste great raw and stored nicely overnight. The bell peppers and carrots held up well when tossed with the hot pasta and vinaigrette (they took on some of the vinaigrette flavor), but we found it necessary to sprinkle the cherry tomatoes over the top of the warm salad in order to prevent them from becoming too smashed.

Finally, we tested various ratios of oil to vinegar for the dressing. Using less vinegar and more oil made the salad taste greasy and dull, while using more vinegar and less oil tasted harsh; equal amounts of oil and vinegar were ideal. While most recipes we found called for just vinegar, we preferred to cut the vinegar with lemon juice for a fuller, more balanced flavor. Including some basic aromatics, such as shallots, mustard, garlic powder, and herbs, also added welcome flavor.

We ran into some trouble when testing various amounts of dressing per pound of pasta. The pasta has an incredible thirst for the dressing, especially since it is tossed with the dressing while still hot, and the salad consistently tasted dry the next day. Simply adding more dressing to the salad didn't solve this problem, but rather it made the salad taste harsh and greasy. Looking for ways to add moisture to the salad without ruining the dressing's balance of flavor, we landed on the idea of the pasta cooking water. Already seasoned and slightly thickened by the pasta starch, the pasta cooking water was able to increase the volume of the dressing without wrecking its flavor. Also, we found it crucial to toss just half the dressing with the salad before chilling, then add the remaining dressing as needed before serving, to refreshen the salad's texture and flavor.

Lastly, we noted that these salads taste best when served at room temperature rather than slightly chilled. While we thought bringing the pasta salad to room temperature was a no-brainer—just let it sit on the counter—we were surprised to find that it actually took a few hours. To speed this process up, we simply microwaved the salad for a minute or two with no ill effects.

Summer Garden Pasta Salad with Olives and Feta
SERVES 12 TO 14
We like the size of farfalle (bow-tie) pasta here, however, you can substitute any small pasta, such as rotini or penne. If using a different pasta shape, note that the yield may change significantly. Cooking the pasta until it is completely tender is crucial here—undercooked pasta becomes tough as it sits in the salad overnight.

DRESSING
6 tablespoons extra-virgin olive oil
3 tablespoons red wine vinegar
3 tablespoons juice from 2 lemons
1 medium shallot, minced
1 tablespoon Dijon mustard
1 tablespoon minced fresh oregano, or ½ teaspoon dried
1 teaspoon salt
¼ teaspoon garlic powder
¼ teaspoon ground black pepper

SALAD
Salt
1 pound farfalle pasta
2 medium carrots, peeled and grated over the large holes of a box grater
1 large yellow bell pepper, stemmed, seeded, and cut into ¼-inch-thick strips
8 ounces feta, crumbled (about 2 cups)
1 cup pitted kalamata olives (about 6 ounces), chopped coarse
½ cup minced fresh parsley leaves
1 pint cherry tomatoes (about 12 ounces), quartered

1. FOR THE DRESSING: Whisk all of the ingredients together in a medium bowl; set aside.

2. FOR THE SALAD: Bring 4 quarts of water to a boil in a large pot. Stir in 2 tablespoons salt and the pasta and cook until completely tender. Reserve 1 cup of the pasta cooking water, then drain the pasta in a colander. Transfer the hot pasta to a large bowl.

3. Stir the reserved pasta water into the dressing. Pour half of the dressing over the pasta and toss to

coat. Stir in the carrots, bell pepper, feta, olives, and parsley. Scatter the tomatoes on top of the pasta (do not mix in).

4. To store: Cover the pasta salad tightly with plastic wrap and poke several vent holes in the plastic. Transfer the remaining dressing to an airtight container. Refrigerate the pasta salad and reserved dressing separately for up to 2 days.

5. To serve: Microwave the pasta salad on high power to remove the chill, 1 to 2 minutes. Shake the reserved dressing to recombine, then pour half of the dressing over the salad and toss to combine. Add the remaining dressing as needed to keep the salad moist.

TO SERVE RIGHT AWAY

Refrigerate the pasta salad as described in step 4 until just slightly chilled, about 1 hour, before tossing with the reserved dressing.

➤ VARIATION

Summer Garden Pasta Salad with Asiago, Capers, and Basil

Follow the recipe for Summer Garden Pasta Salad with Olives and Feta, omitting the feta, olives, and parsley. Add 3 ounces Asiago cheese, grated (about 1½ cups), and 3 tablespoons capers, rinsed, to the pasta with the carrots in step 3. Stir in ½ cup coarsely chopped fresh basil leaves just before serving.

INGREDIENTS: Red Wine Vinegar

The source of that notable edge you taste when sampling any red wine vinegar is acetic acid, the chief flavor component in all vinegar and the by-product of the bacterium Acetobacter aceti, which feeds on the alcohol in wine. The process of converting red wine to vinegar once took months, if not years, but now, with the help of an acetator (a machine that speeds the metabolism of the bacteria), it can be made in less than 24 hours.

Does this faster, cheaper method—the one used to make most supermarket brands—produce inferior red wine vinegar? To find out, we included in our tasting vinegars made using the fast process (acetator) and the slow process.

We first tasted 10 nationally available supermarket brands in two ways: by dipping sugar cubes in each brand and sucking out the vinegar and by making a simple vinaigrette with each and tasting it on iceberg lettuce. We then pitted the winners of the supermarket tasting against four high-end red wine vinegars.

Although no single grape variety is thought to make the best red wine vinegar, we were curious to find out if our tasters were unwittingly fond of vinegars made from the same grape. We sent the vinegars to a food lab for an anthocyanin pigment profile, a test that can detect the 10 common pigments found in red grapes. Although the lab was unable to distinguish specific grape varieties, it did provide us with an interesting piece of information: Some of the vinegars weren't made with wine grapes (known as Vitus vinifera), but with less expensive Concord-type grapes, the kind used to make Welch's grape juice.

The taste-test results were both shocking and unambiguous: Concord-type grapes not only do just fine when it comes to making vinegar, they may be a key element in the success of the top-rated brands in our tasting. Spectrum, our overall winner, is made from a mix of wine grapes and Concord grapes. Pompeian, which came in second among the supermarket brands, is made entirely of Concord-type grapes.

What explains why Spectrum and Pompeian won the supermarket tasting and beat the other gourmet vinegars? Oddly enough, for a food that defines sourness, the answer seems to lie in its sweetness. It turns out that Americans like their vinegar sweet (think balsamic vinegar).

The production of Spectrum is outsourced to a small manufacturer in Modena, Italy, that makes generous use of the Trebbiano grape, the same grape used to make balsamic vinegar. The Trebbiano, which is a white wine grape, gives Spectrum the sweetness our tasters admired. Pompeian vinegar is finished with a touch of sherry vinegar, added to give the red vinegar a more fruity, well-rounded flavor. Also significant to our results may be that both Spectrum and Pompeian start with wines containing Concord grapes, which are sweet enough to be a common choice when making jams and jellies. When pitted against gourmet vinegars, Spectrum and Pompeian still came out on top, so skip the specialty shop and head to the supermarket.

THE BEST RED WINE VINEGARS

Pompeian and Spectrum vinegars are available in supermarkets and bested gourmet brands costing eight times as much.

SIMPLE MAKE-AHEAD VEGETABLES

BLANCHING AND SHOCKING VEGETABLES IS A HANDY TRICK TO KNOW. NOT ONLY DOES IT save you lots of last-minute work if you're having a large dinner party, but it makes throwing together a last-minute midweek supper easier, too. The trick is to boil the vegetables in well-salted water until mostly tender (not completely tender), then shock them in ice water to stop the cooking and preserve their color. The blanched and shocked vegetables can be refrigerated in an airtight container for up to 3 days. To serve as a side dish, you can toss them with a vinaigrette (see page 82) and serve cold, or reheat them briefly in the microwave, tossing them with either a vinaigrette or compound butter (see page 83). The cooked vegetables also make great additions to salads, casseroles, soups, stews, curries, and stir-fries. To make things more interesting, try blanching two vegetables, one after the other, for a nice contrast in colors, flavors, and textures.

HOW TO BLANCH VEGETABLES

To Cook: Bring 4 quarts of water to a boil in a large pot over high heat. Fill a large bowl with ice water; set aside. Add 1 tablespoon salt and the vegetables to the boiling water, and cook until the vegetables are mostly tender (but still have a little crunch in the center), following the times in the chart. Drain the vegetables in a colander, then transfer them immediately to the ice water. Let the vegetables cool completely in the ice water for about 5 minutes, then drain and pat dry with paper towels.

To Store: Transfer the vegetables to an airtight container and refrigerate for up to 2 days.

To Serve Cold: Drain away any accumulated water from the vegetables, and toss with a vinaigrette (see page 82). Season the vegetables with salt and pepper to taste and serve either chilled or at room temperature.

To Serve Hot: Transfer them to a microwave-safe bowl, cover with plastic wrap, and microwave on high until hot and steaming, 2 to 4 minutes. Drain away any accumulated water, and toss with a vinaigrette (see page 82), compound butter (see page 83), or a cheese sauce (see page 84). Season the vegetables with salt and pepper to taste before serving.

VEGETABLE	AMOUNT AND YIELD	PREP	BOILING TIME
ASPARAGUS	1 bunch (1 pound) serves 4	tough ends trimmed	2 to 4 minutes
BROCCOLI	1 bunch (1½ pounds) serves 4	florets cut into 1-inch pieces, stalks peeled and sliced ¼ inch thick	2 to 4 minutes
BRUSSELS SPROUTS	1 pound serves 4	trimmed, discolored leaves removed	6 to 8 minutes
CARROTS	1 pound serves 4	peeled and sliced ½ inch thick on the bias	3 to 4 minutes
CAULIFLOWER	1 medium head (2½ pounds) serves 4 to 6	cored and florets cut into 1-inch pieces	5 to 7 minutes
GREEN BEANS	1 pound serves 4	stem ends trimmed	3 to 5 minutes
SNAP PEAS	1 pound serves 4	stems and strings removed	about 3 minutes
SNOW PEAS	1 pound serves 4	tips and strings removed	about 2 minutes

FLAVORING SIMPLE VEGETABLES

VINAIGRETTES ARE QUICK TO PREPARE AND VERSATILE. KEEP THEM ON HAND TO JAZZ UP simple blanched vegetables, or use them to dress just about any salad. Our compound butter is incredibly versatile, too, and can be used in place of a pan sauce for steak or fish or simply added to flavor a baked potato or creamy polenta. The butter can be rolled into a log, wrapped tightly with plastic wrap, and stored in the freezer, so big flavor is just a slice away.

Bistro-Style Mustard Vinaigrette

MAKES ABOUT ½ CUP, ENOUGH FOR ABOUT 2 POUNDS OF VEGETABLES

This hearty dressing is a perfect complement to green beans and cauliflower.

⅓	cup extra-virgin olive oil
2	tablespoons coarse-grain mustard
1	tablespoon red or white wine vinegar
1	small shallot, minced
1	teaspoon minced fresh thyme leaves
1	small garlic clove, minced or pressed through a garlic press (about ½ teaspoon)
¼	teaspoon salt
⅛	teaspoon ground black pepper

Shake all the ingredients together in a jar with a tight-fitting lid. The dressing can be refrigerated for up to 2 days; bring to room temperature, then shake vigorously to recombine before using.

Soy-Ginger Vinaigrette

MAKES ABOUT ½ CUP, ENOUGH FOR ABOUT 2 POUNDS OF VEGETABLES

Toasted sesame seeds make a nice garnish for vegetables tossed with this dressing. This dressing works well with any of the vegetables in the chart on page 81.

3	tablespoons soy sauce
3	tablespoons juice from 3 limes
2	tablespoons sesame oil
2	scallions, minced
1	tablespoon honey
1	tablespoon minced or grated fresh ginger
1	small garlic clove, minced or pressed through a garlic press (about ½ teaspoon)

Shake all the ingredients together in a jar with a tight-fitting lid. The dressing can be refrigerated for up to 2 days; bring to room temperature, then shake vigorously to recombine before using.

FREEZE IT

Herb Compound Butter

MAKES ½ CUP, ENOUGH FOR ABOUT 4 POUNDS OF VEGETABLES

Add a few tablespoons of grated parmesan for a cheese-flavored compound butter.

8	tablespoons (1 stick) unsalted butter, softened
3	tablespoons minced fresh basil or parsley leaves, or chives
2	tablespoons minced fresh tarragon leaves
2	teaspoons minced fresh tarragon, mint, oregano, or thyme leaves
1	medium garlic clove, minced or pressed through a garlic press (about 1 teaspoon)
¾	teaspoon salt
⅛	teaspoon ground black pepper

1. Beat the butter in a bowl with a large fork until light and fluffy, then stir in the remaining ingredients. Wrap with plastic wrap and let rest to blend the flavors, about 10 minutes.

2. To STORE: Roll the butter into a log, wrap tightly with plastic wrap, and refrigerate for up to 4 days, or freeze for up to 2 months.

3. To SERVE: If chilled, slice the log into table-spoon-sized pieces. Toss the butter with the hot vegetables and let melt (you will need roughly 2 tablespoons of the butter per pound of vegetables).

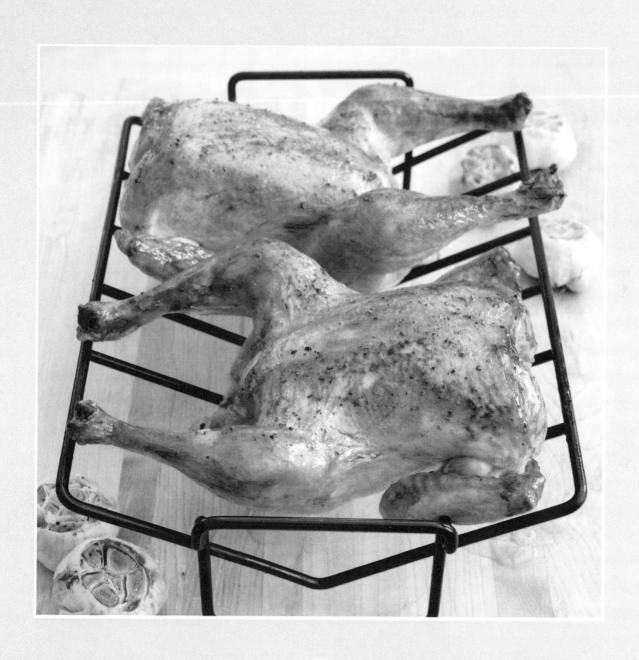

3

DOUBLE-DUTY COOKING

Double-Duty Cooking

WE KNOW THAT FOR TIME-CRUNCHED COOKS, leftovers can be a good thing. But admit it, who really wants to eat warmed-over sliced chicken, beef, or pork? What we wanted was to transform leftovers into a host of entirely new dishes. It was with this concept in mind that we designed this chapter, which we call double-duty cooking. Our goal was simple: Develop eight primary recipes (roast chicken, beef brisket, roast pork loin, and the like)—and put the leftovers to work into two or three secondary recipes. Thus, such leftovers as braised brisket with onions was reinvented into a hearty meat sauce for rigatoni and roast pork loin teamed up with vegetables in a spicy stir-fry.

Because the point of using leftovers is to give the cook a head start into preparing second meals, we made sure to streamline ingredient lists and replace hard-to-find ingredients with pantry staples. Take the complex-flavored Mexican meat stew mole (pronounced moh-lay) which we developed to incorporate our leftover roasted turkey and vegetables. Moles typically contain various dried whole chiles and grated chocolate. We replaced the whole chiles with chili powder and grated chocolate with cocoa powder. Similarly, we used a kitchen cabinet mainstay, ramen noodles—minus the spice packets—to turn our leftover pork loin into a tasty dinner.

For the main recipes, we didn't want to limit ourselves to plainly seasoned chicken or meat—we wanted lots of flavor at the outset for our secondary meals. We relied on the likes of roasted garlic, maple syrup, and bold spice rubs to pack flavor into the meat, and then tailored the leftover recipes accordingly. For example, with the leftovers from Crispy Asian-Flavored Chicken Thighs (page 97), which are flavored with a ginger and five-spice butter, we developed Asian-inspired recipes like Moo Shu Chicken (page 99) and Cold Sesame Noodles (page 98).

We also added more interest to our primary recipes like simple roast turkey breast by cooking carrots and potatoes alongside it, which we could then use with the turkey in the leftovers recipes, such as Skillet Turkey Pot Pie (page 102) and Turkey Curry in a Hurry (page 102)—no peeling, cutting, or cooking vegetables required for the second meal.

TESTING NOTES

ROASTING TWO CHICKENS

Roasting two chickens at once is easy but ensuring crispy skin and moist, tender meat requires the right equipment and attention to technique.

1. Pan Size Matters

A large roasting pan is essential—if the chickens are crowded together in a small roasting pan, they won't roast evenly. If you don't have a large roasting pan, we found that a disposable pan supported by a baking sheet makes an adequate substitute.

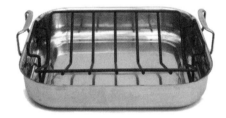

2. Use a V-Rack and a Hot Oven

The chickens need to be raised off the bottom of the pan by a turkey-sized V-rack to allow the air to circulate around the birds and the skin to crisp. A 450-degree oven ensures that the skin will be crisp on both chickens.

3. Start the Birds Wing Side Up Then Turn Twice

For evenly cooked meat, we start roasting the birds on one side, then switch to the other side, and finish roasting breast side up.

Similarly, using the some of the sauce from Onion-Braised Beef Brisket (page 117) and Pot Roast with Root Vegetables (page 113), we were able to give our leftovers recipes—like French Dip Sandwiches (page 118) and Hearty Beef and Barley Soup (page 115)—long-simmered flavor in short order.

We found that there are several key points to keep in mind when devising a new meal using leftover meat. The first trick is brining, a method in which lean cuts of meat like pork loin and chicken are soaked in a salt and water solution and sometimes fortified with a little sugar. We found that brining not only seasons the meat, but it ensures that it will remain moist and juicy when reheated. Another important trick is to understand that leftover meat has already been cooked once, and excessive cooking, especially if the meat is lean like chicken, will only dry it out and ruin its flavor. Therefore, in most instances the leftover meat is simply heated through toward the end of preparing the recipe.

A final note when you're working with leftovers: You want a substantial meal, so be sure to reserve the specified amount of meat, sauce, and/or vegetables. Although we've come across some recipes that claim you can stretch a 4-ounce piece of leftover steak into dinner for four, it's just not true. All of the recipes in this chapter that rely on leftovers are based on 10 ounces (about 2 cups) of shredded, diced, or thinly sliced meat, which is plenty for four people, when sauce, vegetables, pasta, rice, and the like are incorporated.

TWO ROAST CHICKENS

AN EXTRA ROAST CHICKEN PROVIDES A HOST of possibilities for second meals. Sure you can pick up a rotisserie chicken at the supermarket, but why not roast a second chicken while you're already roasting one for dinner? Plus, home-roasted chicken is going to taste far better (and fresher) than anything you could buy at the market. Our goal, therefore, was as follows: Roast two chickens—one for today's meal, complete with pan sauce, and a second for a meal later in the week. And we wouldn't be simply recycling our second chicken into a plain chicken salad—we aimed to come up with

appealing, interesting ways to transform our chicken.

To start, we prefer to brine our chickens. Brining involves soaking the chicken in a mixture of water, sugar, and salt, which results in moister, better seasoned meat. That said, you could start with a kosher bird, which undergoes a similar process.

Our method for roasting chicken is not difficult. In fact, it's easier than most. We dispense with trussing the bird—trussing makes it more difficult for the inner thigh to cook, since it's not exposed to the heat as much as the other parts. By the time the thigh meat is done, the breast is overcooked. Lesson learned? No trussing. Multiple basting? Forget it. We found that brushing the bird multiple times (many recipes suggest every 15 minutes) results in

CHECKING CHICKEN DONENESS

Taking a chicken's temperature can be tricky, no matter how good your thermometer. For the most precise readings, follow the procedures below. Also, it's important to test both breasts and both thighs in multiple spots.

White Meat: Insert the thermometer into the thickest part of the breast from the neck end, keeping it parallel to the breastbone. The white meat is done when the temperature reaches 160 degrees.

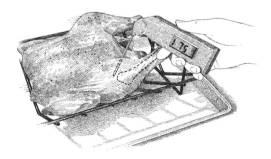

Dark Meat: Insert the thermometer at an angle into the thickest part of the thigh—located between the drumstick and breast—taking care not to hit bone. The dark meat is done when the temperature reaches 175 degrees.

TWO TYPES OF SALT FOR BRINING

You can use either kosher or regular table salt for brining. Kosher salt is ideal because its large, airy crystals dissolve so quickly in water. Unfortunately, the salt crystals of the two major brands of kosher salt—Morton and Diamond Crystal—are not equally airy, and therefore measure differently. This inconsistency between the two brands makes precise recipe writing a challenge. Because there's no way to tell which brand of kosher salt you might have on hand, we list table salt in our brining recipes. If you use kosher salt in your brine, keep the following in mind when making the conversions from table salt in our brining recipes:

¼ cup Table Salt = ½ cup Diamond Crystal Kosher Salt
OR ¼ cup plus 2 tablespoons Morton Kosher Salt

chewy, greasy skin. Instead, we brush the chicken with melted butter—just once—before it goes in the oven. For evenly cooked meat, we start roasting the bird on its side, then switch to the other side, and finish roasting breast side up. Preheating the pan is key too and so is using a roasting rack or V-rack, which allows the air to circulate all around the bird, resulting in crispy, not soggy skin. All in all, our simple method yields fully cooked, juicy chicken with golden brown, crisp skin—exactly what a roast chicken should be.

Is it any more difficult to roast two chickens? After testing, we found that the only difference between roasting one chicken and two is the equipment (and a slightly higher oven temperature). In early tests, we found that if the chickens are crowded together in a small roasting pan, they won't roast evenly. So when roasting two chickens, you need a large roasting pan (or a disposable pan supported by a baking sheet).

For our pan sauce, we zeroed in on a garlicky sauce that relies on roasted garlic (we'd reserved some of the roasted garlic to incorporate into secondary recipes). Now what about those secondary recipes?

No one wants to eat thinly disguised leftovers, so we aimed to create entirely new dishes with our second chicken.

Armed with 10 ounces (about 2 cups) of reserved cooked chicken and ½ cup roasted garlic, we first thought Italian. Taking the lead from the Italian-American restaurant classic ziti with chicken and broccoli, we developed our own version with broccoli rabe. We made a flavorful sauce from the roasted garlic, vermouth, and chicken broth, and thickened it lightly with cornstarch so it clung beautifully to the ziti. A drizzle of extra-virgin olive oil and grated Parmesan finished off the dish, leaving no indication that it was made with leftover chicken.

For our next recipe, we created an Italian-style chef's salad, tossing our chicken with crisp romaine lettuce and fennel, spicy salami, sweet roasted red peppers, and Asiago cheese. We used the roasted garlic as the flavorful base of a zesty salad dressing. The roasted garlic also gave the dressing a thick and creamy consistency.

Lastly, we developed our own easy version of the classic comfort food Chicken and Dumplings. We made a quick stew flavored with carrot, onion, celery, and sherry, and then stirred in the leftover shredded chicken. The roasted garlic fortified the stew with its deep caramelized flavor—a role that browning the chicken normally would play. For the dumplings, we made a simple batter, plopped it on top of the stew, and covered the pan to let them cook through.

What more could we ask for? We had one old-fashioned roasted chicken to enjoy one day and enough leftovers so that we could choose among three quick and fresh-flavored dinners for a second meal.

Two Roast Chickens with Roasted Garlic and Herb Jus

SERVES 4 WITH LEFTOVERS

If using kosher chickens, skip step 1. To use kosher salt in the brine, see above for conversion information. If you're not planning on reserving leftovers for another recipe and would like to serve the entire recipe, which feeds 6 to 8, you will need to make some adjustments. Roast only 3 heads of garlic and increase the amount of broth in step 7 to 1 cup.

LEFTOVER REMINDER

To make the recipes on pages 90–91, remember to reserve ½ cup of the roasted garlic paste and 10 ounces of the cooked chicken, which can be white meat, dark meat, or a combination of the two.

CHICKEN AND ROASTED GARLIC

I	cup sugar
	Table salt (see note)
2	(4- to 4½-pound) whole chickens, giblets discarded
5	heads garlic
I	tablespoon olive oil
2	tablespoons unsalted butter, melted
	Ground black pepper
I	cup low-sodium chicken broth

CHICKEN JUS

½	cup low-sodium chicken broth
¾	cup dry vermouth or dry white wine
2	large shallots, minced (about ½ cup)
2	bay leaves
I	fresh thyme or rosemary sprig
2	tablespoons unsalted butter
	Salt and ground black pepper

1. FOR THE CHICKEN AND GARLIC: Dissolve the sugar and 1 cup salt in 1 gallon cold water in a large container. Add the chickens and submerge completely. Cover and refrigerate for 1 to 1½ hours.

2. Meanwhile, following the illustrations below, slice off the top ½ inch from each head of garlic to expose the cloves, but leave the heads intact (pull away and discard any loose papery skin). Place the garlic heads, cut side up, on a large piece of foil, and drizzle with the oil. Wrap the garlic tightly in the foil; set aside.

3. Adjust an oven rack to the middle position, place a large roasting pan on the rack, and heat the oven to 450 degrees. Spray a turkey-sized V-rack with vegetable oil spray. Remove the chickens from the brine, rinse, and pat dry with paper towels. Brush the butter over the chickens, and season with pepper. Following the photo on page 86, place the chickens on their sides in the V-rack. Place the V-rack in the preheated roasting pan, and the wrapped garlic on the rack beside it. Pour the broth into the roasting pan, and roast for 25 minutes.

4. Remove the roasting pan from the oven (leaving in the garlic). Using 2 large wads of paper towels, rotate the chickens so that the opposite wing sides are facing up. Return the roasting pan to the oven and roast for another 25 minutes.

5. Using 2 large wads of paper towels, rotate the chickens again so that the breast sides are facing up, and continue to roast until the thickest part of the thigh registers 170 to 175 degrees on an instant-read thermometer, about 30 minutes longer.

6. Remove the chicken and garlic from the oven. Tip the chickens to let the juices flow from the cavities into the roasting pan, then transfer the chickens to a carving board and let rest, uncovered, while making the jus. Set the roasting pan with the pan juices aside. Open the package of garlic and

ROASTING GARLIC

1. Cut ½ inch from the top end of the head of garlic so that the clove interiors are exposed.

2. Place each head of garlic, cut side up, in the center a large piece of aluminum foil. Drizzle the garlic with oil, then gather and twist the foil to seal.

3. After the garlic has roasted, open the foil package and cool. With your hand or the flat edge of a chef's knife, squeeze the garlic from the skins, starting from the root end and working up.

TEST KITCHEN TIP:
Crunchy Crumbs

We like to sprinkle freshly toasted bread crumbs over such pasta dishes as Ziti with Chicken, Broccoli Rabe, and Parmesan (below) and Linguine with Chicken, Artichokes, and Peas in Garlic Cream Sauce (page 95) for extra flavor and texture. To make toasted bread crumbs, simply pulse 2 slices high-quality sandwich bread to coarse crumbs using a food processor, about 6 pulses. Toss the crumbs with 2 tablespoons olive oil and a pinch salt, and toast in a large nonstick skillet over medium-high heat, stirring often, until crisp and brown, about 4 minutes; transfer them to a small bowl until needed.

let cool. When the garlic is cool enough to handle, squeeze the garlic from the skins into a bowl, then mash the garlic into a paste with a rubber spatula. *To make one of the recipes on pages 90–91, reserve 10 ounces of the chicken in an airtight container and refrigerate for up to 2 days. Reserve half of the garlic paste (about ½ cup) and refrigerate in a separate airtight container for up to 4 days.*

7. **FOR THE JUS:** While the chicken rests, skim the fat from the juices in the roasting pan, then stir in the broth and scrape up any browned bits. Transfer the pan juices to a medium saucepan, stir in the vermouth, shallots, bay leaves, and thyme, and simmer over medium-high heat until flavorful, 10 to 15 minutes. Strain the sauce and return it to the saucepan, discarding the solids. Whisk in half of the garlic paste (about ½ cup), followed by the butter, and season with salt and pepper to taste; set aside, covered, to keep warm until serving. Carve the chickens and serve immediately, passing the sauce separately.

Ziti with Chicken, Broccoli Rabe, and Parmesan
SERVES 4

The roasted garlic paste and chicken in this recipe are from Two Roast Chickens with Roasted Garlic and Herb Jus (page 88). Other short pasta shapes, like penne, farfalle, and fusilli, can be substituted for the ziti. Freshly toasted bread crumbs make a nice addition to this dish (see the Test Kitchen Tip above). If desired, make the crumbs while

waiting for the water to boil, then wipe out the skillet with paper towels and proceed to make the sauce in step 2.

4	tablespoons extra-virgin olive oil
½	cup roasted garlic paste (see note)
¼	teaspoon red pepper flakes
½	cup dry vermouth or dry white wine
2	cups low-sodium chicken broth
2	teaspoons cornstarch
	Salt
1	bunch broccoli rabe (about 14 ounces), trimmed and cut into 1-inch pieces
1	pound ziti
10	ounces cooked chicken, shredded (about 2 cups; see note)
1	ounce Parmesan cheese, grated (about ½ cup)
	Ground black pepper

1. Bring 4 quarts of water to a boil in a large pot.

2. Meanwhile, combine 1 tablespoon of the oil, roasted garlic, and pepper flakes in a large nonstick skillet over medium-high heat and cook, stirring frequently, until fragrant, about 1 minute. Add the vermouth and cook until evaporated, about 1 minute. Whisk the broth and cornstarch together, then stir into the skillet and simmer the sauce until slightly thickened, about 2 minutes. Remove the skillet from the heat, cover, and set aside until the ziti is cooked.

3. Add 1 tablespoon salt and the broccoli rabe to the boiling water and cook until the broccoli rabe is almost tender, 1 to 2 minutes. Remove the broccoli rabe from the pot using a slotted spoon and transfer it to a colander. Return the water to a boil, add the ziti, and cook, stirring often, until al dente. Reserve ½ cup of the pasta cooking water, then drain the pasta in the colander with the broccoli rabe, and return the ziti and broccoli rabe to the pot.

4. While the pasta finishes cooking, add the chicken to the sauce, and return the sauce to a simmer over medium-high heat until heated through, about 2 minutes. Stir the hot sauce mixture, remaining 3 tablespoons oil, and the Parmesan into the ziti, adding the pasta cooking water as needed to thin the sauce. Season with salt and pepper to taste and serve immediately.

Italian-Style Chef's Salad with Chicken, Fennel, and Asiago

SERVES 4

The roasted garlic paste and chicken in this recipe are from Two Roast Chickens with Roasted Garlic and Herb Jus (page 88).

¾ cup extra-virgin olive oil
½ cup roasted garlic paste (see note)
5 tablespoons juice from 2 lemons
4 teaspoons Dijon mustard
½ teaspoon salt
½ teaspoon ground black pepper
2 romaine lettuce hearts, torn into bite-sized pieces
1 fennel bulb, top discarded, bulb cored and sliced thin (see the illustrations on page 47)
4 medium jarred roasted red peppers, drained, rinsed, patted dry, and cut into ½-inch-wide strips (about 1 cup)
10 ounces cooked chicken, shredded (about 2 cups; see note)
4 ounces salami, cut into matchsticks
2 ounces Asiago cheese, shaved

1. Whisk the oil, roasted garlic, lemon juice, mustard, salt, and pepper together in a small bowl until combined.

2. Toss the romaine and fennel with 6 tablespoons of the dressing and arrange on a platter (or individual plates). Arrange the peppers on top of the greens. Toss the chicken with 2 tablespoons of the dressing and arrange on top of the peppers. Top with the salami and cheese and drizzle with the remaining dressing. Serve immediately.

Streamlined Chicken and Dumplings

SERVES 4

The roasted garlic paste and chicken in this recipe are from Two Roast Chickens with Roasted Garlic and Herb Jus (page 88). Don't substitute low-fat or nonfat milk for the whole milk in this dish. Be sure you mix the dumpling batter just before you're ready to use it; if made too far in advance, the dumplings will be heavy and dense.

STEW
2 tablespoons unsalted butter
2 carrots, peeled and sliced ¼ inch thick
1 celery rib, sliced ¼ inch thick
½ medium onion, minced
1 teaspoon minced fresh thyme leaves, or ¼ teaspoon dried
3 tablespoons unbleached all-purpose flour
2¼ cups low-sodium chicken broth
½ cup roasted garlic paste (see note)
2 tablespoons dry sherry
10 ounces cooked chicken, shredded (about 2 cups; see note)
½ cup frozen peas
1 tablespoon minced fresh parsley leaves
Salt and ground black pepper

DUMPLINGS
1 cup (5 ounces) unbleached all-purpose flour
1½ teaspoons baking powder
½ teaspoon salt
½ cup whole milk
2 tablespoons unsalted butter

1. FOR THE STEW: Melt the butter in a large saucepan over medium-high heat. Add the carrots, celery, onion, and thyme and cook until softened, about 7 minutes. Stir in the flour until incorporated. Whisk in the broth, roasted garlic, and sherry. Simmer until slightly thickened, about 5 minutes.

MAKING CHEESE SHAVINGS

Thin shavings of hard cheeses, such as Asiago or Parmesan, can be used to garnish salads as well as side dishes. Simply run a sharp vegetable peeler along the length of a piece of cheese to remove paper-thin curls.

2. FOR THE DUMPLINGS: While the stew simmers, whisk the flour, baking powder, and salt together in a medium bowl. Microwave the milk and butter together in a microwave-safe bowl on high until the butter melts (do not overheat), about 1 minute. (Alternatively, heat the milk and butter together in a small saucepan over medium-low heat until the butter has melted and the milk is warmed through.) Stir the warmed milk mixture into the flour mixture with a wooden spoon until incorporated and smooth.

3. Stir the chicken, peas, and parsley into the stew and season with salt and pepper to taste. Return the stew to a simmer, then drop golf ball–sized dumplings onto the stew, about ¼ inch apart (you should have about 8 dumplings). Reduce the heat to low, cover, and cook until the dumplings have doubled in size, 15 to 18 minutes. Serve immediately.

PAN-ROASTED CHICKEN BREASTS

TENDER AND JUICY WHITE-MEAT CHICKEN IS always welcome on the dinner table. And leftovers can easily be transformed into second meals. Our goal was simple: We wanted to determine the best technique for pan-roasting bone-in chicken breasts and come up with interesting dishes for using the leftover meat.

Pan-roasting is a technique typically used in restaurants, in which food is browned in a skillet on the stovetop and then placed in a hot oven to finish cooking. We often employ this technique to cook a whole cut-up chicken and thought we should adapt it to chicken breasts for moist, tender meat, and crispy skin. In addition, we wanted a pan sauce to serve with the chicken and then to incorporate into our secondary meals.

A note about shopping for split chicken breasts: We find it best to buy whole chicken breasts and split them ourselves. Why? Sloppy butchering often means that you end up with chicken pieces where just shreds of skin cover the split chicken breasts, leaving large areas of the meat exposed. Also, the breasts within any given package can differ greatly in size (we found 9-ounce and 13-ounce breasts in one package). Obviously, smaller pieces cook more quickly, so when cooking pieces of divergent sizes, we were forced to monitor them closely and pull the smaller breasts out earlier. Not ideal. And curiously, split breasts are often sold three to a package. All in all, you'll have more control over condition, size, and quantity by avoiding packaged split breasts.

Next, we turned to brining the chicken—soaking it in a saltwater solution—before cooking it. Chicken breasts are prone to drying out and brining helps the meat stay moist and seasons it as well. For the sake of convenience, we went with a quick and concentrated brine—½ cup table salt dissolved in 2 quarts water—and a brine time of 30 minutes to 1 hour. Before cooking, we found it necessary to rinse the brined chicken; otherwise, the skin was unpalatably salty.

When it came to browning a large number of split breasts, we found that it was almost as easy to cook six as it was to cook four. While six breasts fit snugly in a large skillet, we decided to cook them in batches to prevent overcrowding and promote even browning. We heated 2 teaspoons vegetable oil in the skillet until it was smoking and then browned both sides of the chicken breasts before transferring them to a baking dish on the middle rack of the oven. We tried oven temperatures ranging from 375 up to 500 degrees. At 500 degrees we noted profuse smoking and sometimes singed drippings, which imparted an acrid flavor to our pan sauce. Temperatures on the lower end meant prolonged cooking times. At 450 degrees, however, the skin was handsomely browned and cracklingly crisp, and the chicken cooked swiftly to the internal temperature of 160 degrees, which translated to about 18 minutes for 12-ounce breasts.

An added bonus of pan-roasting is the caramelized drippings, or fond, left behind in the skillet. While the chicken roasted in the oven, we sautéed shallots in the fond in the skillet, then added chicken broth and herbs and let the sauce (or pan jus) simmer until it reduced by about one quarter. After the chicken came out of the oven and rested, we poured any accumulated juice from the baking dish into the skillet for more chickeny flavor. We then strained the mixture of solids and reserved half (about 1½ cups) for our secondary recipes, and returned the other half to the skillet and enriched it with butter, lemon juice, and parsley. This easy sauce added flavor and moisture to our chicken in short order.

We reserved 10 ounces of the chicken and 1½ cups of the sauce for our secondary recipes. Chicken and rice is a suppertime favorite, but we elevated this classic to a new level. Using the pan sauce, along with water and heavy cream, to cook the rice, we made a subtly creamy casserole with shreds of tender chicken, sweet carrots, tender asparagus, and a toasted cracker-crumb topping. Flavored with lemon, Parmesan, and tarragon, this recipe took comfort food upscale.

For an alternate recipe, we thought of combining the chicken with naturally quick-cooking couscous and North African flavors like cinnamon, cayenne, raisins, and toasted almonds. We simply sautéed the onion and added the spices, chicken, and couscous. Then we poured in the pan jus and brought the whole dish to a simmer. We then let the mixture sit off the heat until the couscous absorbed the jus and was evenly plump and tender, which took just five minutes. To finish, fresh cilantro added brightness and toasted almonds gave the dish some nutty crunch.

Last, we created a lively pasta dish with our chicken and jus—Linguine with Chicken, Artichokes, and Peas in Garlic Cream Sauce. We began by sautéing thawed frozen artichoke hearts in butter until golden brown. Then, we stirred in a generous amount of garlic (six cloves) and red pepper flakes for bite. The sauce, made up of the pan jus and heavy cream, went into the skillet next. We also added a little cornstarch to thicken the sauce so that it would cling nicely to the linguine. Before serving we stirred the chicken and peas into the artichoke mixture and tossed it with the hot pasta to warm through, along with lemon juice for brightness and basil for a hit of freshness. Who knew that we could come up with a host of interesting ways to transform a few chicken breasts?

Pan-Roasted Chicken Breasts with Lemon Jus
SERVES 4 WITH LEFTOVERS
If using kosher chickens, skip step 1. To use kosher salt in the brine, see page 88 for conversion information. If you're not planning on reserving leftovers for another recipe and would like to serve the entire recipe, which makes enough for 6, you will need to make some adjustments. Follow the recipe, decreasing the broth to 3 cups and reducing it in the skillet to 2 cups, about 15 minutes. After straining the reduced broth, stir in ¼ cup juice from 2 lemons and 3 tablespoons unsalted butter.

LEFTOVER REMINDER
To make the recipes on pages 94–95, remember to reserve 1½ cups of the roast chicken jus and 2 cooked chicken breast halves.

	Table salt (see note)
3	whole bone-in, skin-on chicken breasts (about 1½ pounds each), split (see the illustrations on page 94)
	Ground black pepper
4	teaspoons vegetable oil
1	medium shallot, minced (about 3 tablespoons)
4	cups low-sodium chicken broth
2	bay leaves
1	fresh thyme sprig
2	tablespoons unsalted butter
3	tablespoons juice from 1 lemon
1	tablespoon minced fresh parsley leaves

1. Dissolve ½ cup salt in 2 quarts cold water in a large container. Add the chicken breasts and submerge completely. Cover and refrigerate for 30 to 60 minutes. Remove the chicken from the brine, rinse, and pat dry with paper towels. Season the chicken with pepper.

2. Adjust an oven rack to the middle position and heat the oven to 450 degrees. Heat 2 teaspoons of the oil in a 12-inch skillet over medium-high heat until smoking. Brown half of the chicken, skin side down, until deep golden, about 5 minutes. Turn the chicken over and brown lightly on the second side, about 3 minutes longer. Transfer

SPLITTING WHOLE BREASTS

1. With the whole breast skin side down on the cutting board, center the knife on the breastbone, then apply pressure to cut through and separate the breast into halves.

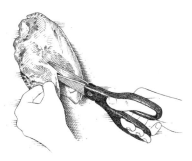

2. Note that some bone-in breasts contain a rib section, which will need to be trimmed with kitchen shears.

the chicken, skin side up, to a 13 by 9-inch baking dish. Repeat with the remaining 2 teaspoons oil and chicken breasts. Roast all the chicken in the oven until the thickest part of the breasts register 160 degrees on an instant-read thermometer, 15 to 18 minutes.

3. While the chicken roasts, add the shallot to the fat in the now-empty skillet and cook over medium heat until softened, about 1 minute. Stir in the broth, bay leaves, and thyme, scraping up any browned bits from the bottom of the pan. Simmer until reduced to about 3 cups, about 15 minutes; set aside until needed.

4. Remove the chicken from the oven, transfer it to a serving platter, and let rest, uncovered, while finishing the jus. *To make one of the recipes on pages 94–95, reserve 2 chicken breast halves and refrigerate in an airtight container for up to 2 days.*

5. Add any accumulated chicken juices from the baking dish to the jus, then strain the jus through a fine-mesh strainer into a large liquid measuring cup, discarding the solids. *To make one of the recipes on pages 96–97, reserve 1½ cups of the jus and refrigerate in an airtight container for up to 2 days.* Return the remaining 1½ cups jus to the skillet, bring to a simmer, and whisk in the butter. Off the heat, stir in the lemon juice and parsley and season with salt and pepper to taste. Serve the chicken, passing the jus separately.

Chicken and Rice Casserole with Lemon and Parmesan
SERVES 4

The chicken and chicken jus in this recipe are from Pan-Roasted Chicken Breasts with Lemon Jus (page 93).

2	tablespoons unsalted butter
2	medium carrots, peeled and sliced thin
1	medium onion, minced
3	medium garlic cloves, minced or pressed through a garlic press (about 1 tablespoon)
1	cup long-grain white rice
2	cups water
1½	cups chicken pan jus (see note)
½	cup heavy cream
	Salt and ground black pepper
10	ounces cooked chicken, shredded (about 2 cups; see note)
8	ounces asparagus (about ½ bunch), tough ends trimmed, cut into 1-inch lengths
1½	ounces grated Parmesan cheese (¾ cup)
3	tablespoons juice from 1 lemon
1	tablespoon minced fresh tarragon leaves
25	Ritz crackers, crushed to coarse crumbs (about 1 cup) or 1 cup Fresh Bread Crumbs (page 90)

1. Adjust an oven rack to the middle position and heat the oven to 400 degrees. Melt the butter in a large nonstick skillet over medium-high heat until the foaming subsides. Add the carrots and onion and cook until lightly browned, about 6 minutes.

2. Stir in the garlic and cook until fragrant, about 30 seconds. Add the rice and stir until evenly coated. Add the water, chicken jus, cream, ¼ teaspoon salt, and ¼ teaspoon pepper and bring to a simmer. Turn the heat to low, cover, and cook, stirring often, until

the rice has absorbed most of the liquid and is just tender, 20 to 25 minutes.

3. Stir in the chicken, asparagus, Parmesan, lemon juice, and tarragon and season with salt and pepper to taste. Pour the mixture into an 8-inch-square baking dish and sprinkle the Ritz crumbs evenly over the top. Bake until the top is browned, about 10 minutes. Cool for 10 minutes before serving.

Chicken and Couscous with Chickpeas, Raisins, and Toasted Almonds

SERVES 4

The chicken and chicken jus in this recipe are from Pan-Roasted Chicken Breasts with Lemon Jus (page 93).

2	tablespoons extra-virgin olive oil
1	medium onion, minced
¾	cup raisins
½	teaspoon ground cinnamon
	Pinch cayenne
3	medium garlic cloves, minced or pressed through a garlic press (about 1 tablespoon)
1	(15.5-ounce) can chickpeas, drained and rinsed
10	ounces cooked chicken, shredded (about 2 cups; see note)
1	cup couscous
1½	cups chicken pan jus (see note)
¼	cup minced fresh cilantro leaves
¼	cup sliced almonds, toasted
2	tablespoons juice from 1 lemon
	Salt and ground black pepper

1. Heat 1 tablespoon of the oil in a large skillet over medium heat until just shimmering. Add the onion, raisins, cinnamon, and cayenne and cook until the onion is softened, about 4 minutes. Stir in the garlic and cook until fragrant, about 30 seconds. Stir in the chickpeas, chicken, and couscous until evenly combined.

2. Add the chicken jus and bring to a simmer. Cover the skillet and let sit off the heat until the liquid is absorbed, about 5 minutes.

3. Gently fold the cilantro, almonds, lemon juice,

and remaining 1 tablespoon oil into the couscous with a fork and season with salt and pepper to taste. Serve immediately.

Linguine with Chicken, Artichokes, and Peas in Garlic Cream Sauce

SERVES 4

The chicken and chicken jus in this recipe are from Pan-Roasted Chicken Breasts with Lemon Jus (page 93). Freshly toasted bread crumbs are a nice addition to this pasta (see the Test Kitchen Tip on page 90). Make the crumbs while waiting for the water to boil, then wipe out the skillet with paper towels and proceed to make the sauce in step 2.

2	tablespoons unsalted butter
1	(9-ounce) package frozen artichoke hearts, thawed and patted dry
	Salt
6	medium garlic cloves, minced or pressed through a garlic press (about 2 tablespoons)
	Pinch red pepper flakes
1½	cups chicken pan jus (see note)
½	cup heavy cream
2	teaspoons cornstarch
1	pound linguine
10	ounces cooked chicken, shredded (about 2 cups; see note)
1	cup frozen peas
¼	cup minced fresh basil leaves
3	tablespoons juice from 1 lemon
	Ground black pepper
	Grated Parmesan cheese (for serving)

TEST KITCHEN TIP: Toasting Nuts

To toast a small amount of nuts (under 1 cup), put them in a dry skillet and toast over medium heat, shaking the skillet occasionally, until lightly browned and fragrant, 3 to 8 minutes. Watch the nuts closely because they can go from golden to burnt very quickly. To toast a large quantity of nuts, spread them in a single layer on a rimmed baking sheet and toast in a 350-degree oven, shaking the baking sheet every few minutes, until lightly browned and fragrant, 5 to 10 minutes.

1. Bring 4 quarts of water to a boil in a large pot.

2. Meanwhile, melt the butter in a 12-inch nonstick skillet over medium heat until the foaming subsides. Add the artichokes and ¼ teaspoon salt and cook until lightly browned and tender, about 6 minutes. Stir in the garlic and pepper flakes and cook until fragrant, about 30 seconds. Stir in the chicken jus. Whisk the cream and cornstarch together, then stir into the skillet and simmer until thickened slightly, about 2 minutes. Remove the skillet from the heat, cover, and set aside.

3. Add 1 tablespoon salt and the linguine to the boiling water and cook, stirring often, until al dente. Reserve ½ cup of the pasta cooking water, then drain the pasta in a colander and return the linguine to the pot.

4. While the pasta finishes cooking, add the chicken and peas to the sauce and bring to a simmer over medium-high heat until the chicken and peas are heated through, about 2 minutes. Pour the sauce mixture over the linguine and add the basil and lemon juice. Stir to evenly combine, adding the pasta cooking water as needed to thin the sauce. Season with salt and pepper to taste. Serve, passing the grated Parmesan separately.

ROASTED CHICKEN THIGHS

WHEN PROPERLY PREPARED, ROASTED CHICKEN thighs have moist, well-seasoned meat and crispy skin. In contrast to chicken breasts, dark-meat chicken thighs don't require brining, making them relatively fuss-free. An added bonus is that it's virtually effortless to throw a few extra pieces in the pan so that you have enough for leftovers. Like many recipes, however, chicken thighs can have problems. The meat can be bland and the skin can be pale and rubbery. We wanted to determine the best way to season the thighs, the optimal oven temperature for roasting them, and then we wanted to come up with some interesting recipes using the leftover meat.

We chose to roast only bone-in, skin-on chicken. First, we like the contrast of crisp skin with moist meat, and we know that skin helps to keep the

ENSURING CRISPY SKIN

Make three diagonal slashes in the skin of each chicken piece to help render the fat.

meat from drying out. Second, chicken cooked with the bone in seems to have a better flavor.

From prior discoveries in the test kitchen, we knew that brining chicken thighs wasn't necessary, so we moved on to finding the best way to bake them.

We quickly discovered that the difficulties with roasting chicken thighs relate directly to the level of heat. If the oven is too hot, achieving crispy skin can be a problem because it is not given time to slowly render its fat, but if the oven is too low, the meat will cook through before the skin is browned and crisped. The thighs baked in a 450-degree oven were the best of the bunch. The meat was perfectly moist and tender after just 30 minutes, and the skin was golden brown, although it wasn't quite crispy enough for our liking. To solve this problem, we tried finishing the chicken under the direct heat of the broiler. The skin caramelized beautifully and was certainly crispy, but we still found it a touch too thick. Remembering a technique used in cooking duck, we tried slashing the skin a few times before placing it in the oven. This worked quite well. The skin rendered just a little more fat because of the extra surface area exposed to the heat, and was thin and crisp.

Although the roasted thighs were delicious seasoned simply with salt and pepper, we wanted to jazz them up a bit with a spiced butter. Mixing minced ginger and five-spice powder into softened unsalted butter was a snap. We then simply rubbed the butter on the meat (under the skin) before slashing the skin. The spiced butter imparted a complex, lightly spicy flavor to the meat that tasters loved. We also came up with a quick sweet-and-sour dipping sauce with ginger, garlic, red pepper flakes, and scallions. With our primary recipe down, we turned to coming up with ways to incorporate the leftover chicken thighs and some of the sauce into a second meal. And because our chicken was seasoned with Asian flavors, we looked specifically to Asian-style recipes.

Cold sesame noodles are an easy dinner to pull together and a perfect canvas to show off our seasoned chicken thighs. For silky, separate strands of noodles, rinse them immediately after cooking under cool, running water—this washes away excess starch, which can cause noodles to stick. And tossing the rinsed noodles with sesame oil not only flavors the noodles but also further ensures that they won't clump. Cold sesame noodles are seasoned and bound together with a nutty-flavored sauce, which is easily made in a blender with the reserved sweet-and-sour sauce, soy sauce, peanut butter, and sesame seeds. Once you've got your sauce pureed and the noodles cooked, this dish is not much more than assembly. Simply toss the noodles with the shredded chicken, grated carrot, and sliced red pepper, toss with the sauce, and dinner is ready.

For our next recipe, we turned to developing a streamlined version of moo shu, a saucy stir-fried dish of chicken (or pork) and shredded cabbage, which is spooned into thin crêpes and rolled up. The leftover sweet-and-sour sauce already contained garlic, ginger, and scallions, which are given seasonings in moo shu. Tasters also liked the filling enriched with meaty shiitake mushrooms. We found that we liked the cabbage best when it still had a distinct texture, so we added it with the chicken and cooked it just until it began to wilt. (It's important to just stir-fry the chicken until it's warm through, otherwise it will dry out since it's precooked.)

A common problem with moo shu is that the filling is often overseasoned and oversauced, making the crêpes soggy. Wary of this, we made just enough sauce to coat the vegetables—a simple mixture of soy sauce, cornstarch, and a little hoisin sauce was simply added to the sweet-and-sour sauce for additional sweetness and depth. While Chinese crêpes are available at specialty Asian markets, we were happy to roll our moo shu up in easier-to-find flour tortillas, which we quickly softened in the microwave while preparing the filling.

For our third option, we turned to developing a Southeast Asian–style chicken salad. We bound the salad together with a vinaigrette, made with the sweet-and-sour sauce balanced by salty fish sauce and a little vegetable oil. Shredded cabbage, carrots, and chopped peanuts added some welcome crunch and a hefty dose of cilantro and mint gave the salad some brightness. Shreds of our Asian-style chicken thighs fit right in to this sweet and tangy combination of flavors.

Crispy Asian-Flavored Chicken Thighs with Sweet-and-Sour Sauce
SERVES 4 WITH LEFTOVERS

Five-spice powder, a blend of spices—most often Sichuan pepper, cinnamon, anise, ginger, and cloves—is available in jars in the spice aisle of the supermarket. The sauce can be spooned over the thighs when serving, or divided among diners and used as a dipping sauce for the chicken. Steamed rice and a stir-fried vegetable, like green beans or broccoli, make a nice accompaniment to the chicken.

LEFTOVER REMINDER

To make the recipes on pages 98–99, remember to reserve ½ cup of the sweet-and-sour sauce and 4 cooked chicken thighs.

CHICKEN

6	tablespoons unsalted butter, softened
4	teaspoons grated fresh ginger
1½	teaspoons five-spice powder
	Salt
12	bone-in, skin-on chicken thighs (about 4½ pounds)
	Ground black pepper

SAUCE

1	tablespoon vegetable oil
6	medium garlic cloves, minced or pressed through a garlic press (about 2 tablespoons)
2	tablespoons grated fresh ginger
½	teaspoon hot red pepper flakes
½	cup packed light brown sugar
½	cup rice vinegar
4	scallions, sliced thin

1. **FOR THE CHICKEN:** Adjust one oven rack to the middle position and a second rack to be 8 inches from the broiler element. Heat the oven to 450 degrees. Line a broiler-pan bottom with foil and lay the slotted broiler pan on top.

2. Mix 4 tablespoons of the butter, ginger, five-spice powder, and ¼ teaspoon salt together in a small bowl. Pat the chicken dry with paper towels and rub the butter mixture underneath the skin of the chicken. Arrange the chicken, skin side up, on the broiler-pan top. Following the illustration on page 96, make 3 diagonal slashes in the skin of each thigh with a sharp knife (do not cut into the meat).

3. Melt the remaining 2 tablespoons butter. Brush the chicken with the melted butter and season with salt and pepper. Bake the chicken on the middle rack until the thickest part of the meat registers 165 degrees on an instant-read thermometer, 30 to 40 minutes.

4. Turn the oven to broil, transfer the chicken to the upper rack, and broil the chicken until the skin is crisp and the thighs register 175 degrees on an instant-read thermometer, 5 to 10 minutes.

5. **FOR THE SAUCE:** While the chicken bakes, cook the oil, garlic, ginger, and pepper flakes together in a small saucepan over medium heat until fragrant and softened, 3 to 4 minutes. Stir in the sugar and vinegar and simmer until the sugar is dissolved, about 2 minutes. Transfer the mixture to a medium bowl and refrigerate until cooled. Stir the scallions into the sauce. *To make one of the recipes on pages 98–99, reserve half of the sauce (about ½ cup) and refrigerate in an airtight container for up to 4 days.*

6. Transfer the chicken to a carving board and let rest for 5 minutes. *To make one of the recipes on pages 98–99, reserve 4 thighs and refrigerate in an airtight container for up to 2 days.* Serve the chicken, passing the sauce separately.

~≈~

Southeast Asian Chicken Salad
SERVES 4

The chicken and sweet-and-sour sauce in this recipe are from Crispy Asian-Flavored Chicken Thighs with Sweet-and-Sour Sauce (page 97). If pressed for time, use preshredded cabbage.

12	ounces shredded green cabbage (about 6 cups)
10	ounces Asian-flavored cooked chicken, shredded (about 2 cups; see note)
2	carrots, peeled and shredded
1	red bell pepper, stemmed, seeded, and sliced thin
¼	cup minced fresh cilantro leaves
¼	cup minced fresh mint or basil leaves
½	cup sweet-and-sour sauce (see note)
1	tablespoon fish sauce
1	tablespoon vegetable oil
¼	cup chopped unsalted roasted peanuts

1. Toss the cabbage, chicken, carrots, bell pepper, cilantro, and mint together in a large bowl. In a separate bowl, whisk the sweet-and-sour sauce, fish sauce, and vegetable oil together.

2. Pour the dressing over the cabbage mixture and toss to coat; let stand for 10 minutes. Sprinkle with the peanuts just before serving.

~≈~

Cold Sesame Noodles
SERVES 4

The chicken and sweet-and-sour sauce in this recipe are from Crispy Asian-Flavored Chicken Thighs with Sweet-and-Sour Sauce (page 97). We prefer the flavor and texture of chunky peanut butter here; however, creamy peanut butter can be used. If you cannot find fresh Chinese egg noodles, substitute 1 pound dried spaghetti or linguine. Garnish with thinly sliced scallions, if desired.

½	cup sweet-and-sour sauce (see note)
6	tablespoons soy sauce
5	tablespoons chunky peanut butter
5	tablespoons sesame seeds, toasted
½	cup hot water
1	tablespoon salt
2	(9-ounce) packages fresh Chinese egg noodles (see note)
2	tablespoons toasted sesame oil
10	ounces Asian-flavored cooked chicken, shredded (about 2 cups; see note)
2	carrots, peeled and grated
1	red bell pepper, stemmed, seeded, and sliced thin

1. Bring 4 quarts of water to a boil in a large pot.

2. Meanwhile, puree the sweet-and-sour sauce, soy sauce, peanut butter, and 4 tablespoons of the sesame seeds in a blender (or food processor) until smooth, about 30 seconds. With the machine running, add the hot water, 1 tablespoon at a time, until the sauce has the consistency of heavy cream (you may not need all the water). Set the sauce aside.

3. Add the salt and noodles to the boiling water and cook, stirring often, until tender, about 4 minutes. Drain the noodles and rinse under cold water until cool. Shake out the excess water and transfer the noodles to a large bowl. Add the sesame oil and toss to coat.

4. Toss the noodles with the chicken, carrots, bell pepper, and pureed sauce to combine. Sprinkle with the remaining 1 tablespoon sesame seeds before serving.

Moo Shu Chicken

SERVES 4

The chicken and sweet-and-sour sauce in this recipe are from Crispy Asian-Flavored Chicken Thighs with Sweet-and-Sour Sauce (page 97).

½ cup sweet-and-sour sauce (see note)
2 tablespoons hoisin sauce, plus extra for serving
2 tablespoons soy sauce
2 teaspoons cornstarch
1 tablespoon vegetable oil
8 ounces fresh shiitake mushrooms, brushed clean and sliced thin
8 (6-inch) flour tortillas
10 ounces Asian-flavored cooked chicken, shredded (about 2 cups; see note)
8 ounces shredded green cabbage (about 4 cups)

1. Mix the sweet-and-sour sauce, hoisin sauce, soy sauce, and cornstarch together in a medium bowl and set aside.

2. Heat the oil in a large nonstick skillet over medium-high heat until just shimmering. Add the mushrooms and cook until lightly browned, about 4 minutes.

3. Meanwhile, stack the tortillas on a plate, cover with plastic wrap, and heat in the microwave on high until soft and hot, 30 seconds to 2 minutes. Keep covered until serving. (Alternatively, stack the tortillas on a large sheet of aluminum foil, seal tightly, and heat in a 350-degree oven until soft and hot, about 15 minutes. Remove from the oven and keep the packet sealed until serving.)

4. Stir the chicken and cabbage into the skillet and cook until the cabbage begins to wilt, about 1 minute. Whisk the sauce to recombine, add to the pan, and bring to a simmer. Cook until the sauce thickens, 1 to 2 minutes. Serve with the warm tortillas and additional hoisin sauce.

ROASTED TURKEY BREAST

A ROASTED TURKEY BREAST IS A MUCH MORE manageable alternative to a behemoth roast turkey—and there will still be plenty of leftovers, since the average turkey breast serves anywhere from eight to 10 people. The downside of the turkey breast is that the meat can be dry and somewhat flavorless if not prepared correctly. It can also be a challenge to get the breast to develop a crisp, golden-brown skin. We wanted to develop a technique that would give us both moist, flavorful meat and tasty, crispy skin. We also wanted to turn it into a complete meal with some roasted vegetables and cranberry sauce, and create recipes using the leftovers that were more interesting than the usual turkey sandwich.

We started by brining the turkey breast in a sugar-salt solution. This process produced delicately seasoned, tender, and juicy meat. We also discovered that slow roasting at 325 degrees did the most to produce tender meat with just a trace of chew. However, the problem with slow roasting a turkey breast is that it does nothing for the skin; the skin on our turkey breast was pale and rubbery. Boosting the heat to 425 degrees for the first 30 minutes of roasting and brushing the skin with butter did the trick—we now had a beautifully browned and crisped bird. (Additionally, we rubbed softened butter, seasoned with thyme, under the skin for moist, herby flavor.)

When it came to the vegetables, we chose to keep things simple—just red potatoes and carrots. We tossed them with a little melted butter, thyme, salt, and pepper and roasted them in the pan with the turkey. The juices from the turkey flavored the vegetables, and the vegetables were just tender when the turkey was ready to come out of the oven. Tasters had only one complaint—they wanted the vegetables to have a more caramelized exterior. Fortunately, this problem was easily solved. While the turkey rested, we cranked the oven to 500 degrees and put the vegetables back in until they were a stunning golden brown.

Instead of a long-simmered cranberry sauce, we decided to make a quick cranberry relish that didn't require any cooking. We simply pulsed the cranberries in a food processor with an apple, an orange, sugar, ground ginger, and a pinch of salt. The flavors in this sweet, sour, and a bit spicy relish really developed after it sat for a while, so we made it while the turkey brined and refrigerated it until we were ready to eat. Now, with the sauce resolved, we were ready to tackle the recipes we'd make from the leftovers.

Leftover turkey can be incredibly tired and dull, so we developed recipes with bold flavors, like a rich and deeply flavored Mexican mole and an Indian curry with lots of complexity. In addition, we created a speedy skillet version of the classic turkey pot pie—all of which we developed to use our leftover roast turkey and vegetables.

Our mole is a simplified version of the traditional Mexican preparation, which typically relies on a laundry list of ingredients. We pared the ingredients back by swapping in chili powder for the various types of dried chiles the recipe usually includes. We also replaced ground chocolate with cocoa powder and ground nuts with peanut butter. We simmered the mixture with chicken broth and tomatoes until it was thick and flavorful, pureed it until it was silky smooth, and returned it to the skillet, at which point we stirred in the vegetables and turkey and simmered them just until warmed through. Cilantro sprinkled over the top just before serving added color and freshness to the finished dish.

Next, we worked on our curry recipe, which takes little time to prepare and delivers complex flavor. We built the sauce using onion, curry powder, ginger, and garlic. We liked the sweetness that raisins imparted, though we found it necessary to cook them with the onion so they had a chance to plump up and soften. We added the roasted vegetables and canned chickpeas (often found in curries) to the aromatics and simmered the mixture briefly before stirring in the turkey and sweet green peas to heat through. Lastly, we finished the sauce with yogurt, to enrich the sauce and temper the spicy flavors. It's important to add the yogurt off the heat to prevent curdling.

For our streamlined turkey pot pie, we zeroed in on a biscuit topping instead of the typical pie dough. We found that biscuits made with cream were a lot quicker to mix together than those made with butter, and baking them while assembling the turkey stew on the stovetop in a skillet allowed us to pull this family favorite together in record time. For the filling, we constructed the sauce using onion, celery, thyme, vermouth, and chicken broth. Flour thickened the liquid to the proper pot-pie consistency, and heavy cream added richness and a velvety texture. Once the sauce was properly thickened and flavorful, all that was left to do was stir in the vegetables and turkey, warm through, and top with the baked biscuits.

With these options, you can choose something a lot more interesting than the usual turkey sandwich.

Roasted Turkey Breast with Roasted Root Vegetables and Cranberry Relish
SERVES 6 WITH LEFTOVERS

If using a kosher turkey breast, skip step 1. To use kosher salt in the brine, see page 88 for conversion information. Don't let the turkey sit in the brine in step 1 for longer than 1½ hours or else it will taste quite salty. If the breast has a pop-up timer, just ignore it (they pop too late) and follow the times and temperatures in the recipe. (Do not remove the timer before cooking.)

LEFTOVER REMINDER

To make the recipes on pages 101–102, remember to reserve 2 cups of the roasted vegetables and 10 ounces of the cooked turkey.

TURKEY AND VEGETABLES

1	cup sugar
	Table salt (see note)
1	(6- to 8-pound) bone-in turkey breast
3	tablespoons unsalted butter, softened, plus 3 tablespoons unsalted butter, melted and cooled
2	teaspoons minced fresh thyme leaves
	Ground black pepper
2	pounds red potatoes (about 7 medium), scrubbed and cut into 1-inch chunks
2	pounds carrots, peeled and sliced 1 inch thick

CRANBERRY RELISH

1½	cups fresh or thawed frozen cranberries
1	large apple, peeled, cored, and chopped coarse
1	orange, peeled, seeded, and chopped coarse
½	cup sugar
½	teaspoon ground ginger
	Pinch salt

1. FOR THE TURKEY: Dissolve the sugar and 1 cup salt in 1 gallon cold water in a large container. Add the turkey breast and submerge completely in the brine. Cover and refrigerate for 1 to 1½ hours.

2. FOR THE RELISH: Meanwhile, pulse the cranberries, apple, orange, sugar, ginger, and salt together in a food processor until the mixture resembles coarse meal, about ten 1-second pulses. Transfer to a serving bowl, cover, and refrigerate until needed. (The relish can be made up to 3 days ahead.)

3. Adjust an oven rack to the middle position and heat the oven to 425 degrees. Remove the turkey from the brine, rinse, and pat dry with paper towels. Mix the softened butter with 1 teaspoon of the thyme, and rub the butter mixture underneath the skin of the turkey breast. Spray a V-rack with vegetable oil spray, set it inside a roasting pan, and lay the turkey breast in the rack, skin side up. Brush the skin of the turkey breast all over with 1 table-spoon of the melted butter. Season with pepper.

4. Toss the potatoes and carrots with the remaining 2 tablespoons melted butter, remaining 1 teaspoon thyme, ½ teaspoon salt, and ½ teaspoon pepper. Scatter the vegetables around the turkey breast in the roasting pan. Roast the turkey and vegetables for 30 minutes.

5. Reduce the oven temperature to 325 degrees and continue to roast until the turkey registers 160 to 165 degrees on an instant-read thermometer and the vegetables are tender, about 1 hour longer. Transfer the turkey to a carving board and let rest, uncovered, while finishing the vegetables.

6. While the turkey rests, increase the oven temperature to 500 degrees. Return the vegetables to the oven and continue to roast until browned, about 10 minutes. *To make one of the recipes on pages 101–102, reserve 2 cups of the roasted vegetables and 10 ounces of the turkey and refrigerate in separate airtight containers for up to 2 days.* Slice the turkey thinly, and serve with the vegetables, passing the cranberry relish separately.

Quick Turkey Mole

SERVES 4

The roasted vegetables and turkey in this recipe are from Roasted Turkey Breast with Roasted Root Vegetables and Cranberry Relish (page 100).

3	tablespoons vegetable oil
1	medium onion, minced
2	tablespoons chili powder
2	tablespoons unsweetened cocoa powder
½	teaspoon ground cinnamon
⅛	teaspoon ground cloves
3	medium garlic cloves, minced or pressed through a garlic press (about 1 tablespoon)
2	cups low-sodium chicken broth, plus extra as needed
1	(14.5-ounce) can diced tomatoes, drained
¼	cup raisins
2	tablespoons peanut butter
2	cups roasted vegetables (see note)
10	ounces cooked turkey, shredded (about 2 cups; see note)
	Salt and ground black pepper
¼	cup minced fresh cilantro leaves

1. Heat the oil in a large skillet over medium-high heat until just shimmering. Add the onion, chili powder, cocoa powder, cinnamon, and cloves and cook until the onion is softened, 5 to 7 minutes. Stir in the garlic and cook until fragrant, about 30 seconds.

2. Stir in the broth, tomatoes, raisins, and peanut butter and cook, stirring occasionally, until thickened, about 20 minutes.

3. Puree the sauce in a blender (or food processor) until smooth. Return the sauce to the skillet, stir in the roasted vegetables and simmer until heated through, about 5 minutes. Stir in the turkey and cook until heated through, about 2 minutes more, adding additional broth as needed to thin the sauce. Season with salt and pepper to taste. Sprinkle with the cilantro and serve immediately.

Turkey Curry in a Hurry

SERVES 4

The roasted vegetables and turkey in this recipe are from Roasted Turkey Breast with Roasted Root Vegetables and Cranberry Relish (page 100). Don't substitute low-fat or nonfat yogurt here, or the sauce will be too thin and have an off-flavor.

3	tablespoons vegetable oil
1	medium onion, sliced thin
¼	cup raisins
2	tablespoons curry powder
	Salt
4	medium garlic cloves, minced or pressed through a garlic press (about 4 teaspoons)
4	teaspoons grated fresh ginger
2	cups roasted vegetables (see note)
1	(15.5-ounce) can chickpeas, drained and rinsed
1	cup water
10	ounces cooked turkey, shredded (about 2 cups; see note)
1	cup frozen peas
1	cup plain whole-milk yogurt
¼	cup minced fresh cilantro leaves

1. Heat the oil in a large skillet over medium-high heat until just shimmering. Add the onion, raisins, curry powder, and ½ teaspoon salt and cook until the onion is softened, 5 to 7 minutes. Stir in the garlic and ginger and cook until fragrant, about 30 seconds.

2. Stir in the roasted vegetables, chickpeas, and water and cook, stirring frequently, until heated through, about 5 minutes. Stir in the turkey and

peas and cook until heated through, about 2 minutes more.

3. Off the heat, stir in the yogurt and cilantro. Season with salt to taste and serve immediately.

Skillet Turkey Pot Pie

SERVES 4

The roasted vegetables and turkey in this recipe are from Roasted Turkey Breast with Roasted Root Vegetables and Cranberry Relish (page 100). We prefer the flavor of Pillsbury Golden Home-Style Biscuits, but you can use your favorite brand (you will need anywhere from 4 to 8 biscuits, depending on their size). Serve the pot pie straight from the skillet or transfer the mixture to a large pie dish.

1	package refrigerator biscuits (see note) or Quick Homemade Biscuits (recipe follows)
2	tablespoons unsalted butter
1	medium onion, minced
1	large celery rib, sliced thin
1	teaspoon minced fresh thyme leaves, or ¼ teaspoon dried
	Salt
¼	cup unbleached all-purpose flour
¼	cup dry vermouth or dry white wine
2½	cups low-sodium chicken broth
½	cup heavy cream
2	cups roasted vegetables (see note)
10	ounces cooked turkey, shredded (about 2 cups; see note)
1	cup frozen peas
	Ground black pepper

1. Adjust an oven rack to the middle position and heat the oven according to the biscuit package instructions; bake the biscuits as directed.

2. Meanwhile, melt the butter in a large skillet over medium heat until the foaming subsides. Add the onion, celery, thyme, and ½ teaspoon salt and cook until the onion is softened, about 5 minutes. Stir in the flour and cook, stirring constantly, until incorporated, about 1 minute.

3. Stir in the vermouth and cook until evaporated, about 30 seconds. Slowly whisk in the broth and cream and bring to a boil. Reduce to a

simmer, add the vegetables, and cook until the sauce is thickened and the vegetables are heated through, about 5 minutes.

4. Stir in the turkey and peas and continue to simmer until heated through, about 2 minutes more. Season with salt and pepper to taste. Place the baked biscuits on top of the stew in the skillet or place on individual servings. Serve immediately.

Quick Homemade Biscuits
MAKES 8 BISCUITS

Contrary to popular belief, we found that kneading the biscuit dough briefly actually produces taller, fluffier biscuits. See the illustrations on page 332 for cutting the biscuits.

2	cups (10 ounces) unbleached all-purpose flour, plus extra for dusting the counter
2	teaspoons sugar
2	teaspoons baking powder
½	teaspoon salt
1½	cups heavy cream

1. Adjust an oven rack to the upper-middle position and heat the oven to 450 degrees.

2. Whisk the flour, sugar, baking powder, and salt together in a large bowl. Stir in the cream with a wooden spoon until a dough forms, about 30 seconds. Turn the dough out onto a lightly floured counter and gather into a ball. Knead the dough briefly until smooth, about 30 seconds. Pat the dough into a ¾-inch-thick circle. Cut the biscuits into rounds using a 2½-inch biscuit cutter or 8 wedges using a knife. Place the biscuits on a parchment-lined baking sheet and bake until golden brown, about 15 minutes. Use as directed in the recipe above.

MAPLE-GLAZED PORK LOIN

SWEET MAPLE, WITH ITS DELICATE FLAVOR notes of smoke, caramel, and vanilla, makes an ideal foil for pork, which has a faint sweetness of its own. However, maple-glazed pork often falls short of its savory-sweet promise. Many times the roasts are dry (a constant concern when cooking today's leaner pork), but we were surprised to discover that most of the glazes were either too thin to coat the pork properly or overly sweet, and none of the glazes had a pronounced maple flavor. We wanted to develop a glistening maple-glazed pork roast, which, when sliced, combined the juices from tender, well-seasoned pork with a rich maple glaze to create complex flavor in every bite. In addition, we wanted to create recipes using the leftovers that would showcase the pork in a moist and juicy light.

Good maple-glazed roast pork starts out as good, plain roast pork. We wanted a boneless cut and so tested four options. Tasters preferred the blade or center-cut loin roast for flavor and juiciness. As with our basic recipe for roasting this cut, we found that brining was optional depending on the type of pork (see page 303 for more information on enhanced and natural pork) and a stovetop sear followed by roasting in a moderate oven was key.

With the roast in the oven, it was time to get serious about developing maple flavor. The recipes we had researched touted dozens of glaze concoctions and methods for marrying them to the pork. Flavoring ingredients added to the maple syrup, like soy sauce, lemon juice, vinegar, and mustard, either diluted it (so that it was too thin to use as a glaze) or were simply unwelcome. Everyone agreed, however, that small amounts of complementary spices added subtle dimension to the maple; thus cinnamon, ground cloves, and cayenne all found their way into the glaze recipe. Still, we wanted more maple flavor and a glaze thick enough to adhere to the meat. We hit upon a simple solution to intensify the maple flavor by reducing it in the skillet—the same skillet that we had used to brown the roast. This method also allowed us to use the drippings (called fond) that had formed in the pan when the meat seared and eliminated an extra pan to reduce the syrup.

Instead of a roasting pan, we transferred the seared pork to a 13 by 9-inch baking dish and roasted it at 375 degrees for 25 minutes before adding the glaze. The smaller surface area of the baking dish prevented the glaze from spreading out and burning, as did adding the glaze after the pork roasted for 25 minutes. The baking dish also made it easier to coat the pork thoroughly because it was sitting right in the glaze. The roast emerged from the oven with a thick, uniform, glistening coating of glaze and an impressive, concentrated maple flavor.

Glazed pork has a fairly neutral flavor, giving it great versatility when it comes to leftovers. We immediately thought of south Florida's most popular sandwich, the Cubano. Made with a combination of roast pork, ham, Swiss cheese, and pickles on crusty French bread, the Cubano is brushed with melted butter, pressed, and grilled. For our version, we split 6-inch sub rolls in half and spread the insides with mayonnaise and spicy brown mustard. Then we simply layered the leftover roast pork and some ham with a mixture of diced dill pickles and jarred banana peppers (a tasty addition we found in a few recipes), and finally Swiss cheese. To cook the sandwiches, we found that we could mimic the effects of a sandwich press using a preheated heavy pot or Dutch oven to weight the sandwiches and crisp up the rolls.

For our next recipe, we changed gears and developed a ramen noodle dish with the leftover pork. Picking up a couple of packs of instant ramen noodle soups, we pitched the sodium-heavy seasoning packets and created our own flavorful hot-and-sour broth (made with fresh garlic, ginger, Asian chili sauce, and cider vinegar). We simmered the noodles in the broth so that they soaked up the liquid and became tender and well seasoned. To enrich our dish and turn it into a hearty meal, we chose to partner the sliced pork with shiitake mushrooms and spinach (a classic Asian combination).

Having had such success combining the pork with Asian flavors in our ramen recipe, we turned to developing a stir-fry dish. We found that it was important to add the longer-cooking carrots and bok choy stalks to the pan first, and then the quick-cooking bok choy leaves. We also discovered that when stir-frying the garlic and ginger, which can easily burn, it is best to take the precaution of mixing them with oil and stir-frying them after the vegetables are tender. For the sauce, we relied on a combination of low-sodium chicken broth, oyster sauce, soy sauce, toasted sesame oil, and cornstarch to thicken the sauce to just the right consistency. And to keep the leftover pork from drying out, we added it to the skillet with the tender bok choy greens, and cooked it just until it was heated through.

Maple-Glazed Roast Pork Loin
SERVES 4 WITH LEFTOVERS

If using enhanced pork (see page 303 for more information), do not brine. Manufacturers don't use the terms "enhanced" or "natural" on package labels, but if the pork has been enhanced it will have an ingredient list. Natural pork contains pork and no other ingredients. To use kosher salt in the brine, see page 88 for conversion information. If the glaze begins to dry up and burn in the oven, stir about ¼ cup warm water into the pan.

LEFTOVER REMINDER
To make the recipes on pages 105–106, remember to reserve 10 ounces of the cooked pork loin.

I	cup sugar
	Table salt (see note)
I	3-pound boneless pork loin roast, tied
	Pepper
I	tablespoon vegetable oil
I	cup maple syrup
½	teaspoon ground cinnamon
¼	teaspoon ground cloves
⅛	teaspoon cayenne pepper

1. Dissolve the sugar and salt in 2 quarts cold water in a large container. Add the pork and submerge it completely in the brine. Cover and refrigerate for 1 to 1½ hours. Remove the pork from the brine, rinse, and pat dry with paper towels. Season the pork with pepper.

2. Adjust an oven rack to the lower-middle position and heat the oven to 375 degrees. Heat the oil in a large skillet over high heat until just smoking. Brown the roast on all sides, reducing the heat if the fat begins to smoke, 8 to 10 minutes. Transfer the roast to a 13 by 9-inch baking dish. Roast the pork in the oven until the thickest part of the roast registers about 85 degrees on an instant-read thermometer, about 25 minutes.

3. Meanwhile, pour off the fat left in the skillet. Add the maple syrup, cinnamon, cloves, and cayenne to the skillet and simmer until slightly thickened and fragrant, scraping up any browned bits, about 30 seconds; set aside.

4. After the pork has roasted for about 25 minutes, pour the glaze over the pork and turn the roast to coat with the glaze. Continue to roast until the thickest part of the roast reaches 140 degrees on an instant-read thermometer, 15 to 25 minutes more, turning once halfway through to recoat it with the glaze.

5. Transfer the roast to a carving board, tent with foil, and let rest until the pork reaches an internal temperature of 150 degrees, about 15 minutes. Transfer the glaze to a small saucepan.

6. Before slicing the pork, pour any accumulated juices from the roast into the glaze, and warm the glaze over low heat. *To make one of the recipes on pages 105–106, reserve a 10-ounce piece of the roast and refrigerate in an airtight container for up to 2 days. Remove the twine and cut the roast into ¼-inch slices. Spoon the glaze over the top of the sliced pork before serving.*

Cubano Sandwiches

SERVES 4

The pork loin in this recipe is from Maple-Glazed Roast Pork Loin (page 104). If you can't fit all 4 sandwiches in the skillet at once, cook them in batches and hold the first batch in a warm oven. Yellow mustard can be used here instead of spicy brown mustard, and soft potato rolls can be used instead of sub rolls.

2	tablespoons mayonnaise
4	teaspoons spicy brown mustard
4	(6-inch) soft sub rolls, halved lengthwise
10	ounces cooked pork loin, sliced thin (see note)
4	ounces thinly sliced ham, preferably Virginia or Black Forest
⅓	cup chopped dill pickles
⅓	cup chopped jarred banana peppers
4	ounces deli-sliced Swiss cheese
2	tablespoons unsalted butter, melted

1. Spread the mayonnaise and mustard evenly inside the rolls. Layer the pork, ham, pickles, peppers, and cheese on the bottom half of each roll. Place the top halves of the rolls on the sandwiches and press down to flatten.

2. Heat both a large nonstick skillet and a large Dutch oven over medium-low heat for 4 minutes.

3. Brush the tops of the sandwiches with half of the melted butter and place them in the skillet, top sides down. Brush the bottoms of the sandwiches with the remaining butter and, using the preheated pot, press down on the sandwiches for 15 to 20 seconds. Continue to cook with the pot on the sandwiches (but not pressing down), until the first side is golden brown, 4 to 5 minutes.

4. Remove the pot, flip the sandwiches over, and continue to cook with the pot on the sandwiches (but not pressing down) until the second side is golden brown, 3 to 4 minutes. Serve immediately.

Ramen Noodles with Pork, Shiitakes, and Spinach

SERVES 4

The pork loin in this recipe is from Maple-Glazed Roast Pork Loin (page 104). The sauce will seem a bit brothy when finished, but the liquid will be quickly absorbed by the noodles when serving.

4	teaspoons vegetable oil
3	medium garlic cloves, minced or pressed through a garlic press (about 1 tablespoon)
1	tablespoon grated fresh ginger
8	ounces fresh shiitake mushrooms, brushed clean and sliced thin
3½	cups low-sodium chicken broth
2	teaspoons Asian chili sauce
4	(3-ounce) packages ramen noodles, seasoning packets discarded
3	tablespoons cider vinegar
2	tablespoons soy sauce
2	teaspoons sugar
10	ounces cooked pork loin, sliced into thin strips (about 2 cups; see note)
1	(6-ounce) bag baby spinach

1. Mix 1 teaspoon of the oil, garlic, and ginger together in a small bowl and set aside. Heat the remaining 1 tablespoon oil in a large skillet over high heat until just shimmering. Add the mushrooms and cook until lightly browned, about 4 minutes.

2. Clear the center of the pan and add the garlic mixture. Cook, mashing the garlic mixture into the pan with the back of a spatula, until fragrant, about 30 seconds. Stir in the broth and chili sauce. Break the ramen into small chunks and add to the skillet. Bring to a simmer and cook, tossing the ramen constantly with tongs to separate, until the ramen are just tender but there is still liquid in the pan, about 2 minutes.

3. Add the vinegar, soy sauce, and sugar. Stir in the pork and the spinach, a handful at a time, and cook until the pork is warmed through and the spinach is wilted, about 3 minutes. Serve immediately.

Stir-Fried Pork and Bok Choy with Ginger-Oyster Sauce

SERVES 4

The pork loin in this recipe is from Maple-Glazed Roast Pork Loin (page 104). Serve with steamed white rice.

⅔	cup low-sodium chicken broth
3	tablespoons oyster sauce
1	tablespoon soy sauce
2	teaspoons toasted sesame oil
2	teaspoons cornstarch
4	teaspoons vegetable oil
2	tablespoons minced fresh ginger
3	medium garlic cloves, minced or pressed through a garlic press (about 1 tablespoon)
1	medium head bok choy (about 1½ pounds), stalks chopped medium and greens sliced thin
3	carrots, peeled and cut into matchsticks
10	ounces cooked pork loin, sliced into thin strips (about 2 cups; see note)
1	tablespoon sesame seeds, toasted

1. Mix the broth, oyster sauce, soy sauce, sesame oil, and cornstarch together in a medium bowl and set aside. Mix 1 teaspoon of the vegetable oil with the ginger and garlic in a small bowl and set aside.

TEST KITCHEN TIP: Preventing Burned Garlic and Ginger
Because garlic and ginger can easily burn in a hot skillet when stir-frying, we like to take the added precaution of mixing them with oil before adding them to the skillet.

2. Heat the remaining 1 tablespoon vegetable oil in a large nonstick skillet over high heat until just smoking. Add the bok choy stalks and carrots and cook, stirring occasionally, until almost tender, 3 to 4 minutes.

3. Clear the center of the skillet and add the ginger mixture. Cook, mashing the ginger mixture into the pan with the back of a spatula, until fragrant, about 30 seconds. Stir the ginger mixture into the vegetables. Stir in the pork and bok choy greens, a handful at a time, and cook until the bok choy leaves begin to wilt, about 1 minute.

4. Whisk the sauce to recombine, add to the pan, and bring to a simmer. Cook, stirring frequently, until the sauce is thickened and the vegetables and pork are coated with sauce and heated through, 1 to 2 minutes. Sprinkle with the sesame seeds before serving.

SPICE-RUBBED PORK TENDERLOIN

WE'LL TAKE SLICES OF MOIST, RICH PORK roast any day. But leaner pork tenderloin isn't always so appealing. This is partly due to the fact that this incredibly lean cut dries out so quickly, but mostly because it can be so flavorless. Over the years, we have found that pork tenderloin is especially suited to the grill because a hot charcoal fire adds flavor. But for our workaday pork tenderloin recipe, we wanted an indoor cooking method that delivered big flavor. And while we were in the kitchen, we wanted to cook extra meat and come up with some great ways to use the leftovers.

Working with three 1-pound tenderloins, we figured that oven temperature was the key to success. We started out with a moderate oven (375 degrees) and worked our way up (475 degrees) and down (250 degrees) the temperature scale. Unfortunately, none of these temperatures was a winner. Cooler ovens produced evenly cooked tenderloins, but they had a pallid, spongy appearance. The tenderloins fared little better in a moderate oven. Confident that a blast of intense heat would give us the seared, crusted exterior we were looking for, we placed the tenderloins inside the oven, closed the door, and waited expectantly. We got color, but it was spotty at best. Even worse, these boneless tenderloins had managed to become as dry as a bone. Having been let down by the oven, we thought we would try the stovetop. We tried sautéing the tenderloins and were heartened by the brilliant crust that formed on the exterior of the pork. But when we cut into the meat, it was nearly raw.

A marriage of pan-searing and roasting has worked well for us in the past (it's the best way to cook bone-in chicken breasts), and it was clearly time to revisit this method. We heated up a little oil in our skillet, cooked the tenderloins to golden perfection, then slid the pan into a 425-degree oven to finish cooking. The tenderloins came out of the oven deeply colored and evenly cooked, but the meat was on the dry side. Tests subsequently revealed that it was best to take the pork out of the oven when the internal temperature was 140 degrees. After a 10-minute rest, the temperature climbed to 150, and the meat retained lots of juices. (Note that the U.S. Department of Agriculture suggests a final temperature of at least 150 degrees and up to 160 degrees. The choice is yours, but we think that 160-degree pork is dry and flavorless.)

Although the golden crust now contributed flavor, we wanted more. Our first thought was brining or marinating, but we wanted a method that delivered big flavor quickly, so we turned to a dry rub.

We tried dry rubs with various combinations of salt and spices. Our favorite was a mixture of cocoa powder, cumin, allspice, black pepper, and salt. While many recipes for spice rubs call for toasting the spices, we found this step to be unnecessary. The intense heat of the skillet does the toasting for you. Taking a bite of the warm-spiced pork, we realized that a cool and fruity salsa would be a natural complement. While the tenderloins were in the oven, we had ample time to make the salsa, a simple combination of mango, red onion, jalapeño, lime juice, and cilantro. In less than 30 minutes we had spice-rubbed, juicy pork tenderloins (with enough pork to turn into another meal) and a brightly flavored salsa.

For our secondary recipes, we immediately turned to Mexican-influenced dishes to best showcase the complex flavors of the spice-rubbed pork. We based our first recipe on the traditional Mexican dish sopa seca, which translates literally as "dry soup." It begins with an aromatic tomato-based broth built in a skillet (the soup part), which is then simmered with thin strands of pasta until the liquid is absorbed and the pasta is tender (the dry part). Traditionally, this dish is prepared with fideos, thin strands of coiled, toasted noodles, but they are difficult to come by. We found that vermicelli, toasted in a skillet until golden brown, were the closest match. To add more heft to the dish, canned black beans went into the mixture along with the pork. A sprinkling of shredded Monterey Jack cheese melted to form a gooey layer over the noodles, and a little chopped cilantro for freshness, color, and authenticity put the finishing touches on the dish.

Next, we created a recipe for everyone's favorite—burritos. Unlike other recipes that roll canned refried beans, jarred salsa, and rice up in a tortilla, we made a fresh-tasting and flavorful filling by simmering pinto beans and tomatoes with onion, garlic, and chipotles. Then we combined cooked rice with the leftover pork, a generous amount of shredded cheddar, and cilantro. We mashed the bean mixture lightly and spread it over the tortillas, then mounded the pork and rice on top, and rolled them up. While other recipes call it quits at this point, we sprinkled our burritos with more cheddar and baked them in a 450-degree oven until the cheese melted and the filling was piping hot throughout.

Lastly, we developed a recipe that is a cross between pork tinga and pozole—both Mexican-style stews. To start, we browned spicy chorizo sausage and then sautéed onion in its rendered fat. The broth was comprised mostly of canned diced tomatoes and chicken broth, but we seasoned it liberally with garlic, chipotles, oregano, and a little brown sugar to balance all the flavors. Canned hominy (dried field corn kernels treated with lime and boiled until tender) is a traditional ingredient in pozole, so that went into the pot as well. We added the pork toward the end of cooking, just to heat it through and then just before serving, we added some cilantro for freshness and color. Our pozole was so good that we forgot we'd been working with leftovers.

Spice-Rubbed Pork Tenderloins with Mango Salsa
SERVES 4 WITH LEFTOVERS

If your tenderloins are larger than 1 pound and you have trouble fitting all 3 into the skillet at once, you can brown them in 2 batches—just add 1 more tablespoon of oil to the skillet for the second batch. If ripe mangos are not available, use 2 cups of frozen mangos, thawed and chopped coarse. Depending on the sweetness of the frozen mango, you might need to season the salsa with sugar to taste.

LEFTOVER REMINDER
To make the recipes on pages 108–110, remember to reserve 10 ounces of the cooked pork tenderloin.

PORK
4 teaspoons ground cumin
4 teaspoons ground black pepper
1 tablespoon unsweetened cocoa powder
2 teaspoons ground allspice
2 teaspoons salt
3 pork tenderloins (about 1 pound each), trimmed of silver skin (see the illustration on page 109)
1 tablespoon vegetable oil

SALSA
2 medium mangos, peeled, pitted, and cut into ¼-inch dice (see note)
¼ cup minced red onion
2 tablespoons minced fresh cilantro leaves
½ jalapeño chile, stemmed, seeded, and minced
1 tablespoon juice from 1 lime
   Salt and ground black pepper

1. FOR THE PORK: Adjust an oven rack to the middle position and heat the oven to 425 degrees. Mix the cumin, pepper, cocoa, allspice, and salt together in a small bowl. Pat the tenderloins dry with paper towels and thoroughly rub them with the spice mixture.

2. Heat the oil in a 12-inch skillet over high heat until just smoking. Brown the tenderloins on all sides, reducing the heat if the fat begins to smoke, about 6 minutes. Transfer the tenderloins to a 13 by 9-inch baking dish.

3. Roast the tenderloins in the oven until an instant-read thermometer registers 140 degrees, 15 to 18 minutes. Remove the pork from the oven, transfer it to a carving board, tent with foil, and let rest until the internal temperature registers 150 degrees on an instant-read thermometer, about 10 minutes. *To make one of the recipes on pages 108–110, reserve a 10-ounce piece of the tenderloin and refrigerate in an airtight container for up to 2 days.*

4. FOR THE SALSA: Meanwhile, mix all of the salsa ingredients together in a medium bowl and season with salt and pepper to taste.

5. Cut the tenderloins crosswise into thin slices. Serve, passing the salsa separately.

Speedy Sopa Seca (Mexican-Style Skillet Vermicelli)
SERVES 4

The pork tenderloin in this recipe is from Spice-Rubbed Pork Tenderloins with Mango Salsa (page 108). If you like your food spicy, use 1 tablespoon minced chipotle chile in adobo sauce.

8 ounces vermicelli, broken in half
2 tablespoons vegetable oil
1 medium onion, minced
2 medium garlic cloves, minced or pressed through a garlic press (about 2 teaspoons)
2 teaspoons minced chipotle chile in adobo sauce
   Salt and ground black pepper
2 cups low-sodium chicken broth
1 (15.5-ounce) can black beans, drained and rinsed
1 (14.5-ounce) can diced tomatoes

10 ounces cooked pork tenderloin, sliced into thin strips (about 2 cups; see note)

2 ounces Monterey Jack cheese, shredded (about ½ cup)

¼ cup minced fresh cilantro leaves
Sour cream (for serving)

1. Toast the vermicelli with 1 tablespoon of the oil in a 12-inch skillet over medium-high heat, stirring frequently, until golden, about 4 minutes; transfer to a paper towel–lined plate and set aside.

2. Add the remaining 1 tablespoon oil, onion, garlic, chipotle, ½ teaspoon salt, and ¼ teaspoon pepper to the skillet and cook over medium heat until the onion is softened, 5 to 7 minutes.

3. Stir in the broth, beans, tomatoes with their juice, and toasted vermicelli. Cover and cook over medium-low heat, stirring often, until all the liquid is absorbed and the vermicelli is tender, about 10 minutes. Season with salt and pepper to taste.

4. Stir in the pork and cook until heated through, about 2 minutes longer. Off the heat, sprinkle the cheese over the top. Cover and let sit off the heat until the cheese melts, about 1 minute. Sprinkle with the cilantro before serving and pass sour cream at the table.

Cheesy Pork, Rice, and Bean Burritos

SERVES 4

The pork tenderloin in this recipe is from Spice-Rubbed Pork Tenderloins with Mango Salsa (page 108). Garnish with diced avocado and sour cream, if desired. If you don't have cooked rice on hand, you can use Uncle Ben's Ready Rice.

2 tablespoons vegetable oil

1 medium onion, minced

3 medium garlic cloves, minced or pressed through a garlic press (about 1 tablespoon)

2 teaspoons minced chipotle chile in adobo sauce

1 (15.5-ounce) can pinto beans, drained and rinsed

1 (14.5 ounce) can diced tomatoes

½ cup water
Salt and ground black pepper

1 cup cooked rice (see note)

10 ounces cooked pork tenderloin, sliced into thin strips (about 2 cups; see note)

8 ounces cheddar cheese, shredded (about 2 cups)

¼ cup minced fresh cilantro leaves

4 (10-inch) flour tortillas

1. Adjust an oven rack to the middle position and heat the oven to 450 degrees. Heat the oil in a large nonstick skillet over medium-high heat until shimmering but not smoking. Add the onion and cook until softened, 5 to 7 minutes. Stir in the garlic and chipotle and cook until fragrant, about 30 seconds. Add the beans, tomatoes with their juice,

TRIMMING SILVER SKIN

To quickly remove the silver skin from a pork tenderloin (it is tough and chewy), simply slip the tip of a sharp paring or boning knife under the silver skin, angle it slightly upward, and use a gentle sawing motion to remove it.

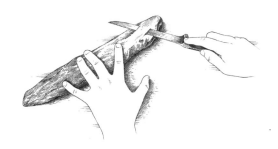

BREAKING LONG-STRAND PASTA IN HALF

Though we don't normally recommend breaking pasta strands in half, this step makes it easier to toast vermicelli in a skillet.

Roll up the bundle of pasta in a kitchen towel that overlaps the pasta by 3 or 4 inches at both ends. Holding both ends firmly, center the rolled bundle over the edge of a table or counter. Push down with both hands to break the pasta in the middle of the bundle.

HOW TO ROLL A TIGHT BURRITO

1. Spread the bean mixture 1½-inches from the bottom of each tortilla, leaving a 2-inch border at the ends, then mound the rice mixture on the beans.

2. Roll the bottom edge of the tortilla up over the filling to cover it completely. Using the tortilla for leverage, press the filling back onto itself into a tight, compact log.

3. Fold the sides of the tortilla over the filling. Continue to roll the burrito into a tidy bundle. Place on a foil-lined baking sheet, seam side down. If the ends come unfolded, simply tuck them under the burrito.

and water and cook until the liquid has evaporated and the beans are softened, about 8 minutes. Using a potato masher, mash the beans lightly. Season with salt and pepper to taste.

2. Place the rice in a medium microwave-safe bowl, cover with plastic wrap, poke holes in the plastic, and microwave on high power until hot, about 90 seconds. Stir in the pork, 1 cup of the cheese, and the cilantro.

3. Line a baking sheet with foil and spray a second large sheet of foil with vegetable oil spray;

set aside. Following the illustrations at left, spread one-quarter of the bean mixture across the center of each tortilla, leaving a 1½-inch border at the bottom edge and a 2-inch border at each end. Mound the rice mixture on the beans and fold the tortillas into burritos. Transfer the burritos, seam sides down, to the prepared baking sheet, sprinkle with the remaining 1 cup cheese, and cover with the oiled foil. Bake until the cheese is melted, 5 to 10 minutes. Serve immediately.

Mexican-Style Pork and Chorizo Stew

SERVES 4

The pork tenderloin in this recipe is from Spice-Rubbed Pork Tenderloins with Mango Salsa (page 108). If you like spicy food, use the higher amount of chipotle. Serve with lime wedges and sour cream.

1	tablespoon vegetable oil
8	ounces chorizo, quartered lengthwise and cut crosswise into ¼-inch pieces
1	medium onion, minced Salt
4	medium garlic cloves, minced or pressed through a garlic press (about 4 teaspoons)
1–2	teaspoons minced chipotle chile in adobo sauce
3	tablespoons unbleached all-purpose flour
4	cups low-sodium chicken broth
1	(15-ounce) can hominy, drained and rinsed
1	(14.5-ounce) can diced tomatoes, drained
1	tablespoon brown sugar
1	teaspoon minced fresh oregano leaves, or ½ teaspoon dried
10	ounces cooked pork tenderloin, cut into medium dice (about 2 cups; see note)
¼	cup minced fresh cilantro leaves Ground black pepper

1. Heat the oil in a large saucepan over high heat until just smoking. Add the chorizo and cook, stirring frequently, until lightly browned, about 3 minutes. Add the onion and ½ teaspoon salt and cook, stirring frequently, until softened, about 5 minutes. Stir in the garlic and chipotle and cook

until fragrant, about 30 seconds. Stir in the flour until incorporated.

2. Add the broth, hominy, tomatoes, sugar, and oregano and bring to a simmer. Reduce the heat to medium-low and continue to simmer until the flavors have melded, about 20 minutes. Stir in the pork and cook until heated through, about 2 minutes. Stir in the cilantro and season with salt and pepper to taste. Serve immediately.

Pot Roast with Root Vegetables

A GOOD POT ROAST BY DEFINITION ENTAILS the transformation of a tough (read: cheap), nearly unpalatable cut of meat into a tender, rich, flavorful main course by means of a slow, moist cooking process called braising. A slow-food survivor of generations past, economical pot roast has stubbornly remained in the repertoire of Sunday-night cookery, despite the fact that the meat can often turn stringy and dry. We wanted to turn this classic into a tasty, complete meal—a one-pot dinner with tender meat, sweet and earthy root vegetables, and a deeply flavored sauce. After that, we wanted to come up with some appealing ways to put those leftovers back on the table in entirely new meals.

The meat for pot roast should be well marbled with fat and connective tissue to provide the dish with the necessary flavor and moisture. Recipes typically call for roasts from the sirloin (or rump), round (leg), or chuck (shoulder). When all was said and done, we found that three of the chuck cuts—seven-bone roast, top-blade roast, and chuck-eye roast—were our favorites because they cooked up the most tender with an incredibly beefy flavor.

Before we began addressing how we braised the pot roast, we needed to deal with the aesthetics of the dish. Because pot roast is traditionally cooked with liquid at a low temperature, the exterior of the meat will not brown sufficiently unless it is first sautéed in a Dutch oven on the stovetop. Medium-high heat and a little oil were all that were needed to caramelize the exterior of the beef and boost both the flavor and the appearance of the dish.

Using water as the braising medium, we found that the moistest meat was produced when we added liquid halfway up the sides of the roast (depending on the cut, this amount could be between 2 and 4 cups). We also found it necessary to cover the Dutch oven with a piece of foil before placing the lid on top. The added seal of the foil kept the liquid from escaping (in the form of steam) by means of the loose-fitting lid and eliminated any need to add more liquid to the pot.

Next we tested different liquids, hoping to add flavor to the roast and sauce. Red wine had a startling effect on the meat, penetrating it with a potent flavor that most tasters agreed was "good, but not traditional pot roast." However, tasters did like the flavor of a little red wine added to the sauce after the pot roast was removed from the pan. In the end, we found that equal amounts of chicken and beef broths did the job, with the beef broth boosting the depth of flavor and the chicken broth rounding things out. Because different amounts of liquid would have to be added to the pot depending on the size and shape of each individual roast, we chose to be consistent in the amount of chicken and beef broth used—1 cup each—and to vary the amount of water to bring the liquid level halfway up the sides of the roast.

We found that starting the pot roast on the stove, and then transferring it to a low oven (300 degrees) maintained a slow, steady simmer. This method required no supervision, just a turn of the meat every 30 to 40 minutes to ensure even cooking. To achieve our goal of fall-apart tenderness, we cooked the pot roast to 210 degrees, the point at which the fat and connective tissue begin to melt, and then maintained that temperature for a full hour. Nearly all the fat and connective tissue had dissolved into the meat, giving each bite a soft, silky texture and rich, succulent flavor. In other words, cook the pot roast until it's done—and then keep on cooking!

With the details of cooking the roast resolved, we focused on the vegetables. Carrots and potatoes were the obvious choices, though tasters also liked the addition of parsnips for their rich, sweet, and assertive flavor. Cooking the vegetables was easy—we simmered them with the roast for the last 20 minutes or so, and then transferred the roast to a carving board to rest while we continued to cook the vegetables until they were completely tender. We found that cooking the vegetables with the lid off for the last 5 or 10 minutes also allowed the sauce to concentrate its flavors and thicken slightly.

The moist meat, tender vegetables, and richly flavored sauce were all exceptional the first time around; however, with pot roast leftovers are to be expected (unless, of course, you are serving a crowd). We aimed to reincarnate the leftover meat, vegetables, and sauce into interesting new meals. Using 10 ounces of pot roast, 2 cups of cooked vegetables, and ½ cup of the sauce, we developed quick and easy recipes that could result in either Beef Hash with Root Vegetables and Poached Eggs or Hearty Beef and Barley Soup.

Our hash recipe is perfect for breakfast or brunch, but here in the test kitchen, we are also big fans of eggs for dinner. To make this recipe quick, we parcooked diced potatoes before frying

them with the leftover root vegetables and beef in rendered bacon fat until golden brown and crusty. While eggs for hash are usually poached and placed on top of the hash just before serving, we made this a one-pot affair. We "poached" the eggs in the same pan by nestling them into indentations in the hash and cooking them over low heat. The results were perfect: eggs with runny yolks conveniently set in the hash and ready to be served.

For the Hearty Beef and Barley Soup, we developed deep, rich flavor quickly by using intensely flavored ingredients like dried porcini mushrooms, tomato paste, and the already richly flavored pot roast sauce. For the soup's broth, we liked the way that beef and chicken broth balanced one another. To speed things up even further, we tried instant barley in our soup. As it turned out, it was worth the extra simmering time required for regular barley since the instant barley turned to an unidentifiable, flavorless mush in the soup. After about 35 minutes, the regular barley was almost tender

HOW TO TIE A TOP-BLADE ROAST

Most top-blade roasts are sold already tied, but if the one you buy is not, here's how to do it.

1. Slip a 6-foot piece of twine under the roast and tie a double knot.

2. Hold the twine against the meat, and loop the long end under and around the meat.

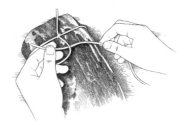

3. Run the long end through the loop.

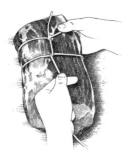

4. Repeat the procedure down the length of the roast.

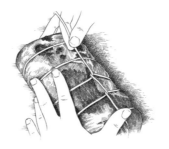

5. Roll the roast over and run the twine under and around each loop.

6. Wrap the twine around the end of the roast, flip the roast, and tie to the original knot.

and we stirred in the leftover meat and vegetables so they could heat through without overcooking. Minced parsley provided the perfect finishing touch, and tasters had no idea that this was a soup made from last night's pot roast.

Pot Roast with Root Vegetables

SERVES 4 WITH LEFTOVERS

Our favorite cut for pot roast is a chuck-eye roast. Because chuck roast contains several pieces of muscle, most markets sell the roast with twine tied around the center; however, if necessary, tie it yourself referring to the illustrations on page 112. Seven-bone and top-blade roasts are also good choices for this recipe. If using a top-blade roast, you will also need to tie it to keep it from falling apart during cooking.

LEFTOVER REMINDER

To make the recipes on pages 114–115, remember to reserve ½ cup of the sauce, 2 cups of the cooked root vegetables, and 10 ounces of the cooked pot roast.

I	boneless chuck-eye roast (about 3½ pounds; see note)
	Salt and ground black pepper
2	tablespoons vegetable oil
I	medium onion, chopped medium
I	carrot, peeled and chopped medium
I	celery rib, chopped medium
2	medium garlic cloves, minced or pressed through a garlic press (about 2 teaspoons)
2	teaspoons sugar
I	cup low-sodium chicken broth
I	cup low-sodium beef broth
I	thyme sprig
I½	cups water, or as needed
I½	pounds carrots (about 8 medium), peeled and sliced ½ inch thick
I½	pounds red potatoes (about 5 medium), scrubbed and cut into ¾-inch chunks
I	pound parsnips (about 5 medium), peeled and sliced ½ inch thick
¼	cup dry red wine

1. Adjust an oven rack to the middle position and heat the oven to 300 degrees. Pat the roast dry with paper towels and season with salt and pepper. Heat the oil in a large Dutch oven over high heat until just smoking. Brown the roast on all sides, reducing the heat if the fat begins to smoke, 8 to 10 minutes. Transfer the roast to a large plate.

2. Add the onion, chopped carrot, and celery to the fat left in the pot and cook over medium heat until lightly browned, about 8 minutes. Stir in the garlic and sugar and cook until fragrant, about 30 seconds. Add the chicken and beef broths and thyme, scraping up any browned bits from the bottom of the pan.

3. Return the roast and any accumulated juices to the pot. Add the water until it measures halfway up the sides of the roast (you may not need it all) and bring to a simmer. Place a large piece of foil over the pot, cover with the lid, and transfer it to the oven. Cook, turning the roast every 30 minutes, until the roast is almost tender (a sharp knife should meet little resistance), 3 to 3½ hours.

4. Add the sliced carrots, potatoes, and parsnips to the pot, submerging them in the liquid, then re-cover, and continue to cook in the oven until the vegetables are almost tender, 20 to 30 minutes more.

5. Transfer the roast to a carving board, tent with foil, and let rest while finishing the vegetables and sauce. Let the liquid in the pot settle for about 5 minutes, then skim any fat off the surface using a spoon. Discard the thyme sprig and add the wine. Over medium-low heat, simmer, uncovered, until the vegetables are tender, 5 to 10 minutes. Season with salt and pepper to taste. *To make one of the recipes on pages 114–115, reserve ½ cup of the sauce and 2 cups of the vegetables and refrigerate in separate airtight containers for up to 2 days.*

6. Remove the twine and cut the pot roast into ½-inch-thick slices or pull apart into large pieces. *To make one of the recipes on page 114–115, reserve 10 ounces of the pot roast and refrigerate in an airtight container for up to 2 days.* Arrange the meat and vegetables on a platter and pour ½ cup of the sauce over the top. Serve, passing the remaining sauce separately.

Beef Hash with Root Vegetables and Poached Eggs

SERVES 4

The sauce, root vegetables, and pot roast in this recipe are from Pot Roast with Root Vegetables (page 113). If you like it spicy, serve with additional hot sauce.

2	pounds russet potatoes (4 medium), peeled and cut into ½-inch dice
	Salt
4	slices bacon (4 ounces), chopped fine
1	medium onion, minced
2	medium garlic cloves, minced or pressed through a garlic press (about 2 teaspoons)
½	teaspoon minced fresh thyme leaves, or ¼ teaspoon dried
10	ounces cooked pot roast, cut into ¼-inch dice (about 2 cups; see note)
2	cups cooked root vegetables (see note)
½	cup pot roast sauce (see note)
½	cup heavy cream
¼	teaspoon hot sauce
4	large eggs
	Ground black pepper

1. Cover the potatoes by 1 inch of cold water in a medium saucepan, add ½ teaspoon salt, and simmer until the potatoes are tender, about 5 minutes. Drain the potatoes.

2. Cook the bacon in a large nonstick skillet over medium-high heat until the fat has partially rendered, about 4 minutes. Add the onion and cook until browned at the edges, about 5 minutes. Stir in the garlic and thyme and cook until fragrant, about 30 seconds.

3. Stir in the diced pot roast, root vegetables, and parcooked potatoes and lightly press the mixture into the pan. Pour the pot roast sauce, cream, and hot sauce over the hash, and cook undisturbed for 6 minutes. Using a spatula, invert the hash a portion at a time and lightly repack it into the pan. Repeat this process every few minutes until the hash is partly crisp and the potatoes are thoroughly cooked, about 6 minutes longer.

4. Make 4 shallow indentations in the hash and crack an egg into each indentation. Sprinkle the eggs with salt and pepper. Reduce the heat to medium-low, cover, and cook until the eggs are just set, about 5 minutes. Serve the hash and eggs immediately.

CHUCK ROASTS

SEVEN-BONE POT ROAST

TOP-BLADE POT ROAST

CHUCK-EYE ROAST

The seven-bone pot roast (left) is a well-marbled cut with an incredibly beefy flavor. It gets its name from the bone found in the roast, which is shaped like the number seven. Because it is only 2 inches thick, less liquid and less time are needed to braise the roast. Do not buy a seven-bone pot roast that weighs more than 3½ pounds, as it will not fit into a Dutch oven. This roast is also sometimes referred to as a seven-bone steak.

The top-blade pot roast (middle) is also well marbled with fat and connective tissue, which make this roast very juicy and flavorful. Even after thorough braising, this roast retains a distinctive strip of connective tissue, which is not unpleasant to eat. This roast may also be sold as a blade roast.

The chuck-eye roast (right) is the fattiest of the three roasts and the most commonly available. The high proportion of fat gives pot roast great flavor and tenderness which makes this cut our top choice for pot roast.

Hearty Beef and Barley Soup
SERVES 4

The sauce, root vegetables, and pot roast in this recipe are from Pot Roast with Root Vegetables (page 113).

2	tablespoons vegetable oil
1	medium onion, minced
½	ounce dried porcini mushrooms, rinsed and minced
2	tablespoons tomato paste
3	medium garlic cloves, minced or pressed through a garlic press (about 1 tablespoon)
1	teaspoon minced fresh thyme leaves, or ¼ teaspoon dried
4	cups low-sodium chicken broth
4	cups low-sodium beef broth
½	cup pot roast sauce (see note)
½	cup pearl barley
10	ounces cooked pot roast, shredded (about 2 cups; see note)
2	cups cooked root vegetables (see note)
	Salt and ground black pepper
1	tablespoon minced fresh parsley leaves

1. Heat the oil in a large saucepan over medium heat until just shimmering. Add the onion and mushrooms and cook until softened, about 5 minutes. Stir in the tomato paste, garlic, and thyme, and cook until fragrant, about 30 seconds.

2. Add the chicken and beef broths, pot roast sauce, and barley and bring to a simmer. Cook until the barley is almost tender, about 35 minutes. Stir in the shredded pot roast and root vegetables and continue to simmer until the barley is tender, 10 to 15 minutes longer. Season with salt and pepper to taste. Stir in the parsley before serving.

BRAISED BRISKET

BRAISED BEEF BRISKET IS A WORKHORSE MEAL. It can serve many people (or just a few with great leftovers) for reasonable cost, and is usually cooked with straightforward, universally appealing flavors. The all-too-common problem with brisket, however, is that the meat can turn out extraordinarily dry and chewy if not prepared correctly. Our goal was to develop a recipe for braised brisket that was both moist and tender, with a simple sauce that complemented this naturally flavorful cut. And along the way, we wanted to develop a couple of recipes that turned the leftovers into something extraordinary.

The method for braising brisket is the same as for other stews and braises. The meat is first browned, and then set off to the side while the browned bits left behind in the pot are used to make a flavorful sauce. The browned beef is nestled back into the pot with the sauce, the liquid is brought to a gentle simmer, and the meat is cooked until tender.

When we followed this basic method we were disappointed to discover that while tender, the brisket was quite dry and had an unappealing boiled flavor, and the sauce was thin and greasy. Last, the meat appeared to cook unevenly; by the time the center of the brisket was tender, the outer layers of meat were falling apart in shreds.

Looking for a better way to braise, we tested an assortment of cooking vessels and techniques. We came across an unusual recipe that called for searing the brisket in a skillet before cooking it in a wrapper of aluminum foil along with the broth used to deglaze the pan. The good news was that this brisket cooked evenly—the meat was always in contact with liquid. But the meat was still dry.

If we couldn't keep the moisture from leaving the meat in the first place, could we get the meat to reabsorb some of the liquid after cooking? Until this point, we had been removing the brisket from the sauce and letting it rest briefly on a carving board before attempting—and failing—to cut it into thin, neat slices. (Like a flank steak, brisket has long muscle fibers and must be sliced against the grain to avoid being chewy. These same long fibers, however, turn into shreds once the connective tissue has been dissolved, making the meat difficult to slice.) Now we tested letting the meat rest in the sauce for a good hour before slicing it, in hopes that it would reabsorb some of the flavorful liquid it had lost. After an hour-long rest, the brisket was noticeably better. But now the sauce needed work.

Many brisket recipes we researched base the sauce around the flavor of caramelized onions (the meat is almost smothered by the onions as it cooks).

Giving this idea a try, we found it easy to lightly caramelize some onions in the drippings left over from browning the meat. To build a flavorful, well-rounded sauce around the onions, we added both brown sugar and tomato paste to develop the sweet onion flavor. A combination of chicken broth and red wine also proved crucial, as did the addition of cayenne pepper, paprika, bay leaves, and fresh thyme. Lastly, we refreshed the flavor of this long-cooked sauce by adding a dash of cider vinegar just before serving. With an ample amount of sauce and onions to serve alongside the sliced brisket (and enough to save for leftovers), no one will ever complain that this version tastes chewy or dry.

Now onto our recipes for using the leftovers. With 10 ounces of brisket, 1 cup of flavorful sauce, and 1 cup of caramelized onions, we couldn't help but think of French dip sandwiches. When building the sandwiches, we quickly dipped the brisket slices into the warmed sauce before layering them with the caramelized onions and cheese (we like provolone, but Swiss cheese works, too) on buttered and toasted sub rolls. Then we broiled the sandwiches until the cheese melted, and served them with the extra sauce for dipping. These French dip sandwiches are so tasty that you might even find yourself making Onion-Braised Beef Brisket just for the leftovers!

Next, we took a completely different route and developed a recipe for Rigatoni with Beef Ragù. The brisket, onions, and sauce were packed with so much deep, rich, beefy flavor, that it was easy to make a quick ragù that tasted like it had cooked for hours. The leftover brisket, caramelized onions, and sauce formed the base of the sauce, along with garlic, tomato paste, red wine, and diced tomatoes. After fifteen minutes of simmering, we had a full-fledged beef ragù, which we then tossed with the rigatoni and finished with a touch of heavy cream to enrich the dish and round out the flavors.

SCIENCE: Making a Tender Brisket

Most cooked briskets are dry, but they are not tough. In contrast, if you cook a steak the way you cook a brisket (that is, until very well done), it will be dry and tough. What makes brisket different?

To find out, we used a Warner-Bratzler meat shear (see photo), a device designed to measure tenderness in meat. It uses a motor to push a piece of meat across a dull blade while a simple scale measures the required force. We first cooked very tender meat (tenderloin) in a 3½-hour braise until very well done. Tender when raw, the meat was, according to the meat shear, 188 percent—2.9 times—tougher after braising. Next we cooked the brisket, which, unlike the tenderloin, was tough to begin with. By the end of the first hour of braising time, the meat had become even tougher. But further cooking reversed this trend. When the brisket was ready to come out of the oven (after 3½ hours of braising), it was 28 percent more tender than when raw. What was happening?

The muscle fibers in meat contract and tighten soon after cooking commences. When the muscle fibers contract, they expel moisture and the meat becomes tougher. As the internal temperature of the meat climbs, a second process begins that helps reverse this trend. A tough connective tissue, collagen, begins to melt, turning into soft gelatin. In some cuts of meat, most of the toughening of the muscle is counterbalanced by the conversion of collagen to gelatin. We could see this when we used the meat shear on the brisket. Early measurements showed large variations, and if we looked at the blade after getting a high reading, we almost invariably saw white material—the collagen—streaked along the side. Once the temperature of the meat passed 200 degrees, however, these streaks had disappeared, and the meat had not only softened but also become more uniform in texture.

Extended cooking destroys tender cuts with little collagen (like the tenderloin) as they steadily give up their juices and become drier and tougher. But extended cooking actually improves the texture of tough cuts with lots of sinuous collagen (like brisket). Yes, they lose juices and become dry, but they also become tender as the collagen melts. So if your brisket seems a little tough, put it back in the oven!

This device, called a Warner-Bratzler meat shear, cuts core samples from meat and measures tenderness.

WORTH THE WAIT

Sliced straight from the pot, brisket almost invariably shreds (left). Letting the cooked brisket rest for one hour in the braising liquid allows the meat to absorb some of these juices, and the result is meat that slices neatly and tastes better (right).

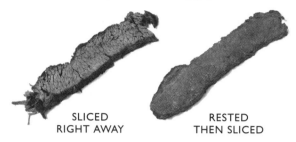

SLICED
RIGHT AWAY

RESTED
THEN SLICED

Onion-Braised Beef Brisket

SERVES 4 WITH LEFTOVERS

Note that brisket is sold in two cuts: flat cut and point cut. We prefer the flat cut for braising. This recipe requires a few hours of unattended cooking. You will need 18-inch-wide heavy-duty foil for this recipe. If you own an electric knife, it will make easy work of slicing the cold brisket.

LEFTOVER REMINDER

To make the recipes on page 118, remember to reserve 1 cup of the sauce, 1 cup of the cooked onions, and 10 ounces of the cooked brisket.

I	(4- to 5-pound) beef brisket, flat cut preferred
	Salt and ground black pepper
	Vegetable oil
3	pounds large onions (about 4), halved and sliced ½ inch thick
I	tablespoon light brown sugar
3	medium garlic cloves, minced or pressed through a garlic press (about I tablespoon)
I	tablespoon tomato paste
I	tablespoon paprika
⅛	teaspoon cayenne pepper
2	tablespoons unbleached all-purpose flour
I	cup low-sodium chicken broth
I	cup dry red wine
3	bay leaves
3	thyme sprigs
2	teaspoons cider vinegar

1. Adjust an oven rack to the lower-middle position and heat the oven to 300 degrees. Line a 13 by 9-inch baking dish with two 24-inch-long sheets of 18-inch-wide heavy-duty foil, positioning the sheets perpendicular to each other and allowing the excess foil to extend beyond the edges of the pan. Place the brisket fat side up on a cutting board. Using a dinner fork, poke holes in the meat through the fat layer about 1 inch apart. Pat the brisket dry with paper towels and season with salt and pepper.

2. Heat 1 teaspoon oil in a 12-inch skillet over high heat until just smoking. Place the brisket fat side up in the skillet (the brisket may climb up the sides of the skillet) and place a heavy Dutch oven or cast-iron skillet on top of the brisket to weight it down. Cook until well browned on both sides, about 14 minutes, flipping the brisket over and replacing the Dutch oven halfway through cooking. Transfer the brisket to a platter.

3. Pour off all but 1 tablespoon of the fat from the pan (or add oil to the skillet to equal 1 tablespoon). Add the onions, sugar, and ¼ teaspoon salt and cook over medium-high heat, stirring occasionally, until the onions are softened and golden brown, 10 to 12 minutes.

4. Stir in the garlic and cook until fragrant, about 30 seconds. Stir in the tomato paste and cook until darkened, about 2 minutes. Add the paprika and cayenne and cook until fragrant, about 1 minute. Sprinkle the flour over the onions and cook, stirring constantly, until well combined, about 2 minutes. Add the broth, wine, bay leaves, and thyme, stirring to scrape up any browned bits from the pan. Simmer until thickened, about 5 minutes.

5. Pour the sauce and onions into the foil-lined baking dish. Nestle the brisket, fat side up, into the sauce and onions. Fold the foil extensions over and seal (but do not tightly crimp the foil because the foil must later be opened to test for doneness). Cook until a fork can be inserted into and removed from the center of the brisket with no resistance, 3½ to 4 hours (when testing for doneness, open the foil with caution as the contents will be steaming).

6. Remove from the oven, reseal the foil, and let the brisket cool at room temperature for 1 hour.

When cool, strain the onion mixture, reserving the onions and sauce in separate bowls. Discard the bay leaves and thyme from the onions. Let the sauce settle for about 5 minutes, then skim any fat from the surface using a spoon. *To make one of the recipes below, reserve 1 cup of the onions and 1 cup of the sauce and refrigerate in separate airtight containers for up to 2 days.*

7. Warm the sauce in a medium saucepan over medium heat, skimming any fat on the surface using a spoon. Transfer the brisket to a carving board. *To make one of the recipes below, reserve 10 ounces of the brisket and refrigerate in an airtight container for up to 2 days.* Cut the brisket against the grain into ¼-inch-thick slices, discarding any excess fat, and transfer the slices to a platter. Stir the onions and vinegar into the warmed sauce and season with salt and pepper to taste. Spoon the sauce over the sliced brisket and serve immediately.

French Dip Sandwiches

SERVES 4

The sauce, onions, and brisket in this recipe are from Onion-Braised Beef Brisket (page 117).

1	cup brisket sauce (see note)
2	tablespoons unsalted butter, softened
4	(6-inch) sub rolls, halved
10	ounces cooked brisket, sliced thin (about 2 cups; see note)
1	cup cooked onions (see note)
8	slices provolone cheese, each slice cut in half

1. Adjust an oven rack about 6 inches from the broiler element, and heat the broiler. Warm the brisket sauce in a small covered saucepan over medium-low heat.

2. Meanwhile, spread the butter evenly inside the rolls. Place them on a baking sheet, buttered sides up, and broil until golden brown, 1 to 3 minutes. Remove the top half of each roll from the baking sheet and set aside.

3. Using tongs, dip the brisket slices into the warmed sauce and place them on the bottom half of each roll. Spoon the onions over the beef and arrange the provolone on top. Broil until the cheese is melted, 1 to 3 minutes.

4. Place the top halves of the rolls on the sandwiches and serve with the remaining sauce for dipping.

Rigatoni with Beef Ragù

SERVES 4

The sauce, onions, and brisket in this recipe are from Onion-Braised Beef Brisket (page 117). If you don't have heavy cream on hand, substitute 3 tablespoons unsalted butter.

2	tablespoons olive oil
3	medium garlic cloves, minced or pressed through a garlic press (about 1 tablespoon)
1	tablespoon tomato paste
½	teaspoon dried oregano
1	cup cooked onions (see note)
½	cup dry red wine
1	(28-ounce) can diced tomatoes
10	ounces cooked brisket, shredded (about 2 cups; see note)
1	cup brisket sauce (see note)
	Salt and ground black pepper
1	pound rigatoni
3	tablespoons heavy cream
	Parmesan cheese, grated (for serving)

1. Bring 4 quarts of water to a boil in a large pot.

2. Meanwhile, heat the oil and garlic in a 12-inch skillet over medium heat until light golden brown, about 2 minutes. Stir in the tomato paste and oregano and cook until fragrant, about 1 minute. Stir in the cooked onions and red wine and cook until the wine is evaporated, about 2 minutes. Stir in the tomatoes with their juice, shredded brisket, and brisket sauce and simmer until thickened, stirring frequently, about 15 minutes. Season with salt and pepper to taste.

3. Add 1 tablespoon salt and the rigatoni to the boiling water, and cook, stirring often, until al dente. Reserve ½ cup of the pasta cooking water, then drain the pasta in a colander and return the rigatoni to the pot. Toss the rigatoni with the sauce and cream, adding the reserved pasta cooking water as needed to thin the sauce. Serve immediately, passing the Parmesan separately.

4

SLOW-COOKER FAVORITES

Slow-Cooker Favorites

SLOW COOKERS PROMISE HOME COOKS THE ultimate make-ahead meal: Simply put your ingredients in the pot in the morning and eight to 10 hours later, dinner (and the credit for it) can be yours simply by walking in the door at 6 p.m. The catch, however, is that to extract a really good meal from your slow cooker, you can't just dump a bunch of raw ingredients in the crock and walk away; you must commit some time to prep work either the night before or in the early morning hours (when most people have better things to do with their time).

For this chapter, we were looking for hearty and practical recipes that would be packed with flavor but would not require much in the way of advance prep—plus we hoped to have the option of doing most, if not all, of the prep work the night before, thereby minimizing early-morning cooking. After all, we understand that anyone using a slow cooker has a hectic life; slow-cooker recipes are meant to be a life raft, not a complicated project. And we wanted recipes that could withstand a full workday in the slow cooker. With these goals in mind, we set out to find ways to streamline recipes without sacrificing flavor.

For meat-based recipes such as Beef Stew (page 142), Beef and Barley Soup (page 132), Texas Chili (page 136), or Southwestern-Style Pot Roast (page 144), the biggest question we faced was: Is it truly crucial to brown the meat before adding it to the slow cooker? While conventional cooking wisdom (and the little voice in our culinary school–trained heads) screamed yes, we wondered if, after hours in a slow cooker, tasters would really notice if the meat had been dutifully browned or not. We did extensive testing and tastings, and you may be surprised with the results (see pages 139–141). When stews with browned meat were pitted against stews where the meat had not been browned, few could tell the difference. We found that there were techniques and ingredients which essentially made up for the flavor lost by not browning the meat (see page 140). With these tricks alone, we solved what we considered the biggest obstacle dividing great slow-cooker recipes from those just not worth eating.

In this chapter you'll also find some vegetarian options like Lentil and Swiss Chard Stew (page 130), Curried Chickpea Stew (page 128), and Vegetarian Black Bean Soup (page 126). For these recipes, our efforts were focused on coming up with a few tricks for replacing the complex flavor that meat brings to the pot, namely through the use of ingredients like dried porcini mushrooms and canned chipotle chiles. Even the most ardent meat eaters among us were happy with these healthy, full-flavored vegetarian alternatives.

The recipes in this chapter all have a range of cooking times based on our testing. Establishing cooking times for slow-cooker recipes is not an exact science, so take our guidelines as a good approximation of how long the cooking will likely take rather than as an absolute. The bottom line is that you need to get to know your slow cooker by trying it with a variety of recipes.

Well-marbled cuts of meat are especially ideal for the slow cooker—during a long gentle simmer on a low setting, the fat melts and the meat becomes tender. Any of the recipes in this chapter can be made in advance in the slow cooker, then reheated on the stovetop, like Meaty Tomato Sauce (page 138), Barbecued Brisket (page 149), or Beef Stew (page 142); most of them can also be frozen. In most cases, these recipes will taste even better the next day after the meat has even more time to absorb the flavorful cooking liquid.

SLOW-COOKER SPLIT PEA SOUP

MADE FROM DRIED GREEN PEAS, VEGETABLES, and the obligatory ham bone, split pea soup is a natural for the slow cooker. The problem with many of the recipes we tried was that they were either too thin and watery, or as thick as wallpaper paste. Many had no flavor after eight hours in the slow cooker, and tasted more like pureed canned peas than anything else. Our goal was a pea soup with a substantial—but not gluey—texture. We wanted the subtle flavor of the split peas to come out, and be enhanced rather than overshadowed by the smoky flavor that a ham bone can add.

Other than around Easter or maybe Christmas, we rarely have a ham bone available to add to the soup pot. So in testing this recipe, we first tried adding chunks of deli ham, both at the beginning of cooking, and at the end as a stand-in for the ham bone. Not surprisingly, the ham added at the beginning of the lengthy cooking time turned

rubbery and flavorless. Adding it at the end was not a bad option (especially if you like a meaty soup), but we found a better alternative with smoked ham hocks. These meaty morsels packed lots of flavor into our soup as it simmered, and instead of turning rubbery during the long cooking time, they became more tender. To add more flavor to the soup, we added the classic trio of mirepoix ingredients (carrot, celery, and onion) as a flavor base. We

EQUIPMENT: Slow Cookers

Slow cookers (better known as Crock-Pots, a name trade-marked by the Rival company) may be the only modern kitchen convenience that saves the cook time by using more of it rather than less. But gone are the days of merely picking out what size you need. We found 40 different models online, which begs the question: Is one slow cooker better than another? To find out, we rounded up eight leading models and put them through some very slow tests in the kitchen.

We prepared a simple beef chili on the low temperature setting for six hours in each model and, frankly, each chili was pretty good. We also prepared pot roast (see page 143) on the high temperature setting in each model, leaving the meat in the cooker until the roast maintained an internal temperature of 200 degrees for an hour. All but one slow cooker managed this task, albeit at different lengths of time, ranging from seven to nine hours. Time, however, is not really the name of this game. It turns out that what matters is size, at least with our pot roast recipe. We recommend buying a slow cooker with a minimum capacity of 6 quarts. Anything smaller and a modest 5-pound roast, pork loin, or brisket won't fit.

Shape also matters. We found the round crock styles to be deeper than the oval crocks, and they heated more evenly. That said, while the depth and shape of these round cookers made them perfect for submerging a roast in braising liquid, it proved a

hindrance with recipes requiring bulky, layered ingredients, such as chicken parts or ribs. Oval-shaped slow cookers, such as the Farberware Millennium ($44.99) and the West Bend Versatility ($54.99), have more surface area for cooking and are better suited to these kinds of recipes. Because oval cookers also work when making chilis, stews, or roasts, they are the more versatile choice. However, if you're going to use your slow cooker only for stews and chilis, the Proctor Silex round cooker ($32) is a great option.

In addition to differences in size and shape, we noted a variety of features on slow cookers, some of which are quite helpful. A "keep warm" setting is sensible (it turns the heat down once the food is done), but only when paired with a timer. This way, if you are late getting home from work, dinner will still be fine. Without a timer, the keep-warm function seems useless. We also liked models with power lights—without one, it's hard to tell if the slow cooker is on. As might be expected, a dishwasher-safe crock and lid are desirable, but neither of our two favorite oval cookers, the Farberware and the West Bend, offered this feature.

In the end, we can recommend three of the eight models tested. Perhaps best of all, we found that spending more money didn't necessarily buy a better slow cooker.

THE BEST SLOW COOKERS

The Farberware Millennium (left) and the Proctor Silex (center) were the best basic models tested. The West Bend Versatility cooker (right) has a stovetop-worthy pot made of aluminum rather than the classic ceramic.

tried first to get away with adding them raw, but sautéing them brought out their sweet flavors and ensured they wouldn't be crunchy at the end of the simmering time.

The next challenge was to address the texture of the soup, which had a tendency to be overly (and unattractively) viscous and unsoup-like. From the very beginning of the process, we debated amongst ourselves just how much liquid to add to the slow cooker so that the peas were cooked but so that we didn't end up with pea Spackle. Many recipes called for up to 12 cups of water, which turned out, not surprisingly, a very thin soup. After several tests, we settled on 8 cups of liquid to provide the ideal thickness. We tested soup made with all water, all chicken broth, and a little of each. In the end, we preferred half water and half chicken broth. This combination let the delicate flavor of the dried peas come through, without imparting a chickeny flavor overall. Many tasters felt the soup needed a little something to brighten the flavors. We found that a bit of fresh lemon juice, added right before serving, was just the ticket.

Slow-Cooker Split Pea Soup
SERVES 6 TO 8
Dried green peas can often contain small stones, so make sure to pick them over carefully.

2	tablespoons vegetable oil
2	medium onions, minced
2	medium carrots, chopped medium
2	celery ribs, chopped medium
	Salt
4	cups water
4	cups low-sodium chicken broth
1	pound green split peas (2½ cups), picked over and rinsed
2	medium smoked ham hocks
3	bay leaves
1	tablespoon minced fresh thyme leaves, or 1 teaspoon dried
¼	teaspoon red pepper flakes
2	tablespoons juice from 1 lemon
	Ground black pepper

1. Heat the oil in a 12-inch nonstick skillet over medium heat until shimmering but not smoking. Add the onions, carrots, celery, and ¼ teaspoon salt and cook until softened and lightly browned, 10 to 15 minutes.

2. Transfer the vegetables to the slow cooker insert and stir in the water, broth, split peas, ham hocks, bay leaves, thyme, and pepper flakes until evenly combined. Cover and cook on low until the soup has thickened and the peas are tender, 10 to 11 hours. (Alternatively, cover and cook on high for 6 to 7 hours.)

3. Remove and discard the bay leaves. Remove the ham hocks and transfer them to a plate to cool; when cool enough to handle, remove any meat, discarding the skin, fat, and bones, and add the meat back to the soup. Stir in the lemon juice, season with salt and pepper to taste, and serve.

PREP-AHEAD TIPS
You can store all the ingredients below together.
- Cook the vegetables as described in step 1, then transfer them to an airtight container and refrigerate.
- Pick over and rinse the split peas and refrigerate.

SLOW-COOKER BLACK BEAN SOUP

BLACK BEANS, ALSO CALLED TURTLE BEANS, are widely eaten in Latin America, and they often are served up in the form of black bean soup. This peasant-style soup is robust, hearty, and earthy-tasting. Black beans have a creamy texture, and their jet-black color provides a beautiful backdrop for a colorful array of garnishes. The problem is that black beans on their own don't have a lot of flavor. Plus slow-cooker recipes compound the problem by washing out flavor. We knew that we had to front-load the seasoning for this soup if we wanted full flavor after hours of simmering.

Our first test was to determine whether or not our beans needed to be soaked overnight, as many recipes suggested. We made one batch of soup with soaked beans and one with unsoaked beans. The first thing we noticed, before we even plugged the slow cooker in, was that the water in which the beans had been soaking had turned a dark grey, muddy color. As it turned out, the soup made with these beans was a much paler color, and the flavor was much more muted than the soup made with the unsoaked beans. Furthermore, the unsoaked beans cooked up tender. Not only was our prep streamlined, we could eliminate the hassle of remembering to soak beans the night before. Next we moved on to the liquid component of our soup. As in other soup recipes, we tested various amounts of broth and water, and were most pleased with the combination of half water and half low-sodium chicken broth. The chicken broth adds just the right amount of flavor, and the addition of water prevents the broth from overpowering the other flavors of the soup.

Now that we had discovered how to cook the beans, it was time to discover the best way to build more layers of flavor onto this base without drowning the earthy flavor of the beans. We determined that meat gave the beans a necessary depth of flavor. We tested cooking the beans with smoked ham hocks, bacon, ham, and even kielbasa. We liked the flavor of all four, and each gave the beans a slightly different flavor; the ham hock provided a smooth background taste, while bacon and ham produced soup with a more assertive and salty flavor. We didn't care for the texture of either the bacon or kielbasa after 10 hours in the slow cooker, however. They were both slippery and unappetizing. Ham hocks proved to be our favorite. (For our vegetarian version, we simply substituted canned chipotle chiles for the ham hocks and vegetable broth for the chicken broth.) With a nice smoky base to build on, we simply added onion, celery, carrot, and a good amount of garlic, all of which contributed a nice sweetness to the soup. To give our soup a decidedly Latin bent, we liked the slightly nutty flavor of ground cumin, which we sautéed along with the vegetables to bring out its full flavor. To finish the soup and add a touch of brightness, we stirred in minced fresh cilantro.

Slow-Cooker Black Bean Soup
SERVES 6 TO 8
Serve this soup with minced red onion, sour cream, and hot sauce, if desired. If the soup becomes too thick as it sits, thin to the desired consistency with either water or broth.

2 tablespoons vegetable oil
3 medium onions, minced
3 celery ribs, chopped medium
2 medium carrots, chopped medium
6 medium garlic cloves, minced or pressed through a garlic press (about 2 tablespoons)
5 teaspoons ground cumin
½ teaspoon red pepper flakes
Salt
3 cups water
3 cups low-sodium chicken broth
1 pound dried black beans (2¼ cups), picked over and rinsed
2 medium smoked ham hocks
2 bay leaves
¼ cup minced fresh cilantro leaves
Ground black pepper

1. Heat the oil in a 12-inch nonstick skillet over medium heat until shimmering but not smoking. Add the onions, celery, carrots, garlic, cumin, pepper flakes, and ¼ teaspoon salt and cook until the vegetables are softened and lightly browned, 10 to 15 minutes.

2. Transfer the vegetables to the slow cooker insert and stir in the water, broth, black beans, ham hocks, and bay leaves until evenly combined. Cover and cook on low until the soup has thickened and the beans are tender, 8 to 10 hours. (Alternatively, cover and cook on high for 6 to 7 hours.)

3. Remove and discard the bay leaves. Remove the ham hocks and transfer them to a plate to cool. Meanwhile, puree 2 cups of the soup in a blender until smooth, then stir back into the slow cooker insert. When the hocks are cool enough to handle, remove any meat, discarding the skin, fat, and bones, and add the meat back to the soup. Stir in the cilantro, season with salt and pepper to taste, and serve.

PREP-AHEAD TIPS

You can store all the ingredients below together.

• Cook the vegetables as described in step 1, then transfer to an airtight container and refrigerate.

• Pick over and rinse the black beans and refrigerate.

➤ VARIATION

Slow-Cooker Vegetarian Black Bean Soup

Follow the recipe for Black Bean Soup, omitting the ham hocks. Substitute 6 cups vegetable broth for the water and chicken broth. Add 2 tablespoons minced chipotle chile in adobo sauce along with the bay leaves in step 2.

SLOW-COOKER TUSCAN WHITE BEAN SOUP

BECAUSE OF ITS SIMPLICITY, WHITE BEAN soup is often poorly prepared, suffering from mushy beans and a thin tasteless broth (or beans that are too hard and pebble-like). But when made correctly, Tuscan white bean soup is delicious. And it can be easy to make. A testament to restraint, this soup requires few ingredients: tender, creamy beans and a soup base perfumed with the fragrance of garlic and rosemary. We surmised that a soup so simple would be easy to adapt to the slow cooker. We had no idea how wrong this assumption would prove to be.

We based our initial research on Italian recipes that used navy, great Northern, or cannellini (white kidney) beans. After cooking a few batches, we found that we preferred the larger size and appearance of the cannellini beans, so we centered our testing on them. Many of these recipes came with tips and warnings on how to achieve a cooked bean with perfect texture. "Always soak the beans overnight to ensure even cooking" and "Never salt the beans while they are cooking or they will become tough or split open" were common counsel. Surely these "rules" were established for a reason. They couldn't be merely myths, could they?

We knew from our testing for our Slow-Cooker Black Bean Soup (page 125) that it wasn't necessary to soak black beans overnight; that said, we also knew from other testing that black beans soften faster than white beans (and chickpeas) so we suspected that soaking might be in order here. Proceeding with our testing, we cooked up three batches of beans. Prior to cooking, we soaked one batch overnight and another according to the "quick-soak" method (water and beans simmer for two minutes, then are taken off the heat, covered, and allowed to sit in the water for one hour). We didn't presoak the third batch at all. Nearly everyone preferred the texture of the beans that had been soaked overnight. The unsoaked beans were tender in some spots, but hard in others. And it seemed to matter where the beans were located in the slow cooker. Those toward the perimeter of the slow cooker were more tender than the unfortunate beans that were in the middle of the cooker. The beans that were presoaked overnight fared much better than the unsoaked or quick-soaked beans. They were evenly cooked, tender, and creamy.

Now we took on rule number two: Never salt the beans during cooking. Recipes that warned against salting stated that it would cause the outer shell of the bean to toughen. We tested beans cooked in water and chicken broth (low-sodium, but still containing some salt), and the beans cooked in broth were indeed slightly more firm on the outside. However, these beans were not any less cooked on the inside than the unsalted beans. In addition, the small amount of resistance that the salted beans had developed on the outside seemed to keep them from bursting. The beans were now softly structured on the outside and tender on the inside.

One other advantage of using a salted cooking medium is flavor. The seasoned beans were simply much tastier than those cooked in just water. We reasoned that by adding other ingredients to the cooking liquid, we could improve the flavor of the beans that much more. In our initial testing, tasters preferred the beans flavored with pork rather than chicken. But because meat is not called for in the finished soup (only the extracted flavor of the meat is used), we didn't want to use expensive cuts of pork, such as loin chops, only to throw out the meat later. We tried an unsmoked ham hock, but the flavor lacked the punch that we were looking for. We then tried pancetta, a salt-cured, unsmoked

Italian bacon. The pancetta gave the beans a welcome sweet-and-sour flavor and the rendered fat boosted the pork flavor of the broth. Finely mincing the pancetta allowed it to sufficiently break down in the soup, making its appearance undetectable while its flavor made a strong presence. Onion, garlic, and bay leaves are the other traditional additions; their flavors permeated the beans. Also traditional in many Italian recipes is a Parmesan rind. If you have one, it adds great flavor to this minimalist soup (and the grated cheese from which you get the rind makes a tasty garnish too).

So now we had perfectly cooked beans full of flavor from the pork, broth, and aromatics. But we still needed to work in the flavor of rosemary, an herb traditional to white bean soup. We tried cooking the rosemary with the beans, but that produced a bitter, medicinal broth. Recalling a technique that we often use with slow-cooker recipes, we allowed the herb to steep in the hot soup for just a few minutes at the finish of our recipe. It worked—just the right amount of bright, fresh rosemary flavor was infused into the soup. We suggest garnishing this soup with a fruity extra-virgin olive oil and freshly grated Parmesan cheese.

Slow-Cooker Tuscan White Bean Soup

SERVES 6 TO 8

For a more authentic soup, place a small slice of lightly toasted Italian bread in the bottom of each bowl and ladle the soup over it. If you can't find pancetta, substitute 6 ounces bacon, finely minced.

2 tablespoons vegetable oil
6 ounces pancetta, minced
3 medium onions, minced
8 medium garlic cloves, minced or pressed through a garlic press (about 8 teaspoons)
  Salt
3 cups water
3 cups low-sodium chicken broth
1 pound dried cannellini beans (2¼ cups), picked over, rinsed, soaked overnight, and drained
1 Parmesan rind (optional)

2 bay leaves
½ teaspoon red pepper flakes
1 sprig fresh rosemary
  Ground black pepper
  Grated Parmesan cheese (for serving, optional)
  Extra-virgin olive oil (for serving, optional)

1. Heat the oil in a 12-inch nonstick skillet over medium heat until shimmering but not smoking. Add the pancetta and cook until golden, about 10 minutes. Stir in the onions, garlic, and ¼ teaspoon salt and cook until the onions are softened and lightly browned, 10 to 15 minutes.

2. Transfer the pancetta and onion mixture to the slow cooker insert and stir in the water, broth, beans, Parmesan rind (if using), bay leaves, and pepper flakes until evenly combined. Cover and cook on low until the beans are tender, 10 to 12 hours. (Alternatively, cover and cook on high for 8 to 9 hours.)

3. Add the rosemary sprig, cover, and continue to cook until lightly fragrant, about 15 minutes longer. Remove and discard the bay leaves, rosemary, and Parmesan rind (if using). Season the soup with salt and pepper to taste, and serve, sprinkling individual portions with the Parmesan and olive oil (if desired).

PREP-AHEAD TIPS
Store the ingredients below separately.
• Cook the pancetta and onion mixture as described in step 1, then transfer it to an airtight container and refrigerate.
• Pick over, rinse, and soak the cannellini beans (drain before cooking).

SLOW-COOKER CURRIED CHICKPEA STEW

CREATING A VEGETARIAN STEW FOR THE slow cooker proved more of a challenge than we had anticipated. First of all, there aren't that many vegetarian recipes to choose from as a starting point, other than chili recipes; and the few we did find simply removed the meat and substituted vegetable broth for chicken or beef broth, making no accommodation for the resulting loss of flavor. Making matters worse was the slow cooker environment, which tends to mute flavors during the long simmering time. So taking all these issues into account, we set out to develop a recipe for a substantial, stick-to-your-ribs chickpea stew that would appeal to vegetarians and carnivores alike. We started our testing with the chickpeas themselves, wondering whether we'd need to soak them overnight first; we found in our very first tests that unsoaked chickpeas just took far too long to become edible in the slow cooker.

So with the soaking issue settled, we moved on to the broth, making three soups: one with water, one with all vegetable broth, and one with half water, half broth. Tasters unanimously favored the well-balanced flavor of the soup made with all vegetable broth. The soup made with only water, not surprisingly, lacked complexity while the one made with half water and half broth was just not as good as the all-broth version. The next quandary we faced was sorting out the vegetables. Our first thought was to add potatoes but, when coupled with the chickpeas (we tried both sweet and white potatoes), the soup was just too starchy. Taking the potatoes out produced a cleaner soup, and let the flavors of the aromatics and curry powder come through. We added a hefty amount of curry powder (sautéing it first to bloom its flavor), diced tomatoes for body, and carrots for slight sweetness.

Although we wanted a chunky stew packed with vegetables, we found that if we added them all at the beginning of cooking, our stew ended up with a uniform texture—which is to say soft and mushy. The solution was simply to add some of the vegetables to the slow cooker at the very end of the cooking time. Frozen peas were a natural in this recipe and frozen cauliflower also complemented the flavors perfectly (and made things easy as well—no need to wrestle with cutting the florets from a head of cauliflower).

The only problem remaining was the thickness of the stew. At this point it was more of a soup than

a stew. Tasters wanted a thicker consistency, one that would make this recipe feel more substantial and more like a meal than a first course. We found that if we pureed 2 cups of the soup before we added the cauliflower and peas, it gave this recipe the "coat the spoon" body we were looking for, definitely elevating it to the "stew" category. To brighten the flavor still more, we stirred in fresh cilantro, and garnished the stew with tangy plain yogurt.

Slow-Cooker Curried Chickpea Stew
SERVES 6 TO 8

This vegetarian stew is great served on its own, but it's also nice served over rice or couscous. Garnish with plain yogurt.

2	tablespoons vegetable oil
3	medium onions, minced
8	medium garlic cloves, minced or pressed through a garlic press (about 8 teaspoons)
2	tablespoons curry powder
	Salt
1	(28-ounce) can crushed tomatoes
6	cups vegetable broth
1	pound carrots, cut into 1-inch chunks
½	pound dried chickpeas (1 cup), picked over, rinsed, soaked overnight, and drained
1	pound frozen cauliflower florets, thawed
2	cups frozen peas, thawed
¼	cup minced fresh cilantro leaves
	Ground black pepper

1. Heat the oil in a 12-inch nonstick skillet over medium heat until shimmering but not smoking. Add the onions, garlic, curry powder, and ¼ teaspoon salt and cook until the onions are softened and lightly browned, 10 to 15 minutes. Stir in the tomatoes, scraping up any browned bits.

2. Transfer the onion and tomato mixture to the slow cooker insert and stir in the broth, carrots, and chickpeas until evenly combined. Cover and cook on low until the chickpeas are tender, 10 to 12 hours. (Alternatively, cover and cook on high for 6 to 8 hours.)

3. Puree 2 cups of the stew in a blender until

smooth, then stir back into the slow cooker insert. Stir in the cauliflower and peas. Turn the slow cooker to high, cover, and cook until the cauliflower is tender and heated through, about 15 minutes. Stir in the cilantro, season with salt and pepper to taste, and serve.

PREP-AHEAD TIPS

Store the ingredients below separately.

- Cook the onion and tomato mixture as described in step 1, then transfer it to an airtight container and refrigerate.
- Prep the carrots and refrigerate (you can store them with the onion–tomato mixture).
- Pick over, rinse, and soak the chickpeas (drain before cooking).
- Let the cauliflower and peas thaw overnight in the refrigerator.

INGREDIENTS: Vegetable Broth

We gathered nine popular brands of vegetable broth and tasted them three different ways: warmed, in vegetable stew, and in asparagus risotto. The winner of the straight broth tasting was Swanson, which had one of the highest sodium levels, with 970 mg per cup, compared with 330 mg per cup for Kitchen Basics, which had the lowest sodium level. Pitting the winner (Swanson) against the lower-sodium option (Kitchen Basics) in a vegetable stew tasting yielded mixed results. Swanson eked out a win, but neither stew was bad. In the asparagus risotto, we threw in what we thought would be a ringer—Swanson reduced-sodium chicken broth, the winner of our canned chicken broth tasting—to compete against the Swanson and Kitchen Basics vegetable broths. Surprisingly, Swanson vegetable broth was the tasters' favorite. The chicken broth came in second, and Kitchen Basics ended up in last place. Which vegetable broth should you buy? Swanson's is the winner, but the differences among brands when used in cooking (rather than tasting them straight) are more subtle than we would have thought.

THE BEST VEGETABLE BROTH

Swanson Vegetable Broth had the most flavor of the nine brands we tested. It also contains the most sodium, which partly explains its strong showing in our tasting.

SLOW-COOKER LENTIL AND SWISS CHARD STEW

LENTIL STEW IS QUICK AND ECONOMICAL to make, and when made well, tastes great (and it's even better the next day). We were determined to develop a slow-cooker recipe for our vegetarian repertoire that would be a keeper. We wanted a hearty lentil soup worthy of a second bowl—not the tasteless variety we have so often encountered with other slow-cooker lentil soups.

We started by preparing five representative recipes, and two discoveries quickly came to light. First, garlic, herbs, onions, and tomatoes are common denominators. Second, texture is a big issue. None of our tasters liked the soup that was brothy or, at the other extreme, thick as porridge. They also gave a big thumbs down to those that looked like brown split pea soup. Consequently, recipes that included tomatoes, herbs, and visible vegetables were rewarded for their brighter colors (and flavors). The next step was to determine what sort of liquid to use as the base for our soup. We prepared three batches: one with water, one with vegetable broth, and one with half water, half broth. Water produced a soup that was not as rich in flavor as desired, while the broth-only version had a richer, more balanced flavor. With the cooking medium out of the way, we moved on to the best legume for the job.

Brown, green, and red lentils are the most common choices on supermarket shelves. At specialty markets and natural foods stores, you can also find black lentils and French green lentils (lentils du Puy), the latter being the darling of chefs everywhere. In addition to color differences, lentils can be divided according to their size—large or small—and to whether they are split, like peas, or not. Ordinary brown and green lentils are large, while red, black, and lentils du Puy are small. Red lentils are often sold split and are used most frequently in Indian dishes such as dal.

To make some sense of all of this, we made five pots of lentil soup, each one using a different colored lentil. We knew from previous stovetop lentil soup testings that red lentils, often sold split, could not stand up to a long cooking time without turning to mush and that was our finding in the slow cooker as well. Lentils du Puy, however, worked fine in our stovetop lentil soup but because they are small, they overcooked in the slow cooker, turning mushy by the end. All three remaining choices produced an acceptable texture, however, the larger green and brown lentils fared the best. Despite the extensive amount of time they spent in the slow cooker, they still retained a desirable texture.

However, one issue concerning texture remained with the soup overall. Tasters wanted a chunkier soup and did not like the brothy base. We tried regular button mushrooms, but they turned slimy. Turning to portobellos, we found that they retained their texture and felt almost like pieces of meat. To enhance the now-earthy flavor of the soup, we found that adding ½ ounce of dried porcini mushrooms was key. To give the soup more body, we tried pureeing a few cups of the soup and then adding it back to the pot. Tasters praised the contrast between the creamy base and the remaining whole lentils and found the entire soup more interesting. Bay leaves and thyme rounded out the other flavors, but the soup was a rather muddy color. To remedy the problem, and add yet more flavor (not to mention color), we stirred in chopped chard

leaves after the soup was basically done. The contrast of the bright chard with the earthy tones of the soup was perfect, except there remained one last issue: The chard stems were tough and stringy. We decided to sauté the stems along with the onions and add them to the soup at the onset of cooking, which solved the problem.

Many recipes called for the addition of vinegar or lemon juice just before the soup is served. We stirred a touch of balsamic vinegar into the pot at completion, and tasters gave this soup a perfect 10.

Slow-Cooker Lentil and Swiss Chard Stew
SERVES 6 TO 8

Be sure to choose large green or brown lentils and avoid red lentils or lentils du Puy, both of which will overcook. Carefully sort through the lentils to remove small stones and pebbles and then rinse.

- 2 tablespoons vegetable oil
- 3 medium onions, minced
- 1 pound Swiss chard, stems and leaves separated; stems cut into ¼-inch pieces and leaves chopped coarse
- 6 medium garlic cloves, minced or pressed through a garlic press (about 2 tablespoons) Salt
- 6 cups vegetable broth
- 1 pound carrots, cut into 1-inch chunks
- 1 (15-ounce) can tomato sauce
- 12 ounces portobello mushroom caps, gills removed, cut into ½-inch chunks
- 7 ounces brown or green lentils (1 cup), rinsed and picked over
- 2 bay leaves
- 1 tablespoon minced fresh thyme leaves, or 1 teaspoon dried
- ½ ounce dried porcini mushrooms, rinsed and minced
- 1 tablespoon balsamic vinegar Ground black pepper Grated parmesan cheese (for serving, optional) Extra-virgin olive oil (for serving, optional)

REMOVING GILLS FROM PORTOBELLO MUSHROOMS

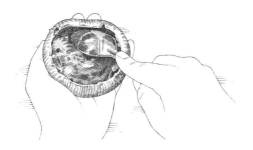

We found that it was necessary to remove the black gills from the portobello mushrooms because they made the stew muddy in appearance. Using a soup spoon, scrape and discard the dark-colored gills from the underside of each mushroom.

1. Heat the oil in a 12-inch nonstick skillet over medium heat until shimmering but not smoking. Add the onions, chard stems, garlic, and ¼ teaspoon salt and cook until the vegetables are softened and lightly browned, 10 to 12 minutes.

2. Transfer the onion mixture to the slow cooker insert and stir in the broth, carrots, tomato sauce, portobello mushrooms, lentils, bay leaves, thyme, and porcini mushrooms until evenly combined. Cover and cook on low until the soup is thickened and the lentils are tender, 8 to 10 hours. (Alternatively, cover and cook on high for 5 to 7 hours.)

3. Remove and discard the bay leaves. Puree 2 cups of the soup in a blender until smooth, then stir back into the slow cooker insert. Stir in the chard leaves, cover, and continue to cook until the leaves are wilted and tender, 10 to 15 minutes longer. Stir in the vinegar, season with salt and pepper to taste, and serve.

PREP-AHEAD TIPS

You can store all the ingredients below together with the exception of the chard leaves.

• Cook the onion–chard stem mixture as described in step 1, then transfer the mixture to an airtight container and refrigerate; prep the chard leaves and refrigerate.
• Prep the carrots and refrigerate.
• Prep the portobellos and refrigerate.
• Pick over and rinse the lentils and refrigerate.

CLEANING A GARLIC PRESS

Garlic presses make quick work of garlic but are notoriously hard to clean. Recycle an old toothbrush with a worn brush for this job. The bristles will clear bits of garlic from the press and are easy to rinse clean.

SLOW-COOKER BEEF AND BARLEY SOUP

BEEF AND BARLEY SOUP IS THE PERFECT COLD-weather comfort food. What could be better than tender beef married with vegetables, flavorful broth, and toothsome barley? It is the ultimate "good for what ails you" soup. There were problems, though, with many of the recipes we tested, including a lack of flavor, minuscule amounts of beef, and textures that were either thin and watery or overly thick. We knew we'd need to come up with a recipe that yielded lots of beef, an intensely flavored broth, and just the right amount of barley to make this a satisfying one-pot meal.

We started with blade steak, which is cut from the chuck, or shoulder of the cow, trimming it into ½-inch pieces. Following the technique we discovered while developing our beef stew recipe we built a flavorful base for our soup by sautéing onions and carrots along with tomato paste, and then deglazing the pan with a good-quality dry red wine, scraping up the tasty browned bits from the bottom. Many recipes contained either tomato puree (which we thought was too sweet) or canned diced tomatoes. But the texture of the soup made with diced tomatoes left us cold. We didn't care for long-cooked, flavorless bits of tomatoes floating on the top of our soup, so we opted to pulse the tomatoes in the blender first, which worked perfectly. Then we turned our attention to the remaining liquid component of our soup, which had been water in many recipes.

A great soup deserves good stock, not water, but because of the time involved in making homemade stock, it was not an option. As this was a beef soup, we naturally tested canned beef broth, but disliked its tinny aftertaste. When we combined it with an equal amount of chicken broth, the results were far better. Chicken broth, beef broth, and the flavor added by the vegetables and soy sauce gave us the deep flavors we wanted (see page 140 for more about adding soy sauce to slow-cooker beef recipes).

The final component of our soup was the barley. Pearl barley, the most commonly available variety, has had its tough outer hulls removed, which makes it a fairly quick-cooking grain. Since pearl barley can absorb two to three times its volume of cooking liquid, we knew that we needed to be judicious in the quantity we added to the soup. After all, we were making soup, not a side dish. After some experimenting, we found that ¼ cup was the ideal amount; it lent a pleasing texture to the soup without overfilling the slow cooker with swollen grains. A final sprinkling of fresh parsley added a bright finish to this simple yet satisfying soup.

Slow-Cooker Beef and Barley Soup

SERVES 6 TO 8

The barley, cooked over a long period of time, adds a velvety texture as well as a nutty flavor to the soup. Try substituting 2 tablespoons minced fresh dill for the parsley.

2	tablespoons vegetable oil
3	medium onions, minced
2	carrots, chopped medium
¼	cup tomato paste
	Salt
½	cup dry red wine
2	pounds blade steak, trimmed and cut into ½-inch pieces
1	(28-ounce) can diced tomatoes, pureed with their juice until smooth in a blender or food processor
2	cups low-sodium beef broth
2	cups low-sodium chicken broth
⅓	cup soy sauce
¼	cup pearl barley
1	tablespoon minced fresh thyme leaves, or 1 teaspoon dried
¼	cup minced fresh parsley leaves
	Ground black pepper

1. Heat the oil in 12-inch nonstick skillet over medium heat until shimmering but not smoking. Add the onions, carrots, tomato paste, and ¼ teaspoon salt and cook until the vegetables are softened and lightly browned, 10 to 15 minutes. Stir in the wine, scraping up any browned bits.

2. Transfer the vegetable mixture into the slow cooker insert and stir in the meat, pureed tomatoes, broths, soy sauce, barley, and thyme until evenly combined. Cover and cook on low until the meat is tender, 9 to 11 hours. (Alternatively, cover and cook on high for 5 to 7 hours.)

3. Gently tilt the slow cooker insert and degrease as much fat as possible off the surface of the soup using a large flat spoon. Stir in the parsley, season with salt and pepper to taste, and serve.

PREP-AHEAD TIPS

You can store all the ingredients below together with the exception of the meat, which must be stored separately.
- Cook the vegetable mixture as described in step 1, then transfer it to an airtight container and refrigerate.
- Trim and cut the meat and refrigerate.
- Puree the tomatoes and refrigerate.

TRIMMING BLADE STEAKS

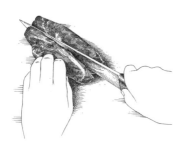

1. Halve each steak lengthwise, leaving the gristle on one half.

2. Cut away the gristle from the half to which it is still attached.

3. Cut the trimmed meat crosswise into 1-inch pieces.

SLOW-COOKER GROUND BEEF CHILI

GROUND BEEF CHILI IS A NATURAL FOR THE slow cooker but, despite the myriad recipes for it, most that we tested turned out watery and bland. How hard could it be to produce a great chili in a slow cooker? We were looking for a hearty all-American chili, with rich flavors and a thick, substantial texture—perfect as a foil for all those wonderful accompaniments such as a dollop of sour cream or a sprinkling of cheese (which are half the reason for making chili in the first place).

Most recipes begin by cooking and draining ground meat, then sautéing onions, garlic, and peppers. Always on the lookout for ways to shorten prep time, our first order of business was to see if we needed to cook the meat before it went into the slow cooker. We learned some tricks in our beef stew testing that allowed us to bypass browning (see page 140) by creating a faux fond with sautéed aromatics and tomato paste, so we followed that method here. Pitting chili made with browned beef against one made with raw beef and the faux-fond method, we found little discernable difference between the two.

Now ready to zero in on flavors, we tried varying amounts of onion, garlic, peppers (which turned slimy in the slow cooker), celery, and carrots. Tasters liked a hefty quantity of onion and garlic, but put the kibosh on the peppers, celery, and carrots. They made the chili taste too vegetal and sweet. After this first step, things became less clear. The most pressing concerns were the spices (how much and what kind) and the meat (how much ground beef and what fat content). There was also the cooking liquid (what kind, if any) to resolve and the proportions of tomatoes and beans to consider.

Our first experiments with these ingredients followed a formula we had seen in lots of recipes: 2 pounds ground beef, 3 tablespoons chili powder, 2 teaspoons ground cumin, and 1 teaspoon each red pepper flakes and dried oregano. Many recipes add the spices after the beef has been browned, but we knew from work done in the test kitchen on curry

that ground spices taste better when they have direct contact with hot cooking oil.

To see if these results would apply to chili, we set up a test with two pots of chili: one with the ground spices added right to the slow cooker and one with the spices toasted with the aromatics. The batch made with untoasted spices tasted harsh, bitter, and weak. The batch made with spices toasted with the aromatics was far better, with a more fully developed spice flavor.

Although we didn't want a chili with killer heat, we did want real warmth and depth of flavor. Commercial chili powder is typically 80 percent ground dried red chiles and 20 percent a mix of garlic powder, onion powder, oregano, ground cumin, and salt. To boost flavor, we increased the amount of chili powder from 3 to 4 tablespoons, added more cumin and oregano, and added chipotle chiles (smoked jalapeños) for heat and a smoky background flavor. We tried some more exotic spices, including cinnamon (which was deemed "awful"), allspice (which seemed "out of place"), and coriander. In the end, we settled on the classic combination of chili powder, cumin, and oregano, opting to garnish the chili with fresh cilantro.

It was now time to consider the meat. The quantity (2 pounds) seemed ideal when paired with two 15-ounce cans of beans. Because we knew we weren't going to be able to drain any grease from the beef, we naturally started out with the leanest beef we could find, which was 90 percent lean. The chili turned out dry, sandy, and largely devoid of flavor. Trying the 80 percent lean beef, we were left with an orange pool of grease floating on top of the chili that was difficult to remove, but the chili had good flavor. Turning to 85 percent lean beef, we found our winner since it had enough fat to carry the flavor of the spices throughout the chili, and although there was a slick of grease on top, it was a manageable amount and easy enough to skim off before serving. And taking a cue from our beef stew testing, we added a little soy sauce for both flavor and color (see page 140).

Some of us have made chili with beer and been satisfied with the results. Nodding to the expertise of others, we tried batches made with water (too watery), chicken broth (too chickeny and dull), beef broth (too tinny), wine (too acidic), and no liquid at all except for that in the tomatoes (beefy tasting and by far the best). When we tried beer, we were surprised to find that it subdued that great beefy flavor. The bottom line? Keep the beer on ice for drinking with dinner.

Tomatoes were definitely going into the pot, but we had yet to decide on the type and amount. We first tried two (14.5-ounce) cans of diced tomatoes. Clearly not enough tomatoes. What's more, the tomatoes were too chunky, and they were floating in a thin sauce. We tried two 28-ounce cans of diced tomatoes, pureeing the contents of one can in the food processor to thicken the sauce. Although the chunkiness was reduced, the sauce was still watery. Next we paired one can of tomato puree with one can of diced tomatoes and, without exception, tasters preferred the thicker consistency. The test kitchen generally doesn't like the slightly cooked flavor of tomato puree, but this recipe needed the body it provided. In any case, after the long simmering time, any such flavor was hard to detect.

Most recipes add the beans toward the end of cooking so that they will heat through without falling apart. But this method often makes for very bland beans floating in a sea of highly flavorful chili. After testing several options, we found it best to add the beans with the tomatoes. The more time the beans spent in the pot, the better they tasted. In the end, we preferred dark red kidney beans or black beans because both keep their shape better than light red kidney beans, the other common choice.

With our recipe basically complete, it was time to try some of those offbeat additions that other cooks swear by, including cocoa powder, ground coffee beans, raisins, chickpeas, mushrooms, olives, and lima beans. Our conclusion? Each of these ingredients either tasted out of place or was too subtle to make much difference. Lime wedges, passed separately at the table, both brightened the flavor of the chili and accentuated the heat of the spices. Our chili was now done.

Slow-Cooker Ground Beef Chili
SERVES 8 TO 10

Do not use beef any leaner than 85 percent or its texture will turn dry and sandy as it cooks. For a milder chili, use the smaller amount of chipotle chiles; if you like yours spicy, use the full 4 tablespoons. Be sure to stir the chili ingredients well before turning on the slow cooker. When the chili is done, break up any large pieces of beef with the back of a spoon if desired.

2	tablespoons vegetable oil
3	medium onions, minced
6	medium garlic cloves, minced or pressed through a garlic press (about 2 tablespoons)
¼	cup chili powder
¼	cup tomato paste
1	tablespoon ground cumin
½	teaspoon red pepper flakes
	Salt
1	(28-ounce) can diced tomatoes
2	pounds (85 percent lean) ground beef
2	(15.5-ounce) cans dark red kidney beans, rinsed and drained
1	(28-ounce) can tomato puree
2–4	tablespoons minced chipotle chile in adobo sauce
3	tablespoons soy sauce
1	tablespoon minced fresh oregano leaves, or 1 teaspoon dried
1	tablespoon brown sugar
	Ground black pepper
	Lime wedges, for serving

1. Heat the oil in a 12-inch nonstick skillet over medium heat until shimmering but not smoking. Add the onions, garlic, chili powder, tomato paste, cumin, pepper flakes, and ¼ teaspoon salt and cook until the onions are softened and lightly browned, 10 to 15 minutes. Stir in the diced tomatoes with their juice, scraping up any browned bits.

2. Transfer the onion and tomato mixture to the slow cooker insert and stir in the beef, beans, tomato puree, chipotles, soy sauce, oregano, and sugar until evenly combined. Cover and cook on

low until the meat is tender and the chili flavorful, 8 to 9 hours. (Alternatively, cover and cook on high for 5 to 6 hours.)

3. Gently tilt the slow cooker insert and degrease as much fat as possible off the surface of the chili using a large flat spoon. Season with salt and pepper to taste and serve with the lime wedges.

PREP-AHEAD TIPS

You can store all the ingredients below together.

• Cook the onion and tomato mixture as described in step 1, then transfer it to an airtight container and refrigerate.

• Rinse and drain the beans and refrigerate.

SLOW-COOKER TEXAS CHILI

HERE IN THE TEST KITCHEN, WE LOVE ALL forms of chili, but our favorite is Texas chili (aka "bowl of red"). Featuring big chunks of tender beef in a fiery red sauce, this Lone Star–state classic seemed like a natural for the slow cooker.

Your typical Texas chilihead believes there is one and only one true recipe for chili: Large pieces of cubed beef browned and then simmered with dried chiles in stock or water—no tomatoes or beans in sight. Many authentic chili recipes demand a mix of dried chiles, which must be toasted, seeded, and ground, in place of the all-purpose supermarket chili powder. Tomatoes and onions are a matter of preference, although the former are not accepted in true Texas chili circles. And beans are strictly for amateurs, or so we've been told. But since Texas chili is all about the meat, that's where we started our testing.

In the test kitchen, we've found that precut stew meat usually makes dry, dull chili. These scraps often come from pretty lean parts of the cow, and for chili you want something with some fat and flavor. A chuck-eye roast is our top choice for chili; it takes just 10 minutes to trim the meat and cut it into chunks. To save on prep time, we went with our new technique (see page 140) of not browning the meat (but sautéing aromatics and tomato paste), knowing that we could augment the flavor with soy sauce; maybe a tad unconventional for chili, but it worked.

INGREDIENTS: Tomato Paste

A celebrated ingredient in its post-WWII heyday, when long-cooked tomato sauce was king, tomato paste has fallen by the wayside as discerning cooks have favored fresher, more brightly flavored tomato sauces. These days, our use of tomato paste comes with a more conservative hand. We reserve it for occasions when a deep tomato flavor is warranted, such as in a chili or our Bolognese sauce.

Given this limited use, we wondered if it mattered which brand we used. To find out, we went to local supermarkets to gather seven brands for a tasting: six American brands in small cans and an Italian import in a toothpaste-like tube. We asked our tasters to taste the tomato paste as is—no cooking, no sauce.

Every brand did well in providing a big tomato punch, but the Amore brand, imported from Italy, was the unanimous winner, owing to its "intense" and "fresh" flavor. Amore is the only tomato paste tested that contains fat, which could account for its bigger flavor. The Amore brand also scored points because

of its tube packaging. Just squeeze out what you need and store the rest in the refrigerator. No fuss, no waste.

How did the flavor of this tomato paste hold up in cooking? We tasted it, along with Hunt's, the brand that came in last, in our Bolognese recipe, to see if we could detect a difference. We did indeed pick out (and downgrade) the distinct dried herb flavor of the Hunt's paste. On the other hand, we liked the sauce made with the Amore tomato paste for its deep, round tomato flavor.

THE BEST TOMATO PASTE
An Italian import, Amore was our tasters' favorite brand. They described this paste-in-a-tube as "intense" and "fresh." The no-fuss, no-waste packaging is also appealing.

With the cut of meat decided, we moved on to seasonings. We sautéed onion and then added our ground spices to the skillet. Chili powder and cumin blossomed in the hot oil, bringing a depth of flavor to the chili that was missing when we had added it to the mixture later. Canned chipotle chiles added even more complexity of flavor, and tasters preferred chili made with (gasp) tomatoes. Tomato puree plus a small amount of tapioca gave our chili just the right texture and kept it from being too thin or watery. (True, tapioca is a bit unconventional, but its thickening effect worked perfectly.) We were getting close to the perfect chili, but it was still a little dry, so we added chicken broth, which also helped carry the flavor of the spices throughout the chili.

At this point, we were happy with the flavor, but some tasters were left wondering about beans. While research confirmed that a real Texas "bowl of red" doesn't include beans (they're often served on the side), we liked the creaminess that they brought to the dish, and their starch helped balance its fiery heat. We tested stirring them in at the beginning of the cooking time as well as during the last half hour and found that the beans held up like chili champs and had the best flavor when we added them at the onset of cooking.

Slow-Cooker Texas Chili

SERVES 6 TO 8

Chuck-eye roasts are notoriously fatty, so don't be surprised if you trim off 1 to 1½ pounds of fat. Avoid precut beef labeled "beef for stew"—it could be beef round or boneless shoulder roast, which will turn out dry and tough. For a milder chili, use the lower amount of chipotle chiles; for a spicy chili, use the higher amount of chipotle. Serve with chopped fresh cilantro, minced onion, diced avocado, shredded cheddar or Jack cheese, and sour cream.

2 tablespoons vegetable oil
3 medium onions, minced
8 medium garlic cloves, minced or pressed through a garlic press (about 8 teaspoons)
¼ cup chili powder
¼ cup tomato paste

2 tablespoons ground cumin
  Salt
1 (28-ounce) can tomato puree
1 (5-pound) chuck-eye roast, trimmed and cut into 1½-inch chunks
2 (15.5-ounce) cans pinto or kidney beans, drained and rinsed
2 cups low-sodium chicken broth
¼ cup Minute tapioca
2–4 tablespoons minced chipotle chile in adobo sauce
3 tablespoons soy sauce
2 tablespoons dark brown sugar, plus extra to taste
1 tablespoon minced fresh oregano leaves, or 1 teaspoon dried
  Ground black pepper

1. Heat the oil in a 12-inch nonstick skillet over medium heat until shimmering but not smoking. Add the onions, garlic, chili powder, tomato paste, cumin, and ¼ teaspoon salt and cook until the onions are softened and lightly browned, 10 to 15 minutes. Stir in the tomato puree, scraping up any browned bits.

2. Transfer the onion and tomato mixture to the slow cooker insert and stir in the beef, beans, broth, tapioca, chipotles, soy sauce, the 2 tablespoons of sugar, and oregano until evenly combined. Cover and cook on low until the meat is tender, 9 to 11 hours. (Alternatively, cover and cook on high for 5 to 7 hours.)

3. Gently tilt the slow cooker insert and degrease as much fat as possible off the surface of the chili using a large flat spoon. Season with salt, pepper, and brown sugar to taste, and serve.

PREP-AHEAD TIPS
You can store all the ingredients below together with the exception of the meat, which must be refrigerated separately.
• Cook the onion and tomato mixture as described in step 1, then transfer it to an airtight container and refrigerate.
• Drain and rinse the beans and refrigerate.
• Trim and cut the meat and refrigerate.

SLOW-COOKER VEGETARIAN CHILI

MANY VEGETARIAN CHILI RECIPES SUFFER from a common problem, namely a lack of flavor. Consisting of little more than beans and tomatoes, the recipes we tried were flat and one dimensional. Most seemed to simply take ground beef out of a typical recipe, and do little to compensate for its absence. To compound the problem, the slow cooker tends to dilute what little flavor there may be due to the excess moisture that collects under the lid.

First, however, we took a moment to consider whether or not to use canned beans. Dried beans are usually thought to have superior flavor, but we all agreed that in the case of chili, a dish packed with seasonings and aromatics, canned beans would be just fine. But since canned beans aren't exactly bursting with flavor on their own, we knew that the medium in which they were cooked had to be highly flavored. To that end, we sautéed a hefty amount of onion and garlic and then added our spices (chili powder and cumin) to the skillet to bring out their flavor.

We knew that we wanted a tomato base for our chili, so we tested tomato puree, crushed tomatoes, and diced tomatoes. Tomato puree tasted too thick and sweet and it overpowered the more delicate, vegetable flavors (this was not a problem in our meat-based chilis). Crushed tomatoes also turned out to be a disappointment; the various brands of crushed tomatoes have dramatically different textures, from watery to super-thick, and they produced wildly different chilis. To our surprise, the diced tomatoes had the best flavor and we found that we could perfect their texture if we pureed them slightly before adding them to the slow cooker. This gave the chili texture and a bit of sweetness (while eliminating floating chunks of tomatoes).

Moving on to the "meat" of the chili, we tested batch after batch made with varying combinations of beans, and even tested tempeh (a fermented soybean cake). Tasters all preferred a combination of beans, rather than just one variety, and nixed the soy protein idea. While the tempeh did provide a texture similar to that of ground beef, tasters found its presence unappealing and somewhat bitter, so we stuck with our combination of pinto, black, and red kidney beans.

To pump up the flavor, we added chipotle chiles for their heat and smoky flavor. A little bit of sugar helped to balance the heat and acidity of the chili. As a finishing touch, we added thawed corn kernels and a hefty amount of fresh cilantro to brighten the flavor. We think this chili is just as good as its meat-packed counterpart, and good for you too.

Slow-Cooker Vegetarian Bean Chili

SERVES 6 TO 8

We prefer to use a combination of pinto, black, and/or dark red kidney beans in this chili. For a milder chili, use the smaller amount of chipotle chiles; if you like yours spicy, use the full 3 tablespoons. The texture of the pureed diced tomatoes with their juice is very important here—do not substitute crushed tomatoes or tomato puree.

2	(28-ounce) cans diced tomatoes
2	tablespoons vegetable oil
3	medium onions, minced
8	medium garlic cloves, minced or pressed through a garlic press (about 8 teaspoons)
¼	cup chili powder
2	tablespoons ground cumin
	Salt
4	(15.5-ounce) cans pinto, black, and/or dark red kidney beans, drained and rinsed (see note)
1–3	tablespoons minced chipotle chile in adobo sauce
4	teaspoons sugar
2	cups frozen corn, thawed
½	cup minced fresh cilantro leaves
	Ground black pepper

1. Pulse the tomatoes with their juice in a food processor until slightly chunky, about 5 pulses; set aside. Heat the oil in a 12-inch nonstick skillet over medium heat until shimmering but not smoking. Add the onions, garlic, chili powder, cumin, and ¼ teaspoon salt and cook until the onions are softened and lightly browned, 10 to 15 minutes. Off the heat, stir in the processed tomatoes, scraping up any browned bits.

2. Transfer the onion and tomato mixture to the slow cooker insert and stir in the beans, chipotles, and sugar until evenly combined. Cover and cook on low until the chili is flavorful, 7 to 8 hours. (Alternatively, cover and cook on high for 4 to 5 hours.)

3. Stir in the corn and cilantro, cover, and continue to cook until the corn is heated through, about 5 minutes longer. Season with salt and pepper to taste and serve.

PREP-AHEAD TIPS

You can store all the ingredients below together.
- Cook the onion and tomato mixture as described in step 1, then transfer it to an airtight container and refrigerate.
- Drain and rinse the beans and refrigerate.

Slow-Cooker Meaty Tomato Sauce

NOTHING COULD BE MORE WELCOMING ON A cold night than coming home to a rustic, flavor-packed meat sauce ready to toss with some stick-to-your ribs pasta. Made from canned tomatoes, pork, and aromatics, we wondered if this classic Sunday "gravy" could transition from the stovetop to the slow cooker. It seemed like it would be ideally suited to the walk-away cooking medium that the slow cooker provides. Our initial tests proved that to be far from the truth. The sauce was watery and puddled on our plate, sliding off the pasta into a disappointing mess. We decided to focus first on the cut of meat to use, and then deal with the consistency of the sauce.

In classic recipes, the meat (often a pork chop) is browned, the fat drained, and the sauce built in the empty pan. The browned meat is added back to the sauce, the pan covered, and the sauce simmered slowly until the meat is fall-off-the-bone tender. The meat is then shredded and stirred into the sauce, at which point it is served over rigatoni with a good sprinkling of grated cheese. We tried pork chops from the blade, loin, and sirloin. But even

the fattiest chops were dry and tough after eight hours in the slow cooker. We wanted the meat to be meltingly tender, and not stringy. We needed a piece of meat with more marbling so that it would not dry out during the extended cooking time in the slow cooker.

We thought about a cut from the shoulder—either picnic or Boston butt—because this part of the pig has more fat than the loin, where most chops come from. The problem with these shoulder roasts was their size; the smallest one at the market was 4 pounds. Nevertheless, we cut a pound of this meat into stew-like chunks and proceeded. This meat was more yielding when cooked and had a better flavor. However, the sauce tasted a bit wan; the meat had not done a really good job of flavoring the tomato sauce.

At this point, we turned to boneless country-style ribs and we were able to find a small packet with just 3 pounds of meat—perfect for one batch of sauce. This sauce had a great meaty flavor. And at just $1.99 a pound, this was our meat of choice.

But we still had to address the issue of the watery sauce; we knew that we had to do something to compensate for the fact that there is no opportunity for liquid to evaporate from the slow cooker. To arrive at the perfect texture, we settled on a trilogy of tomato products: tomato paste, crushed tomatoes, and diced tomatoes. Now the sauce coated the pasta perfectly, with no unsightly pool of liquid at the bottom of our plate.

Slow-Cooker Meaty Tomato Sauce

MAKES 9 CUPS,
ENOUGH FOR 3 POUNDS OF PASTA

If you prefer a beefy sauce, 3 pounds of boneless chuck, cut into 1½-inch pieces, can be substituted for the pork. This recipe makes enough for a hungry crowd or to freeze leftovers for later.

2 tablespoons vegetable oil
2 medium onions, minced
12 garlic cloves, minced or pressed through a garlic press (about ¼ cup)

¼   cup tomato paste

¼   teaspoon red pepper flakes

     Salt

¾   cup dry red wine

3   pounds boneless country-style pork ribs, trimmed and cut into 1½-inch chunks

1   (28-ounce) can crushed tomatoes

1   (28-ounce) can diced tomatoes, drained

⅓   cup soy sauce

2   tablespoons minced fresh oregano leaves, or 2 teaspoons dried

2   bay leaves

¼   cup minced fresh parsley leaves

     Ground black pepper

1. Heat the oil in a 12-inch nonstick skillet over medium heat until shimmering but not smoking. Add the onions, garlic, tomato paste, pepper flakes, and ¼ teaspoon salt and cook until the onions are softened and lightly browned, 10 to 15 minutes. Stir in the wine, scraping up any browned bits.

2. Transfer the onion mixture to the slow cooker insert and stir in the ribs, crushed tomatoes, diced tomatoes, soy sauce, oregano, and bay leaves until evenly combined. Cover and cook on low until the meat is tender, 8 to 9 hours. (Alternatively, cover and cook on high for 5 to 7 hours.)

3. Gently tilt the slow cooker insert and degrease as much fat as possible off the surface of the sauce using a large flat spoon. Use a wooden spoon or spatula to break up the pieces of meat. Discard the bay leaves and stir in the parsley. Season with salt and pepper to taste and serve.

PREP-AHEAD TIPS

You can store all the ingredients below together with the exception of the meat, which must be refrigerated separately.

• Cook the onion mixture as described in step 1, then transfer it to an airtight container and refrigerate.

• Puree the tomatoes and refrigerate.

• Trim and cut the meat and refrigerate.

SLOW-COOKER BEEF STEW

RECIPES FOR SLOW-COOKER BEEF STEWS ARE divided into two camps. In one, the meat, vegetables, and seasoning are simply dumped into a pot and left to their own devices. Effortless, yes. But flavorful? We'd have to say no. The more flavorful stew falls into the second camp, the one in which the meat is browned before it goes into the slow cooker. Here the foundation for flavor is built by the flavorful browned bits left behind, which are the backbone of the sauce that is added to the slow cooker.

But in developing a recipe for slow-cooker beef stew for this make-ahead cookbook, where our goal was to minimize advance prep work, we wanted to streamline our kitchen work, not spend 45 minutes getting a stew ready for the slow cooker. Could we skip browning the meat and still end up with a richly flavored beef stew? Browning meat had been so ingrained into our culinary educations that we never considered it an option until now, when necessity dictated that we give it a try. Needless to say, we had reservations.

To begin our testing, we decided to prepare two recipes. For one, we browned the meat (beef chuck) as we've always done. For the other, we skipped the browning step and simply dumped everything raw into the slow cooker. Once the cooking time was up, we lifted the lids and, to our surprise, found that we couldn't tell the two stews apart—that is visually. But flavor is what really matters and, after tasting each one, we found that the stew with the browned meat was indeed beefier and richer. We knew that in order to successfully justify jettisoning the browning step, we needed to come up with a flavor replacement for the fond. We tried an array of "browning sauces," like Gravy Master and Kitchen Bouquet, as well as bouillon cubes and different combinations of beef and chicken broth. After extensive testing, we landed on a winning solution. We used a combination of soy sauce (its salty elements reinforced the beefy flavor and added deep color) and tomato paste (which we browned along with the onions and which added additional flavor notes). Satisfied, we addressed one

TESTING NOTES

REPLACING THE FOND

Fond—the browned bits left behind in the pan after searing meat—is crucial for flavor in meat stews and braises. But for those of us who use slow cookers, the act of browning the meat presents a problem if you value prepping the recipe the night before. Browned meat that is still raw in the center doesn't hold well overnight. Not wanting to brown the meat at the last minute, we set out to find a reasonable fond replacement. Here's what we tried.

CONVENTIONAL FLAVOR ENHANCERS FALL SHORT

Browning Sauces
We tried adding sauces like Gravy Master and Kitchen Bouquet to the sauce (as well as marinating the meat in them) but they didn't add much besides a brownish color and a slightly sour, vegetal flavor.

Bouillon Cubes
Stirring bouillon cubes into the sauce sounded good in theory—we thought it would fortify the beefy flavor of the broth. In actuality, however, it added a metallic, salty flavor that tasters loathed.

Porcini Mushrooms
The flavor of mushrooms is often referred to as beefy, so we tried adding dried porcini. Although the resulting stew had a nice flavor and good color, it also boasted a too distinctive mushroom flavor.

A THREE-STEP APPROACH DELIVERS GREAT MEATY FLAVOR

Triple the Aromatics
Tripling the aromatics (such as onion and garlic) and sautéing them until lightly browned creates a highly flavorful vegetable fond.

Tomato Paste
Adding tomato paste to a meat stew or braise is quite common, and we found that adding a little more than usual (¼ cup in most cases) helped make up for the lack of fond—especially when it is sautéed along with the aromatics.

Soy Sauce
We found that adding soy sauce to the stew helped the flavor dramatically. Besides adding color, it made the sauce taste deeper and rounder without adding any distinctive flavor of its own.

troubling issue that was a result of not browning: greasiness. Because browning helps to render fat (and we were not browning), our stew had a grease slick on top that tasters found disturbing.

Up until now, we had been using a beef chuck-eye roast that we trimmed and cut into 1½-inch chunks. Wondering if leaner roasts would solve our problem, we tested five stews made with different cuts of beef: top round, bottom round, eye round, rump roast, and top sirloin. After all that work, it turned out that none were as flavorful and tender as the chuck roast. All of the others were too lean, resulting in flavorless, dry meat. We decided that we didn't mind using a spoon to skim a bit of grease from the stew, so we returned to the chuck roast.

There were, however, still those in the test kitchen who were having a hard time coming to grips with this unconventional approach to a full-flavored stew. To make sure that everyone was on board with our new technique, we conducted a blind taste test of three stews, side by side: browned beef stew (browned the night before and refrigerated), unbrowned stew (with no flavor replacement), and unbrowned stew with our fond replacement of sautéed aromatics and tomato paste plus soy sauce. We were happy that taste buds, rather than preconceived notions, settled the controversy. Unaware of the different methods used, the majority of tasters favored the third stew. The flavors were rich and full-bodied, and although it was hard to admit, we were pleased with how much time we had saved. Knowing that our test cooks are a tough crowd to please, we were satisfied that we had landed on a reliable way to save valuable prep time, without sacrificing flavor.

More testing (with the goal to trim even more time), proved that while we could get away with unbrowned beef, the test kitchen still favored the flavor of cooked onion over onion that had been thrown in raw. Without this step, the stew tasted vegetal and the onions sour.

The next dilemma was how to thicken our stew. Many recipes turn to a slurry (a starch stirred together with liquid) of either flour or cornstarch, which has to be stirred into the stew at the end of the cooking time. While both of these options ultimately worked

to thicken the stew, they also made more work for the cook at the last minute, and required a lag time to allow the starch to fully thicken the stew. We found that instant tapioca, stirred in at the onset of cooking, worked like magic. Our stews were thick without being tacky, with no raw starchy aftertaste, and no last-minute fussing.

Moving on, next we wanted to find a way to perk up the vegetables that seemed to suffer dramatically in the slow cooker. To keep our vegetables tasting fresh, we tried roasting carrots and potatoes separately and adding them to the pot just before serving. The roasted veggies tasted great, but an hour of roasting time pushed our stew closer to bedtime than we would have liked. Stealing a trick often used in grilling, we made a "hobo pack" by wrapping the potatoes and carrots in a foil packet. Then we placed the packet on top of the beef in the slow cooker. It may have looked a bit odd, but when we opened that packet and poured the tender vegetables and their juices back into the stew, the results were amazing. The carrots actually tasted like carrots, and the potatoes were not the same color as the beef. And their texture was perfect. Finally, we had a slow-cooker beef stew that was easy to make and tasted great.

SCIENCE: Why Do Onions Make You Cry?

The problem is caused by the sulfuric compounds in onions. When an onion is cut, the cells that are damaged in the process release sulfuric compounds as well as various enzymes, notably one called sulfoxide lyase. Those compounds, which are separated in the onion's cell structure, activate and mix to form the real culprit, a volatile new compound called thiopropanal sulfoxide. When thiopropanal sulfoxide evaporates into the air, it irritates the eyes, causing us to cry.

To combat this problem in the test kitchen, we found that protecting our eyes, covering them with goggles (yes, we know that sounds silly) or contact lenses, worked. The goggles and contact lenses form a physical barrier that keeps the gases from irritating our eyes. Introducing a flame from either a lit candle or a gas burner will also change the activity of the thiopropanal sulfoxide by completely oxidizing it.

Slow-Cooker Beef Stew
SERVES 6 TO 8

You'll need 18-inch heavy-duty aluminum foil or a large oven-ready foil bag to make the vegetable packet. If you're going to be away from your slow cooker for more than 10 hours, cutting the vegetables into larger, 1½- to 2-inch pieces will help them retain their texture. Feel free to add a pound of parsnips, peeled and cut into 1-inch chunks, to the foil packet along with the carrots and potatoes. The stew will thicken further as it sits; add broth or water to thin to the desired consistency before serving.

2	tablespoons vegetable oil
4	medium onions, minced
¼	cup tomato paste
6	medium garlic cloves, minced or pressed through a garlic press (about 2 tablespoons)
	Salt
1½	cups low-sodium chicken broth
1½	cups low-sodium beef broth
1	(5-pound) boneless beef chuck-eye roast, trimmed and cut into 1½-inch chunks
⅓	cup soy sauce
2	tablespoons Minute tapioca
2	bay leaves
1½	pounds red potatoes, cut into 1-inch chunks
1	pound carrots, cut into 1-inch chunks
2	teaspoons minced fresh thyme leaves (do not use dried)
2	cups frozen peas, thawed
	Ground black pepper

1. Heat 1 tablespoon of the oil in a 12-inch nonstick skillet over medium heat until shimmering but not smoking. Add the onions, tomato paste, garlic, and ¼ teaspoon salt and cook until the onions are softened and lightly browned, 10 to 15 minutes. Stir in the chicken broth, scraping up any browned bits.

2. Transfer the onion mixture to the slow cooker insert and stir in the beef broth, meat, soy sauce, tapioca, and bay leaves until evenly combined. Toss the potatoes, carrots, 1 teaspoon of the thyme, and the remaining 1 tablespoon oil together and season with salt and pepper. Following the illustrations below, wrap the vegetables in a foil packet. Set the vegetable packet on top of the stew in the slow cooker insert.

3. Cover and cook on low until the meat is tender, 9 to 11 hours. (Alternatively, cover and cook on high for 5 to 7 hours.)

4. Transfer the vegetable packet to a plate. Let the stew settle for 5 minutes then gently tilt the slow cooker insert and degrease as much fat as possible off the surface of the stew using a large

---

FOILED AGAIN

WE DISCOVERED THAT THE BEST WAY TO KEEP VEGETABLES FROM DISINTEGRATING AFTER 10 or more hours in the slow cooker was to wrap them in a foil packet, or "hobo pack." Keeping the vegetables out of the stewing liquid slows down their cooking time, and keeps their flavors distinct. Here's how you do it:

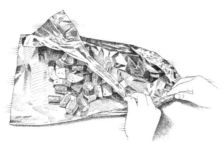

Place the vegetables on one side of a large piece of foil. Fold the foil over, shaping it into a packet that will fit into your slow cooker, then crimp to seal the edges.

Place the foil packet directly on top of the stew, pressing gently as needed to make it fit inside the cooker.

flat spoon. Remove and discard the bay leaves. Carefully open the foil packet (watch for steam), then stir the vegetables along with any accumulated juices into the stew. Stir in the remaining 1 teaspoon thyme and the peas and let stand until the peas are heated through, about 5 minutes longer. Season with salt and pepper to taste and serve.

PREP-AHEAD TIPS

Store the ingredients below separately.

• Cook the onion mixture as described in step 1, then transfer it to an airtight container and refrigerate.

• Trim and cut the meat and refrigerate.

• Prepare the carrots and refrigerate.

SLOW-COOKER POT ROAST

POT ROAST RECIPES APPEAR IN EVERY COOKbook featuring slow cookers and are touted as "starter" recipes in the ubiquitous manuals that come with the appliance. Pot roast is a natural for the slow cooker when done right. The problem is that many slow-cooker pot roasts turn out dry and stringy, floating in a vat of greasy, flavorless, watery liquid. Yet another issue is size; yes, it does matter what size roast you start out with. We found many recipes that called for 2½- to 3-pound roasts pulled a virtual disappearing act. After 10 hours in the slow cooker, the catch phrase "Where's the beef?" took on new meaning. We had our work cut out for us.

Our initial testing showed that the average chuck roast shrank by as much as two pounds during the prolonged cooking time, quickly eliminating the smaller roasts. To compensate for this shrinkage, we decided to use roasts that weighed 5½ to 6 pounds. Previous pot roast tests had shown that reaching and sustaining an internal temperature of 200 to 210 degrees was necessary for a meltingly tender piece of meat. To determine how long it would take a 5- or 6-pound roast to reach that point in the slow cooker, we conducted tests using temperature probes inserted into the center of roasts cooked on both low and high. The ideal time (in our 6-quart slow cooker) was 9 to 10 hours on low or 5 to 6 hours on high. Next, we moved on to flavoring our pot roast.

As with our other slow-cooker recipes for this book, we wanted to skip browning the meat before adding it to the slow cooker. We were worried that this would have an adverse affect with such a large cut of meat, but we were actually pleased to find that after 10 hours in the slow cooker, both the flavor and exterior color of the roast were fine. That said, to make up for the loss of flavor that comes with browning meat and deglazing the pan, we added soy sauce to the mix. Combined with sautéed aromatics, chicken broth, red wine, tomato paste, and crushed tomatoes, our braising liquid was now full flavored, and was at a good jumping-off point for our final "gravy." After all, what's pot roast without gravy? We wanted our gravy to be thick enough to coat the slices of pot roast, without being pasty. To that end, we tried cornstarch, flour (neither of which could be added at the onset of cooking), and even corn tortillas. In the end, instant tapioca proved to be the ideal thickener since it could be added at the beginning of cooking without imparting an off-flavor to the dish. Finished with a hefty amount of chopped fresh parsley, this was a tender pot roast with a flavorful gravy.

Slow-Cooker Pot Roast

SERVES 6 TO 8

In most markets, you will have to special order a large 5½- to 6-pound chuck roast. Alternatively, you can use two 3-pound roasts (which are common in most markets). The pot roast will shrink significantly as it cooks. Serve with rice or mashed potatoes.

2	tablespoons vegetable oil
3	medium onions, minced
2	carrots, cut into 1-inch chunks
8	medium garlic cloves, minced or pressed through a garlic press (about 8 teaspoons)
¼	cup tomato paste

Salt
¾ cup dry red wine
I (28-ounce) can crushed tomatoes
I (5½- to 6-pound) boneless beef chuck-eye
    roast, tied at 1-inch intervals
¾ cup low-sodium chicken broth
6 tablespoons Minute tapioca
⅓ cup soy sauce
I tablespoon fresh thyme leaves,
    or I teaspoon dried
¼ cup minced fresh parsley leaves
    Ground black pepper

1. Heat the oil in a 12-inch nonstick skillet over medium heat until shimmering but not smoking. Add the onions, carrots, garlic, tomato paste, and ¼ teaspoon salt and cook until the vegetables are softened and lightly browned, 10 to 15 minutes. Stir in the wine and tomatoes, scraping up any browned bits; set aside.

2. Lay the roast in the slow cooker insert. Add the broth, tapioca, soy sauce, and thyme to the onion and tomato mixture, then pour it over the roast. Cover and cook on low until the meat is tender, 9 to 11 hours. (Alternatively, cover and cook on high for 6 to 7 hours.)

3. Transfer the roast to a carving board; set aside to rest. Let the cooking liquid settle for 5 minutes then gently tilt the slow cooker insert and degrease as much fat as possible off the surface of the sauce using a large flat spoon. Stir in the parsley and season with salt and pepper to taste.

4. Untie the roast and slice into ½-inch-thick pieces. Arrange the meat on a warmed serving platter and pour 1 cup of the sauce over the top. Serve, passing the remaining sauce separately.

PREP-AHEAD TIPS
You can store all the ingredients below together with the exception of the meat, which must be refrigerated separately.
• Cook the onion and tomato mixture as described in step 1, then transfer it to an airtight container and refrigerate.
• Trim and tie the roast and refrigerate.
• Prep the carrots and refrigerate.

➤ VARIATION
Slow-Cooker Southwestern-Style Pot Roast
For a milder flavor, use the smaller amount of chipotle chiles.

Follow the recipe for Slow-Cooker Pot Roast, adding 3 tablespoons chili powder and 2 tablespoons ground cumin with the onions in step 1. Eliminate the wine, increase the chicken broth to 1½ cups, and add 2 to 4 tablespoons minced chipotle chile in adobo sauce with the broth in step 2. Substitute 1 tablespoon chopped fresh oregano (or 1 teaspoon dried) for the thyme. Replace the parsley in step 4 with 2 tablespoons minced fresh cilantro leaves.

SLOW-COOKER BEEF GOULASH

GOULASH IS A HUNGARIAN STEW, MADE with chunks of beef, flavored with Hungarian paprika, and finished with sour cream. When made correctly, it's rich and satisfying. The problem is that it's not easy to get it right in the slow cooker, and our first attempts turned out watery and bland.

Beef, onions, garlic, and paprika are the constants in this dish. Other possible ingredients include potatoes, tomatoes, and bell peppers. Our goal was to create a very simple stew with tender, flavorful beef and browned onions in a rich, intensely flavored sauce. The sauce would be thick red in color, both from the paprika and from the good browning that the onions would receive.

As with our beef stew (page 142), we found that chuck roast is the best choice because it cooks up tender and flavorful. And, in keeping with our findings from our beef stew testing, the meat for the goulash went into the slow cooker unbrowned, so we knew that replacing the brown fond would be no less important in this recipe. To begin with, we cooked the onions to a nice golden brown and then stirred in tomato paste and a hefty quantity of good-quality Hungarian paprika, cooking it until it reached a deep brown. This pretoasting of the tomato paste and paprika added the traditional deep rust color that we were looking for and which, to our surprise, withstood the time in the slow cooker. Then we added the unusual ingredient that had served us well in previous stew recipes: soy sauce, for its salty, beef-like flavor.

Although onions are a must, the recipes we looked at were divided on the question of garlic. Tasters, however, were not. Everyone in the test kitchen liked garlic in this stew. Six cloves added depth and also balanced the sweetness of the paprika and onions. The quantity of paprika was the next problem to solve. Too much and the goulash tasted bitter, almost burned. Too little and what we ended up with was a goulash that paled in comparison to our standard stovetop recipe. We settled on ¼ cup, which provided the perfect flavor and color without being overpowering.

Recipes uncovered in our research used an assortment of liquids, including water, beef broth, and chicken broth. We found that water created a bland stew, and canned beef broth, in conjunction with the large volume of paprika, contributed a bitter edge to the goulash. Chicken broth proved to be the best option, lending the stew solid body and just enough richness without competing with the other flavorings. Some recipes also include wine in the mix, although authentic recipes do not. We tried varying amounts of red wine, and tasters felt that its flavor was overpowering. Goulash should be soft and mellow; while red wine added complexity, it also made the stew acidic and a bit harsh. A few sources suggested white wine, but tasters were again unimpressed. Our recipe was coming together: beef and onions, garlic, tomato paste, paprika, soy for flavor, and chicken broth as the liquid.

Many Hungarian goulash recipes do not include sour cream, which seems more popular in German and Austrian versions. But our tasters all felt that sour cream mellows and enriches this stew. To prevent the sour cream from curdling, we combined it with a little hot stewing liquid to temper it and then stirred the mixture back into the slow cooker.

Goulash is traditionally served over buttered egg noodles or spaetzle. Egg noodles require almost no effort to cook and are our first choice. Mashed potatoes are not traditional, but they make an excellent accompaniment, too.

Slow-Cooker Beef Goulash
SERVES 6 TO 8

If you like things spicy, feel free to add a pinch of cayenne pepper or hot paprika. Serve over buttered egg noodles and garnish with some minced fresh parsley just before serving.

2	tablespoons vegetable oil
3	medium onions, minced
6	medium garlic cloves, minced or pressed through a garlic press (about 2 tablespoons)
¼	cup sweet paprika
¼	cup tomato paste
1	teaspoon caraway seeds
	Salt
2	cups low-sodium chicken broth
1	(5-pound) boneless beef chuck-eye roast, trimmed and cut into 1½-inch chunks
⅓	cup soy sauce
¼	cup Minute tapioca
2	bay leaves
½	cup sour cream
	Ground black pepper

1. Heat the oil in a 12-inch nonstick skillet over medium heat until shimmering but not smoking. Add the onions, garlic, paprika, tomato paste, caraway seeds, and ¼ teaspoon salt and cook until the onions are softened and lightly browned, 10 to 15 minutes. Stir in the chicken broth, scraping up any browned bits.

2. Transfer the onion mixture to the slow cooker insert and stir in the meat, soy sauce, tapioca, and bay leaves until evenly combined. Cover and cook on low until the meat is tender, 9 to 11 hours. (Alternatively, cover and cook on high for 5 to 7 hours.)

3. Discard the bay leaves. Gently tilt the slow cooker insert and degrease as much fat as possible off the surface of the stew using a large flat spoon. Stir 1 cup of the stewing liquid into the sour cream to temper, then stir the sour cream mixture back into the stew. Season with salt and pepper to taste and serve.

SLOW-COOKER BEEF STROGANOFF

BEEF STROGANOFF IS A CLASSIC RUSSIAN dish marrying beef and mushrooms in a creamy pan sauce. It can be a quick skillet dinner, made with strips of beef tenderloin, fit for company, or it can be a long-simmering braise made with more flavorful (though tougher) cuts of meat. Could we replicate the flavors in a slow cooker? Many of the slow-cooker recipes we tried had little mushroom flavor, with beef that was dry and chewy. We wanted a slow-cooker recipe with tender beef and mushroom flavor that was still apparent after 9 to 10 hours of simmering. We also wanted to keep prep time to a minimum, yet still maintain the authenticity of the dish.

We started our testing with a chuck-eye roast that we judiciously trimmed of excess fat. Following the classic recipe, we cut the beef into strips, and proceeded to make the dish in the slow cooker. Right off the bat, we knew that strips of meat weren't the right choice. We'd need to cut the meat into chunks; otherwise, it would be tough and flavorless after hours in a slow cooker. Following the method we established for beef stew (see page 140), we skipped the browning step, sautéed the onion, then browned tomato paste and added soy sauce for deep flavor. Then we added instant tapioca as our thickening agent.

Our next challenge was how to treat the mushrooms. In the past, we had always sautéed mushrooms until brown to reduce their moisture and bring out their flavor. But this took a good 10 minutes and, while we were willing to sauté onions, we didn't want to complicate things any further. We tried adding them raw and, to our surprise, they maintained their flavor and texture.

The only issue was that they didn't impart as much mushroom flavor to the broth as we would have liked. To bump up the mushroom flavor, as well as deepen the color of the stroganoff, we added ½ ounce dried porcini mushrooms. Their intense, woodsy flavor gave the broth just the flavor it had been lacking.

For the stew's braising liquid, we tried varying combinations of beef and chicken broth. We settled solely on chicken broth for its clean and rather neutral flavor, especially since the dish already had a deep flavor foundation and we worried about adding yet another element in the form of beef broth. That said, the stew needed some brightening up so we added a little dry white wine, which fit the bill perfectly.

Now our stroganoff was nearly done—with the exception of the creamy sauce that is its hallmark. We found it was easy to replicate this sauce by tempering sour cream with some of the cooking liquid and then stirring it back into the pot to finish. (Don't be tempted to simply add the sour cream to the hot mixture without this step or you'll end up with a curdled mess.) Served on top of a bed of buttered egg noodles, no one will know this is a recipe you left alone for hours in a slow cooker.

Slow-Cooker Beef Stroganoff

SERVES 6 TO 8

Serve this classic Russian stew with buttered egg noodles. When buying egg noodles, looked for the thinnest noodles possible, since wider noodles make the finished dish too heavy.

2	tablespoons vegetable oil
3	medium onions, minced
¼	cup tomato paste
	Salt
¾	cup dry white wine
1	(5-pound) boneless beef chuck-eye roast, trimmed and cut into 1½-inch chunks
10	ounces white button mushrooms, wiped clean, trimmed, and quartered
2	cups low-sodium chicken broth
⅓	cup soy sauce
¼	cup Minute tapioca

½ ounce dried porcini mushrooms, rinsed and minced
½ cup sour cream
2 teaspoons Dijon mustard
Ground black pepper

1. Heat the oil in a 12-inch nonstick skillet over medium heat until shimmering but not smoking. Add the onions, tomato paste, and ¼ teaspoon salt and cook until the onions are softened and lightly browned, 10 to 15 minutes. Stir in the wine, scraping up any browned bits.

2. Transfer the onion mixture to the slow cooker insert and stir in the meat, white mushrooms, broth, soy sauce, tapioca, and porcini mushrooms until evenly combined. Cover and cook on low until the meat is tender, 9 to 11 hours. (Alternatively, cover and cook on high for 5 to 7 hours.)

3. Gently tilt the slow cooker insert and degrease as much fat as possible off the surface of the stew using a large flat spoon. Stir 1 cup of the stewing liquid into the sour cream to temper, then stir the sour cream mixture back into the stew. Stir in the mustard, season with salt and pepper to taste, and serve.

PREP-AHEAD TIPS
Store the ingredients below separately.
• Cook the onion mixture as described in step 1, then transfer it to an airtight container and refrigerate.
• Trim and cut the meat and refrigerate.
• Prep the white mushrooms and refrigerate.

SLOW-COOKER BARBECUED BRISKET

MOST PEOPLE (TEXANS ANYWAY) WILL TELL you there's no way that good barbecue can come from a slow cooker. Traditional recipes require that you cook the brisket low and slow, on a real outdoor grill with charcoal and wood chips, and spend lots of time tending the fire. The brisket comes out tender, juicy, and full of that smoky flavor that is the essence of the real deal. But what if you want

SLICING BRISKET

Use a long, sharp knife to cut the meat against the grain into thin slices. Slicing it with the grain will result in tough, stringy slices.

barbecued brisket in winter and you don't care much for tending a grill in the snow? We wondered if this summer favorite could be made indoors, in the slow cooker. It was worth a shot.

Classic recipes for brisket call for a spice rub that is added to the meat, which then sits overnight in the refrigerator so that the flavors permeate the meat. We cobbled together a simple spice rub of brown sugar, paprika, onion powder, garlic powder, cumin, and cayenne, rubbed the meat thoroughly with it, and let it sit overnight. In the morning, it was time to cook the spice-rubbed brisket. We then moved on to choosing what kind of liquid (and how much of it) should be added to the slow cooker.

While the environs of a grill are similar to a sauna, the slow cooker is more like the steam room across the hall, with moisture rather than dry heat as the cooking medium. For our first test, we tried adding 2 cups of beef broth to the slow cooker, an amount that barely covered the brisket. Hours later, when we lifted the lid, we were surprised at what we found. The brisket was literally floating in liquid, a whopping 7 cups of it. And this liquid had a very diluted beef flavor. We wondered if we could cut back on the broth, and thereby concentrate the flavor. We tested quantities all the way down to ½ cup, and were still disappointed with the wateriness of the sauce. Then we wondered what would happen if we replaced the broth with something a bit more flavorful and viscous, like barbecue sauce. Unwilling to take time to make our own, we reached for our favorite store-bought brand and ladled some over the top of the brisket. We were initially concerned that we weren't adding enough liquid to the slow cooker, but when the brisket was done, we realized we needn't have worried. So much juice comes out of the brisket that there was plenty of liquid in the slow cooker (about 4 cups), and what was there was packed with flavor. The slight smokiness of the barbecue sauce imparted just the right amount of smoke flavor to the brisket—a flavor that we thought could compete with that of a brisket cooked outdoors. We knew we were getting closer to a great indoor brisket, but the meat was still not as tender as we felt it should be.

All slow-cooked meat suffers from the same catch-22 situation. For the normally tough meat to become tender, its connective tissues must be broken down, which requires hours of low-temperature cooking. As the meat cooks, the muscle fibers slowly contract, expelling moisture and often leaving the meat dry. The amount and

LOCATING THE BRISKET

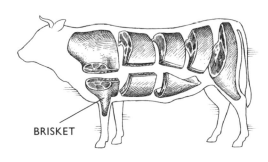

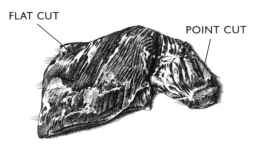

Butchers often separate the whole brisket into two parts, the flat cut (left portion) and the point cut (right portion). The point cut is a bit thicker and contains more fat. It is more tender than the flat cut and is our first choice.

distribution of the fat in the meat can make a big difference. A chuck roast will taste succulent after a proper braise because of its relatively high and even distribution of fat. In a brisket, however, most of the fat is located in an exterior cap and in a few thick layers; it is not marbled throughout. As a result, fat renders into the sauce rather than basting the interior of the meat, which is rather lean. We knew we couldn't keep moisture from leaving the meat, but wondered if there was a way to get the meat to reabsorb some of the liquid after cooking.

Up until this point, we had been removing the brisket from the sauce and letting it rest on a carving board before attempting to cut it into thin, neat slices. (Like a flank steak, brisket has long muscle fibers and must be sliced against the grain to avoid being chewy. These same long fibers, however, turn into shreds once connective tissue has been dissolved, making the meat difficult to slice.) We decided to try letting the meat rest in the sauce before slicing it, in hopes that it would reabsorb some of the flavorful liquid it had lost. This time the brisket was noticeably better. Then it occurred to us that maybe if we poked some holes in the brisket, that would allow even more flavor to return to the meat. This worked like a charm. Now the meat was tender, moist, and packed with flavor. We also found that the brisket tasted even better if we sliced it and poured some of the sauce from the slow cooker over the meat. Taking a closer look at the sauce, we found it necessary to degrease it, then season it with a little vinegar, salt, pepper, and sugar before serving.

Now that we had successfully developed a fantastic slow-cooker version of barbecued brisket, we began to wonder if this method would work with another barbecue classic: pulled pork. Using the traditional roast used for pulled pork—a boneless pork Boston butt—we gave the recipe a whirl with great success. After cooking, the pork roast fell apart into tender, juicy shreds. To serve, we found it easiest to remove the tender, falling-apart roast from the sauce. This gave us time to shred the pork properly (ridding it of any gristle) and degrease and season the sauce. The meat and sauce could then be combined and served on hamburger buns.

Slow-Cooker Barbecued Brisket

SERVES 6 TO 8

Brisket is sold as either the first (flat) cut or second (point) cut. Either cut will work fine in this recipe, but if you can find a point-cut brisket, it is ideal because it is fattier and will be even more tender after slow cooking. You can make your own barbecue sauce or use your favorite store-bought brand—we like Texas Best Original Rib Style or Bull's Eye Original.

¼	cup packed light brown sugar, plus extra to taste
¼	cup paprika
1	tablespoon onion powder
1	tablespoon garlic powder
1	tablespoon ground cumin
1	teaspoon cayenne
	Salt
1	(4- to 5-pound) beef brisket
1	cup barbecue sauce (see note)
	Cider vinegar
	Ground black pepper

1. Together in a small bowl, toss the ¼ cup sugar, paprika, onion powder, garlic powder, cumin, cayenne, and ½ teaspoon salt together. Massage the spice rub all over the brisket, then wrap it tightly in plastic wrap and refrigerate for up to 12 hours.

2. Unwrap the brisket and lay it, fat side up, in the slow cooker insert. Spread the barbecue sauce evenly over the brisket. Cover and cook on low until the meat is tender and a dinner fork can be slid in and out of the brisket with little resistance, 9 to 11 hours. (Alternatively, cook on high for 5 to 7 hours.)

3. Transfer the brisket to a 13 by 9-inch baking dish and cover with foil; set aside. Let the cooking liquid settle for 5 minutes then gently tilt the slow cooker insert and degrease as much fat as possible off the surface of the sauce using a large flat spoon. Season the sauce with additional sugar and vinegar, salt, and pepper to taste. Poke the brisket all over with a fork and then pour 1 cup of the sauce over the brisket and let it rest, covered, for 10 to 15 minutes.

4. Following the illustration on page 147, slice the brisket thinly across the grain. Arrange the meat on a warmed serving platter and serve, passing the remaining sauce separately.

➤ VARIATION

Slow-Cooker Pulled Pork

A 5- to 6-pound pork Boston butt is quite big—we like to cut the roast in half lengthwise to provide more surface area for the spice rub and ensure even cooking.

Follow the recipe for Slow-Cooker Barbecued Brisket, substituting 1 (5- to 6-pound) boneless pork Boston butt, cut in half lengthwise, for the brisket. After cooking, transfer the pork to a 13 by 9-inch baking dish, then degrease and season the sauce as directed in step 3. Using 2 dinner forks, shred the pork while still hot, discarding any fat. Toss the shredded pork with the sauce to taste and serve on hamburger buns, passing the remaining sauce separately.

SPICY SLOW-COOKER CHICKEN AND CHORIZO STEW

THIS HEARTY STEW FEATURES CHICKEN, chorizo, chipotle chiles, and garlic in a spicy tomato-based sauce. We thought this recipe should be fairly easy to adapt to the slow cooker, but we couldn't have been more wrong. Our biggest obstacle turned out to be the chicken. Many recipes we found cautioned against letting the chicken cook for more than five hours, but we were hoping for a chicken stew that could be left in the slow cooker for most of the day. After eight hours, chicken breasts were as dry as dust. Hoping that dark meat might fare better, we tried boneless chicken thighs and were heartened by the results. The thighs withstood the long cooking much better than chicken breasts but still, eight hours in a slow cooker was too long: These thighs were just a little too tough. Determined to find a way to prepare a chicken stew in the slow cooker, we decided to try a rather unorthodox approach: chilled broth and tomatoes. We simply put our chicken broth and canned tomatoes in the refrigerator the night before. This trick worked perfectly. The cold ingredients bought us the time to leave the chicken in the slow cooker for the span of a workday and now the chicken was perfectly cooked after eight hours in a slow cooker.

But we still needed to work on the flavor of the stew. We wanted it to have a spicy kick, but we didn't want it to be overwhelmingly hot. Smoky canned chipotle chiles added just the right level of heat and kept their kick for the long haul. As for the chorizo, we tried sautéing it with the onion and garlic, but found it really wasn't necessary—just adding it to the stew worked fine.

We also wanted black beans and corn in our stew. We tried dried black beans first, assuming that they would be fine here, as they were in our Black Bean Soup (page 125). As it turned out, they were actually a huge problem—their black pigment turned the chicken an unsightly gray color. That prompted us to go with canned black beans, which we simply stirred in along with the corn at the end of the cooking time. To give the stew a bit more body, we added instant tapioca rather than cornstarch or flour. It could be added at the onset of cooking time, which made it a convenient choice. For a final hit of brightness and flavor, we added fresh cilantro right before serving, stirring it into the pot.

Spicy Slow-Cooker Chicken and Chorizo Stew

SERVES 4 TO 6

Be sure to use chicken broth and tomatoes that have been refrigerated overnight or the stew will cook too fast. For a mild flavor, use the lower amount of chipotle chiles; for a spicy flavor, use the higher amount of chipotle. This thick stew is great on its own, but is also good served over rice, with tortillas, or with a crusty loaf of bread.

2   tablespoons vegetable oil
3   medium onions, minced
8   medium garlic cloves, minced or pressed
    through a garlic press (about 8 teaspoons)
    Salt

3   pounds boneless, skinless chicken thighs, trimmed
2   cups low-sodium chicken broth, chilled
1   (15.5-ounce) can diced tomatoes, drained and chilled
8   ounces chorizo, cut into ½-inch chunks
¼   cup Minute tapioca
1–3 tablespoons minced chipotle chile in adobo sauce
1   tablespoon brown sugar
2   cups frozen corn, thawed
1   (14-ounce) can black beans, drained and rinsed
¼   cup minced fresh cilantro leaves
    Ground black pepper

1. Heat the oil in a 12-inch nonstick skillet over medium heat until shimmering but not smoking. Add the onions, garlic, and ¼ teaspoon salt and cook until the onions are softened and lightly browned, 10 to 15 minutes.

2. Transfer the onion mixture to the slow cooker insert and stir in the chicken, broth, tomatoes, chorizo, tapioca, chipotles, and sugar until evenly combined. Cover and cook on low until the chicken is tender, 7 to 9 hours. (Alternatively, cover and cook on high for 4 to 5 hours.)

3. Gently tilt the slow cooker insert and degrease as much fat as possible off the surface of the stew using a large flat spoon. Stir in the corn, beans, and cilantro and let stand until the corn and beans are heated through, about 15 minutes. Season with salt and pepper to taste and serve.

PREP-AHEAD TIPS

You can store all the ingredients below together with the exception of the chicken, which must be refrigerated separately.

• Cook the onion mixture as described in step 1, then transfer it to an airtight container and refrigerate.
• Trim the chicken and refrigerate.
• Refrigerate the broth.
• Drain and refrigerate the tomatoes.
• Drain and rinse the beans.

SUMMER GARDEN PASTA SALAD WITH OLIVES AND FETA **PAGE 79**

CHEESE STRAWS **PAGE 13**

RIGATONI WITH BEEF RAGÙ **PAGE 118**

153

MAKE-AHEAD MASHED POTATOES **PAGE 59**

HEARTY MEAT LASAGNA **PAGE 230**

ANYTIME DINNER ROLLS **PAGE 334**

BREADED CHICKEN BREASTS WITH GOAT CHEESE AND THYME FILLING   **PAGE 276**

RUSTIC CARAMELIZED ONION TART WITH BLUE CHEESE AND WALNUTS **PAGE 35**

ALL-AMERICAN BEEF CHILI **PAGE 197**

159

STUFFED PLUM TOMATOES   **PAGE 41**

160

FLANK STEAK STUFFED WITH SPINACH, PROVOLONE, AND RED PEPPER PESTO   **PAGE 299**

BAKED MANICOTTI **PAGE 238**

RED ONION JAM–STUFFED PORK CHOPS WITH PORT, PECANS, AND DRIED FRUIT   **PAGE 302**

INDIVIDUAL BLACKBERRY-WALNUT BUCKLES **PAGE 355**

OVERNIGHT SOUR CREAM COFFEECAKE **PAGE 328**

165

CRÈME BRÛLÉE **PAGE 349**

5

STEWS, CHILIS, AND SAUCES

Stews, Chilis, and Sauces

STEWS AND CHILIS ARE PERFECT MAKE-ahead meals—all the ingredients go into the pot to cook, and then the finished dish can be served from the same pot as many as three days later. Better yet, the flavor of these recipes often improves with time, so it really makes sense to prepare them in advance. But perhaps what we like best about these recipes is the ease with which you can make stews and chilis in large batches. You can cook a batch on the weekend and simply reheat a portion for an easy weeknight dinner. Or make a big batch and stock your freezer so that a slow-cooked meal can be just minutes away. With little to no last-minute preparation, these recipes are also great for entertaining, whether you're having an intimate dinner for two or a crowd of 20.

Although most of the recipes in this chapter are naturally make-ahead, we did learn a few tricks along the way. Cooling the stews and chilis at room temperature before storing them in the refrigerator is important—a big pot of hot stew or chili will cause your refrigerator temperature to rise significantly, putting all of the other food in there at risk of spoiling. And when reheating stews and chilis a day or two later, it is important to do so slowly and gently, over medium-low heat and stirring frequently. Vigorous simmering can cause the meat to toughen and the vegetables to overcook.

When it came to making big batches, we searched for ways to streamline the process without compromising the integrity of the finished dish. Cooking vessels were our first obstacle. While recipes that simmer on the stovetop were easily adapted for a large stockpot (see White Chicken Chili on page 200 and Classic Bolognese Sauce on page 206), most of the stews require the slow, gentle heat of the oven, where a stockpot isn't ideal. Safe transport to and from the oven was another concern. Stew straight from the oven is hot, and these recipes serve as many as 20 people, so it is also heavy. A turkey-sized roasting pan was our solution to both problems. With more surface area, the stew can cook more evenly in a roasting pan than in a narrow stockpot and it is also sturdy and easy to carry. We browned the meat in a Dutch oven and transferred it to the roasting pan, and then we deglazed the Dutch oven, adding all the liquid until it was simmering. Then, everything went into the roasting pan, and the roasting pan went into the oven.

We also realized that there are no set rules when it comes to making big batches of stews. For our beef stews (pages 173–183), we found that it wasn't necessary to brown all of the meat, which would take as long as 45 minutes for the largest batch. Instead, we browned only half or two-thirds of the meat, developing great beef flavor in a fraction of the time. Conversely, the flavor of Chicken Tagine (page 192) greatly benefited from browning all of the chicken. The resulting browned bits left behind in the pot (also known as fond) were needed for depth and full chicken flavor. For the tagine as well as the White Chicken Chili, we were able to speed up the cooking process by doing two things at once—starting the onions in the stockpot while the chicken browned.

Finally, we were reminded that when scaling recipes up, it isn't always necessary to increase all ingredients proportionally. For instance, All-American Beef Chili (page 197) was unbearably spicy when we increased the amount of cayenne pepper to the same degree as we did the other ingredients. Likewise, for Beef Burgundy (page 177), we kept the amounts of aromatics in the vegetable and herb bouquet the same for the larger batches—a little went a long way. But in some cases, like the Chicken Tagine, we needed the full force of all the spices with our large batch, as anything less changed the integrity of the dish.

Because these recipes are so conducive to freezing, we determined the best containers in which to freeze them and the best way to reheat the contents. In general, the quality of frozen stews, chilis, and sauces that are thawed completely before reheating is superior to those that are reheated from their frozen state, but we understand that there are times when you may not be able to plan that far ahead. For this reason, we have also included reheating instructions for dinners straight from the freezer (see pages 182–183 for freezing and reheating information). We found that the consistency of stews and chilis can change after some time in the freezer (or refrigerator). We recommend adjusting the consistency with water or broth after reheating and before serving (see

"Why Do Stews and Chilis Thicken Over Time?," page 196).

In this chapter you'll also find recipes for pasta sauces and pestos, as well as a variety of simmering sauces meant to take the place of store-bought jarred sauces. Like stews and chilis, these recipes are easy to make ahead—they freeze well or can sit in the refrigerator for a few days until ready to use. Simply warm them right before serving and pour over your favorite pasta or protein for a quick, easy meal.

BEEF STEWS

BEEF STEW IS THE QUINTESSENTIAL MAKE-ahead dish for lots of reasons: It freezes and reheats well; it's easy to scale up into large batches; and it can be fancy enough to serve to company. Unfortunately, though, many of the beef stew recipes we tested weren't very successful and resulted in tough, dry meat in a watery, bland sauce. Our goal was to nail down some beef stew basics so that the meat would always turn out tender and the sauce would have great flavor and a rich, smooth consistency. Then with these basics in hand, we wanted to round out the ingredient lists to create a few flavorful and interesting beef stew variations—from a humble classic beef stew to a couple of dressed-up options.

Starting with the beef itself, we set out to determine the ideal cut for stews. We browned 12 different cuts of beef, marked them for identification, and cooked them in the same kind of pot. The biggest disappointment came from the packages labeled "stew meat," because they contained misshapen and small bits of meat along with scraps from various parts of the animal—basically, the butcher's leftovers. Chuck proved to be our cut of choice—flavorful, tender, and juicy with a moderate price tag. The names given to different cuts of chuck vary, but the most commonly used names for retail chuck cuts include boneless chuck-eye roasts, cross-rib roasts, blade steaks and roasts, shoulder steaks and roasts, and arm steaks and roasts. We particularly like chuck-eye roast, but all chuck cuts work well when trimmed and braised.

We next focused on braising liquids. We tried water, wine, homemade beef stock, store-bought beef broth, store-bought chicken broth, and combinations of these liquids. Water made the stews taste, well, watery. Stew made with homemade beef stock tasted great, but we decided that beef stew has plenty of other hearty ingredients to give it flavor and therefore doesn't require such a time-consuming ingredient. Store-bought beef broth, unfortunately, wasn't an acceptable substitute for the homemade beef stock, because it gave the stew an odd, tinny flavor. We did, however, have excellent results with store-bought chicken broth; but note that low-sodium chicken broth works best, or else the resulting braise may be too salty. Stew made solely with chicken broth can taste a little flat and one dimensional, but the addition of red wine adds just the right touch of brightness and balance.

As for building the stew itself, the traditional method for making a stew involves first browning the meat, then using the leftover browned bits as a base for building the sauce along with basic aromatics like onions, garlic, and tomato paste and a little flour for thickening. The meat is then cooked in the sauce with other stew vegetables and flavorings until it's tender (and the sauce is thick and rich). This traditional method of making the sauce and assembling the stew needed little revision from us as it is already quite sensible and streamlined; we were more interested in the actual cooking of the stew once everything was in the pot.

After a little testing, we noted that the temperature of the stewing liquid during cooking is crucial. We found it essential to keep the temperature of the liquid below boiling (212 degrees Fahrenheit) as boiled meat turns tough and the exterior of the meat becomes especially dry. Keeping the liquid at a simmer (rather than a boil) allows the internal temperature of the meat to rise slowly. By the time the meat is fork-tender, much of the connective tissue will have turned to gelatin. The gelatin, in turn, helps to thicken the stewing liquid.

To determine whether stews cook best on the stovetop or in the oven, we tried both simmering a basic beef stew on the stovetop over low heat (with and without a flame-tamer device to protect the pot from direct heat) and in a moderate oven. The flame-tamer device worked too well in distancing the pot from the heat; the stew juices tasted raw and boozy. Putting the pot right on the burner worked better, but we found ourselves constantly adjusting the burner to maintain a gentle simmer, and this method is prone to error. We had the most consistent results in the oven. We found that putting a covered Dutch oven in a 325-degree oven ensured that the temperature of the stewing liquid remained below the boiling point, at about 200 degrees. (The oven must be kept at a temperature higher than 200 degrees because ovens are not completely efficient in transferring heat; a temperature of 325 degrees recognizes that some heat will be lost as it penetrates through the pot and into the stew.)

Finally, we tested the best way to make a stew ahead of time without losing the integrity of the meat or sauce. This wasn't a great challenge as stews are naturally make-ahead worthy, but we found a few tricks along the way. First, it is important to add all the green ingredients just before serving; this way peas, parsley, and other fresh herbs don't lose their vibrant color and fresh flavor. Second, it is crucial to reseason the stew before serving as certain flavors lose their impact after a stay in the freezer (see "Waking Up a Stored Stew" above). Finally, we noted that stews stored in the freezer or refrigerator tend to be thicker when reheated and need to be thinned out with a little additional broth before serving (see "Why Do Stews and Chilis Thicken Over Time?," page 196).

Scaling up these beef stews to feed a crowd of 12 to 14 or 18 to 20 seemed easy enough, but we soon discovered it wasn't quite as straightforward as we thought. Our first attempt took several hours to assemble and the results were not promising—the rich, lovely sauces all turned into thin, watery broths as the stew simmered.

Part of our problem turned out to be a matter of equipment. To accommodate the larger volume, we had switched from a Dutch oven to a large stockpot—at a whopping 12 quarts, it was the only pot that could handle more than seven quarts of stew. Although this pot was perfect for simmering chili on the stove, inside the oven the dimensions worked against us. In this pot, given that it had less surface area, it took hours for the heat of the oven to properly cook the meat, at which point the

> **TEST KITCHEN TIP:**
> **Waking Up a Stored Stew**
> Certain flavors lose their impact after a stay in the refrigerator or freezer (especially with the big batches). To wake up the flavor of a stew, chili, or sauce that has been stored, try adding an extra dash of wine, lemon or lime juice, fresh herbs, and/or salt and pepper. It may also be necessary to add a little extra broth to adjust the consistency.

sauce was still thin. The solution turned out to be a roasting pan—the larger surface area exposed more of the stew to the oven's heat, thereby keeping the entire stew at the proper simmering temperature for the duration of the cooking time.

Perhaps our most interesting (and timesaving) discovery came when we realized that we could simply brown a portion of the meat from these large batches rather than all of it. Of course the browned bits (fond) left in the pot after browning the meat are important for flavoring the sauce, but two to three batches of browned meat will provide plenty of flavor for even our largest stew. The remaining unbrowned meat then gets added to the stew raw; after the stew is cooked, you'll be hard pressed to note any difference between the browned and unbrowned meat.

Finally, we noted that as the size of the batch got bigger, the corresponding sauces became more and more watery—in part because the unbrowned meat releases a lot more moisture as it cooks. In fact, most of our big batch stew testing centered around this very issue and we tried various liquid and flour amounts until we got it just right; our final results were surprising. In order to achieve the ideal sauce consistencies, we found it necessary to use far less liquid and far more flour than we first imagined.

HEARTY BEEF STEW

CLASSIC HEARTY BEEF STEW RELIES ON A rich, beefy sauce to carry the flavor of the entire dish. In other words, a dull or bland sauce makes a dull or bland stew. Vegetables are also integral to classic beef stew, but the classics—potatoes, carrots, and peas—can often become mushy and flavorless during the long simmer. Our goals for classic hearty beef stew were as follows: Develop a rich, beefy sauce for a stew with great flavor and coordinate the cooking times of the vegetables to prevent their flavors and textures from being compromised.

For the sauce, we found that the fond (the browned meaty bits left over from browning the meat) combined with chicken broth and a modest amount of red wine makes for a meaty-flavored sauce. (From prior testing, we'd learned that beef broth doesn't hold the same quality as chicken broth, making a sauce with off-flavors.) To further highlight the beef flavor without overpowering it, we added a variety of aromatics—but only the regulars need apply here. Onion, garlic, thyme, bay leaves, and tomato paste provided just enough seasoning without detracting from the beef.

Next, it was on to the vegetables. The peas (we use frozen) taste best when stirred in just a few minutes before serving. They heat through quickly and retain their bright green color. The carrots and potatoes, on the other hand, weren't so simple and required further testing. We ultimately determined that if we cut the carrots into large enough pieces they could withstand the total stew cooking time along with the meat; also, cooking the carrots in the stew for the entire time gives the sauce a sweet, earthy bonus of flavor. The potatoes, however, should be added halfway through the stew's cooking time. Any longer and they fell apart. While our method isn't toss-it-all-in-the-pot and simmer, it's not complicated and the fresh-flavored results are well worth the effort.

FREEZE IT

Hearty Beef Stew

SERVES 6 TO 8

A $7 to $10 bottle of medium-bodied red table wine made from a blend of grapes, such as a Côtes du Rhône, will work well here. Make this stew in a Dutch oven, preferably with a capacity of 8 quarts but nothing less than 6 quarts. If you plan on freezing the stew in small or even individual containers for last-minute meals, you might want to add the peas and parsley before storing so they won't be left out or forgotten when reheating.

4	pounds boneless beef chuck-eye roast, trimmed and cut into 1- to 1½-inch chunks (see the illustrations on page 178) Salt and ground black pepper
3	tablespoons vegetable oil
2	tablespoons unsalted butter
2	medium onions, chopped medium
3	medium garlic cloves, minced or pressed through a garlic press (about 1 tablespoon)
¼	cup unbleached all-purpose flour
1	tablespoon tomato paste
1	cup dry red wine (see note)
2½	cups low-sodium chicken broth, plus extra as needed for reheating
1	pound carrots (about 6 medium), peeled and sliced 1 inch thick
2	bay leaves
1	tablespoon minced fresh thyme leaves, or 1 teaspoon dried
1½	pounds red potatoes (about 4 medium), scrubbed and cut into 1-inch chunks
1	cup frozen peas (for serving)
3	tablespoons minced fresh parsley leaves (for serving)

1. Adjust an oven rack to the lower-middle position and heat the oven to 325 degrees. Pat the beef dry with paper towels and season with salt and pepper. Heat 2 tablespoons of the oil in a large Dutch oven over medium-high heat until just smoking. Add half of the meat and cook, stirring occasionally, until well browned, 7 to 10 minutes, reducing the heat if the pot begins to scorch. Transfer the browned beef to a medium bowl. Repeat with the remaining 1 tablespoon oil and the remaining beef; transfer to the bowl.

2. Add the butter to the pot and melt over medium-low heat. Add the onions and 1 teaspoon salt and cook, stirring often, until softened, 5 to 7 minutes. Stir in the garlic and cook until fragrant, about 30 seconds. Stir in the flour and tomato paste and cook, stirring constantly, until golden, about 1 minute. Slowly whisk in the wine, scraping up any browned bits. Gradually whisk in the broth until smooth and bring to a simmer.

3. Stir in the browned meat, carrots, bay leaves, and thyme and bring to a simmer. Cover, place the

pot in the oven, and cook for 1 hour. Stir in the potatoes and continue to cook in the oven, covered, until the meat is just tender, 1½ to 2 hours longer. Remove the bay leaves and season with salt and pepper to taste.

4. TO STORE: Let the stew cool, uncovered at room temperature, for 45 minutes. Transfer to an airtight container(s) and refrigerate for up to 2 days. For freezing instructions, see page 182.

5. TO SERVE: Spoon off and discard any hardened fat from the top and transfer the stew to a Dutch oven. Cover and bring to a simmer over medium-low heat, gently stirring occasionally, about 30 minutes (adding additional broth as needed to adjust the sauce consistency). Off the heat, stir in the peas and let them heat through, about 5 minutes. Season with salt and pepper to taste. Sprinkle the parsley over individual portions before serving.

TO SERVE RIGHT AWAY

After seasoning with salt and pepper to taste in step 3, stir in the peas, cover, and let sit for 10 minutes. Sprinkle the parsley over individual portions before serving.

To Make a Big Batch

Adjust the Hearty Beef Stew recipe as follows using the ingredient amounts listed in the chart on page 175. You will need a turkey-sized roasting pan that measures about 18 by 13 inches with 4-inch high sides. (Alternatively, you can use 2 disposable aluminum roasting pans with these same dimensions, one nested inside the other and supported by a baking sheet.) A big batch of stew in one vessel can be heavy—up to 25 pounds for the largest batch—so use caution when handling.

TO SERVE 12 TO 14

- Following the directions in step 1, brown only half of the meat in 2 batches.
- Transfer the browned meat, remaining unbrowned meat, carrots, bay leaves, and thyme to a large roasting pan (roughly 18 by 13 inches with 4-inch sides).
- Cook the onions as described in step 2, increasing the cooking time to 7 to 10 minutes.

- Continue to build the sauce as described in step 2. Bring the sauce to a simmer, then pour over the meat in the roasting pan.
- Cover the roasting pan tightly with foil and cook in the oven as directed in step 3, increasing the cooking time to 1½ hours.
- Stir in the potatoes as directed in step 3 and continue to cook, covered, for 2 to 2½ hours longer.
- Finish the stew as directed in step 3.
- Store the stew as directed in step 4.
- Reheat as directed in step 5, using a large stockpot (at least 12 quarts), 50 to 60 minutes. (You can also reheat the stew in a 425-degree oven, using a roasting pan covered with foil, 1½ to 2 hours.)
- Stir in the peas, season, and serve as directed in step 5.

TO SERVE 18 TO 20

- Following the directions in step 1, brown two-thirds of the meat in 3 batches. You may need to deglaze the pan before browning the third batch to prevent the browned bits in the pot from burning (see page 179). Use up to 2 tablespoons more oil as needed when browning the third batch of meat.
- Transfer the browned meat, remaining unbrowned meat, carrots, bay leaves, and thyme to a large roasting pan (roughly 18 by 13 inches with 4-inch sides).
- Cook the onions as described in step 2, increasing the cooking time to 10 to 13 minutes.
- Continue to build the sauce as described in step 2. Bring the sauce to a simmer, then pour over the meat in the roasting pan.
- Cover the roasting pan tightly with foil and cook in the oven as directed in step 3, increasing the cooking time to 2 hours.
- Stir in the potatoes as directed in step 3 and continue to cook, covered, for 2 to 2½ hours longer.
- Finish the stew as directed in step 3.
- Store the stew as directed in step 4.
- Reheat as directed in step 5, using a large stockpot (at least 12 quarts), about 1½ hours. (You can also reheat the stew in a 425-degree oven, using a roasting pan covered with foil, 2 to 2½ hours.)
- Stir in the peas, season, and serve as directed in step 5.

MAKING A BIG BATCH OF HEARTY BEEF STEW

INGREDIENTS	SERVES 12 TO 14	SERVES 18 TO 20
BEEF CHUCK ROAST	7 pounds	10 pounds
VEGETABLE OIL	3 tablespoons	5 tablespoons
UNSALTED BUTTER	4 tablespoons (½ stick)	6 tablespoons (¾ stick)
ONIONS	4 medium	5 medium
GARLIC	5 medium cloves (5 teaspoons)	7 medium cloves (7 teaspoons)
ALL-PURPOSE FLOUR	¾ cup	1¼ cup
TOMATO PASTE	2 tablespoons	3 tablespoons
DRY RED WINE	1½ cups	2½ cups
LOW-SODIUM CHICKEN BROTH	4 cups	5½ cups
CARROTS	1¾ pounds	2½ pounds
BAY LEAVES	3 leaves	4 leaves
MINCED FRESH THYME (DRIED THYME)	1½ tablespoons (1½ teaspoons)	2 tablespoons (2 teaspoons)
RED POTATOES	2⅔ pounds (about 7 medium)	3¾ pounds (about 10 medium)
FROZEN PEAS	1½ cups	2¼ cups
MINCED FRESH PARSLEY	⅓ cup	½ cup

BEEF BURGUNDY

BEEF BURGUNDY IS A REFINED, COMPLEX-flavored stew comprised of large chunks of tender beef coated with a velvety, voluptuous, red wine sauce. And instead of the chunks of potatoes and carrots along with green peas, typical in a hearty beef stew, beef Burgundy contains earthy mushrooms and elegant pearl onions. Understandably, this stew is a bit more complex and we wanted to devise ways to streamline its cumbersome methods.

Classic recipes for beef Burgundy require that you marinate the beef in red wine and herbs overnight prior to cooking. But in testing this method, we found no difference between marinated and unmarinated meat in our finished dish. One step we can cross off our list.

Also, the beef is typically cut into larger chunks than in a hearty beef stew—a good 1½ to 2 inches. The large chunks give the stew a welcome luxurious character. It's important to note that in cutting bigger pieces of meat, it is necessary to take extra care to trim off as much fat and silver skin as possible; larger pieces of beef also mean larger, more detectable bites of these undesirables.

Each beef Burgundy recipe we researched begins with either salt pork or bacon cut into small, thick strips (aka lardons) and fried to a crisp; the fat that results is used to brown the beef chunks. The crisped pork is added to the pot to simmer alongside the beef so that it can relinquish its flavors to the braise, providing a subtle, sweet underpinning and lending the sauce roundness and depth. We tried both bacon and salt pork and favored the cleaner, purer flavor of salt pork; thick-cut bacon (blanched to remove its smoky flavor, see page 178) can be substituted if salt pork is unavailable.

> **TEST KITCHEN TIP: Watch It!**
> When testing these stews, we noted that the meat passes from the tough to tender stage fairly quickly. Oftentimes a 15-minute time lapse is all it takes for chewy meat to turn tender. Check the meat often as the stew nears completion to judge when it's just right.

INGREDIENTS:
Does It Have To Be Burgundy?

Beef Burgundy is rightfully made with true Burgundy wine. This means a red wine made from the Pinot Noir grape grown in the French province of Burgundy. Characteristically, these wines are medium-bodied but also deep, rich, and complex, with earthy tones and a reticent fruitiness. They also tend to be expensive, so we went with the cheapest one we could find—a $12 bottle. Quite frankly, it made outstanding beef Burgundies. Nonetheless, we then tried more costly, higher-quality Burgundies and found that they bettered the dish—a $30 bottle gave a stellar, rousing performance. We thought it worth exploring other wines, but wanting to remain faithful to the spirit of the dish, we limited ourselves to Pinot Noirs made on the West Coast of the United States, which are slightly less expensive than French Burgundies. We made beef Burgundies with domestic Pinot Noirs at three different price points, and even the least expensive wine—a $9 bottle—was perfectly acceptable, although its flavors were simpler and less intriguing than those of its Burgundian counterparts.

Both the Burgundies and the Pinot Noirs exhibited the same pattern—that is, as the price of the wine increased, so did the depth, complexity, and roundness of the sauce. We can advise with some confidence to set your price, then seek out a wine—either Burgundy or Pinot Noir—that matches it. But if your allegiance is to true Burgundy, be warned that they can be difficult to find because production is relatively limited. We also caution you to beware of several very inexpensive mass-produced wines from California of questionable constitutions that are sold as "Burgundy." They are usually made from a blend of grape varieties and whether or not they actually contain so much as a drop of Pinot Noir is a mystery. We made beef Burgundy with one of these wines, and it resulted in a fleeting, one-dimensional, fruity, sweet sauce that, though palatable, lacked the deep, lavish flavors we have come to expect in a beef Burgundy.

$9 CALIFORNIA PINOT NOIR   **$30 FRENCH BURGUNDY**

Classically, the salt pork is served in the stew as "garnish" but some tasters objected to the fatty pieces dotting the dish. Instead of fishing out pieces of pork fat before serving, we found our answer in how we handled the aromatics.

The refined nature of this stew requires that the aromatics (onion, carrot, garlic, bay leaves, parsley, and thyme) be sautéed, cooked in stewing liquid, and then strained out to make an absolutely smooth and silky sauce. In testing, we found that skipping the straining step did give the stew an unappealing rustic character, but straining the sauce seemed like a hassle. We looked for a better way. We found it in bundling the aromatics in cheesecloth to make a little sack. This way, we'd be able to drop the sack into the sauce (where the aromatics could still impart their seasoning), and when finished, the sack could easily be removed. To further the richness of the sauce, we added dried porcini mushrooms to the aromatics for their distinctive meaty flavor. True, we were also omitting the step of sautéing the aromatics, but tasters couldn't tell the difference. And as a bonus, this method gave us a solution to the salt pork problem—we simply added the salt pork to the sack along with the aromatics after it had given up its fat in sautéing.

Beef Burgundy recipes are always heavy handed with the red wine (usually one from the French region of Burgundy) because it is the highlighted flavor of this dish. After numerous experiments, we concluded that anything less than a whole bottle left the sauce lacking in personality and that a Burgundy, or at least a decent Pinot Noir, is indeed the wine of choice (see left for more information). Though most recipes indicate that all of the wine should be added at the outset, one recipe, as well as one wine expert, recommended saving a bit of the wine to add at the very end, just before serving. This late embellishment of raw wine vastly improved the sauce, brightening its flavor and giving it resonance. To gussy up the flavor a bit more, we added a splash of brandy just before serving—it further embellished this elegant stew with just the right amount of richness and warmth.

Focusing finally on the mushroom and pearl onion garnish, we noted that it was impossible to cook them in the stew alongside the beef because they turned mushy. The convenience of already peeled frozen pearl onions was too great to ignore, and a brisk simmer in a separate pan (a skillet) with some water, butter, and sugar was all they needed to take on some flavor and life. Giving the mushrooms a quick sauté also worked well and created glazed beauties that were ready to grace the stew, along with a sprinkle of fresh parsley. By adjusting a few ingredients and adding a few more steps, a basic beef stew really can be elegant enough for company.

● FREEZE IT ●

Beef Burgundy

SERVES 6 TO 8

If you can't find salt pork, substitute blanched bacon (see Salt Pork Substitution on page 178). If not enough fat is rendered from the salt pork for browning the meat, add vegetable oil. Boiled potatoes are the traditional accompaniment, but mashed potatoes or buttered noodles are nice as well. If you plan on freezing the stew in small or even individual containers, you might want to add the brandy, extra wine, and parsley before storing so they won't be forgotten.

AROMATIC BOUQUET

4	ounces salt pork, cut into ¼-inch-thick matchsticks
10	sprigs fresh parsley, torn into pieces
6	sprigs fresh thyme
2	medium onions, chopped coarse
2	medium carrots, chopped coarse
1	medium head garlic, cloves separated and crushed but unpeeled
2	bay leaves, crumbled
½	ounce dried porcini mushrooms, rinsed (optional)

STEW

4	pounds boneless beef chuck-eye roast, trimmed and cut into 1½- to 2-inch chunks (see the illustrations on page 178) Salt and ground black pepper
3	tablespoons unsalted butter, cut into 3 pieces
⅓	cup unbleached all-purpose flour
1	tablespoon tomato paste
1	(750-ml) bottle red Burgundy or Pinot Noir (about 3⅛ cups)

2¾	cups low-sodium chicken broth, plus extra as needed for reheating

ONION AND MUSHROOM GARNISH

2	tablespoons unsalted butter
1	pound medium white mushrooms, halved Salt
7	ounces frozen pearl onions
½	cup water
1	tablespoon sugar
2	tablespoons brandy (for serving)
3	tablespoons minced fresh parsley leaves (for serving)

1. FOR THE BOUQUET: Cook the salt pork in a Dutch oven over medium heat until lightly browned and crisp, about 12 minutes. With a slotted spoon, transfer the salt pork to a plate. Pour off and reserve the fat. Following the illustrations below, assemble the salt pork and remaining bouquet ingredients into a double-layer cheesecloth pouch and tie securely with kitchen twine; set aside.

MAKING THE AROMATIC BOUQUET

1. Lay a double layer of cheesecloth (14-inch square) in a medium bowl. Place the designated ingredients in the cheesecloth-lined bowl.

2. Gather together the edges of the cheesecloth and fasten them securely with kitchen twine. Trim any excess cheesecloth with scissors if necessary.

2. FOR THE STEW: Adjust an oven rack to the lower-middle position and heat the oven to 325 degrees. Pat the beef dry with paper towels and season with salt and pepper. Return 2 tablespoons of the rendered pork fat to the pot and heat over medium-high heat until just smoking. Add half of the meat to the Dutch oven and cook, stirring occasionally, until well browned, 7 to 10 minutes, reducing the heat if the pot begins to scorch. Transfer the browned beef to a medium bowl. Repeat with 1 more tablespoon of the reserved fat and the remaining beef; transfer to the bowl.

3. Add the butter to the pot and melt over medium-low heat. Stir in the flour and tomato paste and cook, stirring constantly, until golden, about 1 minute. Gradually whisk in 3 cups of the wine, scraping up any browned bits. Whisk in the broth until smooth and bring to a simmer.

4. Stir in the browned meat and submerge the aromatic bouquet in the liquid. Bring to a simmer. Cover, place the pot in the oven, and cook until the meat is just tender and the sauce is thickened and glossy, 2½ to 3 hours.

5. FOR THE GARNISH: While the stew cooks, melt 1 tablespoon of the butter in a large skillet over medium heat. Add the mushrooms and ¼ teaspoon salt, cover, and cook until the mushrooms have released their liquid, about 5 minutes. Uncover and cook until the liquid has evaporated and the mushrooms are golden brown, about 5 minutes. Transfer to a medium bowl, cover, and set aside.

6. Add the pearl onions, water, remaining 1 tablespoon butter, sugar, and ¼ teaspoon salt to the skillet and bring to a boil over high heat. Cover, reduce to medium-low heat, and simmer, shaking the pan occasionally, until the onions are tender, about 5 minutes. Uncover, increase the heat to high, and simmer until all the liquid evaporates and the onions are golden brown, about

CUTTING BEEF STEW MEAT

You simply can't make good stew from bad meat. And to get the best stew meat possible (regularly shaped, evenly cut, and all from the chuck), you should really cut it up yourself. We like to use a beef chuck-eye roast, but any boneless beef roast from the chuck will work. The trick is not to cut the pieces of meat too small while trimming away the fat—the fat will render into the stew and be easy to skim off later. That said, however, don't be surprised if you have a good amount of trim—count on roughly ½ pound trim for every 4 pounds of meat.

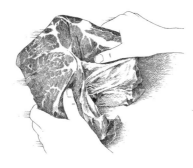

1. Pull apart the roast at its major seams (delineated by lines of fat and silver skin); use a knife as necessary.

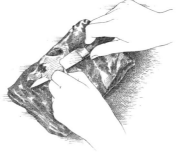

2. With a sharp, thin-tipped knife, trim off the excess fat and silver skin.

3. Cut the meat into cubes or chunks as directed in specific recipes.

TEST KITCHEN TIP:
Stop Scorching

If your pan gets too hot while you are browning the meat, the flavorful browned bits (fond) on the bottom will burn and ruin the flavor of your stew. To avoid this, you should take note of the pan between browning the batches of meat. If the bottom of the pan looks dark and on the edge of burning, use some broth (or water) to help dissolve the fond, while scraping up the brown bits with a wooden spoon; transfer the liquid with bits to a small bowl and reserve. The pot will now be clean enough to continue browning the next batch of meat. Be sure to incorporate the reserved brown bits and accompanying liquid to the stew for flavor.

3 minutes. Transfer the onion mixture to the bowl with the mushrooms, season with salt to taste, and set aside.

7. When the stew is finished cooking, stir in the mushroom and onion mixture and season with salt and pepper to taste.

8. To store: Let the stew cool, uncovered at room temperature, for 45 minutes. Transfer to an airtight container(s) and refrigerate for up to 2 days. For freezing instructions, see page 182.

9. To serve: Spoon off and discard any hardened fat from the top and transfer the stew to a Dutch oven. Cover and bring to a simmer over medium-low heat, gently stirring occasionally, about 30 minutes (adding additional broth as needed to adjust the sauce consistency). Stir in the remaining 2 tablespoons wine and the brandy and season with salt and pepper to taste. Sprinkle the parsley over individual portions before serving.

TO SERVE RIGHT AWAY

After stirring in the mushrooms and onions in step 7, stir in the remaining 2 tablespoons wine and the brandy. Season with salt and pepper to taste and let the stew sit for 10 minutes. Serve, sprinkling the parsley over individual portions.

To Make a Big Batch

Adjust the Beef Burgundy recipe as follows using the ingredient amounts listed in the chart on page 180. You will need a turkey-sized roasting pan that measures about 18 by 13 inches with 4-inch high sides. (Alternatively, you can use 2 disposable aluminum roasting pans with these same dimensions, one nested inside the other and supported by a baking sheet.) A big batch of stew in one vessel can be heavy—up to 25 pounds for the largest batch—so use caution when handling.

TO SERVE 12 TO 14

- Following the directions in step 2, brown only half of the meat in 2 batches.
- Transfer the browned meat, remaining unbrowned meat, and aromatic bouquet to a large roasting pan (roughly 18 by 13 inches with 4-inch sides).
- Build the sauce as described in step 3, using 4½ cups of the wine. Bring the sauce to a simmer, then pour over the meat and bouquet in the roasting pan.
- Cover the roasting pan tightly with foil and cook in the oven as directed in step 4, increasing the cooking time to 3¼ to 3¾ hours.
- While the stew cooks, prepare the mushrooms as directed in step 5, using 2 tablespoons of butter and increasing the uncovered cooking time to 10 minutes.
- Cook the pearl onions as directed in step 6, increasing the covered cooking time to 7 minutes, and the uncovered cooking time to 7 minutes.
- Finish the stew as directed in step 7.
- Store the stew as directed in step 8.
- Reheat as directed in step 9, using a large stockpot (at least 12 quarts), 50 to 60 minutes. (You can also reheat the stew in a 425-degree oven, using a roasting pan covered with foil, 1 to 1½ hours.)
- Stir in the remaining 2½ tablespoons wine and the brandy, then season and serve as directed in step 9.

TO SERVE 18 TO 20

- Following the directions in step 2, brown two-thirds of the meat in 3 batches. You may need to deglaze the pan before browning the third batch to prevent the browned bits in the pot from burning (see above). Use up to 2 tablespoons fat as needed when browning the third batch of meat.

MAKING A BIG BATCH OF BEEF BURGUNDY

INGREDIENTS	SERVES 12 TO 14	SERVES 18 TO 20
SALT PORK	6 ounces	8 ounces
PARSLEY	12 sprigs	15 sprigs
THYME	9 sprigs	12 sprigs
ONIONS	3 medium	3 medium
CARROTS	3 medium	3 medium
GARLIC	2½ medium heads	3 medium heads
BAY LEAVES	3 leaves	4 leaves
DRIED PORCINI MUSHROOMS	¾ ounce	1 ounce
BEEF CHUCK ROAST	7 pounds	10 pounds
UNSALTED BUTTER	6 tablespoons (¾ stick)	8 tablespoons (1 stick)
ALL-PURPOSE FLOUR	1 cup	1⅔ cups
TOMATO PASTE	2 tablespoons	3 tablespoons
RED BURGUNDY WINE	1½ (750-ml) bottles (4⅔ cups)	2 (750-ml) bottles (6¼ cups)
LOW-SODIUM CHICKEN BROTH	4 cups	5 cups
UNSALTED BUTTER	3 tablespoons	4 tablespoons
WHITE MUSHROOMS	1½ pounds	2¼ pounds
PEARL ONIONS	14 ounces	20 ounces
WATER	¾ cup	1 cup
SUGAR	2 tablespoons	3 tablespoons
BRANDY	3 tablespoons	¼ cup
MINCED FRESH PARSLEY	⅓ cup	½ cup

- Transfer the browned meat, remaining unbrowned meat, and aromatic bouquet to a large roasting pan (roughly 18 by 13 inches with 4-inch sides).
- Build the sauce as described in step 3, using 6 cups of the wine. Bring the sauce to a simmer, then pour over the meat and bouquet in the roasting pan.
- Cover the roasting pan tightly with foil and cook in the oven as directed in step 4, increasing the cooking time to 3¼ to 3¾ hours.
- While the stew cooks, prepare the mushrooms as directed in step 5, cooking the mushrooms in 2 batches, using 1 tablespoon of butter for each batch.
- Cook the pearl onions as directed in step 6 (in 1 batch) using 2 tablespoons of butter, increasing the covered cooking time to 10 minutes, and the uncovered cooking time to 10 minutes.
- Finish the stew as directed in step 7.
- Store the stew as directed in step 8.
- Reheat as directed in step 9, using a large stockpot (at least 12 quarts), about 1½ hours. (You can also reheat the stew in a 425-degree oven, using a roasting pan covered with foil, 1½ to 2 hours.)
- Stir in the remaining ¼ cup wine and the brandy, then season and serve as directed in step 9.

EQUIPMENT: Storage Containers

Homemade stews, chilis, and sauces store well in the fridge or freezer—a boon for the make-ahead cook. To store these dishes, we prefer plastic food storage containers to Styrofoam cups (hard to stack and not reusable) or zipper-lock bags (apt to puncture, especially when pushed up against sharp corners in the freezer). In fact, we found out the hard way that zipper-lock bags are not suitable for storing wet foods when we defrosted a bag of chili and liquid leaked out the puncture holes and made a mess in our microwave. As for sizes of our food storage containers, we prefer two: family-size, enough to hold four to six 1½-cup servings, and individual-size, enough to contain a single 1½-cup portion.

Does the brand of plastic food-storage container make a difference? It sure does, especially if you want a tight seal. To test the seal, we came up with several reliable, if slightly unconventional, methods. The "sink test" was first. We filled each container with 2¼ pounds of pie weights topped with a layer of sugar and, with the lid in place, submerged the whole thing in water. Then we fished out the container, dried it, and inspected the sugar inside. Any leaking was immediately revealed by sugar clumps. To further assess the seal, we devised the "shake test." We filled each container with 2 cups of canned chicken barley soup, fixed the lid in place, and shook vigorously. If we ended up wearing soup, the seal wasn't tight enough.

The seal between container and lid is also responsible for preventing the transfer of food odors To gauge odor protection, we conducted "stink tests" by loading slices of white sandwich bread into each container, closing the lid, and storing them in the fridge with a huge, uncovered bowl of diced raw onions. Over the course of five days, we sniffed the bread daily to see if we could detect any onion scent.

We chose chili to test stain resistance, refrigerating it in the containers for three days, microwaving it to serving temperature (about three minutes), and then immediately running the containers through the dishwasher. Finally, to replicate the ravages of time, we ran the containers through 100 cycles in the dishwasher and then repeated every test.

Our lineup of containers included Tupperware, two Rubbermaid models (Seal'n Saver and Stain Shield), several competing plastic containers, two inexpensive disposable containers, and two vacuum-sealing models.

The Genius VakSet container, with its pump-operated vacuum seal, performed impressively in the sink, shake, and stink tests, both brand new and after 100 washes. Nonetheless, we have reservations about it, owing largely to the extra step of pumping. Some testers considered this a hassle, with some finding the vacuum release system confusing. The good news is that several other containers with tight-fitting lids, particularly the Tupperware and both Rubbermaid models, held their own against the vice grip of the Genius.

The stink tests produced no clear pattern among the odor control champs, including the Genius, GladWare, Tupperware, Betty Crocker, and the Rubbermaid Seal'n Saver, which just edged out the Rubbermaid Stain Shield.

The results of the staining tests revealed that those made from hard, clear polycarbonate (the same material used for lightweight eyeglass lenses and compact disks), including the Tupperware, Rubbermaid Stain Shield, Genius, and Snapware, resisted stains best in our tests. The remaining plastic containers were made of polypropylene, which is a somewhat softer polymer that seems more susceptible to staining.

To our surprise, several containers matched or surpassed the performance of the reigning king of plastic food-storage containers, Tupperware. Strictly speaking, the vacuum-sealed Genius VakSet edged out the Tupperware by one point in the performance tests. Despite this stellar performance, we're still not sold on it. We fear that some cooks will lose the pump, rendering the containers useless. Also, no one in our test kitchen could figure out how to release the vacuum seal without first reading the instruction manual. To put it plainly, storing food shouldn't be any hassle at all. With the Genius, it is.

That's why our nod goes to the Tupperware, followed closely by the two Rubbermaid models. Their performance was excellent and you don't have to think twice to use them. If you want something more high-tech, the Genius is your container.

THE BEST FOOD STORAGE CONTAINERS

The Tupperware Rock 'N Serve (top) and the Rubbermaid Stain Shield (bottom) are the containers to reach for when divvying up that big batch of stew or chili to store in your fridge or freezer.

FREEZING, THAWING, AND REHEATING 101

IT'S EASY TO STOCK YOUR FREEZER WITH SAUCES, STEWS, AND CHILIS TO PULL OUT AND reheat whenever you like. In the chart on the facing page, we offer guidelines for storing and reheating in sizes we think you will most often freeze: family-sized portions, serving 6 to 8, and single-serving portions, about 1½ cups of stew or chili or ¼ to ½ cup sauce. Here are the steps you need to follow so that your dishes heat up just as flavorful as freshly made.

Cool and Store. To speed up the cooling process for big batches of chilis, stews, and sauces, first divide the hot dish into the portions you want to freeze. We like freezing in airtight plastic storage containers (for our testing of food storage containers, see page 181). Remember to leave a little room at the top of the container(s) to prevent the lid(s) from popping off. Store in the refrigerator for up to 2 days or store in the freezer for up to 1 month.

Thaw. For safety reasons, we recommend thawing frozen food in the refrigerator, never at room temperature. That said, if you've forgotten to plan ahead, you can heat frozen foods directly in the microwave or on the stovetop, but note that the texture of meat and vegetables may suffer slightly.

For single-serving portions, thaw in the refrigerator, covered, at least 8 hours or overnight.

For 6 to 8-serving portions, thaw in the refrigerator, covered, 24 to 48 hours.

Reheat. For stews and chilis, we prefer a slow steady simmer on the stovetop or the gentle heat of the oven, but you can also reheat in the microwave and so we provide instructions for all three in the chart on the facing page. Because sauces heat through fairly quickly, we prefer reheating them on the stovetop or in the microwave.

Choose the right pot. Depending on what reheating method you choose, you'll need to also choose the right pot to use. Here are our recommendations.

- FOR REHEATING IN THE OVEN: A Dutch oven with a lid or a deep baking dish covered tightly with foil are your best bets. Each conduct heat evenly and can contain the food comfortably.

- FOR REHEATING ON THE STOVETOP: A Dutch oven with a lid or a large heavy-bottomed saucepan with a tight-fitting lid work best for stovetop simmering. These sturdy pots will conduct heat evenly and are not apt to scorch during a long simmer, as could happen with a flimsy, thin-bottomed pot.

- FOR REHEATING IN THE MICROWAVE: Avoid microwaving your stew, chili, or sauce in the same container used to store it. Not all storage containers are microwave-safe and the space inside the container will be too tight for you to comfortably stir the food during the heating process. Instead, we recommend that you transfer the food to a microwave-safe dish with a lid and be sure it's somewhat larger than the storage container. If you don't have a lid, cover the dish with plastic wrap and poke several holes in the wrap to allow for some steam to escape.

PROVENÇAL BEEF STEW

MOST BEEF STEWS HAVE A PERSONALITY-defining ingredient, like the red wine in beef Burgundy. In contrast, Provençal beef stew relies on a complex blend of ingredients typical of the region, such as garlic, olives and olive oil, tomatoes, oranges, mushrooms, anchovies, thyme, and bay leaves—each of which provides a role in distinguishing this stew's sunny flavor. Preparing Provençal beef stew is not difficult. There are just a few differences between making a Provençal stew and a classic hearty beef stew or beef Burgundy.

For example, we noted that several recipes in our research called for browning the beef in olive oil, rather than a vegetable oil, canola oil, or rendered pork fat (all of which have a higher smoke point, ideal for browning). Testing the difference between these fats in our Provençal stew, we found

that we too liked the flavor of olive oil here. And while not typical of the region, tasters liked the addition of salt pork to this stew. Instead of sautéing it as we did in beef Burgundy, we simple wrap it in kitchen twine and drop it into the stew, where its fat cooks down, melting into the stew. Because it's wrapped, it can easily be fished out before serving. Don't be tempted to omit the salt pork. We made stews with and without it and when omitted, its rich flavor was sorely missed. Anchovies, too, might seem like an ingredient you can do without, but we think that you'll miss the depth of flavor that just a few fillets provide to the finished dish.

A final note on ingredients: Canned tomatoes simply work best here. Fresh tomatoes simmered in the stew broke down too much and were unrecognizable beyond the pieces of skin we spooned up throughout the sauce. Canned tomatoes work better

REHEATING STEWS, CHILIS, AND SAUCES

	1 SERVING (THAWED)	6 TO 8 SERVINGS (THAWED)	1 SERVING (FROZEN)	6 TO 8 SERVINGS (FROZEN)
*Stews and chilis**				
TO REHEAT IN THE MICROWAVE	Heat, covered, at high power for 3 to 5 minutes, stirring once.	Heat, covered, at high power, for 8 to 12 minutes, stirring every 2 minutes.	Heat, covered, at high power for 5 to 8 minutes, stirring every 2 minutes.	Heat, covered, at high power, for 30 minutes, stirring every 5 minutes.
TO REHEAT IN THE OVEN	Bake, covered, in a 350-degree oven for 20 to 22 minutes, stirring once.	Bake, covered, in a 350-degree oven for 30 minutes, stirring twice.	Add ¼ cup water to the pot and bake, covered, in a 350-degree oven for 30 to 40 minutes, stirring once.	Add 1 cup water to the pot and bake, covered, in a 350-degree oven for 1 hour 15 minutes, stirring twice during the last 15 minutes.
TO REHEAT ON THE STOVETOP	Heat, covered, over medium-low heat for 10 to 12 minutes, stirring once.*	Heat, covered, over medium-low heat for 30 minutes, stirring twice.	Add ¼ cup water to the pot and heat, covered, over medium-low heat, for 18 to 20 minutes, stirring twice.	Add 1 cup water to the pot and heat, covered, over medium-low heat, for 35 to 40 minutes, stirring twice during the last 15 minutes.
*Sauces**				
TO REHEAT IN THE MICROWAVE	Heat, covered, at high power, for 2 to 4 minutes, stirring every minute.	Heat, covered, at high power, for 5 to 10 minutes, stirring every 2 minutes.	Heat, covered, at high power, for 5 to 10 minutes, stirring every 2 minutes.	Heat, covered, at high power, 15 to 20 minutes, stirring every 5 minutes.
TO REHEAT ON THE STOVETOP	Heat, covered, over medium-low heat, for 2 to 4 minutes, stirring once.	Heat, covered, over medium-low heat, for 5 to 10 minutes, stirring twice.	Add 1 tablespoon water to the pot and heat, covered, over medium-low heat, for 5 to 10 minutes, stirring once.	Add 2 tablespoons water to the pot and heat, covered, over medium-low heat for 15 minutes, stirring twice.

* Note that it may be necessary to add extra broth or water to adjust the consistency

not only because they are skinless, but also because they already have a slightly cooked flavor and softened texture thanks to the canning process. Adding the canned tomatoes just a few minutes before serving was perfect—they were visually apparent yet not raw tasting. But we urge you to dice the tomatoes yourself—meatier whole canned tomatoes have a superior texture to canned diced tomatoes.

While not as familiar to the American palate as beef Burgundy, beef Provençal, with its large chunks of tender meat and bold, brash flavors, is a terrific addition to the typical stew repertoire.

⬭ FREEZE IT ⬭
Provençal Beef Stew
SERVES 6 TO 8

If you can't find salt pork, substitute blanched bacon (see Salt Pork Substitution on page 178); be sure to tie the

bacon into a tidy bundle than can easily be removed. If niçoise olives are not available, kalamata olives, though not authentic, can be substituted. Serve this bold beef stew with soft polenta, egg noodles, or simple boiled red potatoes. If you plan on freezing the stew in small or even individual containers for last-minute meals, you might want to add the tomatoes and parsley before storing so they won't be left out or forgotten.

4   pounds boneless beef chuck-eye roast, trimmed and cut into 1½- to 2-inch chunks (see the illustrations on page 178) Salt and ground black pepper

5   tablespoons olive oil

2   medium onions, halved and cut into ⅛-inch-thick slices

¾   ounce dried porcini mushrooms, rinsed and minced

⅓ cup unbleached all-purpose flour

2 tablespoons tomato paste

1 (750-ml) bottle dry red wine (3⅛ cups)

2¾ cups low-sodium chicken broth, plus extra as needed for reheating

1 pound carrots (about 6 medium), peeled and sliced 1 inch thick

3 ounces salt pork, rind removed (see page 179), tied tightly with kitchen twine for retrieval purposes

4 (3-inch-long) strips orange zest from 1 orange, cut into thin matchsticks

1 cup pitted niçoise olives, rinsed and chopped coarse (see note)

4 medium garlic cloves, sliced thin

3 anchovy fillets, rinsed and minced (about 1 teaspoon)

5 sprigs fresh thyme, tied together with kitchen twine

2 bay leaves

1 (14.5-ounce) can whole tomatoes, drained and cut into ½-inch dice (for serving)

3 tablespoons minced fresh parsley leaves (for serving)

1. Adjust an oven rack to the lower-middle position and heat the oven to 325 degrees. Pat the beef dry with paper towels and season with salt and pepper. Heat 2 tablespoons of the oil in a large Dutch oven over medium-high heat until just smoking. Add half of the meat and cook, stirring occasionally, until well browned, 7 to 10 minutes, reducing the heat if the pot begins to scorch. Transfer the browned beef to a medium bowl. Repeat with 1 more tablespoon of the oil and the remaining beef; transfer to the bowl.

2. Add the remaining 2 tablespoons oil to the pot and place it over medium heat until shimmering. Add the onions, porcini, and 1 teaspoon salt and cook until softened, 5 to 7 minutes. Stir in the flour and tomato paste and cook, stirring constantly, for 1 minute. Slowly whisk in the wine, scraping up any browned bits. Whisk in the broth until smooth and bring to a simmer.

3. Stir in the browned meat, carrots, salt pork, orange zest, half of the olives, garlic, anchovies, thyme bundle, and bay leaves. Bring to a simmer.

Cover, place the pot in the oven, and cook until the meat is just tender and the sauce is thickened and glossy, 2½ to 3 hours.

4. Remove the salt pork, thyme, and bay leaves. Stir in the remaining olives. Season with salt and pepper to taste.

5. To STORE: Let the stew cool, uncovered at room temperature, for 45 minutes. Transfer to an airtight container(s) and refrigerate for up to 2 days. For freezing instructions, see page 182.

6. To SERVE: Spoon off and discard any hardened fat from the top and transfer the stew to a Dutch oven. Cover and bring to a simmer over medium-low heat, gently stirring occasionally, about 30 minutes (adding additional broth as needed to adjust the sauce consistency). Stir in the tomatoes and season with salt and pepper to taste. Sprinkle the parsley over individual portions before serving.

TO SERVE RIGHT AWAY

After seasoning with salt and pepper to taste in step 4, stir in the tomatoes, cover, and let sit for 10 minutes. Sprinkle the parsley over individual portions before serving.

To Make a Big Batch

Adjust the Provençal Beef Stew recipe as follows using the ingredient amounts listed in the chart on page 186. You will need a turkey-sized roasting pan that measures about 18 by 13 inches with 4-inch high sides. (Alternatively, you can use 2 disposable aluminum roasting pans with these same dimensions, one nested inside the other and supported by a baking sheet.) A big batch of stew in one vessel can be heavy—up to 25 pounds for the largest batch—so use caution when handling.

TO SERVE 12 TO 14

- Following the directions in step 1, brown only half of the meat in 2 batches.
- Transfer the browned meat, remaining unbrowned meat, carrots, salt pork, orange zest, half of the olives, garlic, anchovies, thyme bundle, and bay leaves to a large roasting pan (roughly 18 by 13 inches with 4-inch sides).

EQUIPMENT: Dutch Ovens

A good Dutch oven (variously called a stockpot, round oven, or casserole by manufacturers) is a kitchen essential. They are heavier and thicker than a stockpot, allowing them to retain and conduct heat more effectively, and deeper than a skillet, so they can handle large cuts of meat and cooking liquid. Dutch ovens are the best choice for braises, pot roasts, stews, and chilis, as they can go on the stovetop to sear foods and then into the oven to finish with steady, slow cooking. Their tall sides also make them useful for deep-frying, and many cooks press Dutch ovens into service for jobs like boiling pasta. But with prices for these kitchen workhorses ranging from $40 on the low end to six times as much at the other end of the spectrum, we wondered if more money buys you a better pot. We rounded up nine Dutch ovens and brought them into the test kitchen to find out.

For our first test, we prepared a beef stew that starts on the stovetop and then moves to the oven. In each pan, we browned cubes of beef in batches and observed whether the pan heated evenly and consistently without burning the drippings. After the long, slow cooking in the oven, we tasted the stew to see if the meat had become fork-tender and the broth had reduced to an intense flavor. Of all the tests we did, this was the most important, because it focused on the unique abilities of Dutch ovens. As expected, the pricey Le Creuset and All-Clad pots sailed through with flying colors. Surprisingly, so did a few of the others.

We noticed a few trends. Our favorite pots from All-Clad and Le Creuset measure 9¾ inches across, enabling them to brown 3½ pounds of beef in three batches, something narrower pots couldn't do—the narrowest one required five batches of browning, a serious flaw. A couple of the pots were also too light and browned the meat unevenly.

Next we tested heat transfer and retention by frying a pound of frozen french fries. The best pans retain heat well enough to prevent the temperature of the oil from dropping too precipitously when food is added. Those where the temperature dropped too much or took too long to recover produced soggy, greasy fries.

For our last test, we steamed a triple batch of white rice in each Dutch oven to see how they simmered on very low heat. All but one pot made fluffy rice with intact grains.

When all the smoke and steam and sizzling fry oil cleared, the most expensive pots came out on top. Other than price, it's hard to argue with the pots made by All-Clad and Le Creuset. (Most of our test cooks prefer the sturdiness of the latter, but some opt for the lighter, easier-to-manage All-Clad pot.)

Although we weren't surprised by our winners, we were shocked at their narrow margin of victory. The $40 Target Chefmate Casserole held its own and kept up with the winners in every test. The Chefmate looks like a slightly smaller Le Creuset, down to the shape of the handles and the knob on the top. Because the Chefmate casserole is smaller than our top choices, you will need to brown meat for stew in three batches rather than two, and the biggest pot roasts will be a tight fit. While our test cooks are not ready to trade in their favorite Dutch ovens, the Chefmate is a real find for budget-minded cooks.

If you're willing to spend $100 on a Dutch oven, and you have the biceps to handle it, the Mario Batali pot is comparable in size to the Le Creuset and All-Clad pots and performs nearly as well. Yes, the browning wasn't perfect, but that seems like a minor quibble that most cooks would never notice. These are two other good choices, and both reasonably priced. Now that's good news.

THE BEST DUTCH OVENS

The 7¼-quart Le Creuset Round French Oven ($230) is our top choice, while the All-Clad Stainless 8-quart Stockpot ($260) is the best choice for cooks who prefer a lighter pot. For those looking for a less expensive alternative, the Chefmate Round Enameled Cast-Iron Casserole for Target ($40) and the Mario Batali Italian Essentials Pot by Copco ($100) are both solid choices and are our best buys.

LE CREUSET ROUND FRENCH OVEN

ALL-CLAD STAINLESS

CHEFMATE ROUND ENAMELED CAST-IRON CASSEROLE

MARIO BATALI ITALIAN ESSENTIALS POT BY COPCO

- Cook the onions as described in step 2, using the remaining 5 tablespoons oil and increasing the cooking time to 7 to 10 minutes.
- Continue to build the sauce as described in step 2. Bring the sauce to a simmer, then pour over the meat in the roasting pan.
- Cover the roasting pan tightly with foil and cook as directed in step 3, increasing the cooking time to 3¼ to 3¾ hours.
- Finish the stew as directed in step 4.
- Store the stew as directed in step 5.
- Reheat as directed in step 6, using a large stockpot (at least 12 quarts), 50 to 60 minutes. (You can also reheat the stew in a 425-degree oven, using a roasting pan covered with foil, 1 to 1½ hours.)
- Stir in the tomatoes, season, and serve as directed in step 6.

TO SERVE 18 TO 20

- Following the directions in step 1, brown two-thirds of the meat in 3 batches. You may need to deglaze the pan before browning the third batch to prevent the browned bits in the pot from burning (see page 179). Use up to 2 tablespoons oil as needed when browning the third batch of meat.
- Transfer the browned meat, remaining unbrowned meat, carrots, salt pork, orange zest, half of the olives, garlic, anchovies, thyme bundle, and bay leaves to a large roasting pan (roughly 18 by 13 inches with 4-inch sides).
- Cook the onions as described in step 2, using the remaining 7 tablespoons oil and increasing the cooking time to 10 to 13 minutes.
- Continue to build the sauce as described in step 2. Bring the sauce to a simmer, then pour over the meat in the roasting pan.

MAKING A BIG BATCH OF PROVENÇAL BEEF STEW

INGREDIENTS	SERVES 12 TO 14	SERVES 18 TO 20
BEEF CHUCK ROAST	7 pounds	10 pounds
OLIVE OIL	½ cup	¾ cup
ONIONS	4 medium	5 medium
DRIED PORCINI MUSHROOMS	1 ounce	1½ ounces
ALL-PURPOSE FLOUR	1 cup	1⅔ cups
TOMATO PASTE	¼ cup	6 tablespoons
DRY RED WINE	1½ (750-ml) bottles (4⅔ cups)	2 (750-ml) bottles (6¼ cups)
LOW-SODIUM CHICKEN BROTH	4 cups	5 cups
CARROTS	2 pounds	3 pounds
SALT PORK	6 ounces, cut into 2 pieces	8 ounces, cut into 2 pieces
ORANGE ZEST	7 strips (1 orange)	10 strips (2 oranges)
NIÇOISE OLIVES	1½ cups	2¼ cups
GARLIC	7 medium cloves	10 medium cloves
ANCHOVY FILLETS	5 fillets	8 fillets
FRESH THYME	8 sprigs	12 sprigs
BAY LEAVES	3 leaves	4 leaves
CANNED WHOLE TOMATOES	1 (28-ounce) can	3 (14.5-ounce) cans
MINCED FRESH PARSLEY	⅓ cup	½ cup

- Cover the roasting pan tightly with foil and cook as directed in step 3, increasing the cooking time to 3¼ to 3¾ hours.
- Finish the stew as directed in step 4.
- Store the stew as directed in step 5.
- Reheat as directed in step 6, using a large stockpot (at least 12 quarts), about 1½ hours (You can also reheat the stew in a 425-degree oven, using a roasting pan covered with foil, 1½ to 2 hours.)
- Stir in the tomatoes, season, and serve as directed in step 6.

PORK STEW

YEARS AGO WHILE VISITING FRANCE, WE were introduced to a rustic dish of braised pork combined with carrots, prunes, brandy, and a touch of cream. The pork was fall-apart-tender, its flavor enhanced by the sweetness of the carrots and the prunes, yet savory with a stock and cream broth—a luxurious blend of flavors and textures. Elegant without being fussy, it's the perfect dish for entertaining. We've tried many times over the years to recreate this dish from memory, but never quite got it right. After describing it to some fellow test cooks, however, we were convinced to give this dish another shot. We wanted a rich, satisfying pork stew with a careful balance of savory and sweet, and we wanted this dish to be versatile—one that you might prepare for a Tuesday night or make ahead to feed a crowd.

We already knew from our experience with stewing beef that the shoulder, or chuck, is the best cut for braising, and so we assumed that pork shoulder would also make the best pork stew. To test this proposition, we stewed various cuts of pork from both the shoulder and loin, including several kinds of chops. The shoulder cuts were indeed far superior to those from the loin. Like beef chuck, pork shoulder has enough fat to keep the meat tender and juicy during the long cooking process.

But which cut from the shoulder works best? Pork shoulder is called Boston butt or Boston shoulder in most markets. The picnic roast also comes from the shoulder, but includes the skin and bone, which

means more prep work. As with beef, we recommend buying a boneless roast and cutting it into cubes yourself (you can use a picnic roast, but the bone, skin, and thick layer of fat will need to be removed with a knife and discarded). Once the pork was cubed and seasoned with salt and pepper, we browned it to enhance its flavor and that of the overall stew. After setting aside the meat, leeks were added to the pot and "melted" in oil until they softened, providing a sweet aromatic backdrop for the stew.

With the cut of meat and aromatic settled, we moved on to the braising liquid. We needed a full 5 cups of liquid to properly braise the pork and provide ample liquid for serving the stew. Brandy would be the defining flavor of our braising liquid, complemented by chicken broth for a savory element, and cream for richness. We knew this would require a careful balancing act. Starting with 1 cup of brandy (enough to generously deglaze the pan and shine through the other ingredients in this flavorful braise without overwhelming them), we added 2 cups each of the chicken broth and cream. But this was too heavy. And because this stew requires a significant amount of time in the oven, the sweetness of the cream was also now a bit cloying, which in turn dulled the flavor of the brandy (like our beef stews, we start this pork stew on the stovetop to brown the meat and start cooking the vegetables, but the bulk of the cooking happens in the oven for gentle, all-encompassing heat). The obvious fix was to decrease the amount of cream (to 1 cup) and increase the amount of chicken broth (to 3 cups). This was an improvement, but the cream still had that overly sweet, "cooked" flavor. Holding the cream and adding it at the end of cooking allowed the cream to retain its fresh flavor without overpowering the other ingredients.

We already knew prunes and carrots would play an integral role in our stew, but we thought another vegetable might further round out the flavors. We settled on fennel—with its subtle anise notes, it perfectly complemented the other flavors of the stew. Combined with the cream, the brandy, and the pork, it was a hit. Because fennel and carrots cook at a much faster pace than pork, we added them halfway through cooking so they could coast to the finish line together. The prunes were best added at the very end of cooking to prevent them from breaking down and disintegrating into the stew. Freshly minced tarragon and parsley, as well as some lemon juice, all added a welcome complexity to the finished dish.

With our master recipe in place, we wondered what adjustments, if any, would need to be made to increase the recipe to serve up to 20 people. We were happy to discover that the only change we needed to make also saved us some time. It is not necessary to brown all the meat when doubling or tripling this stew.

FREEZE IT

Pork Stew with Fennel, Leeks, and Prunes

SERVES 6 TO 8

You can substitute veal shoulder for the pork. Boneless pork butt roast is often labeled Boston butt in the supermarket. Don't substitute dried tarragon or parsley here. While 1 cup of brandy may seem like a lot for this recipe, we recommend using an inexpensive brand and not skimping on the amount—it provides just the right balance of flavors. Serve this stew with buttered egg noodles or rice pilaf.

3½–4	pounds boneless pork butt roast, trimmed and cut into 1- to 1½-inch pieces
	Salt and ground black pepper
¼	cup vegetable oil
1	large leek, white and light green parts only, halved lengthwise and sliced ¼ inch thick, rinsed thoroughly (about 1 cup)
3	medium garlic cloves, minced or pressed through a garlic press (about 1 tablespoon)
3	tablespoons unbleached all-purpose flour
1	cup brandy
3	cups low-sodium chicken broth
2	bay leaves
1	large fennel bulb (about 1 pound), trimmed of stalks, cored, and cut into ½-inch-thick strips (see the illustrations on page 47)
1	pound carrots (about 6 medium), peeled and sliced 1 inch thick
1	cup heavy cream (for serving)
1	cup prunes, halved (for serving)

	Water, as needed for reheating
2	tablespoons minced fresh tarragon leaves (for serving)
2	tablespoons minced fresh parsley leaves (for serving)
1	tablespoon juice from 1 lemon (for serving)

1. Adjust an oven rack to the lower-middle position and heat the oven to 325 degrees. Pat the pork dry with paper towels and season with salt and pepper. Heat 2 tablespoons of the oil in a large Dutch oven over high heat until just smoking. Add half of the pork and cook, stirring occasionally, until well browned, 7 to 10 minutes, reducing the heat if the pot begins to scorch. Transfer the browned pork to a medium bowl. Repeat with 1 more tablespoon of the oil and the remaining pork; transfer to the bowl.

2. Add the remaining 1 tablespoon oil to the pot and return to medium heat until shimmering. Add the leeks and 1 teaspoon salt and cook, stirring often, until wilted and lightly browned, 5 to 7 minutes. Stir in the garlic and cook until fragrant, about 30 seconds. Stir in the flour and cook, stirring constantly, until golden, about 1 minute. Slowly whisk in the brandy, scraping up any browned bits. Gradually whisk in the broth until smooth and bring to a simmer.

3. Stir in the browned pork and bay leaves and bring back to a simmer. Cover, place the pot in the oven, and cook for 1 hour. Stir in the fennel and carrots and continue to cook in the oven, covered, until the meat is just tender, 45 to 50 minutes more. Remove the bay leaves and season with salt and pepper to taste.

4. TO STORE: Let the stew cool, uncovered at room temperature, for 45 minutes. Transfer to an airtight container(s) and refrigerate for up to 2 days. For freezing instructions, see page 182.

5. TO SERVE: Spoon off and discard any hardened fat from the top and transfer the stew to a Dutch oven. Cover and bring to a simmer over medium-low heat, gently stirring occasionally, about 30 minutes. Stir in the cream and prunes, and continue to simmer gently until the prunes are softened, 5 to 10 minutes (adding water as needed to adjust the sauce consistency). Off the heat, stir in the tarragon, parsley, and lemon juice and season with salt and pepper to taste.

TO SERVE RIGHT AWAY

After seasoning with salt and pepper to taste in step 3, add the cream and prunes, cover, and let sit for 5 minutes. Stir in the tarragon, parsley, and lemon juice before serving.

To Make a Big Batch

Adjust the Pork Stew with Fennel, Leeks, and Prunes recipe as follows using the ingredient amounts listed in the chart below. You will need a turkey-sized roasting pan that measures about 18 by 13 inches with 4-inch high sides. (Alternatively, you can use two disposable aluminum roasting pans with these same dimensions, one nested inside the other and supported by a baking sheet.) A big batch of stew in one vessel can be heavy—up to 25 pounds for the largest batch—so use caution when handling.

TO SERVE 12 TO 14

• Following the directions in step 1, brown only half of the pork in 2 batches. Transfer the browned

pork and remaining unbrowned meat to a large roasting pan (roughly 18 by 13 inches with 4-inch sides).

• Build the sauce as directed in step 2, bring to a simmer, then pour over the meat in the roasting pan.

• Cover the roasting pan tightly with foil and cook as directed in step 3, increasing the cooking time to 1½ hours.

• Stir in the fennel and carrots and continue to cook, covered, as directed in step 3, increasing the cooking time to 1 to 1½ hours.

• Store the stew as directed in step 4.

• Reheat as directed in step 5, using a large stockpot (at least 12 quarts), 50 to 60 minutes. (You can also reheat the stew in the oven, using a roasting pan covered with foil, for 1 to 1½ hours at 425 degrees.)

TO SERVE 18 TO 20

• Following the directions in step 1, brown only two-thirds of the meat in 3 batches. Transfer the

MAKING A BIG BATCH OF PORK STEW WITH FENNEL, LEEKS, AND PRUNES

INGREDIENTS	SERVES 12 TO 14	SERVES 18 TO 20
BONELESS PORK BUTT ROAST	6½ to 7 pounds	9½ to 10 pounds
VEGETABLE OIL	4 tablespoons	5 tablespoons
LEEKS	2 large (2 cups)	3 large (3 cups)
GARLIC	6 medium cloves (about 2 tablespoons)	9 medium cloves (about 3 tablespoons)
ALL-PURPOSE FLOUR	6 tablespoons	9 tablespoons
BRANDY	1½ cups	2 cups
LOW-SODIUM CHICKEN BROTH	6 cups	9 cups
BAY LEAVES	3 leaves	4 leaves
FENNEL BULBS	2 large	3 large
CARROTS	2 pounds	3 pounds
HEAVY CREAM	2 cups	3 cups
PRUNES	2 cups	3 cups
MINCED FRESH TARRAGON	3 tablespoons	¼ cup
MINCED FRESH PARSLEY	3 tablespoons	¼ cup
LEMON JUICE	2 tablespoons (1 lemon)	3 tablespoons (2 lemons)

browned pork and remaining unbrowned meat to a large roasting pan (roughly 18 by 13 inches with 4-inch sides).

- Build the sauce as directed in step 2, bring to a simmer, then pour over the meat in the roasting pan.
- Cover the roasting pan tightly with foil and cook as directed in step 3, increasing the cooking time to 1½ hours.
- Stir in the fennel and carrots and continue to cook, covered, as directed in step 3, increasing the cooking time to 1 to 1½ hours.
- Store the stew as directed in step 4.
- Reheat as directed in step 5, using a large stockpot (at least 12 quarts), about 1½ hours. (You can also reheat the stew in the oven, using a roasting pan covered with foil, for 1½ to 2 hours at 425 degrees.)

CHICKEN TAGINE

WHEN MOST PEOPLE THINK OF MOROCCO, they envision dusty souks, spindly minarets, and men in flowing djellabas. Not us—we think with our stomachs and see tagine. Tagines are exotically spiced, assertively flavored stews slow-cooked in earthenware vessels of the same name. They can include all manner of meats, vegetables, and fruit, though our hands-down favorite combines chicken with olives and lemon. The briny bite of the olives and clarifying tartness of the lemon bring out the best in the meat and the spices.

While we love tagine, it's not a dish we ever conceived of as American home cooking. Why? The few traditional recipes we had seen required time-consuming, labor-intensive cooking methods (some that were entirely foreign to us), a special pot (the tagine), and hard-to-find ingredients (preserved lemon). Although usually game for a day in the kitchen or a hunt for exotica, we realized tagine, at its most elemental level, is just stew.

A little research proved that we weren't the first to take a stab at making tagine accessible. We collected a number of recipes for chicken with olives and lemon, some clearly more ersatz than others. Of the recipes we tried, most lacked the depth of

> **TEST KITCHEN TIP:**
> **Raising the Braise**
> When braising chicken parts, it can be hard to keep the white meat from turning dry and stringy. We solved this problem by layering the dark meat into the pot first, adding a layer of carrots, then setting the white meat on top of the carrots. The propped-up white meat sits above the braising liquid and cooks at a gentler pace than the dark meat below the surface.

an authentic tagine, but they held promise nonetheless. They proved first that a western cooking method—braising (brown the chicken, sauté the aromatics, add broth, and simmer)—was a serviceable substitution. Second, that a Dutch oven worked fine—no special equipment necessary. And finally, that the flavors associated with Moroccan cooking weren't necessarily "exotic"—they were more a strategic blending of common ingredients and spices already in the cupboard.

Almost all of the recipes we collected specified a whole chicken—broken down into pieces—and we soon found out why. Batches made entirely with white meat lacked the depth and character of those made with a blend of dark and white. But for the purposes of turning this recipe into a stew for as many as 20 people, we felt that breaking whole chickens into parts was too time-consuming. We also wanted this stew to be easy to eat, so we chose boneless, skinless breasts and thighs (that we could easily shred into bite-sized pieces) for a more streamlined approach.

But when we cooked the white and dark meat in the same way—simmered partially submerged in broth until fork-tender—the white meat turned dry and stringy. (Existing recipes had largely ignored this fundamental problem.) Pulling out the white meat when it had just cooked through solved matters, but the close attention required was bothersome. There had to be an easier way. If we could somehow raise the white meat pieces above the simmering broth in which the dark meat braised, it could gently steam until just cooked.

That's when we thought of carrots. They were added to many of the recipes we had found and provided just enough bulk to elevate the white meat above the broth. We piled sliced carrots (cut ½ inch thick so that they wouldn't overcook) into the bottom of the pot around the dark meat pieces and set the white meat on top. In this fashion, both dark meat and white meat pieces were perfectly cooked—and ready at the same time.

Some recipes called for rubbing the chicken with lemon and salt and letting the meat marinate (for hours or overnight) before cooking; others employed salt alone or blended with spices. After tasting the options, we found that salt and pepper alone were the best option; adding spices at this point resulted in a muddy-flavored broth.

A large sliced onion and a few minced garlic cloves rounded out the basic flavors of the tagine, and we finally felt ready to tackle the defining ingredients: spices, olives, and lemon. Many recipes called for a spice blend called ras el hanout, which may contain upward of 30 spices. As with many spice blends—curry and garam masala come to mind—ras el hanout is more a matter of taste than rigid formula. We experimented with a broad range of spices in batch after batch until we landed on a blend that was short on ingredients but long on flavor. Cumin and ginger lent depth, cinnamon brought warmth to temper a little cayenne heat, and citrusy coriander boosted the stew's lemon flavor. Paprika added sweetness and, perhaps more important, colored the broth a deep, attractive red. Thoroughly toasting the spices brought out the full depth of flavors.

Finding the right olive proved harder than we anticipated. Big, meaty, green Moroccan olives were the obvious choice, but they were a rarity at any of our local markets. Other big green olives, like Manzanilla, Cerignola, or Lucques, were the right size, but the flavors were either too mild or too assertive to match the other flavors in the tagine. Greek "cracked" olives, however, tasted great and were easy to find (see page 193). But when we added the olives to the stew too soon, their flavor leached out into the broth, rendering them bland and bitter. Stirring in the olives at the end of the stew's simmering time proved a much better approach, as they retained more of their flavor and firm texture.

The lemon flavor in authentic tagines comes from preserved lemon, a long-cured Moroccan condiment that's hard to find outside of specialty stores. "Quick" preserved lemons can be produced at home in a few days, but we wanted to keep the tagine simple and fast. Part tart citrus, part pickled brine, preserved lemon provides a unique taste impossible to imitate. So we chose not to try; instead, we aimed to add a rich citrus backnote to the broth. We added a few broad ribbons of lemon zest along with the onions, and the high heat coaxed out the zest's oils and mellowed them. Adding two lemons' worth of juice just before serving reinforced the bright flavor.

A couple spoonfuls of honey further balanced the broth, and minced cilantro freshened things, but we felt the stew still lacked a certain spark. A last-minute addition of raw garlic and finely chopped lemon zest seemed to clinch it, as the sharpness brought out the best in each of the stew's components.

Tagine is an elegant dish perfect for entertaining, so with the master batch in order, we wanted to increase the recipe to serve a crowd. When cooking large quantities of stew in the oven, we use a roasting pan to accommodate the increased volume. But because our chicken tagine is cooked entirely on the stovetop, we decided to enlist the help of our largest stockpot, giving us ample room to cook the tagine. We found that the spices didn't really need much adjustment—in other big batch recipes, the spices seem to get exponentially stronger when doubling or tripling a recipe, so normally we'd cut back. But with tagine the true nature of this dish is the spices, so we needed their full force. And unlike some of our other big batch stews, in which only a portion of the meat needs to be browned to give the stew a rich meaty taste, this chicken tagine really benefited from browning all of the chicken, no matter how big the batch. That meant up to six batches of browned chicken for our largest quantity. In an attempt to save time elsewhere, we started cooking the onions in the stockpot at the same time the chicken was browning in the Dutch oven. This worked great. With these minor adjustments we now had a recipe that could serve up to 20 people—and because it can be made ahead of time and stored, it's a perfect choice for a gathering any night of the week.

FREEZE IT

Chicken Tagine

SERVES 6 TO 8

If your chicken breasts and thighs are on the large size, you may need to increase their corresponding cooking times. If the olives are particularly salty, give them a rinse. If you cannot find pitted olives, and don't want to pit them yourself, substitute pimiento-stuffed green olives, being sure to rinse them very well under cold running water. We recommend serving this dish with couscous.

1½	pounds boneless, skinless chicken breasts, trimmed (about 4 medium breasts)
1½	pounds boneless, skinless chicken thighs, trimmed (about 6 medium thighs)
	Salt and ground black pepper
½	cup unbleached all-purpose flour
5	tablespoons olive oil
2	large onions, halved and sliced ¼ inch thick
4	(2-inch-long strips) lemon zest from 2 lemons
8	medium garlic cloves, minced or pressed through a garlic press (about 8 teaspoons)
2½	teaspoons sweet paprika
1	teaspoon ground cumin
½	teaspoon ground ginger
½	teaspoon ground coriander
½	teaspoon ground cinnamon
¼	teaspoon cayenne pepper
4	cups low-sodium chicken broth
2	tablespoons honey
1	pound carrots (about 6 medium), peeled and sliced ½ inch thick
2	cups Greek green olives, pitted and halved
1	cup dried apricots, chopped
	Water, as needed for reheating
6	tablespoons juice from 2 lemons (for serving)
2	medium garlic cloves, mashed to a fine paste (for serving)
½	teaspoon grated lemon zest from 1 lemon (for serving)
¼	cup minced fresh cilantro leaves (for serving)

1. Pat the chicken dry with paper towels and season with salt and pepper. Coat the chicken with the flour, shaking to remove the excess. Heat 2 tablespoons of the oil in a large Dutch oven over medium-high heat until just smoking. Add half of the chicken and cook until golden brown on both sides, 6 to 9 minutes. Transfer the browned chicken to a plate. Repeat with 2 more tablespoons of the oil and the remaining chicken; transfer to the plate.

2. Add the remaining 1 tablespoon oil to the pot and return to medium heat until shimmering. Add the onions, lemon zest strips, and 1 teaspoon salt and cook, stirring often, until the onions are browned at the edges, about 7 minutes (add 1 tablespoon of water if the pan gets too dark). Stir in the minced garlic, paprika, cumin, ginger, coriander, cinnamon, and cayenne and cook until fragrant, about 30 seconds. Slowly whisk in the broth and honey, scraping up any browned bits.

3. Add the browned chicken thighs, bring to a simmer, and cook for 5 minutes. Add the carrots and then arrange the breasts in a single layer on top of the carrots. Return to a simmer, cover, and cook until an instant-read thermometer inserted into the thickest part of a breast registers 160 degrees, 10 to 15 minutes.

4. Transfer all of the chicken to a clean plate and tent with foil. Stir in the olives and apricots, return to a simmer, and cook, uncovered, until the liquid has thickened slightly and the carrots are tender, about 6 minutes. Meanwhile, shred the chicken into bite-sized pieces (alternatively, the breasts and thighs can be left whole). Remove the strips of lemon zest, stir in the shredded chicken, and season with salt and pepper to taste.

5. To STORE: Let the tagine cool, uncovered at room temperature, for 45 minutes. Transfer to an airtight container(s) and refrigerate for up to 2 days. For freezing instructions, see page 182.

6. To SERVE: Spoon off and discard any hardened fat from the top and transfer the tagine to a Dutch oven. Cover and bring to a simmer over medium-low heat, gently stirring occasionally, about 30 minutes (adding additional water as needed to adjust the sauce consistency). Off the heat, stir in the lemon juice, mashed garlic, and grated lemon zest and let stand for 5 to 10 minutes. Season with salt and pepper to taste. Sprinkle the cilantro over individual portions before serving.

TO SERVE RIGHT AWAY

Stir the lemon juice, mashed garlic, and grated lemon zest into the tagine with the shredded chicken in step 4 and let sit off the heat for 5 to 10 minutes. Sprinkle the cilantro over individual portions before serving.

To Make a Big Batch

Adjust the Chicken Tagine recipe as follows using the ingredient amounts listed in the chart on page 194. You will need a 12-quart stockpot.

TO SERVE 12 TO 14

- Following the directions in step 1, brown the chicken in a 12-inch skillet in 4 batches, using 2 tablespoons of oil per batch. Add some of the broth and scrape up the browned bits as needed to prevent them from burning between batches (see page 179); pour off and reserve the broth with bits.
- Cook the onions in a 12-quart stockpot as directed in step 2, using the remaining 2 tablespoons of oil and increasing the cooking time to 10 minutes.

- Continue to build the sauce as directed in step 2.
- Simmer the thighs as directed in step 3, increasing the cooking time to 10 minutes.
- Add the carrots and chicken breasts and continue to cook as directed in step 3, increasing the cooking time to 10 minutes.
- Finish the stew as directed in step 4, increasing the cooking time to 10 minutes.
- Store the stew as directed in step 5.
- Reheat as directed in step 6, using a large stockpot (at least 12 quarts), 50 to 60 minutes.

TO SERVE 18 TO 20

- Following the directions in step 1, brown the chicken in a 12-inch skillet in 6 batches, using 2 tablespoons of oil per batch. Add some of the broth and scrape up the browned bits as needed to prevent them from burning between batches (see page 179); pour off and reserve the broth with bits.
- Cook the onions in a 12-quart stockpot as directed in step 2, using the remaining 2 tablespoons of oil and increasing the cooking time to 10 minutes.

INGREDIENTS: Green Olives

Until we began developing our recipe for Chicken Tagine (page 192), we were unaware of just how many green olive varietals were out there—from the $1.99-a-jar cocktail garnish to the $12.99-per-pound French import. Our curiosity (and taste buds) piqued, we scoured local supermarket shelves and returned with nearly two dozen jars and deli containers. We tried all of the olives plain, then cooked them in our Chicken Tagine. Straight from the container, the hands-down favorites were the imported (and somewhat expensive) French samples—Lucques and Picholines—for their buttery, bright flavor and al dente texture. The brawny Spanish Queens/Gordals were lackluster and mealy to some, "pleasantly mild" and soft to others. The Manzanillas (of martini fame) were faulted for an overwhelming pungency but praised for their meatiness. There were two styles of Greek Conservolea—spice brined and salt brined—and both styles were "cracked," a method of curing that involves breaking the olive's flesh to extract a bitter compound called oleuropein. Tasters thought this curing method left the spice-brined Conservoleas lacking in olive flavor but found the salt-brined variety bright and full. When incorporated into a cooked dish, most of the olives maintained their initial characteristics, with one exception. Rather than tainting our recipe with their initially unpleasant pungency and bitterness, the Manzanillas gained points for a newfound depth of flavor and meaty texture. Still superior in both categories, however, were the cracked, salt-brined Conservoleas (Divina was our favorite brand), which topped the charts for being "bright" and "snappy"—and which, at $3.79 a jar, left a little green in our wallets.

CONSERVOLEAS
Bright and snappy

LUCQUES
Crisp and buttery

MANZANILLAS
Pungent and meaty

PICHOLINES
Tiny and bright

SPANISH QUEENS
Brawny and mild

MAKING A BIG BATCH OF CHICKEN TAGINE

INGREDIENTS	SERVES 12 TO 14	SERVES 18 TO 20
BONELESS, SKINLESS CHICKEN BREASTS	3 pounds (about 8 medium breasts)	4½ pounds (about 12 medium breasts)
BONELESS, SKINLESS CHICKEN THIGHS	3 pounds (about 12 medium thighs)	4½ pounds (about 18 medium thighs)
ALL-PURPOSE FLOUR	½ cup	¾ cup
OLIVE OIL	10 tablespoons	14 tablespoons
ONIONS	3 large (about 4½ cups)	4 large (about 6 cups)
LEMON ZEST STRIPS	7 strips (3 lemons)	10 strips (4 lemons)
GARLIC, MINCED	14 medium cloves (about ¼ cup)	21 medium cloves (about 7 tablespoons)
SWEET PAPRIKA	1½ tablespoons	2½ tablespoons
GROUND CUMIN	2 teaspoons	2½ teaspoons
GROUND GINGER	1 teaspoon	1½ teaspoons
GROUND CORIANDER	1 teaspoon	1½ teaspoons
GROUND CINNAMON	1 teaspoon	1½ teaspoons
CAYENNE PEPPER	½ teaspoon	¾ teaspoon
LOW-SODIUM CHICKEN BROTH	8 cups	12 cups
HONEY	¼ cup	6 tablespoons
CARROTS	2 pounds	3 pounds
GREEN OLIVES	4 cups	6 cups
DRIED APRICOTS	2 cups	3 cups
FRESH LEMON JUICE	⅔ cup (4 lemons)	¾ cup (4 lemons)
GARLIC, MASHED TO A PASTE	3 medium cloves	5 medium cloves
GRATED LEMON ZEST	1 teaspoon	1½ teaspoons
MINCED FRESH CILANTRO	6 tablespoons	½ cup

- Continue to build the sauce as directed in step 2.
- Simmer the thighs as directed in step 3, increasing the cooking time to 10 minutes.
- Add the carrots and chicken breasts and continue to cook as directed in step 3, increasing the cooking time to 10 to 15 minutes.

- Finish the stew as directed in step 4, increasing the cooking time to 15 minutes.
- Store the stew as directed in step 5.
- Reheat as directed in step 6, using a large stockpot (at least 12 quarts), about 1½ hours.

BASIC CHILI

CHILI IS A NATURAL MAKE-AHEAD MEAL—ITS flavor actually improves after a day or two in the refrigerator. However, of all the chili recipes we have tried, most are either incredibly bland and watery or overly spicy. We wanted a thick chili made with ground meat, tomatoes, beans, and chili powder; one that was spiced but not spicy. And because chili is so popular at Super Bowl parties and the like, we wanted to successfully scale up the recipe to feed a crowd.

Most recipes for basic chili begin by sautéing onions and garlic. Tasters liked red bell peppers added to these aromatics but rejected other options, including green bell peppers, celery, and carrots. After this first step, things became less clear. The most pressing concerns were the spices (how much and what kind) and the meat (how much ground beef and whether or not to add another meat). There were also the cooking liquid (what kind, if any) and the proportions of tomatoes and beans to consider.

Addressing the spices first, we started with a basic formula of 2 pounds ground beef, 4 tablespoons chili powder, 2 teaspoons ground cumin, and 1 teaspoon each red pepper flakes and dried oregano. While many recipes add the spices to the pot after the beef has been browned, we found that the ground spices added in this manner were harsh and bitter. We preferred to add the spices with the aromatics—they developed their flavors fully when they had direct contact with the hot cooking oil.

To find the perfect balance of spices and heat level, we used chili powder—typically 80 percent ground dried red chiles, with the rest a mix of garlic powder, onion powder, oregano, ground cumin, and salt—and supplemented it with more cumin and oregano, and tossed in some cayenne for heat. We also tried other spices, such as cinnamon, allspice, and coriander, but only the coriander was welcomed as part of our working recipe—cinnamon and allspice were both out of place.

With the spices resolved, we focused on the meat. Starting with 2 pounds, we made batches of chili with 90 percent, 85 percent, and 80 percent lean ground beef. As it turns out, we decided that

there is such a thing as too much fat. An orange pool of fat floated to the top of the chili made with ground chuck (80 percent lean beef). At the other end of the spectrum, the chili made with 90 percent lean beef was a tad bland—not bad, but not as full-flavored as the chili made with 85 percent lean beef, which was our final choice.

We wondered if our chili would benefit from the addition of another type of meat in place of some of the ground beef. After trying batches of chili made with ground pork, diced pork loin, sliced sausage, and sausage removed from its casing and crumbled, tasters preferred the hearty flavor and slightly creamy texture of an all-beef chili.

For the liquid component, we tried beer, water, chicken broth, beef broth, wine, and no liquid at all except for that in the tomatoes—the last chili was beefy tasting and by far the best. Since we knew that tomatoes were definitely going into our chili, we first added two small (14.5-ounce) cans of diced tomatoes. Not only was this clearly not enough, the tomatoes were also too chunky, and they were floating in a thin sauce. We then tried two 28-ounce cans of diced tomatoes, pureeing the contents of one can to reduce the chunkiness and thicken the sauce. The chunkiness was reduced, but the sauce was still watery. Next we tried one can of tomato puree and one can of diced tomatoes, and

---

INGREDIENTS: Chili Powder

While there are numerous applications for chili powder, its most common use is in chili. Considering that most chili recipes rely so heavily on chili powder (ours uses a whopping ¼ cup), we thought it was necessary to gather up as many brands as possible to find the one that made the best chili. To focus on the flavor of the chili powder, we made a bare-bones version of our chili and rated each chili powder for aroma, depth of flavor, and level of spiciness. Tasters concluded that Spice Islands Chili Powder was the clear winner. This well-known supermarket brand was noted by one taster as having "a big flavor that stands out among the others."

THE BEST CHILI POWDER
Spice Islands Chili Powder is our favorite chili powder, with its perfect balance of chili flavor and spiciness.

tasters unanimously preferred the thicker consistency of this combination.

We tried cooking the chili with the lid on, with the lid off, and with the lid on in the beginning and off at the end. The chili cooked with the lid on was too soupy; that cooked with the lid off too dense. Keeping the lid on for half of the cooking time and then removing it was ideal—the consistency was rich but not too thick. Just under two hours of gentle simmering was sufficient to meld the flavors; shorter cooking times yielded chili that was soupy or bland—or both.

Our attention now turned to the beans. Two 15-ounce cans proved to be the right amount, and tasters liked dark red kidney beans or black beans because both keep their shape better than light red kidney beans, the other common choice. As for when to add the beans, many chili recipes add them at the end of cooking, with the goal of letting them heat through without causing them to fall apart. We found that this method makes for tasteless beans floating in an extremely flavorful chili. We prefer to add the beans with the tomatoes. We found that the more time the beans spent in the pot, the better they tasted.

With our recipe basically complete, it was time to make some big batches. Careful not to disturb our perfect ratio of meat to beans to tomatoes, we scaled the chili up to serve 12 to 14 and 18 to 20. We quickly found out that the chili was well suited to big batch cooking and only required a few minor adjustments. Using a 12-quart stockpot to accommodate the augmented amounts of ingredients, we increased the simmering time to give the larger volumes of chili time to concentrate flavors and thicken properly. Most importantly, we found it necessary to hold back some of the red pepper flakes and cayenne—batches made with the greater amounts were a little too spicy for our liking. This chili freezes exceptionally well, so even if you are not planning on serving a crowd, you can still make a big batch and freeze half.

SCIENCE: Why Do Stews and Chilis Thicken Over Time?

We simmered, stored, reheated, and tasted a lot of stews and chilis for this chapter, and one recurring theme throughout was the necessity of adding liquid to the pot during the reheating phase—whether our dish came out of the refrigerator or the freezer.

To find out why this step was essential, we contacted our food science expert. We explained our procedure—carefully ladling our stews and chilis (with no spilling!) into airtight containers and placing some in the refrigerator and some in the freezer to await reheating. He first explained that true airtight containers with well-fitting snap-on lids lose very little moisture to the outside of the container, but the contents can lose moisture to the airspace inside the container. Therefore, it is helpful to select a container that you can fill close to the top. In a fairly full container, not much moisture will be lost to the airspace inside the container (only 5 to 10 percent).

But there are other forces at work here. During storage, the contents will increase in thickness, depending on the nature and concentration of solids in the stew. Any source of starch, such as flour, rice, potatoes, and many vegetables (tomatoes, onions, carrots), will slowly leach out polysaccharides, like starch molecules, pectins, and other soluble fibers. These substances will continue to thicken the stew over time, especially at low temperatures, by binding water. In addition, any gelatin formed by the breakdown of collagen (connective tissue) in the meat will also continue to thicken the stew.

Gradually, as the stew becomes thicker, a process known as syneresis sets in. Syneresis is a process in which the polysaccharide and gelatin molecules form a tighter and tighter molecular network, gradually squeezing out excess moisture. This freed moisture can evaporate into the airspace above the stew, and eventually condense and freeze on the inside of the lid, thus lowering the moisture content of the stew. The extent of syneresis is time dependent. In other words, the more time the stew sits, the more syneresis takes place.

The bottom line? Fill the airtight container close to the top to minimize the loss due to evaporation. (If you are freezing the stew, you will need to leave a little additional room to allow for the contents to expand.) And to restore the original thickness of the sauce, add liquid—either water or chicken broth—in small, incremental amounts to compensate for both the thickening affect of the ingredients and the evaporation of moisture.

FREEZE IT

All-American Beef Chili

SERVES 6 TO 8

Serve with lime wedges, diced fresh tomatoes, diced avocado, sliced scallions, chopped red onion, minced cilantro, sour cream, and/or shredded Monterey Jack or cheddar cheese.

2	tablespoons vegetable oil
2	medium onions, minced
I	red bell pepper, stemmed, seeded, and cut into ½-inch pieces
6	medium garlic cloves, minced or pressed through a garlic press (about 2 tablespoons)
¼	cup chili powder
I	tablespoon ground cumin
2	teaspoons ground coriander
I	teaspoon red pepper flakes
I	teaspoon dried oregano
½	teaspoon cayenne pepper
	Salt
2	pounds (85 percent lean) ground beef
2	(15-ounce) cans dark red kidney beans, rinsed and drained
I	(28-ounce) can diced tomatoes
I	(28-ounce) can tomato puree
	Water, as needed and for reheating

1. Heat the oil in a large Dutch oven over medium heat until shimmering but not smoking. Add the onions, bell pepper, garlic, chili powder, cumin, coriander, pepper flakes, oregano, cayenne, and 1 teaspoon salt and cook, stirring often, until the vegetables are softened, about 10 minutes.

2. Increase the heat to medium-high. Stir in the beef, 1 pound at a time, and cook while breaking up the chunks with a wooden spoon until no longer pink, about 3 minutes per pound.

3. Stir in the beans, tomatoes, and tomato puree, and bring to a boil. Cover and simmer over low heat, stirring occasionally, for 1 hour.

4. Uncover and continue to simmer, stirring occasionally, until the beef is tender and the chili is dark, rich, and slightly thickened, about 45 minutes more. (If the chili begins to stick to the bottom of the pot, stir in ½ cup water and continue to simmer.) Season with salt to taste.

5. To STORE: Let the chili cool, uncovered at room temperature, for 45 minutes. Transfer to an airtight container(s) and refrigerate for up to 2 days. For freezing instructions, see page 182.

6. To SERVE: Spoon off and discard any hardened fat from the top and transfer the chili to a Dutch oven. Cover and bring to a simmer over medium-low heat, gently stirring occasionally, about 30 minutes (adding additional water as needed to adjust the sauce consistency). Season with salt to taste before serving.

TO SERVE RIGHT AWAY

After seasoning with salt to taste in step 4, cover, and let sit for 5 minutes before serving.

To Make a Big Batch

Adjust the All-American Beef Chili recipe as follows using the ingredient amounts listed in the chart on page 198. You will need a 12-quart stockpot.

TO SERVE 12 TO 14

- Cook the vegetables as directed in step 1, increasing the cooking time to 15 to 17 minutes.

TEST KITCHEN TIP: Turkey Chili

This recipe can easily be made with 93 percent lean ground turkey. Follow the recipe for All-American Beef Chili, adding half of the ground turkey, ½ pound at a time, in step 2. To add the second half of the turkey, follow the illustration and pack the meat together into a ball, then pinch off teaspoon-sized pieces and stir them in after the chili has simmered for 1 hour in step 3. (This applies to the big batches as well.) This technique for adding the turkey makes the ground turkey appear crumbled, like ground beef, rather than stringy.

197

MAKING A BIG BATCH OF ALL-AMERICAN BEEF CHILI

INGREDIENTS	SERVES 12 TO 14	SERVES 18 TO 20
VEGETABLE OIL	¼ cup	¼ cup
ONIONS	4 medium	5 medium
RED BELL PEPPER	2 medium	2 medium
GARLIC	12 medium cloves (¼ cup)	15 medium cloves (5 tablespoons)
CHILI POWDER	½ cup	⅔ cup
GROUND CUMIN	2 tablespoons	2½ tablespoons
GROUND CORIANDER	4 teaspoons	1½ tablespoons
RED PEPPER FLAKES	2 teaspoons	2 teaspoons
DRIED OREGANO	2 teaspoons	2½ teaspoons
CAYENNE PEPPER	¾ teaspoon	¾ teaspoon
GROUND BEEF	4 pounds	5 pounds
KIDNEY BEANS	4 (15-ounce) cans	5 (15-ounce) cans
DICED TOMATOES	2 (28-ounce) cans	2 (28-ounce) cans
TOMATO PUREE	2 (28-ounce) cans	3 (28-ounce) cans

- Add the beef, 1 pound at a time, following the directions in step 2.
- Simmer the chili as directed in steps 3 and 4, increasing the uncovered simmering time to 1½ hours.
- Store the chili as directed in step 5.
- Reheat as directed in step 6, using a large stockpot (at least 12 quarts), 50 to 60 minutes.

TO SERVE 18 TO 20
- Cook the vegetables as directed in step 1, increasing the cooking time to 18 to 20 minutes.
- Add the beef, 1 pound at a time, following the directions in step 2.
- Simmer the chili as directed in steps 3 and 4, increasing the uncovered simmering time to 2 hours.
- Store the chili as directed in step 5.
- Reheat as directed in step 6, using a large stockpot (at least 12 quarts), about 1½ hours.

WHITE CHICKEN CHILI

A LIGHTER COUNTERPART TO TRADITIONAL RED-meat chili, white chicken chili contains a chicken and white bean base, simmered in chicken broth and, depending on the recipe, a wide range of ingredients, including diced tomatoes, green salsa, pickled chiles, and chili powder. White chili is a fairly recent creation, which is good news because it allowed us free rein in somewhat new territory, without any risk of breaking the rules. We wanted to develop the ultimate recipe for white chicken chili—one that could be made ahead of time, would freeze well, and could be scaled up to serve a crowd.

White chicken chili is typically made with either diced or ground chicken. We started with ground chicken. Tasters were not sold—they wanted more substance and a meatier texture. We then prepared a batch with diced breast meat chicken that we simmered in chicken broth. This was certainly an improvement, but the cubed meat was reminiscent of the tasteless, dry meat floating in canned chicken soup. Instead, we browned bone-in, skin-on chicken breasts, simmered them in chicken broth just until they were cooked through, and then shredded the meat and returned it to the mix at the end. Tasters raved about the flavor the meat contributed to the chili, and the shredded meat was hearty and moist. But obstacles still remained.

The first few batches we made contained the requisite onions and garlic, but also red bell peppers, tomato paste, diced tomatoes, and chili powder—ingredients found in several of the recipes we researched. The flavor these ingredients contributed was welcomed, but some of our tasters rejected all things red from the start, under the premise that white chili should have nothing in common with red chili. This left us with no flavor base.

We thought about adding green bell peppers, but wanted something that packed a little more punch. We settled on a combination of poblano, Anaheim, and jalapeño chiles. The dark blackish-green poblanos and the long green Anaheims

provided sweetness and depth, while the jalapeños imparted richness and heat. To save ourselves from having to dice lots of onions and chiles, we pulsed them in the food processor until chunky.

Sautéing the onions and chiles before simmering them in the chili contributed an excellent green-chile flavor, but tasters complained that the broth was too thin. We decided to remove a portion of the cooked chiles and puree them with an equal amount of beans and chicken broth. The chiles and beans that were pureed not only added body to the broth, but they melded with the other ingredients and intensified the flavors of the chili. At the same time, the chiles that remained in the chili and the whole beans that were added imparted a nice contrast in texture.

The backbone was in place, but we still needed to iron out the details of seasonings. We knew that we would need to add some spices at the beginning of the cooking process in order to build flavor, but the chili would also benefit from some bright, fresh flavors added just before serving. Using a generous

---

TESTING NOTES

BUILDING A FLAVORFUL WHITE CHICKEN CHILI

We tried a variety of white chicken chili recipes and most were watery and flavorless pots of chili with rubbery chicken. Here are the steps we now take to avoid such problems.

1. Use Bone-in, Skin-on Chicken Breasts
Using bone-in, skin-on chicken breasts (which are browned, poached, and then shredded) produces a chili with a full chicken flavor—ground chicken looks unattractive and tastes rubbery and chewy.

2. Use a Trio of Chiles
To get the most robust green-chile flavor, we found that using a combination of poblanos, Anaheims, and jalapeños was key. A measly can of green chiles, simply does not provide enough chile flavor.

3. Puree the Chile Mixture, Broth, and Beans
Processing I cup each of the sautéed chile mixture, beans, and chicken broth in the food processor deepens the flavor of the chili and thickens the broth to the perfect consistency.

hand with ground cumin and ground coriander produced a mellow yet complex effect on the chili, while scallions, cilantro, and lime juice, along with a little raw minced jalapeño for heat, provided the perfect finish.

When it came to making the chili a day or two ahead of time (or freezing it), we determined that it was best to hold aside some of the lime juice as well as the scallions, cilantro, oregano, and raw minced jalapeño and add them to the chili just before serving so they remained vibrant. Additionally, we found that the chili tends to thicken during storage (see "Why Do Stews and Chilis Thicken Over Time?," page 196), but the consistency can easily be adjusted with additional water or broth when it is reheated. All that was left to do was figure out how to make the recipe in bigger batches, without compromising the chili's great flavor and texture.

For the larger batches, we found that it was best to brown the chicken breasts in batches in a 12-inch skillet. To speed up the cooking process, we sautéed the chile–onion mixture with the garlic

and spices in the stockpot in which we were going to simmer the chili, while the chicken was browning. Aside from these minor adjustments it was just a matter of altering the cooking times to account for the greater volumes of ingredients.

This white chili pleased even the skeptics and self-proclaimed chili aficionados in the test kitchen. Some still refused to categorize it as "chili," preferring to refer to it as a chicken stew, but they gobbled it up nevertheless and were more than happy to take home the leftovers for their freezer.

FREEZE IT

White Chicken Chili
SERVES 6 TO 8

For more heat, include the chile seeds and ribs when mincing. If Anaheim chiles cannot be found, add an additional poblano and jalapeño to the chili. This dish can also be made successfully substituting bone-in, skin-on chicken thighs for the chicken breasts. If using thighs, increase the simmering time in step 4 to about 45 minutes. Serve with sour cream, tortilla chips, and lime wedges.

INGREDIENTS: Chicken Broth

What chicken broth product should you reach for you when you haven't got time for homemade? We recommend choosing a mass-produced, lower-sodium brand and checking the label for evidence of mirepoix ingredients, such as carrots, celery, and onions. Swanson Certified Organic was our clear favorite, but the less expensive, third-place Swanson Natural Goodness was solid as well. And if you don't mind adding water, Better Than Bouillon chicken base came in a very close second and was the favorite of several tasters.

THE BEST CHICKEN BROTHS

SWANSON CERTIFIED ORGANIC CHICKEN BROTH
Swanson's newest broth won tasters over with "very chickeny, straightforward, and honest flavors," a hearty aroma, and restrained "hints of roastiness."

BETTER THAN BOUILLON CHICKEN BASE
We're not ready to switch to a concentrated base for all our broth needs (you have to add water), but the 18-month refrigerator shelf life means it's a good replacement for dehydrated bouillon.

SWANSON "NATURAL GOODNESS" CHICKEN BROTH
Swanson's standard low-sodium broth was full of chicken flavor, but several tasters noted an out-of-place tartness reminiscent of lemon.

IMAGINE ORGANIC FREE RANGE CHICKEN BROTH
This broth had very prominent onion notes, which some tasters loved and others disliked. Some panelists weren't fond of the pale yellow color.

3 pounds bone-in, skin-on split chicken breasts (about 4 breasts, 10 to 12 ounces each)
　Salt and ground black pepper
3 tablespoons vegetable oil
3 medium poblano chiles, seeds and ribs removed, chiles chopped coarse
3 medium Anaheim chiles, seeds and ribs removed, chiles chopped coarse
2 medium jalapeño chiles, seeds and ribs removed, chiles chopped coarse
2 medium onions, chopped coarse
6 medium garlic cloves, minced or pressed through a garlic press (about 2 tablespoons)
1 tablespoon ground cumin
1½ teaspoons ground coriander
2 (15-ounce) cans cannellini beans, drained and rinsed
4 cups low-sodium chicken broth
　Water, as needed for reheating
¼ cup minced fresh cilantro leaves (for serving)
4 scallions, sliced thin (for serving)
3 tablespoons juice from 3 limes, plus extra for serving
1 tablespoon minced fresh oregano leaves (for serving)
1 medium jalapeño chile, seeds and ribs removed, chile minced (for serving)

1. Pat the chicken dry with paper towels and season with salt and pepper. Heat 2 tablespoons of the oil in a large Dutch oven over medium-high heat until just smoking. Brown the chicken, skin side down, until deep golden, about 6 minutes. Transfer the chicken to a plate and remove and discard the skin.

2. While the chicken is browning, pulse the chiles (except the minced jalapeño) and the onions in 2 batches in a food processor to the consistency of chunky salsa, 10 to 12 one-second pulses, stopping to scrape down the sides of the workbowl as needed.

3. Add the remaining 1 tablespoon oil to the pot and return it to medium heat until shimmering. Add the processed chile-onion mixture, garlic, cumin, coriander, and 1 teaspoon salt. Cook, stirring often, until the vegetables are softened, about 10

minutes. Remove the pot from the heat and transfer 1 cup of the chile mixture to the food processor.

4. Process the chile mixture with 1 cup of the beans and 1 cup of the broth until smooth, about 20 seconds. Stir the chile-bean mixture, remaining 3 cups broth, and browned chicken into the pot, and bring to a boil. Cover and simmer over medium-low heat, stirring occasionally, until an instant-read thermometer inserted into the thickest part of a breast registers 160 degrees, 10 to 15 minutes.

5. Transfer the chicken to a clean plate. Stir in the remaining beans and continue to simmer, uncovered, until the beans are heated through and the chili has thickened slightly, about 10 minutes. Shred the chicken into bite-sized pieces, discarding the bones. Stir in the shredded chicken and season with salt and pepper to taste.

6. TO STORE: Let the chili cool, uncovered at room temperature, for 45 minutes. Transfer to an airtight container(s) and refrigerate for up to 2 days. For freezing instructions, see page 182.

7. TO SERVE: Spoon off and discard any hardened fat from the top and transfer the chili to a Dutch oven. Cover and bring to a simmer over medium-low heat, gently stirring occasionally, about 30 minutes (adding water as needed to adjust the sauce consistency). Stir the cilantro, scallions, lime juice, oregano, and minced jalapeño into the chili and season with salt and pepper to taste.

TO SERVE RIGHT AWAY

After stirring in the shredded chicken in step 5, stir in the cilantro, scallions, lime juice, oregano, and minced jalapeño and season with salt and pepper to taste. Cover and let sit for 5 minutes before serving.

To Make a Big Batch

Adjust the White Chicken Chili recipe as follows using the ingredient amounts listed in the chart on page 202. You will need a large skillet and a 12-quart stockpot.

TO SERVE 12 TO 14

• In a large skillet, brown the chicken in 2 batches, following the directions in step 1, using 2 tablespoons of oil for each batch.

MAKING A BIG BATCH OF WHITE CHICKEN CHILI

INGREDIENTS	SERVES 12 TO 14	SERVES 18 TO 20
BONE-IN, SKIN-ON CHICKEN BREASTS	5½ pounds (about 8 breasts, 10 to 12 ounces each)	7½ pounds (about 11 breasts, 10 to 12 ounces each)
VEGETABLE OIL	5 tablespoons	7 tablespoons
POBLANO CHILES	5 medium	7 medium
ANAHEIM CHILES	5 medium	7 medium
JALAPEÑO CHILES	3 medium	5 medium
ONIONS	3 medium	5 medium
GARLIC	9 medium cloves (3 tablespoons)	12 medium cloves (¼ cup)
GROUND CUMIN	1½ tablespoons	2 tablespoons
GROUND CORIANDER	1½ teaspoons	2 teaspoons
CANNELLINI BEANS	3 (15-ounce) cans	4 (15-ounce) cans
LOW-SODIUM CHICKEN BROTH	7 cups	9 cups
MINCED CILANTRO	⅓ cup	⅔ cup
SCALLIONS	7	10
LIME JUICE	5 tablespoons	7 tablespoons
MINCED FRESH OREGANO	1½ tablespoons	2 tablespoons
MINCED JALAPEÑO CHILE	1 medium	1 medium

- Pulse the chiles and onions in 3 batches, as directed in step 2.
- While the chicken browns, cook the processed chile-onion mixture in a 12-quart stockpot, increasing the cooking time to 15 minutes.
- Following the directions in step 4, process 1¾ cups of the beans, 1¾ cups of the chile-onion mixture, and 1¾ cups of the broth until smooth, then add to the stockpot.
- Simmer the chicken as directed in step 4, increasing the cooking time to 20 minutes.
- Simmer the beans as directed in step 5, increasing the cooking time to 20 minutes.
- Store the chili as directed in step 6.
- Reheat as directed in step 7, using a large stockpot (at least 12 quarts), 50 to 60 minutes.

TO SERVE 18 TO 20

- In a large skillet, brown the chicken in 3 batches, following the directions in step 1, using 2 tablespoons of oil for each batch.
- Pulse the chiles and onions in 4 batches, as directed in step 2.
- While the chicken browns, cook the processed chile-onion mixture in a 12-quart stockpot, increasing the cooking time to 20 minutes.
- Following the directions in step 4, process 2½ cups of the beans, 2½ cups of the chile-onion mixture, and 2½ cups of the broth until smooth, then add to the stockpot.
- Simmer the chicken as directed in step 4, increasing the cooking time to 30 minutes.
- Simmer the beans as directed in step 5, increasing

the cooking time to 30 minutes.
• Store the chili as directed in step 6.
• Reheat as directed in step 7, using a large stockpot (at least 12 quarts), about 1½ hours.

BOLOGNESE SAUCE

THERE ARE SCORES OF DELICIOUS MEAT-BASED sauces made in Italy and elsewhere, but we think rich, dense Bolognese (it comes from the city of Bologna, hence the name) is the very best. And, since Bolognese sauce requires hours of slow simmering (unattended, for the most part), it is the perfect thing to make a big batch of on a lazy Sunday afternoon to have on hand—it stores well in the refrigerator and freezer—to toss with pasta for a quick weeknight dinner.

Unlike other meat sauces in which tomatoes dominate (think jars of spaghetti sauce with flecks of meat in a sea of tomato puree), Bolognese sauce is about the meat, with the tomatoes in a supporting role. Bolognese also differs from many tomato-based meat sauces in that it contains dairy—butter, milk, and/or cream. The dairy gives the beef an especially sweet, appealing flavor. We wanted to determine what makes a truly great version of this classic and, while we were at it, we wanted to scale the recipe up so we had enough to serve a crowd, or to freeze and eat later.

All Bolognese recipes can be broken down into three steps. First, vegetables are sautéed in fat. Ground meat is then browned in the pan. The final step is the addition of liquids and slow simmering over very low heat.

Using this process, a good Bolognese sauce should acquire certain characteristics. It must be quite thick in order to heighten the richness and intensity of the beef flavor: Every mouthful should be decadent. The sauce should also be smooth, with the meat disintegrated into tiny pieces, so that it will easily coat the pasta. And finally, it should be complex, with a good balance of flavors—the meat flavor should be first and foremost, but there should be sweet, salty, and acidic flavors in the background.

After an initial round of testing in which we made five different styles of Bolognese, we had a recipe we liked pretty well. We found that we preferred using only onions, carrots, and celery as the vegetables, and that we liked them sautéed in butter rather than oil. We also discovered that a combination of ground beef, veal, and pork made this sauce especially complex and rich tasting. The veal adds finesse and delicacy to the sauce, while the pork makes it sweet.

The liquid element of the recipe, however, proved more difficult to sort out. The secret to a great Bolognese sauce is the sequential reduction of various liquids with the sautéed meat and vegetables. The idea is to build flavor and tenderize the meat, which has toughened during the browning phase. Many recipes insist on a particular order for adding these liquids. The most common liquid choices we uncovered in our research were milk, cream, stock, wine (both red and white), and tomatoes (either fresh, canned diced, crushed, or paste). We ended up testing numerous combinations to find the perfect balance.

Liquids are treated in two ways in Bolognese. In the earlier part of the cooking process, liquids are added to the pan and simmered briskly until fully evaporated, the point being to impart flavor rather than to cook the beef and vegetables. Wine is always treated this way; if the wine is not evaporated, the sauce will be too alcoholic. Milk and cream are often, but not always, treated this way. Later, either stock or tomatoes are added in greater quantity and allowed to cook off very slowly. These liquids add flavor, to be sure, but they also serve as the "cooking medium" for the sauce during the slow simmering phase.

We tested pouring wine over the browned meat first, followed by milk. We also tried them in the opposite order, milk and then wine. We felt that the meat cooked in milk first was softer and sweeter. As the bits of meat cook, they develop a hard crust that makes it more difficult for them to absorb liquid. Adding the milk first, when the meat is not crusty or tough, works better. The milk penetrates the meat, tenderizing it and making it especially sweet.

We tried using cream instead of milk, but felt that the sauce was too rich. Milk provides just enough dairy flavor to complement the meaty flavor. (Some recipes finish the sauce with cream. We found that cream added just before the sauce was done was also overpowering.) So we settled on milk as the first liquid for the sauce. For the second liquid, we liked both white and red wines, but we settled on white wine because it was a bit more delicate.

Now we moved on to the final element in most recipes, the cooking liquid. We did not like any of the recipes we tested with broth. Store–bought beef and chicken broths (we tried both) gave the sauce an odd chemical flavor when reduced so much, and we didn't think homemade stock was worth the effort. As for the tomato paste, we felt that it had

---

INGREDIENTS: Canned Diced Tomatoes

The conventional wisdom holds that canned tomatoes surpass fresh for much of the year because they are packaged at the height of ripeness. After holding side-by-side tests of fresh, off-season tomatoes and canned tomatoes while we were developing recipes for this book, we agree. But with so many brands of canned tomatoes available, there is an obvious question: Which brand tastes best? Having sampled eight brands of canned diced tomatoes, both plain and cooked into a simple sauce, we have the answer.

Depending on the season and the growing location, more than 50 varieties of tomato are used to make these products. Packers generally reserve the ripest, best-colored specimens for use as whole, crushed, and diced tomatoes, products in which consumers demand vibrant color and fresher flavor. Lower-grade tomatoes are generally used in cooked products, such as paste, puree, and sauce.

Before processing, the tomatoes are peeled by means of either steam—always the choice of Muir Glen, the only organic brand in our lineup—or a hot lye bath, which many processors currently favor. Because temperatures in lye peeling are not as high as those in steaming, many processors believe that lye leaves the layer of flesh just beneath the skin in better condition, giving the peeled tomato a superior appearance. Tasters, however, could not detect specific differences in the canned tomatoes based on this aspect of processing. Two of our three highly recommended products, Muir Glen and S&W, use steam, while the third, Redpack, uses lye.

After peeling, the tomatoes are sorted again for color and the presence of any obvious deficiencies, and then they're diced. After the diced tomatoes are sorted, the cans are filled with the tomatoes and topped off with salt and filler ingredients (usually tomato juice, but sometimes puree, which our tasters downgraded). Finally, the lids are attached to the cans and the cans are cooked briefly for sterilization, then cooled and dried so they can be labeled.

The flavor of a ripe, fresh tomato balances elements of sweetness and tangy acidity. The texture should be somewhere between firm and pliant, and certainly not mushy. Ideally, canned diced tomatoes should reflect the same combination of characteristics. Indeed, tasters indicated that excessive sweetness or saltiness (from the salt added during processing), along with undesirable texture qualities, could make or break a can of diced tomatoes. If the tasters thought that any one of these characteristics was out of whack, they downgraded that sample.

Oddly, no single flavor profile dominated. The three highly recommended brands, Muir Glen, S&W, and Redpack, displayed a range of flavor characteristics. Muir Glen led the ratings with a favorable balance of sweetness and saltiness and a notably "fresh" flavor in the sauce. Redpack also ranked high for its fresh flavor in the sauce. The same group of tasters, however, gave the thumbs up to S&W tomatoes, a brand noted for its bracing acidity and powerful, almost exaggerated, tomato flavor.

THE BEST CANNED DICED TOMATOES

MUIR GLEN ORGANIC DICED TOMATOES
"Sweet," "fresh tasting," and "most like fresh tomatoes" were some of the comments that explained why this brand of diced tomatoes received high marks.

S&W "READY-CUT" PREMIUM, PEELED TOMATOES
This West Coast brand was liked for its "tangy," "vibrant" flavor.

REDPACK DICED TOMATOES (known as Redgold on the West Coast)
These tomatoes exhibited a "fresh tomato-y taste" and a texture that "did not break down at all."

little to offer; with none of the bright acidity of canned whole tomatoes and no fresh tomato flavor, it produced a dull sauce.

We tried tomatoes three more ways—fresh, canned crushed, and canned diced. Fresh tomatoes did nothing for the sauce and were a lot of work, since we found it necessary to peel them. (If not peeled, the skins would separate during the long cooking process and mar the texture of the sauce.) Crushed tomatoes were fine but they did not taste as good as canned diced tomatoes that we pulsed in the food processor. Diced tomatoes have an additional benefit—the packing juice. Since Bolognese sauce simmers for quite a while, it's nice to have all that juice to keep the pot from scorching.

Our recipe was finally taking shape, with all the ingredients in place. But we still wanted to know if it was really necessary to cook Bolognese sauce over low heat and, if so, how long the sauce must simmer. We found that long, slow simmering is necessary to tenderize the meat and build flavor. When we tried to hurry the process along by cooking over medium heat to evaporate the tomato juice more quickly, the meat was too firm and the flavors were not melded.

We also tried browning the meat and then simmering it in milk in a separate pan. At the same time, we browned vegetables in another and then quickly reduced the wine and tomatoes over them. When the meat had absorbed all the milk, we added it to the tomato sauce and let it finish cooking for another 30 minutes. The whole process took an hour, start to finish. The sauce was good, to be sure, but the flavor was not nearly as complex and the texture not as smooth and creamy.

We finally concluded that generations of Italian cooks have been right: Low simmering over the lowest possible heat—a few bubbles may rise to the surface of the sauce at one time but it should not be simmering all over—is the only method that allows enough time for flavor to develop and for the meat to become especially tender. In fact, the meat begins to fall apart into a creamy mass when the sauce is done. There is no way to speed up this process.

As for the timing, we found that the sauce was too soupy after two hours on low heat and the meat was still pretty firm. After three to three-and-a-half hours, the meat was much softer, with a melt-in-the-mouth consistency. The sauce was dense and smooth at this point. We tried simmering the sauce for four hours but found no benefit. In fact, some batches cooked this long reduced too much and scorched a bit.

One final test involved browning the meat. Several sources suggest that deep browning builds flavor, a theory that makes some sense. However, other sources caution about overcooking the beef and suggest adding the first liquid to the pan as soon as the meat loses its raw color. We found this latter warning to be true. Sauces made with fully browned meat had a pleasant browned meat flavor, but the meat itself was not as tender and the sauce was not as smooth. When the first liquid was added to the pan as soon as the beef was no longer rosy, the sauce was more delicate and tender.

In the end, great Bolognese sauce is surprisingly simple to prepare—it just takes some time—and we found that it is just as easy to make double and triple batches. The larger batches simply need less butter to keep them from being too fatty, and of course benefit from a longer simmering time. The ingredients are readily available (you probably have most of them on hand) and the results are definitely worth the slow, but not very taxing, cooking process.

SCIENCE: Why Does Milk Make Meat Tender?

Browning adds flavor, but it also causes the protein molecules in ground meat to denature (unwind). As the proteins unwind, they link up to create a tighter network and squeeze out some of the water in the meat. Long simmering allows some of that liquid to be reabsorbed. But if you skip the browning and cook the meat in milk (or any other liquid) at the outset, you limit the temperature of the meat to about 212 degrees (browning occurs in dry heat and at higher temperatures). As a result, meat cooked in milk does not dry out and toughen, but remains tender. This means you can simmer the sauce just until the liquid has reduced to the right consistency rather than waiting for the meat to soften.

FREEZE IT

Classic Bolognese Sauce

MAKES ABOUT 4 CUPS, ENOUGH TO SAUCE
1 POUND OF PASTA

Meatloaf mixes can be very fatty, so be sure to skim the fat from the surface of the sauce as it simmers. Top each serving with a little grated Parmesan and pass additional grated cheese at the table.

3	tablespoons unsalted butter
¼	cup minced onion
¼	cup minced carrot
¼	cup minced celery
	Salt
1	pound meatloaf mix or ⅓ pound each ground beef chuck, ground veal, and ground pork
1½	cups whole milk
1½	cups dry white wine
3	(14.5-ounce) cans diced tomatoes, drained, with 1½ cups of the juice reserved

1. Melt the butter in a large Dutch oven over medium heat. Add the onion, carrot, celery, and 1 teaspoon salt and cook until softened, 6 to 8 minutes. Stir in the ground meat and cook while breaking up the chunks with a wooden spoon until no longer pink, about 3 minutes.

2. Stir in the milk, bring to a simmer, and cook until the milk is evaporated and only clear fat remains, about 25 minutes. Stir in the wine, bring to a simmer, and cook until it has evaporated, about 25 minutes.

3. Meanwhile, pulse the tomatoes in a food processor until slightly chunky, about eight 1-second pulses. Add the tomatoes and reserved tomato juice to the pot and bring to a bare simmer. Cook gently over low heat until the liquid has evaporated, 3 to 3½ hours. Season with salt to taste.

4. To STORE: Let the sauce cool, uncovered at room temperature, for 45 minutes. Transfer to an airtight container(s) and refrigerate for up to 2 days. For freezing instructions, see page 182.

5. To SERVE: Transfer the sauce to a medium saucepan, cover, and warm over medium-low heat.

Season with salt to taste. Thin the sauce with pasta cooking water and butter as needed when tossing it with pasta (see page 227).

TO SERVE RIGHT AWAY

After seasoning with salt to taste in step 3, serve as desired.

To Make a Big Batch

Adjust the Classic Bolognese Sauce recipe as follows using the ingredient amounts listed in the chart on page 207.

To Make a Double Batch

• Cook the vegetables and meat as directed in step 1, increasing the cooking time for the vegetables to 8 to 10 minutes and the meat time to 4 to 6 minutes.

• Add the milk and wine as directed in step 2, increasing the simmering time for each to 45 minutes.

• Simmer the sauce as directed in step 3, increasing the simmering time to 4 to 4½ hours.

To Make a Triple Batch

• Cook the vegetables and meat as directed in step 1, increasing the cooking time for the vegetables to 10 to 12 minutes and the meat time to 6 to 8 minutes.

• Add the milk and wine as directed in step 2, increasing the simmering time for each to 1 hour.

• Simmer the sauce as directed in step 3, increasing the simmering time to 5 to 5½ hours.

MARINARA SAUCE

WE HAVE ALL RESORTED TO CRACKING OPEN a jar of marinara sauce on a busy Tuesday night. While convenient, jarred marinara sauce is usually bland and watery or artificial tasting and cloyingly sweet. Here in the test kitchen, we think marinara is ideal for making in big batches and storing in the refrigerator or freezer. It is tasty tossed with pasta and Parmesan cheese or used as a sauce for pizza

MAKING A BIG BATCH OF CLASSIC BOLOGNESE SAUCE

INGREDIENTS	DOUBLE BATCH	TRIPLE BATCH
UNSALTED BUTTER	4 tablespoons	5 tablespoons
ONION	½ cup	¾ cup
CARROT	½ cup	¾ cup
CELERY	½ cup	¾ cup
MEATLOAF MIX	2 pounds	3 pounds
WHOLE MILK	2¼ cups	3 cups
DRY WHITE WINE	2¼ cups	1 (750-ml) bottle
DICED TOMATOES (RESERVED JUICE)	3 (28-ounce) cans (2½ cups juice)	4 (28-ounce) cans (3½ cups juice)

and Stromboli (page 310). Better yet, it is convenient—it is just as easy to thaw and reheat sauce from the freezer as it is to pop open a jar.

Our goal was to produce a complex sauce that didn't take all day to make. Weeding through hundreds of marinara recipes, we settled on testing not only a variety of "quick" versions, but also some that were cooked for longer than an hour. The differences were readily apparent. The quick sauces were generally thin and lacked depth of flavor. The long-cooked sauces got the complexity right, but most relied on an ambitious laundry list of ingredients to achieve it—not to mention a lot of time. The sauce we were after had to capture some of these robust flavors within the confines of fairly quick cooking.

Because vine-ripened tomatoes are available for such a short time during the year, we opted for canned. But canned tomatoes take up nearly half an aisle at our supermarket. Which one should we choose?

Crushed, pureed, and diced tomatoes offered the ultimate ease in sauce making: open can, dump contents into pan. But all three options have downsides. Pureed tomatoes go into the can already cooked, which imparts a stale, flat flavor to the final sauce. Crushed tomatoes are generally packed in tomato puree, resulting in the same problem. With these, our sauces came out tasting like unremarkable

homemade versions of the jarred spaghetti sauces you buy at the supermarket. With canned diced tomatoes, the problem was texture, not flavor. In the past, we've learned that manufacturers treat diced tomatoes with calcium chloride to keep the perfectly diced shape from turning to mush. That's fine for many dishes, but for recipes where a smooth consistency is desired, calcium chloride does its job too well, making the tomatoes harder to break down in a short amount of time—and the resulting sauces are oddly granular.

The only choice left, then, was canned whole tomatoes. (While whole tomatoes are also treated with calcium chloride, the chemical has direct contact with a much smaller percentage of the tomato.) The big drawback of using whole tomatoes in a sauce is that they have to be cut up. Chopping them on a cutting board was a mess. The solution was to dump the tomatoes into a strainer over a bowl and then hand-crush them, removing the hard core and any stray bits of skin left behind in the packing process.

That's when we made the first of several key decisions that would enable us to get long-simmered complexity in a short amount of time. Most marinara recipes call for simply adding a can (or two) of tomatoes to the pot, juice and all—and some even call for throwing in a can of water. Now that we were separating the solids from the juices anyway, why not experiment with adding less of the reserved liquid? The trick worked: By adding only 2½ cups of the drained juices from two cans of whole tomatoes (rather than the full 3½ cups we had collected) and omitting the extra water, we managed to cut the simmering time by almost 20 minutes.

Up until now we had been following the standard marinara procedure of sautéing aromatics (onions and/or garlic) in olive oil in a saucepan before adding the tomatoes, liquid, and flavorings, then simmering, but we felt that the sauce could use gutsier tomato flavor. Not only was the solution simple, but it also ended up being the single most important step in giving our quick sauce the complexity of a long-simmered one. Before adding the liquids and simmering, we sautéed the tomato meats until they glazed the bottom of the pan. Only then did we add the liquids, a normally routine step that, in our recipe, had become key to flavor as it essentially deglazed the pan. The difference in flavor was dramatic; the sauce now had a much richer tomato flavor.

With the tomato flavor under control, it was time to develop more complexity by introducing other ingredients. Many traditional Italian-American recipes resort to onions, carrots, wine, and sugar to compensate for weak-flavored canned tomatoes, to balance the tomatoes' acidity, or to simply make a more interesting sauce.

Onions added a pleasant sweetness, but carrots, although sweet, also added an earthy flavor that diminished that of the tomatoes. Sugar, added at the end of cooking (as in most recipes) proved to be the working solution to balance the flavors: Too much and our sauce began to taste like it came out of a jar; too little and the acidity overwhelmed the other flavors.

We were worried that wine, another acidic ingredient, would make the sauce unpalatable. We were dead wrong. Tasters loved the robust, complex flavor of the wine, and a mere ⅓ cup was just the right amount. Although red wine was preferred over white, the aging of the wine proved more important than the grape varietal. Wines with a heavy oak flavor rated lower than those with little to no oak presence. Therefore, Chianti and Merlot scored high marks, as did Cabernet Sauvignon.

We now had a good marinara ready to ladle and serve in less than an hour—about half the time of many recipes. Could we further bolster the complexity without adding unwanted minutes? On a hunch, we tried reserving a few of the uncooked

---

EQUIPMENT: Hand Blenders

A hand, or immersion, blender can save time and effort: No need to blend in batches, no need to wash a food processor—just rinse it off and toss it back in the drawer. But which brand is best? To find out, we gathered nine models, priced between $13 and $90, and put them to the test. All nine blenders whirred the chunks out of our marinara sauce easily, so we upped the ante. Pureeing broccoli soup was a more telling task: A few models finished the job in just 30 seconds, while the weaker blenders were still batting around small chunks after a minute. (Several manufacturers advise against continuous running for more than a minute.) What separated the movers from the shakers was pesto. Only three blenders, two Brauns and a KitchenAid, dispatched the herbs and nuts in quick order.

So what makes a better hand blender? The differences aren't obvious. As we've found in past tests, wattage means nothing when it comes to most appliances: The 200- and 400-watt Braun models performed equally well. We did, however, end up with a few design preferences: Stainless-steel shafts (rather than plastic) were not better performers, but they do resist staining and can be used in pots sitting over a flame. And come cleanup time, a removable blade end is best. In the end, KitchenAid's immersion blender ($49.99) was our favorite. Aside from a blending beaker, it offers no extras (some models come with fancy attachments), but it did as good a job at blending as most traditional blenders.

THE BEST HAND BLENDER
The KitchenAid immersion blender has minimal extras, but is as good as many traditional blenders.

canned tomatoes and adding them near the end. When we served this sauce alongside the earlier version, tasters were unanimous in their preference for the new sauce; just six tomatoes pureed into the sauce at the end added enough bright, fresh flavor to complement the deeper, full-bodied essence of the cooked sauce.

So far the sauce had little flavor from herbs beyond oregano. Fresh basil, added just before serving, contributed a floral aroma that complemented the sauce's careful balance of sweet and acid. Adjusting the salt and pepper and adding extra-virgin olive oil rounded things out. Finally, a sauce with complex flavors made in much less time than a traditional version and, aside from longer cooking times, doubling and tripling the sauce was effortless—making this sauce ideal for freezing to have on hand for a quick weeknight meal.

FREEZE IT

Marinara Sauce

MAKES ABOUT 4 CUPS, ENOUGH TO SAUCE
1 POUND OF PASTA

If you prefer a chunkier sauce, give it just three or four pulses in the food processor. Top each serving with a little grated Parmesan and pass additional grated cheese at the table.

2	(28-ounce) cans whole tomatoes packed in juice
3	tablespoons extra-virgin olive oil
1	medium onion, minced
	Salt
2	medium garlic cloves, minced or pressed through a garlic press (about 2 teaspoons)
½	teaspoon dried oregano
⅓	cup dry red wine
	Ground black pepper
	Sugar
2	tablespoons chopped fresh basil leaves (for serving)

1. Pour the tomatoes into a strainer set over a large bowl. Using your hands, open the tomatoes and discard any fibrous cores, skins, and seeds, being careful to keep the tomato meats whole; let the tomatoes drain for 5 minutes. Remove ¾ cup of the tomatoes from the strainer and set aside in a small bowl. Reserve 2½ cups of the tomato juice and discard the remainder of the juice.

2. Heat 2 tablespoons of the oil in a large Dutch oven over medium heat until shimmering but not smoking. Add the onion and 1 teaspoon salt and cook until softened and lightly browned, 5 to 7 minutes. Stir in the garlic and oregano and cook until fragrant, about 30 seconds.

3. Add the tomatoes from the strainer and increase the heat to medium-high. Cook, stirring occasionally, until the tomatoes begin to stick to the bottom of the pan and a brown glaze forms around the pan edges, 8 to 10 minutes. Add the wine and cook until thick and syrupy, about 1 minute. Add the reserved tomato juice and bring to a simmer; reduce the heat to medium-low and cook, stirring occasionally, until the sauce is thick, 8 to 10 minutes.

4. Pulse the sauce with the reserved tomatoes in a food processor (or insert an immersion blender, see page 208) until slightly chunky, about eight 2-second pulses. Return the sauce to the Dutch oven, add the remaining 1 tablespoon oil, and season with salt, pepper, and sugar to taste.

5. TO STORE: Let the sauce cool, uncovered at room temperature, for 45 minutes. Transfer to an airtight container(s) and refrigerate for up to 2 days. For freezing instructions, see page 182.

6. TO SERVE: Transfer the sauce to a medium saucepan, cover, and warm over medium-low heat. Stir in the basil and season with salt, pepper, and sugar to taste. Thin the sauce with pasta cooking water and extra-virgin olive oil as needed when tossing it with pasta (see page 227).

TO SERVE RIGHT AWAY
After seasoning with salt, pepper, and sugar to taste in step 4, serve as desired.

To Make a Big Batch
Adjust the Marinara Sauce recipe as follows using the ingredient amounts listed in the chart on page 210.

MAKING A BIG BATCH OF MARINARA SAUCE

INGREDIENTS	DOUBLE BATCH	TRIPLE BATCH
WHOLE TOMATOES	4 (28-ounce) cans	6 (28-ounce) cans
EXTRA-VIRGIN OLIVE OIL	¼ cup	5 tablespoons
ONIONS	2 medium	3 medium
GARLIC	4 medium cloves (4 teaspoons)	6 medium cloves (2 tablespoons)
DRIED OREGANO	1½ teaspoons	2 teaspoons
DRY RED WINE	⅔ cup	1 cup
CHOPPED FRESH BASIL	¼ cup	6 tablespoons

To Make a Double Batch
- Prep the tomatoes as directed in step 1, reserving 1½ cups of the tomatoes and 4 cups of the juice.
- Cook the onions in 3 tablespoons of the oil as directed in step 2, increasing the cooking time to 10 to 12 minutes.
- Cook the tomatoes as directed in step 3, increasing the cooking time to 10 to 12 minutes.
- Simmer the tomato sauce as directed in step 3, increasing the cooking time to 12 to 14 minutes.

To Make a Triple Batch
- Prep the tomatoes as directed in step 1, reserving 2¼ cups of the tomatoes and 6 cups of the juice.
- Cook the onions in 3 tablespoons of the oil as directed in step 2, increasing the cooking time to 14 to 16 minutes.
- Cook the tomatoes as directed in step 3, increasing the cooking time to 12 to 14 minutes.
- Simmer the tomato sauce as directed in step 3, increasing the cooking time to 18 to 20 minutes.
- Process the sauce in 2 batches.

PESTO

PESTO IS GREAT TO HAVE ON HAND TO transform plain pasta, chicken, a sandwich, or toasted bread into something fresh and thoughtful. Because pesto has so many uses, making big batches that can be stored in the refrigerator or freezer—and used at a moment's notice—makes a lot of sense. Over the years the traditional pesto, a hand-pounded basil and garlic sauce from the Italian province of Liguria, has succumbed to modern appliances and a broader range of ingredients. The term "pesto" now refers not only to a basil-based sauce but also to a multitude of pureed, oil-based sauces. Many of them have the advantage of using ingredients available in the dead of winter, when fresh basil can be very scarce and expensive. We wanted to stick to tradition and develop a recipe for classic pesto, but we also wanted to expand our repertoire to include the likes of toasted nuts and parsley, roasted red peppers, and mushrooms.

For all of our pesto recipes we found that, although we love garlic, the raw article can have a sharp, acrid taste that overwhelms everything else in the sauce. To subdue the garlic, we tried several approaches—roasting, sautéing, and infusing oil with garlic flavor—but found them all lacking. What we did like was toasting whole cloves in a warm skillet. This tamed the harsh garlic notes and loosened the skins from the cloves for easy peeling.

Along with toasting the garlic, the other keys to a flavorful sauce included using extra-virgin olive oil and finely grating a high-quality Parmesan cheese. As for the technique used for making the pesto, we relinquished the laborious, albeit traditional, mortar and pestle. We found that the food processor was the fastest way to produce a consistently good pesto, be it basil, nuts, roasted red peppers, or mushrooms.

With the basics down, we homed in on the details of each specific recipe. For classic pesto, the problem is that it often turns a murky color as it sits for any period of time. Supplementing the basil with parsley helped maintain the pesto's bright green color.

For the pestos with nuts (Classic Pesto and Nut and Parsley), we toasted the nuts in a dry skillet before processing to bring out their full flavor. (We then toasted the garlic in the empty pan.) Almonds are sweet but fairly hard, so they give pesto a coarse, granular texture. Walnuts are softer but still fairly meaty in texture and flavor. Pine nuts yield the smoothest, creamiest pesto. The choice is yours.

We found that deeply flavored roasted red peppers were complemented by the addition of shallot, as was the mushroom pesto, which got its intense mushroom flavor from a combination of roasted white mushrooms and dried porcini mushrooms.

Each of these recipes makes enough to sauce one pound of pasta, although it is virtually as easy to make a double or triple batch and store it in the refrigerator or freezer. The one trick we found when making larger batches of pesto is that it wasn't necessary to increase the garlic to the same degree as the other ingredients—it became harsh-tasting and overpowering. As for storing the pestos, we held out 1 tablespoon of the oil called for in each batch and poured it over the top to prevent it from turning an off-color or drying out.

FREEZE IT

Classic Pesto

MAKES ABOUT ¾ CUP, ENOUGH TO SAUCE
1 POUND OF PASTA

Don't limit yourself to just making pesto for pasta—use it to add a boost of flavor to soups, sandwiches, and pizza. When adding pesto to pasta, be sure to include a little pasta cooking water for proper consistency and even distribution.

¼ cup pine nuts, walnuts, or whole blanched almonds
3 medium garlic cloves, unpeeled
2 cups packed fresh basil leaves
7 tablespoons extra-virgin olive oil
2 tablespoons fresh parsley leaves
 Salt
¼ cup grated Parmesan cheese
 Ground black pepper

1. Toast the nuts in a medium skillet over medium heat, stirring frequently, until just golden and fragrant, 6 to 8 minutes. Transfer the nuts to a plate.

2. Add the garlic to the empty skillet. Toast, shaking the pan occasionally, until fragrant and the color of the cloves deepens slightly, about 7 minutes. Let the garlic cool, then peel and chop coarsely.

3. Process the nuts, garlic, basil, 6 tablespoons of the oil, parsley, and ½ teaspoon salt in a food processor until smooth, stopping to scrape down the sides of the workbowl as needed. Transfer the mixture to a small bowl, stir in the Parmesan, and season with salt and pepper to taste.

4. To store: Transfer to an airtight container(s), pour the remaining 1 tablespoon oil over the top, and refrigerate for up to 4 days or freeze for up to 1 month.

5. To serve: If frozen, thaw in the refrigerator for 24 hours or in the microwave at 50 percent power for 5 to 10 minutes, stirring every 2 minutes. Stir the pesto to recombine and season with salt and pepper to taste. Thin the pesto with pasta cooking water as needed when tossing it with pasta (see note).

TO SERVE RIGHT AWAY

Add all 7 tablespoons of the oil in step 3. After seasoning with salt and pepper to taste in step 3, serve as desired.

To Make a Big Batch

Adjust the Classic Pesto recipe as follows using the ingredient amounts listed in the chart on page 212.

To Make a Double Batch

• Toast all the nuts and garlic in a large skillet as directed in steps 1 and 2.

• Process the pesto as directed in step 3, using all but 2 tablespoons of the oil.

• Store the pesto as directed in step 4, using the remaining 2 tablespoons oil.

MAKING A BIG BATCH OF CLASSIC PESTO

INGREDIENTS	DOUBLE BATCH	TRIPLE BATCH
NUTS	½ cup	¾ cup
GARLIC	5 medium cloves	7 medium cloves
FRESH BASIL LEAVES	4 cups	6 cups
EXTRA-VIRGIN OLIVE OIL	⅔ cup	1¼ cups
FRESH PARSLEY LEAVES	¼ cup	6 tablespoons
PARMESAN CHEESE	1 ounce (½ cup)	1½ ounces (¾ cup)

To Make a Triple Batch

- Toast all the nuts and garlic in a large skillet as directed in steps 1 and 2.
- Process the pesto as directed in step 3, using all but 3 tablespoons of the oil.
- Store the pesto as directed in step 4, using the remaining 3 tablespoons oil.

FREEZE IT

Toasted Nut and Parsley Pesto

MAKES ABOUT 1 CUP, ENOUGH TO SAUCE
1 POUND OF PASTA

This recipe works with nearly any type of nut. When adding pesto to pasta, be sure to include a little pasta cooking water for proper consistency and even distribution.

1	cup pecans, walnuts, whole blanched almonds, skinned hazelnuts, unsalted pistachios, or pine nuts, or any combination thereof
3	medium garlic cloves, unpeeled
½	cup packed fresh parsley leaves
7	tablespoons extra-virgin olive oil
1	small shallot, chopped coarse (about 2 tablespoons)
	Salt
¼	cup grated Parmesan cheese
	Ground black pepper

1. Toast the nuts in a medium skillet over medium heat, stirring frequently, until just golden and fragrant,

4 to 5 minutes. Transfer the nuts to a plate.

2. Add the garlic to the empty skillet. Toast, shaking the pan occasionally, until fragrant and the color of the cloves deepens slightly, about 7 minutes. Let the garlic cool, then peel and chop coarsely.

3. Process the nuts, garlic, parsley, 6 tablespoons of the oil, shallot, and ½ teaspoon salt in a food processor until smooth, stopping to scrape down the sides of the workbowl as needed. Transfer the mixture to small bowl, stir in the Parmesan, and season with salt and pepper to taste.

4. TO STORE: Transfer to an airtight container(s), pour the remaining 1 tablespoon oil over the top, and refrigerate for up to 4 days or freeze for up to 1 month.

5. TO SERVE: If frozen, thaw in the refrigerator for 24 hours or in the microwave at 50 percent power for 5 to 10 minutes, stirring every 2 minutes. Stir the pesto to recombine and season with salt and pepper to taste. Thin the pesto with pasta cooking water as needed when tossing it with pasta (see note).

TO SERVE RIGHT AWAY

Add all 7 tablespoons of the oil in step 3. After seasoning with salt and pepper to taste in step 3, serve as desired.

To Make a Big Batch

Adjust the Toasted Nut and Parsley Pesto recipe as follows using the ingredient amounts listed in the chart above.

MAKING A BIG BATCH OF TOASTED NUT AND PARSLEY PESTO

INGREDIENTS	DOUBLE BATCH	TRIPLE BATCH
NUTS	2 cups	3 cups
GARLIC	5 medium cloves	7 medium cloves
FRESH PARSLEY LEAVES	1 cup	1½ cups
EXTRA-VIRGIN OLIVE OIL	⅔ cup	1¼ cups
SHALLOTS	2 small (¼ cup)	3 small (6 tablespoons)
PARMESAN CHEESE	1 ounce (½ cup)	1½ ounces (¾ cup)

To Make a Double Batch

- Toast all the nuts in a large skillet as directed in step 1.
- Process the pesto as directed in step 3, using all but 2 tablespoons of the oil.
- Store the pesto as directed in step 4, using the remaining 2 tablespoons oil.

To Make a Triple Batch

- Toast all the nuts in a large skillet as directed in step 1.
- Process the pesto as directed in step 3, using all but 3 tablespoons of the oil.
- Store the pesto as directed in step 4, using the remaining 3 tablespoons oil.

FREEZE IT

Mushroom Pesto with Parsley and Thyme

MAKES ABOUT 1½ CUPS, ENOUGH TO SAUCE 1 POUND OF PASTA

Be sure to roast the mushrooms until they are browned and crisp, otherwise they will make the pesto watery. When adding pesto to pasta, be sure to include a little pasta cooking water for proper consistency and even distribution.

10	ounces white mushrooms, wiped clean and sliced ¼ inch thick
9	tablespoons extra-virgin olive oil
	Salt and ground black pepper
3	medium garlic cloves, unpeeled
½	ounce dried porcini mushrooms
½	cup boiling water
1	small shallot, chopped coarse (about 2 tablespoons)
¼	cup packed fresh parsley leaves
1	tablespoon fresh thyme leaves
¼	cup grated Parmesan cheese

1. Adjust an oven rack to the lowest position and heat the oven to 450 degrees. Toss the sliced mushrooms with 2 tablespoons of the oil and season with salt and pepper. Spread evenly on a foil-lined rimmed baking sheet. Roast, stirring occasionally, until browned and crisp, about 25 minutes.

2. Meanwhile, toast the garlic in a medium skillet over medium heat, shaking the pan occasionally, until fragrant and the color of the cloves deepens slightly, about 7 minutes. Let the garlic cool, then peel and chop coarsely. Rehydrate the porcini in the water until softened, about 5 minutes. Strain the hydrating liquid through a fine-mesh strainer or coffee filter and set aside.

3. Process the roasted mushrooms, garlic, porcini and reserved liquid, shallot, parsley, thyme, ½ teaspoon salt, and 6 more tablespoons of the oil in a food processor until smooth, stopping to scrape down the sides of the workbowl as needed. Transfer the mixture to a small bowl, stir in the Parmesan, and season with salt and pepper to taste.

4. TO STORE: Transfer to an airtight container(s),

pour the remaining 1 tablespoon oil over the top, and refrigerate for up to 4 days or freeze for up to 1 month.

5. To serve: If frozen, thaw in the refrigerator for 24 hours or in the microwave at 50 percent power for 5 to 10 minutes, stirring every 2 minutes. Stir the pesto to recombine and season with salt and pepper to taste. Thin the pesto with pasta cooking water as needed when tossing it with pasta (see note).

TO SERVE RIGHT AWAY

Add the remaining 7 tablespoons oil in step 3. After seasoning with salt and pepper to taste in step 3, serve as desired.

To Make a Big Batch

Adjust the Mushroom Pesto with Parsley and Thyme recipe as follows using the ingredient amounts listed in the chart below.

To Make a Double Batch

• Roast the mushrooms as directed in step 1, using 3 tablespoons of the oil and increasing the cooking time to 40 minutes.
• Process the pesto as directed in step 3, using 7 more tablespoons of the oil.

• Store as directed in step 4, using the remaining 2 tablespoons oil.

To Make a Triple Batch

• Roast the mushrooms as directed in step 1, using 3 tablespoons of the oil and increasing the cooking time to 55 minutes.
• Process the pesto as directed in step 3, using 14 more tablespoons of the oil.
• Store as directed in step 4, using the remaining 3 tablespoons oil.

FREEZE IT

Roasted Red Pepper Pesto

MAKES ABOUT 1½ CUPS, ENOUGH TO SAUCE 1 POUND OF PASTA

Although we prefer the flavor of roasted fresh red bell peppers in this pesto, one (12-ounce) jar of roasted red peppers, rinsed, can be substituted. When adding pesto to pasta, be sure to include a little pasta cooking water for proper consistency and even distribution.

2 red bell peppers, prepared according to illustrations 1 through 4 on page 215
3 medium garlic cloves, unpeeled

MAKING A BIG BATCH OF MUSHROOM PESTO WITH PARSLEY AND THYME

INGREDIENTS	DOUBLE BATCH	TRIPLE BATCH
WHITE MUSHROOMS	1¼ pounds	2 pounds
EXTRA-VIRGIN OLIVE OIL	¾ cup	1¼ cups
GARLIC	5 medium cloves	7 medium cloves
DRIED PORCINI MUSHROOMS	1 ounce	1½ ounces
BOILING WATER	1 cup	1½ cups
SHALLOTS	2 small (about ¼ cup)	3 small (about 6 tablespoons)
FRESH PARSLEY LEAVES	½ cup	¾ cup
FRESH THYME LEAVES	2 tablespoons	3 tablespoons
PARMESAN CHEESE	1 ounce (½ cup)	1½ ounces (¾ cup)

7 tablespoons extra-virgin olive oil
1 small shallot, chopped coarse (about 2 tablespoons)
¼ cup packed fresh parsley leaves
1 tablespoon fresh thyme leaves
  Salt
¼ cup grated Parmesan cheese
  Ground black pepper

1. Adjust an oven rack to the top position. The oven rack should be 2½ to 3½ inches from the heating element. If it is not, set a rimmed baking sheet, turned upside down, on the oven rack to elevate the pan. Turn the broiler on and heat for 5 minutes. Lay the peppers, including tops and bottoms, skin side up on a foil-lined rimmed baking sheet. Broil until

the skins are charred and puffed but the flesh is still firm, 8 to 10 minutes, rotating the baking sheet halfway through the broiling time. Cover the peppers with foil and let stand to loosen the skins, about 5 minutes. Remove and discard the skins and cut the peppers into rough 2-inch pieces.

2. Meanwhile, toast the garlic in a medium skillet over medium heat, shaking the pan occasionally, until fragrant and the color of the cloves deepens slightly, about 7 minutes. Let the garlic cool, then peel and chop coarsely.

3. Process the peppers, garlic, 6 tablespoons of the oil, shallot, parsley, thyme, and ½ teaspoon salt in a food processor until smooth, stopping to scrape down the sides of the workbowl as needed. Transfer the mixture to small bowl, stir in the Parmesan, and

PREPARING BELL PEPPERS FOR ROASTING

1. Slice ¼ inch from the top and bottom of the bell pepper, then gently remove the stem from the top lobe.

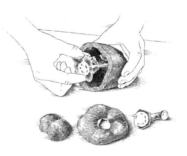

2. Pull the core out of the pepper.

3. Make a slit down 1 side of the pepper, then lay it flat, skin side down, in 1 long strip. Slide a sharp knife along the inside of the pepper to remove all ribs and seeds.

4. Arrange the strips of pepper and the top and bottom lobes skin side up on a foil-lined baking sheet. Flatten the strips with the palm of your hand.

5. Adjust an oven rack to the top position. If the rack is more than 3½ inches from the heating element, set another rimmed baking sheet, upside down, on the rack under the baking sheet with the peppers. Roast the peppers until the skin is charred and puffed up like a balloon but the flesh is still firm.

6. When the peppers are cool enough to handle, start peeling where the skin has charred and bubbled the most. The skin will come off in large strips.

MAKING A BIG BATCH OF ROASTED RED PEPPER PESTO

INGREDIENTS	DOUBLE BATCH	TRIPLE BATCH
RED BELL PEPPERS	4	6
GARLIC	5 medium cloves	7 medium cloves
EXTRA-VIRGIN OLIVE OIL	⅔ cup	1¼ cups
SHALLOTS	2 small (about ¼ cup)	3 small (about 6 tablespoons)
PARSLEY	½ cup	¾ cup
THYME	2 tablespoons	3 tablespoons
PARMESAN CHEESE	1 ounce (½ cup)	1½ ounces (¾ cup)

season with salt and pepper to taste.

4. To STORE: Transfer to an airtight container(s), pour the remaining 1 tablespoon oil over the top, and refrigerate for up to 4 days or freeze for up to 1 month.

5. To SERVE: If frozen, thaw in the refrigerator for 24 hours or in the microwave at 50 percent power for 5 to 10 minutes, stirring every 2 minutes. Stir the pesto to recombine and season with salt and pepper to taste. Thin the pesto with pasta cooking water as needed when tossing it with pasta (see note).

TO SERVE RIGHT AWAY

Add all 7 tablespoons of the oil in step 3. After seasoning with salt and pepper to taste in step 3, serve as desired.

To Make a Big Batch

Adjust the Roasted Red Pepper Pesto recipe as follows using the ingredient amounts listed in the chart above.

To Make a Double Batch

- Broil, steam, and skin the peppers as directed in step 1.
- Toast the garlic as directed in step 2.
- Process the pesto as directed in step 3, using all but 2 tablespoons of the oil.
- Store the pesto as directed in step 4, using the remaining 2 tablespoons oil.

To Make a Triple Batch

- Broil, steam, and skin the peppers in 2 batches as directed in step 1.
- Toast the garlic as directed in step 2.
- Process the pesto as directed in step 3, using all but 3 tablespoons of the oil.
- Store the pesto as directed in step 4, using the remaining 3 tablespoons oil.

MAKE-AHEAD SIMMERING SAUCES

SIMMERING SAUCES ARE A GREAT WAY to add flavor and interest to simply sautéed meats, poultry, and fish, or even shrimp, scallops, tofu, and vegetables. The popularity of jarred or bottled sauces is apparent from one glance at supermarket shelves—they are lined with them. And we understand why: On a busy weeknight, sometimes even making a simple pan sauce for chicken or fish seems like too much. For the time-pressed cook looking for an alternative to plain baked, broiled, or sautéed meat or fish night after night, these simmering sauces seem to be a lifesaver. Unfortunately, most of the supermarket sauces are either insipid or harsh in flavor, and watery or gloppy in texture, plus they are full of chemicals to stabilize for long storage. We knew we could do better.

We wanted to develop our own versions of

these sauces that would offer the same convenience of store-bought. After all, we agree: What could be easier than sautéing some boneless chicken breasts and then adding a creamy or Asian-inspired sauce you'd made days before (or taken out of your freezer)? We headed to the kitchen with three goals in mind: They had to be simple to make, they should use only pantry staples (no fussy ingredients), and they must be freezer friendly.

We started with a basic white wine–cream sauce that we planned to accent with fresh herbs—such as parsley, tarragon, or chives—just before serving. To give the sauce big, bold flavor, we reduced a mixture of chicken broth, white wine vinegar, lemon juice, white wine, and shallot. For richness, we added heavy cream. Tasters liked the fresh flavor of the cream added at the end. We also mixed a little cornstarch in with the cream to thicken the sauce slightly and give it a silkiness that was just right for drizzling over chicken, seafood, or even steamed vegetables.

Next, we wanted to develop a recipe for a tomato-based sauce, but instead of a plain, mild version, we wanted a sauce with some attitude—and a bold puttanesca was just the thing. Chock-full of high-impact ingredients, puttanesca is often dominated by one flavor: it is too fishy, too garlicky, too briny, or just plain too salty and acidic. We made a simple, satisfying version with aggressive but well-balanced flavors. To keep the anchovies from overpowering the sauce, we minced them to a fine paste and added them to the oil in the pan with the garlic, which allowed them to melt into the oil, and their characteristically full, rich flavor blossomed. And to preserve the flavor and texture of the olives, we added them to the sauce at the very last minute. This sauce is excellent tossed with pasta, but equally suited to pork, chicken, and hearty white fish.

Finally, we developed a Chinese-style sauce that could be used as a stir-fry sauce or as a glaze for grilled salmon, or drizzled over virtually any type of protein—pork, beef, chicken, seafood, and tofu. To keep the garlic, ginger, and scallions from burning, we mixed them with oil, started them in a cold saucepan, and cooked them just until fragrant. Then we added low-sodium chicken broth, oyster sauce, soy sauce, toasted sesame oil, and cornstarch, and simmered the mixture just until thickened. A sprinkling of toasted sesame seeds added welcome texture and a nutty flavor.

We wanted a spicy curry to add to the mix, but we knew the yogurt in Indian curry would cause problems when frozen. Instead, we used cream, which is much more resilient. We supplemented the curry powder with onion, garlic, and ginger for even more flavor. Lemon juice replicated yogurt's sour tang, while a little bit of honey rounded things out. We like this sauce best with chicken and tofu, although it is also good with shrimp. Fresh cilantro leaves are the perfect garnish for this sauce.

Finally, we created a rich and deeply flavored Mexican mole. Our mole is a simplified version of a traditional one. Instead of the usual laundry list of ingredients—half of which are typically a variety of chiles—we used pantry staples like chili powder, cocoa powder, cinnamon, onion, garlic, raisins, and peanut butter in our recipe. We simmered the mixture with chicken broth and tomatoes until it was thick and flavorful, and then pureed it until it was silky smooth. This sauce is superb with chicken, turkey, and pork, and a sprinkling of fresh cilantro just before serving will add both color and freshness.

For all of the sauces that follow, with the exception of the puttanesca, 1 cup is enough for 4 servings (about 1½ pounds of boneless chicken, turkey, or pork, fish fillets, or beef). For the puttanesca, because it is chunky, 2 cups is required for 4 servings. After browning the meat, poultry, or fish, simply pour the chosen sauce into the pan, bring to a simmer, and allow the meat, poultry, or fish to cook through.

When it comes down to it, you can use these sauces as you like—they are all quite versatile and certainly better than their store-bought counterparts. These sauces hold for up to two days in the refrigerator in an airtight container, but can also be frozen for up to one month. After reheating, it might be necessary to adjust their consistency with a little water before using. Also, be sure to taste the sauces before serving them—you might need to season them again as flavors can dull in the refrigerator or freezer.

FREEZE IT

White Wine–Cream Sauce

MAKES ABOUT 2 CUPS

In addition to being used as a simmering sauce, a few table-spoons can be drizzled over steamed broccoli, cauliflower, or asparagus. For even more flavor, stir in 2 tablespoons minced fresh parsley, tarragon, or olives before serving.

3	cups low-sodium chicken broth
6	tablespoons white wine vinegar
3	tablespoons juice from 1 lemon, plus extra as needed for serving
3	tablespoons dry white wine or vermouth
2	small shallots, minced (about ¼ cup)
	Salt
2	teaspoons cornstarch
1	cup heavy cream

1. Combine the broth, vinegar, lemon juice, wine, shallots, and ½ teaspoon salt in a medium saucepan over medium heat and simmer until reduced to about 1 cup, about 45 minutes.

2. Whisk the cornstarch into the cream until dissolved, then whisk the mixture into the simmering sauce. Continue to simmer the sauce until it is thickened, about 2 minutes. Season with salt to taste.

3. To STORE: Let the sauce cool, uncovered at room temperature, for 25 minutes. Transfer to an airtight container(s) and refrigerate for up to 2 days. For freezing instructions, see page 182.

4. To SERVE: Warm the sauce in a small sauce-pan over medium-low heat or in the microwave on high power for 5 to 10 minutes, stirring every 2 minutes. Season with salt and additional lemon juice to taste before serving.

TO SERVE RIGHT AWAY

After seasoning with salt to taste in step 2, serve as desired.

FREEZE IT

Puttanesca Sauce

MAKES ABOUT 4 CUPS

This recipe is great for pork, chicken, and hearty white fish like cod and halibut, but of course it also makes a great pasta sauce—this recipe makes enough for 1 pound of pasta.

MINCING A SHALLOT

1. Place the peeled bulb flat side down and make several slices parallel to the work surface, almost to (but not through) the root end. Then make a number of very closely spaced parallel cuts through the top of the shallot down to the work surface.

2. Finish the mincing by making very thin slices perpendicular to the lengthwise cuts.

2	tablespoons olive oil
4	medium garlic cloves, minced or pressed through a garlic press (about 4 teaspoons)
4	teaspoons minced anchovies (8 to 10 fillets)
1	teaspoon red pepper flakes
1	(28-ounce) can diced tomatoes
½	cup black olives, such as Gaeta, Alphonso, or kalamata, pitted and chopped coarse
¼	cup minced fresh parsley leaves
3	tablespoons capers, rinsed
	Salt and ground black pepper

1. Heat the oil, garlic, anchovies, and pepper flakes in a medium saucepan over medium heat. Cook, stirring frequently, until the garlic is fragrant but not browned, 2 to 3 minutes. Stir in the tomatoes and simmer until slightly thickened, about 10 minutes.

2. Stir the olives, parsley, and capers into the sauce and season with salt and pepper to taste.

3. To STORE: Let the sauce cool, uncovered at

room temperature, for 25 minutes. Transfer to an airtight container(s) and refrigerate for up to 4 days. For freezing instructions, see page 182.

4. To SERVE: Warm the sauce in a small saucepan over medium-low heat or in the microwave on high power for 5 to 10 minutes, stirring every 2 minutes. Season with salt and pepper to taste before serving.

TO SERVE RIGHT AWAY

After seasoning with salt and pepper to taste in step 2, serve as desired.

FREEZE IT

Ginger-Sesame Sauce
MAKE ABOUT 2 CUPS

In addition to being used as a simmering sauce, a few tablespoons of this sauce can be brushed on grilled salmon, chicken, pork, or beef, or used as a stir-fry sauce—simply stir-fry all of the meat and vegetables, pour the sauce into the pan, bring to a simmer, and toss to coat.

1½	cups low-sodium chicken broth
¼	cup oyster sauce
2	tablespoons soy sauce
4	teaspoons toasted sesame oil
4	teaspoons cornstarch
1	tablespoon minced scallion
1	tablespoon minced or grated fresh ginger
3	medium garlic cloves, minced or pressed through a garlic press (about 1 tablespoon)
1	teaspoon vegetable oil
1	tablespoon toasted sesame seeds

1. Mix the broth, oyster sauce, soy sauce, sesame oil, and cornstarch together in a medium bowl and set aside. Cook the scallion, ginger, garlic, and vegetable oil in a medium saucepan over medium heat, stirring frequently, until fragrant but not browned, 2 to 3 minutes.

2. Whisk the oyster sauce mixture to recombine, then add to the saucepan and bring to a simmer. Cook, stirring frequently, until the sauce thickens, 1 to 2 minutes. Stir in the sesame seeds.

3. To STORE: Let the sauce cool, uncovered at room temperature, for 25 minutes. Transfer to an airtight container(s) and refrigerate for up to 4 days. For freezing instructions, see page 182.

4. To SERVE: Warm the sauce in a small saucepan over medium-low heat or in the microwave on high power for 5 to 10 minutes, stirring every 2 minutes.

TO SERVE RIGHT AWAY

After stirring in the sesame seeds in step 2, serve as desired.

MINCING ANCHOVIES
Anchovies often stick to the side of a chef's knife, making it hard to cut them into small bits. Here are two better ways to mince them.

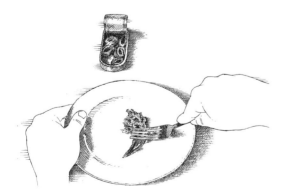

1. Use a dinner fork to mash delicate anchovy fillets into a paste. Mash the fillets on a small plate to catch any oil the anchovies give off.

2. A garlic press will turn anchovies into a fine puree. This method is especially handy when you have already dirtied the press with garlic.

Indian Curry Sauce

MAKES ABOUT 2 CUPS

*We recommend stirring ¼ cup minced fresh cilantro leaves
into the sauce before serving.*

1	small onion, minced
2	tablespoons vegetable oil
3	medium garlic cloves, minced or pressed through a garlic press (about 1 tablespoon)
1	tablespoon minced or grated fresh ginger
1	tablespoon curry powder
2½	cups low-sodium chicken broth
4	teaspoons cornstarch
1	teaspoon honey
½	cup heavy cream
1	tablespoon juice from 1 lemon
	Salt and ground black pepper

1. Cook the onion, oil, garlic, ginger, and curry powder in a medium saucepan over medium heat, stirring often, until fragrant, 2 to 3 minutes. Stir in the broth and simmer until reduced to 1½ cups, about 30 minutes.

2. Whisk the cornstarch and honey into the cream until dissolved, then whisk the mixture into the simmering sauce. Simmer until the sauce thickens, 2 to 3 minutes. Stir in the lemon juice and season with salt and pepper to taste.

3. To STORE: Let the sauce cool, uncovered at room temperature, for 25 minutes. Transfer to an airtight container(s) and refrigerate for up to 4 days. For freezing instructions, see page 182.

4. To SERVE: Warm the sauce in a small saucepan over medium-low heat or in the microwave on high power for 5 to 10 minutes, stirring every 2 minutes. Season with salt and pepper to taste before serving.

TO SERVE RIGHT AWAY

After seasoning with salt and pepper to taste in step 2, serve as desired.

Mole

MAKES ABOUT 2 CUPS

*We recommend stirring ¼ cup minced fresh cilantro leaves
into the sauce before serving.*

3	tablespoons vegetable oil
1	medium onion, minced
2	tablespoons chili powder
2	tablespoons cocoa powder
½	teaspoon ground cinnamon
⅛	teaspoon ground cloves
3	medium garlic cloves, minced or pressed through a garlic press (about 1 tablespoon)
2	cups low-sodium chicken broth
1	(14.5-ounce) can diced tomatoes, drained
¼	cup raisins
2	tablespoons peanut butter
	Salt and ground black pepper

1. Heat the oil in a medium saucepan over medium-high heat until shimmering but not smoking. Add the onion, chili powder, cocoa powder, cinnamon, and cloves and cook until the onion is softened, 5 to 7 minutes. Stir in the garlic and cook until fragrant, about 30 seconds.

2. Stir in the broth, tomatoes, raisins, and peanut butter and cook, stirring occasionally, until thickened and flavorful, about 20 minutes. Season with salt and pepper to taste.

3. Puree the sauce in a blender (or food processor) until smooth, about 20 seconds.

4. To STORE: Let the sauce cool, uncovered at room temperature, for 25 minutes. Transfer to an airtight container(s) and refrigerate for up to 4 days. For freezing instructions, see page 182.

5. To SERVE: Warm the sauce in a small saucepan over medium-low heat or in the microwave on high power for 5 to 10 minutes, stirring every 2 minutes. Season with salt and pepper to taste before serving.

TO SERVE RIGHT AWAY

After pureeing the sauce in step 3, serve as desired.

6

CASSEROLES

CASSEROLES

WHO DOESN'T LOVE THE IDEA OF AN ENTIRE meal in one dish? Pull a casserole from the fridge or freezer, pop it into the oven, and a hot, satisfying dinner is just minutes away. For this chapter, we immediately had visions of stocking our freezer with all our favorites—chicken pot pie, macaroni and cheese, lasagna—the possibilities were endless. The reality however, turned out to be less perfect. As we began to bake our way through our favorite recipes, we found that we couldn't expect these recipes to stand up to the chill of being stored without adverse effect. Pitfalls included pasta turning to mush, vegetables becoming flavorless and drab, and chicken drying out. We needed to rethink the way we prepared these casseroles for the make-ahead cook. At the same time, we wanted to give the cook the option to serve the dishes straight away, if desired.

Because so many casseroles are pasta-based, we were determined to tackle the pasta issue head on. For some pasta casseroles, such as Baked Ziti (page 225) and Creamy Baked Penne and Chicken Casseroles (pages 245–246), we found it was important to cook the pasta just halfway, then combine it with a generous amount of sauce thinned with pasta cooking water or chicken broth. With this method, the undercooked pasta soaked up some sauce in baking, cooking through in the process, yet enough sauce remained to moisten the finished dish. And the formerly thin sauce thickened up nicely during baking.

With make-ahead lasagnas, it was no surprise that we relied on no-boil noodles, as we prefer them in the test kitchen for regular lasagna. What was surprising, was that the flat lasagna noodles held up better upon storage than the curly lasagna noodles. The curly noodles are somewhat thicker and, upon soaking in the tomato sauce, turned chewy. Moreover, the curly noodles made a somewhat warped-looking lasagna, while the flat noodles made perfectly even layers of lasagna.

Frozen vegetables have long been considered a convenient option, but we had no idea how convenient until we used them in our make-ahead casseroles. It was a breeze to simply toss a bag of frozen peas and carrots into our casseroles and pot pies, rather than spending time peeling and cubing carrots. Because frozen vegetables are parcooked, they could be added to our casseroles while still frozen and then could stand up to the simmering or baking time required, coming out bright-colored and toothsome. Using frozen vegetables also helped in our recipes that had a crust on top, like our pot pies or tamale pies (pages 263–264). Placing a crust or batter directly onto piping hot filling can prevent the topping from baking properly, but adding the frozen vegetables to the filling cools it down fast so that the topping bakes up perfectly.

And in our casseroles featuring chicken breasts, we found that to prevent the chicken from drying out, it was important to cook the breasts whole. (Precut white-meat chicken dried out time and again, so in Chicken Enchiladas (page 254) we used rich, dark-meat thighs.) Furthermore, we found that poaching the breasts directly in the sauces boosted the moistness of the chicken and improved the overall flavor of the sauce. The chicken could then be shredded and added back to the filling and still remained tender and juicy.

We don't believe casseroles are necessarily one-size-fits-all, so we scaled our casseroles down and up to suit everyone's needs. While our master recipes were designed to fit a 13 by 9-inch baking dish, serving six to eight, we also understand that's sometimes too much for some households to consume at one time. Our solution? Bake Half, Freeze Half. In this feature, we explain how to divide the dish between two 8 by 8-inch casseroles (each serving four) or among three 9 by 3-inch loaf pans (each serving two to three), along with reheating and freezing instructions, so they bake up perfect every time.

And for occasions that call for feeding a crowd (read: holiday open houses, block parties, church suppers), we scaled up perpetual favorites, such as Baked Ziti (page 225), Lasagna (pages 230–234), Macaroni and Cheese (page 241), and Chicken and Rice (pages 248–250)—all to serve from 16 to 18. If it was as easy as doubling or halving ingredients, we would have left the instructions at that, but in many cases, adjustments for ingredient amounts, assembly, and baking turned out to be a whole lot more particular. After baking more than 50 batches of supersized lasagnas, we know what we're talking about!

Whether your family is large or small, we hope that with our make-ahead casserole recipes and multiple storage instructions, you'll be able to stock your freezer with all your favorites, making your next meal as easy as bake and serve.

BAKED ZITI

WHAT CHURCH SUPPER OR POTLUCK DINNER would be complete without baked ziti? This Italian-American dish sounds simple enough. Combine cooked pasta with tomato sauce, then add cheese and maybe some meatballs, sausage, or even eggplant. But if this dish is so easy to prepare, why are most versions dry, bland, and downright unappealing? And what about making baked ziti ahead? Forget about it. Most of the time, the dish is so dry it cuts into dense, stiff squares, or the pasta absorbs so much sauce that the dish is a bland, mushy mess. We wanted to develop a terrific recipe for baked ziti—tender noodles, tasty tomato sauce, and gooey cheese. And, we wanted to find a way to prepare this dish in advance and still have it taste fresh a few days later.

Mozzarella binds the noodles together and makes this baked casserole incredibly rich. Eight ounces of whole-milk mozzarella was just right for a pound of pasta. More made this dish too gooey. Tasters, however, found the cheesy flavor a bit quiet—after all, mozzarella is very mild, so we added a few ounces of Parmesan for a cheesy flavor boost.

While the mozzarella is the binder in baked ziti, it's the tomato sauce that keeps things moist. You can use your favorite jarred tomato sauce for convenience or you can make the sauce from scratch. We prefer a simple marinara, which relies on pureed whole or diced tomatoes for the best flavor and a smooth texture. (See more about marinara on page 206.) We also found that we had to dilute the tomato sauce with some of the pasta cooking water before tossing it with the pasta—

6 cups of diluted sauce to 1½ pounds of pasta. The extra moisture prevents the pasta from drying out in the fridge.

On the other hand, to conquer any soggy pasta problem, we made sure to undercook our pasta, so that after the casserole had baked the ziti would be perfectly al dente.

This baked ziti was good, but a little dull. The solution? We added a layer of ricotta cheese to the center of the casserole. This also helped keep the pasta moist and added enough interest to please everyone. As discovered in prior testing, we prefer whole milk ricotta to low-fat or nonfat ricotta in make-ahead dishes because whole milk retains its flavor when chilled and stored. Two tablespoons of olive oil stirred into the ricotta gave it some additional richness and flavor. Once assembled, the dish can be baked straight away or wrapped with plastic wrap and stored in the fridge for up to 2 days or frozen for up to 1 month.

We tested a variety of baking dishes and decided on a relatively shallow dish because it allowed the pasta to heat through quickly. More time in the oven only dried out the noodles or made them overly soft. With that in mind, we found that a hot 400-degree oven was best, yielding a casserole with tender pasta with just enough chew. A final step we wouldn't do without: A handful of chopped fresh basil, sprinkled over the top of the casserole, provides a burst of flavor and color to the finished dish.

In addition to our classic version made with mozzarella, ricotta, and marinara, we developed one variation with crumbled sweet Italian sausage.

FREEZE IT

Baked Ziti with Ricotta Cheese

SERVES 6 TO 8

We prefer to make this dish with homemade Marinara Sauce (page 209). For convenience, however, you can substitute jarred tomato sauce—you'll need about 4½ cups (see page 228 for our tasting of supermarket tomato sauces). If you find that your jarred sauce is a little bland, stir in up to 2 tablespoons olive oil for a boost in flavor.

12 ounces whole milk ricotta cheese (about 1½ cups)

4 tablespoons extra-virgin olive oil (see note)
  Salt and ground black pepper

12 ounces fresh whole milk mozzarella cheese, shredded (about 3 cups)

3 ounces Parmesan cheese, grated (about 1½ cups)

1½ pounds ziti or other short, tubular pasta

4½ cups Marinara Sauce (page 209) or jarred tomato sauce (see note)

¼ cup chopped fresh basil leaves (for serving)

1. Bring 6 quarts of water to a boil in a large pot over high heat.

2. Meanwhile, mix the ricotta cheese, 2 tablespoons of the olive oil, ½ teaspoon salt, and ½ teaspoon pepper together; set aside. In a separate bowl, toss the mozzarella and Parmesan together until combined; set aside.

3. Add 1½ tablespoons salt and the pasta to the boiling water and cook, stirring occasionally, until the pasta is just beginning to soften, about 5 minutes. Reserve 1½ cups of the pasta cooking water, then drain the pasta. Return the drained pasta to the pot and stir in the marinara sauce, remaining 2 tablespoons oil, and the reserved pasta cooking water.

4. Pour half of the sauced pasta into a 13 by 9-inch baking dish. Drop large spoonfuls of the ricotta mixture evenly over the pasta, then pour the remaining sauced pasta over the ricotta layer. Sprinkle the top of the ziti evenly with the mozzarella mixture.

5. To STORE: Wrap the dish tightly with plastic wrap and then foil and refrigerate for up to 2 days or freeze for up 1 month. (If frozen, the casserole must be thawed completely in the refrigerator, about 24 hours.)

6. To SERVE: Adjust an oven rack to the middle position and heat the oven to 400 degrees. Remove the plastic wrap and cover the dish tightly with aluminum foil that has been sprayed with vegetable oil spray (or use nonstick foil). Bake until the sauce bubbles lightly around the edges, 30 to 40 minutes. Remove the foil and continue to bake until the cheese begins to brown in spots and the casserole is completely heated through, 25 to 30 minutes longer. Sprinkle with the basil before serving.

TO SERVE RIGHT AWAY

After topping with the mozzarella in step 4, bake the casserole in 400-degree oven, uncovered, until the sauce is bubbling and the cheese is browned, 25 to 35 minutes. Sprinkle with the basil before serving.

Bake Half, Freeze Half

Follow the recipe for Baked Ziti with Ricotta Cheese or Baked Ziti with Italian Sausage, and divide the ingredients between two 8 by 8-inch casserole dishes (each will serve 4), or three 9 by 3-inch loaf pans (each will serve 2 to 3). The casseroles can be baked right away, covered tightly with plastic wrap and refrigerated for up to 2 days, or frozen for up to 1 month. See reheating instructions below:

TO BAKE IMMEDIATELY

Bake the casserole in a 400-degree oven, uncovered, until bubbling and the cheese is browned in spots, 20 to 25 minutes.

TO BAKE IF REFRIGERATED

Unwrap the dish and cover tightly with aluminum foil that has been sprayed with vegetable oil spray (or use nonstick foil). Bake in a 400-degree oven until the sauce bubbles lightly around the edges, about 25 minutes. Remove the foil and continue to bake until hot throughout and the cheese is browned in spots, about 20 minutes longer.

TO BAKE IF FROZEN

Thaw the casserole completely in the refrigerator, about 24 hours, then follow the instructions above for "To Bake if Refrigerated."

To Supersize

SERVES 16 TO 18

Adjust the Baked Ziti with Ricotta Cheese recipe as follows using the ingredient amounts listed in the chart on page 227. A Dutch oven is large enough to accommodate cooking the sauce, but to boil the ziti, you will need an extra-large

SUPERSIZING BAKED ZITI

INGREDIENTS	SERVES 16 TO 18
RICOTTA CHEESE	24 ounces (3 cups)
EXTRA-VIRGIN OLIVE OIL	9 tablespoons
MOZZARELLA CHEESE	18 ounces (4½ cups)
PARMESAN CHEESE	6 ounces (3 cups)
ZITI	3 pounds
MARINARA SAUCE	9 cups
CHOPPED FRESH BASIL	½ cup

stockpot (at least 12 quarts). And to bake the ziti, you will need a large, disposable baking pan (about 16 by 11 inches), supported by a sturdy, rimmed baking sheet.

TO ASSEMBLE AND STORE
• Mix the ricotta with 3 tablespoons of the olive oil, 1 teaspoon salt, and 1 teaspoon pepper.
• Bring 2 gallons water to a boil in an extra-large stockpot, then season with 2 tablespoons salt and cook the pasta as directed in step 3. Reserve 2½ cups of the pasta cooking water before draining.
• Stir the sauce, remaining 6 tablespoons oil, and 2½ cups reserved pasta cooking water into the cooked pasta.
• Assemble the baked ziti in a large disposable aluminum baking pan (about 16 by 11 inches), supported by a sturdy rimmed baking sheet.
• Wrap tightly with plastic wrap and then foil and refrigerate for up to 2 days, or freeze for up to 1 month.

TO BAKE IMMEDIATELY
Unwrap the pan and cover tightly with aluminum foil that has been sprayed with vegetable oil spray (or use nonstick foil). Bake in a 400-degree oven until the sauce is beginning to bubble lightly around the edges, about 15 minutes. Remove the foil and continue to bake until hot throughout and lightly browned on top, about 30 minutes longer.

TO BAKE IF REFRIGERATED
Unwrap the pan and cover tightly with aluminum

foil that has been sprayed with vegetable oil spray (or use nonstick foil). Bake in a 400-degree oven until the sauce is beginning to bubble lightly around the edges, about 1½ hours. Remove the foil and continue to bake until hot throughout and lightly browned on top, 30 to 35 minutes longer.

TO BAKE IF FROZEN
Thaw the casserole completely in the refrigerator, about 48 hours, then follow the instructions above for "To Bake if Refrigerated."

➤ VARIATION
Baked Ziti with Italian Sausage
This variation can easily be supersized to serve 16 to 18. Simply double the amount of sausage below and refer to the chart for Supersizing Baked Ziti (above) for the remaining ingredients as well as for instructions on assembling, storing, and serving the ziti.

Cook 1 pound sweet and hot Italian sausages, casings removed, in a 12-inch nonstick skillet over medium-high heat, breaking the meat into small pieces with a wooden spoon, until the sausage loses its raw color, about 5 minutes. Drain the sausage on a paper towel–lined plate and set aside. Follow the recipe for Baked Ziti with Ricotta Cheese, stirring the sausage into the pasta with the reserved cooking water and marinara.

TEST KITCHEN TIP:
Reserving the Pasta Water

When draining pasta, it's easy to forget to reserve some of the pasta cooking water (for adding to the sauce or to moisten a dry pasta dish), so try this: Before cooking the pasta, set up the colander for draining it in the sink, then place a measuring cup inside the colander. It's sure to nudge your memory at the appropriate moment.

INGREDIENTS:
Supermarket Tomato Sauces

In several of our recipes, jarred pasta sauce can be a real time-saver. But does the brand make a difference? To find out, we collected nine of the nation's top-selling marinara-style sauces, then amassed a new group of tasters—nineteen fifth- and sixth-graders from a local school. With our crack team of test kitchen tasters supplemented by some tasters-in-training, we sampled the sauces plain and on cooked ziti. We found that, whether old or young, our tasters shied away from sauces whose main ingredient was tomato paste or puree. These sauces tasted overly cooked and processed, and their tomato flavor was watered down and bitter. The sauces that performed well typically listed diced or whole tomatoes as the first ingredient, and they maintained a slightly chunky texture even after being heated.

THE BEST JARRED MARINARA SAUCES

Our top contenders were Pasty's Marinara (left), which contains fresh garlic instead of garlic powder; Bertolli Tomato and Basil Pasta Sauce (center), which earned high scores for its fresh flavor and texture; and Barilla Pasta Sauce (right), which was liked by tasters for its good balance, fresh flavor, and chunky texture.

LASAGNA

LASAGNA, LIKE MANY ONE-DISH MEALS, IS terrific for entertaining. Add a salad, maybe some garlic bread, and you're done. The problem is that this dish has multiple components, all of which require their own preparation. And once you've got the lasagna in the oven, your kitchen looks less than pristine. With company arriving any minute, you begin to panic. The answer? Make-ahead lasagna. But why not simply reheat your favorite lasagna recipe when you're ready to serve? The answer is simple—reheating a standard lasagna recipe makes it taste like leftovers. The noodles absorb the sauce and taste mushy and, in storing, the ricotta filling dries out. Even worse is a reheated lasagna's dry, leathery top. Our goal was to develop a lasagna that could be baked right away or stored and baked later and would still taste as good as freshly made—tender noodles layered with a creamy ricotta filling, all blanketed with a rich and meaty tomato sauce and topped with a gooey layer of cheese.

First, we began by simply assembling lasagna using our standard test kitchen recipe. From prior testing, we'd found we preferred no-boil lasagna noodles to regular dried. No-boil noodles are simply more convenient and they taste better too. We'd also found that the secret of no-boil noodles is to leave your tomato sauce a little on the watery side, especially when refrigerating the lasagna overnight. The noodles can then absorb liquid without drying out the dish overall. Our favorite no-boil noodles were flat noodles (as opposed to curly lasagna noodles), because they consistently baked up tender and tasters particularly enjoyed their delicate texture. With this in mind, we got to work on the other components of the lasagna.

For our lasagna sauce, we wanted a complex-flavored meat sauce as rich and thick as the traditional meat sauce, but because time is of the essence these days, we didn't want to simmer our sauce all day to achieve that rich flavor. For complex flavor fast, we turned to meat loaf mix, a combination of ground beef, pork, and veal.

The flavor of the sauce this trio produced was robust and sweet. The texture wasn't right, though; it was still a little thin. We aimed for something richer, creamier, and more cohesive, so our thoughts turned to Bolognese, the classic meat sauce enriched with dairy. Borrowing the notion of combining meat and dairy, we reduced a quarter cup of cream with the meat before adding the tomatoes. The ground meat soaked up the sweet cream and the final product was rich and flavorful.

Because no-boil noodles rely primarily on the liquid in the sauce to rehydrate and soften, we had to get the moisture content just right—especially because our lasagna would be stored in the fridge or freezer before baking. If the sauce was too thick, the noodles would be dry and crunchy; too loose, and they would turn limp and lifeless. We started building the sauce with two 28-ounce cans of pureed tomatoes, but tasters found that this sauce was too heavy for the lasagna and overwhelmed the other flavors. Two 28-ounce cans of diced tomatoes yielded too thin a sauce. We settled on one 28-ounce can of each. The combination of pureed and diced tomatoes yielded a luxurious sauce, with soft but substantial chunks of tomatoes. We added the tomatoes to the meat mixture, warmed it through (no reduction necessary), and in about 15 minutes on the stove the meat sauce was rich, creamy, ultra-meaty, and ready to go.

Most Americans like their lasagna full of cheese. It was a given that we would sprinkle each layer with mozzarella cheese and, after a test of whole milk cheese versus part-skim, we found that whole milk mozzarella was the best for the job. It had a more intense flavor than its part-skim counterpart and better melting qualities, which are crucial to this dish. We also tested preshredded mozzarella, but because it has a very low moisture content, it didn't melt well and was somewhat dry. Shredding a 1-pound block of whole milk mozzarella on a box grater or in a food processor is worth the minimal effort.

Ricotta was the next cheese up for scrutiny. As it turned out, it made little difference whether we used whole milk or part-skim ricotta when we assembled and baked the lasagna right away. But when we made the lasagna ahead and baked later, we found that whole milk retained its flavor and creamy texture far better than cheese with less or no fat. For added sharp, cheesy flavor, we tested the ricotta mixed with Parmesan and Pecorino Romano cheeses. Tasters unanimously rejected the pecorino for the too-strong flavor it gave the lasagna. Grated Parmesan, however, added just enough kick to the mild, milky ricotta. An egg helped to thicken and bind this mixture and some chopped basil added flavor and freshness. Tucked neatly between the layers of lasagna, this creamy ricotta mixture was just what we wanted.

With all the components of the lasagna decided, it was time to concentrate on the layering procedure. Smearing the entire bottom of a 13 by 9-inch baking dish with some of the sauce was the starting point. Next came the first layer of no-boil noodles, which we topped with ricotta, then mozzarella, and, finally, more meat sauce. We built two more layers using this same process. For the fourth and final layer of noodles, we covered them with the remaining meat sauce and remaining mozzarella and then sprinkled the top with grated Parmesan. At this point the lasagna could be baked right away or it could be wrapped tightly with plastic wrap and stored in the refrigerator for up to 2 days or in the freezer for up to 1 month.

In our tests, we found that covering the lasagna with foil from the outset of baking prevented a loss of moisture and helped soften the noodles properly. Removing the foil for the last 25 minutes of baking ensured that the top layer of cheese turned golden brown. An oven temperature of 400 degrees proved ideal. By the time the top was browned, the noodles had softened.

With the basic make-ahead lasagna components sorted out, we were ready to make a few variations. First up was Sausage and Broccoli Rabe Lasagna. We simply replaced the ground meat in the sauce with sausage, which we already knew from previous tests was a tasty alternative. Our major challenge was to find a way to prevent the broccoli rabe from turning army green and mushy. To resolve this, we cut the parboiling time in half, from 2 minutes to 50 to 60 seconds, leaving us with still-crunchy broccoli rabe that then cooked to an ideal texture when we baked the lasagna.

Our third variation was a vegetable lasagna, which makes an excellent vegetarian main course for company. We've found that too many vegetable lasagnas are bland and watery—nothing like our hearty versions with meat. And the good ones require lots of work to achieve great flavor. For example, some vegetarian lasagnas rely on roasting vegetables to intensify their flavor and prevent a watery texture, but roasting multiple baking sheets of vegetables was more than we wanted to do here. Instead, we took a quick route and zeroed in on the classic duo of spinach and mushrooms. We sautéed the mushrooms to intensify their flavor and rid them of excess liquid. Instead of layering the mushrooms in the lasagna, we decided to add them to the sauce, where the earthy slices imparted their meaty flavor. For convenience, we used frozen chopped spinach, which once thawed, is ready to go. We tried layering the spinach, but the leaves dried out, becoming chewy. Instead, we stirred the spinach into the ricotta mixture, where it would be in no danger of drying out. The spinach not only lent flavor to the filling, but its green flecks gave the cheesy mixture a vibrant hue. No one missed the meat in this fresh-flavored and filling lasagna.

There was one final issue left to tackle with lasagna—assembling different sizes. True, we'd supersized our lasagna for serving big crowds, but for everyday, not all households can polish off a 13 by 9-inch pan of this rich casserole. We then thought how helpful it would be to break our lasagna down to fit into 3 small loaf pan–sized lasagnas or 2 medium (8 by 8-inch) lasagnas. That way, cooks could have the option of serving only as much as is needed at a time. The assembly is similar for both sizes. However, in order for the noodles to evenly fit into an 8 by 8-inch pan, it is necessary to break some of the noodles in half, but that is easily done following the instructions on page 236. And, note that the baking times are slightly different to accommodate the sizes of the pans. With these options, smaller households will never have to face too much lasagna at once.

FREEZE IT

Hearty Meat Lasagna

SERVES 8

If you can't find meat loaf mix, you can substitute half 85 percent lean ground beef and half ground pork. Half ground beef and half sweet Italian sausage (casings removed and meat crumbled) is also good. See page 236 for instructions on how to assemble the lasagna into different-sized portions.

SAUCE

2	tablespoons olive oil
1	medium onion, minced
6	medium garlic cloves, minced or pressed through a garlic press (about 2 tablespoons)
1	pound meat loaf mix (see note)
	Salt and ground black pepper
¼	cup heavy cream
1	(28-ounce) can tomato puree
1	(28-ounce) can diced tomatoes, drained

RICOTTA FILLING

24	ounces whole milk ricotta cheese (about 3 cups)
2	ounces Parmesan cheese, grated (about 1 cup)
½	cup chopped fresh basil leaves
1	large egg, lightly beaten
½	teaspoon salt
½	teaspoon ground black pepper

NOODLES AND CHEESE

12	no-boil flat lasagna noodles, preferably Barilla
1	pound whole milk mozzarella cheese, shredded (about 4 cups)
1	ounce Parmesan cheese, grated (about ½ cup)

1. **FOR THE SAUCE:** Heat the oil in a Dutch oven over medium heat until shimmering. Add the onion and cook until softened but not browned, about 3 minutes. Stir in the garlic and cook until fragrant, about 30 seconds. Stir in the meat loaf mix, 1 teaspoon salt, and 1 teaspoon pepper and cook, breaking the meat into small pieces with a wooden spoon, until the meat loses its raw color but has not browned, about 4 minutes.

2. Stir in the cream, bring to a simmer, and cook until the liquid evaporates and only the fat remains, about 5 minutes. Stir in the tomato puree and drained diced tomatoes. Bring to a simmer and cook until the flavors are blended, about 3 minutes. Season with salt and pepper to taste; set aside.

3. **FOR THE RICOTTA FILLING:** Stir all of the ingredients together until combined; set aside.

4. **TO ASSEMBLE THE LASAGNA:** Spread 1 cup of the sauce over the bottom of a 13 by 9-inch baking dish (avoiding large chunks of meat). Place 3 of the noodles in a single layer in the baking dish. Spread ⅓ cup of the ricotta mixture over each noodle, then sprinkle the layer with 1 cup of the mozzarella. Spoon 1 cup of the sauce evenly over the cheeses. Repeat the layering of the noodles,

ricotta, mozzarella, and sauce twice more. Place the remaining 3 noodles on top, cover with the remaining sauce, and sprinkle with the remaining 1 cup mozzarella and the Parmesan.

5. TO STORE: Wrap the dish tightly with plastic wrap and then foil and refrigerate for up to 2 days or freeze for up to 1 month. (If frozen, the casserole must be thawed completely in the refrigerator, about 24 hours.)

6. TO SERVE: Adjust an oven rack to the middle position and heat the oven to 400 degrees. Unwrap the dish and cover tightly with aluminum foil that has been sprayed with vegetable oil spray (or use nonstick foil). Bake until the sauce bubbles lightly around the edges, 30 to 40 minutes. Remove the foil and continue to bake until hot throughout and the cheese is browned in spots, 25 to 30 minutes longer. Let cool for 10 minutes before serving.

TO SERVE RIGHT AWAY

Bake as described in step 6, reducing the covered baking time to 15 minutes.

To Supersize

SERVES 16

Adjust the Hearty Meat Lasagna recipe as follows using the ingredient amounts listed in the chart at right (the sauce simmering time will remain the same). A Dutch oven is large enough to accommodate cooking the sauce, but to bake the lasagna, you will need a large disposable aluminum baking pan (about 16 by 11 inches), supported by a sturdy rimmed baking sheet.

TO ASSEMBLE AND STORE

• Spread 2 cups of the sauce over the bottom of a 16 by 11-inch disposable aluminum baking pan supported by a sturdy rimmed baking sheet. Place 6 of the noodles in a single layer in the pan. Spread ⅓ cup of the ricotta mixture over each noodle, then sprinkle with 2 cups of the mozzarella. Spoon 2 cups of the sauce evenly over the cheeses. Repeat the layering of the noodles, ricotta, mozzarella, and sauce twice more. Place the remaining 6 noodles on top, then cover with the remaining sauce and sprinkle with the remaining 2 cups mozzarella and the Parmesan.

• Wrap the lasagna tightly with plastic wrap and then foil and store in the refrigerator for up to 2 days or in the freezer for up to 1 month.

TO BAKE IMMEDIATELY

Cover the dish tightly with aluminum foil that has been sprayed with vegetable oil spray (or use nonstick foil). Bake in a 400-degree oven until the sauce is bubbling, about 40 minutes. Remove the foil and continue to bake until hot throughout and the cheese is browned in spots, 30 to 35 minutes longer. Let cool for 10 minutes before serving.

SUPERSIZING MEAT LASAGNA

INGREDIENTS	AMOUNTS
Sauce	
OLIVE OIL	2 tablespoons
ONIONS	2 medium
GARLIC	12 medium cloves (¼ cup)
MEAT LOAF MIX	2 pounds
HEAVY CREAM	½ cup
TOMATO PUREE	2 (28-ounce) cans
DICED TOMATOES	2 (28-ounce) cans
Ricotta filling	
RICOTTA CHEESE	3 pounds (about 6 cups)
PARMESAN CHEESE	4 ounces (about 2 cups)
CHOPPED FRESH BASIL	1 cup
EGGS	2 large
SALT	1 teaspoon
GROUND BLACK PEPPER	1 teaspoon
Noodles and cheese	
NO-BOIL FLAT LASAGNA NOODLES	24 noodles
MOZZARELLA CHEESE	2 pounds (about 8 cups)
PARMESAN CHEESE	2 ounces (about 1 cup)

TO BAKE IF REFRIGERATED

Unwrap the pan and cover tightly with aluminum foil that has been sprayed with vegetable oil spray (or use nonstick foil). Bake in a 400-degree oven until the sauce bubbles lightly around the edges, about 1½ hours. Remove the foil and continue to bake until hot throughout and the cheese is browned in spots, 30 to 35 minutes longer. Let cool for 10 minutes before serving.

TO BAKE IF FROZEN

Thaw the casserole completely in the refrigerator, about 48 hours, then follow the instructions above for "To Bake if Refrigerated."

FREEZE IT

Sausage and Broccoli Rabe Lasagna

SERVES 8

See page 236 for instructions on how to assemble the lasagna into smaller portions.

SAUCE
Salt

I	pound broccoli rabe, trimmed and cut into 1-inch lengths (see the illustrations below)
2	tablespoons olive oil
I	medium onion, minced
6	medium garlic cloves, minced or pressed through a garlic press (about 2 tablespoons)
I½	pounds hot or sweet Italian sausage,

casings removed
Ground black pepper

I	(28-ounce) can tomato puree
I	(28-ounce) can diced tomatoes, drained

RICOTTA FILLING

24	ounces whole milk ricotta cheese (about 3 cups)
2	ounces Parmesan cheese, grated (about I cup)
½	cup chopped fresh basil leaves
I	large egg, lightly beaten
½	teaspoon salt
½	teaspoon ground black pepper

NOODLES AND CHEESE

12	no-boil flat lasagna noodles from one box, preferably Barilla
I	pound whole milk mozzarella cheese, shredded (about 4 cups)
I	ounce Parmesan cheese, grated (about ½ cup)

1. FOR THE SAUCE: Bring 2 quarts of water to a boil in a large pot over high heat. Add 1 tablespoon salt and the broccoli rabe. Cook the broccoli rabe until bright green and the stems are still crisp, 50 to 60 seconds, and then drain and rinse under cold water until cool; set aside to drain.

2. Heat the oil in a Dutch oven over medium heat until shimmering. Add the onion and cook until softened but not browned, about 3 minutes.

PREPARING BROCCOLI RABE

Broccoli rabe, also known as rapini, is actually a type of turnip green. It is made up mostly of leaves and stems, but broccoli rabe has a much stronger flavor than broccoli.

1. The thick stalk ends of broccoli rabe should be trimmed and discarded. Use a sharp knife to cut off the thickest part (usually the bottom 2 inches) of each stalk.

2. Cut the remaining stalks and florets into bite-sized pieces about I inch long.

INGREDIENTS:
Supermarket Mozzarella Cheese

We selected five widely available brands of low-moisture block mozzarella cheese and sampled those made with part-skim or whole milk in both block and preshredded forms. Fifteen members of the test kitchen tasted these cheeses both raw (all block cheeses were tasted shredded) and melted in our lasagna. Separate tests were performed in this manner, one for the category of preshredded cheeses and the other for block cheeses. We found the block cheeses to be better than the preshredded cheeses in flavor and texture. Among brands tested, Dragone Low-Moisture Mozzarella came out on top.

THE BEST SUPERMARKET MOZZARELLA CHEESE

If you don't mind shredding a block of cheese yourself, we think you'll get the best flavor and texture with Dragone Low-Moisture Mozzarella (whole milk) in block form.

Stir in the garlic and cook until fragrant, about 30 seconds. Stir in the sausage, 1 teaspoon salt, and 1 teaspoon pepper and cook, breaking the meat into small pieces with a wooden spoon, until the meat loses its raw color but has not browned, about 4 minutes. Stir in the broccoli rabe, tomato puree, and diced tomatoes and bring to a simmer. Cook until thickened slightly, about 3 minutes. Season with salt and pepper to taste; set aside.

3. FOR THE RICOTTA FILLING: Stir all of the ingredients together until uniform; set aside.

4. Follow steps 4, 5, and 6 of Hearty Meat Lasagna (page 230) to assemble, store, and serve.

TO SERVE RIGHT AWAY
Bake as described in step 6 of Hearty Meat Lasagna, reducing the covered baking time to 15 minutes.

To Supersize
SERVES 16

Adjust the Sausage and Broccoli Rabe Lasagna recipe as follows using the ingredient amounts listed in the chart below (the sauce simmering time will remain the same). Assemble and bake as directed in "Supersizing Meat Lasagna" on page 231. A large stockpot is big enough to cook the broccoli rabe and a Dutch oven is large enough to accommodate cooking the sauce. However, to bake the lasagna, you will need a large disposable aluminum baking pan (about 16 by 11 inches), supported by a sturdy rimmed baking sheet.

SUPERSIZING SAUSAGE AND BROCCOLI RABE LASAGNA

INGREDIENTS	AMOUNTS
Sauce	
BROCCOLI RABE	2 pounds
OLIVE OIL	2 tablespoons
ONIONS	2 medium
GARLIC	12 medium cloves (¼ cup)
SAUSAGE	3 pounds
TOMATO PUREE	2 (28-ounce) cans
DICED TOMATOES	2 (28-ounce) cans
Ricotta filling	
RICOTTA CHEESE	3 pounds (6 cups)
PARMESAN CHEESE	4 ounces (about 2 cups)
CHOPPED FRESH BASIL	1 cup
EGGS	2 large
SALT	1 teaspoon
GROUND BLACK PEPPER	1 teaspoon
Noodles and cheese	
NO-BOIL FLAT LASAGNA NOODLES	24 noodles
MOZZARELLA CHEESE	2 pounds (about 8 cups)
PARMESAN CHEESE	2 ounces (about 1 cup)

Mushroom and Spinach Lasagna

SERVES 8

Cremini mushrooms are particularly good in this dish, but regular button mushrooms will work as well. Smoked mozzarella or fontina can be substituted for the mozzarella. See page 236 for instructions on how to assemble the lasagna into smaller portions.

SAUCE

¼	cup olive oil
1½	pounds cremini mushrooms, wiped clean and sliced thin
1	medium onion, minced
	Salt
6	medium garlic cloves, minced or pressed through a garlic press (about 2 tablespoons)
1	(28-ounce) can tomato puree
1	(28-ounce) can diced tomatoes, drained
	Ground black pepper

RICOTTA FILLING

24	ounces whole milk ricotta cheese (about 3 cups)
1	(10-ounce) package frozen chopped spinach, thawed and squeezed dry
2	ounces Parmesan cheese, grated (about 1 cup)
1	large egg, lightly beaten
½	teaspoon salt
½	teaspoon ground black pepper

NOODLES AND CHEESE

12	no-boil flat lasagna noodles from one box, preferably Barilla
1	pound whole milk mozzarella cheese, shredded (about 4 cups)
1	ounce Parmesan cheese, grated (about ½ cup)

1. FOR THE SAUCE: Heat the oil in a Dutch oven over medium heat until shimmering. Add the mushrooms, onion, and 1 teaspoon salt. Cover and cook until the mushrooms have released their liquid, about 10 minutes. Uncover, increase the heat to medium-high, and continue to cook until the mushrooms are dry and browned, 5 to 10 minutes.

2. Stir in the garlic and cook until fragrant, about 30 seconds. Stir in the tomato puree and diced tomatoes, bring to a simmer, and cook until thickened slightly, about 3 minutes. Season with salt and pepper to taste; set aside.

3. FOR THE RICOTTA FILLING: Stir all of the ingredients together until uniform; set aside.

4. Follow steps 4, 5, and 6 of Hearty Meat Lasagna (page 230) to assemble, store, and serve.

TO SERVE RIGHT AWAY

Bake as described in step 6 of Hearty Meat Lasagna, reducing the covered baking time to 15 minutes.

TESTING NOTES

CHOOSING THE RIGHT RICOTTA

Ricotta comes in three forms: fat-free, part-skim, and whole milk. We usually reach for the part-skim ricotta here in the test kitchen because we like its clean, slightly leaner flavor. We have also had good results with fat-free when developing low-fat lasagna. But when it comes to make-ahead dishes, we found that whole milk ricotta is best because it retains its flavor and creamy texture in a stored casserole far better than part-skim or fat-free (especially if the casserole is frozen).

Whole Milk Ricotta

Make-ahead lasagna made with whole milk ricotta (rather than low-fat or nonfat) stored well in the refrigerator and freezer without any loss in flavor or texture.

To Supersize
SERVES 16

Adjust the Mushroom and Spinach Lasagna recipe as follows using the ingredient amounts listed in the chart below (it will take up to 5 minutes longer to cook the mushrooms, but the sauce simmering time will remain the same). Assemble and bake as directed in "Supersizing Meat Lasagna" on page 231. A Dutch oven is large enough to accommodate cooking the sauce, but to bake the lasagna, you will need a large disposable aluminum baking pan (about 16 by 11 inches), supported by a sturdy rimmed baking sheet

SUPERSIZING MUSHROOM AND SPINACH LASAGNA

INGREDIENTS	AMOUNTS
Sauce	
OLIVE OIL	½ cup
CREMINI OR WHITE BUTTON MUSHROOMS	3 pounds
ONIONS	2 medium
GARLIC	12 medium cloves (¼ cup)
TOMATO PUREE	2 (28-ounce) cans
DICED TOMATOES	2 (28-ounce) cans
Ricotta filling	
RICOTTA CHEESE	3 pounds (6 cups)
FROZEN SPINACH	2 (10-ounce) packages
PARMESAN CHEESE	4 ounces (about 2 cups)
EGGS	2 large
SALT	1 teaspoon
GROUND BLACK PEPPER	1 teaspoon
Noodles and cheese	
NO-BOIL FLAT LASAGNA NOODLES	24 noodles
MOZZARELLA CHEESE	2 pounds (about 8 cups)
PARMESAN CHEESE	2 ounces (about 1 cup)

TESTING NOTES

CHOOSING THE RIGHT NO-BOIL NOODLE

We found that the type of no-boil lasagna noodle can make the difference between a delicately textured dish and a chewy, uneven mess.

No-boil lasagna noodles are a convenient alternative to using regular dried lasagna noodles. And in our make-ahead lasagnas, no-boil noodles performed well, retaining their delicate texture, while regular lasagna noodles became bloated from absorbing the sauce and turned mushy. We tested different varieties of no-boil noodles and discovered that some held up better than others. No-boil curly-edged noodles are slightly thicker than their flat counterparts and thus tended to absorb more sauce, resulting in a chewier texture. Curly-edged noodles also tended to bake up in unattractive, uneven layers—some areas of the lasagna rose up, while others sank in. Flat-edged noodles, on the other hand, retained their delicate texture—which some compared to fresh pasta—and these noodles also baked into even layers. Of the flat noodles tested, the test kitchen preferred Barilla brand.

No-Boil Curly-Edged Noodles

Curly-edged noodles are somewhat thick, and when used in our make-ahead lasagna, tended to absorb more sauce, bloating the noodles, resulting in chewy pasta and unattractive uneven layers.

No-Boil Flat Noodles

Tasters preferred no-boil flat noodles for their delicate texture resembling fresh pasta. And unlike curly-edged noodles, no-boil flat noodles made a lasagna with even, attractive layers.

HOW TO ASSEMBLE SMALLER LASAGNAS

IF A 13 BY 9-INCH PAN OF LASAGNA IS TOO MUCH FOR YOUR HOUSEHOLD, IT IS EASY ENOUGH TO BREAK down our recipe to fit into multiple smaller-sized pans. You can then bake just what you need at one time and store the rest. Simply follow the lasagna recipes on pages 230–234 and assemble and bake as described below.

TO MAKE 3 SMALL LASAGNAS
EACH SERVES 2 TO 3

Spread ⅓ cup sauce into the bottom of three 9 by 3-inch loaf pans. Place 1 noodle into each loaf pan. Spread ⅓ cup of the ricotta mixture onto each noodle and sprinkle each with ⅓ cup of the mozzarella. Spoon ⅓ cup of the sauce evenly over the cheeses. Repeat the layering of the noodles, ricotta, mozzarella, and sauce twice more for each pan. Place the remaining noodles on top, cover with the remaining sauce, and then sprinkle with the remaining ⅓ cup mozzarella and the Parmesan. The lasagnas can be baked right away, or covered tightly with plastic wrap and then foil and stored in the refrigerator for up to 2 days or in the freezer for up to 1 month.

- **TO BAKE IMMEDIATELY:** Cover the dish tightly with aluminum foil that has been sprayed with vegetable oil spray (or use nonstick foil). Bake in a 400-degree oven until the sauce bubbles lightly around the edges, about 10 minutes. Remove the foil and continue to bake until hot throughout and the cheese is browned in spots, about 20 minutes longer. Let cool for 10 minutes before serving.

- **TO BAKE IF REFRIGERATED:** Unwrap the pan and cover tightly with aluminum foil that has been sprayed with vegetable oil spray (or use nonstick foil). Bake in a 400-degree oven until the sauce bubbles lightly around the edges, about 25 minutes. Remove the foil and continue to bake until hot throughout and the cheese is browned in spots, about 20 minutes longer. Let cool for 10 minutes before serving.

- **TO BAKE IF FROZEN:** Thaw the casserole completely in the refrigerator, about 24 hours then follow the instructions above for "To Bake if Refrigerated."

TO MAKE 2 MEDIUM LASAGNAS
EACH SERVES 4

Spread ½ cup of the sauce into the bottom of two 8 by 8-inch baking dishes. Place 1½ noodles into each baking dish, following the illustrations below. Spread ½ cup of the ricotta mixture over the noodles in each dish, then sprinkle with ½ cup of the mozzarella. Spoon ½ cup of the sauce evenly over the cheeses. Repeat the layering of the noodles, ricotta, mozzarella, and sauce twice more for each pan. Place the remaining noodles on top, cover with the remaining sauce and then sprinkle with the remaining ½ cup mozzarella, and the Parmesan. The lasagnas can be baked right away, or covered tightly with plastic wrap and then foil and stored in the refrigerator for up to 2 days or in the freezer for up to 1 month.

- **TO BAKE IMMEDIATELY:** Cover the dish tightly with aluminum foil that has been sprayed with vegetable oil spray (or use nonstick foil). Bake in a 400-degree oven until the sauce bubbles lightly around the edges, about 10 minutes. Remove the foil and continue to bake until hot throughout and the cheese is browned in spots, about 20 minutes longer. Let cool for 10 minutes before serving.

- **TO BAKE IF REFRIGERATED:** Unwrap the dish and cover tightly with aluminum foil that has been sprayed with vegetable oil spray (or use nonstick foil). Bake in a 400-degree oven until the sauce bubbles lightly around the edges, about 25 minutes. Remove the foil and continue to bake until hot throughout and the cheese is browned in spots, about 20 minutes longer. Let cool for 10 minutes before serving.

- **TO BAKE IF FROZEN:** Thaw the casserole completely in the refrigerator, about 24 hours, then follow the instructions above for "To Bake if Refrigerated."

PREPARING NOODLES FOR TWO MEDIUM LASAGNAS

Although you can fit 2 no-boil lasagna noodles into the bottom of an 8 by 8-inch baking dish, the noodles will expand and crowd during cooking, making for a dense, chewy layer. Our solution? Place 1½ noodles per layer and the noodles will bake up just right. The trick is to break the noodle cleanly and fit it into the lasagna pan correctly. Here's how.

1. Using a paring knife, score the noodle in half lengthwise. Snap the noodle in half alongside the scored mark.

2. Place the half noodle into the pan alongside the whole noodle. The noodles will expand during cooking, covering the bottom of the dish.

In developing our recipes for lasagna, we noticed that unless we sprayed the foil with vegetable oil spray, it would stick to the lasagna's cheesy top. But could we skip the spraying step if we used Reynolds Wrap Release Nonstick Aluminum Foil, which is coated on one side (the dull side) with a foodsafe nonstick material? We covered our pan of lasagna with the foil, shiny side up (the dull side is nonstick), before baking our lasagna. Once the hot lasagna was ready to uncover for its final browning time in the oven, we peeled the foil away from the normally sticky, cheesy top with ease. So for potentially sticky recipes, we now keep a roll of this special foil in the test kitchen.

MANICOTTI

WELL-MADE VERSIONS OF THIS ITALIAN-American classic—pasta tubes stuffed with rich ricotta filling and blanketed with tomato sauce—can be eminently satisfying. And having this casserole prepared ahead, so all you need to do is slide it into the oven to heat through, is a very attractive proposition. So what's not to love? Putting it all together. For such a straightforward collection of ingredients (after all, manicotti is just a compilation of pasta, cheese, and tomato sauce), the preparation is surprisingly fussy. Blanching, shocking, draining, and stuffing slippery pasta tubes require more patience (and time) than we usually have. In addition, a survey of manicotti recipes proved that most don't get the filling right; too often, the ricotta-based mixture turns out bland and runny. And make-ahead manicotti sitting in tomato sauce overnight comes with its own issues. We wanted a foolproof manicotti that could be assembled ahead of time and baked just before serving. And, we wanted tender, not mushy, pasta, a rich and thick cheese filling, and just enough sauce to lend moisture and flavor to the dish.

To start, we followed a "quick" recipe on the back of one of the manicotti boxes we had in the kitchen. It called for stuffing uncooked pasta tubes with ricotta, covering them with a thin tomato sauce, then baking. We surmised that the uncooked noodles would absorb some of the thin sauce during baking and the rest of the sauce would thicken around the noodles. Filling raw pasta tubes with cheese was marginally easier than stuffing limp and slippery parboiled noodles, but it wasn't without missteps: A few shattered along the way. Still, we followed the recipe through, watering down a jar of tomato sauce with a cup of boiling water and pouring it over the manicotti. After 45 minutes in the oven, this manicotti was inedible, with some of the pasta shells remaining uncooked, and the pink, watered-down sauce tasting, well, watery.

Frustrated, we decided to first zero in on the noodles. We thought back to our lasagna and thought to try no-boil lasagna noodles. We softened the noodles in boiling water, then spread them with the cheese filling. For the filling, we focused on whole milk ricotta, which retains its flavor and texture in make-ahead dishes better than low-fat or nonfat ricotta. We also added shredded mozzarella and grated Parmesan for flavor and further richness. We like eggs in our manicotti filling, too—eggs not only provide richness, but they help bind the cheeses together, so the filling doesn't become runny once baked. Two whole eggs mixed into the ricotta did the trick. After we spread the noodles with the mixture, we simply rolled the pasta sheets up. This method of assembly was a cinch!

Next, we wanted a simple, brightly flavored tomato sauce for our pasta, so we turned to one made with olive oil, garlic, and diced canned tomatoes pureed in a food processor to give the sauce body quickly. Keeping in mind that this manicotti would be made ahead and stored overnight or longer, we made sure that the tomato sauce was on the thin side so that the pasta wouldn't absorb all the moisture when left soaking for a couple of days. We also gave the sauce a flavor boost with fresh basil leaves and a dash of red pepper flakes.

After we assembled the manicotti, we topped each one with sauce, being sure to cover them completely to prevent them from drying out. A final scattering of cheese over the manicotti finished things off. We baked this batch of manicotti right away and tasters raved. We then made additional batches to test how well the manicotti stored in the refrigerator and freezer. For one, we wrapped the dish with plastic wrap and stored it in the fridge for 2 days. And for the other, we stored the wrapped dish in the freezer for 1 month. Baking these stored manicottis along with a freshly prepared version, we called in tasters. Once baked, all the dishes came out just as we'd hoped: tender tubes of pasta with a rich cheesy filling. The tomato sauce lent just enough saucy moistness and the Parmesan and mozzarella topping melted into a golden brown gooey layer. This, at last, was a manicotti that won our complete affection—great tasting and easy to prepare.

FREEZE IT

Baked Manicotti

SERVES 6 TO 8

We prefer Barilla no-boil noodles for their smooth, delicate texture resembling fresh pasta. Note that Pasta Defino and Ronzoni brands contain only 12 no-boil noodles per package; our recipe requires 16 noodles. For a spicier sauce, use the higher amount of red pepper flakes.

2	(28-ounce) cans diced tomatoes
2	tablespoons extra-virgin olive oil
3	medium garlic cloves, minced or pressed through a garlic press (about 1 tablespoon)
	Pinch to ½ teaspoon red pepper flakes
	Salt
2	tablespoons chopped fresh basil leaves
	Ground black pepper
24	ounces whole milk ricotta cheese (about 3 cups)
4	ounces Parmesan cheese, grated (about 2 cups)
10	ounces whole milk mozzarella cheese, shredded (about 2½ cups)
2	large eggs, lightly beaten
2	tablespoons minced fresh parsley leaves
16	no-boil flat lasagna noodles, preferably Barilla

1. Pulse the tomatoes with their juices, 1 can at a time, in a food processor until coarsely chopped with pieces measuring about ¼ inch, about 3 pulses; set aside.

2. Heat the oil, garlic, and pepper flakes in a large saucepan over medium heat until fragrant but not brown, 1 to 2 minutes. Stir in the tomatoes and ½ teaspoon salt, and simmer until slightly thickened, about 15 minutes. Off the heat, stir in the basil and season to taste with salt and pepper; set aside.

3. Stir the ricotta, 1 cup of the Parmesan, 2 cups of the mozzarella, eggs, parsley, ½ teaspoon salt, and ½ teaspoon pepper together; set aside.

4. Pour 1 inch of boiling water into a 13 by 9-inch baking dish and slip the noodles into the water, 1 at a time. Let the noodles soak until pliable, about 5 minutes, separating the noodles with the tip of a knife to prevent sticking. Remove the noodles from the water and place in single layer over clean kitchen towels. Discard the water in the baking dish and pat it dry.

5. Spread 1½ cups of the sauce over the bottom of the baking dish. Use a soup spoon to spread ¼ cup of the ricotta cheese mixture evenly over the bottom three-quarters of each noodle. Roll the noodles up around the filling and lay, seam-side down, in the baking dish. Spoon the remaining sauce evenly over the rolled noodles, covering the pasta completely. Sprinkle with the remaining Parmesan and mozzarella.

6. To store: Wrap the dish tightly with plastic wrap and then foil and refrigerate for up to 2 days or freeze for up 1 month. (If frozen, the casserole must be thawed completely in the refrigerator, about 24 hours.)

7. To serve: Adjust an oven rack to the middle position and heat the oven to 400 degrees. Unwrap the dish and cover tightly with aluminum foil that has been sprayed with vegetable oil spray (or use nonstick foil). Bake until the sauce is bubbling and the cheese is melted, 30 to 40 minutes. Remove the foil and continue to bake until the cheese is browned in spots, 25 to 30 minutes longer.

TO SERVE RIGHT AWAY

Bake as described in step 7, reducing the covered baking time to just 15 minutes.

➤ VARIATIONS

Baked Manicotti with Prosciutto

Follow the recipe for Baked Manicotti, arranging 1 piece of very thinly sliced prosciutto (you will need 16 slices, about 8 ounces total) on each noodle before spreading the cheese filling and rolling the manicotti.

Baked Manicotti Puttanesca

Follow the recipe for Baked Manicotti, sautéing 3 finely minced anchovies with the garlic and ½ teaspoon red pepper flakes in step 2. Proceed as directed, adding ¼ cup pitted and quartered kalamata olives and 2 tablespoons capers, drained, to the cheese mixture in step 3.

Bake Half, Freeze Half

Follow any of the manicotti recipes and divide the ingredients between two 8 by 8-inch casserole dishes (each will serve 4) or three 9 by 3-inch loaf pans (each will serve 2 to 3), following the illustration at right. The casseroles can be baked right away or covered tightly with plastic wrap and then foil and refrigerated for up to 2 days or frozen for up to 1 month. See reheating instructions below.

TO BAKE IMMEDIATELY

Cover the dish tightly with aluminum foil that has been sprayed with vegetable oil spray (or use nonstick foil). Bake in a 400-degree oven until the sauce is bubbling and the cheese is melted, about 10 minutes. Remove the foil and continue to bake until the cheese is browned in spots, about 20 minutes longer.

TO BAKE IF REFRIGERATED

Unwrap the pan and cover tightly with aluminum foil that has been sprayed with vegetable oil spray (or use nonstick foil). Bake in a 400-degree oven until the sauce is bubbling and the cheese is melted, about 25 minutes. Remove the foil and continue to bake until the cheese is browned in spots, about 20 minutes longer.

TO BAKE IF FROZEN

Thaw the casserole completely in the refrigerator, about 24 hours, then follow the instructions above for "To Bake if Refrigerated."

PREPARING LOAF-PAN MANICOTTI

To fit our manicotti into loaf pans, arrange them widthwise (not lengthwise) for a perfect fit.

BAKED MACARONI AND CHEESE

AT ITS FINEST, BAKED MACARONI AND CHEESE emerges from the oven with a golden crumb topping, underneath which a creamy cheese sauce gracefully cloaks tender pasta elbows and fills their curves. But when made ahead and reheated, its texture becomes dense and dried out. We wanted a mac and cheese that could stand up to storage and come out as creamy and cheesy as one that was fresh-baked.

Before diving into the testing, however, we tried several existing recipes to get the lay of the land. Most recipes use a similar technique: a flour-and-milk-based sauce (aka béchamel), enriched with the cheese, mixed with the cooked pasta, and baked. A few nontraditional recipes use eggs rather than flour to thicken the sauce (making it more like a custard) or replace the milk with evaporated milk. Although none of these recipes produced the creamy mac and cheese of our dreams, we did learn a thing or two. First, casseroles cook very unevenly in the oven—the edges of the casserole are often done long before the center is even warm. Because of this phenomenon, we noted that egg-thickened recipes just don't work. The egg at the edges becomes overcooked and solidified by the time the center is hot. Second, the hot air of the oven will quickly dry out a casserole unless it is either covered with foil or has quite a loose texture to begin with. Therefore it is no surprise that the sauces made with evaporated milk—which is essentially milk with some of the water taken out—baked up to a dry, goopy mess; using foil to protect it simply prevented the bread-crumb topping from toasting. The most promising recipes from this initial testing used a béchamel, yet none of them turned out great either. Overall, they tasted bland, dry, and grainy.

Setting the issue of flavor aside, we began by focusing on the béchamel. Testing how much béchamel we needed for 1 pound of pasta (which fills a 13 by 9-inch casserole dish perfectly), we made three sauces using 3, 4, and 5 cups of milk. Although they produced casseroles that were decreasingly dry, we found that even the sauce made with 5 cups of milk was not enough, especially because the pasta tended to absorb some sauce overnight. Increasing the amount of milk seemed the obvious answer; yet as we added more, we noted that the sauce began to turn sticky and taste, well, too milky. As the casserole baked in the oven, the sauce lost some of its moisture but none of the milk fat or flavor. We then tried replacing some of the milk with water or chicken broth. While eliminating some of the milk loosened the sauce up significantly so that it could withstand the evaporation in the oven, adding water made the sauce taste somewhat bland. However, using chicken broth was fantastic. It helped the sauce remain creamy without harming its flavor. Testing various amounts of milk and broth to flour (the sauce thickener), we found 3½ cups of milk and 2¼ cups of chicken broth to 6 tablespoons of all-purpose flour was perfect. Any less liquid and the casserole dried out.

Up until now, we had been adding a pound of cheddar to the sauce as a baseline, but wondered if either less or more would be better. Testing casseroles with amounts of cheese ranging from 12 to 24 ounces, we found the tasters' penchant for cheese was simply insatiable. At 24 ounces (8 cups), we cried uncle—the casserole tasted sufficiently cheesy. A problem that had been annoying us since the beginning, however, was now impossible to ignore—the grainy texture of the cooked cheddar. To get around this, many recipes mix cheddar with other types of cheese. We tried replacing some of the cheddar with Gruyère, but its potent flavor—an acquired taste—did not sit well with all the tasters. Monterey Jack helped to smooth out the sauce, but it also was too bland for a dish where the cheese was so critical. Gouda, Havarti, and fontina were all given a shot; however, none tasted just right. Last, we tried colby and hit the jackpot. Offering a cheddar-like flavor and an unbelievably silky texture when melted, colby was clearly the answer. Trying various ratios of colby to cheddar, we found that the best balance of flavor and texture was 2 parts colby to 1 part extra-sharp cheddar. Adding a pinch of cayenne, dry mustard, and a single clove of garlic also did wonders to enhance the cheesiness of the dish.

As for the topping, we immediately canned the idea of using store-bought bread crumbs, finding their flavor stale and lifeless. Rather, we preferred the fresh, somewhat sweet flavor of sliced sandwich bread, ground into crumbs using a food processor. Tossed with a little melted butter, these crumbs browned nicely in a 400-degree oven in about the same time it took for the sauce and macaroni to bind together. The crumbs can be sprinkled on top, then the casserole could be wrapped with plastic wrap and stored in the refrigerator up to 2 days or frozen for up to 1 month.

When baking our macaroni and cheese, we found that covering the casserole for most of the cooking time helped to keep the heat and moisture in. We then removed the foil to allow the crumb topping to crisp up. We did, however, run into an issue in cooking our Supersized Macaroni and Cheese, which is baked in a 16 by 11-inch baking pan.

This very large casserole just wouldn't heat evenly. In our first test it took 2½ hours to heat through to the center, and by that time the edges were curdled. We resolved to leave the crumb topping off, and stir the mac and cheese while it cooked, so that the hot sides would be mixed with the cooler middle. But during the first hour of cooking, the mac and cheese was simply too firm to stir. But once it did loosen up (after an hour), we stirred and it finally heated through without curdling. With recipe and heating thoroughly tested, we were ready to feed the hungriest of crowds.

FREEZE IT

Baked Macaroni and Cheese

SERVES 6 TO 8

Although the classic pasta shape for this dish is elbow macaroni, any small, curvaceous pasta will work.

I	recipe (about 2¾ cups) Toasted Bread Crumb Topping (page 242)
	Salt
I	pound elbow macaroni
6	tablespoons (¾ stick) unsalted butter
I	medium garlic clove, minced or pressed through a garlic press (about I teaspoon)
I	teaspoon dry mustard
¼	teaspoon cayenne pepper
6	tablespoons unbleached all-purpose flour
2¼	cups low-sodium chicken broth
3½	cups whole milk
I	pound colby cheese, shredded (about 4 cups)
8	ounces extra-sharp cheddar cheese, shredded (about 2 cups)
	Ground black pepper

1. Make the topping and set aside. Bring 4 quarts of water to a boil in a Dutch oven over high heat. Stir in 1 tablespoon salt and the macaroni and cook, stirring occasionally, until just beginning to soften, about 5 minutes. Drain the pasta and leave it in the colander; set aside.

2. Wipe the pot dry, add the butter, and set it over medium heat until melted. Stir in the garlic, mustard, and cayenne and cook until fragrant, about 30 seconds. Stir in the flour and cook, stirring constantly, until golden, about 1 minute. Slowly whisk in the chicken broth and milk. Bring to a simmer and cook, whisking often, until large bubbles form on the surface and the mixture is slightly thickened, about 15 minutes. Off the heat, gradually whisk in the colby and cheddar until completely melted. Season with salt and pepper to taste.

3. Stir the drained pasta into the cheese sauce, breaking up any clumps, until well combined. Pour into a 13 by 9-inch baking dish and sprinkle with the crumb topping.

4. To STORE: Wrap the dish tightly with plastic wrap and then foil and refrigerate for up to 2 days

---

TESTING NOTES

MAKE-AHEAD MACARONI AND CHEESE

When made ahead, macaroni and cheese tends to dry out and become bland. We had to take special steps to ensure a fresh-tasting, creamy mac and cheese.

1. Build a thin sauce and cut the dairy with chicken broth

Most make-ahead macaroni and cheese baked up too firm and had to be sliced like lasagna, so for a thinner sauce, we increased the milk from 2 cups to 3½ cups. For a boost in flavor, we added chicken broth to the mix. This made for a thin sauce that baked up thick and creamy with balanced flavors.

2. Use 2 types of cheese

We like cheddar cheese for flavor, but cheddar alone made for a grainy sauce, so we replaced some of the cheddar with colby. Colby offered a mild cheddar-like flavor and gave the sauce a super-silky texture.

3. Intensify the flavor

To highlight the cheesy flavors in our mac and cheese, we added dry mustard, cayenne pepper, and fresh garlic.

Toasted Bread Crumb Topping

MAKES 2¾ CUPS; ENOUGH FOR ONE
13 BY 9-INCH CASSEROLE

4   slices white sandwich bread, quartered
2   tablespoons unsalted butter, melted
2   tablespoons minced fresh parsley
     leaves
     Salt and ground black pepper

Adjust an oven rack to the middle position and heat the oven to 300 degrees. Pulse the bread and butter in a food processor to coarse crumbs, about 6 pulses. Spread the crumbs out over a rimmed baking sheet. Bake, stirring occasionally, until golden and dry, 20 to 30 minutes. Let the crumbs cool, then toss with the parsley; season with salt and pepper to taste.

Ritz Cracker Topping

Because the crackers are already crisp and salty, there is no need to toast them in the oven or season them with salt.

Follow the recipe for Toasted Bread Crumb Topping, substituting 50 Ritz crackers (1½ sleeves) for the bread. Pulse with the butter to coarse crumbs, about 10 pulses. Toss the crumbs with the parsley and season with pepper. Set aside until needed.

Corn Chip Topping

Because the chips are already crisp and salty, there is no need to toast them in the oven or season them with salt.

Follow the recipe for Toasted Bread Crumb Topping, substituting 6 ounces corn tortilla or Frito corn chips for the bread. Pulse with the butter to coarse crumbs, about 10 pulses. Toss the crumbs with the parsley and season with pepper. Set aside until needed.

or freeze for up to 1 month. (If frozen, the casserole must be thawed completely in the refrigerator, about 24 hours.)

5. To SERVE: Adjust an oven rack to the middle position and heat the oven to 400 degrees. Unwrap the dish and cover tightly with aluminum foil. Bake until the filling is hot throughout, 40 to 45 minutes. Remove the foil and continue to bake until the crumbs are crisp, 15 to 20 minutes longer.

TO SERVE RIGHT AWAY
Bake the casserole in a 400-degree oven, uncovered, until the sauce is bubbling and the crumbs are crisp, 25 to 35 minutes.

Bake Half, Freeze Half

Follow the recipe for Baked Macaroni and Cheese and divide the ingredients between two 8 by 8-inch casserole dishes (each will serve 4) or three 9 by 3-inch loaf pans (each will serve 2 to 3). The casseroles can be baked right away or covered tightly with plastic wrap and then foil and refrigerated for up to 2 days or frozen for up to 1 month. See reheating instructions below.

TO BAKE IMMEDIATELY
Bake the casserole in a 400-degree oven, uncovered, until the sauce is bubbling and the crumbs are crisp, 20 to 25 minutes.

TO BAKE IF REFRIGERATED
Unwrap the dish and cover tightly with aluminum foil. Bake in a 400-degree oven until the filling is hot throughout, 20 to 25 minutes. Remove the foil and continue to bake until the crumbs are crisp, 15 to 20 minutes longer.

TO BAKE IF FROZEN
Thaw the casserole completely in the refrigerator, about 24 hours, then follow the instructions above for "To Bake if Refrigerated."

To Supersize

SERVES 16 TO 18

Adjust the Baked Macaroni and Cheese recipe as follows using the ingredient amounts listed in the chart on page 243. (But if refrigerating or freezing the casserole, be sure to store the crumb topping separately and add partway through baking.) A Dutch oven is large enough to accommodate cooking the cheese sauce, but to boil the macaroni you will need an extra-large stockpot (at least 12 quarts). And to bake the casserole, you will need a large disposable aluminum baking pan (about 16 by 11 inches), supported by a sturdy rimmed baking sheet.

SUPERSIZING BAKED MACARONI AND CHEESE

INGREDIENTS	SERVES 16 TO 18
TOASTED BREAD CRUMB TOPPING	2 recipes (5½ cups)
ELBOW MACARONI	2 pounds
UNSALTED BUTTER	12 tablespoons (1½ sticks)
GARLIC	2 medium cloves (about 2 teaspoons)
DRY MUSTARD	1 tablespoon
CAYENNE PEPPER	½ to ¾ teaspoon
UNBLEACHED ALL-PURPOSE FLOUR	¾ cup
LOW-SODIUM CHICKEN BROTH	4½ cups
WHOLE MILK	7 cups
COLBY CHEESE	2 pounds
EXTRA-SHARP CHEDDAR CHEESE	1 pound

TO ASSEMBLE AND STORE

• Store the crumb topping separately in an airtight container if refrigerating or freezing the casserole.

• Bring 1½ gallons of water to a boil in a large pot, then season with 1½ tablespoons salt and cook the pasta as directed in step 2.

• After draining the pasta, transfer it to a 16 by 11-inch disposable aluminum baking pan, supported by a sturdy rimmed baking sheet.

• After making the cheese sauce in step 3, pour it over the pasta and stir to combine evenly.

• Wrap the casserole tightly with plastic wrap and then foil. Refrigerate the casserole and crumb topping separately for up to 2 days or freeze for up to 1 month.

TO BAKE IMMEDIATELY

Sprinkle the crumb topping evenly over the casserole. Bake, uncovered, in a 400-degree oven until the filling is hot throughout and the crumbs are crisp, 40 to 45 minutes.

TO BAKE IF REFRIGERATED

Adjust an oven rack to the middle position and heat the oven to 400 degrees. Unwrap the pan and cover (without the crumb topping) tightly with aluminum foil. Bake, stirring occasionally as the sauce begins to warm and loosen, until the filling is hot, about 1½ hours. Remove the foil, sprinkle the crumb topping evenly over the top, and continue to bake until the crumbs are crisp, 20 to 25 minutes longer.

TO BAKE IF FROZEN

Thaw the casserole completely in the refrigerator, about 48 hours, then follow the instructions above for "To Bake if Refrigerated."

BAKED PASTA AND CHICKEN

PASTA AND CHICKEN ARE SUCH POPULAR ingredients on their own that we figured teaming them up in a casserole would be a smash hit. Initially, we were wrong. Dry, rubbery chicken, mushy pasta, and bland sauce turned out to be downsides to this casserole. We'd need to develop a chicken and pasta casserole that turned out juicy chunks of chicken and tender (not mushy!) pasta, all bound together with a creamy, well-seasoned sauce.

We started off with a basic cream sauce—we sautéed aromatics (such as onions and garlic), then added cream and allowed it to simmer, thicken, and reduce before we finished with cheese. This type of sauce worked great at binding the pasta and chicken together, but it tasted a little too rich. We tried replacing some of the heavy cream with chicken broth and found that it not only made the sauce taste lighter, but it boosted the chicken flavor too. A little white wine also helped cut through the sauce's heaviness without diluting its flavor. These additions of broth and wine, however, made the texture of the sauce a bit too thin. Unlike cream, chicken broth and wine don't become dramatically thicker as they reduce. In order to make the sauce thick enough to properly coat the chicken and penne, we found it necessary to add some flour.

We then tried flavoring the sauce with several different types of cheese and noted that Italian cheeses fit the bill. Giving Parmesan, fontina, and pecorino a whirl, we found that we didn't care for a sauce flavored with just one type of cheese (too boring and one-dimensional) but rather preferred a sauce flavored with a combination of cheeses. For the sake of convenience, we found that a bag of preshredded blended Italian cheeses (usually containing mozzarella, Parmesan, fontina, pecorino, and/or Asiago) worked wonderfully.

Up to this point, we had been cooking the pasta to an al dente consistency, tossing it with some cooked chicken and the cream sauce, then spreading it into a casserole dish. The casserole was sprinkled with a little extra cheese and baked until bubbling and browned. By serving time, unfortunately, the al dente pasta overcooked to a mushy consistency. To solve the problem, we undercooked the pasta, testing a variety of boiling times to get it just right. In the end, we found that the pasta only required about 5 minutes of boiling (at which point pasta still seems quite raw). Once drained, we tossed the pasta with the remaining ingredients and baked it. In the oven, the pasta absorbs some of the sauce and cooks through, but still retains some of its texture.

While the casserole baked, we surveyed the two pots on the stove—one to boil the pasta and one to prepare the cream sauce. To cut out a pot, we found we could boil the pasta in one pot, then set it aside in a colander while we used the same pot for the sauce. To prevent the pasta from sticking together as the sauce cooked, we found it necessary to toss it with a little oil. We had been using ziti in these initial casseroles (chicken and ziti are a classic combo) but luckily we ran out of it one day

and substituted penne. The tasters raved over the smaller, more elegant size of the penne and found it to be a more appropriate pairing with the chicken and cream sauce.

Moving next to the chicken, we found it easiest to use boneless, skinless breasts. Wanting to prevent the chicken from overcooking and turning tough, we first tried tossing small pieces of raw chicken with the sauce and undercooked penne and letting it cook through in the oven. This method, unfortunately, didn't work. It took far too long for the chicken to cook through in the oven, by which time the pasta was overdone and the sauce had dried out. Testing a variety of ways to precook the chicken, we tried broiling, sautéing, and poaching it in the pasta water. Broiling turned the edges of the chicken unappealingly crisp, while poaching in water resulted in a bland, washed-out flavor. Sautéing the chicken in a skillet with a little oil worked well, but it required an extra pan, which we were loathe to use. Working with the poaching idea, we then tried poaching the chicken right in the sauce. This method worked like a charm—the chicken took on some of the sauce's flavor and vice versa.

During our final chicken cooking tests, we learned that how the chicken is cut is nearly as important as its cooking method. Rather than cutting the raw chicken into pieces before poaching, we found it best to poach the boneless breasts whole, then shred them into bite-sized pieces. When the chicken was poached and then shredded, it tasted much more moist and kept its tender texture regardless of how the casserole was stored and reheated.

Now we just needed to fine-tune the casserole's flavors. Although everything was perfectly cooked, the dish was a bit bland. We tried adding some herbs but, although they tasted good (we kept them in the recipe), alone they weren't enough. Turning to mushrooms, we found their distinctive, earthy flavor shined through and began to give this casserole some well-needed oomph. A combination of both fresh mushrooms (we like cremini mushrooms for their color and flavor) and dried porcinis worked perfectly. In developing a variation, we found that artichoke hearts with lemon and tarragon also worked nicely with the pasta, chicken, and cream sauce and made for a very elegant, company-worthy casserole indeed.

Testing the durability of these casseroles, we found that they held well in the refrigerator for up to 2 days, beyond which time the flavors became too muted and the texture of undercooked pasta began to turn a bit funky. Throwing a batch into the freezer, we were surprised to find that it reheated quite well if thawed completely before baking. A combination of covered and uncovered baking times in a 400-degree oven is ideal for reheating this chilled casserole and browning the cheese on top. A final sprinkling of fresh herbs over the top before serving adds both color and a fresh flavor.

FREEZE IT

Creamy Baked Penne and Chicken with Mushrooms

SERVES 8

Shredded Italian cheese blend is a mix of cheeses, including mozzarella, provolone, Parmesan, fontina, and Asiago.

	Salt
1	pound penne
4	tablespoons olive oil
1½	pounds cremini mushrooms, wiped clean and sliced ¼ inch thick
1	medium onion, minced
½	ounce dried porcini mushrooms, rinsed and minced
8	medium garlic cloves, minced or pressed through a garlic press (about 8 teaspoons)
1	tablespoon minced fresh thyme leaves, or 1 teaspoon dried
¼	cup unbleached all-purpose flour
2	cups low-sodium chicken broth
1	cup dry white wine
1	cup heavy cream
2	pounds boneless, skinless chicken breasts (about 5 breasts), trimmed
8	ounces shredded Italian cheese blend (about 2 cups)
¼	teaspoon ground black pepper
2	tablespoons minced fresh parsley leaves (for serving)

1. Bring 4 quarts of water to a boil in a Dutch oven over high heat. Stir in 1 tablespoon salt and the pasta and cook, stirring occasionally, until just beginning to soften, about 5 minutes. Drain the pasta through a colander and toss with 1 tablespoon of the oil; leave it in the colander and set aside.

2. Wipe the pot dry, add the remaining 3 tablespoons oil, and set over to medium-low heat until shimmering. Add the cremini mushrooms, onion, porcini mushrooms, and 1 teaspoon salt. Cover and cook, stirring often, until the mushrooms have released their liquid, about 10 minutes. Uncover, increase the heat to medium-high, and continue to cook, stirring often, until the mushrooms are dry and browned, 5 to 10 minutes.

3. Stir in the garlic and thyme and cook until fragrant, about 30 seconds. Stir in the flour and cook, stirring constantly, until golden, about 1 minute. Slowly whisk in the broth, wine, and cream.

4. Add the chicken breasts, partially cover, and bring to a simmer. Reduce the heat to low, cover completely, and cook until the thickest part of the chicken registers 160 degrees on an instant-read thermometer, 10 to 15 minutes.

5. Remove the pot from the heat. Remove the chicken and set aside to cool; keep the sauce covered. When the chicken is cool enough to handle, shred it into bite-sized pieces. Stir the shredded chicken and 1 cup of the cheese into the sauce with the cooked pasta until well combined. Season with salt and pepper to taste. Transfer to a 13 by 9-inch baking dish and sprinkle with the remaining 1 cup cheese.

6. To STORE: Wrap the dish tightly with plastic wrap and then foil and refrigerate for up to 2 days or freeze for up to 1 month. (If frozen, the casserole must be thawed completely in the refrigerator, about 24 hours.)

7. To SERVE: Adjust an oven rack to the middle position and heat the oven to 400 degrees. Unwrap the dish and cover tightly with aluminum foil that has been sprayed with vegetable oil spray (or use nonstick foil). Bake until the sauce is bubbling around the edges, 30 to 40 minutes. Remove the foil and continue to bake until hot throughout and browned on top, 25 to 30 minutes longer. Sprinkle with the parsley before serving.

TO SERVE RIGHT AWAY

Bake the casserole in a 400-degree oven, uncovered, until the sauce is bubbling and the top is browned, 25 to 35 minutes. Sprinkle with the parsley before serving.

Bake Half, Freeze Half

Follow the recipes for Creamy Baked Penne and Chicken with Mushrooms or Creamy Baked Penne and Chicken with Artichokes, Tarragon, and Lemon and divide the ingredients between two 8 by 8-inch casserole dishes (each will serve 4) or three 9 by 3-inch loaf pans (each will serve 2 to 3). The casseroles can be baked right away or covered tightly with plastic wrap and then foil and refrigerated for up to 2 days or frozen for up to 1 month. See reheating instructions below.

TO BAKE IMMEDIATELY

Bake the casserole in a 400-degree oven, uncovered, until bubbling and browned, 20 to 25 minutes. Sprinkle with the parsley before serving.

TO BAKE IF REFRIGERATED

Unwrap the dish and cover tightly with aluminum foil. Bake in a 400-degree oven, covered, until the sauce is beginning to bubble lightly around the edges, 30 minutes. Remove the foil and continue to bake until hot throughout and browned, 20 minutes longer. Sprinkle with the parsley before serving.

TO BAKE IF FROZEN

Thaw the casserole completely in the refrigerator, about 24 hours, then follow the instructions above for "To Bake if Refrigerated."

➤ VARIATION

Creamy Baked Penne and Chicken with Artichokes, Tarragon, and Lemon

If you can't find frozen artichokes, you can substitute 3 (14-ounce) cans artichoke hearts; you will need to drain, rinse, and pat them dry thoroughly before using. Shredded Italian cheese blend is a mix of 4 to 5 cheeses, often including mozzarella, provolone, Parmesan, fontina, and Asiago.

Salt

1	pound penne
4	tablespoons olive oil
3	(9-ounce) boxes frozen artichokes, thawed, patted dry, and chopped coarse
1	medium onion, minced
8	medium garlic cloves, minced or pressed through a garlic press (about 8 teaspoons)
¼	teaspoon grated zest from 1 lemon
¼	cup unbleached all-purpose flour
2	cups low-sodium chicken broth
1	cup dry white wine
1	cup heavy cream
2	pounds boneless, skinless chicken breasts (about 5 breasts), trimmed
3	bay leaves
1½	cups frozen peas
8	ounces shredded Italian cheese blend (about 2 cups)
3	tablespoons juice from 2 lemons Ground black pepper
3	tablespoons minced fresh tarragon leaves (for serving)

1. Bring 4 quarts of water to a boil in a Dutch oven over high heat. Stir in 1 tablespoon salt and the pasta and cook, stirring occasionally, until just beginning to soften, about 5 minutes. Drain the pasta through a colander and toss with 1 tablespoon of the oil; leave in the colander and set aside.

2. Wipe the pot dry, then add the remaining 3 tablespoons oil, and set it over medium heat until shimmering. Add the artichokes, onion, and 1 teaspoon salt and cook until the artichokes are lightly browned, 8 to 10 minutes.

3. Stir in the garlic and lemon zest and cook until fragrant, about 30 seconds. Stir in the flour and cook, stirring constantly, until golden, about 1 minute. Slowly whisk in the broth, wine, and cream.

4. Add the chicken breasts and bay leaves, partially cover, and bring to a simmer. Reduce the heat to low, cover completely, and cook until the thickest part of the chicken registers 160 degrees on an instant-read thermometer, 10 to 15 minutes.

5. Remove the pot from the heat and discard the bay leaves. Remove the chicken and set aside

to cool; keep the sauce covered. When the chicken is cool enough to handle, shred it into bite-sized pieces. Stir the shredded chicken back into the sauce with the cooked pasta, peas, 1 cup of the cheese, and lemon juice; stir until well combined. Season with salt and pepper to taste. Transfer to a 13 by 9-inch baking dish and sprinkle with the remaining 1 cup cheese.

6. To STORE: Wrap the dish tightly with plastic wrap and then foil and refrigerate for up to 2 days or freeze for up to 1 month. (If frozen, the casserole must be thawed completely in the refrigerator, about 24 hours.)

7. To SERVE: Adjust an oven rack to the middle position and heat the oven to 400 degrees. Unwrap the dish and cover tightly with aluminum foil that has been sprayed with vegetable oil spray (or use nonstick foil). Bake until the sauce is bubbling around the edges, 30 to 40 minutes. Remove the foil and continue to bake until hot throughout and browned on top, 25 to 30 minutes longer. Sprinkle with the tarragon before serving.

TO SERVE RIGHT AWAY
Bake the casserole in a 400-degree oven, uncovered, until the sauce is bubbling and the top is browned, 25 to 35 minutes. Sprinkle with the tarragon before serving.

CHICKEN AND RICE CASSEROLE

CHICKEN AND RICE CASSEROLE RARELY HITS the mark. Heavy and dull, the dish is too often a tired concoction of dry chicken and mushy rice bound together with a pasty sauce (often built from a canned cream soup). Kids may like the cheesy aspect this dish often sports, but the adult palate needs more refined allure. Add a make-ahead component to the mix and the results can border on inedible. First, we wanted to develop a chicken and rice casserole with fresh flavors—one that's hearty, but not heavy. And, we wanted to find a way to make this weeknight workhorse ahead, so that even the busiest families could prepare and enjoy it.

We began by preparing a cooked, flour-thickened sauce (rather than using a can of cream soup), which allowed us to incorporate the flavors of sautéed fresh aromatics like onions and garlic. Then, we cooked the rice in another pot. We combined the chicken, rice, and sauce in a casserole and then baked it in a hot oven until bubbling. The results were good—the chicken imparted a nice flavor to the sauce as it cooked and vice versa—but did we really need two pots to make this dish? If the rice was cooked directly in the sauce, it might be more flavorful, we reasoned.

It was a good plan, but not a simple one. The biggest hurdle was learning how best to coordinate the cooking times of both the rice and chicken. We knew we needed to cook the chicken through completely (before storing the casserole) for obvious food-safety reasons, and were curious how much cooking time the rice could handle (both before storing and during the reheat) before it would turn mushy.

We made a few more batches, adding the rice and chicken to the sauce to cook at various stages in order to determine the overall timing, but came to realize that there were two main issues preventing the rice from cooking through alongside the chicken. The first issue is that rice cooks more slowly in flour-bound sauce than it does in pure water or straight broth because much of the water is trapped by swollen starch granules, which prevents the rice grains from absorbing the liquid. Also, we noted that the rice cooks quickly at first (when the sauce is a bit more loose), but slows down considerably (as the sauce becomes thicker). Second, we noted that as the chicken cooks in the sauce, it releases its own juice while simultaneously absorbing heat from the sauce; this makes for a truly uneven cooking atmosphere (with pockets of liquid and heat) for the somewhat fussy rice.

The answer to our timing issue came when we figured that we could cook both the chicken and rice in the sauce, but at completely separate times. By poaching whole breasts of chicken in the sauce first, we found it easy to fish them out once cooked, then stir in the rice. This two-step method worked like a charm; the chicken and rice cooked through absolutely evenly, while each absorbed the sauce's flavor and lent their own key attributes to the sauce. This method also boasted a big bonus—the poached, then shredded, chicken held much better in the stored casserole and tasted juicer when reheated than the chicken of our previous tests.

Throughout all of the previous batches, we had noted that this casserole required lots of sauce in order to cook the chicken and rice, but also to prevent the casserole from drying out while being stored in the refrigerator or freezer. Requiring 7 cups of liquid to make enough sauce for the casserole, we tested a variety of flour amounts and found that a mere ¼ cup was plenty to thicken the liquid to a creamy consistency because the rice leaches a fair amount of its starch into the liquid as it cooks. We experimented with sauces made with chicken broth, milk, and cream in varying proportions and found that tasters preferred a broth-based sauce enriched with just a hint of cream (6 cups broth to 1 cup cream). We didn't want to forgo cheese, so after preparing sauces with various types and amounts, tasters gave their thumbs-up to 2 cups shredded cheddar.

The final components of the casserole included vegetables and a simple bread-crumb topping. To keep the ingredient and prep lists short and easy, we liked the convenience of a frozen pea and carrot medley. The peas and diced carrots heat through quickly, so they do not need to be thawed. And fresh lemon juice stirred into the creamy casserole brightened its flavors.

Baked straightaway, we had no problems with producing a freshly flavored, hot casserole topped with golden brown crumbs. But when stored in the refrigerator (or freezer) and then heated, our bread crumbs burned. To prevent burned crumbs, we landed on a combination of covered and uncovered cooking times in a moderately hot 400-degree oven. Note also that while this casserole holds well in the freezer, it must be thawed completely before being baked. This casserole is a great one to scale up to serve a crowd (see our supersized version, page 250), but it does need to be stirred throughout baking so that it heats through evenly.

For a variation on the classic chicken and rice dish, we turned to Southwestern flavors. Frozen corn and canned black beans stood in for the peas and carrots and we swapped in spicy pepper Jack cheese for the cheddar. For some additional heat, we added jalapeño chiles, while fresh cilantro and lime juice lent some tang. And while not authentic, tasters didn't complain about our corn chip crumb topping made from crushed Fritos.

FREEZE IT

Creamy Chicken and Rice Casserole with Peas, Carrots, and Cheddar

SERVES 8

After adding the rice, be sure to stir the sauce often for the first few minutes, using a heatproof rubber spatula; this is when the rice is most likely to clump and stick to the bottom of the pot. Serve with lemon wedges, if desired.

4	tablespoons (½ stick) unsalted butter
I	medium onion, minced
	Salt
3	medium garlic cloves, minced or pressed through a garlic press (about I tablespoon)
⅛	teaspoon cayenne pepper
¼	cup unbleached all-purpose flour
6	cups low-sodium chicken broth
I	cup heavy cream
2	pounds boneless, skinless chicken breasts (about 5 breasts), trimmed
1½	cups long-grain white rice
I	(I-pound) bag frozen pea and carrot medley (about 3 cups)
8	ounces sharp cheddar cheese, shredded (about 2 cups)
2	tablespoons juice from I lemon
	Ground black pepper
I	recipe (about 2¾ cups) Toasted Bread Crumb Topping (page 242)
3	tablespoons minced fresh parsley (for serving)

1. Melt the butter in a Dutch oven over medium heat. Add the onion and 1 teaspoon salt and cook until softened and lightly browned, 5 to 7 minutes. Stir in the garlic and cayenne and cook until fragrant, about 30 seconds. Stir in the flour and cook, stirring constantly, until golden, about 1 minute.

Slowly whisk in the broth and cream.

2. Add the chicken breasts, partially cover, and bring to a simmer. Reduce the heat to low, cover completely, and cook until the thickest part of the chicken breast registers 160 degrees on an instant-read thermometer, 10 to 15 minutes.

3. Remove the chicken and set aside to cool. Stir the rice into the pot, cover, and continue to cook over low heat, stirring often, until the rice has absorbed much of the liquid and is just tender, 20 to 25 minutes. When the chicken is cool enough to handle, shred it into bite-sized pieces.

4. Remove the pot from the heat and stir in the shredded chicken, peas and carrots, cheddar, and lemon juice. Season with salt and pepper to taste. Pour the mixture into a 13 by 9-inch baking dish and sprinkle with the crumb topping.

5. To STORE: Wrap the dish tightly with plastic wrap and then foil and refrigerate for up to 2 days or freeze for up to 1 month. (If frozen, the casserole must be thawed completely in the refrigerator, about 24 hours.)

6. To SERVE: Adjust an oven rack to the middle position and heat the oven to 400 degrees. Unwrap the dish and cover tightly with aluminum foil. Bake until the casserole is bubbling and hot throughout, about 1 hour. Remove the foil and continue to bake until the crumbs are crisp, 15 to 20 minutes longer. Sprinkle with the parsley before serving.

TO SERVE RIGHT AWAY
Bake the casserole in a 400-degree oven, uncovered, until the sauce is bubbling and the crumbs are crisp, 25 to 35 minutes. Sprinkle with the parsley before serving.

Bake Half, Freeze Half
Follow the recipes for Creamy Chicken and Rice Casserole with Peas, Carrots, and Cheddar or Chicken and Rice Casserole with Chiles, Corn, and Black Beans and divide the ingredients between two 8 by 8-inch casserole dishes (each will serve 4) or three 9 by 3-inch loaf pans (each will serve 2 to 3). The casseroles can be baked right away or wrapped tightly with plastic wrap and then foil and refrigerated for up to 2 days or frozen for up to 1 month. See reheating instructions below.

TO BAKE IMMEDIATELY
Bake the casserole in a 400-degree oven, uncovered, until the sauce is bubbling and the crumbs are crisp, 20 to 25 minutes. Sprinkle with the parsley before serving.

TO BAKE IF REFRIGERATED
Unwrap the dish and cover tightly with foil. Bake in a 400-degree oven until the casserole is bubbling and hot throughout, 40 to 50 minutes. Remove the foil and continue to bake until the crumbs are crisp, 15 to 20 minutes longer. Sprinkle with the parsley before serving.

TO BAKE IF FROZEN
Thaw the casserole completely in the refrigerator, about 24 hours, then follow the instructions above for "To Bake if Refrigerated."

To Supersize
SERVES 16 TO 18
Adjust the Creamy Chicken and Rice Casserole with Peas, Carrots, and Cheddar recipe as follows using the ingredient amounts listed in the chart on page 250. A Dutch oven is large enough to accommodate cooking the sauce, chicken, and rice. To bake the casserole, you will need a large disposable baking pan (about 16 by 11 inches), supported by a sturdy rimmed baking sheet.

TO ASSEMBLE AND STORE
- Store the crumb topping separately in an airtight container if refrigerating or freezing the casserole.
- After the cooked chicken has been shredded in step 3, transfer it to a 16 by 11-inch disposable aluminum pan, supported by a sturdy rimmed baking sheet.
- After removing the pot from the heat in step 4, stir in the cheese until melted, then pour the mixture over the chicken in the aluminum pan. Stir in the frozen peas and carrots and lemon juice until evenly combined.
- Wrap the casserole tightly with plastic wrap and then foil. Refrigerate the casserole and crumb topping separately for up to 2 days or freeze for up to 1 month.

TO BAKE IMMEDIATELY

Sprinkle the crumb topping over the casserole and bake in a 400-degree oven, uncovered, until the sauce is bubbling and the crumbs are crisp, 40 to 45 minutes. Sprinkle with the parsley before serving.

TO BAKE IF REFRIGERATED

Unwrap the dish and cover (without the crumb topping) tightly with aluminum foil. Bake in a 400-degree oven, stirring occasionally as the sauce begins to warm and loosen, until the filling is hot throughout, about 1½ hours. Remove the foil, sprinkle the crumb topping evenly over the top, and continue to bake until the crumbs are crisp, 20 to 25 minutes longer. Sprinkle with the parsley before serving.

TO BAKE IF FROZEN

Thaw the casserole completely in the refrigerator, about 48 hours, then follow the instructions above for "To Bake if Refrigerated."

SUPERSIZING CHICKEN AND RICE CASSEROLE WITH PEAS, CARROTS, AND CHEDDAR

INGREDIENTS	INGREDIENTS
UNSALTED BUTTER	6 tablespoons (¾ stick)
ONIONS	2 medium
GARLIC	6 medium cloves (2 tablespoons)
CAYENNE PEPPER	¼ teaspoon
UNBLEACHED ALL-PURPOSE FLOUR	½ cup
LOW-SODIUM CHICKEN BROTH	3 quarts (12 cups)
HEAVY CREAM	2 cups
BONELESS, SKINLESS CHICKEN BREASTS	4 pounds (about 10 medium breasts)
LONG-GRAIN WHITE RICE	3 cups
FROZEN PEA AND CARROT MEDLEY	2 (1-pound) bags (about 6 cups)
SHARP CHEDDAR	1 pound (4 cups)
LEMON JUICE	¼ cup, from 2 lemons
TOASTED BREAD CRUMB TOPPING	2 recipes (5½ cups)
MINCED FRESH PARSLEY	6 tablespoons

FREEZE IT

Chicken and Rice Casserole with Chiles, Corn, and Black Beans

SERVES 8

Don't skip the rinsing of the black beans or the sauce will turn gray. Unlike other frozen vegetables, frozen corn tends to throw off more liquid and can make this dish a bit soupy if not thawed first. While the corn chip topping tastes great here, you can also use a simple bread-crumb topping. After adding the rice, be sure to stir the sauce often for the first few minutes, using a heatproof rubber spatula; this is when the rice is most likely to clump and stick to the bottom of the pot.

1	recipe (about 2¾ cups) Corn Chip Crumb Topping (page 242)
4	tablespoons (½ stick) unsalted butter
2	medium red bell peppers, stemmed, seeded, and chopped medium
1	medium onion, minced
2	medium jalapeño chiles, seeds and ribs removed, chile minced
	Salt
3	medium garlic cloves, minced or pressed through a garlic press (about 1 tablespoon)
1	teaspoon ground cumin
¼	cup unbleached all-purpose flour
6	cups low-sodium chicken broth
1	cup heavy cream
2	pounds boneless, skinless chicken breasts (about 5 breasts), trimmed
1½	cups long-grain white rice
8	ounces pepper Jack cheese, shredded (about 2 cups)
1	(15.5-ounce) can black beans, rinsed and drained
1½	cups frozen corn, thawed and drained
3	tablespoons juice from 2 limes
	Ground black pepper
¼	cup minced fresh cilantro leaves (for serving)

1. Make the topping; set aside. Melt the butter in a Dutch oven over medium heat. Add the bell peppers, onion, jalapeños, and 1 teaspoon salt and cook until softened, 8 to 10 minutes. Stir in the

garlic and cumin and cook until fragrant, about 30 seconds. Stir in the flour and cook, stirring constantly, until golden, about 1 minute. Slowly whisk in the broth and cream.

2. Add the chicken breasts, partially cover, and bring to a simmer. Reduce the heat to low, cover completely, and cook until the thickest part of the chicken registers 160 degrees on an instant-read thermometer, 10 to 15 minutes.

3. Remove the chicken and set aside to cool. Stir the rice into the pot, cover, and continue to cook over low heat, stirring often, until the rice has absorbed much of the liquid and is just tender, 20 to 25 minutes. When the chicken is cool enough to handle, shred it into bite-sized pieces.

4. Remove the pot from the heat and stir in the shredded chicken, cheese, black beans, corn, and lime juice and season with salt and pepper to taste. Pour the mixture into a 13 by 9-inch baking dish and sprinkle with the crumb topping.

5. To STORE: Wrap the dish tightly with plastic wrap and then foil and refrigerate for up to 2 days or freeze for up to 1 month. (If frozen, the casserole must be thawed completely in the refrigerator, about 24 hours.)

6. To SERVE: Adjust an oven rack to the middle position and heat the oven to 400 degrees. Unwrap the dish and cover tightly with aluminum foil. Bake until the casserole is bubbling and hot throughout, about 1 hour. Remove the foil and continue to bake until the crumbs are crisp, 15 to 20 minutes longer. Sprinkle with the cilantro before serving.

TO SERVE RIGHT AWAY

Bake the casserole in a 400-degree oven, uncovered, until the sauce is bubbling and the crumbs are crisp, 25 to 35 minutes. Sprinkle with the cilantro before serving.

To Supersize

SERVES 16 TO 18

Adjust the Chicken and Rice Casserole with Chiles, Corn, and Black Beans recipe as follows using the ingredient amounts listed in the chart at right. (But if refrigerating or freezing the casserole, be sure to store the crumb topping separately and add partway through baking.) A Dutch oven is large enough to accommodate cooking the sauce, chicken, and rice. To bake the casserole, you will need a large disposable aluminum baking pan (about 16 by 11 inches), supported by a sturdy rimmed baking sheet.

SUPERSIZING CHICKEN AND RICE CASSEROLE WITH CHILES, CORN, AND BLACK BEANS

INGREDIENTS	SERVES 16 TO 18
CORN CHIP CRUMB TOPPING	2 recipes (5½ cups)
UNSALTED BUTTER	6 tablespoons (¾ stick)
RED BELL PEPPERS	4 medium
ONIONS	2 medium
JALAPEÑO CHILES	4 medium
GARLIC	6 medium cloves (about 2 tablespoons)
CUMIN	2 teaspoons
UNBLEACHED ALL-PURPOSE FLOUR	½ cup
LOW-SODIUM CHICKEN BROTH	3 quarts (12 cups)
HEAVY CREAM	2 cups
BONELESS, SKINLESS CHICKEN BREASTS	4 pounds (about 10 medium breasts)
LONG-GRAIN WHITE RICE	3 cups
PEPPER JACK CHEESE	1 pound (4 cups)
BLACK BEANS	2 (15.5-ounce) cans
FROZEN CORN	3 cups
LIME JUICE	6 tablespoons, from 6 limes
MINCED FRESH CILANTRO	½ cup

TO ASSEMBLE AND STORE

- Store the crumb topping separately in an airtight container if refrigerating or freezing the casserole.
- After the cooked chicken has been shredded in step 3, sprinkle it evenly into a 16 by 11-inch disposable aluminum pan, supported by a sturdy rimmed baking sheet.
- After removing the pot from the heat in step 4, stir in the cheese until melted, then pour the mixture over the chicken. Add the beans, corn, and lime juice and stir until evenly combined.

• Cover the casserole tightly with plastic wrap and then foil. Refrigerate the casserole and crumbs separately for up to 2 days or freeze for up to 1 month.

TO BAKE IMMEDIATELY

Sprinkle the crumb topping over the casserole and bake in a 400-degree oven, uncovered, until the sauce is bubbling and the crumbs are crisp, 40 to 45 minutes. Sprinkle with the cilantro before serving.

TO BAKE IF REFRIGERATED

Unwrap the dish and cover (without the crumb topping) tightly with aluminum foil. Bake in a 400-degree oven, stirring occasionally as the sauce begins to warm and loosen, until the filling is hot throughout, about 1½ hours. Remove the foil, sprinkle the crumb topping evenly over the top, and continue to bake until the crumbs are crisp, 20 to 25 minutes longer. Sprinkle with the cilantro before serving.

TO BAKE IF FROZEN

Thaw the casserole completely in the refrigerator, about 48 hours, then follow the instructions above for "To Bake if Refrigerated."

CHICKEN ENCHILADAS

ENCHILADAS ARE QUITE POSSIBLY THE MOST popular Mexican casserole in the world; a softened tortilla rolled around a savory, cheesy filling (often chicken) and baked in a spicy chili sauce. Traditional methods require a whole day of preparation. Could we streamline the preparation and still retain the authentic flavor of the real thing? And if we made them in advance, would refrigerated or frozen enchiladas taste as good as fresh-baked?

We began by preparing various simplified recipes. All of them produced disappointing results. Mushy tortillas, bland or bitter sauces, uninspired fillings, too much cheese, and lackluster flavor left tasters yearning for something tastier and more authentic. We had our work cut out for us.

To start, we did a side-by-side tasting of corn and wheat-flour tortillas. Tasters came out clearly in favor of the corn, with its more substantial texture that held up better when made in advance. Tasters also preferred the small 6-inch corn tortillas to the larger 8-inch size. The smaller size provided the best proportion of tortilla to filling to sauce and fit neatly into a 9-inch baking pan.

We tried rolling the corn tortillas around the filling straight out of the package but they were tough and cracked easily (see photo on page 254). Most recipes prep the tortillas before rolling in order to make them soft and pliable. The traditional approach is to dip each tortilla in hot oil (to create a moisture barrier) and then in the sauce (to add flavor) prior to assembly. Although this technique works well, it is time-consuming, tedious, and messy. Heating a stack of tortillas in the microwave also proved disappointing. The tortillas had softened, but the resulting enchiladas were mushy. Next we tried wrapping the tortillas in foil and steaming them on a plate over boiling water. These tortillas turned wet and soggy when baked.

Thinking back to the traditional first step of dipping the tortilla in oil gave us an idea. Using the modern-day convenience of oil in a spray can, we placed the tortillas in a single layer on a baking sheet, sprayed both sides lightly with vegetable oil, and warmed them in a moderate oven. This proved to be the shortcut we were hoping to find. The oil-sprayed, oven-warmed tortillas were pliable and their texture after being filled, rolled, and baked was just perfect.

Moving onto the sauce next, we prepared a half dozen traditional recipes and compared them to store-bought cans of enchilada sauce. Convenience was the only thing the store-bought sauces had going for them; the tasters hated their harsh, tinny flavors. The homemade sauces, on the other hand, were smooth and somewhat thick, with a truly satisfying, deep chile flavor. The only problem was that whole dried chiles played a central role in all of these homemade sauces. Not only are whole chiles difficult to find in some areas, but they also require substantial preparation time, including toasting, seeding, stemming, rehydrating, and processing in a blender. Our sauce would need to depend on store-bought chili powder if we wanted to keep the recipe streamlined.

The obvious question now was how to augment the flavor of the usually bland chili powder available in the supermarket. Our first thought was to heat the chili powder in oil, a process that intensifies flavors. We began by sautéing onions and garlic and then added the chili powder to the pan. This indeed produced a fuller, deeper flavor. We enhanced the flavor further by adding ground cumin, coriander, and sugar—tasters gave this combo a thumbs-up.

Many traditional recipes incorporate tomatoes for substance and flavor. Keeping convenience in mind, we explored canned tomato products first. We tried adding diced tomatoes and then pureeing the mixture. The texture was too thick and too tomatoey. Canned tomato sauce—which has a very smooth, slightly thickened texture and mild tomato flavor—turned out to be a better option.

We had been playing with various fillings up to this point and noted that a chicken-based filling was by far the favorite. It wasn't clear to us, however, how we should cook the chicken. We tried the common method of poaching in broth or water, but tasters said this chicken tasted bland and washed out. We tried roasting both white and dark meat and although it was extremely time-consuming, tasters really liked the flavor of the dark meat. Obsessed with speed and flavor, we had an idea. Why not use boneless, skinless thighs and poach them right in the sauce? Cutting the thighs into thin strips across the grain, we added them to the pan after the spices were fragrant. The chicken cooked in less than 10 minutes and it was nicely seasoned. Cooking the chicken in the sauce also lent the sauce a wonderful richness. To separate the chicken from the sauce, we poured the contents of the pot through a medium-mesh strainer.

With the chicken cooked and ready for the filling, we needed to add just a few complementary ingredients. Cheese topped our list. Queso fresco, the traditional choice, is a young, unripened cheese with a creamy color, mild flavor, and crumbly texture. Because it is not readily available in many parts of the United States, we tried farmer's cheese. Tasters liked this cheese for its creamy texture and mellow flavor. But it was Monterey Jack and sharp white cheddar that made the top of the list. The Jack is mellow while the cheddar adds a sharp, distinctive flavor. In the end, tasters preferred the sharp flavor of the cheddar. (Cheese, we discovered, also helps to bind the filling ingredients.)

Looking for more heat, we taste-tested the addition of fresh jalapeños, chipotles in adobo sauce, and pickled jalapeños. The fresh jalapeños were too mild. Chipotles (smoked jalapeños stewed in a seasoned sauce) added a distinctive, warm heat and smoky flavor that some tasters enjoyed but that most found too spicy and overwhelmingly smoky. Everyone was surprised to find that the very convenient pickled jalapeños (sold in both cans and jars) were the favorite. The vinegar pickling solution added spicy, bright, and sour notes to the filling.

The enchiladas now tasted perfect when assembled and served right away, but we had some trouble adapting them to a make-ahead time schedule. The biggest issue was that the tortillas soften substantially when in contact with liquid for longer periods of time. When the enchiladas were sauced, refrigerated, and baked a day or two later, the flavors tasted fine, but the tortillas were quite mushy and the sauce had nearly disappeared. To fix this, we found it best to lay the filled enchiladas into a dry dish and store them separately from the sauce. Partway through baking, the sauce can simply be poured over the top of the enchiladas. We found that covering the dish with foil and a moderate 350-degree oven quickly reheated the enchiladas in about 30 minutes.

Not surprisingly, freezing the enchiladas works well when the sauce is frozen separately. Before marrying the sauce and enchiladas, however, we learned a crucial defrosting tip. When we tried to defrost the enchiladas on the counter, in the fridge, or in the microwave, we found that they turned seriously mushy. We tried saucing the enchiladas while still frozen and letting them thaw in the oven, but once the frozen enchiladas were heated through, the entire dish was a uniform mush. To solve this issue, we found it necessary to bake the frozen enchiladas uncovered without any sauce. The moisture thrown off from thawing evaporates into the oven. And once the enchiladas are thawed, the hot oven toasts up the outside of the tortillas nicely. Once the enchiladas are thawed and the tortillas are slightly crisp, we poured the sauce over the top and continued to bake them, covered, until the filling was piping hot.

Making a big batch of enchiladas presented no problems, but we did learn two good tricks. First, you want to make sure the enchiladas are always in a single layer in the serving dish—this way, all the enchiladas get the maximum amount of sauce and cheese. Second, you want to arrange the enchiladas in rows that are easy to serve from (and obvious for self-serve if on a buffet). Avoid cramming extra enchiladas alongside the edges of the rows, or the enchiladas may fuse together or break apart upon serving. And for making a supersized batch, we found it best to use several rectangular disposable aluminum baking pans with flat bottoms (stay away from the big, rounded turkey-sized pans that have uneven bottoms meant to catch the turkey drippings.)

TESTING NOTES

ROLLING TORTILLAS MADE EASY

Straight from the refrigerator, a corn tortilla is too stiff to roll and will tear at the edges as seen in the top photograph. Spraying the tortilla with oil and heating it for 2 to 4 minutes in a 300-degree oven will make the tortilla pliable and easy to manage as shown in the bottom photograph.

COOL AND STIFF

WARM AND PLIABLE

FREEZE IT

Chicken Enchiladas

SERVES 4 TO 6

If you prefer, Monterey Jack can be used instead of cheddar or, for a mellower flavor and creamier texture, try substituting an equal amount of farmer's cheese. Serve with sour cream, diced avocado, shredded romaine lettuce, and lime wedges.

2	tablespoons vegetable oil
1	medium onion, minced (about 1 cup)
3	tablespoons chili powder
3	medium garlic cloves, minced or pressed through a garlic press (about 1 tablespoon)
2	teaspoons ground coriander
2	teaspoons ground cumin
2	teaspoons sugar
½	teaspoon salt
1	pound boneless, skinless chicken thighs (about 4 thighs), trimmed and cut into ¼-inch-wide strips
2	(8-ounce) cans tomato sauce
⅓	cup water
½	cup minced fresh cilantro leaves
1	(4-ounce) can pickled jalapeños, drained and chopped (about ¼ cup)
10	ounces sharp cheddar cheese, shredded (about 2½ cups)
10	(6-inch) corn tortillas

1. Adjust an oven rack to the middle position and heat the oven to 300 degrees. Heat the oil in a large saucepan over medium-high heat until shimmering. Add the onion and cook until softened and lightly browned, 5 to 7 minutes. Stir in the chili powder, garlic, coriander, cumin, sugar, and salt and cook, stirring constantly, until fragrant, about 30 seconds. Stir in the chicken and coat thoroughly with the spices, about 30 seconds.

2. Stir in the tomato sauce and water and bring to a simmer. Reduce the heat to medium-low and continue to simmer, stirring occasionally, until the chicken is cooked through and the flavors have melded, 8 to 10 minutes.

3. Pour the mixture through a medium-mesh strainer into a medium bowl, pressing on the strained chicken mixture to extract as much sauce

as possible. Transfer the chicken mixture to a large plate and freeze for 10 minutes to cool; when cool, combine the chicken with the cilantro, jalapeños, and 2 cups of the cheddar in a medium bowl. Transfer the sauce to an airtight container.

4. Following the illustrations at right, spray both sides of the tortillas with vegetable oil spray. Place 5 of the tortillas onto a baking sheet. Bake until the tortillas are soft and pliable, 2 to 4 minutes. Transfer the tortillas to a clean work surface. Place a heaping ⅓ cup filling onto the center of each warm, softened tortilla, and roll it up tightly following the illustrations at right. Arrange the enchiladas, seam side down, in a single layer in a 13 by 9-inch baking dish. Repeat with the remaining tortillas.

5. TO STORE: Cover the dish tightly with plastic wrap and then foil. Refrigerate the enchiladas, sauce, and remaining ½ cup cheese separately for up to 3 days or freeze separately for up to 1 month. (Frozen enchiladas should not be thawed before reheating.)

6. TO SERVE: Adjust an oven rack to the middle position and heat the oven to 400 degrees. Unwrap the dish and spray the top of the enchiladas with vegetable oil spray. Bake uncovered (without the sauce) until lightly toasted on top, 10 to 20 minutes. (Meanwhile if the sauce is frozen, thaw it completely in the microwave on medium-high, 3 to 5 minutes, stopping to break apart any large ice crystals with a fork.)

7. Pour the sauce over the enchiladas, covering the tortillas completely, then sprinkle the remaining ½ cup cheese down the center of the enchiladas, following the illustrations at right. Cover the dish with aluminum foil that has been sprayed with vegetable oil spray (or use nonstick foil) and bake until the sauce is bubbling and the cheese is melted, 20 to 25 minutes more.

TO SERVE RIGHT AWAY
Cover the enchiladas with the sauce and cheese and bake as directed in step 7.

Bake Half, Freeze Half
Follow the recipe for Chicken Enchiladas and divide the enchiladas between two 8 by 8-inch

ASSEMBLING ENCHILADAS

1. Place the tortillas on 2 baking sheets. Spray both sides lightly with cooking spray. Bake until the tortillas are soft and pliable, about 4 minutes.

2. Place the warm tortillas on a work surface. Place a heaping ⅓ cup filling down the center of each tortilla.

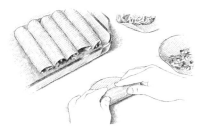

3. Roll each tortilla tightly by hand. Place them in a baking dish, side by side, seam side down.

4. Pour the sauce over the top of the enchiladas. Use the back of a spoon to spread the sauce so it coats the top of each tortilla.

5. Sprinkle the remaining ½ cup cheese down the center of the enchiladas.

casserole dishes (each will serve 2). Divide the sauce between 2 separate covered containers and divide the remaining ½ cup cheese between 2 small storage bags. The casseroles can be baked right away, or covered tightly with plastic wrap and then foil and stored separately from the sauce and cheese for up to 2 days in the refrigerator or frozen for up to 1 month. See reheating instructions below.

TO BAKE IMMEDIATELY

Top the enchiladas with the sauce and cheese, following the illustrations on page 255, and cover the dish tightly with aluminum foil that has been sprayed with vegetable oil spray (or use nonstick foil). Bake in a 350-degree oven until the enchiladas are heated through and the cheese is melted, 15 to 20 minutes.

TO BAKE IF REFRIGERATED OR FROZEN

Unwrap the dish, spray the tops with vegetable oil spray, and bake uncovered (without the sauce) in a 400-degree oven until warmed through and lightly toasted on top, 10 to 15 minutes. (If the sauce is frozen, thaw it in the microwave on medium-high, 3 to 5 minutes.) Pour the sauce over the enchiladas, covering the tortillas completely, then sprinkle the remaining ½ cup cheese down the center of the enchiladas, following the illustrations on page 255. Cover the dish with aluminum foil that has been sprayed with vegetable oil spray (or use nonstick foil) and bake until the sauce is bubbling and the cheese is melted, 15 to 20 minutes more.

To Supersize

MAKES 30 ENCHILADAS, SERVING 12 TO 15

Adjust the Chicken Enchiladas recipe as follows using the ingredient amounts listed in the chart above. A Dutch oven is large enough to accommodate cooking the sauce. As for baking the enchiladas, we don't recommend packing them into 1 (or even 2) large casserole dishes because they will steam as they bake and turn very soggy. Rather, it is better to assemble them into three 13 by 9-inch baking dishes.

SUPERSIZING CHICKEN ENCHILADAS

INGREDIENTS	AMOUNTS
VEGETABLE OIL	¼ cup
ONIONS	3 medium
CHILI POWDER	6 tablespoons
GARLIC	9 medium cloves (3 tablespoons)
GROUND CORIANDER	4 teaspoons
GROUND CUMIN	4 teaspoons
SUGAR	4 teaspoons
SALT	1 ½ teaspoons
BONELESS, SKINLESS CHICKEN THIGHS	3 pounds (about 12 thighs)
TOMATO SAUCE	48 ounces (six 8-ounce cans, or three 15-ounce cans)
WATER	1 cup
MINCED FRESH CILANTRO	1 ½ cups
PICKLED JALAPEÑOS	2 (4-ounce) jars
SHARP CHEDDAR CHEESE	24 ounces (6 cups)
6-INCH CORN TORTILLAS	30

TO ASSEMBLE AND STORE

- Add 24 ounces (6 cups) of the cheddar to the chicken filling in step 3. (The remaining 6 ounces of cheddar is for the topping.)
- Assemble the enchiladas as described in step 4 (5 at a time) and arrange into three 13 by 9-inch casserole dishes following the illustrations on page 255.
- Wrap the dishes tightly with plastic wrap and then foil. Refrigerate the enchiladas, sauce, and cheese topping separately for up to 3 days or freeze separately for up to 1 month.

TO BAKE

- Bake the casseroles at the same time on the upper-middle and lower-middle racks as directed in step 6.
- If frozen, the sauce will need to be thawed in the microwave on medium-high for 8 to 12 minutes (stopping to break apart any large ice crystals with a fork) before spreading over the enchiladas in step 7.

CHICKEN POT PIE

MOST EVERYONE LOVES A GOOD CHICKEN pot pie—juicy chunks of chicken, fresh vegetables, and a full-flavored sauce covered with warm pastry—though few seem to have the time or energy to make one on a weeknight. Given the many time-consuming steps it can take to make a traditional pot pie, we wanted to develop an easier make-ahead version so that we could stock our freezer with pot pies to pull out at a moment's notice any night of the week.

We began by determining the best way to cook the chicken, using legs and thighs for this initial round of tests. Steaming the chicken took a lot of time, requiring about one hour, and the steaming liquid didn't make a strong enough stock for the pot-pie sauce. Roasting a chicken also required an hour in the oven and by the time we took off the skin and mixed the meat in with the sauce and vegetables, the roasted flavor was lost. We had similar results with braised chicken. It lost its delicious flavor once the browned skin was removed.

Next we tried poaching, the most traditional cooking method. Of the two poaching liquids we tried, we preferred the chicken poached in wine and broth to the one poached in broth alone. The wine infused the meat and made for a richer, fuller-flavored sauce. Now we were ready to test a cut-up chicken against quicker cooking boneless, skinless chicken breasts.

Because boneless, skinless breasts cook so quickly, sautéing is generally a good cooking method for them. So before comparing poached parts versus poached breasts, we tried cooking the breasts three different ways. We cut raw breast meat into bite-sized pieces and sautéed them; we sautéed whole breasts, shredding the breast meat once it was cool enough to handle; and we poached whole breasts in broth, also shredding the meat. For simplicity's sake, we had hoped to like the sautéed whole breasts but, once again, poaching was our favorite method. Sautéing caused the outer layer of meat to turn crusty, a texture we did not like in the pie. The sautéed chicken pieces also floated independently in the sauce; their surfaces were too smooth for the sauce to adhere to. By contrast, the tender, irregularly shaped poached chicken pieces mixed well with the vegetables and, much like textured pasta, caused the sauce to cling.

Our only concern with the poached boneless, skinless breasts was the quality of the broth. In earlier tests, we found that bone-in parts could be poached in store-bought broth (rather than homemade stock) without much sacrifice in flavor. But we wondered how quick-cooking boneless, skinless breasts would fare in canned broth. The answer? Not as bad as we feared. In our comparison of the pies made with boneless breasts poached in homemade stock and store-bought broth, we found little difference in quality. Evidently, it's not the cooking time of the chicken but the abundance of ingredients in a pot pie that makes it possible to use store-bought broth with no ill consequences.

Then we decided to make things even easier by poaching the chicken directly in the sauce. Not only was the sauce more flavorful—since it benefited from the juices the chicken yielded while cooking—but the chicken absorbed more flavor as well. Ultimately, we were able to shave half an hour off the cooking time (10 minutes to cook the breasts compared with 40 minutes to cook the parts) and lots of mess and cleanup by poaching directly in the sauce.

Our experiences with making pot pie also made us aware of another difficulty: the vegetables tend to overcook. A filling that is chock-full of bright, fresh vegetables going into the oven looks completely different after 40 minutes of high-heat baking under a blanket of dough. Carrots become mushy, while peas and fresh herbs fade from spring green to drab olive. We wanted to preserve the vegetables' color as long as it didn't require any unnatural acts to do so.

We began by making pies with the classic peas and carrots combination, using raw vegetables, sautéed vegetables, frozen vegetables, and parboiled vegetables. After comparing the pies, we found that the frozen vegetables—the most convenient option—held their color and flavor best, the parboiled ones less so. The raw vegetables were not fully cooked at the end of the baking time and gave off too much liquid, watering down the flavor and thickness of the sauce.

TESTING KITCHEN TIP:
Ensuring Juicy, Moist Chicken

Many pot-pie recipes (and chicken casseroles) call for cutting the chicken into pieces prior to cooking. Sure, smaller pieces of chicken cook faster, but the result is a pie with dry, chewy pieces of meat. We found a better way—cook whole breasts, then shred them into pieces. Poaching whole chicken breasts directly in the sauce not only resulted in juicy chicken, but the chicken also imparted its meaty flavor to the sauce, resulting in a better flavor overall.

Next we wanted to develop a sauce that was flavorful, creamy, and had the proper consistency. Chicken pot pie sauce is traditionally based on a roux (a mixture of butter and flour sautéed together briefly), which is thinned with chicken broth and often enriched with cream. Because of the dish's inherent richness, we wanted to see how little cream we could get away with using. We tried three different pot-pie fillings, using 1½ cups cream, 2 cups half-and-half, and 2½ cups milk. Going into the oven, all of the fillings seemed to have the right consistency and creaminess; when they came out, however, it was a different story. Vegetable and meat juices diluted the consistency and creaminess of the milk and half-and-half sauces. To achieve a creamy-looking sauce, we needed to stick to cream. Next, we tested different amounts of cream: 1½ cups, 1 cup, and ¾ cup. The ¾ cup made a sauce that wasn't rich enough; the 1½-cup filling was too heavy, while the cream overpowered the other flavors. The 1-cup filling was just right; silky on the tongue and it let the other flavors in the filling come through.

We had worked out the right consistency, but the sauce still tasted a little bland. Lemon juice, a flavor heightener we had seen in a number of recipes, had the same dulling effect on the color of the vegetables as wine. We tried vermouth and it worked perfectly. Because vermouth is more intensely flavored than white wine, it gave us the flavor we were seeking without having to use large amounts.

Last, we wondered if we could place pie dough directly onto a hot filling, and then place the whole casserole in the refrigerator or freezer until we were ready to bake it—without adverse consequences. Not a chance. Once baked, the crust turned dense instead of flaky. But how could we cool the filling quickly? Our solution was to add the frozen peas and carrots at the last minute—the chill from the frozen vegetables quickly brought down the temperature of the filling. The trick worked like magic and our pie crust baked just like we wanted it to—golden brown and flaky.

One final note: As with any juicy pie, it's important to seal the sides, so the sauce doesn't leak out and make a mess of your oven. We also opted not to make ventilation holes for our chicken pie to keep all the juices inside the pie—where they belong.

FREEZE IT

Chicken Pot Pie

SERVES 6 TO 8

While we think the best pot pies are those with homemade pie crust, you can substitute store-bought pie dough (see page 260 for more information); you will need to buy 2 crusts.

6	tablespoons (¾ stick) unsalted butter
2	medium onions, minced
3	small celery ribs, sliced ¼ inch thick
	Salt
¾	cup unbleached all-purpose flour
¾	cup dry vermouth
4	cups low-sodium chicken broth
1	cup heavy cream
2	teaspoons minced fresh thyme leaves, or ½ teaspoon dried
3	pounds boneless, skinless chicken breasts (7 to 8 breasts), trimmed
1	(1-pound) bag frozen pea and carrot medley (about 3 cups; do not thaw)
	Ground black pepper
1	recipe Savory Pie Dough (page 259), chilled (see note)

1. Melt the butter in a Dutch oven over medium-high heat. Stir in the onions, celery, and 1 teaspoon salt and cook until softened and lightly browned, 5 to 7 minutes. Stir in the flour and cook, stirring constantly, until lightly browned, about 1 minute.

2. Gradually whisk in the vermouth and cook until evaporated, about 30 seconds. Slowly whisk in the broth, cream, and thyme. Add the chicken, partially cover, and bring to a simmer. Reduce the heat to low, cover completely, and cook until the thickest part of the chicken registers 160 degrees on an instant-read thermometer, 10 to 15 minutes.

3. Remove the pot from the heat. Remove the chicken and set it aside to cool. When the chicken is cool enough to handle, shred it into bite-sized pieces. Stir the shredded chicken back into the sauce with the peas and carrots and season with salt and pepper to taste.

4. Pour the mixture into a 13 by 9-inch baking dish. Following the illustrations on page 260, roll out the pie dough, fit it over the baking dish, and crimp the edges tightly to seal.

5. To STORE: Wrap the dish tightly in plastic wrap and then foil and refrigerate for up to 2 days or freeze for up 1 month. (It is not necessary to thaw the frozen pot pie before baking.)

6. To SERVE: Adjust an oven rack to the middle position and heat the oven to 375 degrees. Unwrap the dish and place the pot pie on a foil-lined rimmed baking sheet. Bake until the filling is hot and the crust is golden, about 1¼ hours if refrigerated or about 1¾ hours if frozen.

TO SERVE RIGHT AWAY
Bake as directed in step 6, reducing the baking time to 1 hour.

Bake Half, Freeze Half
Follow the recipe for Chicken Pot Pie and divide the filling between two 8 by 8-inch casserole dishes (each will serve 4) or three 9 by 3-inch loaf pans (each will serve 2 to 3); top each with pie dough. The casseroles can be baked right away or wrapped tightly with plastic wrap and then foil and refrigerated for up to 2 days or frozen for up to 1 month. It is not necessary to thaw the pot pies before baking. See reheating instructions below.

TO BAKE IMMEDIATELY
Place the pot pie on a foil-lined rimmed baking sheet. Bake in a 375-degree oven until the filling is hot and the crust is golden, 30 to 40 minutes.

TO BAKE IF REFRIGERATED
Unwrap the dish and place the pot pie on a foil-lined rimmed baking sheet. Bake in a 375-degree oven until the filling is hot and the crust is golden, 40 to 50 minutes.

TO BAKE IF FROZEN
Unwrap the dish and place the pot pie on a foil-lined rimmed baking sheet. Bake in a 375-degree oven until the filling is hot and the crust is golden, 1¼ to 1¾ hours.

Savory Pie Dough

MAKES ENOUGH FOR 1 POT-PIE RECIPE

For best results, be sure to use chilled vegetable shortening and chilled butter.

1½	cups (7½ ounces) unbleached all-purpose flour, plus extra for dusting the work surface
½	teaspoon salt
4	tablespoons vegetable shortening, chilled
8	tablespoons (1 stick) unsalted butter, chilled and cut into ¼-inch cubes
3–5	tablespoons ice water

1. Process the flour and salt in a food processor until combined. Add the shortening and process until the mixture has the texture of coarse sand, about 10 seconds. Scatter the butter cubes over the top and pulse until the mixture is pale yellow and resembles coarse crumbs, with butter bits no larger than small peas, about ten 1-second pulses. Turn the mixture into a medium bowl.

2. Sprinkle 3 tablespoons of the ice water over the mixture. With a rubber spatula, use a folding motion to mix. Press down on the dough with the broad side of the spatula until the dough sticks together, adding up to 2 tablespoons more ice water if necessary. Press the dough into a 5 by 4-inch rectangle (see the illustration on page 260) and wrap tightly with plastic wrap. Refrigerate until chilled, at least 30 minutes. Roll out the pie dough, top the pot pie, and seal the edges following the illustrations on page 260.

Most store-bought pie dough has already been rolled out and cut into a round shape that works great if you're making a round pie, but is very awkward if topping a 13 by 9-inch baking dish for a pot pie. Our solution to this problem is simple—divide the filling between two 9-inch deep-dish pie plates or round 8 by 8-inch casserole dishes. The pie dough can then simply be laid over the top and sealed to the edges of the dishes, following the illustrations at right. For baking times, refer to the "Bake Half, Freeze Half" instructions on pages 259 and 262.

INGREDIENTS:
Store-Bought Pie Dough

A flaky, buttery homemade pie crust is the ultimate crown for our Chicken and Beef Pot Pies, but it's also a fair amount of work. How much would we sacrifice by using a store-bought crust instead? To find out, we tried several types and brands—both dry mixes (just add water) and ready-made crusts, either frozen or refrigerated.

The dry mixes, including Betty Crocker ($1.69), Jiffy ($0.99), Krusteaz ($3.28), and Pillsbury ($1.39), all had problems. Some were too salty, some were too sweet, and all required both mixing and rolling—not much work saved. Frozen crusts, including Mrs. Smith's (also sold as Oronoque Orchards, $2.69) and Pillsbury Pet-Ritz ($2.69), required zero prep, but tasters found them pasty and bland, and it was nearly impossible to pry them from the flimsy foil "pie plate" in which they are sold. The one refrigerated contender, Pillsbury Just Unroll! Pie Crusts, wasn't bad. Though the flavor was somewhat bland, the crust baked up to an impressive flakiness. Better yet, this fully prepared product comes rolled up and is flexible enough to top a pie or line one of your own pie plates.

THE BEST STORE-BOUGHT PIE DOUGH
Pillsbury Just Unroll! Pie Crusts, $2.79 for two 9-inch crusts—the hard part is over, and the flavor and texture are fine.

ROLLING OUT AND ARRANGING HOMEMADE PIE DOUGH ON A POT PIE

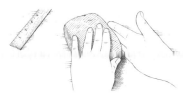

1. Press the dough into a 5 by 4-inch rectangle and wrap tightly with plastic wrap. Refrigerate until chilled, at least 30 minutes.

2. When the pot-pie filling is ready and the dough is chilled, roll the dough on a floured surface to a 15 by 11-inch rectangle, about ⅛ inch thick. (If making two 8 by 8-inch casseroles or 3 loaf pans, divide the dough into 2 or 3 portions before rolling it out.)

3. Roll the dough loosely over the rolling pin and unroll it evenly over the baking dish.

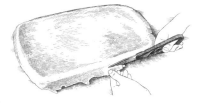

4. Trim the dough, leaving ½ inch hanging over the pan lip.

5. Press the dough firmly to seal it to the lip of the pan. (For a decorative border, press the edges of the pie with the tines of a fork.)

BEEF POT PIE

PLAINLY STATED, BEEF POT PIE IS BEEF STEW baked under a crusty topping. After hours of slow simmering, the stew is ladled into a baking dish, topped with biscuits or a pastry crust, and cooked even longer. It is an all-day affair, requiring hours of diligent attention. To us, it begs the question: Why? Certainly there's nothing wrong with such a labor of love, but we wanted a simpler, faster alternative that could linger in the refrigerator or freezer for a couple of days before its time in the oven.

We commenced the testing process with our primary concern: the choice of meat. Beef stew develops its rich flavor through a slow, deliberate simmering of inexpensive yet flavorful cuts of beef. Our favorite cut happens to be chuck roast, a marbled, collagen-rich roast that contains a good deal of flavor, as long as it is cooked slowly over low heat. But, cooked quickly and over high heat, chuck roast is as tough and bland as a tire. How could we hasten its cooking and turn the tough meat tender? Trimming the meat into smaller cubes than our stew specified—petite 1-inch as opposed to 2-inch pieces—seemed like a logical next step. After browning the meat and simmering it slowly on the stovetop, we found that it was both tender and flavorful within 45 minutes—a far cry from the multihour simmer required for the stew. In addition, the meat continued to tenderize when baked under a crust for another 40 minutes.

With the meat chosen, we could now work on finessing the pie's flavor. Sticking to the basics, we included onions, carrots, peas, and garlic. But tasters wanted a less old-fashioned filling, so we upped the amount of onions and garlic to make a more flavorful stew and we added portobello mushrooms for their rich, meaty flavor and the toothsome heft they added to the mixture.

For the broth, we tried both chicken and beef broth. Chicken broth yielded a weakly flavored stew, while beef broth made the stew taste metallic. Our solution was to fortify the flavor of the chicken broth by adding rosemary, tomato paste, cream, and a cup of sherry. The end result was a rich brown sauce, which tasters found as satisfying as classic beef stew, yet more interesting.

To further enrich the flavor, we borrowed a trick from Cajun cooking and lightly toasted the flour that is used as a thickener. Subjected to dry heat (with or without oil or butter), flour browns and develops a nutty, malty flavor. Cajun cooks brown the flour to a dark mahogany when making gumbo; we took it to a light chestnut for our pot-pie filling.

We had learned from our chicken pot pie tests (page 258), that we needed our filling to be close to room temperature before we placed the crust on top in order for it to bake properly. So, we used the same trick of adding the frozen peas and carrots to the beef stew mixture when it came off the heat, to help bring the temperature down quickly. We also used the same procedure for sealing the crust to the sides and refraining from ventilation marks, to prevent puddles of sauce from forming on top of the pot pie. The end result was a pleasing mix of creamy, rich beef stew and flaky pie crust.

FREEZE IT

Beef Pot Pie

SERVES 6 TO 8

For the best flavor, buy a chuck roast and trim and cut it yourself rather than purchasing prepackaged stew meat. To speed things up, look to see if your local grocery store sells chuck steaks, which are easier to cut, and need less time to prepare. While we think the best pot pies are those with homemade pie crust, you can substitute a store-bought pie dough (see page 260 for more information); you will need to buy 2 crusts.

3   pounds chuck roast, trimmed and cut into
     1-inch cubes
     Salt and ground black pepper
3   tablespoons vegetable oil
4   tablespoons (½ stick) unsalted butter
12 ounces portobello mushroom caps (about
     4 large caps), wiped clean and cut into
     ½-inch pieces
2   medium onions, minced
2   tablespoons tomato paste
4   medium garlic cloves, minced or pressed
     through a garlic press (about 4 teaspoons)
2   teaspoons minced fresh thyme leaves,
     or ½ teaspoon dried

1 teaspoon minced fresh rosemary,
or ¼ teaspoon dried
¾ cup unbleached all-purpose flour
1 cup dry sherry
4 cups low-sodium chicken broth
1 cup heavy cream
1 (1-pound) bag frozen pea and carrot medley
(about 3 cups; do not thaw)
1 recipe Savory Pie Dough (page 259), chilled
(see note)

1. Pat the beef dry with paper towels and season with salt and pepper. Heat 2 tablespoons of the oil in a large Dutch oven over medium-high heat until shimmering. Add half of the meat and cook, stirring occasionally, until well browned, 7 to 10 minutes, reducing the heat if the pot begins to scorch. Transfer the browned beef to a medium bowl. Repeat with the remaining 1 tablespoon oil and beef and transfer to the bowl.

2. Add the butter to the Dutch oven and melt over medium-low heat. Add the portobellos, onions, and 1 teaspoon salt. Cover and cook, stirring often, until the mushrooms have released their liquid, about 10 minutes. Uncover, increase the heat to medium-high, and continue to cook, stirring often, until the mushrooms are dry and browned, 5 to 10 minutes longer.

3. Stir in the tomato paste, garlic, thyme, and rosemary and cook until fragrant, about 30 seconds. Stir in the flour and cook, stirring constantly, about 1 minute. Gradually stir in the sherry, scraping up any browned bits. Slowly whisk in the broth and cream.

4. Add the browned meat with any accumulated juices and bring to a simmer. Reduce the heat to low, partially cover, and continue to simmer, stirring occasionally, until the meat is tender, about 45 minutes.

5. Off the heat, stir in the peas and carrots and season to taste with salt and pepper. Pour the mixture into a 13 by 9-inch baking dish. Following the illustrations on page 260, roll out the pie dough, fit it over the baking dish, and crimp the edges tightly to seal.

6. To store: Wrap the dish tightly in plastic wrap and then foil and refrigerate for up to 2 days or freeze for up 1 month. (It is not necessary to thaw the frozen pot pie before baking.)

7. To serve: Adjust an oven rack to the middle position and heat the oven to 375 degrees. Unwrap the dish and place the pot pie on a foil-lined rimmed baking sheet. Bake until the filling is hot and the crust is golden, about 1¼ hours if refrigerated or about 1¾ hours if frozen.

TO SERVE RIGHT AWAY

Bake as directed in step 7, reducing the baking time to 1 hour.

Bake Half, Freeze Half

Follow the recipe for Beef Pot Pie and divide the filling between two 8 by 8-inch casserole dishes (each will serve 4) or three 9 by 3-inch loaf pans (each will serve 2 to 3); top each with pie dough. The casseroles can be baked right away or covered tightly with plastic wrap and then foil and refrigerated for up to 2 days or frozen for up to 1 month. See reheating instructions below.

TO BAKE IMMEDIATELY

Place the pot pie on a foil-lined rimmed baking sheet. Bake in a 375-degree oven until the filling is hot and the crust is golden, 30 to 40 minutes.

TO BAKE IF REFRIGERATED

Unwrap the dish and place the pot pie on a foil-lined rimmed baking sheet. Bake in a 375-degree oven until the filling is hot and the crust is golden, 40 to 50 minutes.

TO BAKE IF FROZEN

Unwrap the dish and place the pot pie on a foil-lined rimmed baking sheet. Bake in a 375-degree oven until the filling is hot and the crust is golden, 1¼ to 1½ hours.

TAMALE PIE

TAMALE PIE HAS ITS ROOTS IN SOUTHWESTERN cooking. Although time and fashion have altered the recipe from decade to decade, the basic idea remains the same: a good pie contains a juicy, spicy mixture of meat and vegetables encased in or topped with a cornmeal crust. The flavors please adults and children alike, making it a popular weeknight supper option. Bad tamale pies, however, are dry and bland and usually have too much or too little filling. We wanted to develop a really good tamale pie—one with just the right proportion of filling to topping and we wanted it all to taste great. We also wanted to be able to pull this casserole from the fridge or freezer and have it bake up as fresh tasting as one freshly prepared.

We did have a number of questions about how to prepare the cornmeal topping. For starters, did we want it to taste like the exterior of real tamales (made from masa) or should it be more like cornbread (as we'd seen in so many other recipes)? The tamale-style topping was a bit bland and just didn't warrant the efforts of multiple trips around town to locate the masa. The slightly sweet, spongy cornbread was toothsome and had nice corn flavor. Tasters also preferred the clean, simple flavor of cornbread in contrast with the spicy meat filling; it was clearly the winner.

But could we pour a raw batter over a casserole and then let it sit for a day or two in the refrigerator (or even longer in the freezer) and still have it bake into a puffy bread topping? We were doubtful. But pleasantly our fears were not realized. The batter baked into tasty cornbread every time we baked the casserole, whether from the freezer or from the refrigerator. With the cornbread topping in place, we moved on to the filling.

Most recipes use either ground beef or ground pork as the base. We tested both and the all-beef pie was preferred for being rich and flavorful, whereas the all-pork pie was simply too mild in flavor. Most tamale pie fillings call for tomatoes, corn, and black beans. We found that this simple recipe easily accommodates canned tomatoes and beans and frozen corn with no ill effect on the final flavor. Seasoned with onion, garlic, jalapeño, lime juice, cilantro, and a little fresh oregano, the tamale filling tasted fresh and spicy. But, we still found that the filling needed a binder, so rather then sprinkling the cheese on top of the beef mixture, we decided to mix it in with the filling. This solution made a moist, thick filling.

Putting together the filling and topping was simple. We poured the filling into a large baking dish and topped it with cornbread batter, which, as loose as it was, was easy to spread into an even layer to the edges of the dish. A moderately high oven temperature did the best job of getting a golden, light crust and heating the filling.

Tasters liked this combination so much, that they insisted that we create a vegetarian version. So with that in mind we took out the beef and instead bulked up our filling with more beans and zucchini. For some heat and great smoky flavor, we added chipotle chiles. The result was so loved that it is still debated whether the vegetarian or beef tamale pie is better. We hope you'll test them both and decide for yourself.

FREEZE IT

Beef Tamale Pie
SERVES 6 TO 8

For more heat, include the jalapeño seeds and ribs when mincing. Don't mix the cornbread topping until you are ready to spread it over the tamale pie filling. You can substitute 2 (6.5- to 8.5-ounce) packages of cornbread mix for our Homemade Cornbread Topping; mix the batter according to the package instructions and dollop over the pie as directed in step 3. Serve with sour cream, chopped green onions, minced cilantro, and lime wedges.

I	tablespoon vegetable oil
I½	pounds (90 percent lean) ground beef
I	medium onion, minced
I	medium jalapeño chile, seeds and ribs removed, chile minced (see note)
	Salt
2	tablespoons chili powder
4	medium garlic cloves, minced or pressed through a garlic press (about 4 teaspoons)
I	tablespoon tomato paste
I	tablespoon minced fresh oregano leaves, or I teaspoon dried
I	teaspoon ground cumin
¼	teaspoon cayenne pepper
I	(28-ounce) can diced tomatoes
I	(15.5-ounce) can black beans, rinsed and drained

1½ cups frozen corn (do not thaw)
8 ounces Monterey Jack cheese, shredded (about 2 cups)
¼ cup minced fresh cilantro leaves
4 teaspoons juice from 2 limes
Ground black pepper
1 recipe Homemade Cornbread Topping (recipe follows)

1. Heat the oil in a large skillet over medium-high heat until shimmering. Add the beef and cook, breaking up large clumps of meat with a wooden spoon, until it is no longer pink, about 5 minutes. Stir in the onion, jalapeño, and 1 teaspoon salt and cook until softened and lightly browned, 5 to 7 minutes. Stir in the chili powder, garlic, tomato paste, oregano, cumin, and cayenne and cook until fragrant, about 30 seconds.

2. Stir in the diced tomatoes with their juices, scraping up any browned bits. Off the heat, stir in the black beans, corn, cheese, cilantro, and lime juice and season with salt and pepper to taste.

3. Transfer the beef mixture to a 13 by 9-inch baking dish. Spread the cornmeal topping evenly over the filling, pushing it to the edges of the baking dish.

4. To STORE: Wrap the dish tightly with plastic wrap that has been sprayed with vegetable oil spray and then foil and refrigerate for up to 2 days or freeze for up to 1 month.

5. To SERVE: Adjust an oven rack to the middle position and heat the oven to 375 degrees. Unwrap the dish. If refrigerated, bake, uncovered, until the filling is bubbly and the crust is baked through and golden, 50 to 60 minutes. If frozen, unwrap the dish and let the casserole sit at room temperature for 30 minutes while the oven heats, then cover tightly with aluminum foil and bake for about 30 minutes. Remove the foil and bake until the filling is bubbly and the crust is baked through and golden, 50 to 60 minutes longer.

TO SERVE RIGHT AWAY

Bake, uncovered, as directed in step 5, reducing the baking time to 45 minutes.

Homemade Cornbread Topping

MAKES ENOUGH TO TOP ONE
13 X 9-INCH TAMALE PIE

1½ cups unbleached all-purpose flour
1 cup yellow cornmeal
6 tablespoons sugar
2 teaspoons baking powder
¾ teaspoon salt
¼ teaspoon baking soda
1 cup buttermilk
8 tablespoons (1 stick) unsalted butter, melted and cooled
2 large eggs

1. Whisk the flour, cornmeal, sugar, baking powder, salt, and baking soda together in a large bowl.

2. In a separate bowl, whisk the buttermilk, butter, and eggs together. Stir the buttermilk mixture into the flour mixture until uniform. Use as directed in Beef Tamale Pie (page 263) and Vegetable and Bean Tamale Pie (below).

➤ VARIATION

Vegetable and Bean Tamale Pie

Don't mix the cornbread topping until you are ready to spread it over the tamale pie filling. You can substitute 2 (6.5- to 8.5-ounce) packages of cornbread mix for our Homemade Cornbread Topping; mix the batter according to the package instructions and dollop over the pie as directed in step 3.

3 tablespoons vegetable oil
1 medium onion, minced
Salt
2 (28-ounce) cans diced tomatoes, well drained, with 2 cups juice reserved
2 teaspoons sugar
2 tablespoons chili powder
4 medium garlic cloves, minced or pressed through a garlic press (about 4 teaspoons)
2–4 teaspoons minced chipotle chiles in adobo sauce

2 teaspoons minced fresh oregano leaves, or 1 teaspoon dried

1 teaspoon ground cumin

1 (15.5-ounce) can black beans, rinsed and drained

1 (15.5-ounce) can kidney or pinto beans, rinsed and drained

1½ cups frozen corn (do not thaw)

1 medium zucchini (about 12 ounces), cut into ½-inch cubes

8 ounces Monterey Jack cheese, shredded (about 2 cups)

¼ cup minced fresh cilantro leaves

4 teaspoons lime juice from 2 limes
Ground black pepper

1 recipe Homemade Cornbread Topping (page 264)

1. Heat the oil in a large Dutch oven over medium-high heat until shimmering. Add the onion and ½ teaspoon salt and cook until softened and lightly browned, 5 to 7 minutes. Stir in the tomatoes and sugar and cook, stirring often, until the tomatoes are very dry and browned, 10 to 15 minutes.

2. Stir in the chili powder, garlic, chipotles, oregano, and cumin and cook until fragrant, about 1 minute. Stir in the reserved tomato juice, scraping up any browned bits. Off the heat, stir in the black beans, kidney beans, corn, zucchini, cheese, cilantro, and lime juice and season with salt and pepper to taste.

3. Transfer the bean mixture to a 13 by 9-inch baking dish. Spread the cornmeal topping evenly over the filling, pushing it to the edges of the baking dish.

4. To STORE: Wrap the dish tightly with plastic wrap that has been sprayed with vegetable oil spray and then foil and refrigerate for up to 2 days or freeze for up to 1 month.

5. To SERVE: Adjust an oven rack to the middle position and heat the oven to 375 degrees. Unwrap the dish. If refrigerated, bake, uncovered, until the filling is bubbly and the crust is baked through and golden, 50 to 60 minutes. If frozen, unwrap the dish and let the casserole sit at room temperature for 30 minutes while the oven heats, then cover tightly with aluminum foil and bake for about 30 minutes.

Remove the foil and bake until the filling is bubbly and the crust is baked through and golden, 50 to 60 minutes longer.

TO SERVE RIGHT AWAY
Bake, uncovered, as directed in step 5, reducing the baking time to 45 minutes.

Bake Half, Freeze Half
Follow the recipes for Beef Tamale Pie or Vegetable and Bean Tamale Pie and divide the ingredients between two 8 by 8-inch casserole dishes (each will serve 4) or three 9 by 3-inch loaf pans (each will serve 2 to 3). The casseroles can be baked right away or covered tightly with plastic wrap that has been sprayed with vegetable oil spray and then foil and refrigerated for up to 2 days or frozen for up to 1 month. See reheating instructions below.

TO BAKE IMMEDIATELY
Bake the casserole in a 375-degree oven, uncovered, until the filling is bubbly and the crust is baked through and golden, about 30 minutes.

TO BAKE IF REFRIGERATED
Unwrap the dish and bake in a 375-degree oven, uncovered, until the filling is bubbly and the crust is baked through and golden, 40 to 45 minutes.

TO BAKE IF FROZEN
While the oven heats to 375 degrees, unwrap the dish and let the casserole sit at room temperature for 30 minutes. Then, cover the dish tightly with aluminum foil and bake for about 20 minutes. Remove the foil and continue to bake until the filling is bubbly and the crust is baked through and golden, about 40 minutes longer.

SHEPHERD'S PIE
NOTHING MORE THAN A RICH LAMB STEW blanketed under a mashed-potato crust, shepherd's pie is a hearty casserole originally from northern Britain. Today, it is as much a part of American cookery as British, best eaten on a blustery winter

day while sidled up to a roaring fire with a frothy pint of stout. It's arguably America's favorite lamb dish.

Like numerous other dishes in this book, shepherd's pie was a meal traditionally made on Monday with Sunday night's leftovers—the remnants of the roast, vegetables, and mashed potatoes. In this day and age, few of us have such delicious Sunday dinners, much less leftovers, so we aimed to create an assertively flavored, but simple to prepare make-ahead shepherd's pie from scratch.

Our first step was to figure out which cut of lamb worked best. To save on prep time, we hoped to use ground lamb. Shepherd's pie made with ground lamb was pretty good, but a bit bland, so we had to figure out how to heighten the flavor. We added a bit of tomato paste to bring out the sweeter meaty tones and then a dab of Worcestershire sauce to bring forth the lamb's more subtle flavors.

With the basic lamb flavors adequately elevated, we turned to choosing vegetables to complement the lamb. Sautéed onions added sweetness and depth, while a touch of garlic added a little zest. And sweet frozen peas and carrots—characteristic of many British-style meat stews—brought bright color to an otherwise drab-looking dish.

For herbs, we wanted big flavors strong enough to stand up to the lamb's richness. Rosemary and thyme are traditional lamb flavorings, and they tasted great in this instance. Fresh, not dried, herbs provided the best flavor.

As for the liquid in the stew, we settled on chicken broth enriched with red wine. Beef broth clashed with the lamb's earthy flavors, while chicken broth was neutral. After testing a variety of red wines, we liked a medium-bodied Côtes du Rhône best because it is well rounded and low in tannins—traits that allow it to marry well with the rich flavors in the dish. With the stew assembled and cooked, we were ready to top it off with a mashed-potato crust. We quickly found out that simple mashed potatoes would not do; they crumbled and broke down while baking. We started our adjustments by reducing the amount of butter and dairy we usually add to mashed potatoes, so that when placed on top of the lamb sauce they would stay there instead of sinking into the lamb mixture.

We felt that cream, rather than whole milk or half-and-half, made mashed potatoes that held together better when refrigerated or frozen.

Assembling was as easy as pouring the filling into a 13 by 9-inch dish. A large rubber spatula was the best tool for spreading the potatoes evenly across the top of the stew. We found that it was important to completely cover the stew and seal the edges of the dish with the potato topping; otherwise the stew sometimes bubbled out of the dish.

Because the lamb is already tender when it goes into the casserole, the baking time is short. Once the potato crust begins to turn golden brown, the shepherd's pie is ready to come out of the oven.

FREEZE IT

Shepherd's Pie

SERVES 6 TO 8

To add a little color, sprinkle the dish with some minced parsley before serving. Ground beef chuck (or even ground turkey) can be substituted for the ground lamb. For a beef or turkey version, use 2 tablespoons of vegetable oil for the reserved lamb drippings in step 2.

3	pounds ground lamb
2	medium onions, minced
	Salt
4	medium garlic cloves, minced or pressed through a garlic press (about 4 teaspoons)
2	tablespoons tomato paste
⅓	cup unbleached all-purpose flour
3	cups low-sodium chicken broth
¾	cup dry red wine such as Côtes du Rhône
2	teaspoons minced fresh thyme leaves, or ½ teaspoon dried
I	teaspoon Worcestershire sauce
I	teaspoon minced fresh rosemary, or ¼ teaspoon dried
I	(1-pound) bag frozen pea and carrot medley (about 3 cups; do not thaw)
	Ground black pepper
3	pounds russet potatoes (about 6 medium), peeled and sliced ¾ inch thick
I½	cups heavy cream, warmed
4	tablespoons (½ stick) unsalted butter, softened

1. Cook the lamb in a large Dutch oven over medium-high heat, breaking the meat into small pieces with a wooden spoon, until the meat is no longer pink and the fat has rendered, about 5 minutes. Drain the lamb through a fine-mesh strainer, reserving the drippings.

2. Return 2 tablespoons of the reserved lamb drippings to the pot and heat over medium-low heat until shimmering. Add the onions and 1 teaspoon salt and cook until softened and lightly browned, 5 to 7 minutes. Stir in the garlic and tomato paste and cook until fragrant, about 30 seconds. Stir in the flour and cook, whisking constantly, until incorporated, about 1 minute. Whisk in the broth and wine, scraping up any browned bits. Stir in the drained lamb, thyme, Worcestershire sauce, and rosemary and cook until the mixture begins to thicken, about 2 minutes. Off the heat, stir in the peas and carrots and season with salt and pepper to taste. Transfer the mixture into a 13 by 9-inch casserole dish; set aside.

3. Meanwhile, place the potatoes in a large Dutch oven and cover by 1 inch of water. Bring to a boil over high heat, then reduce to a simmer and cook until the potatoes are tender (a paring knife can be slipped into and out of the center of the potatoes with very little resistance), about 20 minutes. Drain the potatoes, return them to the pot set over low heat, and mash to a smooth consistency. Stir in the cream, followed by the butter. Season with salt and pepper to taste.

4. With a large spoon, dollop the mashed potatoes over the lamb filling. Using a rubber spatula, smooth the potatoes out into an even layer and push to the edges of the baking dish.

5. To STORE: Wrap the dish tightly with plastic wrap that has been sprayed with vegetable oil spray and then foil and refrigerate for up to 2 days or freeze for up to 1 month. (If frozen, the casserole must be thawed completely in the refrigerator, about 24 hours, before baking.)

6. To SERVE: Adjust an oven rack to the middle position and heat the oven to 400 degrees. Unwrap the dish and place the casserole on a foil-lined rimmed baking sheet. Bake until the sauce is bubbling and the top is browned, about 1 hour.

TO SERVE RIGHT AWAY
Bake as directed in step 6, reducing the baking time to 35 minutes.

Bake Half, Freeze Half
Follow the recipe for Shepherd's Pie and divide the pie between two 8 by 8-inch casserole dishes (each will serve 4) or three 9 by 3-inch loaf pans (each will serve 2 to 3). The casseroles can be baked right away or covered tightly with plastic wrap and then foil and refrigerated for up to 2 days or frozen for up to 1 month. See reheating instructions below.

TO BAKE IMMEDIATELY
Place the casserole on a foil-lined rimmed baking sheet. Bake, uncovered, in a 400-degree oven until the sauce is bubbling and the top is browned, 20 to 25 minutes.

TO BAKE IF REFRIGERATED
Unwrap the dish and place the casserole on a foil-lined rimmed baking sheet. Bake, uncovered, in a

---

EQUIPMENT: Potato Mashers

For home-style spuds in a hurry, we eschew fancy gadgets and turn to a traditional hand-held potato masher. These come in two forms: wire-looped mashers with a zigzag presser or disk mashers with a perforated round plate. Although elbow grease is the main mashing factor, we found that without exception disk mashers were preferred for achieving a fast and even mash. Our favorite is the Profi Plus Masher ($15.99), whose comfortable grip, small holes, and oval mashing plate turned out mashed potatoes with a minimum of lumps and effort.

THE BEST POTATO MASHER

The Profi Plus Masher turned out mashed potatoes with a minimum of lumps.

400-degree oven until the sauce is bubbling and the top is browned, 40 to 45 minutes.

TO BAKE IF FROZEN

Thaw the casserole completely in the refrigerator, about 24 hours, then unwrap the dish and place the casserole on a foil-lined rimmed baking sheet. Bake, uncovered, in a 400-degree oven until the sauce is bubbling and the top is browned, 1¼ hours.

LAMB AND EGGPLANT MOUSSAKA

A WORKHORSE OF FINE GREEK RESTAURANTS and diners alike, moussaka is a rich casserole of roasted eggplant, meat-enriched (usually ground lamb) tomato sauce, and creamy béchamel. It is similar to lasagna in that it is a layered casserole, with sheets of eggplant instead of noodles sandwiching the filling and sauce. Moussaka can be a delicate, nuanced casserole, but more often than not, it's a heavy-handed, one-dimensional affair. The eggplant is rife with oil and the filling and sauce are cloyingly rich yet disappointingly bland. We wanted to make a version worth all the effort (it can be time-consuming to prepare each of the components) and could also be make-ahead.

Eggplant is the Achilles' heel of moussaka. Most of the recipes we found either pan-fried or roasted the eggplant before assembling the casserole. Fried eggplant was, across the board, greasy. We found that roasted eggplant wasn't nearly as greasy, requiring a minimum amount of oil to brown, and had a superior texture and flavor, so roasting it was.

Once the eggplant was cut and ready for the oven, we tossed it in a small amount of olive oil to promote browning and experimented with temperatures ranging between 375 and 500 degrees. Roasted too hot, the edges of the eggplant burned before the center cooked. Too low, and the slices took an eternity to brown and consequently turned mushy. We finally settled on 450 degrees for 45 minutes because the eggplant slices browned evenly without turning too soft.

But we were in for a rude surprise. We had cooked two sheet pans' worth of eggplant slices (from 4 pounds of eggplant), the most the oven could accommodate at one time—which we thought would be plenty. But when we went to assemble the moussaka, we found that there were barely enough eggplant slices for two layers in an 8 by 8-inch baking dish, or just four dinner-sized servings. We wanted the recipe to serve double that. So, to fill a 13 by 9-inch baking dish, we would have to prepare a staggering 8 pounds of eggplant, requiring a minimum of two hours to roast it all (two baking sheets a batch, the most home ovens will cook evenly). Coupling the extensive cooking time with the effort required for the filling and sauce, this was quickly becoming a long-winded recipe.

We decided to revisit how we were preparing the moussaka and whether or not there was a way to streamline things. Instead of slicing the eggplant into broad planks, we opted to cut it into chunky cubes, which allowed us to squeeze a slightly higher volume of eggplant onto each of the baking sheets. We placed these chunks of eggplant on the bottom of the casserole to be blanketed in filling, which was then capped with béchamel. Unconventional, perhaps, but it was a simple solution that minimized the work and time required.

The best lamb-and-tomato fillings we have tasted are rich, slightly sweet, and perfumed with cinnamon and oregano. Unlike ground beef that is sold with the fat content marked on the package, ground lamb is generally unmarked and almost always pretty fatty. We quickly realized that the meat needed to be browned and the excess fat drained off before we could add the filling's other ingredients.

A good quantity of onions and garlic was a given, their sweetness and piquancy lending the filling a solid base of flavor. We experimented with the usual canned tomato products—whole, diced, and pureed—and preferred the latter. Both whole (chopped coarsely) and diced tomatoes failed to break down to the thick, jammy consistency characteristic of our favorite moussaka fillings. To boost the fruity sweetness of the puree, we included a couple of tablespoons of tomato paste and sugar.

Slowly simmered for about half an hour, the filling's excess moisture evaporated and the flavors blended and tightened. After a couple of batches tasted flat, we realized that the filling needed some acidity—any tartness had been cooked out of the tomatoes. We easily settled on red wine as the best option because it provided a fruitiness that intensified the flavor of the tomatoes.

As for seasoning the filling, Greeks tend to include a fairly substantial amount of cinnamon. We found that too much cinnamon easily overpowered the dish's other flavors, so we settled on a modest ¾ teaspoon as the ideal amount. Briefly toasted in a small amount of oil, the spice's flavor was fuller than when left untoasted. And for herbs, oregano lent the right amount of freshness.

We had tested a variety of béchamel-style sauces for other recipes in this book and felt we had a leg up on things. The béchamel for moussaka should ideally form a thick blanket over the top, effectively sealing in the filling. We quickly realized that this béchamel had to be significantly thicker than most of those that we had prepared for other types of recipes. We added additional flour incrementally until we attained a thick, velvety texture that sealed in the bubbling filling and browned attractively.

In classic recipes, the béchamel is often enriched with a crumbly aged cheese called Myzithra. Salty, drier, and richer-tasting than Greece's more common feta cheese, we found that Myzithra's flavor could be approximated with a healthy dose of Parmesan.

Baking the moussaka was a simple matter of watching the filling percolate beneath the béchamel. We found that moussaka cooked quicker from both the refrigerator and the freezer then most of our other casseroles. A moderately hot oven—400 degrees—quickly brought the moussaka up to temperature without burning the béchamel in no time at all.

FREEZE IT

Lamb and Eggplant Moussaka

SERVES 6 TO 8

When buying eggplant, look for those that are glossy, feel firm, and are heavy for their size. Do not substitute low-fat or nonfat (skim) milk in the sauce.

4	pounds eggplant (about 4 medium), peeled and cut into ¾-inch cubes
3	tablespoons olive oil
	Salt and ground black pepper
2	pounds ground lamb
1	medium onion, minced
4	medium garlic cloves, minced or pressed through a garlic press (about 4 teaspoons)
¾	teaspoon ground cinnamon
2	tablespoons tomato paste
1	(28-ounce) can tomato puree
½	cup dry red wine
1	tablespoon minced fresh oregano leaves, or 1 teaspoon dried
1	teaspoon sugar
3	tablespoons unsalted butter
¼	cup unbleached all-purpose flour
2	cups whole milk
2	ounces Parmesan cheese, grated (about 1 cup)
	Pinch ground nutmeg

1. Adjust 2 oven racks to the lower-middle and upper-middle positions and heat the oven to 450 degrees. Line 2 rimmed baking sheets with aluminum foil and spray with vegetable oil spray (or use nonstick foil). Toss the eggplant with the oil, 1 teaspoon salt, and ¼ teaspoon pepper. Spread the eggplant evenly over the prepared baking sheets and bake until light golden brown, 40 to 50 minutes, switching and rotating the pans halfway though the roasting time. Set aside to cool.

2. Meanwhile, cook the lamb in a large Dutch oven over medium-high heat, breaking the meat into small pieces with a wooden spoon, until the meat is no longer pink and the fat has rendered, about 5 minutes. Drain the lamb through a fine-mesh strainer, reserving the drippings.

3. Return 2 tablespoons of the reserved lamb drippings to the pot and set it over medium heat until shimmering. Add the onion and 1 teaspoon salt and cook until softened and lightly browned, 5 to 7 minutes. Stir in the garlic and cinnamon and cook until fragrant, about 30 seconds. Stir in the tomato paste and cook for 30 seconds. Stir in the drained lamb, tomato puree, wine, oregano, and sugar. Bring to a simmer, reduce the heat to

low, cover partially, and cook, stirring occasionally, until the juices have evaporated and the sauce has thickened, 25 to 30 minutes. Season with salt and pepper to taste.

4. While the sauce simmers, melt the butter in a medium saucepan over medium-high heat. Add the flour and cook, stirring constantly, for 1 minute. Gradually whisk in the milk. Bring to a simmer and cook, whisking often, until the sauce thickens and no longer tastes of flour, about 5 minutes. Off the heat, whisk in the Parmesan and nutmeg and season to taste with salt and pepper; cover and set aside.

5. Spread the roasted eggplant evenly into a 13 by 9-inch baking dish. Spread the lamb filling over the eggplant, then pour the sauce evenly over the top.

6. To STORE: Wrap the dish tightly with plastic wrap that has been sprayed with vegetable oil spray and then foil and refrigerate for up to 2 days or freeze for up 1 month. (If frozen, the casserole must be thawed completely in the refrigerator, about 24 hours, before baking.)

7. To SERVE: Adjust an oven rack to the middle position and heat the oven to 400 degrees. Unwrap the dish and cover tightly with aluminum foil that has been sprayed with vegetable oil spray (or use nonstick foil). Bake until the casserole is heated through, 30 to 40 minutes. Remove the foil and continue to bake until the top is lightly golden, 15 to 20 minutes longer.

TO SERVE RIGHT AWAY

Bake the casserole in a 400-degree oven, uncovered, until the top is lightly golden, 25 to 35 minutes.

Bake Half, Freeze Half

Follow the recipe for Lamb and Eggplant Moussaka and divide the casserole between two 8 by 8-inch casserole dishes (each will serve 4) or three 9 by 3-inch loaf pans (each will serve 2 to 3). The casseroles can be baked right away or covered tightly with plastic wrap and then foil and refrigerated for up to 2 days or frozen for up to 1 month. See reheating instructions below.

TO BAKE IMMEDIATELY

Bake the casserole in a 400-degree oven, uncovered, until the sauce is bubbling and lightly golden, 20 to 25 minutes.

TO BAKE IF REFRIGERATED

Unwrap the dish and cover tightly with aluminum foil that has been sprayed with vegetable oil spray (or use nonstick foil). Bake in a 400-degree oven until heated through, 20 to 25 minutes. Remove the foil and continue to bake until lightly golden, 15 to 20 minutes longer.

TO BAKE IF FROZEN

Thaw the casserole completely in the refrigerator, about 24 hours, then follow the instructions above for "To Bake if Refrigerated."

EQUIPMENT: Baking Pans

Here in cake-and-casserole-crazed America, the shallow, rectangular 13 by 9-inch baking dish is a kitchen staple. As you might expect, there is a huge variety of options from which to choose, many with new designs, materials, finish colors, and baking surface textures, all taking aim at the tried-and-true pans of old—Pyrex and stoneware. These "improvements," of course, come at a cost.

Would our grandparents have spent nearly $100 on a baking pan? En route to determining the true value of these pans, we found ourselves knee-deep in cornbread, lasagna, and raspberry squares, all baked in each of 12 pans representing the major designs and materials, both old and new, including rough stoneware and earthenware, ovensafe glass (Pyrex), several nonstick pans, and heavy-gauge aluminum.

It turns out that our story ends almost right where it began, with Pyrex. This pan may not be perfect, but it did have five distinct advantages over the other pans. First, it browned on a par with the dark-colored nonstick pans. Second, it is compatible with metal utensils—nonstick pans failed in this regard. Third, it is nonreactive, unlike aluminum pans—manufacturers recommend against preparing acidic foods (such as tomato-based products) in them because acid and aluminum can react, causing off-flavors. Fourth, while it's no stunning beauty, most people we asked were perfectly willing to set it on a dining table at dinnertime, which allows it to pull double duty. Last, it's inexpensive at $8.95; only two other pans in the lineup cost less.

7

OVEN-READY ENTRÉES

OVEN-READY ENTRÉES

FOR MANY OF US, THE PROSPECT OF COMING home after work and putting a great main course into our oven with little to no fuss is a dream. While supermarket prepared-food counters and butcher cases ingeniously cater to this idea, their quality is generally not worth the convenience they offer. It was with this sentiment in mind that we developed this chapter, Oven-Ready Entrées. Sure, you will have to marinate your own meat and skewer your own kebabs for these recipes, but with a little planning, you can have a couple nights' worth of satisfying and tasty dinners in your refrigerator—ready to cook.

As soon as we started out in the kitchen, it was evident to us that you can't simply prepare standard recipes ahead of time. Unlike stews or chilis, which usually taste better the next day, poultry, meat, and fish can dry out when refrigerated overnight and then cooked a day or two later. For the most part, without some adjustment to the recipe, many poultry, meat, and fish dishes made ahead of time end up tasting just like leftovers—thus we had our work cut out for us.

In this chapter we included some natural make-ahead recipes, like marinated or spice-rubbed meat (pages 288–293), but we fixed all the problems usually associated with it; meat that's been marinated overnight typically turns mealy and mushy due to the harsh effects of the acid contained in the marinade. Our solution? We remove the acid from the marinade, be it citrus juice, vinegar, or yogurt, and instead spike our marinade with salt—essentially making a brine, which both seasons and tenderizes the meat. And, for an extra layer of flavor, we reserve some of the unused marinade and add an acid so that we can pour it over the meat when it comes off the grill or out of the broiler.

Salt plays a part in our spice rubs, too. The salt draws moisture out of the product initially; then, after a few hours, the reverse happens, and the salt and moisture flow back into the flesh. We found that the spice rubs are most effective when applied and allowed to sit on the meat overnight—in addition to making the meat juicy, their flavor penetrates the meat and seasons it throughout. And in a chart on pages 294–295, we give you all the information you need to grill or broil juicy chicken breasts, well-seasoned steaks, moist fish fillets, and the like.

To round out the poultry, meat, and fish dishes in this chapter, we developed some recipes that take on the role of side dish or sauce. Baked chicken takes on a whole new life when paired with cherry tomatoes, fennel, and olives, all of which cook down to become part vegetable side dish, part sauce (page 283). We take a similar approach with our recipe for Baked Fish Provençal (page 309); the fish cooks on a bed of halved cherry tomatoes tossed with wine, olive oil, capers, and aromatics, which become a zesty sauce, without any extra effort—or pans!

Rolled and stuffed items also have a presence in this chapter. They can be quite time-consuming to make, so we did take ease of preparation into consideration. Sure, we included more labor-intensive, special-occasion recipes like stuffed and breaded chicken breasts (see pages 276–278) and Roast Pork Loin with Dried Fruit Stuffing (page 306), but we also offer options that require minimal prep. For example, Easy Stuffed Chicken Breasts (page 280) simply require that you slip a no-cook stuffing under the skin of the chicken (and to help prevent the chicken from drying out in the fridge we brush it with a bit of olive oil). We find that Sole Florentine (page 308), typically a company-worthy and time-consuming dish, can be assembled a lot faster by taking just a few simple shortcuts. Frozen chopped spinach allowed us to skip the fussy cleaning and cooking of fresh spinach and a tasty cornstarch-thickened white wine sauce replaced the longer cooking roux-based sauce the dish typically requires.

A final note: Because all the recipes in this chapter are oven- (or grill-)ready, they should not be frozen, but refrigerated as directed, before cooking.

STUFFED CHICKEN BREASTS

ON THEIR OWN, CHICKEN BREASTS CAN BE pretty boring, but when they're breaded and stuffed with the right filling, the results are impressive— a true "special occasion" entrée. When sliced, the filling oozes out into a creamy, tasty sauce and the crust makes a crunchy counterpoint. We wanted to create the ultimate stuffed chicken breast—one that could be made ahead of time for the perfect dinner party main course.

Stuffed chicken breasts have three distinct components: the chicken, the filling, and the coating. Typically, the stuffed chicken breast is rolled in a coating, then fried up crisp. However, as was clear from the many recipes we tried, getting the filling to survive cooking without leaking was key. So we started there.

Some recipes call for cutting a slit in the thickest part of the breast and inserting the filling. That was easy, but it was impossible to get the pocket deep enough to accommodate more than a paltry amount of filling, and it became clear that giving the filling any path of egress (even the smallest opening) wasn't a good idea. One false move, and the hot filling came streaming out during cooking—a dangerous proposition when frying.

We needed to find a way to encase the filling completely. Some recipes we came across in our research pounded the chicken thin, put the filling on top, then rolled the chicken around it to form a compact package. This method worked much better, but it was hard to pound the chicken thin and wide enough to encase the filling without accidentally tearing the flesh—or leaving awkward ragged edges in the process. Borrowing a trick the test kitchen has used for other recipes, we butterflied the breasts lengthwise first (giving us cutlets twice as wide but half as thick as the original), then pounded just to make them even. Much better—less pounding meant less damage. Experimenting with various thicknesses, we decided ¼ inch was optimal.

Flattened, our chicken cutlets resembled large teardrops. Following the rolling-and-folding technique used in some recipes, we placed the filling just above the tapered end of the "teardrop" and proceeded as if wrapping a burrito: rolling the tapered end completely over the filling, folding in the sides toward the center, then continuing to roll from the tapered end up until we had a fairly tight bundle.

We were on the right track, but occasionally the folded-in sides refused to stay put. We quickly diagnosed the problem. The ¼-inch-thick sides, once folded over, were double the thickness of the rest of the bundle. Easy enough: We simply pounded the outer edges of the cutlets a little thinner (⅛ inch) than the rest. Obsessive precision? Yes, we'll admit it. But the foolproof results—no leaks—were worth it. (That said, getting the cutlets to a uniform ¼-inch thickness is almost as reliable.)

Now, with four compact chicken bundles at the ready, we could focus on the exterior. We began the coating process as most recipes do, by using a standard breading procedure: dusting each stuffed chicken breast with seasoned flour, dipping in beaten egg, and rolling in bread crumbs. But breading the chicken immediately after stuffing was a hazardous affair: The seam sometimes opened up and, while the filling didn't actually fall out, the entire package became less compact (thus undoing the previous antileak-protection work). Once, after leaving the unbreaded, uncovered, stuffed chicken in the refrigerator for an hour while we tended to other tasks, we noticed that the edges had begun to stick together, nearly gluing shut. Much sturdier. From then on, we purposely left the stuffed chicken in the refrigerator to set up.

No matter what type of crumbs we used—fresh or dried, coarse or fine—we found that deep-frying gave the chicken a thin, homogenous quality, almost like a corndog. This was not the texture we were after. By the time the chicken was fully cooked, the exterior was a hard, tan-colored shell that had to be drained thoroughly to prevent greasiness. And forget about making them ahead

MAKE IT A MENU

Breaded Stuffed Chicken Breasts

buttered egg noodles

Simple Blanched Asparagus (page 81) with Herb Compound Butter (page 82)

Individual Cherry-Almond Buckles (page 355)

of time. We didn't want to heat a large pot of oil right before serving and when we fried them a day ahead of time and reheated them, the chicken was overcooked by the time the crumbs recrisped. We wanted to do away with deep-frying altogether. We tried pan-frying the chicken in a small amount of oil just until the crumbs became delicately crisp. Once they were browned, we finished cooking them to the proper internal temperature in the oven. So far, so good—well, mostly. While the tops and bottoms of the chicken were nicely browned, it was hard to get the sides evenly colored without manhandling the chicken, which often resulted in unraveling.

That's when we made the decision that would finally and effectively transform our chicken into an elegant make-ahead dinner showpiece: baking our chicken. To achieve a crunchy, golden coating, we tossed fresh bread crumbs onto a baking sheet with vegetable oil and salt and pepper, for seasoning. They baked up tasty and crisp. We then simply dredged the chicken rolls in seasoned flour, dipped them in egg, and coated them with the browned bread crumbs. The breaded chicken rolls then go into the refrigerator overnight. Just before serving, we transferred them to the oven to bake. No more frying, no more skillet, no more spotty browning. The crisp (but not oily) crust was now a perfect foil for the creamy interior.

All we had left to do was to perk up the plain filling. Traditional recipes stuff the chicken with butter or cream cheese spiked with nothing more

than parsley. Between the two, tasters preferred the cream cheese for its creaminess and tang. Sautéed onion and garlic provided the rich cheese with welcome savory notes. Once we had the basics down, we used this mixture as a base to host other flavor combinations, like goat cheese and herbs, ham and cheddar, gorgonzola with walnuts and figs, and mushrooms with provolone. Lastly, a teaspoon of Dijon mustard whisked into the egg wash (for coating the chicken) provided another layer of flavor to our chicken bundles.

After batches and batches of mediocre stuffed chicken breasts, we were happy with the outcome—beautifully browned, crisp, stuffed chicken breasts with fragrant, herb-speckled filling. Moreover, these visually appealing chicken breasts can be assembled entirely ahead of time, and simply popped into the oven before serving—a surefire way to impress your friends and family.

Breaded Chicken Breasts Stuffed with Cheese Filling
SERVES 4

While homemade bread crumbs taste best, you can substitute 2 cups panko, toasted as directed in the recipe. Don't skimp on the chicken chilling time in step 2 or else the chicken will unravel when breading in step 4. Serve with lemon wedges, if desired.

- 4   boneless, skinless chicken breasts (6 to 8 ounces each), tenderloins removed (see the illustration at left)
       Salt and ground black pepper
- 1   recipe cheese filling (pages 277–278)
- 4–5   slices high-quality white sandwich bread, torn into large pieces
- 2   tablespoons vegetable oil
- 1   cup unbleached all-purpose flour
- 3   large eggs, lightly beaten
- 1   teaspoon Dijon mustard

1. Adjust an oven rack to the lower-middle position and heat the oven to 300 degrees. Following the illustrations on page 277, butterfly each chicken breast and pound as directed between 2 sheets of plastic wrap.

REMOVING THE TENDERLOIN

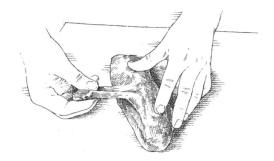

The tenderloin (the long narrow piece of meat attached to each chicken breast) tends to fall off during pounding, so it is best removed and reserved for another use, such as a stir-fry.

2. Pat the chicken dry with paper towels, season with salt and pepper, and place the cutlets cut side up on a clean work surface. Following the illustration below, place a quarter of the filling (about 2 tablespoons) in the center of the bottom half of each breast. Roll the chicken over the filling to form a neat, tight package, pressing on the seam to seal. Repeat with the remaining stuffing and chicken. Refrigerate the chicken, seam side down and uncovered, to allow the edges to seal further, about 1 hour.

3. While the chicken rests, pulse half of the bread in a food processor until coarsely ground, about 16 pulses. Repeat with the remaining bread (you should have 3½ cups of crumbs). Toss the crumbs with the oil, ⅛ teaspoon salt, and ⅛ teaspoon pepper and spread out over a rimmed baking sheet. Bake the crumbs, stirring occasionally, until golden brown and dry, about 25 minutes. Transfer the crumbs to a shallow dish and let cool to room temperature.

4. Combine the flour, ¼ teaspoon salt, and ⅛ teaspoon pepper in a second shallow dish and whisk the eggs and Dijon together in a third shallow dish. Working with 1 chicken roll at a time, dredge in the flour, shaking off the excess, then coat with the egg mixture, allowing the excess to drip off. Finally, coat with the bread crumbs, pressing gently so that the crumbs adhere.

5. To store: Transfer the breaded chicken rolls to an airtight container and refrigerate for up to 24 hours.

6. To serve: Adjust an oven rack to the middle position and heat the oven to 350 degrees. Place the chicken rolls at least 1 inch apart on a wire rack set over a foil-lined rimmed baking sheet. Bake until an instant-read thermometer inserted into the center of the chicken registers 160 degrees, 40 to 45 minutes. Let rest for 5 minutes before serving.

TO SERVE RIGHT AWAY
After breading the chicken in step 4, bake as directed in step 6, until an instant-read thermometer inserted into the center of the chicken registers 160 degrees, 35 to 40 minutes.

Goat Cheese and Thyme Filling
MAKES ENOUGH TO STUFF 4 BONELESS, SKINLESS CHICKEN BREASTS

Parsley or tarragon can be substituted for the thyme.

1	tablespoon unsalted butter
1	small onion, minced
2	teaspoons minced fresh thyme leaves
1	small garlic clove, minced or pressed through a garlic press (about ½ teaspoon)
3	ounces cream cheese, softened (about ⅓ cup)
2	ounces goat cheese, softened (about ¾ cup)
⅛	teaspoon salt
⅛	teaspoon ground black pepper

BUILDING A STUFFED AND BREADED CHICKEN BREAST

1. Starting on the thinnest side, butterfly the breast by slicing it lengthwise almost in half. Open the breast up to create a single, flat cutlet.

2. With the cutlet between sheets of plastic wrap, pound (starting at the center) to ¼ inch thick. Pound the outer perimeter to ⅛ inch.

3. Place the stuffing near the tapered end of the cutlet and roll up the end to completely enclose the stuffing. Fold in the sides and continue rolling to form a cylinder.

1. Melt the butter in a medium skillet over medium heat. Add the onion and cook, stirring occasionally, until well browned, about 10 minutes. Stir in the thyme and garlic and cook until fragrant, about 30 seconds; set aside to cool.

2. Mix the cooled onion mixture, cream cheese, goat cheese, salt, and pepper together until uniform. Spoon the cheese mixture onto the chicken as directed on page 277.

Gorgonzola Filling with Walnuts and Figs

MAKES ENOUGH TO STUFF 4 BONELESS, SKINLESS CHICKEN BREASTS

Two tablespoons dried cherries or cranberries can be substituted for the figs.

1	tablespoon unsalted butter
1	small onion, minced
1	teaspoon minced fresh thyme leaves
1	small garlic clove, minced or pressed through a garlic press (about ½ teaspoon)
2	ounces cream cheese, softened (about ¼ cup)
2	ounces gorgonzola cheese, crumbled (about ½ cup)
¼	cup walnuts, toasted and chopped (see page 95)
3	medium dried figs, chopped (about 2 tablespoons)
1	tablespoon dry sherry
⅛	teaspoon salt
⅛	teaspoon ground black pepper

1. Melt the butter in a medium skillet over medium heat. Add the onion and cook, stirring occasionally, until well browned, about 10 minutes. Stir in the thyme and garlic and cook until fragrant, about 30 seconds; set aside to cool.

2. Mix the cooled onion mixture, cream cheese, gorgonzola cheese, walnuts, figs, sherry, salt, and pepper together until uniform. Spoon the cheese mixture onto the chicken as directed on page 277.

Ham and Cheddar Cheese Filling

MAKES ENOUGH TO STUFF 4 BONELESS, SKINLESS CHICKEN BREASTS

You can substitute Swiss cheese for a cordon bleu–style stuffed chicken breast.

1	tablespoon unsalted butter
1	small onion, minced
1	teaspoon minced fresh thyme leaves
1	small garlic clove, minced or pressed through a garlic press (about ½ teaspoon)
4	ounces cream cheese, softened (about ½ cup)
4	ounces cheddar cheese, shredded (about 1 cup)
⅛	teaspoon salt
⅛	teaspoon ground black pepper
4	slices (about 4 ounces) thin-sliced cooked deli ham

1. Melt the butter in a medium skillet over medium heat. Add the onion and cook, stirring occasionally, until well browned, about 10 minutes. Stir in the thyme and garlic and cook until fragrant, about 30 seconds; set aside to cool.

2. Mix the cooled onion mixture, cream cheese, cheddar cheese, salt, and pepper together until uniform. Place a slice of ham onto each chicken breast, then top with the cheese mixture as directed on page 277.

Mushroom and Provolone Filling

MAKES ENOUGH TO STUFF 4 BONELESS, SKINLESS CHICKEN BREASTS

If you don't plan on using the filling right away, be sure to store the mushrooms and cream cheese mixture separately.

3	tablespoons unsalted butter
10	ounces white mushrooms, wiped clean and quartered
	Salt and ground black pepper
1	small onion, minced
1	tablespoon minced fresh rosemary
1	teaspoon minced fresh thyme leaves
1	small garlic clove, minced or pressed through a garlic press (about ½ teaspoon)
4	ounces cream cheese, softened (about ½ cup)
4	ounces provolone cheese, shredded (about 1 cup)

1. Melt 2 tablespoons of the butter in a medium skillet over medium-high heat. Add the mushrooms

INGREDIENTS: Boneless, Skinless Chicken Breasts

Boneless, skinless chicken breasts are a standard in many home kitchens. And while we've come up with countless recipes to add zip to the chicken, we never stopped to look at the chicken itself. Is there a difference in flavor among the popular brands? To find out, we gathered six brands of boneless, skinless chicken breasts, broiled them without seasoning, and had 20 tasters sample the chickens side by side. Among the contenders were one kosher bird, two "natural," and one "free-range." The remaining two were just "chicken."

The koshering process involves coating the chicken with salt to draw out any impurities; this process, similar to brining, results in moist, salty meat (for this reason, we do not recommend brining kosher birds). "Natural"—in the case of chicken—simply means there are no antibiotics or hormones, and the birds are fed a vegetarian diet. "Free-range" means exactly what it says: The birds are not confined to small cages but are allowed to roam freely.

Last-place finishers (and lowest priced) Perdue and White Gem (our local store brand) were downgraded for poor texture and unnatural flavor. Tasters were also put off by the brash yellow color of the birds. Springer Farms All-Natural and Eberly's Free-Range chickens scored well, but the tie for first place went to Empire Kosher and the all-natural Bell & Evans. The only kosher bird, Empire, won points with tasters for its superior flavor—namely, salt.

and cook until the liquid has evaporated and the mushrooms are golden brown, 10 to 15 minutes. Season with salt and pepper to taste; set the mushrooms aside to cool.

2. Add the remaining 1 tablespoon butter and the onion to the now-empty skillet and cook over medium heat, stirring occasionally, until well browned, about 10 minutes. Stir in the rosemary, thyme, and garlic and cook until fragrant, about 30 seconds; set aside to cool.

3. Mix the cooled onion mixture, cream cheese, provolone cheese, ⅛ teaspoon salt, and ⅛ teaspoon pepper together until uniform. Spread the mushroom mixture onto the chicken, then spoon the cheese mixture on top as directed on page 277.

WEEKNIGHT STUFFED CHICKEN BREASTS

WHILE WE LOVE OUR BREADED AND STUFFED chicken (page 276), sometimes we yearn for an easier approach—one that could be assembled quickly—more weeknight fare than special-occasion dinner. This meant no-fuss fillings and a simple method for stuffing the chicken—without butterflying and pounding chicken breasts or even breading them.

Turning first to boneless, skinless breasts, we wondered if we could construct a filling that we could place on top instead of inside the chicken. Cheese seemed like the obvious starting point, and we tried both shredded and sliced, but both forms tended to slide off the breasts and burn on the baking sheet. Although some of the cheese did adhere, tasters still wanted a more creamy filling. A plain-old chicken breast with cheese melted over the top simply wasn't going to cut it.

Taking a cue from our Breaded Chicken Breasts Stuffed with Cheese Filling (page 276), we whipped up a mixture of cream cheese and goat cheese seasoned with lemon zest, garlic, and herbs—no cooking required. We packed the mixture on top of the chicken breast. As the chicken baked in the oven, the stuffing became molten and, like the cheese we'd tried before, it slid right off the breasts. The stuffing that did remain on the chicken, however, basted the breasts, keeping them moist, and made a creamy, flavorful sauce for the plain chicken. We were onto something. If only we could find a better way to get the mixture to adhere to the chicken.

A little research led us to change gears and try bone-in, skin-on chicken breasts. We had come across several recipes that called for cutting a pocket into the breasts just above the bone and others that stuffed the filling under the skin. First, we tried cutting a pocket into the breast and packing the filling inside. The results were decent, but a significant amount of the filling oozed out and, to be honest, cutting a pocket into the breasts was a bit more effort than we wanted.

Split Breasts versus Whole Breasts

We far prefer to buy whole breasts and split them ourselves (rather than buy split breasts) because the skin is often less damaged, and the breast halves are uniformly sized so that they cook at the same rate. (See page 94 for illustrations on how to split chicken breasts.) If you choose to buy split breasts instead of the whole breasts, inspect the package carefully to make sure they are of similar size with an ample amount of skin to work with.

With high hopes, we tried the under-skin option—after all, there is already a natural pocket in place. Working carefully, we loosened the skin and fit about 1½ tablespoons of the cheese mixture underneath. The skin held the filling in place, and when the chicken emerged from the oven, it was moist and tender, with a creamy, tangy, sauce-like filling. And while we normally brine bone-in, skin-on chicken breasts to keep them from tasting dry, we found that with the creamy filling, which basted the breasts as they cooked, it wasn't necessary—the meat was perfectly moist and juicy. Our results were near flawless, but one problem remained—the skin was flabby and inedible.

We wondered if increasing the oven temperature would help to crisp up the skin. All along we had been baking the chicken breasts at 375 degrees. We tried cooking the chicken at 400 degrees, 425 degrees, and 450 degrees. The skin on the chicken cooked at 450 degrees was golden brown and crispy and the meat was perfectly cooked. Success!

We had the basic filling recipe down, so we tried adding to it a variety of ingredients. We quickly found out that melting cheeses like cheddar and Gruyère, even when mixed with cream cheese, ooze out from under the skin, and that chutney burns. In all of our tests, it was the potent ingredients—like black olives, blue cheese, and Parmesan cheese—mixed into a creamy base that made the most flavorful stuffings, and they all stayed in place under the skin.

Turning these under-skin stuffed chicken breasts into a make-ahead recipe was easy—they baked up just as well after being refrigerated overnight. A final note: When shopping for bone-in, skin-on

chicken breasts for this recipe, it is very important that the skin be intact to secure the stuffing. If possible, we recommend hand selecting the chicken breasts from your butcher's case, rather than buying packaged sets of chicken breasts.

Easy Stuffed Chicken Breasts with Cheese Filling
SERVES 4
It is important to buy chicken breasts with skin still attached and intact, otherwise the stuffing will leak out. We prefer to buy whole breasts and cut them in half ourselves, but you can use already split breasts (see the tip at left). Serve with lemon wedges, if desired.

2   whole bone-in, skin-on chicken breasts (about 1½ pounds each), split (see the illustrations on page 94)
    Salt and ground black pepper
1   recipe cheese filling (page 281)
    Olive oil

1. Pat the chicken dry with paper towels, and season with salt and pepper. Following the illustrations on page 281, use your fingers to gently loosen the center portion of skin covering each breast. Place a quarter of the filling (about 1½ tablespoons) under the skin, directly on the meat in the center of each breast half. Brush the skin with oil.

2. To STORE: Transfer to an airtight container and refrigerate for up to 2 days.

3. To SERVE: Adjust an oven rack to the middle position and heat the oven to 450 degrees. Place the chicken breasts skin side up on a wire rack set over a foil-lined rimmed baking sheet. Bake until an instant-read thermometer inserted into the thickest part of the breast registers 160 degrees, 35 to 40 minutes. Let rest for 5 minutes before serving.

TO SERVE RIGHT AWAY
After brushing the chicken with oil in step 1, bake as directed in step 3, reducing the baking time to 30 to 35 minutes or until an instant-read thermometer inserted into the thickest part of the breast registers 160 degrees.

Lemon–Goat Cheese Filling

MAKES ENOUGH TO STUFF 4 BONE-IN,
SKIN-ON CHICKEN BREASTS

- 3 ounces goat cheese, softened (about ¾ cup)
- 2 ounces cream cheese, softened (about ¼ cup)
- 2 teaspoons minced fresh thyme leaves
- 1 small garlic clove, minced or pressed through a garlic press (about ½ teaspoon)
- ¼ teaspoon grated zest from 1 lemon
- ⅛ teaspoon salt
- ⅛ teaspoon ground black pepper

Mix all the ingredients together until uniform and spread 1½ tablespoons per chicken breast under the skin as directed in the recipe for Easy Stuffed Chicken Breasts on page 280.

Olive and Goat Cheese Filling

MAKES ENOUGH TO STUFF 4 BONE-IN,
SKIN-ON CHICKEN BREASTS

- 3 ounces goat cheese, softened (about ¾ cup)
- 2 ounces cream cheese, softened (about ¼ cup)
- ¼ cup pitted kalamata olives, chopped fine
- 2 teaspoons minced fresh oregano leaves
- 1 small garlic clove, minced or pressed through a garlic press (about ½ teaspoon)
- ⅛ teaspoon salt
- ⅛ teaspoon ground black pepper

Mix all the ingredients together until uniform and spread 1½ tablespoons per chicken breast under the skin as directed in the recipe for Easy Stuffed Chicken Breasts on page 280.

Blue Cheese and Scallion Filling

MAKES ENOUGH TO STUFF 4 BONE-IN,
SKIN-ON CHICKEN BREASTS

- 3 ounces blue cheese, softened (about ¾ cup)
- 2 ounces cream cheese, softened (about ¼ cup)
- 1 scallion, minced

- 1 small garlic clove, minced or pressed through a garlic press (about ½ teaspoon)
- ⅛ teaspoon salt
- ⅛ teaspoon ground black pepper

Mix all the ingredients together until uniform and spread 1½ tablespoons per chicken breast under the skin as directed in the recipe for Easy Stuffed Chicken Breasts on page 280.

Parmesan-Basil Filling

MAKES ENOUGH TO STUFF 4 BONE-IN,
SKIN-ON CHICKEN BREASTS

- 2 ounces Parmesan cheese, grated (about 1 cup)
- 2 ounces cream cheese, softened (about ¼ cup)
- ¼ cup minced fresh basil leaves
- 2 tablespoons extra-virgin olive oil
- 1 small garlic clove, minced or pressed through a garlic press (about ½ teaspoon)
- ⅛ teaspoon salt
- ⅛ teaspoon ground black pepper

Mix all the ingredients together until uniform and spread 1½ tablespoons per chicken breast under the skin as directed in the recipe for Easy Stuffed Chicken Breasts on page 280.

FILLING EASY STUFFED CHICKEN BREASTS

1. Using your fingers, gently loosen the center portion of the skin covering each breast, making a pocket for the filling.

2. Using your fingers or a small spoon, place a quarter of the filling (about 1½ tablespoons) under the loosened skin, directly on the meat in the center of each breast half. Gently press on the skin to distribute the filling over the meat.

EQUIPMENT:
Instant-Read Thermometers

There are two types of commonly sold hand-held thermometers: digital and dial face. While they both take accurate readings, we prefer digital thermometers because they register temperatures faster and are easier to read. After testing a variety of digital thermometers, we preferred the Super-Fast Thermapen ($85) for its well-thought-out design—a long, folding probe and comfortable handle—and speed (about 5 seconds for a reading). If you don't want to spend so much money on a thermometer, at the very least purchase an inexpensive dial-face model. There's no sense ruining a $50 roast because you don't own even a $10 thermometer.

THE BEST INSTANT-READ THERMOMETER

The Super-Fast Thermapen is our top choice for its pinpoint accuracy and quick response time.

BAKED CHICKEN

BAKED CHICKEN IS AN OLD STANDBY, BUT A little ho-hum. Here in the test kitchen, we wanted to turn simple baked chicken into a make-ahead meal, complete with tender, flavorful vegetables and a zesty sauce to accompany the moist, well-seasoned meat. This dish would stand on its own for dinner, perhaps only with the addition of crusty bread to sop up the extra sauce.

We started our kitchen tests by choosing the type of chicken. Bone-in, skin-on breasts were tasters' favorite because the bone and skin protected the meat from drying out in the oven, keeping it moist and tender. (That said, boneless, skinless breasts can be substituted, but the baking time will be slightly shorter.) Next, we had to figure out how to get flavor into the chicken.

Simply brushing the chicken with butter and adding a sprinkling of herbs wasn't giving us the flavor impact we wanted. Instead, we turned to marinating. The only problem, however, is that chicken (or meat) that sits in a marinade for too long—say overnight—will turn mealy and mushy due to the acidic component, such as lemon juice, vinegar, or yogurt, contained in most marinades. As a solution to this problem, we marinated the meat in an acid-free marinade. (After mixing the marinade, we reserved ¼ cup spiked with lemon juice to pour over the chicken just before serving for a fresh hit of flavor.) This technique was perfect for this recipe—the chicken was moist and tender, and nicely permeated by the flavors of the marinade, with a fresh bite from the acid. With the addition of vegetables in mind, we chose a garlic and herb marinade for its bright but neutral flavors.

The chicken was all set, so we focused on the vegetables. We wanted vegetables that required minimal prep that we could throw into the baking dish with the chicken. Cherry tomatoes seemed like an obvious choice. First we tried them cut in half, but found that they broke down too much in the oven. Left whole, the tomatoes softened beautifully, and some even burst, releasing their flavorful juices into the pan to make a sauce, while still maintaining some presence as a vegetable.

We racked our brains to come up with other vegetables that would complement the tomatoes. The flavors of the Mediterranean seemed natural here and we chose fennel for its sweet anise flavor and kalamata olives for their brininess. To ensure that the fennel cooked at the same rate as the chicken and tomatoes, we found that it was important to slice it thinly. The trio of tomatoes, fennel, and olives was excellent with the chicken; our only complaint was that we wanted the vegetables to have more flavor. Instead of chopping more shallots, garlic, and herbs, we simply tossed the vegetables with a few tablespoons of the reserved marinade, which already contained the aforementioned aromatics. The marinade heightened the flavor of the vegetables and pooled in the baking dish with the juice from the tomatoes to make a tasty sauce. To pull the flavors together, we tossed the vegetables with chopped fresh basil leaves before serving.

We were happy with how far we had taken a simple baked chicken dish. All that was left to do was devise the make-ahead and baking logistics. We marinated the chicken per test kitchen standards—in a zipper-lock bag overnight in the refrigerator. After tossing the vegetables with some marinade, we stored them separately from the chicken in an airtight container (or zipper-lock bag). When we were ready to bake the chicken, we poured the vegetables into a baking dish and nestled the chicken on top. How easy is that? Into the oven it went and 45 minutes later, dinner emerged. With moist, tender chicken, fresh vegetables, and a flavorsome but virtually effortless sauce, this dish was certainly better than the sum of its parts!

~✂~

Baked Chicken with Fennel, Tomatoes, and Olives

SERVES 4

Boneless, skinless chicken breasts also work in this recipe—simply decrease the baking time to 40 minutes and use an instant-read thermometer to check for doneness as directed in step 5. Remember to reserve ¼ cup of the unused marinade to pour over the chicken as it rests. If the fennel still has a slight crunch when the chicken is cooked through, return the vegetables to the oven while the chicken rests. Don't cut the basil ahead of time or else it will turn black.

I	recipe Garlic and Herb Marinade (about I cup, page 288)
2	medium fennel bulbs (about 1½ pounds), trimmed of stalks, cored, and sliced thin (see the illustrations on page 47)
I	pint cherry tomatoes (about 12 ounces), stemmed and washed
½	cup pitted kalamata olives
½	teaspoon salt
¼	teaspoon ground black pepper
2	whole bone-in, skin-on chicken breasts (about 1½ pounds each), split (see the illustrations on page 94)
3	tablespoons chopped fresh basil leaves (for serving)

1. Transfer ¼ cup of the marinade to an airtight container; set aside.

2. Add 2 more tablespoons of the marinade to a large zipper-lock bag along with the fennel, tomatoes, olives, salt, and pepper. Seal shut, gently toss to coat, and set aside.

3. Add the remaining marinade to a second large zipper-lock bag along with the chicken breasts. Seal shut and toss to coat.

4. TO STORE: Refrigerate the reserved marinade, vegetables, and chicken separately for up to 2 days, turning the bag of chicken occasionally to redistribute the marinade.

5. TO SERVE: Adjust an oven rack to the middle position and heat the oven to 450 degrees. Transfer the vegetables to a 13 by 9-inch baking dish and lay the chicken breasts on top, skin side up. Bake until an instant-read thermometer inserted into the thickest part of the chicken registers 160 degrees, about 45 minutes. Meanwhile, allow the reserved marinade to sit at room temperature to liquefy, then shake vigorously to recombine.

6. Transfer the chicken and vegetables to a serving platter. Pour the reserved marinade over the chicken, sprinkle with the chopped basil, and serve.

TO SERVE RIGHT AWAY

In step 4, refrigerate the vegetables and chicken separately for at least 30 minutes. Do not refrigerate the reserved marinade. Transfer to the baking dish as described in step 5 and bake until an instant-read thermometer inserted into the thickest part of the chicken registers 160 degrees, about 45 minutes.

➤ VARIATION

Baked Chicken with Spring Vegetables, Capers, and Lemon

Be sure to buy thick asparagus for this recipe—pencil-thin asparagus will overcook. Thaw the artichokes completely and carefully pat them dry before roasting or else they won't brown and might prevent the other vegetables from browning, too. Don't mince the tarragon ahead of time or else it will turn black.

I	recipe Garlic and Herb Marinade (about I cup, page 288)
I	(9-ounce) box frozen artichokes, thawed and patted dry

1   pound asparagus (about 1 bunch), tough ends trimmed, cut in half
1   pint cherry tomatoes (about 12 ounces), stemmed and washed
¼   cup capers, rinsed
½   lemon, sliced ¼ inch thick, end piece discarded
½   teaspoon salt
¼   teaspoon ground black pepper
2   whole bone-in, skin-on chicken breasts (about 1½ pounds each), split (see the illustrations on page 94)
2   tablespoons chopped fresh tarragon leaves (for serving)

1. Transfer ¼ cup of the marinade to an airtight container; set aside.

2. In a large zipper-lock bag, gently toss 2 more tablespoons of the marinade with the artichokes, asparagus, tomatoes, capers, lemon slices, salt, and pepper. Seal shut, gently toss to coat, and set aside.

3. In a second large zipper-lock bag, toss the chicken with the remaining marinade, coating the chicken thoroughly. Seal shut and toss to coat.

4. TO STORE: Refrigerate the reserved marinade, vegetables, and chicken separately for up to 2 days, turning the bag of chicken occasionally to redistribute the marinade.

5. TO SERVE: Adjust an oven rack to the middle position and heat the oven to 450 degrees. Transfer the vegetables to a 13 by 9-inch baking dish and lay the chicken breasts on top, skin side up. Bake until an instant-read thermometer inserted into the thickest part of the chicken registers 160 degrees, about 45 minutes. Meanwhile, allow the reserved marinade to sit at room temperature to liquefy, then shake vigorously to recombine.

6. Transfer the chicken and vegetables to a serving platter. Pour the reserved marinade over the chicken, sprinkle with the chopped tarragon, and serve.

TO SERVE RIGHT AWAY

In step 4, refrigerate the vegetables and chicken separately for at least 30 minutes. Do not refrigerate the reserved marinade. Transfer to the baking dish as described in step 5 and bake as directed.

WEEKNIGHT TURKEY DINNER

THE LABOR-INTENSIVE THANKSGIVING DINNER comes only once a year, but what if you want to enjoy turkey and all that goes with it—rich gravy, savory stuffing, and sweet-tart cranberry sauce—more often? It was with this sentiment in mind that we set out to develop a make-ahead recipe that would offer up the soul of Thanksgiving year-round, but without the hassle.

We had a vision of moist and juicy turkey rolled around stuffing and cranberry sauce and topped with a quick, but flavorful gravy. We scanned our local supermarkets and immediately determined that turkey cutlets fit the bill for cooks in need of a quick, satisfying weeknight Thanksgiving dinner. Cutlets are thin slices of meat, usually no more than about ⅜ inch thick, cut from the breast. The ideal turkey cutlet is of even thickness from end to end. It is cut across the grain of the breast so it won't be stringy when you eat it and it is cut on the diagonal to increase surface area. We tried all the brands of cutlets we could get our hands on and found them to be inconsistent in terms of size, shape, and thickness. Short of butchering your own cutlets, which takes some practice and curtails the speed and ease inherent to this dish, the best you can do is to inspect packages carefully before you buy. We also find that a quick pounding of the cutlets to an even thickness helps to make them more consistent and therefore easier to stuff.

With the turkey component decided, we moved on to the stuffing, with ease of preparation on the forefront of our minds. We tested a variety of bread stuffings, from quick-scratch recipes to store-bought mixes. Surprisingly, tasters didn't find much difference between homemade stuffing and the mixes when rolled up in a moist, tender cutlet. We leave the choice up to you; you can either use your favorite supermarket brand or follow our recipe for Homemade Bread Stuffing (page 286).

In addition to the bread stuffing, we also liked the idea of incorporating cranberry sauce into rolled cutlets. But the cranberry sauce, because of its liquid nature, oozed out of the cutlets before we finished rolling them up. For a similar sweet-and-tart flavor (but without the moisture), we added dried cranberries to the bread stuffing—the perfect solution. And if you find that you really miss the cranberry sauce, serve some on the side.

The next issue to resolve was the gravy. We have never had success with store-bought gravy—tinned flavors, overly salty, too thin, or too gloppy—the drawbacks go on. We knew we would have to make our own. Gravy, by definition, is a thickened sauce made of meat juices and pan drippings, usually left over from a roasted turkey. What if you are limited to just some canned broth and a few vegetables? After extensive testing, we found that gravy can be made very simply with canned broth, an onion, a couple of bay leaves, and a final power ingredient—sausage. The key is to brown the sausage to develop a rich meaty flavor for the base of the gravy. The additions of sautéed onion, bay leaves, and chicken broth, all thickened with flour, result in a very respectable quick sausage gravy—not exactly turkey gravy but tasty just the same.

Our last challenge was to figure out how to best store the stuffed turkey cutlets and gravy overnight and how to cook and serve them the next day. A simple approach ended up being the best. We arranged the stuffed turkey cutlets in a baking dish, covered them with plastic wrap, and placed the dish in the refrigerator. We refrigerated the gravy separately, to pour over the cutlets right before baking. Once baked, the cutlets turned out moist and juicy, enhanced by the cranberry-studded stuffing and meaty gravy. We know this recipe will never take the place of a traditional Thanksgiving dinner, but it certainly is an excellent alternative and a viable option any day of the week, any time of the year.

THE RIGHT CUTLET

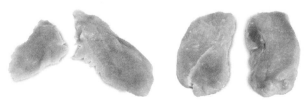

Try to avoid buying packages with ragged, uneven, inconsistently sized cutlets, like those on the left. The even cutlets (right) will be easier to stuff and cook at the same rate.

Stuffed Turkey Cutlets with Sausage Gravy

SERVES 4

We found that store-bought stuffing works just fine in this recipe, but you can also make your own (recipe follows). Serve with cranberry sauce, if desired.

1	tablespoon unsalted butter
4	ounces sweet Italian sausage, casings removed
1	small onion, minced
¼	cup unbleached all-purpose flour
4	cups low-sodium chicken broth
2	bay leaves
8	turkey cutlets (about 3 ounces each), pounded ¼ inch thick
	Salt and ground black pepper
1	cup packaged bread stuffing, prepared following the package instructions, or 1 recipe Homemade Bread Stuffing (recipe follows)
2	tablespoons dried cranberries, chopped

1. Melt the butter in a large saucepan over medium-high heat. Add the sausage and onion and cook, breaking the sausage into small pieces with a spoon, until the onion is softened and lightly browned, about 10 minutes.

2. Stir in the flour and cook, stirring constantly, until golden, about 1 minute. Gradually whisk in the broth and continue to whisk until the liquid is smooth. Add the bay leaves and bring to a boil, skimming off any foam that forms on the surface. Reduce to a simmer and cook, stirring occasionally, until the gravy has thickened and measures about 2¼ cups, about 30 minutes. Remove and discard the bay leaves. Set the gravy aside.

3. Meanwhile, season the turkey cutlets with salt and pepper. Combine the prepared stuffing with the cranberries in a medium bowl. Place 2 tablespoons of the stuffing mixture onto the center of each cutlet and bring up the ends of the cutlet over the stuffing to overlap slightly. Lay the turkey rolls, seam side down, in a 13 by 9-inch baking dish.

4. TO STORE: Wrap the baking dish tightly with plastic wrap and transfer the gravy to an airtight

container. Refrigerate the turkey and gravy separately for up to 24 hours.

5. To SERVE: Adjust an oven rack to the middle position and heat the oven to 400 degrees. Unwrap the baking dish and pour the gravy evenly over the rolled cutlets. Bake, occasionally basting the turkey with the gravy, until an instant-read thermometer inserted into the middle of the rolls registers 165 degrees, 30 to 35 minutes.

TO SERVE RIGHT AWAY

Pour the warm gravy over the turkey rolls and bake as directed in step 5, reducing the baking time to 20 to 25 minutes or until an instant-read thermometer inserted into the middle of the rolls registers 165 degrees.

➤ VARIATION

Turkey Cutlets with Rice Stuffing and Gravy

We like to use Uncle Ben's Ready Rice for this recipe—the Long Grain and Wild Rice Medley is our favorite—but you can use any cooked rice.

INGREDIENTS: Stuffing Mixes

When roasting a turkey, we prefer homemade stuffing to boxed mixes. But in developing our Stuffed Turkey Cutlets (page 285), we decided to give boxed mixes another look. Among the 8 brands we tried, two passed muster: Stove Top Stuffing and Bell's Traditional Stuffing. Come Thanksgiving, we still wouldn't use either of these boxed mixes, but to stuff a turkey cutlet, they were just fine.

THE BEST SUPERMARKET STUFFINGS

For weeknight cooking, tasters found two stuffing mixes to their liking. Stove Top Stuffing (left) was described as tasting "fairly homemade" and Bell's Traditional Stuffing (right) was praised for its "balanced herb flavor."

Toss 1 cup cooked rice with 1 large egg and 1 tablespoon minced fresh parsley leaves. Follow the recipe for Stuffed Turkey Cutlets with Sausage Gravy, substituting the rice mixture for the bread stuffing in step 3.

Homemade Bread Stuffing

MAKES 1 CUP

This stuffing has all the flavors of traditional versions, but it is quick and easy to make, and it yields only 1 cup, the perfect amount for our recipe for Stuffed Turkey Cutlets with Sausage Gravy.

2	tablespoons unsalted butter
½	small onion, minced
1	celery rib, chopped fine
3	slices high-quality white sandwich bread, cut into ½-inch cubes
1	large egg, beaten
¼	teaspoon salt
¼	teaspoon ground black pepper
¼	teaspoon dried sage leaves

1. Melt the butter in a medium skillet over medium heat. Add the onion and celery and cook until softened, 5 to 7 minutes. Transfer to a medium bowl and cool for 5 minutes.

2. Stir the bread, egg, salt, pepper, and sage into the onion mixture until combined. Use as directed in the Stuffed Turkey Cutlets with Sausage Gravy (page 285).

SEASONING MEAT, POULTRY, AND FISH FOR GRILLING AND BROILING

MARINADES AND SPICE RUBS CAN DO A LOT for a boneless, skinless chicken breast or a cheap piece of steak that's headed for the grill or broiler. Supermarkets are catching on to this—just survey the condiments shelf and you're inundated with countless bottles of marinades and jars of spice rubs put out by your favorite celebrity chefs. And as if opening up a bottle wasn't easy enough, you can also buy meat that has been seasoned for you—simply bring it home and throw it on the grill or in the oven! Store-bought seasonings, while not all bad, can be an expensive gamble, especially when a homemade rub or marinade can taste so much better and requires very little effort. And as for meat that's been marinated by the store, its quality depends on how long the meat has been marinated—too long and you end up with a mushy chicken breast or spongy steaks. No thanks—we'd rather spend a couple of extra minutes whipping together our own marinade.

Many marinades contain acids, like citrus juice or vinegar. The theory is that these acids tenderize meat by breaking down its proteins. We've always found this to be a flawed method to attaining tenderness. Even after a short time, acidic marinades can wreak havoc on the meat's texture. Look at a chicken breast that has soaked in an acidic marinade for just 1 hour—you'll see that its edges discolor. And after cooking? The edges of the meat will be spongy. For this reason, we eschew marinades containing acids and instead prefer to rely on salt or salty ingredients like soy sauce, which is essentially a brine. Brining, we've found, is a gentler method toward tenderizing.

In an effort to carry the flavor of the marinades even further, we reserved ¼ cup of each marinade (before adding the protein) to serve as a finishing sauce for the cooked meat. To this reserved marinade we added an acid—be it citrus juice, vinegar, or yogurt. As our meat came off the grill or out of the oven and was set aside to rest, the reserved marinade was poured over the top. This reinforced the flavor of the marinade and the acid brightened the flavors.

For marinades to work effectively, they must come into contact with all surfaces of the meat. The best way to do this is to place the meat in a zipper-lock bag with the marinade. We then squeeze all the excess air from the bag and refrigerate it, turning the bag every 12 hours to redistribute. In our testing, we found that most cuts of poultry and meat can stay in these marinades for two days, with kebabs, shrimp, and fish being the exceptions—the

EQUIPMENT: Food Storage Bags

Here in the test kitchen, we use food storage bags for everything from marinating meats to storing baked goods. To find out which were the best, we tested ten 1-gallon plastic food storage bags, five designed for use in the freezer and five designed for general food storage. We ran the bags through a host of tests and rated them according to the results, as well as design.

First, we determined how well the bags kept moisture from escaping—and odor and air from entering—in a series of tests. For the stinky bread test, five bread-filled bags were refrigerated for two weeks in an airtight container with onion and garlic; tasters sampled the bread for detectable off-tastes or odors. For the water-tightness test, five bags filled with water were stored in an airtight container with five weighed desiccant-drying packets for one week; bags that exuded fewer than 10 grams of moisture were rated highly. For the bread storage test, four bread-filled bags were stored (two in the freezer, two in the refrigerator) for three weeks, with weights recorded daily; bags that lost fewer than 0.4 gram of weight (on average) received the highest marks.

Next, we tested durability. Bags three-quarters full of spaghetti sauce were dropped from a height of 3 feet onto a plastic tarp; bags that survived two drops were rated well. Lastly, we rated the bags on their design, taking into consideration the thickness of the plastic film, as well as seal design and mouth width.

In the end, we had four favorite food storage bags—two freezer and two general storage. For the freezer, the Glad Freezer Zipper Bag, with its double-groove seal, and the Ziploc Freezer Bag, with its wide opening, were our favorites. For general storage bags, the Hefty OneZip Storage Bag was praised for its thickness, while the Ziploc Storage Bag received high marks for its airtight seal.

THE BEST FOOD STORAGE BAGS

In general, sturdy, thick, and airtight bags with a tight seal fared best. For the freezer, the Glad Freezer Zipper Bag, with its double-groove seal, and the Ziploc Freezer Bag, with its wide opening that facilitates mess-free filling, rated the highest. The Hefty OneZip Storage Bag was praised for its water-tight slider seal, while the Ziploc Storage Bag received high honors for its airtight, classic zipper design.

small pieces of meat and delicate seafood become mushy after 24 hours in the marinade.

Spice rubs are a natural make-ahead option and even easier than marinades. Rubs that sit on the meat for 24 hours meld and become complex, seasoning the meat throughout, whereas those immediately rubbed on the meat before grilling tasted raw and harsh because there is little time for the spices to penetrate and flavor the meat.

In all of our testing, we found that 1 tablespoon of rub is enough for 1 portion of poultry or meat, and 1 teaspoon is enough for fish, but this is a vague rule of thumb (with more potent rubs, such as Chile-Cumin Spice Rub, page 291, we use even less). Simply sprinkle on enough rub to cover the meat and gently pat it to adhere. And to keep it from tasting dry, a light coating of vegetable oil spray on the rubbed meat before refrigerating does the trick. Lastly, we found that wrapping the meat portions individually with plastic wrap enabled the spices to sink in while helping to keep them moist.

24-HOUR MARINADES

THE MARINADES BELOW CAN BE REFRIGERATED in an airtight container and stored for up to 4 days. When added to meat, the marinated meat can be refrigerated 1 to 2 days before cooking. Note that we reserve a portion of our unused marinades spiked with an acidic ingredient like citrus juice, vinegar, or yogurt to pour over the cooked meat. This method provides a bright extra layer of flavor to the finished dish. The chart on pages 294–295 provides instructions on grilling or broiling marinated meat.

Garlic and Herb Marinade

MAKES ABOUT I CUP; ENOUGH FOR 2 TO 3
POUNDS POULTRY, MEAT, OR SEAFOOD

This all-purpose marinade is great for chicken, pork, beef, lamb, shrimp, and all types of fish, as well as vegetables.

½   cup extra-virgin olive oil
¼   cup water
¼   cup fresh parsley, tarragon, or basil leaves or
2   tablespoons fresh rosemary or thyme leaves

1   shallot, chopped
6   medium garlic cloves, minced or pressed through a garlic press (about 2 tablespoons)
1   teaspoon salt
¼   teaspoon ground black pepper
2   tablespoons juice from 1 lemon (for serving)

1. Process all of the ingredients, except the lemon juice, in a food processor or blender until smooth, about 20 seconds. Transfer ¼ cup of the marinade to an airtight container, add the lemon juice, and refrigerate until serving time. Pour the remaining marinade over the poultry, meat, or fish in a zipper-lock bag and refrigerate, 1 to 2 days.

2. When ready to cook, remove the meat from the bag and discard the marinade. Cook the poultry, meat, or fish as directed in the chart on pages 294–295. When ready to serve, shake the reserved ¼ cup marinade to recombine and pour over the cooked meat.

Teriyaki Marinade

MAKES ABOUT I CUP; ENOUGH FOR 2 TO 3
POUNDS POULTRY, MEAT, OR SEAFOOD

We like this marinade best for chicken, beef, and shrimp.

½   cup vegetable oil
⅓   cup soy sauce
⅓   cup sugar
¼   cup water
2   scallions, chopped
2   medium garlic cloves, minced or pressed through a garlic press (about 2 teaspoons)
2   tablespoons minced fresh ginger
⅛   teaspoon red pepper flakes
2   teaspoons mirin, sherry, or white wine (for serving)

1. Process all of the ingredients, except the mirin, in a food processor or blender until smooth, about 20 seconds. Transfer ¼ cup of the marinade to an airtight container, add the mirin, and refrigerate until serving time. Pour the remaining marinade over the poultry, meat, or fish in a zipper-lock bag and refrigerate, 1 to 2 days.

2. When ready to cook, remove the meat from the bag and discard the marinade. Cook the poultry, meat, or fish as directed in the chart on pages 294–295. When ready to serve, shake the reserved ¼ cup marinade to recombine and pour over the cooked meat.

Jerk Marinade

MAKES ABOUT 1 CUP; ENOUGH FOR 2 TO 3 POUNDS POULTRY, MEAT, OR SEAFOOD

This Jamaican-inspired marinade is perfect for chicken, although it can also be used for pork, beef, and even fish—red snapper is our favorite.

½ cup vegetable oil
⅓ cup water
6 scallions, chopped
2 medium garlic cloves, peeled
1 tablespoon molasses
½–1 habanero chile, chopped
1 teaspoon dried thyme
1 teaspoon ground allspice
1 teaspoon salt
2 tablespoons juice from 1 or 2 limes (for serving)

1. Process all of the ingredients, except the lime juice, in a food processor or blender until smooth, about 20 seconds. Transfer ¼ cup of the marinade to an airtight container, add the lime juice, and refrigerate until serving time. Pour the remaining marinade over the poultry, meat, or fish in a zipper-lock bag and refrigerate, 1 to 2 days.

2. When ready to cook, remove the meat from the bag and discard the marinade. Cook the poultry, meat, or fish as directed in the chart on pages 294–295. When ready to serve, shake the reserved ¼ cup marinade to recombine and pour over the cooked meat.

Tandoori Marinade

MAKES ABOUT 1 CUP; ENOUGH FOR 2 TO 3 POUNDS POULTRY, MEAT, OR FISH

Use this marinade for chicken, lamb, shrimp, and sturdy white fish, like halibut.

½ cup vegetable oil
¼ cup water
1 tablespoon minced fresh ginger
1 tablespoon ground coriander
1½ teaspoons ground cumin
1 teaspoon ground turmeric
1 teaspoon salt
½ teaspoon ground cinnamon
¼ teaspoon cayenne pepper
3 tablespoons plain yogurt (for serving)

1. Process all of the ingredients, except the yogurt, in a food processor or blender until smooth, about 20 seconds. Transfer ¼ cup of the marinade to an airtight container, add the yogurt, and refrigerate until serving time. Pour the remaining marinade over the poultry, meat, or fish in a zipper-lock bag and refrigerate, 1 to 2 days.

2. When ready to cook, remove the meat from the bag and discard the marinade. Cook the poultry, meat, or fish as directed in the chart on pages 294–295. When ready to serve, shake the reserved ¼ cup marinade to recombine and pour over the cooked meat.

Thai Marinade

MAKES ABOUT 1 CUP; ENOUGH FOR 2 TO 3 POUNDS POULTRY, MEAT, OR SEAFOOD

The spicy, sweet, and salty flavors of this marinade are excellent for chicken, pork, beef, shrimp, and sturdy white fish, like halibut.

½ cup vegetable oil
¼ cup minced fresh cilantro leaves
6 medium garlic cloves, minced or pressed through a garlic press (about 2 tablespoons)
2 tablespoons water
2 tablespoons fish sauce
2 tablespoons ground black pepper
2 tablespoons ground coriander
1 tablespoon brown sugar
1 tablespoon minced fresh ginger
2 tablespoons juice from 1 or 2 limes (for serving)

1. Process all of the ingredients, except the lime juice, in a food processor or blender until smooth, about 20 seconds. Transfer ¼ cup of the marinade to an airtight container, add the lime juice, and refrigerate until serving time. Pour the remaining marinade over the poultry, meat, or fish in a zipper-lock bag and refrigerate, 1 to 2 days.

2. When ready to cook, remove the meat from the bag and discard the marinade. Cook the poultry, meat, or fish as directed in the chart on pages 294–295. When ready to serve, shake the reserved ¼ cup marinade to recombine and pour over the cooked meat.

Southwestern Marinade

MAKES ABOUT I CUP; ENOUGH FOR 2 TO 3
POUNDS POULTRY, MEAT, OR SEAFOOD

Use this marinade for chicken, pork, beef, shrimp, and fish—we like it for swordfish.

½ cup vegetable oil
¼ cup water
3 medium garlic cloves, minced or pressed through a garlic press (about I tablespoon)
I tablespoon dark brown sugar
I tablespoon tomato paste
I tablespoon chili powder
2 teaspoons ground cumin
2 teaspoons salt
¼ teaspoon cayenne pepper
2 tablespoons juice from I or 2 limes (for serving)

1. Process all of the ingredients, except the lime juice, in a food processor or blender until smooth, about 20 seconds. Transfer ¼ cup of the marinade to an airtight container, add the lime juice, and refrigerate until serving time. Pour the remaining marinade over the poultry, meat, or fish in a zipper-lock bag and refrigerate, 1 to 2 days.

2. When ready to cook, remove the meat from the bag and discard the marinade. Cook the poultry, meat, or fish as directed in the chart on pages 294–295. When ready to serve, shake the reserved ¼ cup marinade to recombine and pour over the cooked meat.

Steak Sauce Marinade

MAKES ABOUT I CUP; ENOUGH FOR 2 TO 3
POUNDS POULTRY, MEAT, OR FISH

This marinade was developed for beef, although it can also be used on chicken, pork, and fatty fish, like salmon and tuna.

½ cup soy sauce
⅓ cup olive oil
¼ cup Worcestershire sauce
2 tablespoons dark brown sugar
2 tablespoons minced fresh chives
4 medium garlic cloves, minced or pressed through a garlic press (about 4 teaspoons)
I½ teaspoon ground black pepper
2 teaspoons balsamic vinegar (for serving)

1. Process all of the ingredients, except the vinegar, in a food processor or blender until smooth, about 20 seconds. Transfer ¼ cup of the marinade to an airtight container, add the vinegar, and refrigerate until serving time. Pour the remaining marinade over the poultry, meat, or fish in a zipper-lock bag and refrigerate, 1 to 2 days.

2. When ready to cook, remove the meat from the bag and discard the marinade. Cook the poultry, meat, or fish as directed in the chart on pages 294–295. When ready to serve, shake the reserved ¼ cup marinade to recombine and pour over the cooked meat.

OVERNIGHT KEBABS

MEAT OR CHICKEN AND FRESH VEGETABLE kebabs grilled or broiled to juicy perfection make great summer fare. The problem, however, is that they take quite a bit of time to put together—from cutting up the meat and vegetables, to marinating and skewering them. Supermarket meat counters across the country have made things easier by conveniently offering skewered kebabs for you to take home and throw on the grill or broiler. Unfortunately, most of these versions are either dried out or mushy and salty from sitting in a pool of bottled salad dressing for far too long.

Here in the test kitchen, we wanted to create

24-HOUR SPICE RUBS

SPICE RUBS ARE AN EASY WAY TO IMPART FLAVOR TO MEAT, CHICKEN, AND SEAFOOD AND because they should be applied to the meat 24 hours before cooking, rubs are an ideal flavoring method for the make-ahead cook. To prepare spice-rubbed meat, poultry or seafood: Mix all of the rub ingredients in a small bowl until combined. Sprinkle the rub over the food (1 tablespoon per portion of poultry and meat or 1 teaspoon per portion of seafood; slightly less for more potent rubs like Chile-Cumin Spice Rub). Coat completely and press to adhere. Spray evenly with vegetable oil spray and wrap each portion with plastic wrap. The spice-rubbed poultry, meat, or fish can be refrigerated in an airtight container for up to 24 hours. (The spice rubs themselves can be stored in an airtight container for up to 6 months.) Grill or broil as directed, following the instructions in the chart on pages 294–295.

Chile-Cumin Spice Rub

MAKES ABOUT ⅓ CUP

A little of this potent spice rub goes a long way.

1½	tablespoons chipotle chile powder
1½	tablespoons ancho chile powder
1	tablespoon ground cumin
2	teaspoons salt
2	teaspoons sugar

Coriander and Dill Spice Rub

MAKES ABOUT ⅓ CUP

Try this spice rub on salmon.

2	tablespoons ground black pepper
2	tablespoons ground coriander
1	tablespoon dried dill
2	teaspoons salt
1½	teaspoons red pepper flakes

Cocoa-Cumin-Allspice Rub

MAKES ABOUT ⅓ CUP

This earthy seasoning is especially good on grilled pork tenderloin.

4	teaspoons ground cumin
4	teaspoons ground black pepper
1	tablespoon unsweetened cocoa powder
2	teaspoons ground allspice
2	teaspoons salt

Chinese Five-Spice and Coffee Spice Rub

MAKES ABOUT ⅓ CUP

This spice rub is excellent on grilled or broiled pork chops.

2	tablespoons ground coffee
4	teaspoons Chinese five-spice powder
1	tablespoon ground black pepper
2	teaspoons salt
1	teaspoon sugar

Tarragon-Mustard Rub

MAKES ABOUT ⅓ CUP

We like this rub on grilled or broiled chicken.

3	tablespoons dried tarragon
2	tablespoons dry mustard
2	teaspoons salt
2	teaspoons ground black pepper

Herb Rub

MAKES ABOUT ¼ CUP

This rub works well with chicken and pork.

1	tablespoon dried thyme
1	tablespoon dried rosemary
1	tablespoon ground black pepper
3	bay leaves, crumbled

a make-ahead recipe for kebabs that was far superior to the store-bought versions—succulent, well-seasoned meat, complemented by fruits and vegetables that were equally satisfying—juicy and cooked all the way through but neither shrunken nor incinerated. Sure, for this version you have to cut and skewer the meat and vegetables yourself, but we designed the recipe so that all the work can be done the night before so you can come home from work the next day and fire up the grill (or broiler) for a tasty kebab supper.

When we started our testing, we figured it would be relatively simple. After all, skewered meat is simple food—a standby of every street-corner grill cook from here to China. But after some early attempts, we ran into a few difficulties. When we simply threaded the meat and veggies on skewers, brushed them with a little oil, sprinkled them with salt and pepper, and refrigerated them overnight, we were always disappointed. Sometimes the components cooked at different rates, resulting in dry meat and undercooked vegetables. Even when nicely grilled, quick-cooking kebabs didn't absorb much flavor from the fire and were bland. We decided to attack the flavor problem first, reasoning that once we could produce well-seasoned, juicy meat and chicken chunks, we'd work out the kinks of cooking fruits and vegetables at the same time.

Always thinking that simpler is better, we decided to go with the simplest solution, a spice rub. We'd had success with overnight rubs on steaks and chicken parts, and we saw no reason why rubs wouldn't lend flavor to kebabs as well. But the spice rub treatment was disappointing. The meat and chicken pieces looked and tasted dry. Because the chunks were skinless, there was no fat to dissolve the spices and help form a crispy crust. The surface of the chunks looked and tasted dry, and the spices were a little powdery and raw-tasting. For our kebabs, rubs were out.

Wanting to add a little moisture, we turned to wet preparations, or marinades. We borrowed our Garlic and Herb Marinade recipe (page 288), and soaked the meat in it overnight. We liked the glossy, slightly moist grilled crust that the marinade produced and the way the garlic and herb flavors had penetrated the meat. Then, as we do with all of our marinades, we tossed the meat with some of the marinade after cooking (that we had reserved the day before), spiked with a little lemon juice for a fresh hit of flavor. It is important to note that unlike larger pieces of meat, such as steaks and chicken breasts, small chunks of meat did not fare well in the marinade for 2 days—they became overly mushy and mealy.

Now for the vegetables: It was clear early on that cooking meat and vegetables together enhances the flavor of both. Therefore, we needed to figure out how to prepare the vegetables so that they would cook at the same rate as the meat. Precooking seemed like a hassle, so we eliminated items like potatoes, which take more time to cook through

MAKE IT A MENU

Overnight Kebabs

couscous or warm pita bread

Stuffed Plum Tomatoes (page 41)

mixed green salad with Bistro-Style Mustard Vinaigrette (page 82)

Italian Almond Cake (page 369)

on the grill than meat.

In general, resilient (but not rock-hard) vegetables fared well. Bell peppers and onions were our favorites because they held up in the marinade, cooked thoroughly but stayed moist, and lent good flavor and crunch to the skewers. We had the best results when we skewered the meat and vegetables and marinated them together, overnight.

As for grilling, we found a medium-hot fire to be best. A hotter fire chars the outside before the inside is done; a cooler fire won't give you those appetizing grill marks and may dry out the meat as it cooks. For broiling, we found it best to cook the kebabs 5 inches from the heat element. For the juiciest meat with the strongest grilled or broiled flavor, skewers should be cooked for seven to 12 minutes. Check for doneness by cutting into one of the pieces with a small knife. Remove chicken and pork from the grill or broiler as soon as there is no sign of pink at the center, and cook lamb and beef to the desired doneness.

After experimenting with various sizes and shapes, we chose 1½-inch chunks, small enough for easy eating but big enough to get some good grilled or broiled flavor before they have to come off the fire or out of the broiler. With smaller chunks and thin strips, there's no margin for error; a few seconds too long and you'll wind up with a dry-as-dust dinner.

Overnight Kebabs for the Grill or Broiler

SERVES 4 TO 6

You will need eight 12-inch skewers for this recipe. Remember to reserve ¼ cup of the unused marinade to pour over the kebabs before serving, as directed in the marinade recipes on pages 288–290—the reserved marinade will give the kebabs a bright hit of flavor. Serve the kebabs over rice, quick-cooking couscous, or orzo tossed with a little olive oil.

3   red, yellow, or orange bell peppers, stemmed, seeded, and cut into 1-inch pieces
1   large red onion, cut into ¼-inch pieces
2   pounds boneless beef, pork, lamb, or chicken, trimmed and cut into 1½-inch chunks (see page 292)

1   recipe marinade (pages 288–290)
    Lemon or lime wedges (for serving)

1. Using eight 12-inch metal skewers, thread each skewer with 1 piece of pepper, 3 pieces of onion, and 1 cube of meat. Repeat this sequence 2 more times. Arrange the skewers in a 13 by 9-inch baking dish. Set aside ¼ cup of the marinade and pour the remaining marinade over the top, turning to coat.

2. **TO STORE:** Cover tightly with plastic wrap and refrigerate, turning the skewers once or twice, for up to 24 hours. Refrigerate the reserved marinade separately.

3. **TO SERVE:** Cook as directed on page 295. Pour the reserved marinade over the cooked kebabs. Serve with the lemon wedges.

EQUIPMENT: Skewers

How much "performance" difference is there between one pointed stick and another? Well, we thought not much when we set out to test skewers. Once we surveyed the field—and tried out the designs with our recipes for grilled kebabs—our attitude changed. It really is possible to buy bad skewers.

First of all, forget what most grilling books say: If you're cooking over very high heat, bamboo skewers will burn and break apart—no matter how long you soak them in water beforehand. We had better luck with metal skewers. They may cost more, but they're reusable and they can handle the heartiest kebabs without bending or breaking.

Not all metal skewers are created equal, however. We had a tough time flipping food on round skewers—the skewer itself turned just fine, but the food stayed in place. Flat skewers proved much more effective. Double-pronged skewers turned the food, but some were flimsy and most had a tendency to twist out of their parallel configuration. Other models took the sturdy concept too far, with bulky skewers that severed meat in half.

Our choice: Any flat, thin metal skewer will do. We particularly like Norpro's 12-inch stainless-steel skewers (six skewers for $10), which are just ³⁄₁₆ inch thick.

THE BEST SKEWERS

We like flat, thin, metal skewers for grilling kebabs, like Norpro's 12-inch stainless-steel skewers, which are just ³⁄₁₆ inch thick.

GRILLING AND BROILING POULTRY, MEAT, AND FISH

GRILLING AND BROILING REQUIRE VERY LITTLE EFFORT AND FOR THE MAKE-AHEAD COOK WITH marinated or spice-rubbed poultry, meat, or fish, a juicy, well-seasoned entrée is just a few minutes away. Our instructions below cover both charcoal and gas grills. For broiling, note that our instructions and cooking times were developed with a conventional broiler, not the drawer-style broilers found at the bottom of some ovens. The heating element in drawer-style broilers typically isn't adjustable and you may find cooking times vary. That said, even conventional broilers vary in strength from brand to brand, so use our cooking times as guidelines and check for doneness early. Also, to prevent sticking, be sure to spray the broiler pan top with vegetable oil spray and set over a foil-lined broiler pan bottom.

MEAT AND PREP	CHARCOAL GRILLING INSTRUCTION	GAS GRILLING INSTRUCTION	BROILING INSTRUCTION	DONENESS TEMPERATURE* AND SERVING
BONELESS, SKINLESS CHICKEN BREASTS, TRIMMED	Medium-hot, single-level fire Grill, uncovered, 5 to 6 minutes per side.	With all burners on high, grill, covered, 5 to 6 minutes per side.	Adjust an oven rack about 5 inches from the broiler element. Cook, without flipping, 10 to 15 minutes.	160 degrees Transfer the chicken to a platter or carving board, tent with foil, and let rest for 5 to 10 minutes before serving. (If using a marinade, pour the reserved portion over the chicken before serving.)
BONE-IN, SKIN-ON SPLIT CHICKEN BREASTS, TRIMMED (SKIN SCORED IF BROILING, SEE PAGE 96)	Hot, modified two-level fire Grill over hot side of grill, uncovered, until well browned, 2 to 3 minutes per side. Move to cooler side of grill and grill, uncovered, 5 to 8 minutes per side.	With all burners on high, grill, covered, until well browned, 2 to 3 minutes per side. Turn all burners to medium-low and grill, covered, 5 to 8 minutes per side.	Adjust one oven rack about 13 inches from the broiler element and a second rack about 5 inches from the broiler element. Broil on bottom rack, skin side down, 15 minutes. Flip the chicken and cook until 155 degrees, 5 to 10 minutes. Move to top rack and broil until the skin is crispy, about 5 minutes.	160 degrees Transfer the chicken to a platter or carving board, tent with foil, and let rest for 5 to 10 minutes before serving. (If using a marinade, pour the reserved portion over the chicken before serving.)
BONE-IN, SKIN-ON CHICKEN THIGHS, DRUMSTICKS, AND WHOLE LEGS, TRIMMED (SKIN SCORED IF BROILING, SEE PAGE 96)	Medium-hot, two-level fire Grill over hot side of grill, uncovered, until well browned, 2 to 3 minutes per side. Move to cooler side of grill and grill, uncovered, 6 to 10 minutes per side.	With all burners on high, grill, covered, until well browned, 2 to 3 minutes per side. Turn all burners to medium-low and grill, covered, 6 to 10 minutes per side.	Adjust one oven rack about 13 inches from the broiler element and a second rack about 5 inches from the broiler element. Broil on bottom rack, skin side down, 15 minutes. Flip the chicken and cook until 170 degrees, 10 to 15 minutes. Move to top rack and broil until the skin is crispy, about 5 minutes.	175 degrees Transfer the chicken to a platter or carving board, tent with foil, and let rest for 5 to 10 minutes before serving. (If using a marinade, pour the reserved portion over the chicken before serving.)
BONE-IN OR BONE-LESS PORK LOIN CHOPS, 1 TO 1½ INCHES THICK, TRIMMED	Medium-hot, two-level fire Grill over hot side of grill, uncovered, until well browned, 2 to 4 minutes per side. Move to cooler side of grill and grill, uncovered, 1 to 5 minutes per side.	With all burners on high, grill, covered, until well browned, 2 to 4 minutes per side. Turn all burners to medium-low and grill, covered, 1 to 5 minutes per side.	Adjust an oven rack about 5 inches from the broiler element. Broil, without flipping, for 12 to 17 minutes.	140 degrees Transfer the pork to a platter or carving board, tent with foil, and let rest for 5 to 10 minutes before serving. (If using a marinade, pour the reserved portion over the meat before serving.)

MEAT AND PREP	CHARCOAL GRILLING INSTRUCTION	GAS GRILLING INSTRUCTION	BROILING INSTRUCTION	DONENESS TEMPERATURE* AND SERVING
BONELESS PORK TENDERLOINS (12 OUNCES EACH), TRIMMED OF SILVER SKIN (SEE PAGE 109)	Hot, modified two-level fire Grill over hot side of grill, uncovered, turning several times, until well browned all over, 10 to 12 minutes. Move to cooler side of grill and grill, uncovered, 2 to 5 minutes longer.	With all burners on high, grill, covered, turning several times, until well browned all over, 10 to 12 minutes. Turn all burners to medium-low and grill, covered, 2 to 5 minutes longer.	Adjust an oven rack about 5 inches from the broiler element. Broil, without flipping, 15 to 17 minutes.	140 degrees Transfer the pork to a platter or carving board, tent with foil, and let rest for 5 to 10 minutes before slicing. (If using a marinade, pour the reserved portion over the meat before slicing.)
FLANK STEAK (ABOUT 2 POUNDS), TRIMMED	Medium-hot, modified two-level fire Grill over hot side of grill, uncovered, until well seared on one side, 5 to 7 minutes. Flip steak over and grill, uncovered, 2 to 6 minutes. (Move steak to cooler side of grill if it begins to char.)	With all burners on high, grill, covered, until well seared on one side, 5 to 7 minutes. Flip steak over, and grill, covered, 2 to 6 minutes.	Adjust an oven rack about 5 inches from the broiler element. Broil, without flipping, 7 to 18 minutes.	115 to 120 degrees for rare; 120 to 125 degrees for medium-rare; 130 to 135 degrees for medium; 140 to 145 degrees for medium-well Transfer the steak to a platter or carving board, tent with foil, and let rest for 5 to 10 minutes before slicing. (If using a marinade, pour the reserved portion over the meat before slicing.)
MEDIUM-FIRM TO FIRM-FLESHED FISH STEAKS OR FILLETS, 1 TO 2 INCHES THICK (INCLUDING SALMON, HALIBUT, SWORDFISH, ARCTIC CHAR, BLUEFISH, COD, SNAPPER, AND MAHI-MAHI)	Medium-hot, single-level fire Grill, uncovered (skin side up), until lightly seared, 3 to 5 minutes. Gently flip the fish and grill, uncovered, 3 to 8 minutes longer.	With all burners on high, grill, covered (skin side up), 3 to 5 minutes. Gently flip the fish and grill, covered, 3 to 8 minutes longer.	Adjust an oven rack about 5 inches from the broiler element. Broil, without flipping, 10 to 14 minutes.	Cook until the fish flakes apart easily when prodded with a fork. Transfer the fish to a platter and, if using a marinade, pour the reserved portion over the fish before serving.
EXTRA-LARGE SHRIMP (21 TO 25 PER POUND), PEELED, DEVEINED, AND SKEWERED	Medium-hot, single-level fire Grill, uncovered, turning once, until bright pink, 4 to 6 minutes.	With all burners on high, grill, covered, turning once, until bright pink, 4 to 6 minutes.	Adjust an oven rack about 5 inches from the broiler element. Broil, flipping once, until bright pink, 5 to 6 minutes.	Cook until the shrimp are pink and slightly curled. Transfer the shrimp to a platter and, if using a marinade, pour the reserved portion over the shrimp before serving.
KEBABS (CHICKEN, BEEF, PORK, OR LAMB, CUT INTO 1½ INCH CHUNKS)	Medium-hot, single-level fire Grill, uncovered, turning often, until well browned on all sides, 8 to 12 minutes.	With all burners on high, grill, covered, turning once, until well browned on all sides, 8 to 12 minutes.	Adjust an oven rack about 5 inches from the broiler element. Broil, without flipping, 10 to 14 minutes.	When the meat is well browned, it will be cooked through. Transfer the kebabs to a platter and, if using a marinade, pour the reserved portion over the kebabs before serving.

* The doneness temperature given is the temperature at which the meat should be removed from the grill. The temperature of the meat will continue to rise as it rests before serving. For example, pork can be removed from the grill or broiler once the internal temperature reaches 140 degrees. Once rested, the pork should rise to a final serving temperature of 150 degrees.

Grilling 101

GRILLING IS A VERSATILE TECHNIQUE THAT INVOLVES COOKING FOOD DIRECTLY OVER HEAT, WHETHER generated by charcoal or gas. The goal is to cook the food quickly over a lot of heat. We prefer the flavor that charcoal adds to grilled food; however, there is no disputing that a gas grill is easier to set up. We leave the choice of grill up to you, and we provide directions in our recipes for both charcoal and gas grills.

LIGHTING A CHARCOAL GRILL WITH A STARTER

The easiest way we've found to light a charcoal fire is using a chimney starter (also called a flue starter). To use this simple device, fill the bottom section with crumpled newspaper, set the starter on the bottom grill grate, and fill the chimney with charcoal (a large starter holds about six quarts of charcoal, which is enough to make all the fires listed below). When the newspaper is lit, the flames ignite the charcoal. Once the coals are coated with even layer of fine gray ash, they are ready to be turned out into the grill.

LIGHTING A CHARCOAL GRILL WITHOUT A STARTER

Although a chimney starter is relatively inexpensive (about $15 to $25), you can improvise with this method as a last resort.

1. Place eight crumpled sheets of newspaper beneath the rack on which the charcoal sits.

2. With the bottom air vents open, pile the charcoal on the rack and light the paper. After about 20 minutes, the coals should be covered with fine gray ash and ready for cooking.

LIGHTING A GAS GRILL

It couldn't be easier to light a gas grill. Simply turn all of the burners to high with the lid down for 15 minutes.

ADJUSTING THE HEAT OF THE GRILL TO MEET YOUR NEEDS

It is necessary to arrange the lit coals in a charcoal grill, or adjust the gas burners, to suit the type of food you are cooking. Once the coals have been arranged in the bottom of the grill, put the cooking grate in place and put the cover on for five minutes to heat up the grate.

SINGLE-LEVEL FIRE

A single-level fire is great for foods that cook fairly quickly, such as fish, shellfish, vegetables, and boneless, skinless chicken breasts. This fire delivers even, moderate heat.

Charcoal: Arrange all of the lit charcoal in an even layer across the bottom of the grill.

Gas: Adjust all the burners to the same level.

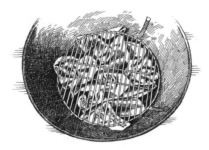

TWO-LEVEL FIRE

This fire creates two cooking zones—a hotter area for searing and a medium area to finish the cooking process. We use this fire for steaks and pork chops.

Charcoal: Arrange one-third of the lit coals in a single layer over half of the grill and pile the remaining coals over the other half.

Gas: Leave one burner on high or medium-high and turn the other(s) to medium or medium-low.

MODIFIED TWO-LEVEL

This fire allows searing over the coals and then slow cooking over indirect heat. We use this fire to grill-roast beef tenderloin, pork loin, and pork tenderloin.

Charcoal: Arrange all of the coals over half of the grill and leave the other half of the grill empty.

Gas: Leave one burner on high and turn the other burner(s) off.

CLEANING AND OILING A COOKING GRATE

Oiling your cooking grate is a must for preventing fish, burgers, and other foods from sticking to the grill. But the cooking grate should be cleaned before it is oiled. Use a grill brush or this improvised method: Once your cooking grate is hot, fashion your own grill brush with a crumpled wad of aluminum foil and long-handled tongs.

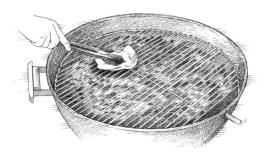

Once your cooking grate is clean, a slick of oil over the grate will further prevent food from sticking. Simply dip a wad of paper towels in vegetable oil, grasp the oiled towels with a pair of long-handled tongs, and rub the oil over the hot cooking grate.

PREVENTING FLARE-UPS FROM THE GRILL

Flare-ups are caused primarily by fats melting into the fire, but you don't need to let a grease fire get out of control and ruin your meal. As a precaution, we keep a squirt bottle or plant mister filled with water near the grill. At the first sign of flames, try to pull foods to a cool part of the grill and douse the flames with water.

GAUGING THE TEMPERATURE OF YOUR GRILL

Use the chart below to determine the intensity of the fire. We use the terms "hot fire," "medium-hot fire," and so forth in our grilling recipes. To take the temperature of the fire, hold your hand 5 inches above the cooking grate and count how many seconds you can comfortably leave it in place.

INTENSITY OF FIRE	TIME YOU CAN HOLD YOUR HAND 5 INCHES ABOVE GRATE
HOT	2 seconds
MEDIUM-HOT	3 to 4 seconds
MEDIUM	5 to 6 seconds
MEDIUM-LOW	7 seconds

GETTING AN ACCURATE READ FROM YOUR INSTANT-READ THERMOMETER

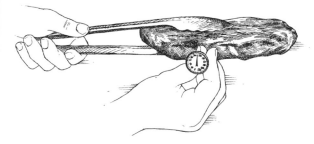

An instant-read thermometer is your best bet for checking the doneness of meat and poultry. The sensor on most thermometers is located an inch or two up from the tip of the shaft, which isn't a problem when you're inserting it through the top of a whole chicken, beef tenderloin, or other thick piece of meat. But if you poke the thermometer straight down into a thinner piece of meat, such as a steak, burger, or even some chicken breasts, you aren't going to get an accurate reading. Instead, insert the tip of the thermometer through the side of the meat until most of the shaft is embedded. Make sure the shaft is not touching any bone, which will throw off the reading. And make sure to check each piece of meat—based on their thickness and location on the grill, some will cook faster than others.

STUFFED FLANK STEAK

ALONGSIDE READY-TO-COOK BREADED CUT-
lets and marinated kebabs, many supermarket meat cases also feature stuffed flank steak—thin steak rolled around a colorful pinwheel filling of spinach and cheese. But the reality is that these overpriced beauties look better than they taste. The steak cooks up dry and the filling turns gummy and bland—not to mention it also often leaks out the sides. At its best, stuffed flank steak is a tasty combination of filling and rosy-red meat in each bite, nicely caramelized on the outside and still moist on the inside. We love the idea of this make-ahead dish—especially for company. We set out to make a truly great stuffed flank steak for our make-ahead arsenal.

So why flank steak? Like other steaks cut from the flank and plate of the cow, it has a rich, full, beefy flavor and its increasing popularity in restaurants has caused it to be more available in supermarkets. It is also easily adaptable to a wide variety of cooking styles, and rolled, stuffed flank keeps well overnight and thus lends itself well to our make-ahead concept.

Perhaps the most difficult part of this recipe is butterflying the flank steak so the stuffing can be added. Butterflying is a fancy term for cutting the steak laterally through the center, stopping ½ inch from the edge to create a hinge. Cut this way, the steak can then be opened like a book. We found that the thicker the flank steak, the easier it was to butterfly. Taking a cue from Chinese chefs, we tried freezing it for 20 minutes. Chilling the meat firms it up and thus prevents the meat from wiggling with the movement of your knife.

Once butterflied, we turned next to the stuffing. The recipes we researched utilized a wide range of ingredients, but we set out to improve upon the most common supermarket version—a combination of spinach and cheese. We also decided to take a few liberties with this classic combination and add roasted red bell peppers to the mix, for their sweet flavor and bright color.

Leaving a 1-inch border around the edges of the steak, we started by layering the cheese onto the steak, followed by the spinach and chopped roasted bell peppers. It was important to blot the chopped peppers on paper towels beforehand to remove as much excess moisture as possible. Otherwise, the excess moisture might have a tendency to steam inside the steak, leading to uneven cooking, and a soggy stuffing that would leak out the sides. Once cooked, the stuffing didn't leak out the sides, but it was a bit soggy. We also noticed that the peppers hadn't been distributed evenly and overall the flavor of the stuffing wasn't as pronounced as we'd hoped. Momentarily stumped, we then thought of replacing the peppers with a red pepper pesto. Containing ingredients like garlic, shallots, thyme, and Parmesan, the pesto provided a strong flavor base without excess moisture and it was easily spooned over the spinach, resulting in well-seasoned flavor in every bite. The addition of Parmesan also helped to bind the stuffing a bit, helping make it stay put inside the rolled steak. (We did try to spread the pesto directly onto the steak, but it soaked into the meat, thus disappearing, and we missed the colorful red layer that makes the presentation of this dish so impressive.)

Once stuffed, we turned to rolling and tying the steak. Starting with the short end, the steak was rolled to form a large pinwheel and tied in three places with kitchen twine. In our early tests, the importance of leaving a 1-inch border on the inside of the steak became apparent. If the filling was too close to the edges when rolling, it would be forced out the top of our pinwheel. Once it was rolled, the two ends of the steak were trimmed off for a neat presentation.

After the steak and filling were wrapped up, we turned our attention to storage and cooking. Taking a tip from a fellow test cook, we brushed the steak with olive oil before wrapping it in plastic wrap. The olive oil protected the meat from drying out while it sits in the refrigerator.

As for cooking, we wanted our steak to have a browned caramelized exterior, medium-rare meat, and a piping hot filling. While some stuffed flank steak recipes sear the steak first in a hot skillet on the stovetop, then slide it into the oven to finish cooking, we wanted a more streamlined approach. A hot oven would be a great start to help caramelize the exterior, so we cranked it up to 450 degrees. We placed the steak on the rack of a roasting pan (allowing the hot air to circulate all around the meat) and into the hot oven until the internal temperature reached 120 degrees, about 45 minutes. We transferred the steak to a carving board, tented it loosely with foil, and allowed it to rest for 10 minutes. During this time, the meat's residual heat finished cooking it to a perfect medium-rare and the juices redistributed. You can also grill the steak for an extra dimension of flavor.

As we set out to do, we had successfully improved upon a butcher's case classic. Although it did take a bit longer than a swipe of the credit card to prepare, the results far outweighed the premade pinwheels. And the stuffing actually made it from the oven to the plate.

Flank Steak Stuffed with Spinach, Provolone, and Roasted Red Pepper Pesto

SERVES 6 TO 8

An instant-read thermometer is a must for this recipe. Brushing the meat with oil both before storing and during cooking helps prevent it from drying out and turning leathery.

1	flank steak (about 2 pounds)
1	(12-ounce) jar roasted red bell peppers, rinsed, drained, and patted dry
5	tablespoons extra-virgin olive oil
½	ounce Parmesan cheese, grated (about ¼ cup)
1	medium shallot, chopped coarse
1	small garlic clove, minced or pressed through a garlic press (about ½ teaspoon)
1	tablespoon minced fresh thyme leaves Salt and ground black pepper
8	ounces thinly sliced deli provolone cheese
3	ounces baby spinach (about 2 cups)

1. Lay the steak on a large plate and freeze until firm, about 20 minutes.

2. Meanwhile, puree the peppers, 2 tablespoons of the oil, Parmesan, shallot, garlic, thyme, and

STUFFING FLANK STEAK

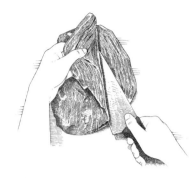

1. Slice the chilled steak horizontally, opening the steak as if it were a book. Slice the steak to within ½ inch of the edge.

2. Layer the cheese and spinach over the steak, then cover with the pesto, leaving a 1-inch border around the edges of the steak.

3. Rotate the steak 90 degrees. Starting with a short edge, roll up the steak tightly.

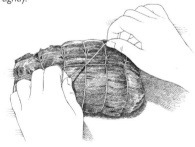

4. Use kitchen twine to tie the steak at 1-inch intervals. Loop a piece of twine around both ends of the steak to prevent the filling from falling out.

⅛ teaspoon salt in a food processor until smooth about 30 seconds, stopping to scrape down the sides of the work bowl as needed; set the pesto aside.

3. Following the illustrations on page 299, slice the chilled steak in half horizontally to within ½ inch of the edge and open it like a book. Pat the steak dry with paper towels and season with salt and pepper.

4. Layer the cheese over the steak, leaving a 1-inch border around the edges, then cover with the spinach. Spoon the roasted red pepper mixture evenly over the spinach. Following the illustrations on page 299, roll the steak up tightly and tie. Brush the steak with 1 more tablespoon of the oil.

5. To STORE: Wrap the steak tightly with plastic wrap and refrigerate for up to 24 hours.

6. To SERVE: Adjust an oven rack to the middle position and heat the oven to 450 degrees. Brush the steak with 1 more tablespoon of the oil and transfer to a wire rack set over a foil-lined baking sheet. Roast until an instant-read thermometer inserted into the middle of the steak registers 120 degrees, 45 to 50 minutes, rotating the steak and brushing it with the remaining tablespoon oil halfway through cooking. Transfer the steak to a carving board, tent with foil, and let rest, about 10 minutes. Remove the twine and slice the steak crosswise.

TO SERVE RIGHT AWAY

After brushing the steak with the oil in step 4, proceed to step 6 and roast as directed. (Note that is not necessary to brush the steak with oil at the start of step 6, but only halfway through cooking as described.)

➤ VARIATIONS
Charcoal-Grilled Stuffed Flank Steak
Follow the recipe for Flank Steak Stuffed with Spinach, Provolone, and Roasted Red Pepper Pesto through step 5. Following the instructions on page 296, build a medium-hot, modified two-level fire. Grill the steak until browned on all sides, about 12 minutes. Move the steak to the cool side of the grill, cover, and cook until an instant-read thermometer inserted into the center

registers 120 degrees, 20 to 30 minutes, rotating and brushing the steak with the remaining tablespoon oil halfway through cooking. Rest and slice the steak as directed.

Gas-Grilled Stuffed Flank Steak
Follow the recipe for Flank Steak Stuffed with Spinach, Provolone, and Roasted Red Pepper Pesto through step 5. Turn all of the burners to high and heat the grill for 15 minutes. Grill the steak until browned on all sides, about 12 minutes. Leave the primary burner on high and turn off all of the other burners. Move the steak to the cool side of the grill, cover, and cook until an instant-read thermometer inserted into the center registers 120 degrees, 20 to 30 minutes, rotating and brushing the steak with the remaining tablespoon oil halfway through cooking. Rest and slice the steak as directed.

Flank Steak Stuffed with Spinach, Provolone, and Raisin–Pine Nut Pesto
If desired, substitute an equal amount of grated pecorino for the Parmesan—its strong flavor works especially well in this sweet, nutty pesto.

Follow the recipe for Flank Steak Stuffed with Spinach, Provolone, and Roasted Red Pepper Pesto, replacing the roasted red peppers and thyme in step 2 with ½ cup raisins, ½ cup toasted pine nuts, ¼ cup minced fresh parsley leaves, and ¼ cup minced fresh basil leaves. Rest and slice the steak as directed.

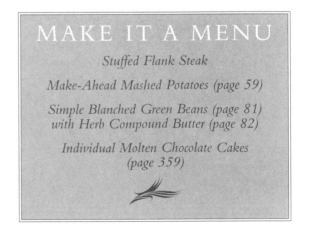

MAKE IT A MENU

Stuffed Flank Steak

Make-Ahead Mashed Potatoes (page 59)

Simple Blanched Green Beans (page 81)
with Herb Compound Butter (page 82)

Individual Molten Chocolate Cakes
(page 359)

STUFFED PORK CHOPS

THE MENTION OF STUFFED PORK CHOPS usually brings to mind those enormous oddities exhibited at the supermarket meat counter: dinosaur chops, split open and barely able to contain their soggy, softball-sized portions of bread crumbs, sausage, and fruit—the sight of which always leaves us wondering how we would cook such a thing, let alone consume it. Stuffing a pork chop is not a bad idea—today's lean pork needs all the help it can get—but it is rarely well executed, as the supermarket variety illustrates. Most recipes insist on treating the chops like a turkey, cramming them full of bulky bread stuffing. This type of stuffing does little for a chop besides take up space that is tight to begin with. What we were after was a thick, juicy pork chop, enhanced with a flavorful stuffing that could be assembled the night before, and cooked for dinner the next day.

Initial tests showed that tasters preferred their stuffed chops on the bone, both for the visual appeal and because the meat stayed juicier. But shopping for bone-in pork chops can be confusing since butchers—and supermarket labels—rarely agree on precisely what is called what. For example: While cuts of beef may come from either the "loin" or the "rib," butchers refer to these two sections of the pig collectively as the "loin." Therefore, the common label "pork loin chop," while technically accurate, is too broad to be of much use. The more precise "center-cut loin chop" should, but does not always, refer to chops cut right from the center of the loin. They are easily identified by the T-shaped bone running through the center, which separates the loin muscle from the adjacent tenderloin.

A much better choice for stuffing is a chop cut from the rib cage, which has a wide, unbroken "eye" of meat and a curved rib bone off to the side and out of the way. This is the chop to buy. We call it a rib chop, but markets often do not make that distinction. Another cut also sold as a "rib chop" (and one that you do not want) is taken from the blade end of the rib cage (near the head and shoulder of the pig) and has a smaller central eye, broken up by threads of tough connective tissue and surrounded by a thick cap of meat that

contracts during cooking. A common approach to stuffing chops is to butterfly them completely open, then stitch them back together with toothpicks or string. Toothpicks are easy enough to use, assuming the cook has some handy in the kitchen, but only marginally effective at holding the seam closed as the meat cooks.

Sewing the chops is effective but also extremely tedious. We much prefer a less invasive technique, in which a sharp paring knife is used to cut a wide pocket whose opening is actually quite small. Care must be taken not to poke straight through the edge of the chop when enlarging the pocket, however. After making this mistake half a dozen times, we learned to guard against it by leaving the thin layer of fat and connective tissue around the edge of the chop untrimmed. Also helpful is to seal the pocket with a citrus wedge.

Some recipes suggested braising the chops, usually covered, with some stock or wine. We knew it was important to keep the chops moist, but simply adding liquid to the recipe was not the way to go about it. In the test kitchen, we frequently turn

---

TEST KITCHEN TIP: Buying the Right Chop

Stuffed pork chops depend on purchasing the right chop. Note that even within the rib chop category, there are good ones cut from close to the center of the loin and not-so-good ones cut from the shoulder or blade end of the loin.

1. Loin Chop: The bone running through this chop makes it difficult to stuff.

2. Blade-End Chop: This chop contracts during cooking and squeezes out the stuffing.

3. Rib Chop: The unbroken eye of meat makes this chop perfect for stuffing.

to brining (a simple saltwater soak) to keep lean, mild-flavored meat and poultry from turning out bland and dry, and this technique worked well in this recipe.

With our chops brined, we turned to high, dry heat to develop the crusty brown exterior we wanted. Roasting the chops in a hot oven failed to deliver the goods and cooking the chops in a skillet from start to finish took quite a while thanks to the thickness of the chops and the rather crowded pan. Transferring the seared chops (still in the skillet) to the oven worked better, but the best results came from first searing the chops in a hot skillet to develop the crust and then transferring them to a preheated baking sheet in a hot oven. Spread out on the hot baking sheet, the chops browned all over and cooked quickly.

Throughout our testing, we had experimented with different departures from a traditional bread-based stuffing. Our priorities were to incorporate moisture, fat, and assertive flavors to enhance the lean, mild pork and to eliminate any bland, starchy fillers. Along the way, we discovered that consistency and texture were also important: Creamy, even sticky, stuffings were much easier to pack into a chop than dry, loose, crumbly ones.

With these guidelines, we settled on our red onion and fruit jam stuffing with dates, sour cherries, orange, pecans, and blue cheese. Tasters raved about the lively combination of flavors—a perfect foil to the juicy pork.

Red Onion Jam–Stuffed Pork Chops with Port, Pecans, and Dried Fruit

SERVES 4

If using enhanced pork (see page 303 for more information), do not brine the pork in step 1. Manufacturers don't use the terms "enhanced" or "natural" on package labels, but if the pork has been enhanced it will have an ingredient list. Natural pork contains pork and no other ingredients. To use kosher salt in the brine, see page 88 for conversion information. One stuffed chop makes for a very generous serving. If desired, the chops can be made to serve 6 by removing the meat from the bone and cutting it into ½-inch-thick slices.

4	bone-in pork rib chops, 1½ inches thick (12 to 14 ounces each)
¾	cup packed light brown sugar
	Salt
2	tablespoons olive oil
1	large red onion, halved and sliced ⅛ inch thick
1	tablespoon granulated sugar
¾	cup ruby port
⅓	cup chopped pitted dates
⅓	cup dried sour cherries
1	medium orange, cut into 4 wedges
3	tablespoons white wine vinegar
2	teaspoons minced fresh thyme leaves
⅓	cup pecans, toasted
	Ground black pepper
3	ounces blue cheese, crumbled (about ¾ cup, for serving)

1. Following the illustrations on page 303, cut a 1-inch opening into the side of each pork chop, then cut a pocket for the stuffing. Dissolve the brown sugar and ¼ cup salt in 6 cups of water in a large bowl or container. Submerge the chops in the brine, cover with plastic wrap, and refrigerate for 1 hour.

2. While the chops brine, heat 1 tablespoon of the oil in a medium saucepan over medium heat until shimmering. Add the onion and granulated sugar and cook, stirring occasionally, until browned, 20 to 25 minutes.

3. Meanwhile, combine the port, dates, and cherries in a microwave-safe bowl, cover with plastic wrap, and microwave on high until simmering, about 1 minute. Set aside until needed. Squeeze ¼ cup of juice from the orange wedges into a small bowl, reserving the juiced wedges for sealing the stuffing pockets in the chops.

4. When the onions are browned, stir in the dried fruit–port mixture, orange juice, 2 tablespoons of the vinegar, and thyme. Cook, stirring occasionally, until thickened and jam-like, 10 to 12 minutes. Stir in the remaining 1 tablespoon vinegar and the pecans. Season with salt and pepper to taste. Cool until just warm, about 15 minutes.

5. Remove the chops from the brine, rinse, and pat dry with paper towels. Place one-quarter of the stuffing (about ⅓ cup) in the pocket of each chop. Trim the reserved orange wedges from the stuffing

recipe to 2-inch lengths. Insert 1 orange wedge into each pocket to contain the stuffing. Season the chops with pepper.

6. **TO STORE:** Cover the chops with plastic wrap and refrigerate for up to 24 hours.

7. **TO SERVE:** Adjust an oven rack to the lower-middle position, place a rimmed baking sheet on the rack, and heat the oven to 450 degrees. Heat the remaining 1 tablespoon oil in a heavy-bottomed large skillet over medium-high heat until just smoking. Add the chops and brown well on both sides, 5 to 6 minutes.

8. Transfer the chops to the preheated sheet in the oven. Cook until an instant-read thermometer inserted into the center of the stuffing registers 140 degrees, 10 to 15 minutes, flipping the chops halfway through the cooking time. Transfer the chops to a platter, tent loosely with foil, and let rest for 10 minutes. Sprinkle with the blue cheese before serving.

TO SERVE RIGHT AWAY

Cook the stuffed chops as directed in steps 7 and 8, until an instant-read thermometer inserted into the center of the stuffing registers 140 degrees, 10 to 15 minutes, flipping the chops halfway through the cooking time.

INGREDIENTS: Enhanced or Unenhanced Pork?

Because modern pork is remarkably lean and therefore somewhat bland and prone to dryness if overcooked, a product called "enhanced" pork has overtaken the market. In fact, it can be hard to find unenhanced pork in some areas. Enhanced pork has been injected with a solution of water, salt, sodium phosphates, sodium lactate, potassium lactate, sodium diacetate, and varying flavor agents to bolster flavor and juiciness, with the total amount of enhancing ingredients adding 7 to 15 percent extra weight. Pork containing additives must be so labeled, with a list of the ingredients. After several taste tests, we have concluded that while enhanced pork is indeed juicier and more tender than unenhanced pork, the latter has more genuine pork flavor. Some tasters picked up unappealingly artificial, salty flavors in enhanced pork. Enhanced pork can also leach juices that, once reduced, will result in overly salty sauces. In the test kitchen, we prefer natural pork, but the choice is up to you.

STUFFING A PORK CHOP

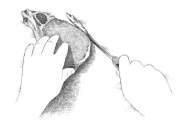

1. Using a sharp boning or paring knife, trim away the excess fat and connective tissue around the edge of the meat.

2. With the knife positioned as shown, insert the blade through the center of the side of the chop until the tip touches the bone.

3. Holding the chop firmly, carefully swing just the tip of the blade through the middle of the chop to create a pocket.

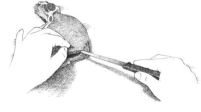

4. Remove the knife from the chop and, if necessary, enlarge the pocket opening slit to measure 1 inch.

5. With your fingers, gently press the stuffing mixture into the pocket, without enlarging the opening.

STUFFED PORK LOIN

STUFFED PORK LOIN IS AN IMPRESSIVE MAIN course that is often overlooked these days. Perhaps stuffed pork loin has fallen out of favor because of the perceived complexity of preparing the dish, or maybe because the effort involved simply doesn't deliver, resulting in dry pork and bland stuffings. This is a shame because a well-stuffed pork loin offers lean, meaty slices with an attractive center for a company-worthy main course. This dish is also particularly suited to the make-ahead cook because it stores wonderfully and allows the flavors of the stuffing to permeate the meat. Our goals were as follows: Develop an approachable method for preparing a make-ahead stuffed pork loin—one with moist, juicy meat and a tasty sauce—and develop a complementary full-flavored stuffing that stays intact, even when sliced.

We started with the choice of pork roast. Boneless loin roasts are the best choice for stuffing because they consist largely of a single, uniformly shaped muscle that is easy to stuff and roast neatly. When we started testing, though, our first few trips to the market revealed that not all boneless loin roasts are the same. Some come from the blade end and have an extra muscle attached, making it cumbersome to butterfly, and others may tend to narrow at one end making them difficult to stuff. We had to communicate clearly and specifically with the supermarket meat manager or butcher to get roasts with a large circumference, which was key for manageable stuffing and roasting.

With our pork loin in hand, we next looked to preparing it for stuffing. There are various ways to do so, but in order to provide a generous amount of stuffing in every bite, we settled on butterflying. Butterflying, or cutting the roast in the center and opening it like a book, allowed it to hold more of the mixture than roasts stuffed by means of the other methods we tried, including boring a hole through the center of the roast with a knife and sharpening steel, making a "Y" cut to create space in the center, slitting the loin from the bottom, and studding the meat with its filling. Pounding the butterflied roast further maximized the amount of stuffing we could use by increasing the meat's surface area. Pounding also helped to even out the thickness of the meat and, in test after test, proved to tenderize it as well.

In an effort to reduce the workload in this recipe, we cut out one very common step in roasting—searing the meat. Searing lends a beautiful caramel color to a roast, as well as a depth of flavor. However, we wanted to reduce the number of pots and pans and store and cook everything in one dish, so we decided to dust the top of the pork with a scant teaspoon of sugar just prior to roasting, to help give the roast a caramelized appearance and add a bit of flavor as well.

We knew from previous testing that roast pork fared best when brined. But, in an effort to reinvent the wheel, we tried brining in a mixture of apple cider and water instead of our usual brine of water, sugar, and salt. We had hoped that this would add another level of flavor to the meat and encourage browning during roasting. No such luck. When compared side by side to our standard brine, the

BUYING A GOOD PORK LOIN ROAST

The pork loin runs from the shoulder of the hog down the back to the ham in the rear. While every hog is different, most whole boneless loins measure roughly 30 inches long and weigh in the range of 8 to 12 pounds when they reach the butcher shop or supermarket meat department. There they are broken down into the 2- to 3-pound roasts typically available in the meat case.

1. Center-Cut Roast: Our top choice, this cut is mild and lean. It butterflies evenly, and its delicate flavor doesn't compete with the stuffing.

2. Blade-End Roast: Our second choice, this cut is moist and flavorful, but the muscle separation makes it hard to butterfly evenly.

difference was negligible. In our quest for ever-tender pork, it is key to avoid overcooking it. As we usually do in the test kitchen, we aimed for a final internal temperature of 150 degrees, at which point the meat would be fully cooked yet retain a slightly rosy hue inside. (This means we'd need to pull the roast from the oven when it reached 140 degrees—after resting, the roast would rise to the final desired temperature.)

Having conquered all issues relating to the meat, we began our search for stuffing recipes. For our pork loin with a relatively small cavity, we were looking for a highly flavored stuffing with very little binder. Dried fruit is often paired with pork (think chutneys and relishes) and in stuffings as well. Because dried fruit possesses a high sugar content, it has a somewhat sticky texture, acting as a binder itself. After trying several combinations of dried fruits and seasonings, we liked apricots and cherries best—one or the other or a combination. Chopped pistachios added some crunch and further flavor to the fruit and we seasoned the mixture with garlic, shallots, thyme, cumin, and cinnamon. Alongside the lean pork, this stuffing won raves.

Our final refinement came in the tying itself. Many cooks (including some in our test kitchen) are all thumbs when it comes to manipulating a single long piece of twine into a series of butcher's knots around a roast. (If you feel like your roast-tying skills need some work, see our tip on page 396, where you can practice with some kitchen twine and a roll of paper towels.)

Even though we brined the pork and it was a juicy, flavorful piece of meat, we felt that it was still missing something—a sauce perhaps. Wanting to keep this dish confined to one pan, we realized that the sauce would have to be made in the oven while the meat cooked. A light and silky sauce made with chicken broth, heavy cream, white wine, and shallots complemented the pork and stuffing without overwhelming it. The flavor was just what we wanted, but the consistency was a little thin. Just 1½ teaspoons of cornstarch helped thicken the sauce to a perfect consistency. This is a company-worthy main course everyone will enjoy.

STUFFING A PORK ROAST

1. Lay the loin on the cutting board and begin to slice laterally through the center, starting at the thinner edge.

2. As you slice, open the meat as you would a book. Stop slicing 1 inch shy of the edge to create a "hinge."

3. Cover the surface with plastic wrap and pound the meat to a 1 inch thickness. Brine the meat as directed on page 306.

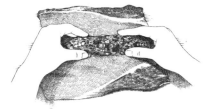

4. Remove the pork loin from the brine, rinse, and pat dry; season with salt and pepper. Form the stuffing into a log and place onto the center of the butterflied pork, over the hinge.

5. Roll up the pork to encase the stuffing. Tie lengths of twine at 4 equal intervals along the roast. Trim the twine before roasting.

Roast Pork Loin with Dried Fruit Stuffing

SERVES 4 TO 6

Pounding the pork into a uniform thickness is key to even cooking. If using enhanced pork (see page 303 for more information), do not brine the pork in step 1. Manufacturers don't use the terms "enhanced" or "natural" on package labels, but if the pork has been enhanced it will have an ingredient list. Natural pork contains pork and no other ingredients. To use kosher salt in the brine, see page 88 for conversion information. For the best flavor, we don't advise preparing the sauce ahead of time. You can use either dried cherries or apricots in the stuffing, although a mixture of both fruits is both tasty and attractive.

PORK AND STUFFING

I	boneless center-cut or blade-end pork loin roast (2 ½ to 3 pounds)
	Salt
¾	cup plus I teaspoon sugar
¾	cup dried cherries or apricots (or a mixture of both fruits)
¼	cup shelled pistachios, toasted
2	small shallots, minced (about ¼ cup)
2	teaspoons extra-virgin olive oil, plus extra for rubbing on the pork
2	teaspoons minced fresh thyme leaves, or ¼ teaspoon dried thyme
I	medium garlic clove, minced or pressed through a garlic press (about I teaspoon)
⅛	teaspoon ground cumin
⅛	teaspoon ground cinnamon
	Ground black pepper

SAUCE

I ¼	cups low-sodium chicken broth
½	cup heavy cream
¼	cup white wine
I	medium shallot, minced (about 3 tablespoons)
I ½	teaspoons cornstarch
2	tablespoons minced fresh parsley leaves

1. FOR THE PORK AND STUFFING: Trim, butterfly, and pound the pork loin to an even 1-inch thickness, following the illustrations on page 305. Dissolve ¾ cup salt and ¾ cup of the sugar in 3 quarts cold water in a large container. Place the pork loin in the brine, cover, and refrigerate for 1½ hours.

2. Meanwhile, pulse the cherries, pistachios, shallots, oil, thyme, garlic, cumin, and cinnamon in a food processor until chunky, about ten 1-second pulses. Season with salt and pepper to taste.

3. Remove the pork from the brine, rinse, and pat dry with paper towels. Season the pork with pepper. Stuff and tie the pork following the illustrations on page 305.

4. TO STORE: Rub the pork roast lightly with 1 teaspoon oil. Cover the pork tightly with plastic wrap and refrigerate for up to 24 hours.

5. TO SERVE: Adjust an oven rack to the middle position and preheat the oven to 450 degrees. Remove the plastic wrap from the pork and sprinkle with the remaining 1 teaspoon sugar. Place the pork in a 13 by 9-inch baking dish, seam side down.

6. FOR THE SAUCE: Whisk the broth, cream, wine, shallot, and cornstarch together, then pour into the baking dish around the roast. Roast the pork until it registers 140 degrees on an instant-read thermometer, about 50 minutes.

7. Transfer the roast to a carving board, tent loosely with foil, and let rest for 10 minutes before carving into ½-inch slices. Stir the parsley into the sauce and season with salt and pepper to taste. Serve, passing the sauce separately.

TO SERVE RIGHT AWAY

After stuffing and tying the pork in step 3, sprinkle it with 1 teaspoon sugar (it is not necessary to rub the pork with oil). Roast the pork with the sauce as described in steps 6 and 7, reducing the roasting time to 40 to 45 minutes or until an instant-read thermometer inserted into the center of the stuffing registers 140 degrees.

STUFFED SOLE

THIN FILLETS OF SOLE ROLLED AROUND A savory stuffing and blanketed with a white sauce are a natural choice for the make-ahead cook, especially one who likes to entertain. Too often, however, this dish tastes like bad banquet fare—overcooked fish, soggy stuffing, and a dull-flavored white sauce. We aimed to create a version of this dish you'd be proud to serve to company: tender, moist fillets, a lively stuffing, and a delicately flavored sauce that pulls the whole dish together. And because the dish has multiple components, we wanted to streamline the prep without compromising this impressive dish.

We started with the filling and dismissed a bread-based stuffing in favor of a Florentine-style filling made with spinach and cheese. Spinach and cheese would pack a lot more flavor than one with bread crumbs, and a spinach stuffing would not get soggy in the fridge overnight—a typical downfall with a bread stuffing. In lieu of cooking fresh spinach, which would involve multiple steps, we turned to frozen spinach. Using frozen prechopped spinach cut out most of the laborious preparation; all we had to do was make sure it was thawed and thoroughly squeezed dry.

For the white sauce, most recipes start with a roux: a combination of butter and flour are cooked together, then cream is added until the sauce is simmered until thickened. We seasoned ours with garlic, shallot, and thyme. Tasted right away, the sauce was rich and delicious, but after an overnight sit in the fridge, it lost some of its fresh flavor. We had a hunch that the long simmer combined with the overnight refrigeration and reheating was giving the sauce a stale flavor. To solve the problem, we omitted the flour and added just 4 teaspoons of cornstarch to the mix—cornstarch thickens the sauce without a long simmer. The result? A sauce with a less "cooked," thus fresher, flavor. We combined some sauce with the spinach and Parmesan cheese, for a moist, rich filling. The remainder would be set aside to pour over the fillets.

Assembling the fish rolls was easy. We lined up the fillets, mounded the filling on each, and folded the end of each fillet over the filling. We then arranged the stuffed fillets seam side down in a baking dish and poured the remaining white sauce over them. After an overnight stay in the fridge, we removed the baking dish and sprinkled the fish with Ritz cracker crumbs. Tasters liked the crumbs for their buttery flavor and crunchy texture—a perfect foil to the tender fillets and creamy sauce. After just 25 minutes in a 475-degree oven, the bundles baked up moist and tender with a piping hot filling and golden, crunchy crumbs—a main course ready to take center stage at any dinner party. And, for an even more upscale version of stuffed sole, we swapped out the spinach and cheese for a stuffing containing crab and corn, seasoned with lemon and tarragon.

MAKING FISH BUNDLES

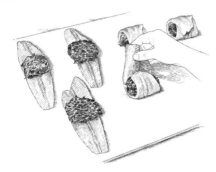

1. Lay the fillets out on a cutting board, smooth sides down. Divide the spinach filling evenly among the fillets and mound it in the center of each fillet. Tightly fold the tapered end of each fillet over the filling, then fold the thicker end of the fillet over the top.

2. Flip the bundles over, transfer them to the baking dish, and press on them lightly to flatten, leaving a small space between each bundle. Pour the sauce evenly over the fish, then sprinkle with the Ritz crumbs.

Sole Florentine
SERVES 4

Try to buy fish fillets of equal size to ensure even cooking. Be sure to squeeze as much moisture out of the frozen spinach as possible or it will water down the sauce. To check the doneness of the fish, use the tip of a paring knife to gently prod the fish—the flesh should be opaque and flaky, but still juicy.

2	tablespoons unsalted butter
1	medium shallot, minced (about 3 tablespoons)
2	teaspoons minced fresh thyme leaves
1	small garlic clove, minced or pressed through a garlic press (about ½ teaspoon)
2	cups heavy cream
4	teaspoons cornstarch
	Salt and ground black pepper
2	(10-ounce) packages frozen chopped spinach, thawed and squeezed dry
1	ounce Parmesan cheese, grated (½ cup)
8	boneless, skinless sole fillets, ¼ to ½ inch thick
15	Ritz crackers, crushed fine (¾ cup)
1	lemon, cut into wedges (for serving)

1. Melt 1 tablespoon of the butter in a medium saucepan over medium-high heat. Add the shallot and cook until softened, about 2 minutes. Stir in the thyme and garlic and cook until fragrant, about 30 seconds. Stir in 1¾ cups of the heavy cream and bring to a simmer. Whisk the remaining ¼ cup heavy cream and cornstarch together, then stir into the saucepan. Continue to simmer until the sauce is thickened, about 2 minutes. Season with salt and pepper to taste. Set aside to cool.

2. Combine 1 cup of the sauce, spinach, and Parmesan in a medium bowl and season with salt and pepper to taste. Pat the fish dry with paper towels and season with salt and pepper. Coat a 13 by 9-inch baking dish with the remaining 1 tablespoon butter.

3. Following the illustrations on page 307, place the fish on a cutting board, smooth side down. Divide the spinach filling equally among the fish fillets, mounding it in the middle of each fillet. Fold the tapered end of the fish tightly over the filling and then fold the thicker end of the fish over the top to make a tidy bundle.

4. Arrange the fish bundles in the baking dish, seam side down (leaving space between each roll). Pour the remaining sauce evenly over the fish.

5. To STORE: Cover tightly with plastic wrap and refrigerate for up to 24 hours.

6. To SERVE: Adjust an oven rack to the middle position and heat the oven to 475 degrees. Sprinkle the fish with the Ritz cracker crumbs and bake until all but the very center of the fish turns from translucent to opaque and the filling is hot, about 20 minutes. Serve with the lemon wedges.

TO SERVE RIGHT AWAY
Bake as described in step 6, reducing the baking time to 12 to 15 minutes.

✒ VARIATION
Crab-Stuffed Sole
We recommend buying fresh or pasteurized crabmeat (usually sold next to the fresh seafood) rather than the canned crabmeat (packed in tuna fish–like cans) found in the supermarket aisles.

Follow the recipe for Sole Florentine, substituting 12 ounces fresh or pasteurized crabmeat, squeezed dry, for the spinach. Omit the Parmesan and add ½ cup frozen corn kernels, thawed, 2 tablespoons minced fresh tarragon leaves, 1 tablespoon juice and ½ teaspoon grated zest from 1 lemon, and a pinch cayenne pepper.

MAKE IT A MENU
Stuffed Sole

white rice or orzo pasta

sliced tomatoes with Bistro-Style Mustard Vinaigrette (page 82)

Orange Pound Cake with Citrus Glaze (pages 366–367)

BAKED FISH

HAVING TACKLED A ROLLED AND STUFFED FISH recipe (page 308), we were on the lookout for another make-ahead fish preparation. But this time, we wanted something with a rustic character and more suitable for weeknight fare. We imagined an easy baked fish dish: one where we could arrange sturdy fish fillets on a bed of vegetables and herbs, store overnight in the fridge, and bake the next day. Once baked, the fillets would turn tender and flaky and the vegetables would cook down into a sauce, lending flavor and additional moisture to the fish.

To start, we turned to our choice of fish and quickly settled on cod. Its mild flavor pairs well with a variety of flavors and the thick fillets would hold up well during baking. For our vegetables, we turned to Provençal flavors such as tomatoes, wine, capers, shallots, thyme, and olive oil. These heady seasonings would imbue our fish with bold character.

We didn't want a precooked sauce—too much trouble. Plus we thought that if the tomatoes and seasonings cooked alongside the fish in the oven, they would better retain their fresh flavors. We began our testing by combining the tomatoes with shallots, capers, garlic, wine, oil, thyme, salt, and pepper and layering the mixture in the bottom of a baking dish. The fish was then nestled into the tomato mixture and cooked. We originally started off using seeded and diced plum tomatoes and while the flavors worked well, the tomatoes cooked down too much and didn't retain the visual appeal we were hoping for. So, next we tried halved cherry tomatoes. These tomatoes still cooked down into a sauce, but cooked up chunkier than the plum tomatoes. Tasters approved.

Tasters had also commented that, while the fish was good, it was definitely missing something; there were no contrasting textures. A flavorful crust seemed like a logical step in the right direction. And because our fish would be sitting on a bed of vegetables, not covered by them, the crust would not be in danger of becoming soggy. We settled on crushed Melba toast for its very sturdy character.

We kept the crumb topping simple, crushing the crackers and combining them with olive oil, lemon zest, salt, and pepper. We brushed the fish with olive oil, then pressed the crumbs to adhere. Even after a night of refrigeration, the crumbs were crispy after baking and coated the fish with a golden brown crust. Paired with the chunky tomato sauce, these crunchy-on-the-outside, tender-on-the-inside fillets made for a dinner we'd be eager to come home to.

A final note: After testing this recipe numerous times, we found that fillets other than cod, such as halibut, haddock, monkfish, and salmon, work well too, so feel free to use what's freshest in your market.

Baked Fish Provençal

SERVES 4

While we prefer thick fillets of cod here, you can also use another fish, such as haddock, halibut, sea bass, monkfish, or salmon. Note that when shopping for fillets, look for those that are at least 1 inch thick—any less and the fillets will cook through before the vegetables have had time to release their juices. Serve this dish with a loaf of crusty bread to sop up the extra sauce.

2½ ounces Melba toast (about 18 crackers), crushed to coarse crumbs (about ½ cup)

4 tablespoons extra-virgin olive oil

½ teaspoon grated zest from 1 lemon
Salt and ground black pepper

2 pints cherry tomatoes (about 1½ pounds), halved

2 medium shallots, minced (about 6 tablespoons)

¼ cup dry white wine or vermouth

2 tablespoons capers, rinsed

2 medium garlic cloves, minced or pressed through a garlic press (about 2 teaspoons)

1 teaspoon minced fresh thyme leaves, or ¼ teaspoon dried

4 boneless, skinless fish fillets, 1 to 2 inches thick (6 to 8 ounces each; see note)

2 tablespoons chopped fresh basil leaves
Lemon wedges (for serving)

1. Toss the Melba crumbs with 1 tablespoon of the oil, lemon zest, ¼ teaspoon salt, and

¼ teaspoon pepper; set aside. Toss the tomatoes, shallots, wine, capers, 2 more tablespoons of the oil, garlic, thyme, ½ teaspoon salt, and ¼ teaspoon pepper together; spread evenly over the bottom of a 13 by 9-inch baking dish.

2. Pat the fish dry with paper towels, and season with salt and pepper. Nestle the fish into the tomato mixture. Brush the tops of the fish with the remaining 1 tablespoon oil, then sprinkle with the Melba crumbs, pressing on the crumbs to adhere.

3. To store: Cover tightly with plastic wrap and refrigerate for up to 24 hours.

4. To serve: Adjust an oven rack to the middle position and heat the oven to 400 degrees. Unwrap the dish and bake until the crumbs are crisp and the fish flakes apart when gently prodded with a paring knife, 20 to 25 minutes. Let rest for 5 minutes, then sprinkle with the basil and serve with the lemon wedges.

TO SERVE RIGHT AWAY
Bake as directed in step 4, reducing the baking time to 15 to 20 minutes.

STROMBOLI

AN OMNIPRESENT STAPLE IN ITALIAN PIZZERIAS, stromboli—a close cousin of the calzone—seemed to us like an ideal make-ahead entrée for a busy weeknight. With their crunchy and golden-brown exterior and flavorful layered meat and cheese fillings, stromboli pair well with salad for a welcome change-of-pace dinner. Less doughy than calzones, stromboli often rely on a sturdy filling of layered deli meats and mozzarella and provolone cheese instead of the typical calzone filling: ricotta cheese and vegetables. The result? Stromboli hold up a lot better overnight than calzones—making them an ideal choice for the make-ahead cook. While we'd never made stromboli, we weren't deterred. Having had plenty of experience with calzones and pizza, we set about creating our ideal recipe.

The first step was the dough. Since we desired an easy weeknight dinner, we hoped that store-bought dough would suffice. Readily available in most grocery stores and some pizzerias, store-

bought dough was a great timesaving option for our stromboli. (Although if you have time to prepare your own pizza dough, that's certainly an option we offer.) Typically sold in 1-pound balls, store-bought dough gave us the option of making four small stromboli or one large one. Four individual stromboli would, theoretically, increase storage space and speed up the cooking time. But we also wondered whether making one large stromboli would be easier and faster. We tried both options. Making four small stromboli definitely took more time and effort. Rolling out four dough balls, layering the filling, and rolling each stuffed dough into a cylinder took a bit of time, and in the end there was no clear advantage. Rolling up one big stromboli gave us more filling per slice and, in the end, was a time-saver. So the big stromboli was in and the little ones were out, but the filling posed some issues.

In our recipe search, we were constantly reminded that a stromboli was a "rolled sandwich," so it seemed natural to include a variety of deli meats and cheese. And to make this recipe as simple as possible, we wanted to avoid any additional cooking—a true quick-and-easy make-ahead dinner. So as we sought out a more adventurous filling, we settled on a combination of salami, capocollo, and provolone cheese. Our first attempt wasn't far off the mark, but it was missing something. Some tasters commented that the filling was too one dimensional. We were up against a wall due to our moisture as well as time restrictions and our flavor options seemed limited. Caramelizing onions or browning mushrooms would simply take too long. One test cook then suggested roasted red bell peppers. We quickly turned to quality jarred peppers for convenience and to avoid any potential problems with these liquid-packed peppers, we thoroughly dried them with paper towels before chopping and adding them to the filling. The results were right on the mark. We had successfully boosted the flavor of our filling without making for a soggy crust.

We next turned to developing flavor variations. First we tried pesto, but it was too oily, and then we tried fresh basil, but the herb turned army green and lifeless. Chopped sun-dried tomatoes were up next, but their strong flavor overpowered the stromboli's other flavors. It seemed like the more creative we tried to get with various fillings, the less successful we were, so we decided to stick with simple variations. Tasters gave thumbs up to a ham and cheddar stromboli and one with pepperoni and mozzarella.

Now that the fillings were done, our focus turned to other details, namely the finishing touches to the crust and baking times. We knew that in order to achieve a golden-brown color, the stromboli would need to be brushed with either an egg wash or olive oil. Both provided the toasty hue we were looking for, but traditional stromboli are coated with either poppy or sesame seeds, and in order for them to adhere, we found that the egg wash worked best.

Switching gears now to the actual baking, we started at 450 degrees. We assumed that a high temperature would be the key to a crispy crust. The crust certainly got crispy, but the inside remained undercooked and doughy. The obvious solution was to lower the oven temperature. When cooked at 400 degrees for 45 minutes, the exterior of the stromboli was still overbrowning, while the interior was insufficiently cooked. We needed to find a way to shield the exterior from direct heat while the inside cooked, so we decided to cover the stromboli with aluminum foil for the first half of the baking. This gave the interior a sufficient head start and after 25 minutes, we removed the foil to allow for proper browning on the outside. Pulling the stromboli from the oven, we allowed it to cool for at least 5 minutes before slicing. This allowed the cheese enough time to set up, and kept it from oozing out when sliced. Tasters could hardly keep their hands off the slices as we served our stromboli in the test kitchen—a good indication of how well this recipe can fit into your repertoire.

Stromboli with Salami, Capocollo, and Provolone

SERVES 4

You can make your own pizza dough (recipe follows), although store-bought dough, dough from your local pizzeria, or one 12-ounce or 13.8-ounce pop-up canister of pizza dough (Pillsbury brand) all work here. Serve with tomato sauce, if desired.

	Olive oil
1	pound pizza dough (see note)
4	ounces thinly sliced deli salami
4	ounces thinly sliced deli capocollo
4	ounces thinly sliced deli provolone cheese
4	ounces jarred roasted red bell peppers, sliced thin, rinsed, and patted dry (about ½ cup)
1	ounce Parmesan cheese, grated (about ½ cup)
1	large egg, lightly beaten
1	teaspoon sesame seeds
	Kosher salt (optional)

1. Brush a rimmed baking sheet lightly with oil; set aside. On a lightly floured work surface, roll the dough into a 12 by 10-inch rectangle, about ¼ inch thick. Place the meat and provolone over the dough, leaving a 1-inch border along the edges. Top with the roasted red bell peppers and Parmesan.

2. Brush the edges of the dough with water. Starting from a long side, roll the dough tightly into a long cylinder, pressing the edges to seal. Transfer the stromboli to the prepared baking sheet, seam side down.

3. To store: Cover with plastic wrap and refrigerate for up to 24 hours.

4. To serve: Adjust an oven rack to the middle position and heat the oven to 400 degrees. Remove the plastic wrap, brush the egg over the top, and sprinkle with the sesame seeds and kosher salt (if using). Cover the stromboli lightly with aluminum foil that has been sprayed with vegetable oil spray (or use nonstick foil) and bake for 25 minutes. Remove the foil and continue to bake until the crust is golden, about 25 minutes. Transfer the stromboli to a wire rack and let cool 5 minutes. Transfer to a carving board and slice into 2-inch pieces.

TO SERVE RIGHT AWAY

Bake as directed in step 4, reducing the covered baking time to 20 minutes. Remove the foil and continue to bake uncovered as directed.

Ham and Cheddar Stromboli

Swiss cheese also works well in this variation.

Follow the recipe for Stromboli with Salami, Capocollo, and Provolone, omitting the roasted red peppers and Parmesan. Substitute 8 ounces thinly sliced deli ham for the salami and capocollo and 4 ounces thinly sliced deli cheddar cheese for the provolone.

Pepperoni Pizza Stromboli

Serve with a simple tomato sauce on the side, if desired.

Follow the recipe for Stromboli with Salami, Capocollo, and Provolone, omitting the roasted red peppers. Substitute 4 ounces thinly sliced pepperoni for the salami and capocollo and 6 ounces mozzarella, shredded (about 1½ cups), for the provolone.

Pizza Dough

MAKES 1 POUND DOUGH; ENOUGH FOR 1 STROMBOLI

All-purpose unbleached flour can be used instead of the bread flour here, but the resulting crust will be a little less crisp and chewy.

- 2 cups (11 ounces) bread flour, plus extra for the work surface
- 1 teaspoon instant or rapid rise yeast
- ¾ teaspoon salt
- 2 tablespoons olive oil, plus extra for the bowl
- 1 cup warm water

1. Pulse the flour, yeast, and salt in a food processor (fitted with a dough blade if possible) to combine. With the food processor running, pour the oil, then the water, through the feed tube and process until a rough ball forms, 30 to 40 seconds. Let the dough rest in the bowl for 2 minutes, then process for 30 seconds longer.

2. Following the illustrations at right, turn the dough out onto a lightly floured work surface and knead by hand to form a smooth, round ball, about 5 minutes, adding additional flour as needed to prevent the dough from sticking. Transfer to a lightly

oiled bowl, cover with plastic wrap, and let rise in a warm place until doubled in size, 1 to 1½ hours.

3. Gently deflate the dough with your fist and turn it out onto an unfloured work surface. Gently reshape the dough into a ball and cover with plastic wrap lightly sprayed with vegetable oil spray. Let the dough rest 15 minutes, but no more than 30 minutes, before shaping as directed in the stromboli recipes on pages 311–312.

PREPARING THE DOUGH FOR STROMBOLI

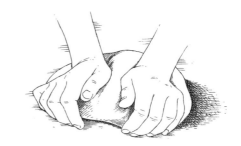

1. Turn the dough out onto a lightly floured surface and knead the dough, using your palms for maximum leverage.

2. Place the dough in a lightly oiled bowl and cover the bowl tightly with plastic wrap. Plastic wrap forms a tighter seal than a damp towel and keeps the dough moister.

3. After the dough has doubled in size, 1 to 1½ hours, deflate it by pressing down on it with your fist. Turn the dough out onto a lightly floured work surface and shape into stromboli as directed.

8

BREAKFAST AND BREADS

Breakfast and Breads

WEEKENDS ARE MADE FOR LEISURELY AND sometimes festive breakfasts, where something other than cereal or a poached egg is in order. The only problem is that it often takes half the morning just to prepare such treats, and by the time breakfast is over and the dishes are being cleaned, it's time for lunch. We wanted to fill this chapter with simple recipes that could be made in advance, so that a weekend breakfast can be special but easy.

With that in mind, we first looked at all of the natural make-ahead dishes such as stratas (pages 320–322) and other breakfast casseroles; these are dishes that are meant to be made in advance. Indeed their success depends upon an overnight soaking of bread and custard, after which time they almost magically turn into a puffed and golden casserole. However, we found that these casseroles couldn't soak in their egg custard for more than 24 hours. We also discovered that tasty make-ahead casseroles depended upon the use of the correct bread. For example, the 24-Hour "Omelet" (page 318) worked best when we used high-quality white sandwich bread, whereas the French Toast Casserole (page 323) needed the stronger crumb of a supermarket French or Italian bread.

In addition to casseroles, this chapter includes both sweet and savory yeasted rolls and leavened quick breads (muffins, coffeecakes, and biscuits). With an eye toward giving maximum flexibility to the home cook, we tested the limits of every recipe hoping to come up with ones that could go from freezer to oven, or refrigerator to oven. So what did we learn? With the cinnamon rolls, sticky buns, and dinner rolls, we found that in order to freeze yeasted dough, we had to let it rise fully twice before freezing it. This was a great discovery, because it meant we could pull rolls out of the freezer and place them in the oven to bake while still frozen, and we could bake any quantity we wanted, virtually guaranteeing dinner rolls any night of the week once we had a batch or two stocked away in our freezer.

We also found that refrigerating yeasted dough was possible, but unlike frozen dough, it needed to be placed in the refrigerator before the second rising. The refrigerator simply retarded the rising, instead of arresting it like the freezer did, so the dough rose very slowly while in the refrigerator. With this approach, you just have to leave time for the dough to finish its second rise on the counter before baking.

Leavened batter also made the journey from the fridge or freezer to the oven successfully—with one exception, biscuits. When left in the refrigerator overnight, the gluten relaxed and the result was flat biscuits. But biscuits were fine in the freezer. We think it's handy to have biscuits stashed in the freezer to top a pot pie or serve with a last-minute stew.

24-Hour "Omelet"

THIS HOMEY CASSEROLE IS NOTHING LIKE THE omelet that you order at your favorite breakfast joint. Nor does it take a day to bake. It's meant to be assembled in the evening—particularly the night before a hectic holiday morning—and then popped into the oven to bake while the coffee brews and the children and houseguests wake up. Cheesy and golden, it puffs impressively above the rim of the baking dish. While similar to a breakfast strata, a 24-hour omelet is more about the eggs and less about the bread; it also usually forgoes the meats and vegetables that often star in a strata.

Consisting of an eggy custard, bread, and cheese, the 24-hour omelet is lighter than the fluffiest scrambled eggs and practically melts in your mouth. Invariably, however, most recipes we found for 24-hour omelets suffered the fate of normal omelets; they were often overstuffed with myriad ingredients, losing their eggy richness in the confusion of vegetables and spices. With the intent of keeping the ingredients and preparation simple, we set out to develop the tastiest 24-hour omelet possible.

We decided to start our tests with the bread, since it plays such an important role in the texture of this dish. We wanted the bread to "melt" into the custard (a simple mixture of eggs and milk or cream). As such, we ruled out rustic loaves with heavy crusts or any bread that was overly chewy. Trying a number of loaves of white bread, we found that a firm, dense loaf provided the best texture (we liked Pepperidge Farm Hearty White). We also learned it was best to avoid really soft loaves, as they had a tendency to break down too much, lending the dish an unpleasant raw, yeasty flavor. In the course of testing, we also discovered that buttering the bread added a richness and flavor to the omelet that was favored among tasters.

The custard was the next component to examine. In past experiences, we found that custard made with 2 parts dairy to 1 part egg provided the best texture and flavor. Bearing in mind the name of the dish, we felt it should have a pronounced egg flavor. We therefore reduced the amount of dairy called for in most recipes, encouraging the egg flavor to dominate. In the end, we settled on a custard consisting of eight whole eggs (about 2 cups) and 3 cups of dairy. When it came to the type of dairy, we tested the recipe with milk, half-and-half, and heavy cream (both on their own and in combinations). Wanting to keep the emphasis on the eggs, we chose milk—as both half-and-half and the cream masked the egg flavor

and made the dish too heavy.

With our strata recipes (see pages 320–322), we found it necessary to weigh down the assembled dish while it rested overnight in order to evenly distribute the custard. Curious as to whether we would have to employ this technique with the assembled 24-hour omelet, we tested a weighted and an unweighted casserole side by side. Because there was more custard in relation to bread in the 24-hour omelet, we found that weighting the dish was an unnecessary step.

The final crucial ingredient to address was the cheese. In the recipes we consulted, the amount of cheese ranged from a scant cup to a whopping 1½ pounds. After several tests, we settled on an amount in between these two figures: 12 ounces. This proportion added a rich flavor but didn't have an adverse effect on the consistency of the omelet. As for the type of cheese, we found it better to use cheeses that were high in moisture and melted well, such as cheddar, Monterey Jack, and Havarti. It

BUYING EGGS

Freshness: Egg cartons are marked with both a sell-by date and a pack date (the latter is also known as the "Julian" date). The sell-by date is the legal limit for when the eggs may be sold and is within 30 days of the pack date. The pack date is the day the eggs were graded and packed, which is generally within a week of being laid but, legally, may be as much as 30 days. In short, a carton of eggs may be up to two months old by the end of the sell-by date. Even so, according to the U.S. Department of Agriculture, they are still fit for consumption for an additional three to five weeks past the sell-by date. Sell-by and pack dates are thus by no means an exact measure of an egg's fitness; they provide vague guidance at best.

How old is too old? We tasted two- and three-month-old eggs that were perfectly palatable. At four months the white was very loose and the yolk "tasted faintly of the refrigerator," though it was still edible. Our advice? Use your discretion. If the egg smells odd or displays discoloration, pitch it. Older eggs also lack the structure-lending properties of fresh eggs, so beware when baking. Both the white and yolk become looser. We whipped four-month-old eggs and found that they deflated rapidly.

Color: The shell's hue depends on the breed of the chicken. The run-of-the-mill Leghorn chicken produces the typical white egg. Larger brown-feathered birds, such as Rhode Island Reds, produce the ecru- to coffee-colored eggs common to New England. Despite marketing hype to the contrary, a kitchen taste test proved that shell color has no effect on flavor.

Grade: Although eggs are theoretically sold in three grades—AA, A, and B—we found only grade A eggs for sale in nearly a dozen markets in Massachusetts and New York. Grade AA eggs are the cream of the crop, possessing the thickest whites and shells, according to the American Egg Board. Grade B eggs are used commercially.

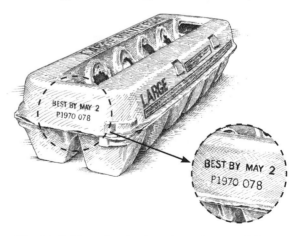

The Pack Date: It is the three-digit code stamped above or below the sell-by date. The numbers run consecutively, starting at 001 for January 1 and ending with 365 for December 31. These eggs were packed on March 19 (078). The number next to the pack date (P1970) is an internal code for egg packers.

proved wise to stay away from firmer cheeses, such as Parmesan and Asiago, which gave the omelet a dry texture.

For other flavors, we concluded that simpler was better. A small amount of onion provided a little pungency, but didn't overwhelm the cheese and eggs. To finish, we experimented with a little dry mustard and Tabasco, which together gave the dish a hint of spiciness and accentuated the creaminess of the eggs.

24-Hour "Omelet"

SERVES 6 TO 8

Be sure to use a hearty white sandwich bread; our favorite is Pepperidge Farm Hearty White bread. The omelet needs to sit in the refrigerator, well covered, for at least 8 hours in order to achieve the desired consistency, and it can be made up to 24 hours in advance.

3	tablespoons unsalted butter, softened, plus extra for the baking dish
10	slices high-quality white sandwich bread
12	ounces cheddar cheese, shredded (about 3 cups)
8	large eggs
3	cups whole milk
1	small onion, grated over the large holes of a box grater
1	teaspoon salt
½	teaspoon ground black pepper
1	teaspoon dry mustard
½	teaspoon hot sauce

1. Butter the bottom and sides of a 13 by 9-inch baking dish (or shallow casserole dish of similar size). Spread the butter evenly over 1 side of each bread slice. Cut the bread into 1-inch pieces. Scatter half of the bread evenly in the prepared dish and sprinkle with half of the cheddar. Repeat with the remaining bread and cheese.

2. Whisk the eggs in a large bowl until combined, then whisk in the milk, onion, salt, pepper, mustard, and hot sauce. Pour the egg mixture evenly over the bread and press lightly on the bread to submerge.

3. TO STORE: Wrap the dish tightly with plastic wrap and refrigerate for at least 8 hours or up to 24 hours.

4. TO SERVE: Adjust an oven rack to the middle position and heat the oven to 350 degrees. Unwrap the casserole and bake until puffed and golden brown, about 1 hour. Serve immediately.

➤ VARIATIONS

24-Hour "Omelet" with Pepper Jack and Chipotle Chiles

Follow the recipe for 24-Hour "Omelet," substituting pepper Jack cheese for the cheddar and 2 to 3 teaspoons minced chipotle chile in adobo sauce for the dry mustard and hot sauce. Sprinkle 3 tablespoons minced fresh cilantro leaves over the top of the omelet before serving.

24-Hour "Omelet" with Sun-Dried Tomatoes and Mozzarella

Follow the recipe for 24-Hour "Omelet," substituting mozzarella cheese for the cheddar, and sprinkling 1 ounce Parmesan cheese, grated (about ½ cup) and ½ cup oil-packed sun-dried tomatoes, patted dry and chopped coarse, between the 2 layers of bread in step 1. Sprinkle 3 tablespoons chopped fresh basil leaves over the top of the omelet before serving.

BREAKFAST STRATA

WHAT'S QUICKER THAN QUICHE, STURDIER than soufflé, and combines the best qualities of both? The answer is strata, a layered casserole that in its most basic form comprises bread, eggs, cheese, and milk or cream. Layered among them are flavorful fillings that provide both substance and character, and the result is, in essence, a golden brown, puffed, hearty, savory bread pudding. One of strata's charms is that it should be assembled well ahead of time.

But strata is not without its pitfalls. In our experience, stratas often suffer from largesse. Many of the recipes we sampled were too rich for breakfast, with a belly-busting overabundance of custard. And then there were the fillings, where an everything-but-the-kitchen-sink approach led to wet, sagging, overwrought stratas. One we sampled early on included mustard, garlic, nutmeg, marinated artichoke hearts, raw green peppers, cherry tomatoes, ham, Parmesan, fontina, and goat cheese! Such overindulgence not only sends unlucky diners scrambling for Maalox but also turns a simple workhorse dish into a self-parody. Our goal was to scale back strata, keeping it just moist enough that it could be made ahead, while choosing flavorings and fillings that would blend into the chorus, not hog the spotlight.

Bread is the foundation of strata. Although sliced white sandwich bread is the most common choice, recipes we found also called for Italian, French, sourdough, multigrain, rye, pumpernickel, challah, focaccia, and even hamburger and hot dog buns. We tried them all and preferred supermarket Italian and French breads for their strong crumb, which allowed the bread to soak for up to 24 hours. While many recipes specified cubes of bread, we preferred slices because they added to the layered effect of the casserole. Half-inch-thick slices were best; anything thicker was too chewy, and thin slices just melted away. We also preferred the texture of stale bread (or fresh bread dried in the oven) and found that it was an imperative step when storing the dish overnight.

Our next consideration was the custard that binds the bread. In a battery of tests, tasters were divided between mixtures with equal parts dairy and egg and those with twice as much dairy as egg. The solution was to meet in the middle, adding a little extra dairy to the 50-50 mixture. As for the dairy, we tested low-fat milk, whole milk, half-and-half, and heavy cream, both alone and in combinations. The half-and-half was the clear winner.

As a basic flavoring, sautéed shallots won over onions and garlic. We had a surprise in store when we tested another flavoring common to a few strata recipes: white wine. It showed promise, lightening the flavor of the whole dish. But it also imparted an unwelcome boozy flavor. We corrected this problem by applying a technique used in sauce making—reduction—that cooked off the alcohol and concentrated the flavor of the wine. The reduced wine brightened the flavor of the whole dish considerably.

Even with the right basic ingredients in the right proportions, test after test proved that high-moisture fillings such as sausage and raw vegetables ruined the strata's texture. Moisture from them leached into the casserole, leaving it wet enough to literally slosh and ooze when cut. To correct this problem, we took to sautéing all filling ingredients until they looked dry in the pan, evaporating moisture that would otherwise end up in the strata. Whatever your filling choice, this critical step will make the difference between a moist, tender dish and one that resembles a wet sponge.

A test kitchen colleague suggested weighing down the assembled strata during its rest and this step had a dramatic effect. Without exception, the weighted stratas had a perfectly even, custardy texture throughout. In stratas rested without the weight, it was not unusual to encounter a bite of bread that had not been fully penetrated with custard.

At this point we wanted to know just how long a strata could sit (obviously the raw egg limited that a bit) before the bread would fall apart. We tested refrigerating stratas for 24 hours (we felt that this was the maximum amount of time raw eggs should sit), eight hours, four hours, one hour, and not at all. The freshly made strata was noticeably less cohesive than the rested versions and failed to make the cut. The stratas rested for one hour and four hours were an improvement, but we decided a minimum of eight hours was ideal to allow the bread ample time to absorb the egg. Once assembled, the strata can be rested anywhere from eight to 24 hours.

Once in the oven, the strata cooked much more evenly in a wide, shallow baking dish than in the deep soufflé dish called for in many recipes. Lowering the baking temperature from the widely recommended 350 degrees to 325 was an additional tactic we adopted to even out the cooking. Baking the strata until the top was crisp and golden brown was another common recommendation, but we found that this often produced an overcooked, overly firm, and even rubbery interior. We found it best to remove the strata from the oven when the top was just beginning to brown, and the center was barely puffed and still slightly loose when the pan was gently jiggled. With just a five-minute rest, the center finished cooking from residual heat, reaching the perfectly set, supple texture we prized.

Breakfast Strata with Spinach and Gruyère

SERVES 6 TO 8

Though each strata calls for a certain type of cheese, feel free to substitute any good melting cheese, such as Havarti, sharp cheddar, or colby. Be sure to use supermarket-style loaf bread with a thin crust and fluffy crumb; artisan loaves with a thick crust and chewy crumb don't work well here (see page 324 for more information). The strata needs to sit in the refrigerator, well covered, for at least 8 hours in order to achieve the desired consistency, and it can be made up to 24 hours in advance.

16–20	(½-inch-thick) slices supermarket French or Italian bread
7	tablespoons unsalted butter, softened, plus extra for the baking dish
2	large shallots, minced (about ½ cup)
2	(10-ounce) packages frozen chopped spinach, thawed and squeezed dry
	Salt and ground black pepper
1	cup dry white wine or vermouth
12	ounces Gruyère cheese, shredded (about 3 cups)
12	large eggs
3½	cups half-and-half

1. Adjust 2 oven racks to the upper-middle and lower-middle positions and heat the oven to 325 degrees. Spread the bread out over 2 baking sheets and bake until dry and light golden brown, about 25 minutes, switching and rotating the baking sheets halfway through the baking time. Let the bread cool completely and then spread butter evenly over 1 side of each bread slice, using 4 tablespoons of the butter.

2. Meanwhile, melt the remaining 3 tablespoons butter in a medium nonstick skillet over medium heat. Add the shallots and cook until softened, about 3 minutes. Stir in the spinach and cook until warm, about 2 minutes. Transfer to a medium bowl and season with salt and pepper to taste. Add the wine to the skillet and simmer over medium-high heat until reduced to ¼ cup, about 5 minutes; set aside to cool.

3. Butter a 13 by 9-inch baking dish and tightly fit half of the bread slices, buttered sides up, into a single layer in the dish. Sprinkle half of the spinach mixture, then 1 cup of the cheese evenly over the bread slices. Repeat with the remaining bread slices, spinach mixture, and 1 more cup of the cheese.

4. Whisk the eggs in a large bowl until combined, then whisk in the reduced wine, half-and-half,

---

TEST KITCHEN TIP:

Weighty Matters

Three 1-pound boxes of brown or confectioners' sugar, laid side by side over the plastic-covered surface, make ideal weights for the assembled strata (see the illustration below). A gallon-size zipper-lock bag filled with about 2 pounds of sugar or rice also works.

ASSEMBLING THE STRATA

1. Layer the bread and the filling in the baking dish.

2. Pour the custard mixture evenly over the assembled layers.

3. Cover the surface flush with plastic wrap and weight the strata.

1 teaspoon salt, and ½ teaspoon pepper. Pour the egg mixture evenly over the bread layers and sprinkle the remaining 1 cup cheese evenly over the top.

5. To store: Wrap the strata tightly with plastic wrap, pressing the wrap flush to the surface of the strata. Weigh the strata down following the illustrations on page 320 and refrigerate for at least 8 hours or up to 24 hours.

6. To serve: Adjust an oven rack to the middle position and heat the oven to 325 degrees. Meanwhile, unwrap the strata and let it sit at room temperature for 20 minutes. Bake the strata, uncovered, until puffed and the edges have pulled away slightly from the sides of the dish, about 1 hour and 20 minutes. Cool on a wire rack for 5 minutes before serving.

Breakfast Strata with Sausage, Mushrooms, and Monterey Jack

SERVES 6 TO 8

Mushrooms contain a lot of water that must be cooked out before they are added to the strata. The mildness of Monterey Jack works well in this dish, but other possible choices are cheddar or Havarti. The strata needs to sit in the refrigerator, well covered, for at least 8 hours in order to achieve the desired consistency, and it can be made up to 24 hours in advance.

16–20	(½-inch-thick) slices supermarket French or Italian bread
4	tablespoons (½ stick) unsalted butter, softened, plus extra for the baking dish
1	pound bulk breakfast sausage
2	large shallots, minced (about ½ cup)
1	pound white button mushrooms, wiped clean and quartered
	Salt and ground black pepper
1	cup dry white wine or vermouth
12	ounces Monterey Jack cheese, shredded (about 3 cups)
12	large eggs
3½	cups half-and-half
3	tablespoons minced fresh parsley leaves

1. Adjust 2 oven racks to the upper-middle and lower-middle positions and heat the oven to 325 degrees. Spread the bread out over 2 baking sheets and bake until dry and light golden brown, about 25 minutes, switching and rotating the baking sheets halfway through the baking time. Let the bread cool completely and then spread butter evenly over 1 side of each bread slice.

2. Meanwhile, cook the sausage in a medium nonstick skillet over medium heat, breaking the meat into small pieces with a wooden spoon, until beginning to brown, about 7 minutes. Stir in the shallots and cook until softened, about 3 minutes. Stir in the mushrooms and cook until their liquid is released, about 10 minutes. Transfer to a medium bowl and season with salt and pepper to taste. Add the wine to the skillet and simmer over medium-high heat until reduced to ¼ cup, about 5 minutes; set aside to cool.

3. Butter a 13 by 9-inch baking dish and tightly fit half of the bread slices, buttered sides up, into a single layer in the dish. Sprinkle half of the sausage mixture, then 1 cup of the cheese evenly over the bread slices. Repeat with the remaining bread slices, sausage mixture, and 1 more cup of the cheese.

4. Whisk the eggs in a large bowl until combined, then whisk in the reduced wine, half-and-half, parsley, 1 teaspoon salt, and ½ teaspoon pepper. Pour the egg mixture evenly over the bread layers and sprinkle the remaining 1 cup cheese evenly over the top.

5. To store: Wrap the strata tightly with plastic wrap, pressing the wrap flush to the surface of the strata. Weigh the strata down following the illustrations on page 320 and refrigerate for at least 8 hours or up to 24 hours.

6. To serve: Adjust an oven rack to the middle position and heat the oven to 325 degrees. Meanwhile, unwrap the strata and let it sit at room temperature for 20 minutes. Bake the strata, uncovered, until puffed and the edges have pulled away slightly from the sides of the dish, about 1 hour and 20 minutes. Cool on a wire rack for 5 minutes before serving.

Breakfast Strata with Potatoes, Rosemary, and Fontina

SERVES 6 TO 8

If you have leftover potatoes, simply skip the second step and add 3 cups of diced cooked potatoes in step 3. The strata needs to sit in the refrigerator, well covered, for at least 8 hours in order to achieve the desired consistency, and it can be made up to 24 hours in advance.

16–20	(½-inch-thick) slices supermarket French or Italian bread
7	tablespoons unsalted butter, softened, plus extra for the baking dish
1½	pounds red potatoes (about 5 medium), scrubbed and cut into ½-inch cubes
	Salt
2	large shallots, minced (about ½ cup)
4	medium garlic cloves, minced or pressed through a garlic press (about 4 teaspoons)
1	tablespoon minced fresh rosemary
	Ground black pepper
1	cup dry white wine or vermouth
12	ounces fontina cheese, shredded (about 3 cups)
12	large eggs
3½	cups half-and-half
3	tablespoons minced fresh parsley leaves

1. Adjust 2 oven racks to the upper-middle and lower-middle positions and heat the oven to 325 degrees. Spread the bread out over 2 baking sheets and bake until dry and light golden brown, about 25 minutes, switching and rotating the baking sheets halfway through the baking time. Let the bread cool completely and then spread butter evenly over 1 side of each bread slice, using 4 tablespoons of the butter.

2. Meanwhile, bring the potatoes, 1 quart of water, and ½ teaspoon salt to a boil in a large saucepan over high heat. Reduce to a simmer and cook until the potatoes are just tender, about 4 minutes. Drain the potatoes.

3. Melt the remaining 3 tablespoons butter in a medium nonstick skillet over medium heat. Add the potatoes and cook until just beginning to brown, about 10 minutes. Stir in the shallots and cook until softened, about 3 minutes. Stir in the garlic and rosemary and cook until fragrant, about 30 seconds. Transfer the mixture to a medium bowl and season with salt and pepper to taste. Add the wine to the skillet and simmer over medium-high heat until reduced to ¼ cup, about 5 minutes; set aside to cool.

4. Butter a 13 by 9-inch baking dish and tightly fit half of the bread slices, buttered sides up, into a single layer in the dish. Sprinkle half of the potato mixture, then 1 cup of the cheese evenly over the bread slices. Repeat with the remaining bread slices, potato mixture, and 1 more cup of the cheese.

5. Whisk the eggs in a large bowl until combined, then whisk in the reduced wine, half-and-half, parsley, 1 teaspoon salt, and ½ teaspoon pepper. Pour the egg mixture evenly over the bread layers and sprinkle the remaining 1 cup cheese evenly over the top.

6. To STORE: Wrap the strata tightly with plastic

SHREDDING SOFT CHEESE

Semisoft cheeses such as Monterey Jack, cheddar, or mozzarella can stick to a box grater and cause a real mess. Here's how to keep the holes on the grater from becoming clogged.

1. Use vegetable oil spray to lightly coat the side of the box grater with the large holes.

2. Shred the cheese as usual. The cooking spray will keep the cheese from sticking to the surface of the grater.

wrap, pressing the wrap flush to the surface of the strata. Weigh the strata down following the illustrations on page 320, and refrigerate for at least 8 hours or up to 24 hours.

7. TO SERVE: Adjust an oven rack to the middle position and heat the oven to 325 degrees. Meanwhile, unwrap the strata and let it sit at room temperature for 20 minutes. Bake the strata, uncovered, until puffed and the edges have pulled away slightly from the sides of the dish, about 1 hour and 20 minutes. Cool on a wire rack for 5 minutes before serving.

FRENCH TOAST CASEROLE

FRENCH TOAST IS BEST RESERVED FOR THOSE leisurely mornings when you have time to toast the bread, make the eggy batter, and carefully cook it in batches on the stovetop. But when you're craving the flavors and richness of French toast without a fuss—enter French Toast Casserole, which is meant to be made the night before and, even better, can serve a crowd all at once, no batches necessary.

After a review of many recipes (and many batches of casseroles later), tasters decidedly favored one style: those that presented as layers of rich, creamy custard and toothsome pieces of bread, all covered by a sweet, candy-like topping of brown sugar, butter, and pecans.

With a clear goal, we set out to closely examine each component of the dish, starting first with the choice of bread. Initially, we tried using tender, butter-enriched loaves of challah and brioche, but found that their soft, spongy crumb disintegrated and left the dish with little texture. Moving on to supermarket loaves, we tried using several different varieties of sliced white bread. The results from these tests, while improved, still left us yearning for something with a denser, heartier texture. So we tried using rustic breads with hearty crusts, but these made the casserole far too dense. Next up were supermarket loaves of French and Italian bread. The dense texture and thin chewy crust of these loaves was exactly what we were looking for.

We also found during our tests that the pudding was better if we dried the bread in a moderately hot oven, allowing it to toast slightly, before assembling the dish. The casserole made with the dried toasted bread had a firmer texture and deeper flavor and was able to withstand a longer stay in the refrigerator before being baked.

For the custard, we tried using milk, half-and-half, heavy cream, and combinations of the three and found that 2½ cups whole milk and 1½ cups cream provided us with a rich, silky liquid base that was neither too cloying nor too bland and watery. We made custards with both whole eggs and with a combination of whole eggs and yolks. Although we liked the richness of the combination of whole eggs and yolks, we preferred the firm consistency and eggy flavor that eight whole eggs gave the custard.

When it came to baking the custard, a relatively low oven temperature of 350 degrees was best. Going above 350 degrees, in order to shorten the baking time, left us with curdled and grainy custards.

The topping of the casserole was the last component to address. In our initial test, tasters had preferred a topping that called for creaming brown sugar and butter with a dash of corn syrup, into which we folded pecans. Considering that the topping was mostly brown sugar, we wondered if the corn syrup might be redundant. To our surprise, we found that the corn syrup wasn't there for sweetness but to keep the sugar and butter from separating during baking. Without the corn syrup, the French toast turned into a greasy mess.

We achieved our goal of a French toast casserole that could be made the day before, fulfilling the sweet breakfast cravings of a whole family in one dish.

French Toast Casserole
SERVES 6 TO 8

Do not substitute low-fat or skim milk for the whole milk in this recipe. Walnuts can be substituted for the pecans. Be sure to use supermarket-style loaf bread with a thin crust and fluffy crumb; artisan loaves with a thick crust and chewy crumb don't work well here (see page 324 for more information). The casserole needs to sit in the refrigerator, well covered, for at least 8 hours in order to achieve the desired consistency, and it can be made up to 24 hours in advance.

CASEROLE

1	(16-ounce) loaf supermarket French or Italian bread, torn into 1-inch pieces
1	tablespoon unsalted butter, softened
8	large eggs
2½	cups whole milk
1½	cups heavy cream
1	tablespoon granulated sugar
2	teaspoons vanilla extract
½	teaspoon ground cinnamon
½	teaspoon ground nutmeg

TOPPING

8	tablespoons (1 stick) unsalted butter, softened
1⅓	cups packed (9⅓ ounces) light brown sugar
3	tablespoons light corn syrup
2	cups pecans, chopped coarse

1. FOR THE CASSEROLE: Adjust 2 oven racks to the upper-middle and lower-middle positions and heat the oven to 325 degrees. Spread the bread out over 2 baking sheets and bake until dry and light golden brown, about 25 minutes, switching and rotating the baking sheets halfway through the baking time. Let the bread cool completely.

2. Coat a 13 by 9-inch baking dish with the butter and pack the dried bread into the dish. Whisk the eggs in a large bowl until combined and then whisk in the milk, cream, granulated sugar, vanilla, cinnamon, and nutmeg. Pour the egg mixture evenly over the bread and press on the bread lightly to submerge.

3. FOR THE TOPPING: Stir the butter, brown sugar, and corn syrup together until smooth, then stir in the pecans.

4. TO STORE: Transfer the topping to an airtight

TESTING NOTES

BREAD FOR BREAKFAST CASSEROLES

While testing our breakfast casserole recipes, we discovered that the bread can make or break the final results. Here are the different breads we tried and what we learned.

Authentic Baguettes and Artisan Loaves

We certainly enjoy authentic crusty breads on their own, drizzled with a bit of olive oil, or as the base for bruschetta, where you want a tight crumb to support the topping. But we found that their thick crusts and chewy crumbs worked against us in our breakfast casseroles, making them overly dense, tough, and dry.

Sliced Bread

Standard white sandwich bread did not work well in dishes that required a hearty texture, like the French Toast Casserole and the Strata. It did, however, work well for some dishes in which we wanted the bread to meld fully with the custard and produce a soft, soufflé-like consistency, such as with the 24-Hour "Omelet." But be sure to stay away from cheap, flimsy sandwich bread (such as Wonder bread) and choose a sturdier loaf (such as Pepperidge Farm Hearty White).

Generic Supermarket Baguettes or Italian Bread

These breads have thin, lightly browned crusts and a fluffy crumb that straddle the line between sandwich bread and rustic breads. We found these generic breads ideal for our French Toast Casserole and our Strata because they kept a bit of texture but were soft enough to fully absorb the eggy custards. Toasting them is essential for both texture and flavor.

container and wrap the dish tightly with plastic wrap. Refrigerate the topping and casserole separately for at least 8 hours or up to 24 hours.

5. TO SERVE: Adjust an oven rack to the middle position and heat the oven to 350 degrees. Unwrap the casserole and sprinkle the topping evenly over the top, breaking apart any large pieces with your fingers. Place the casserole on a rimmed baking sheet and bake until puffed and golden, about 1 hour. Serve immediately.

➤ VARIATION

Rum-Raisin French Toast Casserole

Combine 1½ cups raisins and 1 cup rum in a microwave-safe bowl, cover with plastic wrap, and poke several vent holes with the tip of a paring knife. Microwave on high until the rum comes to a boil, 1 to 2 minutes. Set aside, covered, until the raisins are plump, about 15 minutes. Drain thoroughly, discarding the rum (or save it for another use). Follow the recipe for French Toast Casserole, sprinkling the plumped raisins in between the bread pieces in step 2.

OVERNIGHT YEASTED WAFFLES

RAISED WAFFLES ARE MUCH MORE INTERESTING than basic waffles; they are at once creamy and airy, tangy and salty, refined and complex. Plus, because they can be left to rise overnight, they are just the ticket when you want a homemade waffle on a busy morning but don't have time to start measuring ingredients and dirtying bowls.

Most raised waffle recipes call for the batter (minus the eggs) to be left out at room temperature overnight to rise. A warm kitchen provides a fertile field in which the yeast can feed. During our initial tests, however, we discovered that these recipes had too small a window of time before tangy turned downright sour. Batter left to rise unrefrigerated overnight rose and fell, leaving behind a thin, watery batter that yielded an unpleasantly sharp-tasting waffle. We discovered a more flexible option: the refrigerator. By leaving the

batter to rise—more slowly—in the refrigerator, it could be prepared before dinner and left to sit safely overnight.

Given that we were now refrigerating the batter, adding the eggs the day before was no longer a concern, so we wanted to see if adding them along with the other ingredients affected the batter. We prepared a batch and found that these waffles had the same great texture and flavor as a batch made with eggs added at the last minute. Best of all, adding the eggs at the outset made for even less last-minute work.

Because most home cooks now use instant (rapid-rise) yeast, which does not require proofing, this was our leavener of choice. The question was, how much? A full packet of yeast (2¼ teaspoons) yielded an overly fluffy, insubstantial waffle; the large amount of yeast produced a glut of gas. Waffles made with a scant 1 teaspoon of yeast were too bland, so we settled on 1½ teaspoons, which imparted a pleasant tangy flavor and a texture halfway between airy and earthbound.

Choosing the right flour was confusing because raised waffles are part bread (think yeast bread) and part cake (think griddle cakes). Tests quickly determined that waffles made with bread flour were bready, tough, and chewy. On the other hand, cake flour produced a sour, thin waffle. All-purpose flour lived up to its name and was the flour of choice, providing a solid base for both good flavor and good texture.

Just 1 teaspoon of vanilla added depth of flavor and a full teaspoon of salt complemented the waffle's tangy flavor. A tablespoon of sugar gave the

---

TEST KITCHEN TIP:

Freezing Waffles

Place the cooked waffles on a baking sheet and transfer it to the freezer. Once frozen, put the waffles in a zipper-lock bag; they can be frozen for up to a month. They can be reheated individually in a toaster or toaster oven. To reheat several waffles at once, adjust an oven rack to the middle position and heat the oven to 400 degrees. Place the waffles on a baking sheet and bake until heated through, about 10 minutes.

waffles a sweetness that wasn't cloying.

Tasters overwhelmingly preferred waffles made with milk to those made with heavy cream or buttermilk. The batter made with cream was too heavy for the leavening power of the yeast and the resulting waffles were dense. The waffles made with buttermilk, on the other hand, were thought to taste "like cheese" (the yeast provided more than enough flavor), so we decided to eliminate all sour products. Both sour cream and yogurt were crossed off the list. Too much milk made the waffles fragile; the right amount was 1¾ cups. Whole, reduced-fat, and skim milk all yielded similar results, not a big surprise considering the stick of melted butter. We tested 2 and 4 tablespoons of butter, but tasters preferred the extra-crisp exterior and rich flavor provided by a full stick.

This rich and yeasty batter produces great raised waffles and better yet, it takes only a few minutes and simple ingredients to put together the night before.

EQUIPMENT: Waffle Irons

Waffle irons range in price from less than $20 to almost $100. Is there as wide a range in quality? To find out, we gathered eight classic (not Belgian) models. There were two types of iron: The first group, large and square, yielded huge perforated waffles that can be torn into four smaller squares for individual servings; the second yielded a much smaller, round waffle that serves one.

All of the models tested featured a sensor that lit or dimmed to indicate whether the waffle was ready. All but two models had adjustable temperatures, letting you choose how dark you want your waffles. The two unadjustable models—the Hamilton Beach/Proctor Silex Waffle Baker, priced at $18.99, and the Toastmaster Cool-Touch Waffle Baker, priced at $19.99—produced insipid waffles. Neither model is recommended.

Our favorite irons were those that produced waffles with good height and dark, even browning. Topping the list were two VillaWare models (Uno Series Classic Waffler 4-Square, $89.95, and Classic Round, $59.95); the Cuisinart Classic Waffle Maker, $29.95; and the Black and Decker Grill and Waffle Baker, $56.99. The VillaWare models featured not only a ready light but also a ready bell.

A more meaningful feature on which to base your choice is size. The VillaWare Classic Round and Cuisinart irons are fine if you don't mind making one small waffle at a time. In the end, we preferred the convenience of the VillaWare 4-Square and the Black and Decker Grill and Waffle Baker, which cook four individual waffles at once. While the VillaWare produced a marginally better waffle (which was slightly darker and more evenly colored), the Black and Decker costs $30 less and also features reversible griddle plates.

BEST PERFORMANCE
The VillaWare Uno Series Classic Waffler 4-Square makes the best waffles, and the iron chimes when the waffles are done, but note the high price, around $90.

BEST VALUE
The Black and Decker Grill and Waffle Baker makes big, beautiful waffles and also doubles as a griddle. A great value at about $57.

Yeasted Waffles

MAKES ABOUT SEVEN (7-INCH) ROUND OR
FOUR (9-INCH) SQUARE WAFFLES

We prefer the texture of waffles made in a classic waffle iron, but a Belgian waffle iron will work too—although it will make fewer waffles. The waffles are best fresh from the iron but can be held in an oven until all of the batter is used. See the Test Kitchen Tip on page 326 for more information.

1¾	cups whole, low-fat, or skim milk
8	tablespoons (1 stick) unsalted butter, cut into 8 pieces
2	cups (10 ounces) unbleached all-purpose flour
1	tablespoon sugar
1	teaspoon salt
1½	teaspoons instant yeast
2	large eggs
1	teaspoon vanilla extract

1. Heat the milk and butter in a small saucepan over medium-low heat until the butter is melted, about 4 minutes; let cool until warm. Meanwhile, whisk the flour, sugar, salt, and yeast together in a large bowl.

2. Gradually whisk the warm milk mixture into the flour mixture and continue to whisk until the batter is smooth. Whisk the eggs and vanilla together in a small bowl until combined, then whisk into the batter until incorporated.

3. To store: Scrape down the sides of the bowl with a rubber spatula. Cover the bowl tightly with plastic wrap and refrigerate for at least 12 hours or up to 24 hours.

4. To serve: Following the manufacturer's instructions, heat the waffle iron. Remove the waffle batter from the refrigerator when the waffle iron is hot (the batter will be foamy and doubled in size). Whisk the batter to recombine (the batter will deflate). Bake the waffles according to the manufacturer's instructions (use about ½ cup for a 7-inch round iron and about 1 cup for a 9-inch square iron).

OVERNIGHT SOUR CREAM COFFEECAKE

A SOUR CREAM COFFEECAKE WITH MOUNDS of streusel topping is the king of coffeecakes. Not only does it taste rich and satisfying, but it is easy to make and can be served any time of day—not just at breakfast. We were after a recipe for the ultimate make-ahead coffeecake, one where the batter could be prepared the night before, refrigerated, and then baked in the morning, eliminating all last-minute prep. And we wanted to keep the recipe simple and convenient, preferably made with melted butter (no softening or creaming required) and one that required no complicated layering of streusel.

Since the concept of refrigerating cake batter overnight was rather alien to us, we started our research by looking for coffeecake recipes that were billed as make-ahead. Heading into the kitchen, we tested several of them. But these cakes all ranged from dense to sickly sweet, dull, and sometimes even tough. The streusel topping was most often wet and pasty, and sometimes melted into the cake, while other times it stayed sandy and granular. Realizing that we had our work cut out for us, we took two of our own coffeecake recipes (one made with sour cream and one made with buttermilk) and headed into the kitchen for further tests.

We pitted our sour cream coffeecake (a simple recipe made with all-purpose flour, white and dark brown sugar, eggs, butter, sour cream, baking powder, and baking soda) against our buttermilk coffeecake recipe. Both batters were made the day before (the streusel was placed on top) and then refrigerated overnight. When we baked them the next day, we were surprised to see just how much work they would need to become great make-ahead material. The streusel topping melted into the buttermilk cake and sank into the sour cream cake. Both cakes were chewy and dry and neither had cooked evenly. Tasters showed a preference for the sour cream cake, though, because the streusel had not disappeared, and because it had a moister crumb.

Using this as our working recipe, we turned to making a sturdier cake that could keep the topping afloat. We first tested the amount of egg in the recipe. We had been making the cake with two eggs and decided to try three and four eggs thinking that more eggs would both make a heartier batter and keep the cake moist. The four-egg version was too eggy, and rather then adding richness it tasted like an egg cake. Three eggs was exactly the solution we were hoping for: The cake was moist, the crumb just dense enough, and there was a nice golden color to the cake.

Next we looked at the fat content. We thought the more the better, since this is what makes cake moist, and would hopefully enable us to refrigerate the cake batter without loss of flavor and texture. We had been using 5 tablespoons of butter and wanted to see how more butter would help the texture of the cake, but we were worried that it might also make a thinner batter that would absorb the streusel. We tested cakes made with 12, 10, 8, and 6 tablespoons of butter. The cakes made with 10 and 12 tablespoons of butter were too greasy and rich. The cake made with 8 tablespoons of butter was almost what we wanted, but still a tad too rich, and the 6-tablespoon cake seemed a little too dry. So we settled on a number in the middle: 7 tablespoons.

While the topping was not sinking quite as much as it had previously, we were still plagued by this problem. We tried putting the streusel on top right before baking the coffeecake, but had the same problem with sinking. Then a test kitchen colleague suggested that the cake was too large (too much surface area) to bake evenly when cold. Running with that theory, we divided the batter between two 9-inch cake pans instead of one 13 by 9-inch pan and repeated the overnight refrigerator test. This worked perfectly. The streusel topping stayed proudly on top of the cake, and we had two great-looking coffeecakes.

This, of course, made us wonder if we could push the boundaries even further: What about freezing the batter and then baking it in its frozen state? We were pleased to find that this trick worked well and that only a minimal amount of change was required. We had to extend the baking time slightly, but tasters couldn't discern which cake was from frozen batter and which had been made the same day. Not only did we now have an easy recipe for a very good coffeecake, but our recipe gave us many options: We could bake it right away, refrigerate the batter and bake it hours later, or freeze the batter and bake it at a moment's notice.

FREEZE IT

Overnight Sour Cream Coffeecake

MAKES TWO 9-INCH CAKES, EACH SERVING 6
Do not try to put all of the batter into one large cake pan or else the cake will bake very unevenly (especially if refrigerated or frozen).

STREUSEL
- ⅓ cup packed (2⅓ ounces) light brown sugar
- ⅓ cup (2⅓ ounces) granulated sugar
- ⅓ cup (1½ ounces) unbleached all-purpose flour
- 4 tablespoons (½ stick) unsalted butter, cut into ½-inch pieces and chilled
- 1 tablespoon ground cinnamon
- 1 cup pecans, almonds, or walnuts, chopped

CAKE
- 3 cups (15 ounces) unbleached all-purpose flour
- 1 tablespoon baking powder
- 1 teaspoon baking soda
- 1 teaspoon ground cinnamon
- ¼ teaspoon salt
- 1¾ cups sour cream
- 1 cup packed (7 ounces) light brown sugar
- 1 cup (7 ounces) granulated sugar
- 3 large eggs
- 7 tablespoons unsalted butter, melted and cooled

1. **FOR THE STREUSEL:** Using your fingers, mix the brown sugar, granulated sugar, flour, butter, and cinnamon together in a medium bowl until the mixture resembles coarse meal. Stir in the nuts and set aside.

2. **FOR THE CAKE:** Coat two 9-inch cake pans with vegetable oil spray. Mix the flour, baking powder, baking soda, cinnamon, and salt together

TEST KITCHEN TIP:
Frozen Blueberries

Frozen blueberries can save the day in the dead of winter when fresh ones are hard to come by or outrageously overpriced, but there are a couple of factors to consider. Stirred right from the package into a muffin or cake batter, they cool down the batter so much that the muffins or cake will take too long to cook. Frozen blueberries will also turn the batter an unsightly purple-gray color. Rinsing the berries in a sieve under cool water until the water runs clear eliminates both problems. Be sure to dry them well with paper towels before folding them into the batter.

in a large bowl. In a separate bowl, whisk the sour cream, brown sugar, granulated sugar, eggs, and melted butter together until smooth. Gently whisk the egg mixture into the flour mixture until the batter looks smooth and well combined (do not overmix).

3. Scrape the batter into the prepared pans and smooth the tops. Sprinkle the streusel evenly over the top of both cakes.

4. To STORE: Wrap the pans tightly with plastic wrap and refrigerate for up to 24 hours or freeze for up to 1 month. (Do not thaw the frozen cakes before baking.)

5. To SERVE: Adjust an oven rack to the middle position and heat the oven to 350 degrees. Unwrap the cakes and bake until the tops are golden and a toothpick inserted into the center comes out with just a few crumbs attached, 30 to 35 minutes if refrigerated, or 40 to 45 minutes if frozen. Let the cakes cool on a wire rack for 15 minutes before serving.

TO SERVE RIGHT AWAY
Bake the cake as directed in step 5, reducing the baking time to 25 to 30 minutes.

➤ VARIATIONS
Apricot-Orange Sour Cream Coffeecake
Follow the recipe for Overnight Sour Cream Coffeecake, stirring 1 teaspoon grated orange zest into the flour mixture in step 2 and 1 cup chopped dried apricots into the finished batter in step 2.

Lemon-Blueberry Sour Cream Coffeecake
You can substitute frozen blueberries for the fresh; they must be thawed, rinsed, and dried (see left for more information), but they do not need to be tossed with flour.

Toss 2 cups fresh blueberries with 1 tablespoon all-purpose flour. Follow the recipe for Overnight Sour Cream Coffeecake, stirring 1 teaspoon grated lemon zest into the flour mixture in step 2 and the floured berries into the finished batter in step 2.

Cranberry-Orange Sour Cream Coffeecake
Dried cherries can be substituted for the cranberries.

Follow the recipe for Overnight Sour Cream Coffeecake, stirring 1 teaspoon grated orange zest into the flour mixture in step 2 and 1 cup dried cranberries into the finished batter in step 2.

ANYTIME MUFFINS

MUFFINS ARE THE ULTIMATE AMERICAN breakfast treat. So we knew that we had to include a great recipe for make-ahead muffins in this book. The problem is that with the exception of the rare weekend morning, there just isn't time to make even the simplest of muffin batters. Our goal was to devise a recipe where the batter could be made in advance and baked when we wanted it.

We started by using one of our long-standing muffin recipes. We wanted to adapt this recipe so that we could refrigerate the batter overnight, or freeze muffin-sized batter balls.

The test kitchen favorite muffin recipe calls for creaming (rather than melting) the butter, which results in a tender muffin with nice height. In our original development for this recipe, we tested both cake and all-purpose flours. In the end, we rejected cake flour—it made squat, wet, greasy muffins. All-purpose flour was chosen because it produced shapely and fairly tender muffins, with a nice contrast between crust and crumb. Finally, this recipe calls for plain yogurt as the dairy ingredient. In our previous testing, we had discovered that milk made muffins with flat tops, while thicker liquids delivered muffins with rounded, textured tops. Sour cream and cream made the muffins heavy; yogurt was our first choice, with buttermilk as a backup choice.

Using this recipe, we began the make-ahead testing, starting with the refrigerator. In our first test we made the batter in a mixing bowl and placed it in the refrigerator for 16 hours. The next morning we scooped it into a muffin tin and baked it at the same temperature, and for the same length of time, as when baked immediately. This yielded muffins that were equally as good as those baked right away, and they baked in exactly the same amount of time! To simplify matters even further, we tried putting the batter into the muffin tin and then refrigerating the tin overnight. Again, the results were impressive.

With the refrigerator method under control, we turned to what we felt would be trickier: frozen batter. We made a batch of muffin batter and scooped it into a muffin tin and then placed the tin in the freezer, covering it lightly with plastic wrap just until the batter was frozen. Once frozen, we stored the frozen batter in zipper-lock bags so when we were ready to bake them, all we needed to do was put the frozen batter balls back into a muffin tin. Much to our delight, they baked up nicely, and only took 5 minutes longer than their warmer counterparts.

Knowing that there are some times when you don't want to bake an entire batch of muffins at once, we also tested baking a couple of muffins at a time. Following the same baking instructions, we put one or two frozen batter balls into the muffin tin, and found that they too baked up nicely in about the same amount of time as a full batch.

We now had the perfect anytime muffin. It could be pulled from the freezer and baked within half an hour—no measuring, no mixing, no dirty bowls—just one great muffin you can make while you take a shower and get your day started.

FREEZE IT
Anytime Muffins
MAKES 12 MUFFINS

This is a basic master muffin recipe that is fairly plain, so we recommend adding other flavorings or fruit (see the

variations that follow). This recipe can easily be halved and doubled, if desired. If doubling the recipe, mix the batter in a large bowl and take care to evenly incorporate the flavorings. We prefer whole milk yogurt, although the recipe will work with low-fat or nonfat. When storing the batter overnight in the refrigerator, you can either put it in an airtight container or, if you have space, in a muffin tin covered with greased plastic wrap.

3   cups (15 ounces) unbleached all-purpose flour
1   tablespoon baking powder
½   teaspoon baking soda
½   teaspoon salt
10 tablespoons (1¼ sticks) unsalted butter, softened
1   cup (7 ounces) sugar
2   large eggs
1½ cups plain whole milk yogurt

1. Coat a 12-cup muffin tin with vegetable oil spray; set aside. Whisk the flour, baking powder, baking soda, and salt together in a medium bowl; set aside.

2. Using an electric mixer, beat the butter and sugar together at medium-high speed until light and fluffy, about 2 minutes. Add the eggs, 1 at a time, beating well after each addition.

3. Reduce the mixer speed to medium-low and beat in half of the flour mixture, followed by one-third of the yogurt. Beat in half of the remaining flour mixture, followed by half of the remaining yogurt; repeat with the remaining flour mixture and yogurt. Portion the batter evenly into the prepared muffin tin.

4. TO STORE: Wrap the muffin tin tightly with plastic wrap sprayed with vegetable oil spray and refrigerate for up to 24 hours or freeze for up to 1 month. (After the muffin batter is completely frozen, about 6 hours, the batter balls can be transferred to a zipper-lock bag to save space in the freezer. Transfer the batter balls back to an oiled muffin tin before baking.)

5. TO SERVE: Adjust an oven rack to the lower-middle position and heat the oven to 375 degrees. Unwrap the muffins and bake until golden brown, 25 to 30 minutes if refrigerated, or 35 to 40

minutes if frozen. Let the muffins cool in the pan 5 minutes before serving.

TO SERVE RIGHT AWAY

Bake the muffins for 25 to 30 minutes, as described in step 5.

➤ VARIATIONS

Blueberry Muffins

You can substitute frozen blueberries for the fresh; they must be thawed, rinsed, and dried (see page 329 for more information), but they do not need to be tossed with flour.

Toss 2 cups fresh blueberries with 1 tablespoon all-purpose flour. Follow the recipe for Anytime Muffins, gently folding the floured blueberries into the finished batter in step 3.

Apricot–Almond Muffins

Follow the recipe for Anytime Muffins, stirring 1 cup finely diced dried apricots and ½ teaspoon almond extract into the finished batter in step 3.

Cranberry–Orange Muffins

Follow the recipe for Anytime Muffins, stirring 1½ cups coarsely chopped fresh (or thawed frozen) cranberries and 1 teaspoon grated orange zest into the finished batter in step 3 (being careful not to let the zest clump).

Lemon–Poppy Seed Muffins

Follow the recipe for Anytime Muffins, stirring 2½ tablespoons poppy seeds and 1½ tablespoons grated lemon zest into the flour mixture in step 1.

Banana–Pecan Muffins

Follow the recipe for Anytime Muffins, substituting 1 cup packed light brown sugar for the granulated sugar and adding ½ teaspoon ground nutmeg to the flour mixture in step 1. Stir 1½ cups finely diced bananas and ¾ cup coarsely chopped toasted pecans into the finished batter in step 3.

FREEZER BISCUITS

RICH AND SATISFYING, BISCUITS SHARE WITH muffins the distinction of being among the simplest of all breads. They are made from a mixture of flour, leavener (baking powder or soda), salt, fat (usually butter or vegetable shortening), and liquid (milk, buttermilk, sour milk, yogurt, or cream). They are usually rolled out and cut, although they can also be shaped by hand or dropped onto a baking sheet by the spoonful. Over the years, we have developed a variety of biscuits—buttermilk, cream, and drop biscuits. For the purposes of this book, we were looking for a cut biscuit that was quick and easy to make and that could be frozen and then baked in its frozen state, making it virtually an anytime biscuit, like the bags of frozen biscuits you can buy in the supermarket—only better.

Given these parameters, we used our basic cream biscuit recipe as our starting point. They are rich tasting, can be rolled and cut, and they have an advantage over buttermilk biscuits in that they do not require cutting butter into flour. In fact there is no fat in these biscuits apart from that present in the heavy cream, so they couldn't be simpler. Just whisk together the dry ingredients (flour, sugar, baking powder, and salt), add the cream, form the dough, knead it, cut it, and bake it.

Scaling up our cream biscuit recipe so that it would make 24 biscuits, we followed the procedures we learned when we developed our original cream biscuits. First and foremost, since cream biscuits are less sturdy than those made with butter and can become soft and "melt" during baking, a little more handling is required as this helps build structure. Dough that was more heavily worked produced much higher, fluffier biscuits, while those made from lightly handled dough looked short and bedraggled.

Although we found it easy enough to quickly roll out this dough and then cut it into rounds with a biscuit cutter, a quicker method is to shape the dough by hand, pushing it with your palms until it is ¾ inch thick. The dough can then be cut with a biscuit cutter and pushed back into a disk to be cut again.

We now turned to the big question central to our make-ahead mission. How would our biscuits bake up from the freezer or refrigerator? Those that sat in the refrigerator overnight baked into squat round disks, nothing like those that were made right away. It seemed that the long resting period worked against our kneading, by allowing the gluten in the dough to relax. We tried kneading the dough longer, but after many attempts were forced to give up on refrigerated biscuits. Next up were frozen biscuits. Much to our delight they baked up beautifully straight from the freezer (which halted any chance that the gluten could relax), and took only a few minutes longer to cook than those baked right away.

Now we had the simplest of biscuit recipes, one that could be whipped up on the weekend during a lull in activity and pulled out of the freezer on a weeknight to accompany a savory bowl of soup or stew. And you can bake as many (or as few) biscuits as you need at any given time, making these a lifesaver on those busy weeknights.

FREEZE IT

Freezer Biscuits

MAKES ABOUT 24 BISCUITS

Try to cut out as many biscuits as possible each time the dough is patted out in step 2; each additional batch of cut biscuits will look more rustic. Obviously, these biscuits do not need to be baked at the same time, but rather can be baked as desired. The biscuit dough cannot be held in the refrigerator, or it won't bake well.

6	cups (30 ounces) unbleached all-purpose flour, plus extra for the counter
2	tablespoons sugar
2	tablespoons baking powder
1½	teaspoons salt
4½	cups heavy cream

1. Line a rimmed baking sheet with parchment paper (if your baking sheets are small, you may need to use 2); set aside. Whisk the flour, sugar,

SHAPING CREAM BISCUITS

1. Pat the dough on a lightly floured work surface into a ¾-inch-thick circle.

2. Punch out the dough rounds with a 2½-inch round biscuit cutter.

baking powder, and salt together in a large bowl. Stir in the cream with a wooden spoon until a dough forms, about 30 seconds. Turn the dough out onto a lightly floured counter and gather into a ball. Knead the dough briefly until smooth, about 60 seconds, adding extra flour as needed if the dough is too sticky.

2. Pat the dough into a ¾-inch-thick circle. Following the illustrations above, cut out the biscuits using a 2½-inch round biscuit cutter. Lay the biscuits on the prepared baking sheet, spaced about ½ inch apart. Gather up the scraps of dough and reknead them briefly to combine, then pat the dough again into a ¾-inch-thick round and cut more biscuits; repeat this process again for a third time. You can either discard any remaining bits of dough or gently pat them into rustic hand-formed biscuits.

3. To store: Wrap the baking sheet tightly with greased plastic wrap and freeze the biscuits until frozen solid, about 6 hours. Transfer the frozen biscuits to a large zipper-lock bag and freeze for up to 1 month. (Do not thaw before baking.)

4. To serve: Adjust an oven rack to the upper-

middle position and heat the oven to 450 degrees. Lay the biscuits on a parchment-lined baking sheet, about 2 inches apart, and bake until puffed and golden brown, 20 to 25 minutes. (If baking a large amount of biscuits, spread them out over 2 baking sheets and bake the sheets separately; do not bake both sheets at the same time.) Serve hot.

TO SERVE RIGHT AWAY

After cutting out the biscuits in step 2, spread them out over 2 parchment-lined rimmed baking sheets. Bake the biscuits, 1 sheet at a time, as directed in step 4, reducing the baking time to 15 to 20 minutes.

➤ VARIATIONS

Freezer Biscuits with Fresh Herbs

You can either use just one herb or a combination of them.

Follow the recipe for Freezer Biscuits, whisking 6 tablespoons minced fresh mild herbs (such as tarragon, cilantro, chives, parsley, or dill) or 3 tablespoons minced fresh hearty herbs (such as thyme, sage, or rosemary) into the flour mixture in step 1.

Freezer Biscuits with Cheddar Cheese

Follow the recipe for Freezer Biscuits, tossing 6 ounces cheddar cheese, cut into ¼-inch pieces, into the flour mixture in step 1.

ANYTIME DINNER ROLLS

REALLY GOOD DINNER ROLLS CAN BE HARD to come by unless you are lucky enough to live near a great bakery, preferably one that's on your route home. So if you really want good ones to go with that stew you made in advance, it's best to have a stash in your freezer, ready to bake up at a moment's notice. With this appealing thought in mind, we turned our attention to developing a durable recipe for rich, buttery rolls that could go from freezer to oven.

Almost all of the recipes we gathered for a basic dinner roll had the same ingredients in varying proportions. They were fairly rich, loaded with milk, eggs, butter, and a fair amount of sugar. Each recipe also employed a healthy amount of yeast for a quick rise and big yeasty flavor. So, with this goal, we began a battery of tests.

We wanted this recipe to make a fair amount of rolls, so our working recipe contained 4¼ cups all-purpose flour and 1 envelope (2¼ teaspoons) of yeast. We began by looking at different amounts of milk and settled on 1¼ cups, since the rolls produced were moist, but not overly sticky. Next we moved on to the amount of butter. Tasters were unsatisfied with our first tests, where the rolls contained between 5 and 10 tablespoons of butter. They were finally content in our next butter test with rolls that contained 12 tablespoons of butter.

We were still looking for a richer flavor though, and so we turned to the amount of egg in the dough. Up to this point we had been using one whole egg but thought that we could achieve a better roll if we added some yolks as well. One yolk moved us in the right direction, but we wanted more. Three or more yolks (we tested up to five) produced rolls that were more egg bread or brioche than dinner rolls. With one whole egg and two yolks, we had just the balance we were looking for.

Selecting the ideal kneading time took some experimenting. With a soft, billowy, tender crumb as our goal, we knew a reasonably short knead was in order, but how short was short? We tried times of four to 12 minutes (in a standing mixer at medium speed) and were most pleased with a six-minute knead, followed by a scant minute of hand kneading. With 12 minutes of kneading, the dough's gluten was overdeveloped and too elastic—its texture more like that of a chewy sandwich. With four minutes, the dough lacked structure and collapsed during baking.

With a full envelope of yeast and 4¼ cups flour, we knew a quick rise would not be a problem. Within one to 1½ hours, the dough had doubled in volume. After we divided the dough, we rounded the individual portions on the countertop until they developed a smooth, tight skin and perfect globe shape. Rounding relies on the friction created between the moisture in the dough and the work surface and this process helps the dough rise by redistributing the yeast and sugars.

After spacing the rolls on a baking sheet, we gave them a light brushing of melted butter. They were now ready for their second rise; this was where the make-ahead testing came into play. We placed the rolls in the refrigerator overnight, where the cool temperature slows down but does not stop the yeast activity; these rolls needed to finish rising on the counter before baking and then baked up light and golden and were equally as rich as their non-make-ahead counterparts. Next we tested freezing the rolls after the second rising. They were baked from their frozen state and again baked into rolls we would be proud to serve any night of the week.

We tried baking the rolls in baking dishes and on baking sheets. While we liked the height of the rolls baked in a dish, the rolls in the middle were gummy long after the outer rolls were perfectly baked. A metal baking sheet, however, delivered even heat and got the rolls out of the oven in about 20 minutes. These rolls are best when eaten warm. After a 10-minute rest once out of the oven, they are ready to serve, preferably with a roast and plenty of gravy.

FREEZE IT

Anytime Dinner Rolls

MAKES 24 ROLLS

It's important to keep the pieces of dough covered while rounding them into rolls or else they will quickly dry out and develop a tough "skin." Surprisingly, the baking times for frozen, refrigerated, or fresh rolls are about the same (give or take a few minutes). You will need about 2 tablespoons melted butter for brushing the tops of the rolls prior to baking. We prefer the soft texture of rolls that meld together during baking, which is what will happen when they are spaced ½ inch apart on the baking sheet.

1¼	cups whole milk, warmed to about 110 degrees
12	tablespoons (1½ sticks) unsalted butter, melted and cooled, plus extra for brushing on rolls for serving
2	large yolks, lightly beaten
1	large egg, lightly beaten
4¼	cups (21¼ ounces) unbleached all-purpose flour, plus extra for the counter
2	tablespoons sugar
1	envelope (2¼ teaspoons) instant or rapid-rise yeast
1½	teaspoons salt

1. Whisk the milk, butter, yolks, and egg together in a medium bowl; set aside. Mix 4 cups of the flour, sugar, yeast, and salt together in a standing mixer fitted with the dough hook. With the mixer on low speed, add the milk mixture and mix until the dough comes together, about 1 minute.

2. Increase the speed to medium-low and knead until the dough is smooth and elastic, about 10 minutes. (After 5 minutes, if the dough seems very sticky, add the remaining ¼ cup flour, 1 tablespoon at a time, until the dough clears the side of the bowl but sticks to the bottom.)

3. Turn the dough out onto a clean counter and knead by hand to form a smooth, round ball. Place the dough in a lightly oiled bowl and cover loosely with greased plastic wrap. Let rise in a warm place until the dough has doubled in size, about 1 hour.

4. Line a rimmed baking sheet with parchment paper; set aside. Following the illustrations on page 335, divide the dough into 24 even pieces and cover with greased plastic wrap. Working with 1 piece of dough at a time (keeping the other pieces covered), round the dough into a small roll. Lay the rolls on the prepared baking sheet, spaced about ½ inch apart. Cover the rolls loosely with greased plastic wrap and let rise in a warm place until the rolls have doubled in size, about 1 hour.

5. To STORE: Without pressing on the rolls, wrap the tray tightly with greased plastic wrap. Freeze the rolls until frozen solid, about 6 hours. Transfer the frozen rolls to a large zipper-lock bag and freeze for up to 1 month. (Do not thaw before baking.)

6. To SERVE: Adjust an oven rack to the middle position and heat the oven to 375 degrees. Line a baking sheet with parchment paper and lay the rolls on the sheet, about ½ inch apart. Brush the rolls with melted butter and bake until golden, 15 to 25 minutes. Cool for 10 minutes before serving.

TO MAKE A DAY IN ADVANCE

Immediately after laying the shaped rolls on the baking sheet in step 4, wrap the tray tightly with greased plastic wrap, without pressing on the rolls; refrigerate the rolls for up to 16 hours. Before baking, let the rolls sit on the counter with the plastic wrap loosened until they are softened and puffy, 30 to 60 minutes. Unwrap the rolls, brush with butter, and bake as directed in step 6.

TO SERVE RIGHT AWAY

After the rolls have risen as directed in step 4, unwrap them, brush with butter, and bake as directed in step 6.

➤ VARIATIONS

Food Processor Method

Whisk the milk, butter, yolks, and egg together in a large liquid measuring cup. Pulse 4 cups of the flour, sugar, yeast, and salt in a food processor (fitted with a dough blade if possible) to combine. With the processor running, pour the milk mixture through the feed tube and process until a rough ball forms, 30 to 40 seconds. Let the dough rest in the bowl for 2 minutes, and then process for 30 seconds longer. Turn the dough out onto a clean counter and knead by hand to form a smooth, round ball, about 5 minutes, adding the remaining ¼ cup flour as needed to prevent the dough from sticking to the counter. Transfer to a lightly oiled bowl, cover with greased plastic wrap, and let rise as directed in step 3.

Hand-Mixing Method

Whisk the milk, butter, yolks, and egg in a medium bowl. In a separate large bowl, whisk 4 cups of the flour, sugar, yeast, and salt together. Add the milk mixture and stir with a rubber spatula until the dough comes together and looks shaggy. Turn the dough out onto a clean counter and knead by hand to form a smooth, round ball, 10 to 15 minutes, adding the remaining ¼ cup flour as needed to prevent the dough from sticking to the counter. Transfer to a lightly oiled bowl, cover with greased plastic wrap, and let rise as directed in step 3.

SHAPING DINNER ROLLS

Shaping a blob of dough into a tidy, round dinner roll takes a little practice. Here are some tips: When shaping the dough into rolls (step 3 below), it is important to have some friction between the dough and the counter; don't flour the counter or else you'll lose this friction. Shaping the dough into rolls feels very different than rolling cookie dough into balls or making meatballs. When shaping dinner rolls, the key is to drag the dough in circles over the counter with a cupped palm—the bottom of the roll will stick to the counter, causing the rest of the dough to pull taut and smooth.

1. Divide the dough into 2 equal pieces and, with your hands, pull and shape each piece until it is 18 inches long and about 1 inch across.

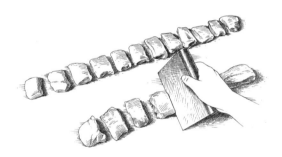

2. With a bench scraper, cut each length of dough into twelve 1½-inch pieces (each piece will weigh about 1 ounce). Loosely cover all 24 pieces with plastic wrap.

3. With a cupped palm, roll each piece of dough into a smooth, tight ball and then loosely cover it with plastic wrap.

CINNAMON ROLLS

A PUFFY CINNAMON ROLL COATED WITH thick white icing brings out the child in all of us, encouraging even the most mature person to greedily uncoil its tight swirls and dig in. Most of us eat them at the mall these days, opting not to take the time to make them, except for the periodic special occasion. Even when we do make them, we end up spending too much time in the kitchen and not enough with our friends and family. Could we come up with a cinnamon roll we could make in advance?

First, we had to define what sort of roll we wanted. Our ideal cinnamon roll is a little more reserved than what we usually find either at the mall or a bakery. We wanted a rich, yeasty dough—one that was soft and rich but not greasy. The filling should be slightly sweet, rather than sugary sweet, and potent with cinnamon. The icing should be creamy and thick and boast a tang sufficient to balance the richness and sweetness elsewhere in the roll.

With our ideal cinnamon roll in mind (along with the requirement that it could be made in advance and baked at the last minute), we collected recipes and started testing. The recipes we found used a variety of dough types, from lean sandwich bread dough to buttery brioche dough (a very rich French dough made with huge amounts of egg yolks and butter). While we were inclined toward recipes using the rich brioche-style dough because they would undoubtedly taste better, after further thought we realized that combining such a rich dough with a cinnamon filling and glaze would be gilding the lily.

We decided to start with a basic recipe for sandwich bread made with buttermilk and a modest amount of butter (just 2 tablespoons). To develop richness, we tried adding varying amounts of eggs, butter, and cream. With too many whole eggs, the dough turned hard, dry, and almost cakey, though it did have an appealing golden hue. More butter gave the dough more flavor and a softer texture. However, with too much butter, the dough practically oozed off the counter and was difficult to work with. Cream, surprisingly, did little at all. Buttermilk was just fine for this dough.

After many attempts, we settled on a soft dough enriched with a good amount of butter (6 tablespoons) as well as three whole eggs. When baked, this dough had a tender crumb, buttery richness, slight golden color, and enough gluten development for a little resiliency. (Gluten is the protein formed when flour is mixed with water and the mixture is kneaded; it gives bread its structure.) The recipe also allowed us to add the butter melted rather than in softened pieces, a trickier method used for brioche. This dough, once made, needs to rise until doubled in size before making cinnamon rolls with it.

With our dough ready, we turned our attention to the filling, which came together easily. Our tasters preferred cinnamon mixed with just enough sugar to temper its bitterness. And they liked rolls with a generous 2 teaspoons of cinnamon. We tested granulated sugar as well as light and dark brown sugars in the filling. Granulated sugar was too dry and added little flavor. Dark brown sugar proved too wet and turned syrupy, like the filling for a sticky bun. And its strong molasses flavor detracted from the cinnamon. Light brown sugar proved the best sweetener, adding moisture and a lighter molasses flavor that complemented the cinnamon. Salt mixed with the cinnamon and sugar helped marry the flavors and sharpen the sugar's sweetness.

Shaping the dough into pinwheel spirals could not have been any easier. The soft dough gracefully yielded to a light touch under the rolling pin as we rolled it out. We then sprinkled it with the filling and rolled it up slowly and tightly so that the rolls would not uncoil while cooking. Now this is where things were going to differ for a make-ahead recipe. Usually cinnamon rolls are left to rise until doubled in size (the second rising for the dough), and then baked. But we knew that for make-ahead cinnamon rolls, this would not work. We could not hold them after they doubled in size since after this point, the yeast would die and the rolls would deflate.

In search of the solution, we let the cinnamon rolls rise fully and then refrigerated them overnight and baked them the next morning still cold, right out of the refrigerator. These rolls had too much time to rise (the refrigerator only slowed the process) and were slightly deflated. Next we tried letting the rolls rise halfway before placing them in the refrigerator. We then baked them right out of the refrigerator the following day. This method worked well, but determining when the rolls were half risen was an impossible task. We were hoping for the least complicated method and tried placing them in the refrigerator without a second rising. We hoped that they would rise in the refrigerator enough overnight and then we would simply bake them directly from the refrigerator. While this worked fairly well, the cinnamon rolls were not as light as the ones made right away. Next we tried refrigerating them overnight and then letting them sit on the counter to come to room temperature, and to finish rising before we baked them. To our delight, this method produced rolls that rivaled those made the same day.

With the refrigerator method resolved, we were ready to conquer the freezer. We knew that placing the cinnamon rolls in the freezer would arrest the rising altogether, so the freezer method would have to be different. We again tried the partial rising method, letting the rolls rise halfway and then freezing them; and we also played with parbaking (baking the cinnamon rolls 90 percent of the way before freezing them). Neither of those options resulted in cinnamon rolls as tasty as those that were baked immediately. Our last hope was to let the cinnamon rolls rise fully, freeze them, and then bake them from their frozen state. To help ensure ovenspring (the final burst of fermentation and expansion which happens in the first five to 10 minutes of baking) we covered the baking dish with foil for the first 20 minutes of baking, so the rolls would stay as moist as possible. These were finally cinnamon rolls worth their effort.

Because there are many sticky bun fans out there, we also made a sticky bun variation. But we found that when baked frozen, the caramel (which is on the bottom of the pan) overcooked and turned so hard that it threatened even the sturdiest teeth. We tried adding more corn syrup and butter to make a looser caramel, but this produced a lighter colored caramel that tasters found lacking.

Turning back to our original recipe, we increased the amount of time that the rolls were covered by 10 minutes and placed two baking sheets underneath the baking dish to guard the caramel from too much direct heat. We had our solution—now the caramel was golden brown and ran smoothly down the sides of the rolls.

Basic Sweet Dough
MAKES ENOUGH DOUGH FOR 12 ROLLS OR BUNS

This dough is used to make Cinnamon Rolls (page 338) and Sticky Buns (page 339).

¾	cup buttermilk, warmed to about 110 degrees
6	tablespoons (¾ stick) unsalted butter, melted and cooled
3	large eggs, lightly beaten
4¼	cups (21¼ ounces) unbleached all-purpose flour
¼	cup (1¾ ounces) granulated sugar
1	envelope (2¼ teaspoons) instant or rapid-rise yeast
1¼	teaspoons salt

1. Whisk the buttermilk, butter, and eggs together in a large liquid measuring cup; set aside. Mix 4 cups of the flour, sugar, yeast, and salt in a standing mixer fitted with a dough hook. With the mixer on low speed, add the buttermilk mixture and mix until the dough comes together, about 1 minute.

2. Increase the speed to medium-low and knead until the dough is smooth and elastic, about 10 minutes. (After 5 minutes, if the dough is sticky, add the remaining ¼ cup flour, 1 tablespoon at a time, until the dough clears the side of the bowl but sticks to the bottom).

3. Turn the dough out onto a clean counter and knead by hand to form a smooth, round ball, about 1 minute. Place the dough in a lightly oiled bowl and cover loosely with greased plastic wrap. Let rise in a warm place until the dough has doubled in size, 2 to 2½ hours.

VARIATIONS

Food Processor Method

Whisk the buttermilk, butter, and eggs together in a large liquid measuring cup. Pulse 4 cups of the flour, sugar, yeast, and salt in a food processor (fitted with a dough blade if possible) to combine. With the processor running, pour the buttermilk mixture through the feed tube and process until a rough ball forms, 30 to 40 seconds. Let the dough rest in the bowl for 2 minutes, then process for 30 seconds longer. Turn the dough out onto a clean counter and knead by hand to form a smooth, round ball, about 5 minutes, adding the remaining ¼ cup flour as needed to prevent the dough from sticking to the counter. Transfer to a lightly oiled bowl, cover with greased plastic wrap, and let rise as directed in step 3.

Hand-Mixing Method

Whisk the buttermilk, butter, and eggs together in a large liquid measuring cup. In a separate large bowl, whisk 4 cups of the flour, sugar, yeast, and salt together. Pour the buttermilk mixture into the flour mixture. Stir with a rubber spatula until the dough comes together and looks shaggy. Turn the dough out onto a clean counter and knead by hand to form a smooth, round ball, 10 to 15 minutes, adding the remaining ¼ cup flour as needed to prevent the dough from sticking to the counter. Transfer to a lightly oiled bowl, cover with greased plastic wrap, and let rise as directed in step 3.

FREEZE IT

Cinnamon Rolls

MAKES 12 ROLLS

These soft rolls bake into each other, but can easily be pulled apart before serving or at the table.

ROLLS

1	tablespoon unsalted butter, melted, plus extra for the baking dish
¾	cup packed (5¼ ounces) light brown sugar
2	teaspoons ground cinnamon
¼	teaspoon ground cloves
	Pinch salt
1	recipe Basic Sweet Dough (page 337)
	Flour (for the counter)

ICING (FOR SERVING)

1½	ounces cream cheese, softened
3	tablespoons buttermilk or whole milk
1½	cups (6 ounces) confectioners' sugar

1. **FOR THE ROLLS:** Butter a 13 by 9-inch baking dish; set aside. Mix the brown sugar, cinnamon, cloves, and salt together in a small bowl. Turn the dough out onto a lightly floured counter and press it into a 16 by 12-inch rectangle. Brush the dough with the melted butter. Following the illustrations on page 339, sprinkle the brown sugar mixture over the dough, leaving a ¾-inch border along the top edge. Press on the sugar mixture to adhere it to the dough.

2. Roll the dough into a tight cylinder and pinch the seam closed. Roll the cylinder over so that it is seam side down. Gently stretch the cylinder until it is 18 inches in length, with an even diameter. Pat the ends of the cylinder to even them. Slice the cylinder into 12 evenly sized rolls using a serrated knife. Arrange the rolls, cut side down, in the prepared baking dish.

3. **TO STORE:** Without pressing on the rolls, wrap the baking dish tightly with greased plastic wrap and refrigerate for up to 16 hours.

4. **TO SERVE:** Remove the rolls from the refrigerator, loosen the plastic wrap, and let sit at room temperature until puffy and pressed against one another, 1 to 1½ hours. Meanwhile, adjust an oven rack to the middle position and heat the oven to 350 degrees. Unwrap the rolls and bake until golden and puffed, 20 to 30 minutes. Flip the rolls out onto a wire rack and let cool for 5 minutes before icing.

5. **FOR THE ICING:** Whisk the cream cheese and buttermilk together in a large bowl until thick and smooth. Sift the confectioners' sugar over the mixture and whisk until smooth, about 30 seconds. Flip the rolls upright and, using a large spoon, drizzle the glaze over the warm rolls, pulling them apart first, if desired.

TO FREEZE

After arranging the rolls in the prepared baking dish in step 2, cover loosely with greased plastic wrap and let rise in a warm place until the rolls have doubled in size and are pressed against one another, 1 to 1½ hours. Wrap the dish tightly with greased plastic wrap, without pressing on the rolls, and freeze for up to 1 month. To bake, adjust an oven rack to the middle position and heat the oven to 350 degrees. Unwrap the dish and wrap tightly with foil. Bake the rolls for 20 minutes, then remove the foil, and continue to bake until golden and puffed, about 30 minutes longer. Unmold, cool, and ice the rolls as directed in steps 4 and 5.

TO MAKE RIGHT AWAY

After arranging the rolls in the prepared baking dish in step 2, cover loosely with greased plastic wrap and let rise in a warm place until the rolls have doubled in size and are pressed against one another, 1 to 1½ hours. To bake, adjust an oven rack to the middle position and heat the oven to 350 degrees. Unwrap the rolls and bake until golden and puffed, 20 to 30 minutes. Unmold, cool, and ice as directed in steps 4 and 5.

FREEZE IT

Sticky Buns

MAKES 12 BUNS

Be careful when turning the buns out of the pan—the caramel will be dangerously hot. For information on toasting nuts, see page 95.

TOPPING

5	tablespoons unsalted butter, plus more for greasing the dish
½	cup (3½ ounces) packed light brown sugar
½	cup light corn syrup
⅛	teaspoon salt
1	teaspoon vanilla extract
2	cups pecans, toasted and chopped coarse

BUNS

¾	cup packed (5¼ ounces) light brown sugar
2	teaspoons ground cinnamon
¼	teaspoon ground cloves
	Pinch salt
1	recipe Basic Sweet Dough (page 337)
	Flour (for the counter)
1	tablespoon unsalted butter, melted

ASSEMBLING CINNAMON ROLLS AND STICKY BUNS

1. Sprinkle the dough with the filling.

2. Roll the dough into a tight cylinder.

3. Firmly pinch the seam to seal.

4. Cut the cylinder into 12 buns, each about 1½ inches thick.

5. Arrange the buns in the prepared dish.

339

1. **FOR THE TOPPING:** Butter a 13 by 9-inch baking dish; set aside. Bring the brown sugar, corn syrup, butter, and salt to a simmer in a small saucepan over medium heat. Stir in the vanilla and pecans. Spread the mixture over the bottom of the prepared baking dish.

2. **FOR THE BUNS:** Mix the brown sugar, cinnamon, cloves, and salt together in a small bowl. Turn the dough out onto a lightly floured counter and press it into a 16 by 12-inch rectangle. Brush the dough with the butter. Following the illustrations on page 339, sprinkle the brown sugar mixture over the dough, leaving a ¾-inch border along the top edge. Press on the sugar mixture to adhere it to the dough.

3. Roll the dough into a tight cylinder and pinch the seam closed. Roll the cylinder over so that it is seam side down. Gently stretch the cylinder until it is 18 inches in length, with an even diameter. Pat the ends of the cylinder to even them. Slice the cylinder into 12 evenly sized buns using a serrated knife. Arrange the buns, cut side down, in the prepared baking dish.

4. **TO STORE:** Without pressing on the buns, wrap the baking dish tightly with greased plastic wrap and refrigerate for up to 16 hours.

5. **TO SERVE:** Remove the buns from the refrigerator, loosen the plastic wrap, and let sit at room temperature until puffy and pressed against one another, 1 to 1½ hours. Meanwhile, adjust an oven rack to the middle position and heat the oven to 350 degrees. Unwrap the buns and bake until golden and puffed, 20 to 30 minutes. Let the buns cool in the pan for 5 minutes before flipping them out onto a large serving platter. Scrape any glaze from the pan and drizzle it over the buns before serving.

TO FREEZE

After arranging the buns in the prepared baking dish in step 3, cover loosely with greased plastic wrap and let rise in a warm place until the buns have doubled in size and are pressed against one another, 1 to 1½ hours. Wrap the dish tightly with greased plastic wrap, without pressing on the buns, and freeze for up to 1 month. To bake, adjust an oven rack to the middle position and heat the oven to 350 degrees. Unwrap the dish, wrap tightly with foil, and set on top of 2 stacked baking sheets (to prevent the topping from burning). Bake the buns for 30 minutes, then remove the foil and continue to bake until golden and puffed, about 20 minutes longer. Cool, unmold, and scrape extra glaze onto the buns as directed in step 5.

TO MAKE RIGHT AWAY

After arranging the buns in the prepared baking dish in step 3, cover loosely with greased plastic wrap and let rise in a warm place until the buns have doubled in size and are pressed against one another, 1 to 1½ hours. To bake, adjust an oven rack to the middle position and heat the oven to 350 degrees. Bake the buns until golden and puffed, 20 to 30 minutes. Cool, unmold, and scrape extra glaze onto the buns as directed in step 5.

SCIENCE: **Yeast and Gluten**

Yeast is a microorganism that is maintained in pure culture. Under proper conditions in liquid, it can multiply continuously until the growth medium is exhausted. Yeast in liquid medium is sold by the tanker-full to commercial food manufacturers. For bakeries, yeast companies remove some of the moisture to create a product called crumbled yeast, which is sold in 50-pound bags. The next processing step extrudes the yeast to make a product that remains fully hydrated yet is fine enough to press into the small cakes you see for sale in supermarkets, labeled cake yeast. Further drying yields dried, powdered yeast, called active dry yeast. The same process is used to make other dry yeasts, including instant yeast, although this product starts with a different strain of yeast. (As a general rule, we prefer instant yeast—also called rapid-rise yeast—to other forms of yeast because it is reliable and works quickly.)

Although yeast does provide the gas (in the form of carbon dioxide) that gives bread lift, it needs long sheets of gluten to trap the gas. What exactly is gluten? When water is mixed with wheat flour, proteins, most importantly the proteins glutenin and gliadin, bind to each other and to the water and become pliable. Gluten is the name given to this combination of proteins. Kneading stretches the gluten into elastic sheets that trap and hold the gases produced by the yeast, which allows the bread to rise.

9
DESSERTS

Desserts

WITH THIS CHAPTER, WE WORKED TO PRESENT a range of desserts, all of which can be made in advance. Some are no doubt obvious (like cheesecake, pound cake, and panna cotta), but they are here to remind you both of their virtues and of the best way to make them, as well as how far in advance they can be made. But others required some substantial testing since we wanted to push the boundaries to see just how far we could go. Is it possible to make a soufflé in advance, freeze it, and then simply bake it? Can you make the batter for berry buckles, freezing it in portions for baking sometime in the future? Or can you make the batter in the morning, refrigerate it, and then simply put the buckles in the oven just as your guests sit down to dinner, ensuring freshly baked dessert with no last-minute fuss? And what about stocking your freezer with the elements of an easy dessert where only a little fresh fruit is needed to complete the picture? The simple answer to all these questions is yes, and with lots of testing under our belts, we're comfortable saying it's not as difficult as we thought.

We had two main goals in mind. First, we wanted to determine if the desserts in this chapter should be baked before storing (and then reheated when ready to serve) or stored raw and simply popped into the oven at a moment's notice. We also wanted to find the best way to store these desserts—in the refrigerator, the freezer, or even on the countertop—until ready to serve, be it an hour, a day, a week, or in some cases a month. And we wanted to do all this without compromising flavor, texture, or quality.

Of course we did have our challenges along the way, particularly when it came time to store these desserts in the freezer. While developing a recipe for crème brûlée, we tried freezing the cooked custard for future use, but when thawed the custard looked like scrambled eggs. We also tried storing the baked blackberry-walnut buckles in the freezer, then thawing them to serve, but ultimately found that they were far better when baked right from the freezer, then served while still warm.

Our challenges led to some discoveries about the best way to store these desserts. We already knew that pound cake becomes drier in the refrigerator and stays moist on the countertop, but we

also found that it freezes perfectly and stays this way for up to a month. And individual molten chocolate cakes freeze better than they refrigerate and the resulting colder batter allows the baker a more relaxed window of opportunity to pull the cakes out of the oven with a still-molten center.

As we know, some desserts must be made ahead of time, such as a cheesecake that needs to set up in the refrigerator overnight, or a flourless chocolate cake that would otherwise fall apart without time in the refrigerator. But who would have guessed these two particular desserts freeze great too? A taste test of both frozen and refrigerated cheesecakes and flourless chocolate cakes revealed no differences between the two storage methods and in fact, some tasters preferred the frozen version. The trick here is to allow them to properly thaw in the refrigerator overnight before serving.

Other desserts are best enjoyed straight from the oven (think molten chocolate cake). Our dilemma here was whether to freeze the cakes raw or to cook them, store them, and then reheat when ready to serve. This required a lot of testing and tasting (not that we were complaining). At the end of all that testing, we concluded that freezing the batter and then putting it into the oven straight from the freezer yields results that are as good as if it were made fresh that day (although if baking the same day, these desserts can sit in the refrigerator for up to eight hours).

In fact, with the exception of chocolate mousse and custards (panna cotta and crème brûlée), *all* the desserts in this chapter last in the freezer for up to one month, suffering no degradation of flavor or texture.

You'll also find some extremely versatile desserts, great to serve with fruit, whipped cream, or just a simple flourish of confectioners' sugar. A prime example is a pound cake with several flavor variations and an assortment of glaze options. And an authentic Italian almond cake is simple and rustic—a great vehicle for your favorite sauce or fruit, but just as enticing with a sprinkling of confectioners' sugar. The only last-minute preparation required is some thawing time in the refrigerator and a brief stint in the oven to take off the chill.

In the end we achieved our goals. Our panel

of tasters and test cooks suffered through countless comparisons of fresh versus frozen desserts, day-after-day tastings of refrigerated sweets, and meticulous judgment of cakes left at room temperature. All of our desserts in this chapter were highly praised for their ability to stand the test of time. We couldn't have asked for a better testament to our hard work. Now we can make our dessert and eat it too—whenever we want!

PANNA COTTA

THOUGH ITS NAME IS LYRICAL, THE LITERAL translation of panna cotta, "cooked cream," does nothing to suggest its ethereal qualities or the actual method by which it is made. In fact, panna cotta is not cooked at all. Neither is it complicated with eggs, as is a custard. Instead, sugar and gelatin are melted in cream and milk, and the whole is poured into individual ramekins and chilled. Even better, this simple-to-prepare dessert *requires* advance preparation—it has to chill in the refrigerator until the gelatin is set—and it can remain in the fridge for a few days until ready to serve. It calls for few ingredients, comes together quickly, and forms a rich but neutral backdrop for any number of accompaniments: strawberry coulis, fresh raspberries, or light caramel or chocolate sauce.

That said, we've certainly had our share of subpar versions that run the gamut from watery and flat-tasting to chewy and tough. With such a simple and short ingredient list, it was clear that a great panna cotta required a careful balancing act. Our mission, therefore, was to determine the correct proportions for the four main ingredients: cream, milk, sugar, and gelatin. Once this careful balance was achieved, we would test the storage limits of this delicate dessert. We knew that the gelatin would play an important role in determining the longevity of this dessert—if we allowed the gelatin to set for too long, a creamy, delicate panna cotta would become an unappealing rubbery disk.

We began by preparing five recipes from well-known Italian cookbooks. Each of them used similar ingredients (in varying proportions) and techniques. But after tasting the recipes, it was clear they fell into two groups. Those with higher proportions of milk were slippery and translucent, their flavor elusive and flat. Those with more cream had a rich texture and creamier, more rounded flavor. What united these recipes most noticeably, however, was a slightly rubbery chew—the result of too much gelatin.

Focusing on the gelatin first, we began to build a working recipe around a single packet, thinking that would simplify matters. The next step was to establish the correct proportion of liquid for this amount of gelatin. Starting with a 3-to-1 ratio of cream to milk (a ratio we found in many recipes) for a total of 4 cups liquid, we made batch after batch of panna cotta.

After making several panna cotta recipes, we were surprised to find textural inconsistencies between batches that should have been identical. Some were flabby, while others were stalwart. Upon closer inspection, we realized that the amount of gelatin in a packet is not at all consistent but varies widely from one packet to another. In fact, in two packages of gelatin (each containing four packets), we found eight different weights. Realizing we would have to measure the gelatin by the teaspoonful, we pressed on.

Starting with 2 teaspoons of gelatin, we gradually increased the amount in increments of ⅛ teaspoon, all the way up to 3 teaspoons. We found that 2½ teaspoons produced a firm enough yet still fragile finished texture after 4 hours. Tasters all agreed that this was a good texture for panna cotta, yet on the looser end of things. Now we

> **TEST KITCHEN TIP:**
> **Measuring Gelatin**
> When making a texture-sensitive dessert like panna cotta, we found measuring the gelatin in teaspoons (instead of by the packet) to be the only reliable way. Envelope packets of gelatin contain imprecise amounts; in fact, in two separate gelatin packages (each containing four individual packets) we found eight different weights with discrepancies as great as 20 percent. We also found that when a recipe calls for an envelope of gelatin, it typically requires 2½ teaspoons. So dump a couple of envelopes into a bowl and get out your measuring spoons.

Gelatin is a flavorless, nearly colorless substance derived from the collagen in connective tissue and bones, extracted commercially and dehydrated. It works on the same principle as in a meat stew that you put in the fridge hot and remove the next day as a solid one-piece mosaic. When you reheat the stew, the collagen melts and the stew reverts to its liquid state. Commercial gelatin begins dry in granular or leaf form and must first be rehydrated in cool liquid—where it absorbs about three times its weight—then melted, and finally cooled. Gelatin has clout when cold. Depending on the length of cooling time and the concentration of the solution, gelatin molecules form anything from a web-like gel—in the case of panna cotta, for example—to a solid block that can be cut with a knife (as illustrated by cafeteria Jell-O cubes).

wanted to see how long panna cotta with this amount of gelatin would hold in the refrigerator before becoming tough and unappealing. Each day, we unmolded a panna cotta, carefully jiggled it on the plate, and tested it for firmness and flavor. After one day the gelatin had tightened noticeably from its first taste (after just four hours), yet tasters all agreed this firmer version was still within the range of acceptability. Each day after that, we followed the same pattern, and each day the texture and flavor of the panna cotta remained exactly the same. That is, until day six, at which point tasters thought this creamy dessert developed a rubbery texture and tasted "off."

Pleased with our large window for storage and with the ratios of the main ingredients determined, we moved on to fine-tuning our technique. Because cold temperatures hasten gelatin's response (firming a liquid to a gel) it seemed reasonable to keep most of the liquid cold. Why heat all the milk and cream when we needed just enough hot liquid to melt the gelatin and sugar? We gave the milk this assignment, pouring it into a saucepan, sprinkling the gelatin over it, and then giving the gelatin 10 minutes to swell and absorb the liquid before heating. We then heated the mixture just enough to melt the gelatin (it sustains damage at high temperatures) and added the sugar off the heat to dissolve.

To do its job, melted gelatin must be mixed with the other recipe ingredients while its molecules have enough heat energy to move through the mixture. By combining ingredients hastily in the past, we had often precipitated gelatin seizures, causing the melted gelatin to harden into chewy strings, which ruined the texture of the dessert. So we stirred the cold cream slowly into the milk to temper it.

Several test cooks in the kitchen have learned to stir gelatin-based desserts over an ice bath—allowing the gelatin to thicken somewhat under gentle agitation—before refrigerating them to set. This process is supposed to produce a finer finished texture. Hoping to avoid this step in a recipe that was otherwise so easy, we presented tasters with side-by-side creams, one stirred first over ice and one simply refrigerated. They unanimously preferred the texture of the panna cotta chilled over ice, describing it as lighter, creamier, and smoother. Given the stellar results, the extra 10 minutes required did not seem unreasonable.

All our panna cotta needed now was a subtle flavor accent, and whole vanilla bean was just the thing. Lemon zest and juice were also bright and refreshing additions, so we decided to make that a variation. At last we had a true make-ahead panna cotta, one that could be made several days in advance. And with our simple, streamlined technique, we can make it whenever the mood strikes.

REMOVING SEEDS FROM A VANILLA BEAN

Place the knife at one end of a bean half and press down to flatten the bean as you move the knife away from you, catching the seeds on the edge of the blade.

Panna Cotta

SERVES 8

If your vanilla bean is shriveled and dried out you will want to use a slightly longer piece; 2 teaspoons of vanilla extract can be substituted for the vanilla bean seeds. Though traditionally chilled in ramekins and then unmolded onto a plate for serving, the panna cotta can also be served in the ramekins (or use wine glasses). Serve panna cotta very cold with Berry Coulis (below) or lightly sweetened berries.

1	cup whole milk
2½	teaspoons unflavored gelatin
1	(2-inch) piece vanilla bean, slit lengthwise with a paring knife
3	cups heavy cream
6	tablespoons (3½ ounces) sugar
	Pinch salt

1. Pour the milk into a medium saucepan. Sprinkle the gelatin evenly over the milk and let stand to hydrate, about 10 minutes.

2. Meanwhile, scrape the seeds from the vanilla bean following the illustration on page 346. Combine the vanilla seeds, vanilla bean pod, and cream together in a large measuring cup; set aside. Set eight 4-ounce ramekins on a baking sheet and set aside. Make a large bowl of ice water using 2 trays ice cubes and 4 cups cold water.

3. Heat the milk and gelatin mixture over high heat, stirring constantly, until the gelatin is dissolved and the mixture registers 135 degrees on an instant-read thermometer, about 1½ minutes. Off the heat, stir in the sugar and salt until dissolved, about 1 minute. Stirring constantly, slowly add the cream and vanilla mixture.

4. Transfer the mixture to a medium bowl and

Berry Coulis

Coulis is simply sweetened fruit pureed into a sauce, and it's an ideal accompaniment to a variety of desserts such as Panna Cotta (above), New York–Style Cheesecake (page 372), Lemon Pound Cake (page 367), or Flourless Chocolate Cake (page 363). Because the types of berries used as well as their ripeness will affect the sweetness of the coulis, the amount of sugar is variable. Start with 5 tablespoons, then add more to taste. Additional sugar should be stirred in immediately after straining, while the coulis is still warm, so that the sugar will readily dissolve. This recipe makes about 1½ cups, enough to accompany any of the desserts mentioned above.

12	ounces (2½ to 3 cups) fresh or thawed frozen raspberries, blueberries, blackberries, or sliced strawberries
¼	cup water, plus extra as needed for serving
5–7	tablespoons sugar
⅛	teaspoon salt
2	teaspoons juice from 1 lemon

1. Bring the berries, ¼ cup water, 5 tablespoons of the sugar, and salt to a simmer in a medium nonreactive saucepan over medium heat. Cook, stirring occasionally, until the sugar is dissolved and the berries are heated through, about 1 minute.

2. Transfer the mixture to a blender or food processor and puree until smooth, about 20 seconds. Strain through a fine-mesh strainer into a small bowl, pressing and stirring the puree with a rubber spatula to extract as much seedless puree as possible. Stir in the lemon juice and additional sugar, if desired.

3. TO STORE: Cover with plastic wrap and refrigerate for up to 4 days or freeze in an airtight container for up to 1 month. (If frozen, thaw the coulis overnight in the refrigerator before serving.)

4. TO SERVE: Stir the coulis to recombine, adding 1 teaspoon of water at a time as needed to adjust the consistency.

TO SERVE RIGHT AWAY

After adding the lemon juice and additional sugar, serve as directed in step 4.

set the bowl gently into the ice water. Let the mixture chill, stirring frequently, until it has thickened to the consistency of eggnog and registers 50 degrees on an instant-read thermometer, about 10 minutes. Strain the mixture into a pitcher, then pour it evenly into the ramekins.

5. To STORE: Cover each ramekin with plastic wrap, making sure that the plastic does not mar the surface of the cream and refrigerate for up to 5 days.

6. To SERVE: Unwrap the panna cotta and run a paring knife between the custard and the side of the ramekin in 1 smooth stroke. Flip the ramekins upside down onto individual serving plates. Shake the ramekins gently to unmold the panna cotta and lift the ramekins from the plate.

TO SERVE RIGHT AWAY
Refrigerate the panna cotta as directed in step 5 until just set and chilled, about 4 hours, then serve as directed in step 6.

➤ VARIATION
Lemon Panna Cotta
The easiest way to make chopped lemon zest is to peel off several strips of lemon zest, then chop them up; be sure that the zest is chopped quite coarse so that it can be easily strained out.

Follow the recipe for Panna Cotta, increasing the amount of gelatin to 2¾ teaspoons. Add 2 tablespoons coarsely chopped lemon zest to the cream with the vanilla seeds and pod in step 2. Stir ¼ cup fresh lemon juice into the thickened mixture before pouring it into the ramekins in step 4.

CRÈME BRÛLÉE
WITH ITS CRACKLE-CRISP CARAMELIZED SUGAR crust and creamy custard, this show stopping dessert (and restaurant classic) is actually quite easy to make at home. And we knew it was a solid make-ahead choice, as the custard requires time to chill and set. But we had some questions nonetheless: How long would it keep? Could it be frozen? Was it possible to form the caramelized crust before storing, thus eliminating any last-minute work?

Before answering these questions, we first wanted to uncover the secrets to a great crème brûlée, one with a rich, smooth, flavorful custard and delicate but crispy crust.

First we turned to the issue of the all-important egg. Firmer custard, like that in crème caramel, is made with whole eggs, which help the custard to achieve a clean-cutting quality. Crème brûlée is richer and softer—with a pudding-like, spoon-clinging texture—in part because of the exclusive use of yolks. With 4 cups of heavy cream as the dairy for the moment, we went to work. The custard refused to set at all with only six yolks; with eight (a common number for the amount of cream we were using) it was better, but still rather slurpy. With 10 yolks we struck gold. It was a surprisingly large number of yolks, but the custard now had a lilting texture and rich flavor.

Moving on to the sugar, we tested quantities ranging from ½ cup to ¾ cup. Two-thirds cup was the winner; with more sugar the crème brûlée was too saccharine, and with less the simple egg and cream flavors tasted muted and dull. We also found that a pinch of salt heightened all of the flavors and that a vanilla bean was superior to extract.

With the proportions in place, we turned our attention to cooking technique. Nearly all crème brûlée recipes instruct the cook to scald the cream before gradually whisking it into the yolks. When compared, a started-cold custard and a scalded-cream custard displayed startling differences. The former had a silkier, smoother texture. Custard research explained that eggs respond favorably to cooking at a slow, gentle pace. If heated quickly, they set only just shortly before they enter the overcooked zone, leaving a very narrow window between just right and overdone. If heated gently, however, they begin to thicken the custard at a lower temperature and continue to do so gradually until it, too, eventually overcooks.

The downside to starting with cold ingredients is that unless the cream is heated, it is impossible to extract all the flavor from a vanilla bean and the sugar will not dissolve. But scalding the cream and sugar, steeping the vanilla, and then refrigerating the mixture until cold seemed like an overwrought process, so we tested a hybrid technique. We heated

THE "BRÛLÉE" IN CRÈME BRÛLÉE

Carefully ignite the torch, then lower it until the end of the flame is about 1 inch from the sprinkled sugar. Hold the flame in place until you see the sugar melt and burn to a caramel color, then move along to the next patch of unburnt sugar repeating the process until the entire custard has a deep golden crust.

only half the cream with the sugar and the vanilla bean. After a 15-minute off-heat steep to extract flavor from the vanilla bean, we added the remaining cold cream to bring the temperature down before whisking it into the yolks. This technique created a custard with a fineness equal to the one started cold—and it baked in less time, too.

We quickly determined that a 300-degree oven and a water bath (which prevents the periphery of a custard from overcooking) were the ideal conditions for baking the custards. The golden rule of custards is that they must not be overcooked lest they lose their smooth, silken texture and become grainy and curdled. An instant-read thermometer will tell you when the custards should come out of the oven, which is between 170 and 175 degrees. (If you do not have a thermometer, look at the center of the custard. It should be barely set—shaky but not sloshy.) The custard will continue to cook from residual heat once out of the oven. Then, a deep chill helps to solidify things.

For the crackly caramel crust, we tried brown sugar, regular granulated sugar, and turbinado and Demerara sugars (the latter two are coarse light brown sugars). Because brown sugar is moist and lumpy, recipes often recommend drying it in a low oven and crushing it to break up lumps. We found that it just isn't worth the effort. Turbinado and Demerara sugars were superior to granulated only because their coarseness makes them easy to

distribute evenly over the custards. A torch accomplishes the task of caramelizing most efficiently. A hardware-store propane torch is the tool of choice, but a small butane kitchen torch, available in cookware stores, can do the job, just at a more leisurely pace.

In the process of being "brûléed," we found that the custard unavoidably warmed a bit. In standard round ramekins, usually only the upper third of the custard is affected. But in shallow dishes (our favorite for their higher ratio of crust to custard), the custard can be completely warmed through. In our opinion, a warm custard can ruin an otherwise perfect crème brûlée. To remedy this problem, we refrigerated the finished crème brûlées and found that the crust maintained its crackly texture for up to 30 minutes—but no longer.

We decided to see how well the cooked custard would hold up in the refrigerator or freezer without its crust. After one day, the refrigerated custard was great—the crust still set up and shattered perfectly. The frozen custard, however, was a disaster. The eggs looked like they had scrambled and the custard became watery, making it difficult to get a good crust. With the freezer option out, we forged ahead with the refrigerated custards and continued to taste them each day for up to one week. Tasters were still raving about the texture and flavor of the crème brûlée through day four, but after that, the custards started showing their age so we stopped there. But now that the only last-minute prep work was caramelizing the sugar, we had an elegant and impressive dessert we could serve at the most hectic of gatherings.

Crème Brûlée

SERVES 8

Two teaspoons of vanilla extract, whisked into the yolks in step 4, can be substituted for the vanilla bean. The best way to judge doneness is with a digital instant-read thermometer. The custards, especially if baked in shallow fluted dishes, will not be deep enough to provide an accurate reading with a dial-face thermometer. For the caramelized sugar crust, we recommend turbinado or Demerara sugar. Regular granulated sugar will work, too, but use only 1 scant teaspoon on each ramekin or 1½ teaspoons on each shallow fluted dish. If your oven has a history of uneven heating, the custards may finish at different rates, so it is advisable to check each one separately rather than take the whole lot out at once.

1	vanilla bean, slit lengthwise with a paring knife
4	cups heavy cream, chilled
⅔	cup (4⅔ ounces) granulated sugar
	Pinch salt
10	large egg yolks
8–12	teaspoons turbinado or Demerara sugar

1. Adjust an oven rack to the lower-middle position and heat the oven to 300 degrees. Place a kitchen towel on the bottom of a large baking dish or roasting pan and arrange eight 4- to 5-ounce ramekins (or shallow fluted dishes) on the towel; set aside. Bring a kettle of water to a boil over high heat.

2. Scrape the seeds from the vanilla bean following the illustration on page 346. Combine the vanilla seeds, vanilla bean pod, 2 cups of the cream, granulated sugar, and salt together in a medium saucepan and bring to a boil over medium heat, stirring occasionally to dissolve the sugar. Remove the pan from the heat and let steep to infuse the flavors, about 15 minutes.

3. After the cream has steeped, stir in the remaining 2 cups cream to cool down the mixture. Whisk the yolks together in a large bowl until uniform. Whisk about 1 cup of the cream mixture into the yolks until loosened and combined; repeat with 1 more cup of the cream. Add the remaining cream and whisk until evenly colored and thoroughly combined. Strain through a fine-mesh strainer into a 2-quart measuring cup or pitcher, discarding the solids. Pour or ladle the mixture evenly into the ramekins.

4. Gently place the baking dish with the ramekins on the oven rack. Pour the boiling water into the baking dish, being careful not to splash any water into the ramekins, until the water reaches two-thirds the height of the ramekins. Bake until the centers of the custards are just barely set and are no longer sloshy and a digital instant-read thermometer inserted in the centers registers 170

to 175 degrees, 30 to 35 minutes (25 to 30 minutes for shallow fluted dishes). Begin checking the temperature about 5 minutes before the recommended time.

5. Transfer the ramekins from the baking dish to a wire rack and let cool to room temperature, about 2 hours.

6. TO STORE: Wrap each ramekin tightly with plastic wrap and refrigerate for up to 4 days.

7. TO SERVE: Unwrap the ramekins; if condensation has collected on the custards, place a paper towel on the surface to soak up the moisture. Sprinkle each custard with about 1 teaspoon turbinado sugar (1½ teaspoons for shallow fluted dishes); tilt and tap the ramekin for even coverage. Ignite a torch and, following the manufacturer's instructions, caramelize the sugar by holding the end of the flame about 1 inch from the surface of the custard until the sugar melts, then burns to a golden brown, proceeding the same way until the entire surface is deeply golden brown and hard. Refrigerate the ramekins, uncovered, to rechill, about 30 minutes (but no longer).

TO SERVE RIGHT AWAY
Chill the baked custards as directed in step 6 until they are set, about 4 hours, before serving as directed in step 7.

TEST KITCHEN TIP: Ensuring Good Grip for Tongs

We recommend the use of tongs to remove ramekins of custard from a water bath. Cooks who worry about the ramekins slipping in the tongs can try this tip: Slip rubber bands around each of the 2 tong pincers, and the sticky rubber will provide a surer grip.

EQUIPMENT: Torches

Fire up a torch to caramelize the sugar on your crème brûlée—it's the best way to put the crowning glory of a crust on the custard. We tested a hardware-store propane torch ($27) against four petite kitchen torches (prices ranged from $30 to $40) fueled by butane.

The propane torch, with its powerful flame, caramelized the sugar quickly and easily, but it's admittedly not for the faint-hearted. Although easy to wield, a propane torch puts out a lot of heat and works in just seconds, so you must work very carefully. (In contrast, the kitchen torches took about one minute to brûlée each custard.) If you opt for a propane torch, make sure to buy a model with a built-in trigger that does not need to be held in place for the torch to remain lit. The most widely available brand, BernzOmatic, worked well in our kitchen tests.

Among the four butane-powered kitchen torches we tested, only one is worth owning. The BernzOmatic Torch ST1100T ($29.95) has a plastic flame adjuster that is clearly marked and stayed cool enough to handle without burning our fingers. This torch was also the most intuitive and easy to operate.

The remaining models had flaws. The safety lock on the RSVP Culinary Butane Torch ($29.95) was difficult to engage, and the air intake port became red-hot with use. The metal flame-width adjuster on the Bonjour Torch ($29.95) must be held in place during use, but it became very hot to the touch. Finally, although the Messermeister Chefflame Culinary Torch ($39.95) generated the most powerful flame of the kitchen torches tested, testers needed to use both hands to switch it on and found its large size awkward.

THE BEST TORCHES

With its powerful flame, the BernzOmatic propane torch (right) will brûlée custard in seconds. If you don't want to use such a powerful torch, the BernzOmatic kitchen torch (left) is the best butane option. Just make sure to purchase a can of butane along with it: otherwise, you'll have more luck "brûléeing" with a book of matches. The smaller torch is available in many cookware stores. Most hardware stores stock the BernzOmatic propane torch.

CHOCOLATE MOUSSE

IN OUR EXPERIENCE, CHOCOLATE MOUSSE IS not a natural make-ahead dessert—its light, airy, and delicate texture is like a ticking time bomb, waiting to deflate. Too many times, we've watched the life cycle of a chocolate mousse barely outpace the dinner guests' stay. It's true there are some chocolate mousses that have lasting power, but they usually have the texture of ganache—much too rich and dense to be a proper mousse. We wanted a recipe for make-ahead mousse that didn't compromise our idea of what chocolate mousse should be: light and meltingly smooth in texture with serious chocolate flavor.

Whisking our way through the gamut of chocolate mousse recipes, we were struck by the wide variations in texture achieved with the same simple ingredients: chocolate, eggs, sugar, and fat (in the form of butter and/or cream). Proportions and handling, apparently, were all that separated thick ganache from fluffy pudding—with the perfect chocolate mousse somewhere in between these two extremes. It seemed logical to start with an average working recipe: Melt chocolate in a double boiler; whisk in egg yolks, butter, and heavy cream (for richness and smoothness); beat egg whites with sugar; then fold the soft peaks into the mixture (for silkiness). After a few hours in the fridge, the resulting mousse was a fine start, but it was still too dense, and the modest 4 ounces of chocolate little more than a tease.

Before embarking on the chocolate rampage we had planned, we decided to take a crack at lightening the dense texture. Of the recipe's six ingredients, butter, chocolate, cream, and egg yolks were all likely culprits for adding heaviness. We already knew we wanted more chocolate, not less, so we focused on the other ingredients—in particular, the butter. Tasters had complained about a residual "waxy slickness" in the first few batches we made, and sure enough, when the butter was incrementally decreased—and, ultimately, eliminated—the texture lightened considerably and the waxiness was gone.

Although our mousse now had a lighter texture, it still retained an unwelcome billowy, marshmallow-like quality. Simply reducing the number of egg whites from four to two took the texture from airy to silky. But now four yolks seemed like too many. By scaling the yolks down to two also, we achieved a lighter, yet still-creamy mousse. Whipping the heavy cream to soft peaks before adding it to the chocolate made up for some of the lost volume without reintroducing the "marshmallow effect."

Armed with a shopping cart's worth of bittersweet chocolate, we set about steadily increasing the amount in search of this mousse's breaking point. Since many recipes we found call for a paltry 4 ounces of chocolate, we started our testing with 6 ounces. Mmm, nice—but nice wasn't good

THE PERFECT MOUSSE TEXTURE

There are as many different mousse textures as there are mousse recipes. Here's how some of them look.

Dense: Butter, unwhipped cream, and too much chocolate are often the culprits in heavy, ganache-like mousse.

Fluffy: Too many whipped egg whites produce an unappealing "marshmallow effect."

Perfect: Going easy on the egg whites, omitting the butter, and adding a small amount of water yield just the right texture.

enough. Seven ounces. Eight ounces. Nine ounces. At 9 ounces, it was time to regroup. The texture was suffering—it had become too thick—and the mousse was now too sweet. We reduced the sugar (beaten with the egg whites) from 2 tablespoons down to 1. Better, but the dramatic increase in chocolate was still wreaking havoc on the texture.

We retreated to 8 ounces but immediately missed the more powerful flavor. Then it hit us: What about a second form of chocolate? Adding 1 ounce of unsweetened chocolate made the mousse starchy and heavy. Two tablespoons of Dutch-processed cocoa powder, on the other hand, gave the mousse a fuller, more vibrant chocolate flavor, but now it had a gritty texture. Having removed the butter and two of the egg yolks from our recipe, the liquid-to-solid ratio had become too heavy on solids, resulting in a grainy texture.

To increase the liquid side of things we started adding water, 1 tablespoon at a time. At 8 tablespoons, we were starting to undo the depth of flavor we had achieved; at 6 tablespoons, the texture was almost perfect—light, ethereal, and chock-full of chocolate. Tinkering once again with the cream, we found that an additional 2 tablespoons further lightened the mousse without masking its deep, dark profile.

All our chocolate mousse needed now was some finessing in terms of flavor notes. In many other chocolate recipes, we have found that a small amount of instant espresso powder intensifies the chocolate experience. The trick worked here as well. One teaspoon added to the chocolate-cocoa-water mixture provided just the right boost. A mere ⅛ teaspoon of salt rounded out the mild sweetness. Tasters rejected vanilla for lending unwelcome floral notes to the mousse, but brandy was popular and favored over rum and bourbon. Just 1 tablespoon of the stuff (replacing an equal amount of water) added complexity without booziness.

With the finishing touches in place, we now had a silky, smooth mousse with a full, rich chocolate flavor. And with all that cocoa butter to lend structure, we knew our mousse would keep well in the refrigerator, but just how long could it hold up? With fingers crossed we tested our final recipe, tasting the mousse each day, all the way up to one week after it had been made. The result? Not bad, but by the end of one week the mousse was starting to show its age. The first four days, however, yielded a perfect mousse every day. This chocolate mousse suffered no textural or flavor changes by being made ahead of time. The only trick to perfect texture was to set the mousse out 10 minutes before serving to come to room temperature. (As for freezing, it took only one attempt to abandon that line of testing—the resulting mousse was a shapeless, separated, gritty mess.) Finally we had exactly the make-ahead chocolate mousse we were looking for. Rich but not dense, chocolaty but not cloying, light and silky but not unsubstantial, and all with time to spare.

Dark Chocolate Mousse

MAKES 3½ CUPS, SERVING 6 TO 8

When developing this recipe, we used our winning supermarket brand of dark chocolate, Ghirardelli bittersweet, which contains about 60 percent cacao. If using a boutique brand of bittersweet chocolate that has a higher percent of cacao, follow the recipe for Premium Dark Chocolate Mousse below. Serve this mousse with very lightly sweetened whipped cream and chocolate shavings.

8	ounces bittersweet chocolate, chopped fine
2	tablespoons Dutch-processed cocoa powder
1	teaspoon instant espresso powder
5	tablespoons water
1	tablespoon brandy
2	large eggs, separated
1	tablespoon sugar
⅛	teaspoon salt
1	cup plus 2 tablespoons heavy cream, chilled

1. Combine the chocolate, cocoa powder, espresso powder, water, and brandy in a medium heatproof bowl set over a saucepan filled with 1 inch of barely simmering water, stirring frequently until smooth. Remove from the heat.

2. Whisk the egg yolks, 1½ teaspoons of the sugar, and salt in a medium bowl until the mixture lightens in color and thickens slightly, about

30 seconds. Pour the melted chocolate into the egg mixture and whisk until combined. Let cool until just warmer than room temperature, 3 to 5 minutes.

3. Using an electric mixer and a clean bowl, whip the egg whites at medium-low speed until frothy, 1 to 2 minutes. Add the remaining 1½ teaspoons sugar, increase the mixer speed to medium-high, and whip until soft peaks form when the whisk is lifted, 1 to 2 minutes. Whisk the last few strokes by hand, making sure to scrape any unwhipped whites from the bottom of the bowl.

4. Using a whisk, stir about one-quarter of the whipped egg whites into the chocolate mixture to lighten it; gently fold in the remaining egg whites with a rubber spatula until just a few white streaks remain.

5. Using an electric mixer, whip the heavy cream at medium speed until it begins to thicken, about 30 seconds. Increase the speed to high and whisk until soft peaks form when the whisk is lifted, about 15 seconds more. Using a rubber spatula, fold the whipped cream into the mousse until no white streaks remain. Spoon the mousse into 6 to 8 individual serving dishes or goblets.

6. TO STORE: Cover the glasses with plastic wrap and refrigerate for up to 4 days.

7. TO SERVE: Unwrap the glasses and allow the mousse to soften at room temperature for 10 minutes before serving.

TO SERVE RIGHT AWAY

Refrigerate the mousse as directed in step 6 until firm, about 2 hours, then serve as directed in step 7.

➤ VARIATION

Premium Dark Chocolate Mousse

This recipe is designed to work with a boutique chocolate that contains a higher percentage (62 to 70 percent) of cacao than the Ghirardelli chocolate recommended in our Dark Chocolate Mousse.

Follow the recipe for Dark Chocolate Mousse, increasing the amount of eggs to 3 and adding 2 additional tablespoons of water and 2 tablespoons of sugar to the chocolate in step 1.

INDIVIDUAL FRUIT BUCKLES

JUST WHAT IS A BUCKLE? IT'S AN AMERICAN classic—a streusel-topped coffeecake, traditionally blueberry. To call it a mere coffeecake, however, is to sell it short. The substance of a fruit buckle is the fruit, not the cake. This rustic confection starts with berries held together in a buttery cake batter, which is then topped with a crisp, sugary streusel. And the name? The cake, burdened as it is with fruit and topping, is said to buckle on the surface as it bakes.

Although typically served for breakfast, a streusel-topped cake filled with fruit sounds like dessert to us, and we wanted to develop the best possible version. We suspected this sort of dessert would hold well in the refrigerator or freezer, but we still had a few questions: Did we really need the sugary streusel topping typically associated with a breakfast cake? How far in advance could we make them? And would we have to bake them before storing, or could we simply store the batter and bake the buckle right before serving?

We collected dozens of recipes for buckle (mostly blueberry) and immediately put six of them to the test. They were a ragtag collection of cakes—some were lean and dry but most dense and greasy. Not to mention bland. The problem? It seemed that an overwhelming berry-to-cake ratio was throwing things out of whack. The moisture released from the berries during baking often added a disagreeable sogginess.

We cobbled together a working recipe, with a batter made in the manner of a cake or cookie: The butter and sugar are creamed, the eggs beaten in, the flour added, and then the berries folded in. Hoping to streamline the process a bit, we tried a melted butter variation, but it had less rise—the result of a lack of aeration, which provides lift. We then thought of a food processor and wondered if we could use it to achieve the same effect as the standard method of creaming with an electric mixer. We processed the butter and sugar together, then added the eggs, followed by the flour. This worked great.

Moving on to the berries, we made a decision to use blackberries, which we felt would stand up to the batter well. We set out to determine just how many were needed to give the cake full berry flavor without weighing it down and making it soggy. The recipes we found called for as little as 1 cup to as many as 4 cups. According to tasters, even 2 cups weren't enough. Two and a half cups? Better. Three? Bingo. Now the berries were the headliner, with the cake in a supporting role. But the cake was still a bit soggy. Looking for a solution, we wondered if the type of flour we were using might be a factor. Up to this point we had been using cake flour, which is low in protein. This was leaving the buckles somewhat structureless, pasty, and sodden. A buckle made with all-purpose flour, however, was drier and cakier, with a sturdy texture that could contend with all the fruit. Problem solved.

Dairy—milk, cream, or sour cream—is often found in buckle recipes. We tested all three and liked the flavor and richness of the cream, which we added to the food processor with the eggs. Sugar was an even simpler matter. The buckle needed some sugar to counter the tart berries and because we were going to be serving ours for dessert rather than breakfast, we upped the amount to a substantial ¾ cup.

With such a generous amount of sugar in the cake, we began to wonder if we really needed the streusel topping. Instead, we tried substituting a sprinkling of chopped nuts on top. Tasters loved this approach, especially since the flavor of the nuts bloomed while they toasted in the oven. We liked it even more because skipping the streusel step allowed us to streamline our recipe. But tasters felt we needed to have some nuts in the batter as well, to tie the flavors together. Blackberries and walnuts are a classic combination, so we pulsed the walnuts in the food processor to grind them. We removed half of them for the topping and left the rest in the food processor to incorporate into the batter. The flavors were now well rounded, but tasters wanted all the nuts toasted. Since we couldn't put toasted walnuts on top of the batter (because they'd over-toast while cooking), we toasted only the nuts that would go into the batter. The other walnuts were chopped with a knife, left untoasted, and sprinkled on top of the cake to toast during the baking process. Now we had the flavor of blackberries and toasted walnuts in every bite.

These buckles baked through and the topping browned perfectly in just 30 minutes at 375 degrees. We found that they could be refrigerated for up to three days. The cakes also had enough structure so that they could be frozen, then thawed and heated, with little change in texture. Unfortunately, the flavors were muted. We tried freezing the batter before it was cooked and then popping them in the oven straight from the freezer, but the exterior of the buckles overcooked by the time the inside was done. This problem was easily solved by letting the buckles rest at room temperature for just 30 minutes. These buckles were a big improvement in flavor. The batter softened enough to cook evenly and it took no extra time to cook these buckles to perfection—surprising yet streamlined.

So there it was. An easy-to-make cake that was strong enough to support a lot of berries. In fact, this buckle didn't really buckle during baking; it could hold its own. Now do we have to change its name?

FREEZE IT

Individual Blackberry-Walnut Buckles

SERVES 8

You can substitute 3 cups of frozen blackberries, thawed, drained, and patted dry, for the fresh berries. The buckles can be served in their ramekins. Serve warm with vanilla ice cream or lightly sweetened whipped cream.

½	cup walnuts, chopped coarse
4	tablespoons (½ stick) unsalted butter, softened
¾	cup (5¼ ounces) sugar
¼	teaspoon salt
⅓	cup heavy cream
2	large eggs
I	teaspoon vanilla extract
¾	cup (3¾ ounces) unbleached all-purpose flour
½	teaspoon baking powder
3	cups (about 16 ounces) fresh blackberries

1. Lightly coat eight 6-ounce ramekins with vegetable oil spray and place on a rimmed baking sheet; set aside. Toast ¼ cup of the walnuts in a small, dry skillet over medium heat until lightly toasted and aromatic, 3 to 4 minutes; let cool.

2. Process the toasted walnuts, butter, sugar, and salt in the food processor until finely ground, 10 to 15 seconds. With the processor running, add the cream, eggs, and vanilla through the feed tube and continue to process until smooth, about 5 seconds. Add the flour and baking powder and pulse until just incorporated, about 5 pulses.

3. Transfer the batter to a large bowl and gently fold in the blackberries. Spoon the batter into the prepared ramekins and sprinkle the top of each cobbler with the remaining ¼ cup walnuts.

4. TO STORE: Wrap each ramekin tightly with plastic wrap and then foil and refrigerate for up to 3 days or freeze for up to 1 month.

5. TO SERVE: Adjust an oven rack to the middle position and heat the oven to 375 degrees. (If frozen, let the buckles sit at room temperature for 30 minutes before baking.) Unwrap the buckles and place them on a baking sheet. Bake until golden and the buckles begin to pull away from the sides of the ramekins, 25 to 35 minutes.

TO SERVE RIGHT AWAY

After portioning the batter into the ramekins, bake the buckles as directed in step 5, reducing the baking time to 20 to 25 minutes.

➤ VARIATIONS

Individual Raspberry-Pistachio Buckles
Don't use frozen raspberries here because they are too mushy.

Follow the recipe for Individual Blackberry-Walnut Buckles, substituting ½ cup pistachios for the walnuts and 3 cups fresh raspberries for the blackberries.

Individual Cherry-Almond Buckles
Fresh pitted cherries or canned cherries, rinsed and patted dry, can be substituted for the frozen cherries.

Follow the recipe for Individual Blackberry-Walnut Buckles, substituting ½ cup sliced or slivered almonds for the walnuts, 3 cups frozen sweet cherries, thawed, drained, and patted dry, for the blackberries and 1 teaspoon almond extract for the vanilla extract.

APPLE TURNOVERS

WHEN YOU EAT A REALLY GOOD APPLE TURN-over, the flaky dough should shatter all over your plate (and yourself). Eating bad apple turnovers—the kind found in the freezer section of your supermarket—may be neater, but the experience couldn't be more disheartening. Bland, mushy filling and a soggy dough are just a couple of the pitfalls we've found. But the straight-from-the-freezer turnover is a great idea, at least in theory. Could we develop our own version—one that would result in a crisp, flaky exterior and warm apple interior? And could we streamline the recipe in the process?

Heading into the kitchen, we quickly made our first decision: We wouldn't be making puff pastry from scratch. Homemade puff pastry is extremely time-consuming to prepare, and we already knew that frozen puff pastry is a great time-saver. But although it makes turnovers easy to prepare, it doesn't ensure success. We tested a dozen apple turnover recipes and were met with mushy, messy, and mediocre results. Apparently, we would need to build our turnover from the inside out, and so we turned our attention to the filling.

Most recipes called for either sliced or shredded apples, but we found both to be unappealing. Sliced apples were undercooked or unevenly cooked, unless they were cut paper-thin—a real headache. Apples shredded on a box grater resulted in a more appealing texture, but unappealing appearance—the filling resembled little worms. Searching for a happy medium, we pulsed the apples and sugar in the food processor until the apples were roughly chopped. The varying chunkiness of the processed apples was great for texture and appearance, but now they exuded too much liquid and waterlogged the pastry.

We tried straining the apple mixture, but this left the filling dry and grainy. Cooking some of the apples created a cohesive filling and helped absorb excess moisture, but we wanted a simpler solution. Could we get away with a shortcut—store-bought applesauce—to produce the "cooked apple" texture? Sure enough, applesauce combined with the strained apple mixture gave us the right consistency and boosted the apple flavor. With a little lemon juice and a pinch of salt, this filling was just right.

We now turned our attention back to the pastry.

Over the years, we've learned that puff pastry works well as long as you play by its rules. For the perfect puff, the pastry must be cold and the oven hot—and since we were planning on pulling our turnovers straight from the freezer, cold pastry wouldn't be a problem. After assembling a batch, we placed them in the freezer for a couple of hours (until they were firm), then began testing oven temperatures. The turnovers baked at 400 degrees were the flakiest, with the nicest amount of rise. But there was still one problem to work out.

Most of the turnovers split at the seams while they baked. What we needed was some sort of "glue" to brush over the edges of the pastry before sealing. After glancing over at the draining apple mixture, we realized that we could use the juice from the apples; we'd been planning to throw it out anyway! The sticky, sugary juice made a great sealant. Taking it further, we brushed more of the apple juice over the top of the turnovers. This helped them to brown and a sprinkle of cinnamon sugar made them look as good as they tasted.

The new "glue" helped when these turnovers were freshly crimped and placed in the oven, but not when they were frozen first. The seams split in places again, allowing molten apple filling to ooze out. But by leaving the frozen turnovers on the counter for 20 minutes, long enough for the dough to soften a bit, we could recrimp them with a fork, reinforcing the seal. After 20 minutes in the oven, our turnovers emerged golden, crisp, and full of bright, tart apple flavor. Now when the desire for a warm apple dessert overcomes us, we can reach for a homemade turnover from our own freezer.

SEALING THE TURNOVERS

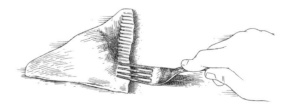

After placing the apple mixture into the center of each pastry square and brushing the edges of the squares with the reserved apple juice, bring one corner over the pastry to meet the opposite corner to form a triangle. Use a fork to crimp the edges and seal the turnovers.

Apple Turnovers

MAKES 8

If you don't have a food processor, grate the peeled apples on the coarse side of a box grater before mixing them with the lemon juice, sugar, and salt. (Grating results in a less attractive appearance, but the texture will be fine.)

¾ cup (5¼ ounces) sugar
I teaspoon ground cinnamon
2 Granny Smith apples, peeled, cored, and chopped coarse
I tablespoon juice from I lemon
⅛ teaspoon salt
½ cup applesauce
2 sheets frozen puff pastry (9 by 9½ inches), thawed overnight in the refrigerator
Flour for dusting the work surface

1. Line a baking sheet (or 2 large plates) with parchment paper and set aside. Combine ¼ cup of the sugar and cinnamon in a small bowl and set aside.

2. Pulse the apples, remaining ½ cup sugar, lemon juice, and salt in a food processor until chopped into pieces no larger than ½ inch, 8 to 10 pulses. Transfer the mixture to a fine-mesh strainer set over a bowl and let drain for 5 minutes, reserving the juices. Transfer the drained apple mixture to a medium bowl and stir in the applesauce.

3. Unfold 1 sheet of puff pastry onto a lightly floured work surface and roll it out to a 10-inch square. Cut the pastry into four 5-inch squares. Place 2 tablespoons of the apple mixture in the center of each square, brush the edges of the squares with the reserved apple juice, then fold and crimp following the illustration on page 356. Brush the tops of the turnovers with the reserved apple juice and sprinkle with the cinnamon sugar. Transfer the turnovers to the prepared baking sheet; repeat with the remaining pastry and apple mixture.

4. To STORE: Freeze the turnovers until firm, about 2 hours. Transfer the turnovers to a zipper-lock bag and freeze for up to 1 month.

5. To SERVE: Adjust 2 oven racks to the upper-middle and lower-middle positions and heat the oven to 400 degrees. Line 2 rimmed baking sheets with parchment paper. Place 4 turnovers on each baking sheet and let them sit at room temperature until the edges have softened, about 20 minutes. Recrimp the edges to seal and bake until well browned, 20 to 26 minutes, rotating and switching the baking sheets halfway through the baking time. Transfer the turnovers to a wire rack and let cool slightly, about 15 minutes, before serving.

TO SERVE RIGHT AWAY

Bake the turnovers as directed in step 5.

INDIVIDUAL MOLTEN CHOCOLATE CAKES

MOLTEN CHOCOLATE CAKE, USUALLY MADE IN individual portions, is a show stopping dessert featuring an intense buttery chocolate cake with an appealingly undercooked chocolate center. This cake became popular after appearing on countless restaurant menus. Having tasted this decadent dessert on a number of occasions, we became intrigued with the notion of turning what has become a restaurant classic into a practical dessert for home cooks—one that would be sure to impress guests at an elegant dinner party. But who wants to fuss with a dessert at the last minute? This restaurant favorite would only be worth creating at home if it could be made ahead of time and then baked just before serving. We knew that the ingredient list was short and figured that the techniques required to make it would be relatively simple, but since restaurant recipes rarely work at home, we suspected that a fair amount of work awaited us.

The first step was to understand exactly what we wanted in a molten chocolate cake. We started by baking three versions of the cake and asked tasters to rate them on taste and texture. One was baked in a tube pan (rather than in the typical individual ramekins) and had a delicate, soufflé-like texture that tasters appreciated, but it lacked intense chocolate richness. The second recipe was the heaviest of the lot, similar to an undercooked brownie. The third cake was the clear favorite, with the most intense chocolate flavor, a relatively light

GETTING THE TEXTURE RIGHT

Although acceptable in a standard cake, this texture is too dry for this recipe.

Just a bit of uncooked batter should ooze out of the center when the cake is cut.

A puddle of uncooked batter flowing out of the cake's center is unappealing.

texture, and a warm, runny center. We wanted a cake with the ethereal lightness of the first recipe, along with the rich chocolate flavor and gooey interior of the third cake.

Knowing the style of cake we were after, we had to decide on the basic preparation method. Melting the chocolate and butter together was a given, but from there we had two choices: We could whip the egg yolks and whites separately and then fold them together, or we could whip whole eggs and sugar to create a thick foam. The latter method proved superior, as it delivered the rich, moist texture we were looking for—and it was simpler. That left us with a recipe that consisted of melting chocolate and butter; whipping whole eggs, sugar, and flavorings into a foam; and then folding the two together.

Our next step was to determine the proper proportions for each ingredient. After considerable testing, we decided that ½ cup of melted butter made the dessert just moist enough. The amount of chocolate was highly variable in recipes

we researched, running from a mere 4 ounces to a whopping 12 ounces. Eight ounces provided a good jolt of chocolate without being overbearing. The eggs, however, were perhaps the most crucial element, affecting texture, richness, and moistness. We tested six whole eggs (giving a light and airy sponge-cake texture), four whole eggs plus four yolks (moist and dark), and the winning combination of four whole eggs plus one yolk (rich but light, moist, intense, and dark). And although some recipes use very little or no flour, we found a modest amount (2 tablespoons) gave the cake some structure and lift—making it less like fudge and more like a cake.

When baking these desserts in ramekins at 450 degrees, as called for in some recipes, we found that the tops were slightly burnt and the center was a bit too runny. At 350 degrees, the dessert took on a more cake-like quality, but was also drier. 400 degrees was best, yielding a light, cake-like perimeter around a moist well of intense, gooey chocolate. (When using a cake pan rather than ramekins, though, we found it best to set the oven at 375 degrees.)

We now had a great working recipe and all that was left to do was determine if it could be made ahead of time and stored—and if so, for how long? After all, if we couldn't do all the prep work in advance and just pop this dessert in the oven before serving, we knew we'd never make it when entertaining. (No one wants to run out to the kitchen during dinner and whip up an egg foam.) We tested pouring the batter into the ramekins, refrigerating them, and then baking them during dinner. This worked, and the batter held well for up to eight hours. But although the filled ramekins can be taken directly from the refrigerator to the oven with good results, we happily discovered that these cakes are foolproof if pulled directly from the freezer. Since the batter cooks from outside to inside, the window of opportunity for achieving a molten center is longer than if the batter went into the oven at room temperature or just chilled. Even better, these cakes can stay in the freezer for up to a month, making them an ideal make-ahead dessert.

Individual Molten Chocolate Cakes

SERVES 8

The whipping time in step 3 will depend on the type of mixer you use; a standing mixer will take about 5 minutes, while a handheld mixer will take about 10 minutes. Serve with lightly sweetened whipped cream, fresh berries, and/or dust the cakes with cocoa or confectioners' sugar.

RAMEKIN PREPARATION

1	tablespoon unsalted butter, softened
1	tablespoon cocoa powder

CAKES

8	ounces semisweet chocolate, chopped coarse
8	tablespoons (1 stick) unsalted butter
4	large eggs
1	large egg yolk
1	teaspoon vanilla extract
¼	teaspoon salt
½	cup (3½ ounces) granulated sugar
2	tablespoons unbleached all-purpose flour

1. FOR THE RAMEKINS: Mix the butter and cocoa together to make a paste. Brush the paste evenly inside eight 6-ounce ramekins; set aside.

2. FOR THE CAKE: Melt the chocolate and butter in a medium heatproof bowl set over a saucepan filled with 1 inch of barely simmering water, stirring frequently until smooth. Remove from the heat and set aside.

3. Using an electric mixer, whip the whole eggs, yolk, vanilla, salt, and sugar together at the highest speed until the volume nearly triples, the color is very light, and the mixture drops from the whisk in a smooth, thick stream, 5 to 10 minutes depending on your mixer (see note).

4. Scrape the egg mixture over the melted chocolate mixture, then sprinkle the flour over the top. Gently fold the egg and flour into the chocolate until the mixture is uniformly colored. Ladle or pour the batter into the prepared ramekins.

5. TO STORE: Cover each ramekin tightly with plastic wrap and then foil and refrigerate for up to 8 hours or freeze for up to 1 month.

6. TO SERVE: Adjust an oven rack to the middle position and heat the oven to 400 degrees. Unwrap the cakes and place them on a rimmed baking sheet (do not thaw before baking). Bake until the cakes have puffed about ½ inch above the rims of the ramekins, have a thin crust on top, and jiggle slightly at the center when they are shaken very gently, 12 to 15 minutes (if refrigerated, the cakes bake in 11 to 14 minutes). Serve in the ramekins or unmold onto individual plates. To unmold, run a paring knife around the inside edges of the ramekins to loosen the cakes, then invert them onto individual plates and let cool for 1 minute before removing the ramekins.

TO SERVE RIGHT AWAY

After portioning the batter into the ramekins, bake as directed in step 6, reducing the baking time to 10 to 13 minutes.

INDIVIDUAL CHOCOLATE SOUFFLÉS

FOR MOST PEOPLE, SOUFFLÉS ARE THE COOKING equivalent of a high-wire act—better left to the deft and practiced hands of a professional. You might order one in a restaurant, but you would never think about adding one (and the stress that accompanies it) to your own menu at home, right? Timing is essential, and anxiety about last-minute whisking and fallen soufflés abound. But the truth is, they are really not that hard to execute—especially if you eliminate the last-minute hurdles like whipping and gently folding in the egg whites. But the idea of making one ahead still seemed totally out of the question—which meant we wanted to find a way to do it. Determined, we headed into the kitchen to develop a make-ahead chocolate soufflé.

But first we needed to define the perfect soufflé. A quick poll in the test kitchen and some mouth-watering conversation revealed a soufflé with a crusty exterior packed with flavor, a dramatic rise above the rim, an airy but substantial outer layer, and a rich, loose center that is not completely set. A great soufflé must also convey a true mouthful of flavor, bursting with the taste of the main ingredient. In a chocolate soufflé, the chocolate high notes should be clear and strong. A balancing act between egg whites, chocolate, yolks, and butter is the essence of a great chocolate soufflé.

A primary consideration when trying to create such a soufflé is what to use as the "base"—the mixture that gives substance and flavor to the soufflé, as opposed to the airiness and "lift" provided by the whipped egg whites. The base can be a béchamel (a classic French sauce made with equal amounts of butter and flour, whisked with milk over heat), pastry cream (egg yolks beaten with sugar and then heated with milk), or flour cooked with milk or water until thickened. After trying several versions of each of these options, we liked the béchamel base the best, but found that the milk in it was muting the chocolate. Taking a new approach, we removed both the milk and the flour from our recipe and reduced the amount of butter. We then more than doubled the amount of chocolate and added six egg yolks (the egg whites were already being folded into the chocolate as part of our working recipe). This approach resulted in a base of egg yolks beaten with sugar until thick. This gave the soufflé plenty of volume and, because we had eliminated the milk, the chocolate now took center stage. Our chocolate soufflé now had the intense flavor we had been looking for. But we still weren't completely happy with the texture, which was a bit cakey on the outside. After several more experiments, we discovered that an additional two egg whites solved the problem, giving the soufflé more lift and a better texture.

We now moved on to check oven temperatures. For most recipes a 25-degree variance in oven temperature is not crucial, so we were surprised to discover the dramatic impact it had on our soufflé. Our initial oven temperature was 400 degrees, but to be sure this temperature was optimum, we tested both 375 and 425 degrees as well. The higher oven temperature resulted in an overcooked exterior and an undercooked interior, while the lower temperature did not brown the exterior enough to provide good flavor and also produced a texture that was too even—a proper soufflé should have a nice contrast between the loose center and slightly crusty exterior. We decided to stick with 400 degrees.

During the course of all this testing, we found a chocolate soufflé will give you three indications for doneness: you can smell the chocolate, it stops rising, and only the very center of the top jiggles when gently shaken. Of course, these are all imprecise methods. If you are not sure if your soufflé is done, simply take two spoons, pull open the top of the soufflé, and peek inside. If the center is still soupy, simply put the dish back in the oven! Much to our surprise, this in no way harmed the soufflé.

With our ideal soufflé recipe in hand, we turned our attention to the real challenge. We tried both refrigerating and freezing the soufflé batter in a single soufflé dish and in individual ramekins—and discovered that individual soufflés hold up much better in the refrigerator or freezer than a full recipe held in a soufflé dish. As we suspected, the refrigerated soufflés were a disaster when we baked them (they hardly rose at all and were very wet inside). But much to our amazement, the frozen versions worked fairly well—though they were cake-like and lacked the requisite loose center.

We tried adding two tablespoons of confectioners' sugar to the whites. This version was a great success, producing a soufflé that was light and airy with an excellent rise and a nice moist center. The actual texture of the whites changed as they were beaten, becoming more stable so they held up better during freezing. We did find that these soufflés ended up with a domed top, but by wrapping foil around each ramekin to form a "collar," our soufflés baked up picture-perfect. Your guests may not believe you made these soufflés ahead of time, but we guarantee they will be impressed with the results.

FREEZE IT

Individual Chocolate Soufflés
SERVES 6 TO 8

The yolk whipping time in step 3 depends on the type of mixer you use; a standing mixer will take about 3 minutes, while a handheld mixer will take about 8 minutes. If using 6-ounce ramekins, reduce the cooking time to 20 to 22 minutes. See our tip on page 361 for making a collar for the ramekins.

RAMEKIN PREPARATION

2   tablespoons unsalted butter, softened

2   tablespoons granulated sugar

SOUFFLÉS

8   ounces bittersweet or semisweet chocolate, chopped coarse

4   tablespoons (½ stick) unsalted butter, cut into ½-inch pieces

⅛   teaspoon salt

½   teaspoon vanilla extract

I   tablespoon Grand Marnier

6   large egg yolks

⅓   cup (2⅓ ounces) granulated sugar

8   large egg whites

¼   teaspoon cream of tartar

2   tablespoons (½ ounce) confectioners' sugar

1. FOR THE RAMEKINS: Grease the inside of eight 8-ounce ramekins with the softened butter, then coat the inside of each dish evenly with the sugar.

2. FOR THE SOUFFLÉS: Melt the chocolate and butter in a medium heatproof bowl set over a saucepan filled with 1 inch of barely simmering water, stirring frequently until smooth. Remove from the heat and stir in the salt, vanilla, and liqueur; set aside.

3. Using an electric mixer, whip the yolks and the granulated sugar at medium speed until the mixture triples in volume and is thick and pale yellow, 3 to 8 minutes (see note). Fold the yolk mixture into the chocolate mixture. Thoroughly clean and dry the mixing bowl and the beaters.

4. Using the clean beaters, whip the egg whites at medium-low speed until frothy, 1 to 2 minutes. Add the cream of tartar, increase the mixer speed to medium-high, and whip until soft peaks form when the whisk is lifted, 1 to 2 minutes. Add the confectioners' sugar and continue to whip at medium-high speed to stiff peaks, 2 to 4 minutes (do not overwhip). Whisk the last few strokes by hand, making sure to scrape any unwhipped whites from the bottom of the bowl.

5. Vigorously stir one-quarter of the whipped egg whites into the chocolate mixture. Gently fold the remaining whites into the chocolate mixture until just incorporated. Carefully spoon the mixture into the prepared ramekins almost to the rim, wiping the excess filling from the rims with a wet paper towel.

6. TO STORE: Cover each ramekin tightly with plastic wrap and then foil and freeze for at least 3 hours or up to 1 month. (Do not thaw before baking.)

7. TO SERVE: Adjust an oven rack to the lower-middle position and heat the oven to 400 degrees. Unwrap the ramekins and spread them out over a baking sheet. Bake the soufflés until fragrant, fully risen, and the exterior is set but the interior is still a bit loose and creamy, about 25 minutes. (To check the interior, use 2 spoons to pull open the top of one and peek inside.) Serve immediately.

TO SERVE RIGHT AWAY

After portioning the batter into the ramekins, bake as directed in step 7, reducing the baking time to 12 to 15 minutes.

➤ VARIATION

Individual Mocha Soufflés

Follow the recipe for Individual Chocolate Soufflés, adding 1 tablespoon instant coffee or espresso powder dissolved in 1 tablespoon hot water to the melted chocolate with the vanilla in step 2.

> **TEST KITCHEN TIP:**
> **Making a Collar**
> Baking our individual chocolate soufflés from the freezer yields a high rise and a domed top, just as we like them. But placing a collar around the ramekins yields an even higher rise with a flat, perfectly iconic rise. To get this look, make a foil collar by securing a strip of foil that has been sprayed with vegetable oil spray (or use nonstick foil) around each ramekin so that it extends about 2 inches above the rim (this is easiest to do after the ramekins have been filled). You can tape the foil collar to the soufflé dish as necessary to prevent it from slipping.

FLOURLESS CHOCOLATE CAKE

TO OUR KNOWLEDGE, FLOURLESS CHOCOLATE cake is the only dessert that is named for a missing ingredient. Even using the word "cake" for this popular dessert is a stretch. Although some recipes replace flour or crumbs with ground nuts, this cake typically contains only chocolate, butter, and eggs—nothing that could conceivably be called a dry ingredient. The result is moist and fudgy, more confection than cake. Because of its texture and lack of dry ingredients, we had doubts that this decadent dessert would hold up well in the refrigerator or freezer. But it is such an elegant, company-worthy dessert, so we figured it was at least worth a shot. First of course, we had to determine the characteristics of our ideal flourless chocolate cake.

Although the ingredient choices are limited—chocolate, butter, and eggs, sometimes sugar, and sometimes liquid such as water, coffee, or liqueur—the proportions, as well as mixing and baking methods, differed considerably in the recipes we researched. We selected and baked six and the results were staggering in their variety. One resembled a flourless fudge brownie; one was more like an ultra-dense, creamy custard; and one was a puffy, fallen soufflé–like affair. Some were very bittersweet, while others were quite sweet. All, however, had the richness and intensity of a confection.

Although almost all the desserts were enticing, we were quickly able to define our criteria for the ultimate flourless chocolate cake. We wanted something dense, moist, and ultra-chocolaty, but with some textural finesse. In short, we wanted an intense bittersweet "adult" dessert, not a piece of fudge or a brownie or a thick chocolate pudding—and certainly nothing fluffy.

Some recipes used unsweetened chocolate instead of semisweet or bittersweet, but we rejected this idea after tasting just one cake made with unsweetened chocolate. The flavor and texture weren't smooth or silky enough for this type of dessert, and there was an unappealing chalkiness. This made sense. Unsweetened chocolate is coarse and needs high heat to blend with the sugar required to sweeten it. It is most successful in desserts with a cakey or fudgy texture, when perfect smoothness is unnecessary. But with flourless chocolate cake, the ingredients are few, they are cooked very gently, and the result must be perfectly smooth. The cakes made with semisweet and bittersweet chocolates, by contrast, were incomparably smooth, owing to the fact that these chocolates have already been blended with sugar.

We were pretty sure that the ultimate cake would need some form of aeration from beaten eggs to achieve the texture that we wanted. In the first test, we whisked the eggs over gentle heat to warm them and then beat them until they had about tripled in volume and were the consistency of soft whipped cream. We then folded the whipped eggs into the warm chocolate and butter in three parts. In the second test, we separated the eggs, whisked the yolks into the warm chocolate and butter, and then beat the whites to a meringue before folding them in. In the third test, we simply whisked the eggs, one by one, into the warm chocolate and butter, as though making a custard.

The cake with beaten whole eggs differed from the one with yolks and meringue more than we expected. Even more surprising, the difference in flavor was greater than the difference in texture. Whole beaten eggs produced a dessert with nicely blended flavors, while the cake with separated eggs tasted as though the ingredients had not been completely integrated. Along the way, we realized that we could eliminate the step of warming the eggs before beating them, since cold eggs produce a denser foam with smaller bubbles, which in turn gave the cake a more velvety texture.

The next decision had to do with the baking temperature and whether or not a water bath was necessary. Some recipes called for baking at a high temperature for a short time without a water bath, but this technique resulted in hard, crumbly edges. We then tried baking the cake again for a short period at a high temperature, but this time in a water bath. This one was creamier by far, but we could taste raw egg. We guessed that, like cheesecake, this dessert required a longer baking time at a lower temperature in a water bath to allow the interior to reach a safe temperature without overcooking the edges. We found that 325 degrees in a water bath was just right.

The trick in baking this cake, however, is knowing when to stop. Flourless chocolate cake must be taken from the oven when the center still jiggles and looks quite underdone, as it continues to cook from residual heat after it comes out of the oven. At first we used a thermometer to make sure that the center of the cake had reached the safe temperature of 160 degrees (to kill any salmonella present in the eggs). But this cake was clearly overbaked; the texture was dry and chalky. Knowing that a temperature of at least 140 degrees held for five minutes also kills salmonella bacteria, we let the cake reach 140 degrees and then left it in the oven for five more minutes. It was overbaked as well. After trying four, three, and two extra minutes in the oven, we finally realized that if we removed the cake at 140 degrees, it would stay at or even above 140 degrees for at least five minutes (thus killing off salmonella) as the heat from the edges of the cake penetrated the center. The results were perfect.

We now hoped that we would be able to completely assemble and bake our flourless chocolate cake before storing. Simply making the batter ahead of time wouldn't do—there was no way we were going to fuss with a water bath and temperature measurements in the middle of a dinner party. Once baked, we tried both refrigerating and freezing the cake. To our pleasant surprise, both storage methods worked beautifully. The refrigerated cake tasted great for the first four days, after which its flavor and texture immediately began to suffer dramatically. The frozen cake was thawed in the refrigerator overnight (sprinkled with confectioners' sugar to hide any flaws from handling) and it also tasted great. As rich and delicate as this cake appears to be, it's strong enough to stand up to the freezer—which means we can enjoy this elegant, rich dessert any night of the week!

FREEZE IT

Flourless Chocolate Cake
SERVES 12 TO 16
The cake will still look quite underdone and liquidy when it is ready to be removed from the oven; be sure to remove it when an instant-read thermometer registers 140 degrees.

It will continue to firm up as it cools and will set completely with an overnight stay in the refrigerator. If using an 8-inch springform pan, increase the cooking time to 22 to 25 minutes. Sprinkle confectioners' sugar or cocoa powder over the cake to decorate and serve with lightly sweetened whipped cream, Berry Coulis (page 347), or fresh berries.

16	tablespoons (2 sticks) unsalted butter, cut into ½-inch pieces, plus extra for greasing the pan
1	pound semisweet or bittersweet chocolate, chopped coarse
¼	cup strong coffee or coffee liqueur (optional)
8	large eggs, cold

1. Adjust an oven rack to the lower-middle position and heat the oven to 325 degrees. Line the bottom of a 9-inch springform pan with parchment paper and grease the pan sides with butter. Wrap the outer bottom and sides of the pan securely with heavy-duty foil. Set the pan in a large roasting pan; set aside. Bring a kettle of water to a boil.

2. Meanwhile, melt the 16 tablespoons butter, chocolate, and coffee (if using) in a medium heatproof bowl set over a saucepan filled with 1 inch of barely simmering water, stirring frequently until smooth. Remove from the heat.

3. Using an electric mixer, whip the eggs at medium-high speed until they turn pale yellow and creamy, about 3 minutes. Increase the speed to high and continue to whip until the volume doubles to approximately 1 quart, 1 to 2 minutes longer.

4. Fold ⅓ of the eggs into the chocolate mixture using a large rubber spatula until only a few streaks of egg are visible. Gently fold in half of the remaining eggs, then the last of the remaining eggs until the mixture is totally homogenous. Scrape the batter into the prepared springform pan and smooth the surface with a rubber spatula.

5. Set the roasting pan on the oven rack and pour enough boiling water to come about halfway up the sides of the springform pan. Bake until the cake has risen slightly, the edges are just beginning to set but still quite jiggly, a thin glazed crust (like a brownie) has formed on the surface, and an instant-read thermometer inserted halfway through the center of the cake registers 140 degrees, 20 to 22 minutes.

6. Remove the cake pan from the water bath, set on a wire rack, and let cool to room temperature.

7. To STORE: Wrap the cake tightly with plastic wrap and then foil and refrigerate for up to 4 days or freeze for up to 1 month. (If frozen, the cake must be defrosted in the refrigerator for 24 hours before serving.)

8. To SERVE: Remove the springform pan sides, invert the cake onto a sheet of waxed paper, peel off the parchment pan liner, and turn the cake right side up on a serving platter. Let the cake soften at room temperature for 20 to 30 minutes before serving.

TO SERVE RIGHT AWAY

Refrigerate the cake as described in step 7 until firm and set, about 8 hours, then serve as directed in step 8.

INGREDIENTS: Dark Chocolate

Dark chocolate sounds simple enough, doesn't it? In reality, though, dark chocolate is anything but simple. Located somewhere between milk chocolate and unsweetened chocolate, dark chocolate is made mostly from two basic ingredients: chocolate liquor (also called cocoa mass or just cocoa on labels) and sugar. Although the term "dark" has no official meaning, it generally refers to chocolates labeled sweet, semisweet, or bittersweet. The only regulation from the U.S. Food and Drug Administration (FDA) that concerns these dark chocolates is that they must contain at least 35 percent chocolate liquor (though most contain more than 55 percent and on rare occasions go as high as 99 percent). The rest consists of sugar and, depending on the manufacturer, emulsifiers, flavorings, extra cocoa butter (for fluidity and smoothness; some cocoa butter exists naturally in the chocolate liquor), and milk fat (if present, in small amounts only).

To complicate matters, many companies sell more than one line of dark chocolate, the difference being in their percentage of chocolate liquor—but these percentages are not always printed on the label. As a result, many labels offer little reliable indication of what the chocolate inside tastes like, leaving us all, as it were, in the dark.

To make sense of this confusing array of dark chocolate options, we gathered nine brands that represent the widely divergent choices available and tasted each one raw, in a sauce, and in flourless chocolate cake.

We found, to our great surprise, that one factor had more influence on the success or failure of a chocolate than any other: sugar. Unfortunately, sugar content is neither readily identifiable on labels, nor is it regulated. The government-mandated nutritional information printed on the back of the labels includes sugar by number of grams but not in percentage terms. That means that not even the terms "semisweet" and "bittersweet" are surefire indicators of a chocolate's sweetness.

To figure out the total sugar content of the contenders in our taste test, we used a little basic mathematics. As it turns out, our top three finishers—Ghirardelli, Callebaut, and Hershey's—had sugar contents of 44 percent, 44 percent, and 49 percent respectively. The less-preferred brands had lower sugar contents that ranged from 28 percent to 35 percent. Though some tasters appreciated the robust and nuanced flavors of the latter high-cocoa chocolates (the premium brands revered by pastry chefs) when tasted raw, their complexity was lost once cooked. The sauces and cakes made with these premium brands were described as "bitter," "sour," "sharp," and simply not sweet enough.

What, then, to buy? Unless you have a rarefied palate (at least when it comes to chocolate), you don't have to shell out a lot of money or search gourmet shops to find a winning brand. Our top choice is the reasonably priced Ghirardelli Bittersweet.

THE BEST DARK CHOCOLATE

GHIRARDELLI BITTERSWEET CHOCOLATE PREMIUM BAKING BAR
With its high percentage of sugar, Ghirardelli Bittersweet chocolate was considered the most balanced—neither too bitter not too sweet. Its smooth, creamy texture won points in the raw and sauce tests, while solid acidity and fruit flavor notes shone through in the cake despite its sweetness. Tasters noted both "flavor bursts" and a flavor range with comments such as "starts sweet and finishes bitter," which explain why this chocolate stood out.

POUND CAKE

IN OUR OPINION, THERE IS NO OTHER CAKE that is as versatile (or as satisfying) as a rich and buttery pound cake, be it plain or flavored, glazed or unglazed. It's endlessly variable and best of all, it is a natural make-ahead dessert—it holds for days at room temperature and freezes perfectly. And at first glance, pound cake also seems like a simple dessert. After all, it's made only of eggs, butter, sugar, and flour mixed together and baked in a loaf pan. But if it's so easy, why do pound cakes often turn out spongy, rubbery, heavy, and dry rather than fine-crumbed, rich, moist, and buttery? In addition, most pound cake recipes call for creaming the butter, a tricky method that demands the ingredients be at just the right temperature to achieve a silken cake batter. We wanted to produce a superior pound cake while making the process as simple and foolproof as possible. We then hoped to double the recipe so you could enjoy one right away and save one (or both) for later. With a pound cake in your freezer, you need only add whipped cream and some berries for a company-worthy dessert.

We started our testing with a pound cake recipe that we knew to be excellent in its results but finicky in its preparation. The cake was top-notch, with a submissive crumb and a golden, buttery interior. In fact, it was everything we wanted from a pound cake except for one thing—the preparation method was anything but foolproof. Made in the traditional style, by creaming the butter and sugar until fluffy and pale, the method was so exacting that even the smallest diversion sent the batter over the edge into a curdled abyss. To achieve perfection, the ingredients had to be at an unforgiving 67 degrees, the butter and sugar beaten together for exactly five minutes to aerate, and the eggs drizzled into the batter over a period of 3 to 5 minutes. All of these precautions were advised to eliminate the danger of "breaking" the batter (a pound cake has so many eggs that keeping them in emulsion can be tricky when using the creaming method), which can make the crust look mottled and leave the cake's interior dense and tough.

We then looked at other cake recipes for ideas on streamlining the preparation. First we tried cutting softened butter into flour using a standing mixer.

After the butter and flour resembled knobby crumbs, we added some of the eggs, beat the mixture until cohesive, then added the rest of the eggs and beat the batter further until thick, fluffy, and lush. We often favor this method for cakes because it produces a velvety texture and a superfine crumb. Although the pound cake batter assembled this way looked great, the baked cake was too open-grained and tender, more like a yellow cake than a pound cake.

Next we tried melting the butter, a method often used in making quick breads. The liquids are combined and the dry ingredients then mixed into the wet by hand. This method was quick and easy. Melting the butter eliminated all of the temperature issues associated with creaming. Best of all, the batter could be pulled together and put into the oven in five minutes.

With a tight grain, a perfect swell and split in its center, and a nice, browned exterior, this cake showed promise. When we made it a second time, however, it sagged in the center. Additional tests yielded varying results. The problem may have been in the mixing method; perhaps inconsistent mixing produced inconsistent cakes. The solution? A food processor would do a better job of emulsification and also standardize the process. We added the eggs, sugar, and vanilla to the food processor bowl, combining them enough to integrate the sugar and eggs, and then drizzled the melted butter in through the feed tube. We transferred the watery base to a large bowl and sifted in flour and salt, whisking these ingredients in by hand. The method was a success. The cake had a split dome that afforded a peek inside at the marvelously yellow color of its interior. Just to be sure, we made the cake again and again, with the same results.

Our next objective was to make the cake just a bit lighter, but not so light as to resemble a yellow cake. (Pound cakes are by definition heavier and more dense than layer cakes.) When we tested cake flour against all-purpose, the former was superior, making the cake more tender. But the cake still needed more lift and less sponginess.

Up to this point we had been using two sticks of melted butter. Thinking that more butter might improve the texture, we increased the amount, but the cake turned out greasy. Next we turned to the eggs. Several recipes we researched called for three eggs plus three yolks, so we tried four whole eggs instead (an equivalent liquid amount), thinking that the additional white might add some lift. The cake was better but still on the dense side. Without success, we tried adding cream (this cake turned out heavy) and reducing the flour (this one was greasy). Four whole eggs had gotten us close, but the texture was still not ideal.

In the oldest of recipes (from the 1700s), eggs were the only ingredient in pound cake that gave it lift. In the 1850s, however, many cooks began adding the new wonder ingredient—baking powder—to achieve a lighter texture and a higher rise. Although traditionalists might scoff at the addition of chemical leavening, we were willing to give it a try. With just 1 teaspoon, we instilled enough breath into the cake to produce a consistent, perfect crumb. Now that we had simplified the method and achieved the right texture, it was time to determine just how far in advance these cakes could be made.

We knew refrigerating the cake would make it drier, so we tried storing the cooled cake (tightly wrapped with plastic wrap) at room temperature, tasting it each day to determine how long it would keep. We found that our cake stayed fresh for up to

GLAZES FOR POUND CAKE

POUND CAKES LOOK AND TASTE GREAT ON THEIR OWN, BUT WILL LOOK AND TASTE even better drizzled with a little glaze. We recommend glazing the pound cake just before serving. Each recipe makes enough for two cakes, but can be halved to glaze one cake.

FOR THE GLAZE: Mix all the ingredients together until smooth, then let sit until thickened, about 25 minutes. Pour the glaze over the top of the cake after it has completely cooled, allowing the glaze to drip down the sides. Let the glaze set for about 10 minutes before serving.

Citrus Glaze

- 1¾ cups (7 ounces) confectioners' sugar
- ¼ cup juice from 2 lemons or oranges
- ½ teaspoon grated zest from 1 lemon or orange
  Pinch salt

Nutty Glaze

- 1¾ cups (7 ounces) confectioners' sugar
- ¼ cup milk
- ¼ teaspoon almond or coconut extract
  Pinch salt

Cream Cheese Glaze

- 1½ cups (6 ounces) confectioners' sugar
- 3 tablespoons cream cheese, softened
- 3 tablespoons milk
- 1 teaspoon juice from 1 lemon
  Pinch salt

Chocolate Glaze

- 1 cup (4 ounces) confectioners' sugar
- 2 ounces bittersweet chocolate, melted
- 3 tablespoons milk
  Pinch salt

Coffee Glaze

- 1¾ cups (7 ounces) confectioners' sugar
- ¼ cup milk
- 1 tablespoon instant espresso or coffee powder
  Pinch salt

four days, after which it became dry and slightly stale-tasting. Next we tested the freezer. After a stay in the freezer, we left the cake on the counter to thaw and tasted it as soon as it was thawed. Not bad—although we thought we could do better. Just 10 to 15 minutes in a moderate oven took the chill off this cake, and that was all it needed to taste freshly baked.

Pound Cake

MAKES TWO 8½ BY 4½-INCH CAKES, SERVING 8 EACH

This batter looks almost like a thick pancake batter and is very fluid.

3	cups (12 ounces) cake flour
2	teaspoons baking powder
1	teaspoon salt
2½	cups (17½ ounces) sugar
1	tablespoon vanilla extract
8	large eggs
1	pound (4 sticks) unsalted butter, melted
1	recipe glaze for pound cake (optional, see page 366)

1. Adjust an oven rack to the middle position and heat the oven to 350 degrees. Spray two 8½ by 4½-inch loaf pans with vegetable oil spray, then line the bottom of the pans with parchment paper; set aside. In a medium bowl, whisk together the flour, baking powder, and salt; set aside.

2. Pulse the sugar and vanilla in a food processor until combined, about 5 pulses. Add the eggs and process until combined, about 5 seconds. With the machine running, slowly add the melted butter through the feed tube in a steady stream (this should take about 30 seconds), until it is all incorporated. Transfer the mixture to a large bowl. Sift the flour mixture over the eggs in 3 batches, whisking gently after each addition, until just combined.

3. Pour the batter into the prepared pans and bake for 15 minutes. Reduce the oven temperature to 325 degrees and continue to bake until the cakes are deep golden brown and a skewer inserted in the center comes out clean, about 35 minutes, rotating

the pans halfway through the baking time.

4. Let the cakes cool in the pans for 10 minutes, then turn them out onto a wire rack. Let the cakes cool completely, 2 to 3 hours.

5. To STORE: Wrap the fully cooled cakes tightly with plastic wrap and then foil and store at room temperature for up to 4 days or freeze for up to 1 month. (If frozen, let the cake thaw completely at room temperature, 2 to 4 hours.)

6. To SERVE: The cake can be served at room temperature or warmed. To warm the cake, unwrap it and place it on a baking sheet in a 350-degree oven for 10 to 15 minutes.

TO SERVE RIGHT AWAY
Follow the recipe through step 4, letting the cake cool for about 1 hour before serving.

➤ VARIATIONS
Ginger Pound Cake
Follow the recipe for Pound Cake, adding 3 tablespoons minced crystallized ginger, 1½ teaspoons ground ginger, and ½ teaspoon mace to the sugar before processing in step 2.

Lemon Pound Cake
Follow the recipe for Pound Cake, adding 2 tablespoons finely grated lemon zest and 2 teaspoons fresh lemon juice to the sugar before processing in step 2.

Orange Pound Cake
Follow the recipe for Pound Cake, adding 1 tablespoon finely grated orange zest and 1 tablespoon fresh orange juice to the sugar before processing in step 2.

ITALIAN ALMOND CAKE

ALMONDS HAVE BEEN A CULINARY STAPLE in Mediterranean countries for centuries, used in place of flour for cakes and for thickening sauces. A base in many Italian desserts, almonds come in two forms: bitter and sweet. The bitter almond is the smaller of the two and has the typical almond taste, which is used to boost the flavor of products made with sweet almonds. It has to be heat-treated before use, however, as otherwise it is toxic. The sweet almond is what we find in our local supermarkets and is the star ingredient in almond cake, a simple and humble Italian dessert. Like pound cake, almond cake is a versatile dessert that is as good plain as it is with a simple sauce, cream, or fresh berries. It is also a natural make-ahead dessert. The batter comes together quickly and simply, then once baked, almond cake will keep at room temperature for days.

There are many types of almond cakes, some using bitter almonds, others using marzipan (sweetened almond paste), and still others using polenta, or cornmeal, to add texture. For our recipe, we wanted simple, easy-to-find ingredients and a procedure to match.

Working with a basic almond cake recipe, we lined up all the ingredients typically used—almonds, sugar, butter, and eggs—as well as a couple of ingredients we found used in a handful of almond cake recipes, such as flour and baking powder, that we thought might lighten the texture of this fairly rich, dense cake. Our first goal was to determine if we were going to add flour to this cake at all, or let the almonds really speak for themselves. Testing different ratios of almonds (ground fine in a food processor) and all-purpose flour, we started with a batter made of half flour and half almonds. Tasters complained that the almond flavor was too faint and the cake too light. Working our way toward more almonds and less flour in ¼-cup increments, the cakes got progressively better. We finally settled on ¾ cup of flour and 3½ cups of ground almonds. Any more flour and the cake lost its appealing rustic texture, but any less and this cake was too moist and heavy. A last-minute substitution of cake flour for the all-purpose flour gave our almond cake a welcome lightness without sacrificing pure almond flavor.

Next we focused our attention on the sugar. We already knew we wanted granulated sugar in this cake recipe, not only for its pure sweetness, but because we knew brown sugar would add moisture that this cake definitely didn't need (it already has

plenty of moisture from the oil in the almonds). Our challenge was to figure out just how much sugar was necessary. Taking a cue from other similar recipes, we started with 1½ cups of sugar. We added some to the almonds when we ground them in the food processor—as this prevents them from turning into nut butter—and just ½ cup did the trick. The remaining 1 cup went into the bowl of the mixer with the butter to be creamed before adding the other ingredients. The resulting cake was flavorful and the sugar really brought out the almond flavor, but the crust that formed was almost like candy. Reducing the sugar by ¼ cup worked perfectly.

We were making progress, but this cake needed a higher rise and so we looked to baking powder. Starting with 1 teaspoon, we worked our way down to ¼ teaspoon. One teaspoon was too much, making the cake dense, while ¼ teaspoon was not enough to contribute much lift. We found that ½ teaspoon baking powder provided just the right lift and texture.

Most almond cakes that we found in our research called for three eggs, but that seemed like a lot for a single-layer cake. After testing one, two, and three eggs, we were surprised to find that three was exactly right after all—any less and the cake sagged in the middle. Now the cake had good structure, with a light spring and tender crumb.

Up to this point, our batter was coming together pretty easily, but the end result was thick and required a spatula to spread it into the pan. Taking a cue from past cake recipes, we started adding liquid to thin the batter out. Water worked great, making the batter pourable and the cake's texture was now also lighter. Unfortunately, a little too light—after all, we'd worked so hard to get the right balance of flavors, so it seemed counterintuitive to now water them down. But substituting milk for water and settling on ½ cup was just right to satisfy all our tasters. This dessert was finally where we wanted it to be.

Finally we could turn our attention to storing the cake. We knew from past experience that cakes often store better at room temperature than they do in the refrigerator, where they tend to quickly dry out. And if you want to keep the cake for longer than a few days, it's best kept in the freezer until ready to serve. Now it was time to put this theory to the test. We baked two cakes, stored one in the freezer, and left one wrapped with plastic wrap on the countertop. The cake on the countertop was still good on the fifth day (served warm or at room temperature), but after that it tasted stale. We let the frozen cake thaw on the countertop and then warmed it up in a 350-degree oven for 10 minutes to take the chill off. Tasters thought this frozen one was just as good as the freshly baked cake. The 10 minutes in the oven brought the crust back to life, and with a sprinkling of confectioners' sugar and a dollop of whipped cream, we had dessert on the table with very little effort.

FREEZE IT

Italian Almond Cake

MAKES ONE 9-INCH ROUND CAKE,
SERVING 8 TO 10

Do not substitute low-fat or nonfat milk for the whole milk. Blanched almonds are almonds without their skin. Be careful not to overtoast the almonds or the cake will have a dry, crumbly texture. You can substitute 3 cups whole blanched almonds for the slivered; increase their oven toasting time to 11 minutes and their processing time to 30 seconds in step 2.

14	ounces blanched, slivered almonds (about 3½ cups) (see note)
1¼	cups (8¾ ounces) sugar
	Pinch salt
¾	cup (3 ounces) cake flour
½	teaspoon baking powder
8	tablespoons (1 stick) unsalted butter, at room temperature
3	large eggs, at room temperature
½	cup whole milk

1. Adjust an oven rack to the middle position and heat the oven to 350 degrees. Spray a 9-inch springform pan with vegetable oil spray, then line the bottom of the pan with parchment paper.

2. Spread the almonds out on a rimmed baking sheet and toast in the oven until very lightly toasted and fragrant, 5 to 7 minutes (do not overtoast); let cool completely. Process the almonds, ½ cup of the sugar, and salt in a food processor until very finely ground with a texture that resembles flour, about 10 seconds. Add the flour and baking powder and pulse to incorporate, about 5 pulses; set aside.

3. Using an electric mixer, cream the butter and remaining ¾ cup sugar until light and fluffy, 3 to 5 minutes. Add the eggs, 1 at a time, beating briefly after each addition to incorporate. Add the ground almond mixture and beat until just incorporated. Add the milk and beat until just incorporated.

4. Transfer the batter to the prepared pan and smooth the top. Bake until the cake is puffed and golden on top and a toothpick inserted comes out clean, 30 to 40 minutes, rotating the pan halfway through the baking time.

5. Let the cake cool in the pan on a wire rack for 15 minutes, then remove the sides of the pan and let the cake cool to room temperature, 2 to 3 hours.

6. TO STORE: Remove the cake pan bottom and wrap the fully cooled cake tightly with plastic wrap and then foil. Store at room temperature for up to 5 days or freeze for up to 1 month. (If frozen, let the cake thaw completely at room temperature, 2 to 4 hours.)

7. TO SERVE: The cake can be served at room temperature or warmed. To warm the cake, unwrap it and place it on a baking sheet in a 350-degree oven for 10 to 15 minutes.

TO SERVE RIGHT AWAY

Let the cake cool at room temperature for about 1 hour before serving.

NEW YORK–STYLE CHEESECAKE

CHEESECAKE IS A MAKE-AHEAD DESSERT BY design—once baked, the cheesecake must go into the refrigerator to "set" or firm up, and this can take as many as three hours. The fact that cheesecake has to be made in advance makes it a great choice when entertaining. So it wasn't a stretch to include this recipe in our book, but we wanted a recipe for the ultimate New York–style cheesecake.

And we wanted to know if we could take the make-ahead component one step further and freeze this dessert.

But first, we needed a great recipe. A quick poll revealed a unanimous opinion of the ultimate New York–style cheesecake: It should be cool, thick, smooth, satiny, and creamy; radiating outward, the texture should go gradually from velvety to suede-like, until finally becoming cake-like and fine-pored at the edges. The flavor should be simple, sweet yet tangy, and rich. It should not be so dry as to make you gag, and it definitely should not bake up with a fault as large as the San Andreas.

We decided to start with the crust. One test was all it took to eliminate a pastry crust, as it only became soggy beneath the filling. Cookie and cracker crumbs were tasty and more practical options. Every taster considered a mere dusting of crumbs on the bottom of the cheesecake insufficient. We wanted a crust with more presence. A graham cracker crust made with a cup of crumbs,

some sugar, and melted butter, pressed into the bottom of the springform pan and prebaked until it was fragrant and browned around the edge, was ideal at a thickness of about ⅜ inch. If served within a day of baking, it retained its crispness. If the cheesecake was held for a couple of days, the crust softened, but tasters didn't seem to mind.

A great New York cheesecake should be of great stature. One made with 2 pounds (four bars) of cream cheese was not tall enough. We threw in another half pound—the springform pan reached maximum capacity, but the cheesecake stood tall and looked right. The amount of sugar was quickly settled upon—1½ cups. The cheesecake now struck a perfect balance of sweet and tangy.

Cheesecakes always require a dairy supplement to the cream cheese, usually either heavy cream or sour cream, or sometimes both. Dairy helps to loosen up the texture of the cream cheese, giving the cake a smoother, more luxurious feel. We found that heavy cream, even when used in the

---

EQUIPMENT: Springform Pans

Although infrequently used, a springform pan is essential for a variety of cakes that would be impossible to remove from a standard cake pan. To find the best model, we baked cheesecakes in six pans, ranging in price from $9 to $32.

An ideal pan, we thought, would release the cakes from the sides and bottom of the pan effortlessly. All six pans tested had acceptable side release, but dislodging a cake from the pan bottom was trickier. Here, the top-performing pans possessed a rimless bottom (just two out of the six tested). These two also proved the easiest to clean.

Another valuable quality in a springform pan is its resistance to leakage when placed in a water bath. To test leakage, we baked cheesecakes in a water bath tinted with green food coloring, our theory being that the less secure the seal of the pan, the more water would seep through, the greener the cheesecake. This was a tough test. Even the best-performing pan in this test thus far showed an edge of green that traveled around one third of the cake. In the worst instances, the green made a complete circle around the outside edge of the cake. These pans were the cheapest we tested, and they were very flimsy.

In this case, price does matter as the two most expensive pans topped the testing. The Kaiser Noblesse ($20) and the

Frieling Glass Bottom ($32) are both well constructed, well designed (flat bottomed and rimless as opposed to the rest tested), and worth the extra money. But the Frieling pan came out on top for its extra features. It has a glass bottom that allows you to monitor the browning of the crust (a feature that does not make it fragile—something we discovered after the pan survived several falls onto the kitchen floor). It also has handles, which are very helpful when removing the pan from a water bath or oven.

THE BEST SPRINGFORM PAN

The Frieling's transparent, sturdy glass bottom and convenient handles are worth the extra cash.

EQUIPMENT: Measuring Spoons

Even cooks who forgo the use of measuring spoons for stovetop recipes know they are considered essential equipment when it comes to baking. But which brand is best?

After filling nine spoons to level, then carefully weighing the contents, we concluded that every brand was sufficiently accurate. So preferences came down to design. We measure dry ingredients by scooping a heaping spoonful, then sweeping it to level (a method we call "dip and sweep"). Easy enough—unless the shape of the spoon hinders either the dipping or the sweeping. Fat spoons, spoons with short handles, overly bulky spoons, and spoons with raised handles all made this task more difficult. When measuring out liquid ingredients, shallow spoons posed a higher risk of spillage than deep spoons.

Where did we end up? The sturdy Cuisipro spoons ($10.95) feature an elongated, oval shape that proved optimal for scooping ingredients from a narrow jar. In addition, the ends of the handles curl down, putting them level with the spoon's base and thereby allowing a full measure to be set down on the counter with no tipping and no mess. Perfection is in the details.

THE BEST MEASURING SPOONS

The oval shape of the Cuisipro Measuring Spoons makes for easy scooping into tall, narrow jars.

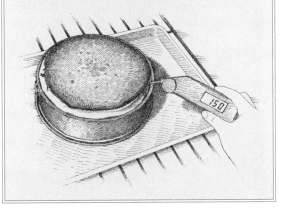
smallest amounts, dulled and flattened the flavor of the cream cheese. Sour cream, with a tartness of its own, supplemented the tangy quality of the cream cheese, but an overabundance made the cheesecake taste sour and acidic. We found that ⅓ cup was just enough to offer a touch of tartness and help give the cheesecake a smoother, creamier texture without advertising its presence.

Eggs help bind the cheesecake and give it structure. Whole eggs are often called for in cheesecakes of non–New York persuasions, but recipes for New York cheesecake seem to agree that a few yolks in addition to whole eggs help to get the velvety, lush texture of a proper New York cheesecake. Our testing bore this out, and ultimately we concluded that a generous amount of eggs—six whole and

two yolks—yielded a cheesecake of unparalleled texture: dense but not heavy, firm but not rigid, and perfectly rich.

Perfecting the flavor of the cheesecake was easy. A little lemon juice helped to perk up the flavors without adding a lemon-flavored hit. Just a bit of salt (cream cheese already contains a good dose of sodium) and a couple of teaspoons of vanilla extract rounded out the flavors.

There are many ways to bake a cheesecake: in a moderate oven, in a low oven, in a water bath, and in accordance with the New York method—500 degrees for about 10 minutes, then 200 degrees for about an hour—now a standard technique. We tried them all, but the New York method was the only one that yielded the nut-brown surface that is a distinguishing mark of an exemplary New York cheesecake. This dual-temperature, no-water-bath baking method also produced a lovely graded texture, soft and creamy at the center and firm and dry at the periphery.

With our recipe ready, we started testing how far in advance this cheesecake could be made. As with many of our other make-ahead desserts, we found that our cheesecake held in the refrigerator for up to four days before the quality began to suffer. But what about freezing? We froze a half dozen cheesecakes and tasted them at different intervals of time—one day, one week, and one month. With the exception of a slightly softer crust (which tasters didn't mind), to our amazement each one emerged from the freezer tasting just as good as a freshly made cake. The only trick to serving it from the freezer is to allow time for the cheesecake to completely defrost in the refrigerator (we recommend overnight). Once properly thawed, a 30-minute stay at room temperature is all that's needed for a cheesecake that's just as creamy, rich, and smooth as one made and served in the same day.

FREEZE IT

New York–Style Cheesecake

MAKES ONE 9-INCH CHEESECAKE,
SERVING 12 TO 16

For a chocolate crust, substitute 14 chocolate wafers (Nabisco Famous) for the graham crackers. The flavor and texture of the cheesecake is best if the cake is allowed to stand at room temperature for 30 minutes before serving. When cutting the cake, have a pitcher of hot tap water nearby; dipping the blade of the knife into the water and wiping it clean with a kitchen towel after each cut helps make neat slices.

GRAHAM CRACKER CRUST

I	cup (4 ounces) graham cracker crumbs (8 whole crackers, broken into rough pieces and processed in a food processor until uniformly fine)
6	tablespoons (¾ stick) unsalted butter, melted
I	tablespoon sugar

CHEESECAKE FILLING

2½	pounds cream cheese, cut into rough 1-inch chunks and left to soften at room temperature for 30 to 45 minutes
1½	cups (10½ ounces) sugar
⅛	teaspoon salt
⅓	cup sour cream
2	teaspoons juice from I lemon
2	teaspoons vanilla extract
2	large egg yolks
6	large eggs
I	recipe Fresh Strawberry Topping (optional, page 373)

1. FOR THE CRUST: Adjust an oven rack to the lower-middle position and heat the oven to 325 degrees. Toss the graham cracker crumbs, 5 tablespoons of the butter, and sugar together with a fork until evenly moistened. Brush the bottom and sides of a 9-inch springform pan with half of the remaining melted butter, making sure to leave enough to brush the pan in step 4. Empty the crumbs into the springform pan and following the illustrations on page 373, press evenly into the pan bottom. Bake until fragrant and beginning to brown around the edges, about 13 minutes. Let cool on a wire rack while making the filling.

2. FOR THE CHEESECAKE FILLING: Increase the oven temperature to 500 degrees. Using an electric mixer, beat the cream cheese at medium-low speed to break it up, 1 to 2 minutes. Scrape the beater and bottom and sides of the bowl well with a rubber spatula, then beat in ¾ cup of the sugar and salt at medium-low speed until combined, 1 to 2 minutes. Scrape the bowl and beat in the remaining sugar until combined, 1 to 2 minutes.

3. Scrape the bowl and beat in the sour cream, lemon juice, and vanilla on low speed until combined, 1 to 2 minutes. Scrape the bowl and beat in the yolks at medium-low speed until thoroughly combined, 1 to 2 minutes. Scrape the bowl and beat in the whole eggs (2 at a time) at medium-low speed, scraping the bowl between additions, until thoroughly combined, 1 to 2 minutes.

4. Brush the sides of the springform pan with the remaining melted butter. Set the pan on a rimmed baking sheet (to catch any spills if it leaks). Pour the

filling into the cooled crust and bake for 10 minutes. Without opening the oven door, reduce the oven temperature to 200 degrees and continue to bake until an instant-read thermometer inserted into the side of the cheesecake (see the illustration on page 371) registers 150 degrees, about 1½ hours.

5. Transfer the cake to a wire rack and let cool for 5 minutes, then (without releasing the sides of the pan) run a paring knife between the cake and the inside of the pan. Let the cake cool until barely warm, 2½ to 3 hours.

6. To store: Wrap the cake tightly with plastic wrap and then foil and refrigerate for up to 4 days or freeze for up to 1 month. (If frozen, allow the cheesecake to thaw in the refrigerator overnight before serving.)

7. To serve: Unmold the cheesecake by removing the sides of the pan. Slide a thin metal spatula between the crust and pan bottom to loosen, then slide the cake onto a serving plate. Let the cheesecake stand at room temperature for about 30 minutes before serving with the strawberry topping (if using).

TO SERVE RIGHT AWAY

Refrigerate the baked cheesecake as described in step 6 until chilled, about 3 hours, then serve as described in step 7.

Fresh Strawberry Topping
MAKES ABOUT 1½ QUARTS

Do not substitute frozen strawberries here. While this topping tastes best when made the same day, it can be made up to 2 days in advance.

2   pounds strawberries, hulled and sliced ¼ inch thick
½   cup (3½ ounces) sugar
     Pinch salt
1   cup strawberry jam (about 11 ounces)
2   tablespoons juice from 1 lemon

1. Toss the berries, sugar, and salt together and let stand, tossing occasionally, until the berries have released juice and the sugar has dissolved, about 30 minutes.

2. Process the jam in a food processor until smooth, about 8 seconds; transfer it to a small saucepan. Simmer the jam over medium-high heat, stirring frequently, until dark and no longer frothy, about 3 minutes. Stir in the lemon juice.

3. Stir the warm jam into the strawberries and let cool. Cover with plastic wrap and refrigerate until cold, at least 2 hours or up to 2 days.

PRESSING THE CRUMBS INTO THE PAN

1. Use the bottom of a ramekin, 1-cup measuring cup, or drinking glass to press the crumbs into the bottom of a springform pan. Press the crumbs as far as possible into the edge of the pan.

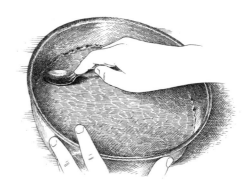

2. Use a teaspoon to neatly press the crumbs into the edge of the pan to create a clean edge.

SHORTCAKES

SHORTCAKES AREN'T JUST FOR STRAWBERRIES (THOUGH THERE'S NOTHING BETTER OR EASIER when they are in season). You can pair these sweet biscuits with any seasonal fruit and a little whipped cream for a simple dessert any time of the year. These shortcakes get their lift from the baking powder, their tenderness from the all-purpose flour, and their sturdiness and rich flavor from eggs and half-and-half, which is important since you are topping them with juicy fruit. We found that baking them first and then cooling them before freezing was the easiest method for guaranteeing perfect biscuits in a flash.

As for the fruit, we use 8 cups of fruit (strawberries, figs, blueberries, peaches, or any other ripe fruit) with about 6 tablespoons of sugar, depending on the sweetness of the fruit for one recipe of shortcakes. We've also found that mashing 3 cups of the fruit and mixing it with the sugar and remaining sliced fruit yields the most attractive presentation and the best flavor. Keep these simple, foolproof biscuits in your freezer and you'll be ready for dessert at a moment's notice.

(FREEZE IT)

Shortcakes

MAKES 8 BISCUITS

After cutting 6 perfect rounds of dough, you can reknead the scraps and repeat the cutting process to get 2 more rounds. These shortcakes will be a little tougher and less attractive than those from the first cutting.

2	cups (10 ounces) unbleached all-purpose flour, plus extra for the counter and biscuit cutter
5	tablespoons (about 2¼ ounces) sugar
1	tablespoon baking powder
½	teaspoon salt
8	tablespoons (1 stick) unsalted butter, cold, cut into ½-inch pieces
½	cup plus 1 tablespoon half-and-half
1	large egg, lightly beaten
1	large egg white, lightly beaten

1. Adjust an oven rack to the lower-middle position and heat the oven to 425 degrees. Line a baking sheet with parchment paper and set aside. Process the flour, 3 tablespoons of the sugar, baking powder, and salt together in a food processor to combine, about 5 seconds. Add the butter and pulse until the mixture looks like coarse cornmeal flecked with pea-sized bits of butter, about 15 pulses.

2. Mix the half-and-half and egg together, then add to the flour mixture and pulse it until large clumps form, about 10 pulses. Turn the mixture onto a floured work surface and lightly knead until the dough comes together.

3. Pat the dough into a 9 by 6-inch rectangle about ¾ inch thick. Flour a 2¾-inch biscuit cutter and cut 6 dough rounds, flouring the cutter as needed. Reknead the scraps and repeat the cutting process to get 2 more rounds. Spread the cakes 1 inch apart on the prepared baking sheet. Brush the dough tops with the egg white and sprinkle with the remaining 2 tablespoons sugar. Bake until golden brown, 12 to 14 minutes.

4. **To STORE:** Let the shortcakes cool completely on a wire rack, then store them in a zipper-lock plastic bag in the freezer for up to 1 month. (Alternatively, you can store them at room temperature for up to 4 days.)

5. **To SERVE:** Adjust an oven rack to the middle position and heat the oven to 350 degrees. Spread the cakes out over a baking sheet. Bake until heated through, 7 to 10 minutes (3 to 5 minutes if not frozen).

SPLITTING SHORTCAKES

When the shortcakes have cooled, look for a natural crack around the circumference. Gently insert your fingers into the crack and split the shortcake in half.

ICE CREAM PIES AND CAKES

IN THE WORLD OF MAKE-AHEAD DESSERTS, anything with ice cream reigns supreme, whether it's softened and pressed into a cookie-crumb crust to make a pie or pressed into layers in a springform pan, emerging from the freezer cake-like and ready to be decorated. The problem of course is that these frozen desserts take time (and some forethought!) to execute at home. But since homemade varieties are worlds better than the store-bought versions most of us remember from our childhood—with one-dimensional flavor and gloppy frosting—we knew homemade ice cream desserts were worth the effort.

We set out with a few goals in mind for these pies and cakes. First, we wanted to steer away from boring all-chocolate or all-vanilla desserts and create some interesting flavor combinations. Second, we wanted to explore various fillings to see which ones held up in the freezer without getting soggy. Finally, we were determined to do away with the overly-sweet, greasy frosting that ice cream shops smother their ice cream cakes with, using a simple sauce or garnish instead.

But first we needed a crust. Since we planned to use chocolate ice cream (but not just chocolate!) in most of our cakes, we felt that a crust of crushed Oreo cookies would be best suited for these cakes. We crushed the Oreos, added some melted butter, and then pressed the crumbs firmly into the pan. Just 15 minutes in the oven hardened the crumbs into a crust. For variety we also tried using Nutter Butter cookies in place of the Oreos and they worked great too (especially with our Double Chocolate and Peanut Butter Cake, page 378).

With our crust in place, it was time to build our desserts. We already knew it was necessary to soften the ice cream first before adding it to the crust, but it took us a few bumpy ice cream cakes and pies to figure out that it not only needs to be softened, but whipped until creamy smooth. We found that a wooden spoon is the best tool for the job. Working quickly, we softened the ice cream by stirring it constantly until all the lumps were worked out, then poured it into the pan. (It's important to work

quickly to soften the ice cream before it starts to melt, but if the ice cream is really hard, you may need to let it sit briefly at room temperature before softening.)

Although the wooden spoon worked great for this step, we needed something perfectly flat to smooth the top. Digging through our drawer of kitchen tools, we came up with a couple of handy tools to get a perfectly smooth top. A meat mallet with a heavy, flat disk was the crowd favorite. In a pinch, however, we realized we could use the flat bottom of a 1-cup measuring cup or a drinking glass.

Finally it was time for the sauce and garnish. Those waxy, greasy frostings found on commercial ice cream cakes were exactly what we did not want, although tasters agreed that a little sauce either spread on top or served with these desserts was a nice touch. We chose a chocolate sauce, which would enhance any of our pies or cakes, as well as a caramel sauce, geared specifically toward the Caramel Turtle Ice Cream Cake (page 378), but delicious with many others.

As for garnishes, the options are endless. We tried nuts, sprinkles, coconut, cookie crumbs, and even cake crumbs—and they all worked great. However, we found that harder crumbs from cookies, for example, held up the best between the ice cream layers. When garnishing the outside of the cake or pie, anything was fair game. Now we had just what we wanted—an easy master recipe for ice cream cake or pie with endless potential for variation. We'll never buy one from the store again.

FREEZE IT

Simple Ice Cream Pie

SERVES 6 TO 8

Use traditional Oreo cookies here—not double stuffed. For a peanut butter–flavored crust, substitute Nutter Butters for the Oreos. This pie can be made with any type of ice cream or sherbet. If you don't have a meat mallet, you can use something else with a flat surface (1-cup measuring cup or drinking glass) to smooth the top of the pie. This easy pie can be decorated with chopped nuts, sprinkles, or maraschino cherries and is also nice when served with a dessert sauce (see pages 376–377).

16   Oreo cookies, broken into rough pieces
2   tablespoons unsalted butter, melted
2   pints ice cream
1½   cups heavy cream, chilled
1½   tablespoons sugar
½   teaspoon vanilla extract

1. Adjust an oven rack to the middle position and heat the oven to 325 degrees. Pulse the cookies in a food processor until coarsely ground, about 15 short pulses, then let the machine run until the crumbs are uniformly fine, about 15 seconds. With the machine running, pour the butter through the feed tube and continue to process until the mixture resembles wet sand.

2. Transfer the crumbs to a 9-inch pie plate. Press the crumbs into an even layer over the bottom and sides of the pie plate. Bake the crust until it is fragrant and beginning to brown, about 15 minutes. Let cool on a wire rack.

3. Scoop the ice cream into a large bowl and use a wooden spoon to soften the ice cream and remove any lumps, working quickly so the ice cream does not melt. With a meat mallet (or other flat surface; see note), spread the softened ice cream evenly into the cooled crust, creating a smooth top.

4. To STORE: Wrap the pie tightly with plastic wrap and then foil and freeze for up to 1 month. (Once the pie is completely frozen, press the plastic wrap directly on the surface to prevent ice crystals from forming.)

5. To SERVE: Whip the cream, sugar, and vanilla together in a chilled bowl until stiff peaks form. Unwrap the frozen pie and spread the whipped cream attractively over the top of the pie. Serve immediately.

TO SERVE RIGHT AWAY
Freeze the pie as directed in step 4 until firm, 4 to 6 hours, then serve as directed in step 5.

➤ VARIATIONS
Grasshopper Pie
Follow the recipe for Simple Ice Cream Pie, using vanilla ice cream. Stir ¼ cup crème de menthe and 3 tablespoons crème de cacao into the softened ice cream before spreading it into the crust. Sprinkle

the top of the pie with ½ cup mini chocolate chips before freezing.

Mud Pie
Store-bought chocolate sauce can be substituted; the chocolate sauce needs to be spreadable, but shouldn't be warm.

Follow the recipe for Simple Ice Cream Pie, using coffee ice cream. Before freezing the pie, spread 1 cup Chocolate Sauce (below) over the top and sprinkle with ½ cup toasted, slivered almonds.

Chocolate Sauce
MAKES 2 CUPS
When whisking the sauce to combine, do so gently so as not to create air bubbles, which will mar its appearance. The recipe can easily be doubled.

1   cup heavy cream, plus extra as needed
¼   cup light corn syrup
4   tablespoons (½ stick) unsalted butter
      Pinch salt
8   ounces bittersweet chocolate, chopped fine

1. Bring the 1 cup cream, corn syrup, butter, and salt to a boil in a small saucepan over medium-high heat. Off the heat, stir in the chocolate, cover, and let stand until the chocolate is melted, about 5 minutes.

2. Uncover and whisk gently until smooth. Adjust the consistency by heating and stirring in additional cream as needed, 1 tablespoon at a time.

3. To STORE: Cool to room temperature then store in an airtight container for up to 3 weeks.

4. To SERVE: Transfer the sauce to a heatproof bowl set over a saucepan of simmering water and heat to the desired temperature. Alternatively, microwave at 50 percent power, stirring once or twice, for 1 to 3 minutes.

Caramel Sauce

MAKES 1½ CUPS

Be careful when adding the cream since the sugar is molten and can burn. Use a large saucepan and keep your hands well above the pan. If you don't have a candy thermometer, follow the times in the recipe.

- ½ cup water
- 1 cup (7 ounces) sugar
- 1 cup heavy cream
- ⅛ teaspoon salt
- ½ teaspoon juice from 1 lemon
- ½ teaspoon vanilla extract

1. Pour the water into a large saucepan. Add the sugar to the center of the pan, taking care not to let the granules adhere to the sides of the pan. Cover and bring to a boil over high heat.

2. Once boiling, uncover and continue to boil until the syrup is straw-colored and registers 300 degrees on a candy thermometer, about 7 minutes. Reduce to medium heat and continue to cook until the syrup is a deep amber color and registers 350 degrees on the thermometer, 1 to 2 minutes.

3. Meanwhile, bring the cream and salt to a simmer in a small saucepan (if the cream simmers before the syrup reaches a deep amber color, remove it from the heat and cover to keep warm).

4. Remove the sugar syrup from the heat. Very carefully, pour about one-quarter of the hot cream into the sugar syrup and let the bubbling subside. Add the remaining cream, vanilla, and lemon juice and let the bubbling subside. Whisk the sauce gently until smooth.

5. To STORE: Let the sauce cool to room temperature, then store in an airtight container for up to 3 weeks.

6. To SERVE: Transfer the sauce to a heatproof bowl set over a saucepan of simmering water and heat to the desired temperature. Alternatively, microwave at 50 percent power, stirring once or twice, for 1 to 3 minutes.

TEST KITCHEN TIP: Smoothing the Surface

A flat surface is important when decorating an ice cream cake, but smoothing the layers of ice cream can be tricky. We suggest smoothing the ice cream with a large, flat-bottomed object such as a meat pounder or metal measuring cup—just run either of these over the top of the cake in a circular motion until you get a perfectly level surface.

FREEZE IT

Ice Cream Cake

SERVES 8 TO 10

If you don't have a meat mallet, you can use something else with a flat surface (1-cup measuring cup or drinking glass) to smooth the ice cream layers. You can easily pipe decorations or a greeting on the top of this cake after it is completely frozen. Instead of decorating the side of the cake with sprinkles, try using chopped nuts, crushed candies or cookies, or mini chocolate chips. Before removing the cake from the springform pan, run your paring knife under hot tap water for 10 seconds or so. The hot knife will slide easily between the cake and the pan, allowing the sides of the pan to be removed quickly.

- 25 Oreo cookies, broken into rough pieces
- 3 tablespoons unsalted butter, melted
- 1 pint strawberry ice cream
- 1 pint vanilla ice cream
- 1 pint chocolate ice cream
- ½ cup rainbow sprinkles (see note)

1. Adjust an oven rack to the middle position and heat the oven to 325 degrees. Pulse the cookies in a food processor until coarsely ground, about 15 short pulses, then let the machine run until the crumbs are uniformly fine, about 15 seconds. With the machine running, pour the butter through the feed tube and continue to process until the mixture resembles wet sand.

2. Transfer ⅔ cup of the crumbs to a 9-inch springform pan and, following the illustrations on page 373, use the bottom of a measuring cup to press the crumbs into an even layer. Bake the crust until it is fragrant and beginning to brown, about 15 minutes. Let cool on a wire rack.

3. Scoop the strawberry ice cream into a large bowl and use a wooden spoon to soften the ice cream and remove any lumps, working quickly so the ice cream does not melt. With a meat mallet (or other flat surface; see note), spread the softened ice cream evenly over the cooled crust, creating a smooth top. Sprinkle another ⅔ cup of the Oreo crumbs over the ice cream and pack them down lightly. Wrap tightly with plastic wrap and freeze until the ice cream is just firm, about 30 minutes. Repeat with the vanilla ice cream and the remaining ⅔ cup Oreo crumbs, and freeze for another 30 minutes. Finish with the chocolate ice cream, spread evenly into the pan, and smooth the top.

4. To STORE: Wrap the cake tightly with plastic wrap and then foil and freeze for up to 1 month.

5. To SERVE: Run a paring knife (see note) between the springform pan and the cake, then remove the sides of the pan. Slide a thin metal spatula between the crust and the pan bottom to loosen, then slide the cake onto a serving platter. Press the sprinkles thoroughly into the side of the cake to cover.

TO SERVE RIGHT AWAY
Freeze the cake as directed in step 4 until firm, 4 to 6 hours, then serve as directed in step 5.

➤ VARIATIONS
Spumoni Cake
Follow the recipe for Ice Cream Cake, substituting cherry ice cream for the strawberry ice cream and pistachio ice cream for the vanilla ice cream. Substitute ground amaretti cookies for the sprinkles and decorate with maraschino cherries.

Double Chocolate and Peanut Butter Cake
If you can find it, use dark chocolate or chocolate fudge ice cream in place of the chocolate ice cream.

Follow the recipe for Ice Cream Cake, substituting Nutter Butter cookies for the Oreos, chocolate ice cream for the strawberry ice cream, and chopped, toasted peanuts for the sprinkles. Make peanut butter ice cream by mixing 1 pint softened vanilla ice cream with ¼ cup chunky peanut butter and use it in place of the vanilla ice cream. Serve with Chocolate Sauce (page 376).

Caramel Turtle Cake
Follow the recipe for Ice Cream Cake, substituting dulce de leche ice cream (made by Häagen-Dazs) for the strawberry ice cream and finely crushed Skor bars for the sprinkles. Sprinkle chopped, toasted pecans over the cake and serve with Caramel Sauce (page 377) and whipped cream.

INGREDIENTS: Chocolate Ice Cream

What's the difference between premium ice creams—the kind sold in small pint- or quart-sized packages—and the mass-market brands sold in half-gallons tubs? And does one taste better than the other?

When ice cream is churned, air is incorporated. If no air were added, the ice cream would be hard and stiff, like an ice cube. Manufacturers can control the amount of air added to the ice cream mixture before it freezes. This air, called overrun, can increase the volume of the ice cream by as little as 20 percent (this is typical of premium brands) or as much as 100 percent (typical of mass-market brands). More overrun produces a fluffy, light ice cream with more air and less of everything else, including fat. Less overrun produces a creamy, dense ice cream with little air and a lot of fat. So when you buy a fluffy ice cream packed in a half-gallon container, you're buying a fair amount of air. But this may not be as bad as it sounds.

When we conducted a blind tasting of seven best-selling brands, two reigned over the rest—one brand, as it turned out, for each style of ice cream. Fans of premium ice cream praised Ben & Jerry's for having a dense, creamy texture and an intense flavor they found reminiscent of fine bittersweet chocolate. Meanwhile, tasters who preferred mass-market Edy's Grand liked it for its fluffy texture and sweet, milk-chocolaty flavor. The other five brands weren't bad—we're talking about ice cream, after all. But tasters did downgrade them for weak flavor and/or icy texture.

THE BEST CHOCOLATE ICE CREAMS

Tasters appreciated the rich flavor and creamy, dense texture of Ben and Jerry's Chocolate Ice Cream (left), while Edy's Grand (right) was praised for its fluffy texture and milk-chocolate flavor.

FLAVORED ICES

FLAVORED ICES ARE SIMPLE TO MAKE, AND THEY'RE LIGHT AND REFRESHING. SOMETIMES referred to as granita, ices are simply a frozen mixture of water, sugar, and liquid flavoring such as fruit juice, wine, or coffee. During the freezing process, ices are generally stirred frequently to produce a slightly granular final texture, but we found a simpler method. By freezing them in small portions (we use ice cube trays) we were able to drop them into a food processor fitted with a metal blade and process until icy and smooth. You can also make popsicles or Italian ices—just pour the mixture into popsicle molds or paper cups, or make multi-flavored popsicles by freezing different layers of flavor one at a time. Just about any fruit juice will work, but here are some of our favorite variations.

FREEZE IT

Lemon (or Lime) Ice

MAKES ABOUT 1 QUART

For the best texture, place the serving bowls in the freezer until ready to serve. Only process as many ice cubes as you need; once processed, the ices must be eaten within an hour or two. Process 3 to 4 ice cubes per person for dessert.

2¼	cups water, preferably spring water
1	cup juice from 6 lemons (or 16 limes)
1	cup sugar
2	tablespoons vodka (optional)
⅛	teaspoon salt

1. Stir all the ingredients together in a nonreactive bowl (glass or pottery) to dissolve the sugar. Pour the mixture into 2 ice cube trays and freeze thoroughly, about 2½ hours.

2. To store: Once frozen, remove the ice cubes from the ice tray and store in a zipper-lock bag for up to 1 month.

3. To serve: Place the desired amount of ice cubes in a food processor and pulse until smooth (if processing all of the ice cubes, you will need to work in 2 batches). Serve immediately.

➤ VARIATIONS

Grapefruit Ice

1¼	cups water, preferably spring water
2½	cups juice from 6 to 8 grapefruits
½	cup sugar
1	tablespoon Campari (optional)
⅛	teaspoon salt

Cranberry Ice

4	cups cranberry juice
½	cup sugar
2	tablespoons juice from 1 lemon or 2 limes
2	tablespoons vodka (optional)
⅛	teaspoon salt

Grape Ice

4	cups grape juice
¼	cup sugar
2	tablespoons juice from 1 lemon
2	tablespoons vodka (optional)
⅛	teaspoon salt

Margarita Ice

2¼	cups water, preferably spring water
½	cup juice from 3 lemons
½	cup juice from 8 limes
1	cup sugar
2	tablespoons tequila
⅛	teaspoon salt

Mimosa Ice

2¼	cups juice from 5 oranges
1½	cups champagne
½	cup sugar
1	tablespoon juice from 1 lime
⅛	teaspoon salt

FRUIT CRISP

WHAT COULD BE BETTER THAN FRESH FRUIT FOR A WARM DESSERT? HOW ABOUT A READY-TO-GO fruit crisp? We found that making this topping for crisp in bulk, then storing it in the freezer gave us the flexibility to have dessert on the table in a flash any night of the week. Our secret? Lay the crisp topping out on a baking sheet and freeze until hard. Then break it apart as it goes into the zipper-lock bag.

We found that two ingredients are essential to a successful crisp—spices (we recommend cinnamon and nutmeg) and nuts (particularly almonds or pecans). The spices add flavor to the topping, while the nuts give it some texture and much-needed crunch. Firm fruits, such as apples, pears, nectarines, peaches, and plums, work best in crisps. Berries are quite watery and will make the topping soggy if used alone—though they will work in combination with firmer fruits.

FREEZE IT

Make-Ahead Fruit Crisp Topping

MAKES 8 CUPS, ENOUGH FOR FOUR 9-INCH
ROUND FRUIT CRISPS

Although almost any unsalted nut may be used in the topping, our preference is for almonds or pecans.

6	tablespoons (2½ ounces) unbleached all-purpose flour
¼	cup packed (1¾ ounces) light brown sugar
¼	cup (1¾ ounces) granulated sugar
¼	teaspoon ground cinnamon
¼	teaspoon ground nutmeg
¼	teaspoon salt
5	tablespoons unsalted butter, cut into ½-inch pieces and chilled
¾	cup pecans or whole almonds, chopped coarse (or chopped fine if mixing topping by hand)

1. Pulse the flour, sugars, cinnamon, nutmeg, and salt in a food processor to combine, 4 to 5 pulses. Add the butter and pulse until the mixture has a coarse cornmeal texture, about 15 pulses. Add the almonds and pulse until the mixture resembles crumbly sand, about 5 pulses. (Do not overprocess or the mixture will take on a smooth, cookie dough–like texture.)

2. TO STORE: Spread the mixture on a rimmed cookie sheet and place in the freezer until frozen, about 1 hour. Transfer the frozen crisp topping to a zipper-lock bag, gently breaking apart the clumps into individual crumbs, and freeze for up to 1 month.

3. TO SERVE: Sprinkle about 2 cups of the frozen crisp topping evenly over prepared fruit (see Fruit Crisp recipe below).

Fruit Crisp

SERVES 4 TO 6

Before assembling a filling, taste the fruit. If the fruit is on the sweet side, add the smaller amount of sugar. If the fruit is more tart, add the larger amount of sugar. When using apples or pears, peel and core them before cutting them into chunks. If using stone fruits like peaches, plums, nectarines, or apricots be sure to remove the pit.

2½–3	pounds apples, pears, nectarines, peaches, apricots, or plums, cut into 1-inch chunks
¼–⅔	cup (1¾ to 2⅓ ounces) sugar
1½	tablespoons juice plus ½ teaspoon zest from 1 lemon
2	cups Make-Ahead Fruit Crisp Topping

1. Adjust an oven rack to the lower-middle position and heat the oven to 375 degrees. Toss together the fruit, sugar, lemon juice, and zest in a medium bowl.

2. Spread the fruit mixture with a rubber spatula into a 9-inch pie plate. Sprinkle the frozen topping evenly over the fruit. Bake for about 40 minutes, until the fruit is bubbling and the topping is deep golden brown. Let cool for 5 minutes before serving.

10

MAKE-AHEAD HOLIDAY MENUS

Make-ahead Holiday Menus

Other Suggested Menus For Make-Ahead Entertaining

Here are some menus featuring recipes from other chapters in this book, which we think will work nicely together. You will need to adjust yields and coordinate preparation of these recipes.

Beef Burgundy (page 177)
buttered egg noodles
Simple Green Beans with Herb Compound Butter (pages 81–82)
Individual Molten Chocolate Cakes (page 359)

Provençal Beef Stew (page 183)
Creamy Polenta (page 67)
mixed green salad
Individual Raspberry Pistachio Buckles (page 355)

Roast Pork Loin with Dried Fruit Stuffing (page 306)
Rice Pilaf (page 64)
Simple Carrots with Herb Compound Butter (pages 81–82)
Fruit Crisp (page 380)

Chicken Tagine (page 192)
couscous
Simple Asparagus with Bistro-Style Mustard Vinaigrette (pages 81–82)
Ginger Pound Cake with Citrus Glaze (pages 366–367)

Overnight Kebabs (page 293)
Rice Pilaf with Currants and Cinnamon (page 65)
Stuffed Plum Tomatoes (page 41)
Grapefruit Ice (page 379)

Crab-Stuffed Sole (page 308)
steamed white rice
sliced tomatoes with Bistro-Style Mustard Vinaigrette (page 82)
Italian Almond Cake (page 369)

Marinara Sauce over Spaghetti (page 209)
Baked Stuffed Onions with Sausage and Chard (page 43)
mixed green salad
Lemon Panna Cotta (page 348)

MAKE-AHEAD TRADITIONAL THANKSGIVING DINNER

⋲ SERVES 12 ⋲

WHEN YOU LOOK AT EACH OF THE INDIVIDUAL dishes we all like to eat on Thanksgiving Day, there is nothing especially difficult about making any single one of them. The problem is that there are so many! Our goal with this menu and timeline was clear: create a crowd-pleasing Thanksgiving menu and organize its preparation so that just one cook can handle this holiday feast.

The menu timeline is built around a big turkey—18 to 22 pounds—because if you're going to the trouble of preparing a traditional Thanksgiving dinner, we think you should have enough turkey (and trimmings) left over to enjoy for days afterward. And since we've roasted nearly 500 turkeys in the test kitchen over the last few years, we can say with confidence that a simple method here works: Choose a Butterball or kosher turkey (for more information see page 386). Just don't pay any attention to the cooking times that come with the turkey. All you need to do is brush it with butter, place it breast side down in a V-rack, and follow our roasting instructions. The result? A perfectly cooked bird.

THE MENU

Classic Roast Turkey with Make-Ahead Gravy

Cranberry Sauce

Savory Bread Stuffing with Sage and Thyme

Make-Ahead Mashed Potatoes

Roasted Carrots with Orange Glaze and Toasted Almonds

Buttery Sautéed Peas with Shallots and Thyme

Spiced Pumpkin Cheesecake

As for the gravy, our recipe doesn't hinge on the turkey neck and giblets and avoids all last-minute roux making, straining, and extra dirty pots. Instead, we rely on roasted turkey parts and vegetables to build the gravy's base. The beauty of our gravy recipe is that it can be made weeks in advance and frozen long before you've purchased your holiday bird.

One of the biggest mistakes people make when planning their menus is to include multiple last-minute side dishes in addition to those that require an hour or more of oven time. Unless you're lucky enough to have two ovens, this is tricky; remember, the turkey is going to be taking up most of the oven. Because we don't cook our stuffing inside our turkey (for food-safety reasons), we developed a make-ahead stuffing prepared in a baking dish that can simply be reheated once the turkey comes out of the oven to rest. And to round out the meal we offer two simple, crowd-pleasing vegetables. Our make-ahead recipe for creamy, fluffy mashed potatoes can be reheated in the microwave. Our roasted, glazed carrot recipe requires zero prep and we designed it so the carrots and stuffing are baked at the same temperature for exactly the same amount of time, so keeping track of them both is a breeze. We also included a sautéed pea recipe that uses frozen peas and a 12-inch nonstick skillet for easy cleanup.

When it comes to dessert, we're assuming the cook is doing everything here, hence our choice of a rich and generous-sized pumpkin cheesecake, which feeds a crowd and can be made several days in advance. Baking multiple pies is needlessly complicated—plus, in our opinion, they are never as good when made the day before. But if you really want pie as part of your Thanksgiving spread, ask your guests to bring one!

THE SHOPPING LIST

PRODUCE

8   pounds russet potatoes (about 12 large; purchase individually, not bagged)

3   pounds baby carrots

2   medium carrots

2   medium shallots

1   medium bunch celery

4   medium onions

2   heads garlic

2   bunches fresh thyme

1   bunch fresh sage

1   bunch fresh parsley

2   (12-ounce) bags cranberries

1   lemon

2   oranges

DAIRY

  Unsalted butter (5½ sticks)

9   large eggs

1   quart heavy cream

2   cups (1 pint) half-and-half

3   (8-ounce) packages cream cheese

MEAT

6   turkey thighs or 9 turkey wings

1   (18- to 22-pound) frozen Butterball or kosher turkey

FREEZER

2   pounds frozen peas

ALCOHOL

  Dry white wine (2 cups)

  Orange liqueur, such as triple sec or Grand Marnier (¼ cup)

PANTRY GOODS

  Vegetable oil spray

  Unbleached all-purpose flour

  Granulated sugar

  Light or dark brown sugar

  Ground ginger

  Ground cinnamon

  Ground cloves

  Ground allspice

  Whole nutmeg

  Cayenne pepper

  Bay leaves

  Vanilla extract

1   (15-ounce) can pumpkin puree

  Graham cracker crumbs (4 ounces, or 8 whole crackers)

  Orange marmalade (⅓ cup)

½   cup sliced almonds

5   quarts low-sodium chicken broth

3   pounds high-quality sliced white sandwich bread

SPECIAL EQUIPMENT

- Large (15 by 12 inches) roasting pan for the gravy and turkey or 2 large disposable aluminum roasting pans (supported by a baking sheet)
- Turkey-sized V-rack
- Instant-read thermometer
- Fat separator
- 9-inch springform pan (for the cheesecake)
- Heavy-duty aluminum foil (for the cheesecake)
- 15 by 10-inch baking dish (or two smaller 8 by 8-inch baking dishes) for the stuffing
- Electric mixer (for the mashed potatoes)

I DAY TO I MONTH AHEAD
- Make the pumpkin cheesecake
- Make the gravy

5 TO 7 DAYS AHEAD
- Thaw the turkey (if necessary). If you forget, quick-thaw your turkey in a bucketful of cold tap water. Plan on 30 minutes per pound and to avoid bacterial growth, change the water every 30 minutes.

I TO 3 DAYS AHEAD
- Make and refrigerate the cranberry sauce

I TO 2 DAYS AHEAD
- Make and refrigerate the mashed potatoes
- Make and refrigerate the stuffing
- Thaw the gravy (if necessary)

4½ TO 5 HOURS BEFORE SERVING
- Prep the turkey for the oven

4 HOURS BEFORE SERVING
- Roast the turkey

I HOUR BEFORE SERVING
- Rest the turkey
- Bake the stuffing
- Roast the carrots
- Bring the cranberry sauce to room temperature
- Prep the sautéed peas (if desired)

30 MINUTES BEFORE SERVING
- Reheat the mashed potatoes
- Reheat the gravy

15 MINUTES BEFORE SERVING
- Sauté the peas
- Carve the turkey

* **NOTE:** About 30 minutes before serving dessert, unmold the cheesecake and let sit at room temperature to soften.

It used to be that when you wanted to cook a turkey you didn't have a choice: They were all frozen. But now there are a variety of fresh kosher and natural birds to choose from. We wondered if there was a difference. After tasting a number of turkeys—both fresh and frozen, all-natural and kosher—we found that most tasters liked the flavor of fresh all-natural turkeys when they were brined but felt that they were dry otherwise. Among unbrined birds, our tasters preferred the "self-basting" Butterball turkey (injected with a salt solution) or a kosher turkey (which is essentially brined by the koshering process). We found both turkeys to be very juicy and flavorful—good options when you're making a really big turkey for a crowd and don't have the space or the inclination to fuss with brining it.

TAKING THE TEMPERATURE OF A TURKEY

To take the temperature of the thigh: Insert an instant-read thermometer into the thickest part of the thigh, away from the bone; when it registers 170 to 175 degrees, the thigh meat is done.

To take the temperature of the breast: Insert the thermometer at the neck end, holding it parallel to the bird; when it registers 165 degrees, the breast meat is done. Confirm the temperature by inserting the thermometer in both sides of the bird.

Spiced Pumpkin Cheesecake

SERVES 12 TO 16

Depending on the oven and the temperature of the ingredients, this cheesecake may bake about 15 minutes faster or slower than the instructions indicate; check the cake 1¼ hours into baking. Although the cheesecake can be made up to 1 month ahead, the crust will begin to lose its crispness after only 1 day. To make slicing easy and neat, it's best to use a knife with a narrow blade, such as a carving knife. Between cuts, dip the blade into a pitcher of hot water and wipe it clean with paper towels. Consider serving the cheesecake with Flavored Whipped Cream (page 397).

CRUST

1	cup (4 ounces) graham cracker crumbs (or 8 whole crackers, broken into rough pieces and processed in food processor until uniformly fine)
3	tablespoons sugar
½	teaspoon ground ginger
½	teaspoon ground cinnamon
¼	teaspoon ground cloves
6	tablespoons (¾ stick) unsalted butter, melted

FILLING

1⅓	cups (9⅓ ounces) sugar
1	teaspoon ground cinnamon
½	teaspoon ground ginger
¼	teaspoon freshly grated nutmeg
¼	teaspoon ground cloves
¼	teaspoon ground allspice
½	teaspoon salt
1	(15-ounce) can pumpkin puree
3	(8-ounce) packages cream cheese, cut into 1-inch chunks, at room temperature
1	tablespoon vanilla extract
1	tablespoon juice from 1 lemon
5	large eggs, at room temperature
1	cup heavy cream

1 DAY TO 1 MONTH AHEAD

1. FOR THE CRUST: Adjust an oven rack to the lower-middle position and heat the oven to 325 degrees. Toss the graham cracker crumbs, sugar, spices, and butter together with a fork until evenly moistened. Spray the bottom and sides of a 9-inch springform pan with vegetable oil spray. Empty the crumbs into the springform pan and press evenly into the pan bottom. Bake until fragrant and beginning to brown around the edges, about 13 minutes. Let cool on wire rack; when cool, wrap the outside of the pan with two 18-inch-square pieces of heavy-duty foil and set inside a roasting pan.

2. FOR THE FILLING: While the crust cools, bring about 4 quarts of water to a simmer in a large saucepan. In a small bowl, whisk the sugar, spices, and salt together; set aside.

3. Line a baking sheet with a triple layer of paper towels and spread the pumpkin on the towels. Cover with a second triple layer of towels and press firmly until the towels are saturated. Peel back the top layer of towels and discard. Grasp the bottom towels and fold the pumpkin in half; peel back the towels. Repeat and flip the pumpkin onto the baking sheet; discard the towels.

4. Using an electric mixer, beat the cream cheese at medium-low speed to break it up, 1 to 2 minutes. Scrape the beaters and bottom and sides of the bowl well with a rubber spatula and then beat in about one-third of the sugar mixture at medium-low speed until combined, 1 to 2 minutes. Scrape the bowl and beat in the remaining sugar mixture in 2 additions, scraping the bowl after each addition.

5. Scrape the bowl and, using low speed, beat in the pumpkin, vanilla, and lemon juice until combined, 1 to 2 minutes. Scrape the bowl and beat in 3 of the eggs at medium-low speed until thoroughly combined, 1 to 2 minutes. Scrape the bowl and beat in the remaining 2 eggs at medium-low speed until thoroughly combined, 1 to 2 minutes. Add the heavy cream and beat at low speed until combined, about 45 seconds. Using a rubber spatula, scrape the bottom and sides of the bowl and give a final stir by hand.

6. Pour the filling into the springform pan and smooth the surface. Set the roasting pan in the oven and pour in enough boiling water to come about halfway up the sides of the springform pan. Bake until the center of the cake is slightly wobbly when the pan is shaken and it registers 150 degrees on an instant-read thermometer, about 1½ hours (see note above).

7. Set the roasting pan on a wire rack and cool until the water is just warm, about 45 minutes. Remove the springform pan from the water bath, discard the foil, and set the pan on the wire rack. Run a paring knife between the cake and the side of the springform pan and let the cake cool until barely warm, about 3 hours. Wrap with plastic wrap and refrigerate until chilled, at least 4 hours. The cake can be refrigerated for up to 3 days or frozen for up to 1 month. (If frozen, allow the cheesecake to thaw in the refrigerator overnight before serving.)

30 MINUTES BEFORE SERVING DESSERT

8. Remove the sides of the pan. Slide a thin metal spatula between the crust and the pan bottom to loosen the cake, then slide the cake onto a serving platter. Let the cheesecake stand at room temperature for about 30 minutes, then cut into wedges and serve.

Make-Ahead Turkey Gravy

MAKES ABOUT 2 QUARTS

Six drumsticks can be substituted for the thighs; however, we found drumsticks to be a bit more unwieldy. Depending on when you make the gravy, you may be able to add the neck (hacked into chunks) and giblets (except the liver) from the turkey to the roasting pan in step 1. You may need to adjust the gravy's consistency when reheating it in step 5; you can use either defatted drippings from the roast turkey or canned chicken broth.

6	turkey thighs, trimmed, or 9 wings, separated at the joints
2	medium carrots, chopped coarse
2	medium celery ribs, chopped coarse
2	medium onions, chopped coarse
1	head garlic, halved
	Vegetable oil spray
12	cups low-sodium chicken broth, plus extra as needed (see note)
2	cups dry white wine
12	sprigs fresh thyme
	Unsalted butter, as needed
1	cup unbleached all-purpose flour

Salt and ground black pepper
Defatted drippings from the Classic Roast Turkey (optional; see step 5 of recipe on page 389)

I DAY TO I MONTH AHEAD

1. MAKE THE GRAVY: Adjust an oven rack to the middle position and heat the oven to 450 degrees. Place the thighs, carrots, celery, onions, and garlic in a roasting pan, spray with vegetable oil, and toss well. Roast, stirring occasionally, until everything is well browned, 1 to 1½ hours.

2. Transfer the contents of the roasting pan to a large Dutch oven. Add the broth, wine, and thyme and bring to a boil. Reduce the heat to low and simmer slowly until the broth is brown and flavorful and measures about 8 cups when strained, about 1½ hours. Strain the broth through a fine-mesh strainer into a large container, pressing on the solids to extract as much liquid as possible; discard the solids. Let the broth sit until the fat has risen to the top, 15 to 20 minutes.

3. Spoon off and reserve ½ cup of the fat (add butter as needed if short on turkey fat). Heat the fat in a Dutch oven over medium-high heat until bubbling. Whisk in flour and cook, whisking constantly, until well browned, 3 to 7 minutes. Slowly whisk in the turkey broth and bring to a boil. Reduce the heat to medium-low and simmer until the gravy is very thick, 10 to 15 minutes. Season with salt and pepper. Transfer the gravy to an airtight container and refrigerate for up to 2 days or freeze for up to 1 month.

I TO 2 DAYS AHEAD

4. THAW THE GRAVY (IF NECESSARY): Transfer the gravy to the refrigerator to thaw overnight.

30 MINUTES BEFORE SERVING

5. REHEAT THE GRAVY: Transfer the gravy to a saucepan and heat over medium heat, stirring often, until bubbling. Add the defatted roast turkey drippings (or additional chicken broth) as needed to adjust the gravy's consistency, then season with salt and pepper to taste.

THE SECRET TO FLAVORFUL GRAVY—IT'S IN THE BAG

Tucked neatly inside the turkey is a turkey neck and a small bag of giblets, which can be added to the gravy for extra flavor. The giblets are three small organs that have been washed and are ready go: the heart, the gizzard, and the liver. We recommend using the heart and gizzard in the gravy, but not the liver— its flavor is just too strong and overpowering.

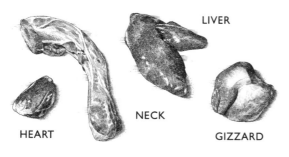

LIVER

NECK

HEART

GIZZARD

Classic Roast Turkey

SERVES 12, WITH LEFTOVERS

Be careful to dry the skin thoroughly before brushing the turkey with butter or else it will have spotty brown skin. Flipping the bird during roasting helps produce evenly cooked meat, but you may opt not to rotate it; in this case, skip the step of lining the V-rack with foil, roast the bird breast side up for the entire cooking time, and be prepared for the cooking time to be extended by ½ hour.

1	(18- to 22-pound) frozen Butterball or kosher turkey
4	tablespoons (½ stick) unsalted butter, melted
1	teaspoon salt
1	teaspoon ground black pepper
1	cup water

5 TO 7 DAYS AHEAD

1. **THAW THE TURKEY (IF NECESSARY):** If the turkey is frozen, place it in a large, disposable aluminum roasting pan supported by a baking sheet and let it thaw in the refrigerator. (Count on 1 day of defrosting for every 4 pounds of turkey; a 20-pound bird will take about 5 days. For last-minute thawing instructions, see page 386.) If desired, remove the neck and giblet packet (discarding the liver) to use in Make-Ahead Turkey Gravy (page 388).

4 TO 5 HOURS BEFORE SERVING

2. **PREP THE TURKEY FOR THE OVEN:** Adjust an oven rack to the lowest position, remove the remaining oven racks, and heat the oven to 425 degrees. Line a large V-rack with heavy-duty foil, poke holes in the foil, and set it inside a 15 by 12-inch roasting pan.

3. Remove and discard any plastic or metal trussing device holding the drumsticks. If you haven't already used them in the gravy, remove and discard the turkey neck and giblet packet. Pat the turkey breast dry with paper towels, then brush with 2 tablespoons of the melted butter and sprinkle with half of the salt and half of the pepper. Set the turkey breast side down on the V-rack. Pat the back dry with paper towels, then brush with the remaining 2 tablespoons of butter and sprinkle with the remaining salt and pepper.

4 HOURS BEFORE SERVING

4. **ROAST THE TURKEY:** Pour the water into the roasting pan. Roast the turkey for 1 hour. Remove the turkey from the oven and, using clean towels or potholders, flip the turkey breast side up in the V-rack. Lower the oven temperature to 325 degrees and continue to roast the turkey, adding more broth as needed to prevent the drippings in the pan from burning, until the legs move freely and an instant-read thermometer inserted into the thickest part of the thigh registers 170 to 180 degrees, about 2 hours longer.

1 HOUR BEFORE SERVING

5. **REST THE TURKEY:** Tip the turkey to drain the juices from the cavity into the roasting pan. Transfer the turkey to a carving board and let it rest until ready to carve, about 45 minutes. (If desired, scrape up any drippings in the roasting pan and pour into a fat separator; let the drippings sit until the fat has separated, about 20 minutes. The defatted drippings may be added to the gravy; see page 388.)

15 MINUTES BEFORE SERVING

6. **CARVE THE TURKEY:** Carve the turkey following the illustrations on page 390 and serve with the gravy.

Cranberry Sauce

MAKES 5 CUPS

If you've got frozen cranberries, do not defrost them before use; just pick through them and add about 2 minutes to the simmering time.

1½	cups water
2	cups sugar
2	tablespoons grated zest from 1 to 2 oranges
½	teaspoon salt
2	(12-ounce) bags cranberries, picked over
¼	cup orange liqueur, such as triple sec or Grand Marnier

1 TO 3 DAYS AHEAD

1. MAKE THE SAUCE: Bring the water, sugar, zest, and salt to a boil in a medium nonreactive saucepan over high heat, stirring occasionally to dissolve the sugar. Stir in the cranberries and return to a boil. Reduce the heat to medium and simmer until saucy and slightly thickened and about two-thirds of the berries have popped open, about 6 minutes.

2. Transfer to a nonreactive bowl, stir in the liqueur, and cool to room temperature. Transfer to an airtight container and refrigerate.

1 HOUR BEFORE SERVING

3. BRING THE SAUCE TO ROOM TEMPERATURE: Remove the sauce from the refrigerator and let stand at room temperature for 1 hour. Stir the sauce thoroughly before serving.

HOW TO CARVE A TURKEY

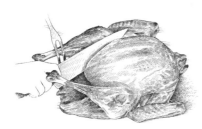

1. Start by slicing the skin between the meat of the breast and the leg.

2. Continue to cut down to the joint, using a fork to pull the leg away from the bird while the tip of the knife severs the joint between the leg and breast.

3. Lay the leg skin side down and use the blade to locate the joint between the thigh and drumstick (where the thigh and drumstick form the sharpest angle). Cut through the joint. If you have properly located it, this should be easy, as you will not be cutting through bone.

4. Use a fork to pull the wing away from the body. Cut through the joint between the wing and the breast to separate the wing from the bird.

5. Using the tip of the knife, cut along the length of the breastbone. Angle the blade of the knife and slice along the line of the rib cage to remove the entire breast half. Use a fork to pull the breast half away from the rib cage in a single piece.

6. Cut thin slices from the breast, slicing across the grain of the meat.

EQUIPMENT: **Carving Boards**

As the centerpiece of the traditional Thanksgiving meal, the turkey—and the bearing of the turkey to the table—inspires in many minds the tableau Norman Rockwell depicted in *Freedom from Want*. What his painting neglects to show, however, is the head of the table struggling to slice that huge bird on its coaster-like china platter. Seasoned cooks know that turkey carving is best done in the kitchen—and requires a sturdy board. We tested eight carving boards to determine which should be entrusted with the holiday bird.

A modest 15-pound turkey measures roughly 16 inches long, a fact that put two 18-inch boards out of the running. After half an hour's rest, our birds shed roughly half a cup of liquid, which flooded the shallow channels on two other boards.

The deeper, wider trenches on the Williams-Sonoma Medium Reversible Carving Board ($58) and the Ironwood Memphis Cutting Board ($79.95) were far more effective at trapping juices. What's more, both boards featured meat-anchoring mechanisms that kept the main course from sliding around en route from countertop to tabletop. The Williams-Sonoma featured a deep, oval-shaped central well,

where the turkey rested snugly, while the Ironwood Memphis had convex rows of pyramid points that gently gripped the turkey. Where the Williams-Sonoma board bested its rival, however, was in its versatility. The Ironwood Memphis, even with its generous surface area (22 by 15 inches) and sturdy, padded feet, was no match for the Williams-Sonoma, which with one flip could be used to accommodate a flank steak or tenderloin roast. And our winning board is elegant enough even for Rockwell's table.

THE BEST CARVING BOARD

The Williams-Sonoma Medium Reversible Carving Board features an oval well that holds the turkey snugly, with ample room for carving.

Make-Ahead Mashed Potatoes

SERVES 12

Bake the potatoes until they are completely tender; err on the side of overcooking rather than undercooking; be sure to use the microwave as instructed, as this is critical to achieving good texture (for more about our method, see "Testing Notes" on page 57). You can use a handheld mixer instead of a standing mixer, but the potatoes will be lumpier. After the potatoes are cooked, it is best to divide them into 2 batches when whipping them and adding the dairy; the smaller batches require less mixing and are therefore less gluey. Although we cut the heavy cream with some half-and-half, you can use all heavy cream, if desired.

8	pounds russet potatoes (about 12 large), scrubbed and poked several times with a fork
4	cups heavy cream, hot
2	cups half-and-half, hot
12	tablespoons (1½ sticks) unsalted butter, melted
	Salt and ground black pepper

1 TO 2 DAYS AHEAD

1. MAKE THE MASHED POTATOES: Adjust an oven rack to the middle position and heat the oven to 450 degrees.

2. Spread the potatoes out over the turntable of the microwave (stacked if necessary). Microwave on high power for 16 minutes, turning potatoes over (and switching them if stacked) halfway through the cooking time.

3. Transfer the potatoes directly onto the hot oven rack. Bake until a skewer glides easily through the flesh, 30 to 45 minutes, flipping them over halfway through the baking time (do not undercook).

4. Remove the potatoes from the oven and cut each potato in half lengthwise. Using an oven mitt or a folded kitchen towel to hold the hot potatoes, scoop out all of the flesh from each potato half into a medium bowl. Break the cooked potato flesh down into small pieces using a fork, potato masher, or rubber spatula. Divide the mashed potatoes into 2 equal batches.

5. Working with 1 batch of the potatoes at time, add half of the batch to the bowl of a standing mixer

fitted with the paddle attachment. Beat the potatoes on high speed until smooth, about 30 seconds, gradually adding the rest of the batch to incorporate, until completely smooth and no lumps remain, 1 to 2 minutes, stopping the mixer to scrape down the sides and bottom of the bowl as needed; transfer each batch to a separate large bowl.

6. Combine the cream and half-and-half. Working with 1 batch of potatoes at a time, fold in 2 cups of the cream mixture, followed by 6 tablespoons of the butter and ¾ teaspoon of salt. Gently fold in additional cream mixture, ¼ cup at time, as needed until you reach desired serving consistency. Once the desired consistency is reached, gently fold in an additional ½ cup of the cream mixture (the potatoes will be quite loose).

7. Combine the 2 batches of mashed potatoes into a large microwave-safe bowl and cover tightly with plastic wrap. Refrigerate for up to 2 days.

30 MINUTES BEFORE SERVING

8. REHEAT THE MASHED POTATOES: Poke lots of vent holes in the plastic wrap with the tip of a knife and microwave at medium-high (75 percent) power until the potatoes are hot, 20 to 30 minutes, stirring gently twice during the reheating time.

✒

Savory Bread Stuffing with Sage and Thyme
SERVES 12, WITH LEFTOVERS

Be sure to use fresh bread for this recipe and do not cut the crusts off (if using store-bought dried bread cubes, see the Test Kitchen Tip at right). We used 1 very large baking dish for this recipe, but you can portion the stuffing into 2 smaller dishes if preferred. In this menu, the stuffing and carrots are baked in the same oven while the roasted turkey rests (the stuffing on the middle rack and the carrots on a lower rack); the cooking times for the stuffing and the carrots are exactly the same, so keeping track of them both as they cook will be easy.

3	pounds high-quality white sandwich bread, cut into ¾-inch cubes
12	tablespoons (1½ sticks) unsalted butter, plus extra for the dish
4	medium celery stalks, chopped fine
2	medium onions, minced
½	cup minced fresh parsley leaves
3	tablespoons minced fresh sage leaves, or 2 teaspoons dried
3	tablespoons minced fresh thyme leaves, or 2 teaspoons dried
5	cups low-sodium chicken broth
4	large eggs, lightly beaten
2	teaspoons salt
2	teaspoons ground black pepper

I TO 2 DAYS AHEAD

1. MAKE THE STUFFING: Adjust 2 oven racks to the upper-middle and lower-middle positions and heat the oven to 300 degrees. Spread the bread out over 2 rimmed baking sheets and bake, stirring occasionally, until the bread is dry, about 1 hour. Let the bread cool completely, about 15 minutes.

2. Melt the butter in a 12-inch nonstick skillet over medium-high heat. Add the celery and onions and cook until softened, about 10 minutes. Stir in the parsley, sage, and thyme and cook until fragrant, about 1 minute. Transfer to a very large bowl.

3. Add the dried, cooled bread, broth, eggs, salt, and pepper to the vegetables and toss to combine. Spread the mixture evenly into a buttered 15 by 10-inch baking dish. Wrap the dish with plastic wrap and refrigerate for up to 2 days.

I HOUR BEFORE SERVING

4. BAKE THE STUFFING: As soon as the turkey is removed from the oven, adjust 2 oven racks to the middle and lowest positions and increase the oven temperature to 425 degrees (the middle rack is for the stuffing, the lower rack is for the carrots; see note above). Unwrap the stuffing, cover it tightly with aluminum foil, and bake on the middle rack for 25 minutes. Remove the foil and continue to bake until the top is golden, 20 to 30 minutes longer.

TEST KITCHEN TIP: Using Store-Bought Dried Bread Cubes
You can substitute three 14-ounce bags of plain, dried bread cubes; however, these bread cubes will be very dry and require more liquid; increase the amount of chicken broth to 7 cups.

Roasted Carrots with Orange Glaze and Toasted Almonds

SERVES 12

A nonstick baking sheet will allow the carrots to get a nice roasted color and make cleanup a breeze. Don't line the baking sheet with foil or you will lose some of the glaze (it will seep underneath the foil) and the carrots will not brown at all. In this menu, the stuffing and carrots are baked in the same oven while the roasted turkey rests (the stuffing on an upper rack and the carrots on a lower rack); the cooking times for the stuffing and the carrots are exactly the same, so keeping track of them both as they cook will be easy.

3	pounds baby carrots
⅓	cup light or dark brown sugar
⅓	cup orange marmalade
4	tablespoons (½ stick) unsalted butter, cut into small pieces
	Salt
	Pinch cayenne pepper
½	cup sliced almonds, toasted
2	tablespoons minced fresh parsley leaves
	Ground black pepper

1 HOUR BEFORE SERVING

1. ROAST THE CARROTS: As soon as the turkey is removed from the oven, adjust 2 oven racks to the middle and lowest positions and increase the oven temperature to 425 degrees (the middle rack is for the stuffing, the lower rack is for the carrots).

2. Spray a nonstick rimmed baking sheet with vegetable oil spray. Spread the carrots over the prepared baking sheet and sprinkle with the sugar, marmalade, butter, ½ teaspoon salt, and cayenne. Cover tightly with foil and bake, stirring occasionally, until the sugar and butter have melted and the sauce is bubbling, about 25 minutes.

3. Uncover the carrots and continue to cook in the oven, stirring occasionally, until tender and glazed, 20 to 30 minutes. Transfer to a serving bowl, stir in the almonds and parsley, and season with salt and pepper to taste.

Buttery Sautéed Peas with Shallots and Thyme

SERVES 12

To make this last-minute side dish a real breeze, prep and measure all the ingredients an hour or two in advance (keep the peas frozen).

4	tablespoons (½ stick) unsalted butter
2	medium shallots, minced
2	teaspoons minced fresh thyme leaves
2	medium garlic cloves, minced or pressed through a garlic press (about 2 teaspoons)
1	tablespoon sugar
	Salt
2	pounds frozen peas (do not thaw)
	Ground black pepper

15 MINUTES BEFORE SERVING

SAUTÉ THE PEAS: Melt the butter in a 12-inch nonstick skillet over medium-high heat. Add the shallots, thyme, garlic, sugar, and ½ teaspoon of salt and cook until softened, about 2 minutes. Stir in the peas and cook, stirring often, until thawed and heated through, 5 to 10 minutes. Season with salt and pepper to taste.

INGREDIENTS: Frozen Peas

In the test kitchen, we have come to depend on frozen peas. Not only are they more convenient than their fresh, in-the-pod comrades, but they taste better. Test after test, we found frozen peas to be tender and sweet while fresh peas tasted starchy and bland. Trying to understand this curious finding, we looked to the frozen food industry for some answers.

Green peas lose a substantial portion of their nutrients within 24 hours of being picked. This rapid deterioration is the reason for the starchy, bland flavor of most "fresh" peas found at the grocery store. These not-so-fresh peas might be several days old, depending on where they came from and how long they were kept in the cooler. Frozen peas, on the other hand, are picked, cleaned, sorted, and frozen within several hours of harvest, which helps preserve their delicate sugars and flavors. Fittingly enough, when commercially frozen vegetables first began to appear in the 1920s and 1930s, green peas were among them. So unless you grow your own or know a reputable local farm stand, you're better off buying frozen peas.

MAKE-AHEAD HOLIDAY
BEEF TENDERLOIN DINNER

⇒ SERVES 12 ⇐

CHOOSING DISHES FOR A THANKSGIVING menu is easy, but when the cold weather sets in and you're looking to celebrate another winter holiday—or just celebrate period—you probably don't want the usual turkey dinner again. That's where beef comes in. And when you really want to impress, a big, buttery beef tenderloin is the way to go. Our goal with this menu was to create an impressive array of make-ahead dishes built around this holiday-worthy main course. And we wanted to coordinate the cooking so that it could easily be made ahead to avoid any last-minute stress typically associated with such a grand dinner.

Because we wanted this dinner to have a slightly formal feel, we thought a first course would be in order. A first course would also help us pace the preparation of the meal, so that while guests sit down to enjoy this dish, the rest of the meal can finish cooking. A rich shrimp bisque would start our tenderloin dinner off on the right note. The broth for the bisque, which is the most time-consuming aspect of its preparation, can be made up to two days ahead and refrigerated. The shrimp, cut into pieces (along with cream and a few seasonings to finish), are added to the broth during reheating, so they cook up plump, juicy, and full of fresh flavor.

The beef tenderloin requires very little prep beyond tying the roast for even cooking and seasoning with olive oil, salt, and pepper. But do note that roasts are sold peeled or unpeeled. A peeled roast has had the outer layer of fat and the tough silver skin removed, while an unpeeled roast will require a fair amount of trimming. Wholesale clubs sell beef tenderloin unpeeled, but the discounted price justifies the extra work—at a wholesale club, you might find yourself paying one-third the price of a roast from a butcher or supermarket (for more information, see page 396). A rich red wine and cherry sauce is the perfect complement to the beef and can be prepared up to two days ahead and simply reheated.

A worthy partner for tenderloin, Potato Gratin with Fennel and Leeks can be assembled and fully baked one to two days ahead. One hour and 15 minutes before serving the gratin is removed from the fridge. And then, while the roasted tenderloin rests, it heats through in the oven for just 30 minutes. For our second side, we chose asparagus seasoned simply with olive oil, salt, and pepper. The asparagus can be blanched up to two days ahead and the dish is easily reheated in the microwave.

As a finale to our sophisticated dinner, we wanted an equally refined dessert. Flourless Chocolate Cake fits the bill—and the best part is that the cake can be made up to four days ahead and refrigerated or even frozen for up to a month. With this festive menu, your guests will think you slaved all day—though you'll know otherwise.

THE MENU

Rich and Velvety Shrimp Bisque

Roast Beef Tenderloin with Port Wine and Cherry Sauce

Potato Gratin with Fennel and Leeks

Simple Steamed Asparagus

Flourless Chocolate Cake

PRODUCE

2	medium carrots
2	medium celery ribs
2	medium leeks
4	bunches asparagus
2	medium fennel bulbs
1	medium onion
2	large shallots
1	medium head garlic
4	pounds russet potatoes (about 8 medium)
1½	pounds sweet potatoes (2 to 3 medium)
1	bunch thyme
1	bunch chives
1	lemon

DAIRY

1	pound (4 sticks) unsalted butter
8	large eggs
1	quart plus ½ cup heavy cream
	Whole milk (1 cup)
6	ounces Gruyère cheese

MEAT AND SHELLFISH

3	pounds extra-large shell-on shrimp
1	whole, unpeeled beef tenderloin (about 6 pounds; see note on page 396)

ALCOHOL

Port (2 cups)
Dry red wine (2 cups)
Dry white wine (3½ cups)
Dry sherry or Madeira (¼ cup)
Bourbon, brandy, or Grand Marnier
(1 tablespoon)

PANTRY GOODS

	Kosher salt
	Coffee
	Vegetable oil
	Olive oil
	Extra-virgin olive oil
	Cornstarch
	Unbleached all-purpose flour
	Granulated sugar
1	pound semisweet chocolate or bittersweet chocolate
1	(32-ounce) carton low-sodium chicken broth
5	(8-ounce) bottles clam juice
1	(28-ounce) can diced tomatoes
	Fennel seeds
	Bay leaves
	Cayenne pepper
5	ounces (1 cup) dried tart cherries

SPECIAL EQUIPMENT

- 9-inch springform pan (for the cake)
- Food processor (for the bisque and the gratins)
- Cheesecloth or a very-fine-mesh strainer (for the bisque)
- Two 2-quart gratin dishes (for the gratins)
- Large roasting pan fitted with a wire rack (for the cake and the tenderloin)

THE TIMELINE

I DAY TO I MONTH AHEAD
- Make the flourless chocolate cake

I TO 2 DAYS AHEAD
- Make the shrimp broth for the bisque
- Make the potato gratins
- Blanch the asparagus
- Make the port wine and cherry sauce

2¼ HOURS BEFORE SERVING
- Let the tenderloin sit at room temperature

1¼ HOURS BEFORE SERVING
- Roast the tenderloin
- Let the potato gratins sit at room temperature

45 MINUTES BEFORE SERVING THE TENDERLOIN
- Finish the bisque

30 MINUTES BEFORE SERVING
- Let the roasted tenderloin rest
- Bake the potato gratins
- Serve the bisque

5 TO 10 MINUTES BEFORE SERVING
- Finish the port wine and cherry sauce
- Reheat the asparagus in the microwave
- Slice the tenderloin

* **NOTE:** Thirty minutes before serving dessert, unmold the flourless chocolate cake and bring to room temperature.

ALL ABOUT BEEF TENDERLOIN

We found that prices of tenderloin range wildly—between $12.60 and $54.84 per pound—and that a high price doesn't always ensure the best quality. After tasting a variety of tenderloins (bought at local supermarkets, at wholesale clubs, and from specialty mail-order sources), we highly recommend buying a whole, untrimmed (unpeeled) tenderloin from a wholesale club, such as BJ's or Sam's Club, and trimming it yourself. See page 403 for illustrations of how to trim and tie a whole tenderloin into a tidy roast. Note that a whole, untrimmed 6-pound tenderloin will weigh roughly 4½ to 5 pounds after you trim it.

TYING WITH THE RIGHT TWINE

What if you don't have a skein of kitchen twine on hand? Are there any worthy substitutes? To find out, we tested tying our roast with household twine (not labeled kitchen twine) from the hardware store along with dental floss. Although it didn't melt or burn, the hardware store twine leached its day-glo yellow dye into our roast. And the floss? Because it's so thin, it cut into our roast during tying. And, after cooking, we found the whitish almost translucent filament nearly invisible and impossible to remove. Our advice? Stick with simple cotton or linen twine labeled kitchen twine.

As for tying your roasts, some cooks have trouble tying properly. If you're one of them, practice with a roll of paper towels and strands of kitchen twine. It's a lot neater than practicing on a roast.

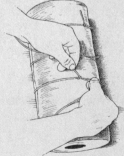

Want to hone your roast-tying skills? Improvise with a roll of paper towels and kitchen twine.

FREEZE IT

Flourless Chocolate Cake

SERVES 12 TO 16

The cake will still look quite underdone and liquidy when it is ready to be removed from the oven; be sure to pull it from the oven when an instant-read thermometer registers 140 degrees. It will continue to firm up as it cools and will set completely with an overnight stay in the refrigerator. If using an 8-inch springform pan, increase the cooking time to 22 to 25 minutes. Sprinkle confectioners' sugar or cocoa powder over the cake, if desired, and serve with Flavored Whipped Cream (recipe follows), Berry Coulis (page 347), or fresh berries.

16	tablespoons (2 sticks) unsalted butter, cut into ½-inch chunks, plus extra for greasing the pan
1	pound semisweet chocolate or bittersweet chocolate, coarsely chopped
¼	cup strong coffee or liquor (optional)
8	large eggs, cold

1 DAY TO 1 MONTH AHEAD

1. MAKE THE CAKE: Adjust an oven rack to the lower-middle position and heat the oven to 325 degrees. Line the bottom of a 9-inch springform pan with parchment paper and grease the pan sides with butter. Wrap the bottom and sides of the pan securely with heavy-duty foil. Set the pan in a large roasting pan; set aside. Bring a kettle of water to a boil.

2. Meanwhile, melt the chocolate, butter, and coffee (if using) in a medium heatproof bowl set over a saucepan filled with 1 inch of barely simmering water, stirring frequently until smooth. Remove from the heat.

3. Using an electric mixer, whip the eggs until they turn pale yellow and creamy, about 3 minutes. Increase the speed to high and continue to whip until the volume doubles to approximately 1 quart, 1 to 2 minutes longer.

4. Using a large rubber spatula, fold one-third of the eggs into the chocolate mixture until only a few streaks of egg are visible. Gently fold in half of the remaining eggs, then the last of the remaining eggs until the mixture is totally homogenous.

Scrape the batter into the prepared springform pan and smooth the surface with a rubber spatula.

5. Set the roasting pan on the oven rack and pour enough boiling water to come about halfway up the side of the springform pan. Bake until the cake has risen slightly, the edges are just beginning to set but are still quite jiggly, a thin glazed crust (like a brownie) has formed on the surface, and an instant-read thermometer inserted halfway through the center of the cake registers 140 degrees, 20 to 22 minutes.

6. Remove the cake pan from the water bath, set on a wire rack, and let cool to room temperature. Wrap the cake tightly with plastic wrap and refrigerate for up to 4 days or freeze for up to 1 month. (If frozen, the cake must be defrosted in the refrigerator for 24 hours before serving.)

30 MINUTES BEFORE SERVING

7. BRING THE CAKE TO ROOM TEMPERATURE: Remove the springform pan sides, invert the cake on a sheet of waxed paper, peel off the parchment pan liner, and turn the cake right side up on a serving platter. Let the cake sit at room temperature for 20 to 30 minutes before serving.

Flavored Whipped Cream

MAKES ABOUT 2 CUPS

This whipped cream is terrific with Flourless Chocolate Cake (above) or Spiced Pumpkin Cheesecake (page 387). If you like your whipped cream only lightly sweetened, reduce the sugar to 1½ teaspoons. Bourbon, brandy, and Grand Marnier are just a few flavorful liquors you could use in this recipe. Prepare this whipped cream just before serving.

1	cup heavy cream, chilled
1	tablespoon sugar
1	tablespoon liquor (see note) or 1 teaspoon vanilla extract
	Pinch salt

Using an electric mixer, whip all the ingredients together at low speed until frothy and the sugar has dissolved, about 1 minute. Increase the speed to high and continue to whip until smooth, thick, and doubled in volume, 1 to 3 minutes.

INGREDIENTS:
White Wines for Cooking

When a recipe calls for "dry white wine," it's tempting to grab whatever open bottle is in the fridge, regardless of grape varietal. Are we doing our dishes a disservice? Sure, Chardonnay and Pinot Grigio may taste different straight from the glass, but how much do those distinctive flavor profiles really come through once the wines get cooked down with other ingredients?

To find out, we tried four different varietals and a supermarket "cooking wine" in five recipes: braised fennel, risotto, a basic pan sauce, a beurre blanc, and chicken chasseur. In our tests, only Sauvignon Blanc consistently boiled down to a "clean" yet sufficiently acidic flavor—one that played nicely with the rest of the ingredients. Differences between the wines were most dramatic in gently flavored dishes, such as the risotto and beurre blanc. In contrast, all five wines produced similar (and fine) results when used in chicken chasseur, no doubt because of all the other strong flavors in this dish.

But what's a cook without leftover Sauvignon Blanc to do? Is there a more convenient option than opening a fresh bottle? To find out, we ran the same cooking tests with sherry and vermouth, wines fortified with alcohol to increase their shelf life. Sherry was too distinct and didn't fare well in these tests, but vermouth was surprisingly good. In fact, its clean, bright flavor bested all but one of the drinking wines. And at $5 a bottle (for Gallo, our top-rated brand of vermouth), you can't argue with the price.

THE BEST WHITE WINES FOR COOKING

Crisp, clean, and bright, Sauvignon Blanc (left) was strong enough to share the spotlight with other ingredients but refused to steal the show. And a pleasing sweet/tart balance made dry vermouth (right) a close second. And, after being opened, it can sit on the shelf for months.

Rich and Velvety Shrimp Bisque
SERVES 12

The shrimp shells contribute a lot of flavor to the bisque, so be sure to purchase shell-on shrimp for the soup base. Straining the soup base in step 4 is the most difficult part of this recipe, and we found it easiest to strain it twice: once using a wide-mesh strainer or colander to remove the large bits, then again through a fine-mesh strainer or strainer lined with cheesecloth to remove the smaller bits. In this menu, the soup is served as a first course; it should be served while the tenderloin rests and the gratins bake.

SHRIMP BROTH

2	medium carrots, peeled and cut into large chunks
2	medium celery ribs, cut into large chunks
1	medium onion, cut into large chunks
3	medium garlic cloves, peeled
2	pounds extra-large shell-on shrimp (21 to 25 per pound)
4	tablespoons (½ stick) unsalted butter
3	sprigs fresh thyme
2	bay leaves
1	teaspoon salt
½	teaspoon sugar
1¼	cups unbleached all-purpose flour
5	(8-ounce) bottles clam juice
3	cups dry white wine
14	ounces low-sodium chicken broth (1¾ cups from one 32-ounce carton)
1	(14-ounce) can low-sodium vegetable broth (1¾ cups)
1	(28-ounce) can diced tomatoes, drained, ¼ cup juice reserved

BISQUE

1½	cups heavy cream
	Salt and ground black pepper
1	pound extra-large shrimp (21 to 25 per pound), peeled and deveined (including tails), each shrimp cut into 3 pieces
¼	cup dry sherry or Madeira
2	tablespoons juice from 1 small lemon
	Pinch cayenne pepper
¼	tablespoons minced fresh chives

1 TO 2 DAYS AHEAD

1. **PREPARE THE SHRIMP BROTH:** Pulse the carrots, celery, onion, and garlic in a food processor until finely chopped, about 5 pulses; transfer to a bowl and set aside. Process 1 pound of the shrimp (with the shells) in the food processor until finely chopped, 10 to 15 seconds; transfer to the bowl with the vegetables and repeat with the remaining pound of shrimp.

2. Melt the butter in a large Dutch oven over medium-high heat. Stir in the chopped vegetables and shrimp, thyme, bay leaves, salt, and sugar. Cover and cook, stirring frequently, until the shrimp are pink and have released their juices and the vegetables are softened, about 10 minutes.

3. Stir in the flour and cook, stirring constantly, until thoroughly combined and lightly browned, about 1 minute. Stir in the clam juice, wine, broths, tomatoes, and ¼ cup reserved tomato juice. Cover and bring to a boil. Uncover, reduce to a simmer, and cook, stirring frequently, until the broth is thickened and flavorful, 50 to 60 minutes.

4. Strain the broth through a colander or wide-mesh strainer, pressing on the solids with the back of a ladle to extract all the liquid (you should have just under 3 quarts). Strain the broth again, to remove any fine bits, through a fine-mesh strainer (or a large-mesh strainer lined with a double layer of damp cheesecloth) into an airtight container and refrigerate for up to 2 days.

45 MINUTES BEFORE SERVING

5. **FINISH THE BISQUE:** Transfer the broth to a large Dutch oven and bring to a simmer over medium heat, about 15 minutes. Meanwhile, whip ½ cup of the cream to stiff peaks and season with salt and pepper to taste; set aside.

6. Stir the remaining 1 cup cream, shrimp, sherry, lemon juice, and cayenne into the broth and simmer until the shrimp are just pink, about 1 minute. Remove from the heat and season with salt and pepper to taste. When serving, dollop individual portions with the whipped cream and sprinkle with the chives.

PEELING SHRIMP

1. Hold the tail end of the shrimp with one hand and the opposite end of the shrimp with the other, then bend the shrimp back and forth and side to side to split the shell.

2. Lift off the tail portion of the shell, then slide your thumb under the legs of the remaining portion and lift it off as well.

DEVEINING SHRIMP

1. With a paring knife, make a shallow slit along the back of each shrimp. With the tip of the blade, lift up and loosen the vein.

2. Because the vein is quite sticky, we like to touch the knife blade to a paper towel on the counter. The vein will stick to the towel and you can devein the next shrimp with a clean knife.

Potato Gratin with Fennel and Leeks

SERVES 12

The gratin is portioned into 2 smaller dishes rather than a single large dish so that it can be reheated more quickly. We like to use shallow 2-quart gratin dishes, which allow for the most surface area (and browned crust), but 8 by 8-inch Pyrex baking dishes also work. Prep and assemble all of the ingredients before slicing the potatoes or else the potatoes will begin to brown (do not store the sliced potatoes in water to prevent this or else the gratin will taste bland and watery). Parmesan cheese can be substituted for the Gruyère, if desired.

4	pounds russet potatoes (about 8 medium), peeled and sliced ⅛-inch thick
1½	pounds sweet potatoes (2 to 3 medium), peeled and sliced ⅛-inch thick
2	cups heavy cream
1	cup whole milk
4	tablespoons (½ stick) unsalted butter
2	medium leeks (about 12 ounces), white and light green parts only, sliced ⅛ inch thick
2	medium fennel bulbs (about 1½ pounds), halved, cored, and sliced ⅛ inch thick
5	teaspoons salt
1	teaspoon fennel seeds
4	medium garlic cloves, minced or pressed through a garlic press (about 4 teaspoons)
1½	teaspoons minced fresh thyme leaves, or ½ teaspoon dried
½	cup dry white wine
½	teaspoon ground black pepper
6	ounces Gruyère cheese, grated (1½ cups)

1 TO 2 DAYS AHEAD

1. MAKE THE GRATINS: Adjust an oven rack to the middle position and heat the oven to 375 degrees. Divide the potatoes and sweet potatoes evenly between 2 large bowls. Divide the cream and milk evenly between the 2 bowls and toss to coat the potatoes; set aside.

2. Melt the butter in a large nonstick skillet over medium-high heat. Add the leeks, fennel, salt, and fennel seeds; cover and cook, stirring occasionally, until the vegetables are wilted and have given off some liquid, 5 to 7 minutes. Uncover and continue to cook until most of the liquid has evaporated, 3 to 5 minutes longer. Stir in the garlic and thyme and cook until fragrant, about 30 seconds. Stir in the wine and pepper and cook until mostly evaporated, about 1 minute. Divide the leek mixture evenly between the 2 bowls of potatoes and toss to combine.

3. Turn each bowl of potatoes into 2 shallow 2-quart gratin dishes, pressing the potatoes into a flat, even layer. Cover the dishes tightly with foil, arrange on a rimmed baking sheet lined with foil (or 2 small baking sheets), and bake side by side on the same oven rack until the potatoes are completely tender and a fork can be inserted easily into the center of both dishes, 1¾ to 2 hours, rotating the baking sheets halfway through baking.

4. Transfer the gratins from the baking sheets to a wire rack, remove the foil, and let cool until just warm, about 45 minutes. Wrap the dishes tightly with plastic wrap and refrigerate for up to 2 days.

1¼ HOURS BEFORE SERVING

5. PREP THE GRATINS FOR REHEATING: Remove the gratins from the refrigerator and let sit at room temperature for 30 to 45 minutes.

30 MINUTES BEFORE SERVING

6. REHEAT THE GRATINS: As soon as the tenderloin is removed from the oven, adjust the oven rack to the middle position and increase the oven temperature to 450 degrees. Unwrap the gratins and sprinkle the Gruyère evenly over the top. Bake the gratins, uncovered and side by side, on the oven rack until the cheese is golden brown and the edges are bubbling, about 30 minutes.

> **TEST KITCHEN TIP:**
> **Potato Slicing Basics**
> The quickest way to slice the potatoes for the gratin is in a food processor fitted with an ⅛-inch-thick slicing blade or by using a mandoline or V-slicer. If using a food processor, you'll need to halve the potatoes crosswise and put them in the feed tube cut side down so that they sit flat to the surface of the blade. If cutting the potatoes by hand, be sure to take your time and cut them uniformly.

Simple Steamed Asparagus

SERVES 12

The simplicity of this dish is a perfect complement to the rich potato gratin and potent red wine–cherry sauce within this menu. Feel free to substitute butter, or even a compound butter (see page 82), for the olive oil. When blanching the asparagus, be sure to leave it slightly underdone; the asparagus will finish cooking in the microwave during reheating.

	Salt
4	bunches asparagus (3½ to 4 pounds), tough ends trimmed
	Extra-virgin olive oil
	Ground black pepper

1 TO 2 DAYS AHEAD

1. BLANCH THE ASPARAGUS: Bring 8 quarts of water to a boil in a large pot over high heat. Fill a large bowl with ice water; set aside. Add 2 tablespoons salt and the asparagus to the boiling water and cook until mostly tender but still underdone, with a little crunch in the center, 2 to 4 minutes.

2. Drain the asparagus, then transfer immediately to the ice water. Let the asparagus cool completely, about 5 minutes, then drain and pat dry with paper towels. Wrap the asparagus loosely in paper towels and store in an airtight container (or large zipper-lock bag) for up to 2 days.

5 TO 10 MINUTES BEFORE SERVING

3. REHEAT AND FINISH THE ASPARAGUS: Transfer the asparagus to a large microwave-safe bowl, cover with plastic wrap, and microwave on high until steaming, 6 to 8 minutes. Drain away any accumulated water and season with the oil, salt, and pepper to taste.

Port Wine and Cherry Sauce

MAKES 3 CUPS

Use a $10 bottle of medium-bodied red wine, such as Côtes du Rhône.

1	tablespoon vegetable oil
2	large shallots, minced
2	cups port

2	cups dry red wine
1½	cups low-sodium chicken broth (from one 32-ounce carton)
1	cup dried tart cherries (5 ounces)
4	sprigs thyme
2	bay leaves
4	teaspoons cornstarch, dissolved in 2 tablespoons water
4	tablespoons (½ stick) unsalted butter, cut into 4 pieces
	Salt and ground black pepper

1 TO 2 DAYS AHEAD

1. MAKE THE SAUCE: Heat the oil in a medium saucepan over medium heat until shimmering. Add the shallots and cook until softened, about 2 minutes. Stir in the port, wine, broth, cherries, thyme, and bay leaves and bring to a boil. Reduce to a simmer and cook until the mixture measures about 3 cups, 50 to 60 minutes.

2. Whisk to dissolve the cornstarch in the water, then stir into the simmering sauce and cook until the sauce has thickened and no longer tastes powdery, about 2 minutes. Remove the thyme sprigs and bay leaves, transfer the sauce to an airtight container, and refrigerate for up to 2 days.

5 TO 10 MINUTES BEFORE SERVING

3. HEAT AND FINISH THE SAUCE: Bring the sauce to a simmer in a medium saucepan over medium heat. Stir in the butter, one piece at a time, and season with salt and pepper to taste.

Roast Beef Tenderloin

SERVES 12

To give the tenderloin a more pronounced pepper crust, increase the amount of pepper to 6 tablespoons and use a mixture of black, white, pink, and green peppercorns. For a consistently even grind of all the peppercorn types, we suggest using a mortar and pestle or heavy-bottomed skillet rather than a pepper or spice grinder. Letting the seasoned roast sit at room temperature for 1 hour before cooking enhances its flavor and helps it cook through more evenly. The tenderloin can be trimmed and tied (but not seasoned) a day in advance.

INGREDIENTS: Black Pepper

For a spice that we use just about every day, and with a wide variety of foods, it's hard not to wonder if we have taken pepper too much for granted. Although most of us tend to think that one jar of black pepper is the same as another, several varieties exist. The most readily available include Vietnamese pepper, Lampong (from the island of Sumatra), and Malabar and Tellicherry (both from India). Among spice experts, each has gained a reputation for its particular attributes. Perhaps we should be seeking out black pepper from a particular region of a particular country.

Or, at the other end of the spectrum, perhaps all this fuss over grinding fresh whole peppercorns is nonsense, not really providing any improved flavor. We decided to hold a blind tasting to sort it all out. We included in our tasting the two preeminent national supermarket brands as well as the above-mentioned varieties, which were ordered from specialty spice and gourmet stores.

All of the peppers were offered plain but with the option of being tasted on plain white rice. Overall, our tasting confirmed that freshly ground pepper is far superior to pepper purchased already ground. The latter carried minimal aroma and tended to taste sharp and dull, lacking in complexity. Those whole peppercorns that were fresh ground just before the tasting contained bold as well as subtle flavors and aromas that were both lively and complex.

As for differences between the varieties of whole peppercorns that were tasted fresh ground, we found them to be distinct yet subtle. All were appreciated for their particular characteristics, receiving high scores within a close range of one another. Based on these results, we concluded that what is important is not so much which variety of pepper you buy but how you buy it.

Why did we find the most noticeable differences in pepper to be between fresh-ground whole pepper and commercially ground pepper? When a peppercorn is cracked, the volatile chemical components that give pepper its bold aroma as well as its subtle characteristics immediately begin to disperse. These more subtle flavors often include pine and citrus. So with time (and cracking), what remains is the predominant nonvolatile compound in black pepper, piperine. Piperine is the source of black pepper's renowned pungency and is what gives it its characteristic hot, sharp, and stinging qualities. It is also said to stimulate saliva and gastric juices, creating the sensation of hunger.

THE BEST BLACK PEPPER

McCormick Whole Black Peppercorns beat out the rest of the supermarket competition as well as several mail-order brands. Note that this "premium" product, sold in glass bottles, also fared better than McCormick peppercorns sold in plastic bottles. This brand is sold under the Schilling label on the West Coast.

---

1   whole, unpeeled beef tenderloin (about 6 pounds), trimmed of fat and silver skin, tail end tucked, and tied at 2-inch intervals (see illustrations on page 403)
2   tablespoons olive oil
1   tablespoon kosher salt
2   tablespoons coarsely ground black pepper (see note)

2¼ HOURS BEFORE SERVING

1. PREP THE TENDERLOIN FOR ROASTING: Remove the tenderloin roast from the refrigerator. Following the illustration on page 403, set the roast on a sheet of plastic wrap and rub it all over with the oil. Sprinkle with the salt and pepper and then lift the wrap to press the excess seasoning into the meat. Let the roast sit at room temperature for 1 hour.

1¼ HOURS BEFORE SERVING

2. ROAST THE TENDERLOIN: Adjust an oven rack to the upper-middle position and heat the oven to 425 degrees. Transfer the tenderloin to a wire rack set in a shallow roasting pan. Roast until an instant-read thermometer inserted into the thickest part of the roast registers about 125 degrees (the meat will range from medium-rare to medium in different areas), about 45 minutes.

30 MINUTES BEFORE SERVING

3. REST THE TENDERLOIN: Transfer the tenderloin to a carving board, tent loosely with foil, and let rest for 20 to 30 minutes.

5 TO 10 MINUTES BEFORE SERVING

4. SLICE THE TENDERLOIN: Cut the meat into ½-inch-thick slices, arrange on a warm platter, and serve with the Port Wine and Cherry Sauce (page 401).

TRIMMING AND TYING A BEEF TENDERLOIN ROAST

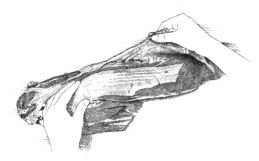

1. Pull away the outer layer of fat to expose the fatty chain of meat.

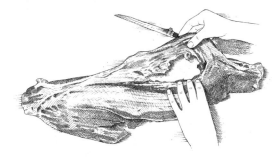

2. Pull the chain of fat away from the roast and cut it off; discard the chain.

3. Scrape the silver skin at the creases in the thick end to expose the lobes.

4. Trim the silver skin by slicing under it and cutting upward.

5. Remove the remaining silver skin in the creases at the thick end.

6. Turn the tenderloin over and remove the fat from the underside.

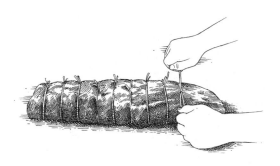

7. Fold the thin tip end of the roast underneath, then tie the roast at 2-inch intervals with kitchen twine.

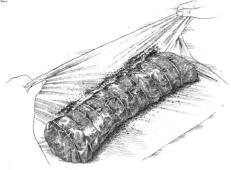

8. One hour before roasting, set the roast on a sheet of plastic wrap, then rub with oil and season with salt and pepper. Lift the plastic wrap up and around the roast and press on the seasonings to adhere.

MAKE-AHEAD
HOLIDAY HAM DINNER

⋛ SERVES 12 ⋖

A GLAZED SPIRAL-SLICED HAM IS A HOLIDAY favorite. Cooks especially appreciate the versatility a ham provides—it can be served hot for a sit-down dinner or warm as part of a buffet. For this menu we aimed to create a make-ahead ham dinner that could be served in either style.

We prefer spiral-sliced hams for their well-seasoned flavor, meaty texture, and ease of serving. There are a few things to keep in mind with spiral-sliced hams. First, choose a shank portion—the bone configuration will make it easier to carve. Use an oven bag to heat the ham. An oven bag creates a tight seal that helps encapsulate the heat and speeds the heat-through process. Third, ditch the overly sweet gloppy glaze that comes with your ham. Instead, make your own tangy, well-seasoned glaze with apple cider, brown sugar, mustard, and a pinch of cloves. If you choose to serve the ham as part of a buffet, you might consider adding sliced dinner rolls alongside for sandwiches. Offering a variety of mustards is also a nice touch.

For one of our side dishes, we chose macaroni and cheese. A traditional Southern accompaniment to ham, macaroni and cheese can easily be made up to two days ahead and then baked just before serving. Most macaroni and cheese casseroles turn dry when reheated. Not ours. We make our mac and cheese with lots of sauce to keep it moist in the fridge. And two kinds of cheeses (colby and cheddar) guarantee a rich flavor.

We keep our other sides fairly simple to counterbalance the rich ham and the macaroni and cheese. Pureed butternut squash can be made up to four days in advance and reheated in the microwave just before serving. If serving the squash as part of a buffet, keep the serving dish covered so it stays warm. Green beans, which can be blanched two days ahead of serving, are dressed with a mustard vinaigrette and can be served warm or at room temperature. And we wanted a refreshing salad as part of our menu so we chose a festive green salad. Composed of arugula, mesclun, radishes, and toasted almonds, the salad is complemented by a festive orange marmalade dressing. The dressing can be made up to two days ahead and the salad can be assembled up to an hour in advance and covered with damp paper towels to prevent the greens from drying out. Dress the salad just before serving.

An easy-to-serve cherry cobbler makes the perfect ending to this holiday meal. Both the biscuits and filling can be made up to two days prior to serving and stored separately. Getting dessert ready is as simple as arranging the biscuits over the filling and sliding the cobbler in the oven to heat through. Serve the cobbler warm with vanilla ice cream or Flavored Whipped Cream (page 397).

THE MENU

*Green Salad with Orange Marmalade Dressing
and Toasted Almonds*

Spiral-Sliced Ham with Cider Glaze

Baked Macaroni and Cheese

Butternut Squash Puree

Green Beans with Bistro Mustard Vinaigrette

Sour Cherry Cobbler

THE SHOPPING LIST

PRODUCE

- 3 medium butternut squash (about 6 pounds)
- 3 pounds green beans
- 8 radishes
- 5 ounces arugula (about 8 cups)
- 5 ounces mesclun greens (about 8 cups)
- Shallots
- Garlic
- 1 bunch parsley
- 1 bunch thyme

DAIRY AND REFRIGERATED JUICE

- Unsalted butter (2½ sticks)
- Half-and-half (6 tablespoons)
- Whole milk (3½ cups)
- Buttermilk (1 cup)
- 1 pound colby cheese
- 8 ounces extra-sharp cheddar cheese
- Apple cider (½ cup)

MEAT

- 1 (7-pound) spiral-sliced bone-in half ham, preferably shank end

ALCOHOL

- Dry red wine (1 cup)

PANTRY GOODS

- High-quality white sandwich bread (4 slices)
- 1 pound elbow macaroni
- 1 cup sliced almonds
- Extra-virgin olive oil (¾ cup)
- Sherry or red wine vinegar (4 tablespoons)
- Dijon mustard (2 teaspoons)
- Whole-grain mustard (3 tablespoons)
- Low-sodium chicken broth (2¼ cups)
- Orange marmalade (3 tablespoons)
- 4 (24-ounce) jars Morello cherries (or seven 15-ounce cans)
- Unbleached all-purpose flour
- Light or dark brown sugar
- Granulated sugar
- Baking powder
- Baking soda
- Cornstarch
- Almond extract
- Ground cloves
- Cayenne pepper
- Dry mustard
- Cinnamon stick (1 stick)

SPECIAL EQUIPMENT

- Three 13 by 9-inch baking dishes (for the cobbler, the macaroni and cheese, and the ham)
- Plastic oven bag (for the ham)

THE TIMELINE

I TO 4 DAYS AHEAD
• Cook the butternut squash

I TO 2 DAYS AHEAD
• Bake the biscuits and prepare the filling for the cobbler
• Make the macaroni and cheese
• Blanch the beans; make the vinaigrette
• Make the dressing for the salad

4½ HOURS BEFORE SERVING
• Let the ham come to room temperature

3 HOURS BEFORE SERVING
• Bake and glaze the ham

I HOUR BEFORE SERVING
• Reglaze and rest the ham
• Bake the macaroni and cheese
• Let the vinaigrette for the beans come to room temperature
• Assemble the salad and let the dressing come to room temperature

20 MINUTES BEFORE SERVING
• Reheat and dress the beans
• Carve the ham

5 TO 10 MINUTES BEFORE SERVING
• Reheat and finish the squash
• Dress the salad

* **NOTE:** About 45 minutes before serving dessert, assemble and bake the cobbler.

ALL ABOUT HAM

Plan on roughly 3 to 4 servings per pound for a bone-in ham. We recommend buying the shank end of the ham, because the bone configuration makes it easier to carve; look for a half ham with a tapered, pointed end (left). The butt end (right) has a rounded blunt end and is awkward to carve. We've tasted many brands of spiral sliced ham here in the test kitchen and we like two in particular: Cook's Spiral Sliced Hickory Smoked Honey Ham and Hillshire Farm Spiral Sliced Brown Sugar Cured Ham.

SHANK END   **BUTT END**

TRIMMING THE OVEN BAG

We like to use an oven bag when heating ham. Unlike foil, an oven bag creates a tight seal that encapsulates the heat and speeds the heat-through process. After tying the oven bag, use scissors to trim the bag, leaving 1 inch above the tie.

Butternut Squash Puree

SERVES 12

Don't be tempted to buy squash that is already peeled and cut—it will have a lot less flavor. You can substitute delicata squash for the butternut squash. If you do not have a microwave-proof bowl large enough to fit all of the squash together in step 1, you can microwave it in 2 batches; if you do so, the cooking time will be 5 to 10 minutes shorter.

3 medium butternut squash (about 6 pounds), peeled, seeded, and cut into 1½-inch chunks (see illustrations on page 49)
6 tablespoons half-and-half
6 tablespoons (¾ stick) unsalted butter
3 tablespoons light or dark brown sugar, plus extra to taste
   Salt and ground black pepper

1 TO 4 DAYS AHEAD

1. COOK THE SQUASH: Place the squash in a large microwave-safe bowl. Cover the bowl tightly with plastic wrap and microwave on high until the squash is tender and easily pierced with a dinner fork, 20 to 25 minutes, stirring the squash halfway through the cooking time.

2. Carefully remove the plastic wrap (watch for scalding steam). Drain the squash in a colander, then transfer it to a food processor. Add the half-and-half, 3 tablespoons of the butter, 3 tablespoons brown sugar, and 1 teaspoon salt. Process until smooth, about 20 seconds, stopping to scrape down the sides

of the workbowl as needed. Transfer the puree to an airtight container and refrigerate for up to 4 days.

10 MINUTES BEFORE SERVING

3. REHEAT AND FINISH THE SQUASH: Transfer the puree to a microwave-safe bowl and cover tightly with plastic wrap. Microwave on high power, stirring occasionally, until hot, about 10 minutes. Stir in the remaining 3 tablespoons butter and season with additional sugar, salt, and pepper to taste.

Sour Cherry Cobbler

SERVES 12

Use the smaller amount of sugar in the filling if you prefer your fruit desserts on the tart side and the larger amount if you like them sweet. You can substitute 7 (15-ounce) cans of Morello cherries (we like the Oregon Fruit Products brand), but do not substitute cans of pie filling (which has added sugars and thickeners). Serve with lightly sweetened whipped cream or vanilla ice cream.

BISCUIT TOPPING
2 cups (10 ounces) unbleached all-purpose flour
8 tablespoons (3½ ounces) sugar
½ teaspoon baking powder
½ teaspoon baking soda
½ teaspoon salt
6 tablespoons (¾ stick) unsalted butter, cold, cut into ½-inch cubes
1 cup buttermilk

EASY MICROWAVE OVEN CLEANING

Cleaning up dried-on spills inside your microwave oven needn't be a time-consuming chore. Here's what we recommend:

1. Place a microwave-safe bowl full of water in the oven and heat it on high for 10 minutes. The steam loosens up any dried food particles, which can then be wiped off with ease.

2. For hard-to-reach corners, a small disposable foam paint brush is just the right size to brush away any crumbs or other residue.

INGREDIENTS: Vanilla Ice Cream

Because it can be served with so many desserts, it's smart to keep a cache of vanilla ice cream in your freezer around the holidays. With so many brands to choose from, we wondered if one brand in particular is better than the rest. And while some supermarket vanilla ice creams attempt to get by on just the basics—"all natural" blends of cream, sugar, vanilla, and little else—many cartons sport labels that read like highlights from a chemistry textbook. Does any of this hocus-pocus deliver a better product? To find out, we tasted 18 varieties, including 10 French-style (with egg yolks) and eight regular (yolkless) vanilla ice creams.

The side-by-side comparison was striking. Some were fluffy and light; others were dense and rich. A few had assertive vanilla notes that reminded tasters of "frozen, boozy eggnog," but several ice creams seemed to be lacking in vanilla flavor altogether. Contrary to expectations, the French vanilla ice creams—prized for the rich flavor and creamy texture that comes from egg yolks—did not sweep the competition. In fact, regular-style Turkey Hill Vanilla Bean just edged out French-style Edy's Dreamery (the winner of our 2001 French vanilla tasting) for first place. Yes, the French-style ice creams (with 12.5 percent to 17 percent butterfat) took five of the six top spots, while leaner eggless vanilla ice creams (with 11.6 percent to 12.3 percent butterfat) took four of the five bottom places. But the top ranking of Turkey Hill Vanilla Bean (with just 12.1 percent butterfat) did not fit the neat pattern of more fat equals better quality.

Just as puzzling were tasters' comments about the texture of this yolkless winner. "What an amazingly gooey, creamy texture!" wrote one taster. "Nice eggy mouthfeel," said another. Double-checking the list of ingredients, we saw no evidence of any egg product. Even stranger, a quick skim through the rest of the comments revealed similar remarks about the "custardy" texture of a few of the other regular (yolkless) samples. We studied the labels again and soon noticed a clear pattern. Every regular-style ice cream that had passed for French vanilla contained substances such as carob bean gum, carrageenan, guar gum, and mono- and diglycerides. Could these additives be mimicking the textural effect of egg yolks?

We were partly correct. Carob bean gum, carrageenan, and guar gum are all stabilizers, added to ice cream to help keep ice crystals from forming and wreaking havoc on texture. Mono- and diglycerides, on the other hand, are emulsifiers, added to ice cream to keep the fat from separating—which, in turn, contributes a luscious, silky texture. Egg yolks, which naturally contain the emulsifier lecithin, serve this same function in French-style ice creams. So it was the mono- and diglycerides that had fooled our panelists into praising the "custardy" texture of the eggless ice creams.

A much clearer picture was emerging: High fat content and egg yolks can give ice cream a rich, creamy texture, but the judicious use of stabilizers and emulsifiers goes a long way toward making up for the absence of either one. The ice creams in our lineup that got the lowest scores for texture have low fat content and no egg yolks, stabilizers, or emulsifiers (that is, the "natural" regular-style ice creams). Our winning ice cream, Turkey Hill Vanilla Bean, contains emulsifiers as well as two stabilizers. And runner-up Edy's Dreamery has egg yolks, stabilizers, and a high fat content. No wonder it received the highest score for texture in the entire lineup.

So what about flavor? Although the occasional ice cream lost points for too-potent vanilla notes, by the end of the tasting it was clear why "vanilla" is often synonymous with "plain." In fact, weak vanilla flavor was the reason cited most often by panelists for awarding an ice cream a low score.

There are three forms of vanilla found in supermarket vanilla ice creams. Natural vanilla extract is made by steeping ground vanilla beans in a solution of alcohol and water to extract more than 240 flavorful compounds, the most dominant of which is called vanillin. Imitation vanilla extract is made by synthesizing vanillin from either eugenol or lignin. The third form is vanilla beans themselves.

Only two of the ice creams—Blue Bunny regular and Blue Bell French—contained imitation vanilla extract. One failed to make it out of the elimination round and the other landed in next-to-last place in the main tasting. Clearly, natural vanilla is a key component in good ice cream.

So where did we come out overall? Turns out it is possible to pull one over on Mother Nature—and, when it comes to vanilla ice cream, some strategic engineering is actually a desirable thing. Our tasters liked both French-style ice creams with stabilizers and regular (yolkless) ice creams with stabilizers and emulsifiers.

THE BEST VANILLA ICE CREAMS

Turkey Hill All Natural Flavor Vanilla Bean (regular-style) earned high scores for its "very clean flavor, and an amazingly creamy, gooey texture." And, runner-up, Edy's Dreamery Vanilla (French-style), was praised for its strong vanilla flavor and "ultra-creamy" texture.

FILLING
4 (24-ounce) jars Morello cherries, drained (about 8 cups), 2 cups juice reserved
¾–1 cup (5¼ to 7 ounces) sugar
3 tablespoons plus 1 teaspoon cornstarch
Pinch salt
1 cup dry red wine
1 cinnamon stick
¼ teaspoon almond extract

1 TO 2 DAYS AHEAD

1. MAKE THE BISCUIT TOPPING AND COBBLER FILLING: Adjust an oven rack to the middle position and heat the oven to 425 degrees. Line a baking sheet with parchment paper.

2. In a food processor, pulse the flour, 6 tablespoons of the sugar, baking powder, baking soda, and salt to combine. Scatter the butter pieces over the mixture and process until the mixture resembles coarse meal, about 15 pulses. Transfer the mixture to a medium bowl and stir in the buttermilk until combined. Using a 2- to 2¼-inch spring-loaded ice cream scoop, scoop 12 biscuits onto the prepared baking sheet, spacing them 1½ to 2 inches apart. (Or spray a ¼-cup measuring cup with vegetable oil spray, fill it with the biscuit dough, and tap the dough out onto the baking sheet.)

3. Sprinkle the biscuits evenly with the remaining 2 tablespoons sugar and bake until lightly browned on the tops and bottoms, about 15 minutes. Transfer the biscuits to a wire rack and let cool completely, about 1 hour. Store the cooled biscuits in a zipper-lock bag at room temperature for up to 2 days.

4. FOR THE FILLING: Meanwhile, spread the drained cherries in an even layer in a 13 by 9-inch glass baking dish; set aside. Combine the sugar, cornstarch, and salt in a medium nonreactive saucepan and whisk in the reserved cherry juice and the wine. Add the cinnamon stick and cook over medium-high heat, whisking frequently, until the mixture simmers and thickens, about 5 minutes. Discard the cinnamon stick and stir in the almond extract. Pour the hot liquid over the cherries in the baking dish and allow to cool. Cover with plastic wrap and refrigerate for up to 2 days.

45 MINUTES BEFORE SERVING

5. ASSEMBLE AND BAKE THE COBBLER: Adjust an oven rack to the middle position and heat the oven to 350 degrees. Unwrap the cobbler and arrange the biscuits in rows over the filling. Cover the dish tightly with foil and bake until the filling bubbles lightly around the edge, 30 minutes. Remove the foil and continue to bake until the filling is hot and the biscuits are crisp, 10 to 15 minutes longer.

Baked Macaroni and Cheese
SERVES 12
Although the classic pasta shape for this dish is elbow macaroni, any small, curved pasta will work. Undercooking the pasta in step 1 helps prevent it from turning mushy when reheated.

1 recipe (about 2¾ cups) Toasted Bread Crumb Topping (page 242)
Salt
1 pound elbow macaroni
6 tablespoons (¾ stick) unsalted butter
1 medium garlic clove, minced or pressed through a garlic press (about 1 teaspoon)
1 teaspoon dry mustard
¼ teaspoon cayenne pepper
6 tablespoons unbleached all-purpose flour
2¼ cups low-sodium chicken broth
3½ cups whole milk
1 pound colby cheese, shredded (about 4 cups)
8 ounces extra-sharp cheddar cheese, shredded (about 2 cups)
Ground black pepper

1 TO 2 DAYS AHEAD

1. MAKE THE MACARONI AND CHEESE: Bring 4 quarts of water to a boil in a Dutch oven over high heat. Stir in 1 tablespoon salt and the macaroni and cook, stirring occasionally, until just beginning to soften, about 5 minutes. Drain the pasta and leave it in the colander; set aside.

2. Wipe the pot dry, add the butter, and set it over medium heat until melted. Stir in the garlic, mustard, and cayenne and cook until fragrant,

INGREDIENTS:
Convenience Green Beans

For those of us without a willing partner to trim and cut pounds of fresh green beans, a package of trimmed and cut beans can look pretty enticing. But how do they taste? We went out and bought eight types of convenience green beans: three canned, four frozen, and one brand that offered packages of trimmed fresh green beans. When used in our Green Beans with Bistro Mustard Vinaigrette, the canned beans were bland and mushy. Slightly better were frozen green beans, though they were somewhat "waterlogged" and "spongy," with a diluted flavor. (These flaws were exaggerated in beans that were "frenched," or cut into long, thin matchsticks.) The trimmed fresh beans sounded promising, but the cut ends of the beans in the five different bags we bought had dried out and needed a retrim once we got them home—not much of a time-saver.

In the end, none of these products warranted an enthusiastic nod. Our recommendation? Spend a few minutes to trim—and blanch—fresh green beans—after all it doesn't really take so long after all.

NO CAN DO
Canned beans were mushy, pale, and bland.

CUT...AND DRIED
We had to retrim the dried-out ends on these trimmed fresh beans.

EMERGENCY ONLY
Frozen beans are passable in a pinch, but steer clear of "frenched" beans.

NO NUKES
Microwaveable frozen beans came out unevenly cooked and olive drab.

about 30 seconds. Stir in the flour and cook, stirring constantly, until golden, about 1 minute. Slowly whisk in the chicken broth and milk. Bring to a simmer and cook, whisking often, until large bubbles form on the surface and the mixture is slightly thickened, about 15 minutes. Off the heat, gradually whisk in the colby and cheddar until completely melted. Season with salt and pepper to taste.

3. Stir the drained pasta into the cheese sauce, breaking up any clumps, until well combined. Pour into a 13 by 9-inch baking dish and sprinkle with the crumb topping. Wrap the dish tightly with plastic wrap and refrigerate for up to 2 days.

1 HOUR BEFORE SERVING

4. BAKE THE MACARONI AND CHEESE: As soon as the ham is removed from the oven, adjust the oven rack to the middle position and increase the oven temperature to 400 degrees. Unwrap the macaroni and cheese and cover the dish tightly with aluminum foil. Bake until the filling is hot throughout, about 40 minutes. Remove the foil and continue to bake until the crumbs are crisp, about 20 minutes longer.

Green Beans with Bistro Mustard Vinaigrette
SERVES 12
Because these beans can be served hot, warm, or at room temperature, we suggest you reheat the beans first, then reheat the squash just before serving time.

BEANS

3	pounds green beans, ends trimmed
	Salt

VINAIGRETTE

6	tablespoons extra-virgin olive oil
4	teaspoons red or sherry vinegar
3	tablespoons whole-grain mustard
1	medium shallot, minced (about 3 tablespoons)
1	small garlic clove, minced or pressed through a press (about ¾ teaspoon)
1½	teaspoons minced fresh thyme leaves
½	teaspoon salt
¼	teaspoon ground black pepper

I TO 2 DAYS AHEAD

1. BLANCH THE BEANS: Bring 8 quarts of water to a boil in a large pot over high heat. Fill a large bowl with ice water; set aside. Add the beans and 2 tablespoons of salt to the boiling water and cook until mostly tender but still underdone, with a little crunch in the center, 2 to 4 minutes.

2. Drain the beans, then transfer immediately to the ice water. Let the beans cool completely, about 5 minutes, then drain and pat dry with paper towels. Wrap the beans loosely in paper towels and store in an airtight container (or large zipper-lock bag) for up to 2 days.

3. MAKE THE VINAIGRETTE: Shake all the ingredients together in a jar with a tight-fitting lid and refrigerate for up to 2 days.

I HOUR BEFORE SERVING

4. Let the vinaigrette sit at room temperature to allow the oil to liquefy.

20 MINUTES BEFORE SERVING

5. HEAT AND DRESS THE BEANS: Transfer the beans to a large microwave-safe bowl, cover with plastic wrap, and microwave on high until hot and steaming, 6 to 8 minutes. Drain away any accumulated water. Shake the vinaigrette to recombine, then toss with the beans to coat. Cover with foil to keep warm until serving.

Green Salad with Orange Marmalade Dressing and Toasted Almonds

SERVES 12

You can toss the salad greens and radishes in a large serving bowl, cover it with damp paper towels, and refrigerate up to 6 hours ahead of time.

DRESSING

6   tablespoons extra-virgin olive oil
3   tablespoons orange marmalade
3   tablespoons sherry or red wine vinegar
I   medium shallot, minced (about 3 tablespoons)
I   teaspoon minced fresh thyme leaves
     Salt and ground black pepper

SALAD

5   ounces lightly packed arugula (about 8 cups)
5   ounces lightly packed mesclun greens (about 8 cups)
8   medium radishes (about 4 ounces), sliced thin
I   cup sliced almonds, toasted

I TO 2 DAYS AHEAD

1. MAKE THE DRESSING: Shake all the ingredients together in a jar with a tight-fitting lid and refrigerate for up to 2 days.

I HOUR BEFORE SERVING

2. PREP THE SALAD: Let the vinaigrette sit at room temperature to allow the oil to liquefy. Toss the salad greens and radishes together in a large bowl, cover with damp paper towels, and refrigerate until needed.

5 MINUTES BEFORE SERVING

3. DRESS AND FINISH THE SALAD: Toss the salad with the dressing and sprinkle the almonds over the top.

Spiral-Sliced Ham with Cider Glaze

SERVES 12, WITH LEFTOVERS

You can put the ham in the oven cold, bypassing the 90-minute standing time, but you'll need to add a couple of minutes per pound to the baking time. You can also forgo the plastic oven bag and place the unwrapped ham cut side down in the baking dish and cover it tightly with foil, but you will need to add 3 or so minutes per pound to the baking time. If using an oven bag, be sure to cut slits in the bag so it does not burst.

I   spiral-sliced bone-in half ham (7 pounds), preferably shank end
½   cup apple cider
I   cup packed brown sugar
2   teaspoons Dijon mustard
       Pinch ground clove

4½ HOURS BEFORE SERVING

1. PREP THE HAM FOR BAKING: Unwrap the ham and remove and discard the plastic disk and/or pad covering the bone. Place the ham in a plastic oven bag, pull tightly for a close fit, tie the bag, and trim the excess plastic (see the illustration on page 406). Set the ham cut side down in a 13 by 9-inch baking dish and cut 4 slits in the top of the bag with a paring knife. Let the ham sit at room temperature for 1½ hours.

3 HOURS BEFORE SERVING

2. BAKE THE HAM: Adjust an oven rack to the lowest position and heat the oven to 250 degrees. Bake the ham until the center registers about 100 degrees on an instant-read thermometer, about 1¾ hours (about 14 minutes per pound).

3. Meanwhile, bring the cider, brown sugar, Dijon, and clove to a boil in small saucepan over high heat. Reduce the heat to medium-low and simmer until the mixture is syrupy and measures about 1 cup, about 5 minutes; set aside. (The glaze will thicken further as it cools; if necessary, reheat it over medium heat before using.)

4. Remove the ham from the oven and roll back the bag to expose the ham (without losing any of the accumulated juices). Increase the oven temperature to 450 degrees. Brush the ham liberally with the glaze and continue to bake until the glaze becomes sticky, about 10 minutes.

1 HOUR BEFORE SERVING

5. REST THE HAM: Remove the ham from the oven, brush thoroughly again with the glaze, and cover loosely with foil. Let the ham rest in the baking dish until the internal temperature registers 115 to 120 degrees on an instant-read thermometer, about 40 minutes.

20 MINUTES BEFORE SERVING

6. CARVE THE HAM: Transfer the ham to a carving board. Pour the juices from the bag into a small bowl and reserve. Slice the ham according to the illustrations at right and arrange on a warm platter. Pour the reserved juices over the ham and cover with foil to keep warm until serving.

CARVING A SPIRAL-SLICED HAM

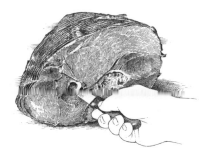

1. With the tip of a paring or carving knife, cut around the bone to loosen the attached slices.

2. Using a long carving knife, slice horizontally above the bone and through the spiral-cut slices, toward the back of the ham.

3. Pull the cut portion away from the bone and cut between the slices to separate them fully.

4. Beginning at the tapered end, slice above the bone to remove the remaining chunk of meat. Flip the ham over and repeat the procedure on the other side.

INDEX

INDEX

A NOTE ON CONVERSIONS

A NOTE ON CONVERSIONS

SOME SAY COOKING IS A SCIENCE AND AN art. We would say that geography has a hand in it, too. Flour milled in the United Kingdom and elsewhere will feel and taste different from flour milled in the United States. So we cannot promise that the loaf of bread you bake in Canada or England will taste the same as a loaf baked in the States, but we can offer guidelines for converting weights and measures. We also recommend that you rely on your instincts when making our recipes. Refer to the visual cues provided. If the bread dough hasn't "come together in a ball," as described, you may need to add more flour— even if the recipe doesn't tell you so. You be the judge. For more information on conversions and ingredient equivalents, visit our Web site at www.cooksillustrated.com and type "conversion chart" in the search box.

The recipes in this book were developed using standard U.S. measures following U.S. government guidelines. The charts below offer equivalents for U.S., metric, and Imperial (U.K.) measures. All conversions are approximate and have been rounded up or down to the nearest whole number. For example:

1 teaspoon = 4.9292 milliliters, rounded up to 5 milliliters

1 ounce = 28.3495 grams, rounded down to 28 grams

Volume Conversions

U.S.	METRIC
1 teaspoon	5 milliliters
2 teaspoons	10 milliliters
1 tablespoon	15 milliliters
2 tablespoons	30 milliliters
¼ cup	59 milliliters
⅓ cup	79 milliliters
½ cup	118 milliliters
¾ cup	177 milliliters
1 cup	237 milliliters
1¼ cups	296 milliliters
1½ cups	355 milliliters
2 cups	473 milliliters
2½ cups	592 milliliters
3 cups	710 milliliters
4 cups (1 quart)	0.946 liter
1.06 quarts	1 liter
4 quarts (1 gallon)	3.8 liters

Weight Conversions

OUNCES	GRAMS
½	14
¾	21
1	28
1½	43
2	57
2½	71
3	85
3½	99
4	113
4½	128
5	142
6	170
7	198
8	227
9	255
10	283
12	340
16 (1 pound)	454

Conversions for Ingredients Commonly Used in Baking

Baking is an exacting science. Because measuring by weight is far more accurate than measuring by volume, and thus more likely to achieve reliable results, in our recipes we provide ounce measures in addition to cup measures for many ingredients. Refer to the chart below to convert these measures into grams.

INGREDIENT	OUNCES	GRAMS
I cup all-purpose flour*	5	142
I cup whole-wheat flour	5½	156
I cup granulated (white) sugar	7	198
I cup packed brown sugar (light or dark)	7	198
I cup confectioners' sugar	4	113
I cup cocoa powder	3	85
Butter†		
4 tablespoons (½ stick, or ¼ cup)	2	57
8 tablespoons (I stick, or ½ cup)	4	113
16 tablespoons (2 sticks, or I cup)	8	227

*U.S. all-purpose flour, the most frequently used flour in this book, does not contain leaveners, as some European flours do. These leavened flours are called self-rising or self-raising. If you are using self-rising flour, take this into consideration before adding leavening to a recipe.

† In the United States, butter is sold both salted and unsalted. We generally recommend unsalted butter. If you are using salted butter, take this into consideration before adding salt to a recipe.

Oven Temperatures

FAHRENHEIT	CELSIUS	GAS MARK (IMPERIAL)
225	105	¼
250	120	½
275	130	1
300	150	2
325	165	3
350	180	4
375	190	5
400	200	6
425	220	7
450	230	8
475	245	9

Converting Temperatures from an Instant-Read Thermometer

We include doneness temperatures in many of our recipes, such as those for poultry, meat, and bread. We recommend an instant-read thermometer for the job. Refer to the table at left to convert Fahrenheit degrees to Celsius. Or, for temperatures not represented in the chart, use this simple formula:

Subtract 32 degrees from the Fahrenheit reading, then divide the result by 1.8 to find the Celsius reading.

EXAMPLE:
"Roast until the juices run clear when the chicken is cut with a paring knife or the thickest part of the breast registers 160 degrees on an instant-read thermometer." To convert:

$160°$ F $- 32 = 128°$
$128° ÷ 1.8 = 71°$ C (rounded down from 71.11)